PSYCHOLOGY OF
CRIMINAL BEHAVIOUR

A CANADIAN PERSPECTIVE

RALPH SERIN
Carleton University

ADELLE FORTH
Carleton University

SHELLEY BROWN
Carleton University

KEVIN NUNES
Carleton University

CRAIG BENNELL
Carleton University

JOANNA POZZULO
Carleton University

Pearson Canada
Toronto

Library and Archives Canada Cataloguing in Publication

Psychology of criminal behaviour: a Canadian perspective / Ralph C. Serin ... [et al.]. — 1st ed.

Includes index.
ISBN 978-0-13-505380-5

1. Criminal psychology—Textbooks. 2. Criminal psychology—Canada—Textbooks. I. Serin, Ralph C. (Ralph Charles), 1953– II. Title.

HV6080.P79 2011   364.3   C2009-904933-3

ISBN 978-0-13-505380-5

Vice-President, Editorial Director: Gary Bennett
Editor-in-Chief: Ky Pruesse
Editor, Humanities and Social Sciences: Joel Gladstone
Marketing Manager: Arthur Gee
Developmental Editor: Rema Celio
Production Editor: Imee Salumbides
Copy Editor: Sally Glover
Proofreaders: Susan Bindernagel, Kelli Howey
Production Coordinator: Sarah Lukaweski
Compositor: Integra
Photo and Permissions Researcher: Terri Rothman
Art Director: Julia Hall
Cover Designer: Miriam Blier
Cover Image: Getty Images/Stone/Eric Tucker

8   14 13

Printed and bound in Canada.

Contents

Preface

Over the past several years, likely spawned by interest in our second-year Forensic Psychology course and popular television shows on criminal behaviour, enrollment in our Criminal Behaviour course has been consistently high. As we prepared each year for teaching, the same question arose among the faculty: which text to use? It seemed we had all used different texts for different reasons, but with similar results. Student response was modest at best. Complaints were that the texts were too dense, too American, too expensive, too British, etc. We even tried a course pack of some of our favourite selected readings, believing this compromise would be successful. Perhaps we were simply delaying the inevitable, because students' comments were equally critical of the course pack. They rightly noted it wasn't a textbook and lacked all the requisite bells and whistles such as a glossary and sample quizzes, and it certainly wasn't inexpensive. This collective experience led to the realization that a new textbook was needed, and that this textbook should highlight the many contributions made by Canadian researchers.

We owe a significant debt of gratitude to numerous Canadian researchers whom we have highlighted in this text. Based on their collective contributions, Canadian corrections research and practice continues to be at the forefront in the United States and abroad. Canadian theory and research is prominently represented in risk and needs assessment, correctional rehabilitation programs, and evaluation strategies throughout the world. We feel it is important that students understand this legacy and that they appreciate the contribution Canadian researchers have made. This textbook also highlights subgroups of offenders, such as Aboriginal and women offenders, for whom specific research is emerging. Also, the importance of a more integrated model of criminal behaviour that considers biology, as well as the person and situation interaction, is emphasized. It is our hope that this textbook intrigues and engages a new generation of corrections researchers and practitioners. Certainly, relentless media coverage, political and ideological debates, fiscal challenges in corrections, and continued public concern regarding safety make this an exciting time in corrections research.

As a group we mused and reflected on the needs of our students and what a new textbook might look like. For instance, of the 1500 or so students that take our Criminal Behaviour course at Carleton each year, very few continue their studies at the graduate level. Also, our students are an interdisciplinary mix of psychology, criminology, sociology, and law students, many of whom aspire to a job in the areas of policing, corrections, probation and parole, and nongovernment organizations such as the John Howard Society and Elizabeth Fry Society. Many of us recruit guest lecturers and often the most popular class is one by senior corrections officials describing work in corrections and how to get a summer job (usually there is a mob scene at the end of class as students clamour for a business card). These experiences meant that our textbook needed to meet a range of needs and interests of our students. It had to highlight Canadian research, both influential and contemporary; it had to link research to practice; and it had to be accessible. We hope that we have achieved these goals with this textbook.

DISTINGUISHING FEATURES

Although the textbook has been written by six different authors, a common outline has been utilized. Key pedagogical aids have been incorporated to promote student learning and to assist instructors in presenting important material. Key features include the following:

■ **Chapter objectives.** Each chapter starts with a list of learning objectives to guide students' learning of the material and closes with a summary linked to the learning objectives.

■ **Vignettes.** Case studies or vignettes are presented at the beginning of each chapter to provide a context for the key concepts reflected in the chapter. These vignettes are real-world cases and scenarios to help students make the link from research to practice.

■ **Key terms and Glossary.** Key terms are highlighted in bold type throughout each chapter and a definition is provided in the glossary at the end of the textbook for easy reference.

■ **Evidence-based practice.** A major focus of the text is the use of empirical research to support key theories and practice. Data reported in original studies is often presented in graph or table form and is cited throughout the textbook.

■ **Profiles of Canadian researchers.** Canadian researchers are among the best in the world and their contributions have been innumerable. Each chapter provides a profile of a key Canadian researcher whose work is relevant to the chapter. These profiles also highlight information such as educational background, research interests, and some aspects of their personal lives.

■ **Boxes.** Boxed features within the chapters provide interesting asides to the main text. These boxes will develop students' appreciation for current assessment techniques and issues.

■ **Discussion questions.** Several discussion questions are provided at the end of each chapter. Instructors can assign these for group discussion in class, or students can consider them in order to examine their understanding of the chapter material.

■ **Additional readings.** At the end of each chapter are several additional readings that reflect the central concepts presented in the chapter. For students especially interested in the chapter material, this is an opportunity to expand their understanding beyond the level presented in the textbook.

■ **Websites.** Several chapters list websites at the end of the chapter for intesrested students to seek additional information regarding correctional research and practice.

- **"Top 10" contemporary issues.** For each chapter a listing of "Top 10" key issues such as theoretical advances, key points, contentious issues, and people to watch is provided.

- **Linking research to practice.** A separate chapter is provided that demonstrates how empirical research and theory are linked to contemporary correctional practice. This should be of interest to students who plan on pursuing careers in the fields of corrections and criminal justice.

- **Career options.** An appendix is provided that highlights graduate training and career options in the field of correctional psychology. This appendix includes current salary information as well as hints to enhance student success.

SUPPLEMENTS

The following supplements specific to this text can be downloaded by instructors from a password-protected location of Pearson Canada's online catalogue (vig.pearsoned.ca). Contact your local sales representative for further information.

Instructor's Manual. The Instructor's Manual is a comprehensive resource that provides chapter outlines, class activities, and summaries of key concepts. We hope our colleagues will use the textbook and Instructor's Manual as a foundation that they can build on in the classroom.

Test Item File. This test bank, offered in Microsoft Word format, contains multiple-choice, true/false, short-answer, and essay questions. Each question is classified according to difficulty level and is keyed to the appropriate page number in the text.

PowerPoint Presentations. PowerPoint slides highlight the key concepts in each chapter of the text.

mysearchlab

MySearchLab offers extensive help to students with their writing and research projects and provides round-the-clock access to credible and reliable source material.

Research

Content on MySearchLab includes immediate access to thousands of full-text articles from leading Canadian and international academic journals, and daily news feeds from The Associated Press. Articles contain the full downloadable text—including abstract and citation information—and can be cut, pasted, emailed, or saved for later use.

Writing

MySearchLab also includes a step-by-step tutorial on writing a research paper. Included are sections on planning a research assignment, finding a topic, creating effective notes, and finding source material. Our exclusive online handbook provides grammar and usage support. Pearson SourceCheck™ offers an easy way to detect accidental plagiarism issues, and our exclusive tutorials teach how to avoid them in the future. MySearchLab also contains AutoCite, which helps to cite sources correctly using MLA, APA, CMS, and CBE documentation styles for both endnotes and bibliographies.

To order this book with MySearchLab access at no extra charge, use ISBN 978-0-13-801340-0.

Take a tour at **www.mysearchlab.com.**

CourseSmart for Instructors

CourseSmart goes beyond traditional expectations, providing instant, online access to the textbooks and course materials you need at a lower cost for students. And even as students save money, you can save time and hassle with a digital eTextbook that allows you to search for the most relevant content at the very moment you need it. Whether it's evaluating textbooks or creating lecture notes to help students with difficult concepts, CourseSmart can make life a little easier. See how when you visit **www.coursesmart.com/instructors.**

CourseSmart for Students

CourseSmart goes beyond traditional expectations, providing instant, online access to the textbooks and course materials you need at an average savings of 50%. With instant access from any computer and the ability to search your text, you'll find the content you need quickly, no matter where you are. And with online tools like highlighting and note-taking, you can save time and study efficiently. See all the benefits at **www.coursesmart.com/ students.**

Acknowledgments

This book would never have come to fruition without assistance from many people. In particular, we would never have been able to complete such a text without the mentoring by outstanding forensic and correctional researchers.

We would like to acknowledge that the forensic program at Carleton University, of which we are part, would not exist without Don Andrews. He is an exceptional and generous colleague whose work has guided the field for decades. As well, Robert Hoge has also been a long-time supportive colleague and important advocate for attending to the issue of juvenile crime in Canada.

We are thankful to the exceptional researchers we profiled in this textbook for giving us permission to give students a glimpse into their lives, and for offering us great insight by reviewing content we provided, specifically Don Andrews, Kelley Blanchette, Joseph Couture, Donald Dutton, Paul Gendreau, Karl Hanson, Sheilagh Hodgins, Martin Lalumière, William Marshall, Marlene Moretti, Vernon Quinsey, and John Weekes. All have made significant contributions to understanding criminal behaviour.

We would like to make special mention of Shannon Gottschall, a graduate student at Carleton University, who tirelessly and carefully reviewed our initial drafts and provided very helpful feedback that better integrated our chapters and strengthened the final work.

We would like to thank the reviewers who provided us with helpful feedback that allowed us to make the textbook stronger. Reviewers of the manuscript and/or the original project proposal include the following:

John S. Conklin, Camosun College

Janne A. Holmgren, Mount Royal University

Amy Johnson, University of the Fraser Valley

Kristine A Peace, Grant MacEwan University

Amy Prevost, University of the Fraser Valley

Julia Shaw, St. Jerome's University, University of Waterloo

We would like to thank the family at Pearson Canada. Ky Pruesse (editor-in-chief) enthusiastically supported the original concept. Rema Celio (developmental editor) kept us focused on timeframes and was patient regarding our transgressions. Sally Glover (copy editor) helped us transform our ideas into a more readable form.

Finally, we would like to thank our many undergraduate and graduate students. The undergraduates prompted us to undertake this challenge and we feel our program will be stronger because of their wish for a real Canadian criminal behaviour textbook. Our graduate students continue to encourage us with their thoughtful discussions regarding the contents of this textbook and challenge us to look forward to the next frontiers of a psychological perspective on criminal behaviour.

Completion of a textbook is a considerable challenge not only to the authors, but to the people in their lives. Ralph Serin would like to thank his wife, Carolan, for her continued patience and support as he spent countless hours hidden away in front of a computer. Joanna Pozzulo would like to thank the employees of Apple for making a reliable computer. She couldn't have written the chapters without her MacBook. Adelle Forth would like to give a huge thanks to her partner, John Logan, for editing her chapters, giving insightful feedback, not getting too frustrated with repeated requests for help, and for generally being supportive, including taking over the care of numerous four-footed critters while the textbook was being written. Shelley Brown would like to thank her husband, Murray, for his unwavering support during the writing of this book that included taking their two small children (William and Lydia) away on the occasional weekend when she desperately needed to write. Craig Bennell would like to thank his wife, Cindy, for her love, patience, and support; Noah, for being such a good boy while Dad had to write; and Elijah, who arrived at the tail end of this book, for being a wonderful baby and a very good sleeper. Kevin Nunes would like to thank his partner, Anne, for her patience with the long hours and for her intellectual and moral support.

Chapter 1
Crime in Canada

Typical Offender Profile

Bill Jones, aged 28, is serving a 36-month sentence for armed robbery. This is not his first incarceration, having served time both in secure custody as a youth and in provincial jails for property crimes (theft, break and enter, drug possession, and a couple of assaults). He dropped out of high school prior to completing Grade 10 and has infrequently held odd jobs. Presentence reports describe a fairly chaotic childhood and family situation, a long history of drug and alcohol abuse, and multiple brief relationships.

Assessments indicate that Bill presents as impulsive with poor problem-solving skills, which, along with his hanging out with antisocial peers, seem related to his fairly consistent involvement with the courts as an adult. He claims to want treatment, but is somewhat unclear regarding what this would entail. Prior involvement in counselling has not been successful in reducing his criminality. He met a woman recently and hopes that this relationship, along with improved employment skills, will help him go straight. Until now, his main form of leisure activity has been going to bars with friends.

Sensational Case Profile

In June 1991, Paul Bernardo kidnapped, raped, and murdered 14-year-old Leslie Mahaffy. He and his girlfriend, Karla Homolka, held Mahaffy for 24 hours, during which time they repeatedly raped her. Homolka and Bernardo taped the assaults; one scene even shows Homolka putting on makeup to look pretty before raping the teen. The two killed Mahaffy with a plan to dismember her body and dispose of it piece by piece after encasing the parts in cement. Two people canoeing in a local lake found Mahaffy's body. The very same day, Homolka and Bernardo were married.

A short time later, in April 1992, with the aid of his wife Homolka, Bernardo kidnapped another teenager, Kristen French. French was also raped and tortured over several days. The pair killed French just before attending Easter Sunday dinner with Homolka's parents.

The Canadian press began calling the couple "the Ken and Barbie" murderers. Homolka would later enter into a plea bargain with the prosecution in return for a lighter sentence, testifying against Paul Bernardo, including information about their part in the killing of Homolka's sister. Bernardo, who claimed to be a fan of serial killer stories, would later change his name to Paul Teale. Bernardo was convicted of three counts of murder on September 1, 1995, and sentenced to life in prison at Kingston Penitentiary in Kingston, Ontario. Reports indicate that Bernardo's parents were not close to one another but cite their son as being a "perfect" child who began a career as an accountant.

Source: © 2008 SerialKillers.ca by WhiteBark Innovations. Used with permission.

Learning Objectives

1   Describe a typical offender, with a discussion of implications for understanding criminal behaviour in general.

2   Provide an interdisciplinary context to understanding criminal behaviour.

3   Describe public perceptions of criminal justice agencies.

4   Describe crime trends throughout Canada.

5   Describe the empirically derived determinants of crime and discuss their implications for assessment and treatment of offenders.

6   Introduce types of crime and their implications for understanding criminal behaviour.

7   Describe variations in rates of crime according to different sources.

8   Describe the financial and social impact of crime on Canadians.

INTRODUCTION

WHILE MEDIA PORTRAYAL OF SENSATIONAL CASES SUCH AS SERIAL MURDERS IS ENGAGING and series crime dramas are highly popular, they often tell us little about understanding crime. With regards to the majority of individuals involved in the criminal justice system, an analysis of sensational cases does not inform us about the most prevalent types of crime, nor the motivations underlying "ordinary" criminal behaviour. Indeed, media depictions of crime may unduly influence public opinion with respect to such issues as the likelihood of being a victim of crime, the most prevalent types of crime, and the merits (or lack) of rehabilitative efforts for offenders. Moreover, understanding criminal behaviour from a single source such as the newspaper or television may limit our knowledge of the complex phenomenon of criminality. This could lead to an understanding of crime that is informed only by sensational cases or ideology rather than empirical sources and an integration of research across the disciplines of law, sociology, and psychology. The importance of research findings in explaining, understanding, and changing criminal behaviour is a significant theme that permeates this text.

Accordingly, this text highlights the significant contributions of Canadian scholars and clinicians to correctional research and practice both in Canada and abroad. There are many excellent books that reflect specific aspects of correctional practice in terms of forensic and risk assessment, motivation, and treatment of offenders, including specific subgroups, but they are not written as university textbooks. In our view, other texts remain either too general (i.e., blur between forensic and correctional psychology) or too American in focus. This book is intended to address such shortcomings, examining Canadian contributions to a psychological understanding of criminal behaviour and reflecting on how empirical research underscores the assessment and treatment of offenders throughout the correctional process, thereby yielding improved correctional outcomes.

The Influence of the Media

Even inmates eat better than seniors in nursing homes. (Wallace 2008: 4)

James Wallace's 2008 story "Even inmates eat better than seniors in nursing homes" in *The Kingston Whig Standard* notes that the Ontario government raised its food allowance for feeding seniors in long-term care facilities by 12 cents a day. This move increased the meal per diem to $5.46, which includes two choices of meals at breakfast, lunch, and dinner each day, as well as snacks and drinks. In contrast, Ontario prisoners receive meals worth more than $10 per day.

Nothing galvanizes public opinion more than the media's portrayal of criminal justice issues. Perhaps it is for this reason that in 2008 the *Toronto Star* undertook to publish a special series highlighting the complexity of crime and criminal justice issues in Canada. Crime and criminal justice issues receive considerable media scrutiny, sensational crimes receive front-page billing, and the public is inundated with facts, figures, and opinions about what to do about crime and how to increase public safety. At times of political change, crime and public safety are typically high on the agenda of issues to discuss. During the federal election in 2008, all three major political parties espoused views on getting tough on crime, especially in terms of sentencing. This is not entirely surprising, given that Canadian surveys indicate that crime is an important concern (Queen's University 2006), albeit below issues of health care, the environment, poor government leadership, unemployment, and the military. Similar research indicates that 44 percent of Canadians believe more money should be spent on the criminal justice system (Queen's University 2006), although survey results do not indicate where the funds should allocated (i.e., courts, police, or prisons). A further goal of this text, then, is to provide a context for understanding crime in Canada and to dispel myths regarding what is working and what is not.

Figure 1.1 illustrates the results of a recent survey regarding how Canadians rate different sources of information about the criminal justice system (Latimer and Desjardins 2007).

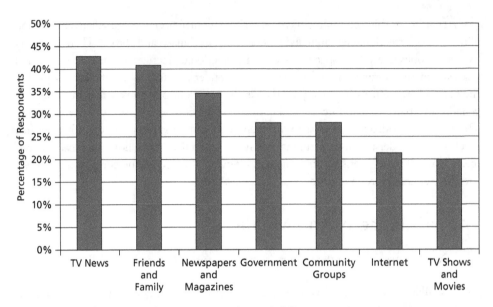

Figure 1.1 Information Sources Rated as Highly Important

Source: Department of Justice (2007)

Researchers surveyed more than 4500 Canadians by telephone regarding their perceptions of crime. The results show government information as having moderate influence and academic contributions as having none, although some academics provide commentaries in newspapers and magazines. Clearly these data confirm the importance of media for Canadians.

Current Context

This text focuses on a psychological understanding of criminal behaviour, with a consideration of individual and intra-individual (i.e., personality) influences. The focus is not intended to ignore broader social influences on criminality but asserts that greater understanding of criminal behaviour comes from psychological explanations that consider individual differences. Psychology is interested in **intra-individual differences** (variations in criminal conduct within an individual across time and situations) as well as **inter-individual differences** (variations in criminal conduct between individuals). It is this latter distinction that has been of greatest interest to sociologists. McGuire (2004) states that the difference between psychology and sociology is the level or focus of comparisons: psychology focuses on individuals, whereas sociology focuses more on groups. He uses the analogy of a microscope, arguing that psychology involves a much higher level of magnification in order to see things (about crime) that are not apparent from a different view. In this manner, broader social context is an insufficient viewpoint from which to understand individual differences (i.e., not all individuals who are poor commit criminal acts, and not all well-off individuals avoid crime).

The terms used to define the study of criminal behaviour vary somewhat across different texts. Broadly speaking, **forensic psychology** refers to any application of psychology to the legal system (Pozzulo, Bennell, and Forth 2008). While some reserve the term for the practice of clinical psychology within the legal system (Huss 2009), this more reflects issues of risk assessment and expert testimony—key activities of psychologists in court, intended to guide legal decision making—than the understanding of criminal behaviour. In the United Kingdom (McGuire 2002), the specific psychological study of criminal behaviour is referred to as criminological psychology; in the United States and Canada, the area would often be described as correctional psychology (Magaletta and Boothby 2002). The latter recognizes that correctional psychologists conduct crisis management and individual and group psychotherapy with general population inmates as well as with offenders with mental disorders and substance abuse problems. The focus of this text is to understand the assessment and management of individuals who engage in criminal behaviour. The idea is to follow dispositions by the court, not the actual issues relating to the operation of justice. Accordingly, our preferred "model" is that of correctional psychology as described by Magaletta and Boothby (2002).

Sociological explanations regarding such factors as age, gender, and social class provide some insight into groups of individuals. For instance, relatively speaking, younger males are more likely to be involved in **criminal behaviour**, and crime decreases with increased age (Blumstein and Cohen 1987). Prisoners tend to be less well educated and have poorer employment histories (Motiuk, Cousineau, and Gileno 2005). However, not all young males commit crimes, and, indeed, some quite elderly males are involved in criminal behaviour. Highly educated citizens (i.e., university professors!) have been known to commit crimes and receive sanctions by the courts.

Juxtaposing correctional psychology with a sociological and criminological explanation underscores the different perspectives and levels of analysis considered (McGuire 2002). As the level of analysis varies, so too does the theoretical explanation. For instance, at the macro level, the objective is to understand crime as a large-scale social phenomenon, reflecting strain theory (Merton 1957). As the perspective narrows, the importance of socialization and the influence of community, family, and peer groups becomes of greater interest, reflecting differential association theory (Sutherland and Cressey 1970). An even narrower focus examines patterns of individual behaviour, first over time and situation and then in terms of the influence of psychological factors such as thoughts, feelings, or attitudes (Andrews and Bonta 2006; McGuire 2002). It is these last two levels of analysis that are of interest to appreciating inter- and intra-individual differences in criminal behaviour.

Notably, as illustrated by our two case examples, offenders comprise a particularly heterogeneous group (Piquero, Blumstein, Brame, Haapanen, Mulvey, and Nagin 2001), such that aggregate age-crime data conceal the distinct trajectories of widely different offenders (Barnett, Blumstein and Farrington 1987; Hussong, Curran, Moffitt, Caspi and Carrig, 2004). Importantly, as many as 70 percent of offenders follow some approximation of the age-crime curve, with only a small percentage maintaining criminal activity well into adulthood (Piquero et al. 2001). This phenomenon of decreased criminal activity is a process referred to as **crime desistance** and group-based explanations of crime acquisition and desistance must be informed by individual difference explanations in order to situate a psychological understanding of crime.

A psychological explanation, then, considers the factors that might influence criminal behaviour (both crime acquisition and cessation). Within a group of males, which younger males are more likely to engage in criminal activity and which older ones are more likely to stop committing crimes? Psychology attempts to refine our understanding of criminal behaviour by considering individual variation in order to account for heterogeneity and provide differentiated assessment and intervention. A psychological understanding is derived from recognizing the variability of criminal behaviour between individuals as well as within an individual over time and across situations. A prominent psychological depiction of the interplay among factors influencing criminality, sometimes referred to as a general personality and social psychology of criminal conduct, is the Personal, Interpersonal and Community-Reinforcement model (PIC–R; Andrews and Bonta 2006). This model posits that criminal behaviour reflects the "immediate situation" in that factors (e.g., temptations, facilitators, inhibitors, and stressors) combine to influence a decision to engage in criminal behaviour. The decision is further influenced by attitudes supportive of crime, a history of criminal behaviour, a balance of the costs and rewards for crime, and the presence of social supports for crime (Andrews and Bonta 2006). Further, Andrews and Bonta's PIC–R highlights the contributions of community (i.e., family of origin, social economic factors), interpersonal (i.e., family/child relations, childhood attachment, neglect, abuse, ties to criminal others), personal (i.e., early conduct problems, biological factors such as temperament and verbal intelligence, gender and age, and cognitions), and consequences (i.e., whether criminal behaviour is rewarded). In this manner, it is an integrative and situational model of criminal behaviour that recognizes the influence of both historical and immediate factors in an individual arriving at the decision to engage in a criminal act and to view such behaviour as appropriate. In this manner, the PIC–R reflects a learning theory of crime that attends to social and cognitive factors as well as behaviour, underscoring it as a contemporary **cognitive social learning theory** of crime.

It is interesting and important to note that this model is quite similar to contemporary criminological viewpoints (Farrington 2003) that consider short- and long-term risk factors as well as cognitive processes and consequences of behaviour. In Farrington's (2003) theory, long-term risk factors (e.g., biological, individual, family, peer, school, community, and society) interact with short-term ones (energizing and inhibiting factors, opportunity, antisocial tendency, and cognitive processes) to influence antisocial behaviour.

DEFINITION OF CRIME

VARIATION IN RATES OF CRIME AND INCARCERATION ACROSS COUNTRIES SUGGESTS differences in definitions and/or tolerance. McGuire (2004) describes a variety of factors that have been used to define crime and in part explain when certain behaviours may be viewed as criminal. These include an individual's motivation, opportunity, politics, social convention, and context. Further, Muncie (2001) has delineated 11 separate definitions of crime, highlighting the challenges in arriving at a perfect description. Types of definitions typically include legal, moral, social, and psychological explanations: legal refers to acts prohibited by the state that are punishable under the law; moral refers to the violation of norms of religion and morality that are punishable by supreme beings; social refers to the violation of certain norms and customs that are punishable by the community; and psychological refers to acts that are rewarding to the perpetrator but harmful to others.

While it is clear that crime is a socially constructed phenomenon, early research (Newman 1976; 1977) has shown that there is consistency across countries regarding what is viewed as criminal. Using brief vignettes to describe situations (e.g., a person forcefully taking money from another, resulting in injury to the victim; a father having sexual relations with his grown-up daughter), he surveyed people in six countries and found there was a high degree of agreement in respondents' perceptions of what is considered a crime. In particular, robbery, theft, and incest were all viewed to be criminal.

For the purposes of this text, our working definition of criminal behaviour comes from Bartol and Bartol (2008). Of note is that it incorporates intent, thereby addressing Canadian concerns regarding criminal responsibility.

> Criminal behaviour refers to intentional behaviour that violates a criminal code; intentional in that it did not occur accidentally or without justification of excuse. (Bartol and Bartol 2008)

The issue of what is considered a crime may seem unwarranted in that the courts adjudicate cases and determine sanctions and it is the responsibility of probation officers/jails/prisons to manage these sentences. A definition of crime is critical in that the specific description will influence prevalence (i.e., a more conservative or restrictive definition will decrease the rate of crime). Further, any definition of crime must concede that there are inter-cultural variations regarding normative and acceptable behaviour, and that acceptable norms can change over time within a culture (e.g., abortion laws in Canada). Further, immigrants to Canada may behave in a manner consistent with the cultural norms of their native country, but such behaviour may be illegal in their newly adopted home (e.g., age of consent for sexual intercourse). Since treatment is often provided by correctional agencies to address the underlying reasons for criminality and to reduce the likelihood of repeating a crime, sensitivity to both legal and cultural issues must be reflected in psychological responses to criminal behaviour.

DETERMINANTS OF CRIME

As noted in the PIC–R model, determinants of crime have often been described as distal (i.e., historical) and proximal (i.e., immediate, situational). From psychology's perspective, it is of interest to identify those factors that are most strongly associated with criminality in order that assessments are developed to reflect these domains and that interventions are derived to address (i.e., change, modify, diminish) them and reduce future re-offending. While literature reviews are helpful in understanding key issues within a field, a more useful strategy to empirically identify determinants of crime is through meta-analysis. Meta-analytic reviews are less biased in that they provide a quantitative estimate of the importance of the results rather than a narrative interpretation by the author. This method of reviewing studies and aggregating the findings in terms of effect sizes (i.e., the strength of the association between independent variables such as substance abuse and a dependent variable such as criminal behaviour) is now considered the standard for reviewing the literature. Moreover, statistical techniques exist to allow differences between groups (percentages, t-scores) to be converted to a Pearson correlation coefficient (r), permitting a common metric for easily understanding the relative importance of independent variables.

Box 1.1

Statistical Information for Understanding Research

In order to understand various tables and terms in this and subsequent chapters, it may be useful to review some key ideas and approaches to presenting and summarizing research findings. This section will briefly describe effect sizes, meta-analysis, and how to measure predictive accuracy.

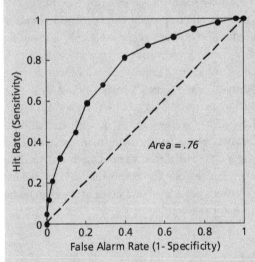

Receiver Operator Characteristic Curve for Violence Risk Assessment Guide (VRAG) for 7-Year Violent Recidivism

Source: Rice and Harris (1995)

Effect Sizes and Meta-Analysis

Most research questions (e.g., Does treatment work? What predicts recidivism?) have been tested in multiple studies, which makes synthesizing the current research a challenging task. For example, by 1990, there were nearly 500 studies evaluating offender treatment (Andrews and Bonta 2006), with some studies concluding that treatment reduced recidivism, others concluding that it increased recidivism, and still others finding no effect. How does one go about interpreting such a large and contradictory body of research?

One way to synthesize the information is meta-analysis, which uses statistics to aggregate the results of individual studies and develop one averaged effect size for

Box 1.1   Continued

all the studies combined. It should be noted that meta-analytic statistics typically do not report an unweighted average (i.e., a straight average from all studies); instead, they give some studies more weight than others. The rationale behind weighted average effect sizes is that more weight can be placed on certain studies, such as those with larger sample sizes.

A note about effect sizes is necessary here. Statistics such as the t test or the F test (ANOVA) tell you whether groups are significantly different from each other, but they do not tell you anything about the magnitude of that difference. Effect sizes, however, provide information about the magnitude of the difference (and they can also be tested for significance). The best effect size to use depends on the type of research question you are asking. Studies involving two dichotomous variables (e.g., assessing the impact of treatment versus no treatment on recidivism) typically use effect sizes such as a phi correlation or an odds ratio. For studies looking at a continuous variable and a dichotomous variable (e.g., risk assessment scores and recidivism), effect sizes are typically reported as the area under the receiver operating characteristic curve (Area Under the Curve [AUC] for Receiver Operating Characteristic [ROC]), a Cohen's d correlation, or the $B1$ coefficient from logistic regression. It is important to be aware of the advantages and disadvantages of these statistics when selecting which effect size to use (for more information, see Hanson 2008; Rice and Harris 2005). For example, correlations are fairly robust when recidivism base rates are roughly 50 percent; they become unreliable, however, for extremely low or high base rates. When using correlations for low base rate research (e.g., sex

offender recidivism), statistical adjustments for correlations are recommended.

Meta-analysis is useful because the aggregated effect size provides a quantitative summary of a large body of research. It also has some other interesting features. Different studies tend to use different statistics to report their results, which makes them difficult to compare directly (e.g., some report ROCs while others might report Cohen's d). In meta-analysis, however, formulae can be used to convert information from one effect size measure into another. This allows you to directly compare individual studies that used different statistics, and to combine studies no matter what statistics they reported.

There are also some limitations to meta-analysis. For example, aggregating data only from published studies is problematic if there is a publication bias (i.e., studies with significant effects are more likely to be published). Seeking out unpublished studies can help provide a more accurate answer to your research question. Another important limitation of meta-analysis is that the conclusions of the meta-analysis are only as strong as the quality of the individual studies that were aggregated. You would not put much faith in a study with poor methodological quality (e.g., a study with threats to its validity or with systematic biases in the results). Likewise, a meta-analysis that aggregates results from 50 poor-quality studies should be interpreted with caution. One way to address this issue is to code study quality (several guidelines exist for this task) and test whether the effect sizes vary based on the quality of the study. For example, in a meta-analysis of sex offender treatment, Hanson, Bourgon, Helmus, and Hodgson (2009) found a trend for smaller effect sizes in better quality studies. Although meta-analysis has certain

Continued >

Box 1.1   Continued

indicates that 80 percent of the time, a randomly selected recidivist will have a higher risk score than a randomly selected non-recidivist. An AUC greater than 0.80 is considered very good. The measure can be directly converted to a Cohen's *d* effect size. (No math required! Just look it up in a table!)

Figure 1.2 uses data from Quinsey et al. (1994) to plot true positives on the Y axis and false positives on the X axis for different scores on a risk scale (in this case, the Violence Risk Assessment Guide—see Chapters 7 and 10) to yield an ROC curve. The area under the curve reflects an index of accuracy. For instance, the area under the diagonal reflects accuracy equal to chance, or 50/50. As the plotted line increases toward the top left corner, the accuracy increases.

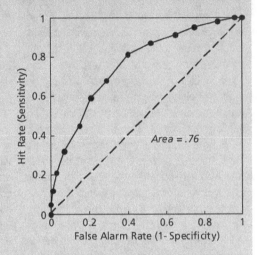

Receiver Operator Characteristic Curve for Violence Risk Assessment Guide (VRAG) for 7-Year Violent Recidivism

Source: Rice and Harris (1995)

First and Second Order Correlates of Criminal Conduct

The work by Andrews and his colleagues ranks variables purported to be related to criminality and identifies the **Central Eight** risk/need factors that are most important in understanding criminal behaviour. Embedded within this group are the **Big Four**, proposed as the major causal variables in the analysis of the criminal behaviour of individuals. Equally significant, a series of meta-analyses have confirmed that certain variables previously considered important correlates of crime in sociological theory have proved to be relatively unimportant. These factors are referred to as **minor risk factors.** Major risk factors are considered first order correlates of crime and are presented in Table 1.1, which illustrates James Bonta's synthesis of this meta-analytic research.

Perhaps the most compelling demonstration of the relative importance of major (first order) and minor (second order) risk factors comes from an ongoing research project and collaboration between the University of New Brunswick and Carleton University (Andrews and Bonta 2006). **Moderate risk factors** are those that are part of the Central Eight but are not major correlates. It should be apparent from Table 1.1 that some risk factors (antisocial history, seriousness of current offence) are **static**, meaning they cannot change, whereas

Table 1.1 An Overview of Meta-Analytic Findings Regarding Correlates of Crime

Type		Factor	Risk
The "Central Eight" Risk Factors	The "Big Four" Risk Factors	History of antisocial behaviour	Early and continuing involvement in a number and variety of antisocial acts in a variety of settings
		Antisocial personality pattern	Adventurous pleasure seeking, weak self-control, restlessly aggressive
		Antisocial cognition	Attitudes, values, beliefs, and rationalizations supportive of crime; cognitive emotional states of anger, resentment, and defiance; criminal versus reformed identity
		Antisocial associates	Close association with criminal others and relative isolation from anticriminal others; immediate social support for crime
		Family and/or marital	Low levels of nurturance and/or caring and poor monitoring and/or supervision
		School and/or work	Low levels of performance and satisfaction in school and/or work
		Leisure and/or recreation	Low levels of involvement and satisfaction in anticriminal leisure pursuits
		Substance abuse	Abuse of alcohol and/or other drugs
Examples of Minor Risk Factors		Personal and/or emotional distress	
		Major mental disorder	
		Physical health issues	
		Fear of official punishment	
		Physical conditioning	
		Low IQ	
		Social class of origin	
		Seriousness of current offence	
		Other factors unrelated to offending	

Source: Bonta (2007)

others (antisocial cognition, substance use) can change and are therefore referred to as **dynamic risk factors.** Approximately 1000 studies were identified from 1970 on, which yielded 372 studies for content analysis and meta-analysis. These 372 studies yielded more than 1770 Pearson correlation coefficients, each of which reflected correlations between purported risk factors and some measure of criminal behaviour. In general, the Central Eight, as reflected in PIC–R, yielded more robust correlations than other factors. Similar findings have also been reported by McGuire (2002). Table 1.2 presents a summary of the findings.

As is clear, the more robust co-variation with criminal behaviour is from variables embedded within a cognitive social learning theory of crime. This means that if the goal is to understand and reduce criminal behaviour, then assessments and treatment must attend to those factors that are most highly correlated with criminal conduct. Specifically, antisocial attitudes and associates are much more important than such factors as social class or mental health symptoms.

Another series of analyses reported by Andrews and Bonta (2006) using eight different datasets from eight independent meta-analyses further reflects the relative importance of the Central Eight and the emergence of the Big Four as the strongest correlates of criminal conduct. These findings are highlighted in Table 1.3.

Two key points are worth highlighting in Table 1.3. First, the eight independent meta-analyses yielded very consistent findings regarding the relative importance of risk factors. Second, the confidence interval for the minor risk factors includes 0.00, which indicates that on average there is no relationship between these predictor variables and criminal behaviour. That is, these minor risk factors cannot explain criminal conduct. In combination, Tables 1.2 and 1.3 provide strong empirical support for a cognitive social learning model of criminal behaviour. These major risk factors are often termed **criminogenic** in that they are empirically related to criminal conduct and, when reduced, lead to reductions in future re-offending. For this reason, **criminogenic needs** typically inform treatment referrals.

Table 1.2 Summary of Correlations Among Risk Factors and Criminal Conduct

Risk Factor	Pearson Correlation	No. of Correlation Coefficients
1. Lower-class origins	0.06	97
2. Personal distress/ psychopathology	0.08	226
3. Personal education/ vocational achievement	0.12	129
4. Parental/family factors	0.18	334
5. Temperament/personality	0.21	621
6. Antisocial attitudes/ associates	0.22	168

Source: Andrews and Bonta (2006)

Table 1.3 Mean Estimates of Correlations Among Risk Factors and Criminal Conduct

Risk Factor	Mean Pearson Correlation	Confidence Interval (95%)
1. Big Four risk factors	0.26	0.19–0.33
2. Moderate risk factors	0.17	0.12–0.21
3. Minor risk factors	0.04	−0.04–0.12

Source: Andrews and Bonta (2006)

Impact of Risk and Need Model of Criminal Conduct

A provincial survey by Hannah-Moffat and Maurutto (2003) for young offender services confirmed that all provinces except Quebec (which declined to participate in the survey given the newly changed Youth Criminal Justice Act) utilize some form of a risk and need assessment modelled after the major risk factors. Most use variants of either the Wisconsin model (Ashford and LeCroy 1988; Baird 1981) or the Level of Service Inventory (Andrews and Bonta 1995). Moreover, adult assessments in **provincial corrections** also reflect the Level of Service Inventory-Revised (LSI-R) or variations. These data are more difficult to ascertain because there is no centralized survey as there was in the case of youth services. The federal correctional system, **Correctional Service of Canada (CSC)**, uses an Offender Intake Assessment (Motiuk 1997) based on the Wisconsin model. This automated assessment was recently refined and renamed as a Dynamic Factor Identification Analysis (Brown and Motiuk 2005). The LSI-R has also been adopted for use internationally, most notably in the United States.

All these assessments are intended to assist in the identification of levels of criminal risk for decision purposes (i.e., security placement, release), specific treatment targets (i.e., criminogenic needs), and treatment planning.

Role of Substance Use

Substance abuse is described as a moderate risk factor, based on a Pearson correlation with criminal conduct (Andrews and Bonta 2006). As well, relative to the targeting of first-order risk factors, meta-analyses show modest effect sizes through intervention (Dowden and Andrews 2000; Lipton, Pearson, Cleland, and Yee 2002). Nonetheless, an inordinate number of offenders report substance abuse as an important precursor to their commission of crimes (Kunic and Grant 2006; McMurran 2003). While numbers vary somewhat according to the sample, for federal offenders, 52.1 percent report regular drug use and 62.7 percent report regular alcohol use (Brochu, Cousineau, Gillet, Cournoyer, Pernanen, and Motiuk 2001). This same research noted that approximately 50 percent of federal offenders report using drugs and/or alcohol prior to or during the commission of their crimes. Kunic and Grant (2006) state that 68 percent of federal offenders have substance abuse problems warranting intervention. Similar findings have been noted by McMurran (2003) in the United Kingdom.

Understanding substance abuse is germane to increasing our understanding of criminal behaviour. The use of alcohol or drugs is related to different types of violent crime, with alcohol being more related to interpersonal conflict (i.e., assaults, homicides) and drugs being related to more acquisitive violence (i.e., robbery) (Kunic and Grant 2006; Pernanen, Cousineau, Brochu, and Sun 2002). McMurran (2003) appropriately cautions that despite the clear link between alcohol and crime, the nature of its influence is unclear. That is, does alcohol cause crime directly through diminished inhibitory control or increased cognitive impairment? If so, then substance abuse is an important treatment target. However, if alcohol is mediated by another factor such as personality or social cues, then such an influence may not be remedied by a program that simply addresses an addiction problem, at least for offenders. Moreover, substance abuse has also been uniquely implicated for sexual offenders, where rapists and child molesters report higher levels of alcohol consumption than non-sexually violent offenders. McMurran and Gilchrist (2008) challenge the field to reconsider the role of substance abuse in domestic violence when determining intervention models. Encouragingly, integrated substance abuse programs are now popular in addressing both the nature of addiction and its impact on offending behaviour (Correctional Service of Canada 1999; McMurran and Priestley 2001).

LINKING THE RESEARCH TO CASE STUDIES

IT MAY BE HELPFUL TO REVIEW THE CASE STUDIES PRESENTED EARLIER TO DETERMINE HOW research regarding determinants of crime actually applies in the real world (see Table 1.4). For instance, in the case of Bill Jones, he is a younger male with prior criminal involvement.

Table 1.4 Case Studies (Bill Jones and Paul Bernardo): Presence of Risk Factors

Risk Factors	Bill	Paul
	Applies	
History of antisocial behaviour	Yes	No
Antisocial personality	Yes	Likely
Antisocial attitudes	Likely	Likely
Antisocial associates	Yes	No (co-accused?)
Family/marital problems	Yes	No
Education/employment problems	Yes	No
Substance abuse	Yes	No
Leisure/recreation problems	Yes	No

Family background is problematic, as are educational achievement and employment history. In addition to these distal risk factors, he presents with self-regulation deficits and substance abuse problems and maintains antisocial peer relationships. These more proximal risk factors have not been satisfactorily ameliorated through treatment. A recent relationship may have the potential to change the contingencies for prosocial behaviour, thus acting as a protective factor.

In the case of Paul Bernardo, less information is provided regarding his background, although it is readily available elsewhere. His co-accused could be viewed as an antisocial associate given the nature of her participation, although her plea bargain asserted she had been a victim of abuse by Bernardo. His family background was dysfunctional in terms of parental modelling and attachment, although he presented as the perfect child. He had a good job as an accountant and there was no evidence of substance abuse, although recreational drug use could have occurred. Independent accounts speculate that Bernardo meets the criteria for a diagnosis of psychopath but court evidence confirming this is unavailable. As well, it is important to note that at the time of his arrest, Bernardo scored low on a variety of standardized sex offender risk scales, further supporting the view that he was atypical of the majority of sex offenders who come in formal contact with the courts.

One noteworthy aspect of this review is that a clearer understanding of typical criminal behaviour comes from a review of primary or first-order risk factors. As will be clear in examining prevalence rates for different types of crimes, the majority of crimes reflect ordinary individuals committing less serious offences. Despite the fascination of the public (and psychology students!) with serial and unusual crimes, most individuals involved in criminal behaviour are ordinary individuals with ordinary problems (i.e., poor self-regulation, substance abuse, lack of employment, or poor choice in friends) whose decision to engage in criminal conduct reflects disinhibition, a failure to consider short- and long-term consequences, support from criminal peers, and attitudes about such behaviour. As support for prosocial behaviour increases, offenders' decisions and behaviours, especially when addressed by intervention, become less criminal.

Crime in Canada Perhaps as a prelude to appreciating public opinion of crime and criminal justice issues in Canada, it will be helpful to review some basic statistics regarding the extent of crime in Canada and trends over time. Some information about sentencing and the differences between provincial and federal corrections will be helpful in situating our understanding of crime in Canada. It is also worth noting that Andrews's original work in the development of a risk and needs assessment instrument involved provincial offenders.

Federal and Provincial Corrections

It should be noted that more data pertaining to **federal corrections** is available than provincial corrections because of the existence of a national electronic dataset. Correctional services are operated by both federal and provincial governments. Offenders who receive sentences of less than two years or who receive community sentences such as fines, community service work, or probation are under ~~provincial jurisdiction~~. Offenders given prison sentences of two years or more are the responsibility of the ~~federal government~~. Young offender services, including pre-trial supervision, community and custody sentences, and extrajudicial sanctions programs, are the responsibility of provincial governments. Offenders serving a sentence of two years or greater are incarcerated in federal prisons. Unlike in the United States, where state and federal prisons have markedly different populations due to sentencing guidelines, in Canada the major difference relates to sentence length. Provincial jails also act as remand centres, so some offenders awaiting trial, who might be subsequently found guilty and sentenced, will eventually be transferred to federal prisons. This means that, typically, a variety of offence categories are represented in both settings but that federal offenders are more likely to have engaged in more violent crime and/or have more serious criminal histories. If federal offenders on supervised release (i.e., parole, statutory release after two-thirds of their sentence is completed) are revoked or commit new crimes and receive sentences of less than two years, they will still return to federal custody. As well, some sex offenders may be given a sentence of less than two years but also be designated a Long-Term Offender, requiring community supervision for up to 10 years. This supervision is completed by federal parole officers following the offender's release from a provincial jail. In some cases (i.e., New Brunswick) there is an exchange of service agreement such that federal corrections manage provincial offenders. In other areas of Canada, an exchange of service agreement exists whereby federal corrections utilizes provincial resources (i.e., halfway house bed space). See Table 1.5 for an overview of Canadian provincial correctional facilities.

Typically, federal prisons are larger facilities with greater numbers of offenders and staff (see Table 1.6 for basic facts), although some provinces such as Ontario have adopted a super-jail model. Both the federal and provincial systems include correctional staff and parole officers. Social workers are more common in provincial facilities and psychologists work in both settings. Licensing is a provincial responsibility, so social workers and psychologists must meet the certification requirements of the province in which they work. This means there is some variation across the country. The CSC is the largest single employer of psychologists in Canada.

CRIME TRENDS

PERHAPS FUELLED BY MEDIA REPORTS AND POLITICAL CALLS TO GET TOUGH ON CRIME, it would be reasonable for Canadians to believe that crime rates, especially for serious gun crimes, are increasing. The data overall are encouraging, however, notwithstanding some specific subgroups for which there is marked concern (i.e., young girls, Aboriginals of all ages). Police-reported crime rates from 1983–2007 are presented in Figure 1.3, showing a general decline since 1991. The highlights include significant reductions (46 percent) since the peak in 1991. Violent crime (defined as homicide, attempted

Table 1.5 Provincial Jails

Alberta: Nine correctional centres, two camps

British Columbia: Six pretrial facilities, three medium correctional centres

Manitoba: Seven adult and two youth correctional centres

New Brunswick: Six correctional centres or detention centres, one youth correctional centre

Newfoundland and Labrador: Three correctional centres, one penitentiary, two lock-ups, two youth facilities

Northwest Territories: Three correctional centres, two youth correctional centres, one wilderness camp

Nova Scotia: Five correctional facilities, one young offender facility

Nunavut: One correctional centre

Ontario: Sixteen correctional centres, seven detention centres, fourteen jails

Prince Edward Island: Two correctional centres, one youth centre

Quebec: Eighteen correctional centres and jails

Saskatchewan: Three multilevel correctional centres, seven community correctional centres and community training residences, one facility for men and women

Yukon: One correctional centre

Source: Provincial corrections websites (2009)

murder, assault, sexual offences, abduction, and robbery) has gradually decreased from a peak in 1992, with a decrease of 2.5 percent in 2007. It is important to note that these figures reflect crimes reported to the police; since not all crimes are reported, the data underestimate actual crime.

Table 1.6 Basic Facts: Correctional Service of Canada

- Responsible for approximately 13 200 incarcerated offenders and 8000 offenders in the community
- 58 institutions (8 maximum, 12 multilevel, 18 medium, 20 minimum security), 16 community correctional centres, 71 parole offices across five regions
- 15 425 staff (15 percent in headquarters, 76.8 percent at institutions, 8.1 percent in the community)
- 40 percent of staff are correctional officers, 15 percent are parole officers or program staff
- 8100 volunteers active in institutions and in the community
- Annual budget of $1.87 billion

Source: Correctional Service of Canada (2008 and 2009)

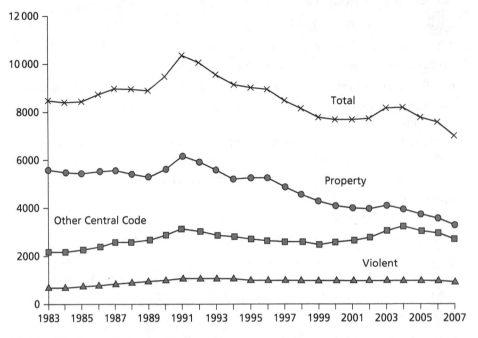

Rate per 100 000 Population

Figure 1.3 Police-Reported Crime Rates

Source: Public Safety Canada (2008)

A similar trend exists for youth-related crime (12 to 17 years) and adult crime (Corrections and Conditional Release Statistical Overview 2008). Further, for both youth and adults, violent crime is less prevalent than property crimes. Administration of justice charges (e.g., failure to appear, breach of probation), impaired driving, and weapons charges are more common for adults. Break and enter, robbery, and sexual assault are more prevalent among youth. It would appear that age has some influence on types of crime committed. Table 1.7 presents a summary of crime statistics for youth and adults.

The pattern of rates of crime between youth and adults in 2007 was consistent with previous years. Overall, youth account for more criminal charges (2923 per 100 000 population) than adults (1792 per 100 000). Among youth, there were more charges for males (4432) than females (1430) for all types of crime (violent, property, or other criminal code).

When combining violent offences, including major assaults, 12 percent of all adult offences are violent. This figure increases to 20 percent when common assault is included and to 23 percent when violence includes possession of weapons charges.

Crime Severity Index

The Crime Severity Index was recently developed for measuring police-reported crime in Canada (Statistics Canada 2009). It tracks changes in the severity of police-reported

Table 1.7 Percentage of Types of Crime Committed by Youth and Adults, 2006–07

Type of Crime	Youth (%)	Adults (%)
Administration of justice	8.8	24.0
Impaired driving	1.9	8.9
Break and enter	9.0	2.7
Theft	13.6	7.5
Fraud	1.4	5.9
Common assault	10.1	7.9
Drugs (possession and trafficking)	6.1	5.8
Robbery	3.9	0.9
Weapons	0	3.4
Sexual assault	2.1	0.8
Homicide and related	0.1	0.04

Source: Public Safety Canada (2008)

crime from year to year by taking into account not only the change in volume of a particular crime (i.e., police-reported crime), but also the relative seriousness of that crime in comparison to others. The traditional "crime rate" provides information on the number of police-reported incidents that occur in a given population. It measures the volume of crime brought to the attention of police. The rate is simply a count of all criminal incidents reported to and by police, divided by the population of interest. Each criminal incident, regardless of the type or seriousness of the offence, counts the same in the rate. For example, one homicide counts the same as one act of mischief.

The Crime Severity Index helps answer such questions as whether the crime coming to the attention of police is more or less serious than before and whether police-reported crime in a given city or province is more or less serious than in Canada overall. The principle behind the Crime Severity Index is to have more serious crimes carry a higher weight than less serious crimes. As a result, changes in more serious offences would have a greater impact on the Index than on the traditional crime rate, allowing the Index to better reflect these changes. It would also minimize the impact of differences in the way the public and police in various jurisdictions report high-volume, less-serious crimes, thereby improving comparisons among provinces and municipalities.

The weights are derived from actual sentences handed down by courts in all provinces and territories. More serious crimes are assigned higher weights; less serious offences are given lower weights. The specific weight for any given type of offence consists of two parts. The first component is the incarceration rate for that offence type. This is the proportion of people convicted of the offence who are sentenced to time in prison.

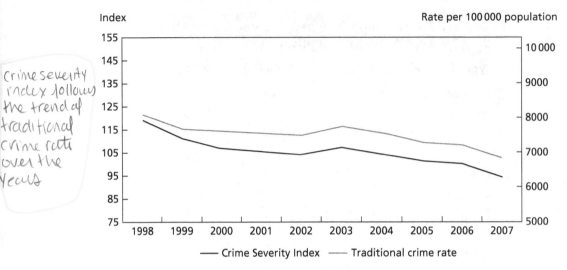

Handwritten note in left margin: Crime severity index follows the trend of traditional crime rate over the years

Note: The crime rate does not include traffic offences, drugs, or other federal statutes.

Figure 1.4 Comparison of the Crime Severity Index and the Traditional Crime Rate, 1998–2007

Source: Statistics Canada (2009)

The second component is the average (mean) length of the prison sentence given, in days, for the specific type of offence. The weights will be updated every five years to ensure that they reflect any changes in sentencing patterns or new legislation. It is not necessary to update them every year, as trends in court data do not tend to change substantially from year to year. Figure 1.4 presents the Crime Severity Index and the traditional crime rate for comparison.

It appears the Index may be a useful tool for analyzing crime trends in Canada. It addresses not only the amount of crime coming to the attention of police, but also the severity of this crime. In addition, it shows whether crime in general is relatively more or less serious than in previous years and helps in determining if reported crime is more or less serious in one jurisdiction than another.

Crime Victimization

Incident-based data (Canadian Centre for Justice Statistics 2007; as cited in Corrections and Conditional Release Statistical Overview 2008) reveal marked variation in the age of crime victims. More than half (54.3 percent) of all victims of violent crime reported in 2007 were under the age of 30, where 37.5 percent of the Canadian population is under the age of 30. Canadians aged 65 and older, who account for 13.5 percent of the general population, represented 1.9 percent of victims. Females aged 20–44 were more likely than males of that age to be victims of a violent crime. Male victims of violent crime tended to be younger. The groups with the highest percentage of recipients of violent crime were ages 15–19 (16.6 percent), ages 20–24 (14.8 percent), and ages 25–29 (11.5 percent). According to the General Social Survey (Statistics Canada 1999; 2004), rates of being a victim of property crime increased from 75 per 1000 population to 93 per 1000 population. Rates for other crimes remained relatively constant during this time (sexual assault: 21 per 1000; robbery: 11 per 1000; assault: 75 per 1000). Combining these rates yields an overall rate of 20 percent.

As noted earlier, police-reported crime does not necessarily reflect the extent of criminal conduct because some crime goes unreported. Victimization surveys present an additional understanding of crime and typically yield higher rates. According to a 2004 survey, 17 percent of Canadians aged 16 and over had been victims of at least one crime measured by the International Criminal Victimization Survey during the previous year (Statistics Canada 2005). This rate was similar to the overall international victimization rate (16 percent). Across all participating countries, slightly more than half the population (53 percent) reported a victimization incident to the police, whereas 48 percent Canadians reported being a victim of one of five offence types: theft from a car, theft of a bicycle, burglary, attempted burglary, or theft of personal property. Interestingly, a recent Canadian survey (Latimer and Desjardins 2007) provides additional insight into crime victimization and its potential impact on Canadians' perceptions of the criminal justice system, specifically their confidence in its various components (police, courts, corrections, and parole). This study utilized a household telephone survey of 4502 Canadians across all 10 provinces (with only a 9 percent response rate, which is consistent with industry norms). The respondents were asked if within the last 10 years they had been an accused, a witness, a juror, a victim, or had worked within the justice system in some capacity. The results are presented in Table 1.8.

While extrapolation of this small sample to the larger Canadian population should be performed with caution because of the small sample size, it is important to note that almost 30 percent of participants reported being a victim of crime. Within this group, 76.2 percent reported a property offence (e.g., break and enter, theft), while 23.8 percent indicated that the offence was violent in nature (e.g., assault). Nonetheless, police-reported violent crime in 2007 in Canada was 930 per 100 000 population (Corrections and Conditional Release Statistical Overview 2008), or approximately 294 000 victimizations annually, roughly

Table 1.8 Involvement in the Criminal Justice System

Involvement	N (%)
Being a victim of a crime	1069 (28.8%)
Being a witness to a crime	435 (9.7%)
Working in the justice system	214 (4.8%)
Being a juror	150 (3.3%)
Being charged with a crime	141 (33.1%)

Source: Department of Justice Canada (2007)

equivalent to the sixteenth-largest city in Canada. Estimates for victimization-related costs in Canada were suggested to be an additional $47 billion in 2003 (National Victims of Crime 2007). These costs must be added to the actual costs of the operation of the criminal justice system to fully appreciate the impact of crime on Canadians. Accordingly, in 2003, crime in Canada cost an estimated $60 billion, $13 billion of which was related to criminal justice system expenditures such as police, courts, and correctional services. This cost is slightly less than half of the direct and indirect costs for health care, which was estimated to be $123 billion in 2003 (Canadian Institute for Health Information 2004).

Public Perceptions of the Criminal Justice System

Latimer and Desjardins's (2007) study reveals interesting insight into Canadians' perceptions of the criminal justice system. For instance, contrary to the evidence, 57.8 percent of Canadians believe that the overall crime rate has gone up (74.4 percent for property crime, 62.7 percent for violent crime). Surprisingly, only 6.5 percent indicated that they believed their neighbourhoods were less safe, despite their view that crime is increasing. Public confidence in the criminal justice system is lower than that for the education, health care, and welfare systems. A quarter of respondents indicated a low level of confidence in the criminal justice system and a third rated their confidence in the youth criminal justice system as low. Figure 1.5 provides a more specific breakdown for different components of the criminal justice system. Parole appears to generate the least confidence in the Canadians who responded to this survey.

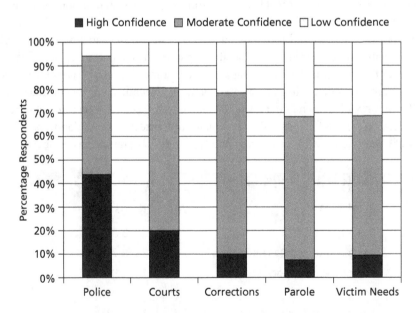

Figure 1.5 Public Perceptions of the Criminal Justice System

Source: Department of Justice Canada (2007)

A further examination of confidence in specific components of the criminal justice system suggests the least confidence in police preventing crime, the courts imposing appropriate sentences, corrections rehabilitating offenders, and parole supervising offenders in the community. Nonetheless, greater confidence was reported in terms of police solving crimes, the courts determining guilt, and corrections preventing escapes. This report also identified characteristics that lead Canadians to be more optimistic about the criminal justice system. Those individuals who value government information, support less punitive sentencing practices, are treatment-oriented, have a university degree, use the Internet as a source of information, and support the government's Tackling Crime agenda (i.e., tougher penalties and crime prevention) are more confident in their views of the criminal justice system. For more specific information regarding Canadians' perceptions of sentencing and other aspects of the criminal justice system, review Latimer and Desjardins's (2007) full report. See also Roberts, Crutcher, and Verbrugge (2007), whose recent research demonstrates that 74 percent of Canadians believe that sentencing is too lenient, although there was support for restorative sentence objectives promoting a sense of responsibility in the offender (84 percent) and securing reparation for the crime victim (66 percent).

Variation in Crime by Source

As alluded to earlier, crime rates vary according to the definition of crime and the source of the information. Police-reported crime is lower than victimization rates. Moreover, if incarceration rates are used as an index of the seriousness of crime in Canada, then crime is less problematic. One method of presenting the attrition in crime is to review the number of crimes reported, the number of convictions, the number of provincial sentences, and the number of federal sentences (the most lengthy sentences, presumably reserved for the more serious offences). Figure 1.6 presents what has been referred to as a crime funnel. Of the 2.7 million crimes reported to the police in 2007, only 5007 resulted in warrants of committal for a federal sentence (2 percent). Some cases were still pending before the courts, but using similar data from the year 2005–06, the total percentages of police-reported offences were 1.7 percent for federal sentences and 2.8 percent for provincial custodial sentences.

Length of Sentences

Over half (54.6 percent) of all custodial sentences imposed by adult courts are less than one month in length. Prison sentences for men tend to be longer than for women. Over two-thirds (69.9 percent) of women and just over half of men (52.9 percent) who are incarcerated upon conviction receive a sentence of one month or less, and 92.1 percent of women and 85.1 percent of men receive a sentence of six months or less. Of all convictions that result in custody, only 4.2 percent result in federal jurisdiction (i.e., a sentence of two or more years).

These figures are very important in terms of the provision of assessment and treatment services to offenders. The shorter the sentence received by the offender, the less time available for comprehensive assessments and participation in prison-based programming prior

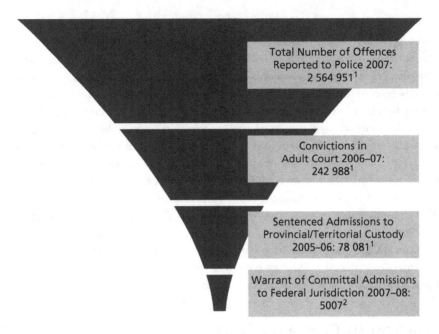

Note: [1]Uniform Crime Reporting Survey, Adult Criminal Court Survey and Adult
Corrections Survey, Canadian Centre for Justice Statistics, Statistics Canada.
[2]Correctional Service of Canada

Figure 1.6 Crime Funnel of Criminal Outcomes

Source: Public Safety Canada (2008)

to their return to the community. The proportion that receives sentences of greater than
12 months, a reasonable time to arrange and complete programming, is relatively small
(men: one to two years (3.6 percent), two years or greater (4.5 percent); women: one to
two years (1.9 percent), two years or greater (2.0 percent)). As we will see later, community-based programming is effective in reducing future re-offending, but some offenders
clearly require prison-based programming if the correctional agencies are to address public
safety concerns. This is not a call for increased sentence lengths but rather recognition that
certain correctional operational realities are linked to sentencing.

Variations Across Provinces

One important consideration in understanding the impact of crime is to consider variations across Canada. Figure 1.7 presents the crime rate by province compared against the
national average. There is a general trend toward increased crime rates the farther west
and north one moves. Most notable is that the Northwest Territories has eight times the
national average crime rate. Underscoring these data is the over-representation of
Aboriginals in the Canadian criminal justice system (see Chapter 12).

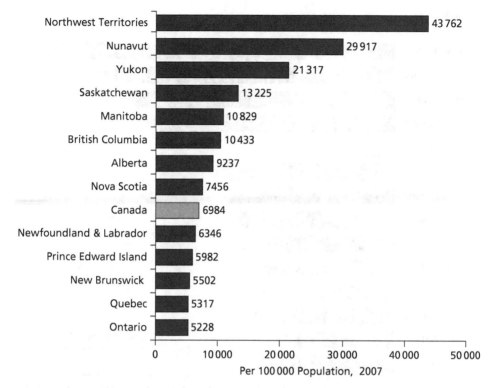

Northwest Territories	43 762
Nunavut	29 917
Yukon	21 317
Saskatchewan	13 225
Manitoba	10 829
British Columbia	10 433
Alberta	9237
Nova Scotia	7456
Canada	6984
Newfoundland & Labrador	6346
Prince Edward Island	5982
New Brunswick	5502
Quebec	5317
Ontario	5228

Per 100 000 Population, 2007

Figure 1.7 Crime Rates by Province

Source: Public Safety Canada (2008)

International Context

The next issue to consider is how Canada compares to other countries regarding crime and, in particular, rates of incarceration. Canada's incarceration is 108 per 100 000 population (about 34 000 people relative to the Canadian population). There has been a slight downward trend in recent years, but Canada's relative ranking remains unchanged. Compared to the United States, our incarceration rate is modest, but clearly there are lessons to be learned from other countries that appear less inclined to incarcerate offenders when they are convicted for criminal offences. Figure 1.8 presents a summary of international incarceration rates.

Impact of Criminal Conduct on Canadians

This chapter highlighted three aspects of crime that specifically impact Canadians: prevalence, cost, and likelihood of being a victim of crime. These influence the public's opinion of and confidence in the effectiveness of the criminal justice system.

In Canada there are 115 provincial correctional facilities and 58 federal facilities. There are approximately 2.6 million reported crimes annually, the greatest proportion of

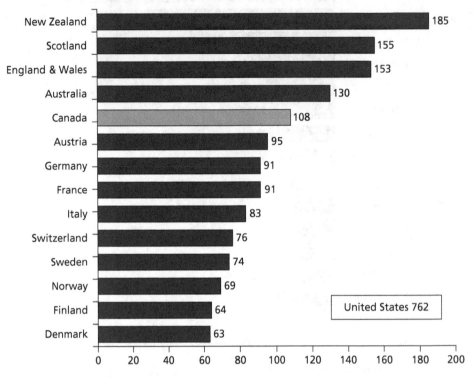

Number of Inmates per 100 000 Population

New Zealand	185
Scotland	155
England & Wales	153
Australia	130
Canada	108
Austria	95
Germany	91
France	91
Italy	83
Switzerland	76
Sweden	74
Norway	69
Finland	64
Denmark	63

United States 762

Figure 1.8 International Incarceration Rates

Source: International Centre for Prison Studies (2008)

which are property crimes. The General Social Survey (Statistics Canada 2004) suggests that 20 percent of Canadians report being a victim of crime in a given year. Other credible estimates range from 28.8 percent (Latimer and Desjardins 2007) to 48 percent (Statistics Canada 2005) when the timeframe is extended beyond one year. Suppose we accept the lowest estimate of 20 percent and further assert that for each victim of a crime, there is a perpetrator, and that both the victim and perpetrator have someone in their life who is negatively affected by the incident. For the victim, this could relate to loss of property, trauma, or fear of future victimization; for the perpetrator, this could relate to a partner or child who is financially or socially disadvantaged by the perpetrator being fined, put on probation, or sentenced to jail time. We can readily appreciate that the scope of negative influence of crime is significant, perhaps affecting close to 80 percent of Canadians. Recall that the financial implication of crime victimization was estimated to be $47 billion. Thus, crime is a major social concern that might be best considered a public policy concern rather than simply a criminal justice issue.

Below is a list of the top 10 issues and people to consider when thinking about crime and criminal justice research in Canada.

Advances to Come, Debates, Ethical Conundrums, and People to Watch

1 Despite compelling evidence regarding researchers' understanding of criminal risk factors, public confidence in corrections is low. Encouragingly, correctional practice is informed by evidence such as the Central Eight.

2 While group-based information such as socioeconomic status is of some interest, only individual difference variables can explain criminal behaviour within groups and highlight factors to target in order to reduce potential for future re-offending.

3 The media focuses on sensational cases, yet this tells us little about criminal behaviour. Academics and corrections researchers need to improve their social marketing.

4 Although it may not be suitable for all situations, alternative approaches to punishment such as restorative justice are gaining popularity, but further research is required.

5 Criminal justice and corrections affects many Canadians (perpetrators, victims, family members), suggesting it is a major public policy concern that has significant fiscal costs. Even minor improvements could yield major benefits to Canadians.

6 Contrary to public perception, crime rates are declining, and violent crime, which accounts for about 12 to 20 percent of all adult convictions, is lower than in many other countries.

7 The crime funnel reveals that the rate of police-reported crime is markedly higher than either the rates of conviction or incarceration. What does this tell us about the federal offender population?

8 The incarceration rate generally increases as one moves from east to west in Canada. What are potential explanations for this?

9 You recently graduated from university and are now working in a correctional agency. You are asked to complete an assessment that fails to consider criminogenic needs or risk. What do you do?

10 People to watch: Serge Brochu, Anthony Doob, Jeff Latimer, Julian Roberts, Irvin Waller.

SUMMARY

As noted by this excerpt from the Speech from the Throne, Canadians are very concerned regarding crime:

> Canadians feel less safe today and rightly worry about the security of their neighbourhoods and the country. There is no greater responsibility for a government than to protect this right to safety and security. (Speech from the Throne, October 16, 2007)

The goal of this introductory chapter was to highlight some key reasons why crime is of concern to Canadians and to provide an empirical setting (Central Eight major risk factors) to understanding criminal conduct upon which the rest of the chapters are based. The book focuses on Canadian data and Canadian contributions. Key studies covered in this chapter illustrate the role of media, Canadians' perceptions of components of the criminal justice system, and rates and types of crimes for youth and adults. Crime and incarceration in Canada have been situated in an international context, showing that relative to the United States we are in fairly good shape, although less so relative to Western Europe. With respect to crime in Canada, there are differences in terms of age and gender—topics that are addressed in Chapters 5 and 11, respectively.

Restricting the text to correctional psychology is intended to inform an explanation and understanding of offending (i.e., criminal) behaviour in a manner that will be of interest and assistance to staff involved in community corrections and prisons, including parole and probation staff and psychologists. The purpose is to highlight key literature regarding offenders such that an **evidence-based practice** is described and supported, allowing its application to yield improved understanding and correctional outcomes (i.e., reduced re-offending). While not a clinical "how to" book, this text is clearly intended to underscore the contribution that correctional psychology can make in addressing concerns about criminal behaviour in Canada.

The balance of the book reviews theory about criminal behaviour, specific chapters on types of offenders, a discussion of how theory informs practice, and some descriptions about different career paths in the field of corrections practice and research. Each chapter is written with a focus on Canadian research, underscoring significant contributions made by Canadian researchers and why Canadian corrections remain the envy of most countries in the world.

Discussion Questions

1. Why does the public have such low confidence in corrections? How could this be improved?
2. How does Canada fare relative to other countries in terms of rates of incarceration? Is this a satisfactory situation?
3. Why should crime be considered a major public policy concern in Canada? What is the impact of crime on Canadians?
4. What role should academics play in informing the Canadian public regarding crime trends?
5. How could the media help Canadians better understand the true picture of crime?

Additional Reading

Andrews, D. A. and Bonta, J. 2006. *The psychology of criminal conduct.* 4th ed. Cincinnati, OH: Anderson.

McGuire, J. 2004. *Understanding psychology and crime: Perspectives on theory and action.* New York: McGraw Hill.

Relevant Websites

The CSC site has research publications as well as program descriptions, policy statements, and links to other criminal justice partners.
www.csc-scc.gc.ca/text/index-eng.shtml

Previously the Solicitor General of Canada site, the Public Safety of Canada website has corrections research publications that highlight initiatives among provincial and territorial criminal justice partners.
www.publicsafety.gc.ca/index-en.asp

The Research Department of the Department of Justice has a number of interesting studies regarding youth and adult crime, as well as public perceptions of the criminal justice system in Canada.
www.justice.gc.ca/eng/index.html

The National Institute of Corrections is part of the U.S. Bureau of Prisons (U.S. federal prison system) and has a wealth of information about offender assessment and programming initiatives in the United States.
www.nicic.org

Chapter 2
Theories of Crime: Biological and Evolutionary Explanations

Bob was recently released from prison after serving a five-year sentence. He has a long history of getting into fights, committing break and enters for "thrill," and drinking to excess. His psychological report indicates that he was abused as a child, is impulsive, and has an anger management problem. Bob participated in a research study while in prison that revealed his MAOA gene was of the "low activity" variety. Immediately upon release, he went to a bar and met a woman. As the evening progressed, Bob became increasingly intoxicated and noticed his new acquaintance was being hit on by another male patron. He informed the man (in a somewhat threatening manner) that his "friend" was taken and that he should look elsewhere. As Bob walked away, the man yelled, "You can have the slut." Bob stopped for a second and resisted the burning urge to punch the man in the face. However, the man persisted and said, "What's the matter, too cowardly to defend your woman?" A crowd had begun to gather. Bob responded immediately and threw the first punch. Within 24 hours, he was back in prison for breaching the conditions of his release and for incurring a new criminal assault charge.

Learning Objectives

1 Describe the range of biological explanations of crime, which include genetics, neurochemistry, hormones, psychophysiology, and more.

2 Explain the basic principles of evolutionary psychology and demonstrate how these principles are used to understand crime in general as well as more specific forms of crime and specific types of criminal offenders.

3 Demonstrate that biological and evolutionary theories of crime are as much about the environment as they are about biology and evolution.

4 Demonstrate that biological and evolutionary explanations are not incompatible with traditional theories of crime (e.g., social learning theory, presented in Chapter 3), but rather are complementary.

INTRODUCTION

HOW WE EXPLAIN BOB'S BEHAVIOUR DEPENDS ON OUR PERSPECTIVE. WE COULD FOCUS ON factors in the immediate situation, such as his alcohol-induced disinhibition or his childhood, where he learned that violence is an effective conflict resolution strategy. These sorts of accounts are addressed in Chapter 3. Alternately, we could focus on Bob's innate nature (his genes), or take an entirely different perspective by asking if his behaviour is part of an adaptation that has been selected over the human's evolutionary history. For example, did defending honour and reputation somehow increase the reproductive success of our ancestors, perhaps by deterring or eliminating competition or by enhancing attractiveness as a worthy mate?

This chapter focuses on biological and evolutionary explanations for antisocial behaviour, crime, and related phenomena. Biological explanations are varied, ranging from genetics as exemplified by twin and adoption studies to brain neurochemistry and the importance of diet. Basic evolutionary psychology principles are described, followed by an illustration of how these principles are used to understand certain types of offenders, such as psychopaths, and specific types of crimes, such as homicide. Paradoxically, it will become evident that this chapter is as much about the environment as it is about biology and evolution. Not only will it become apparent how the environment—our hunter-and-gatherer **ancestral environment**, that is—profoundly shaped the evolution of the human species, but that our environment continues to influence our biology and our biology is constantly influenced by our ever-changing surroundings.

What Makes a Strong Theory?

Numerous textbooks and experts have defined the meaning of theory, particularly strong theory. Thus, our definition represents an amalgamation of perspectives (see Andrews and Bonta 2006; Blanchette and Brown 2006; Pozzulo, Bennell, and Forth 2009; Rappaport 1987). In sum, a theory is simply an explanation of a particular phenomenon, in our case antisocial behaviour. Importantly, a strong theory (1) is parsimonious; (2) clearly identifies the **causal mechanisms** and corresponding **mediators** and **moderators** underlying the phenomenon of interest (3) is testable and hence falsifiable via hypotheses and predictions; (4) is based on empirical data and is modified in response to new data; (5) possesses interdisciplinary compatibility; and (6) respects gender, ethnicity, and culture. Throughout this chapter, it may be helpful to ask, "Does this perspective provide a good theory of crime?" For example, are certain explanations stronger in the sense that the corresponding evidence is stronger—e.g., causal evidence is presented versus correlational evidence?

[handwritten margin note: makes the least # of new assumptions]

BACKGROUND
Historical Context

Franz Gall (1758–1828) was the founding father of phrenology—a theoretical perspective positing that there is a relationship between the shape and size of a person's head

Cesare Lombroso "father of criminology" (1835–1909)

and his/her personality, mental ability, and behaviours. Johann Spurzheim, one of Gall's students, applied the principles of phrenology to explain why 30 women had killed their children. Spurzheim concluded that the women suffered from an underdeveloped part of the brain responsible for loving children. Like most phrenology-oriented researchers at the time, Spurzheim failed to include a comparison group—women who had not killed their children (Niehoff 1999). Although the "science" of phrenology eventually died out, an Italian physician, Cesare Lombroso (1835–1909), took Gall's work one step further and began comparing criminals—both men and women as well as prostitutes—to "normal" segments of the population. Lombroso argued that criminals possess distinctive physical features such as sloping foreheads and twisted lips often not observed in his "normal" subjects. He referred to these features as atavisms, and suggested that criminals were evolutionary throwbacks who had more in common with Neanderthals than modern-day man (Lombroso and Ferrero 2004). Although his theories eventually lost their gusto, Lombroso remains the "father of criminology." Recent and more accurate translations of his works have cast Lombroso's theories and scientific methods in a more positive light than previous accounts (e.g., Lombroso and Ferrero 2004).

Interestingly, Charles Darwin published *On the Origins of Species* in 1859, almost 17 years before Lombroso published the first volume of *The Criminal Man.* Darwin posited that humans had evolved from ancestral species via the mechanisms of **natural selection**. Unfortunately, others began to misuse his work, most notably Darwin's own cousin, Francis Galton. Galton founded **eugenics**—the theory that was ultimately responsible not only for the forced sterilization (or worse) of thousands of individuals deemed "unfit" to reproduce in the United States during the early part of the twentieth century, but also for the atrocities that occurred under Hilter's regime—forced abortion, sterilization, and, ultimately, death camps (Niehoff 1999).

Thus it is not surprising that a number of social scientists, particularly criminologists working from a sociological perspective, have been dismissive and in some instances scornful of biological and/or evolutionary approaches. However, as Anderson (2007) cleverly demonstrates, the tides are changing. The study of biology and evolution has advanced considerably since Darwin and Lombroso. Moreover, it is becoming increasingly clear that biology is not destiny.

RESEARCHING BIOLOGICAL EXPLANATIONS OF CRIME

A NUMBER OF RESEARCHERS WORKING FROM VERY DIFFERENT PERSPECTIVES HAVE STUDIED biological explanations of crime using diverse and complex research methods. Behavioural genetics researchers might employ twin methodology to ask whether identical twins are more likely to commit crime than non-identical twins. Molecular biologists might compare the genetic makeup of a group of "criminals" to one of "non-criminals" to look for distinct genetic differences between the two. Neurochemical approaches might examine how genes actually express themselves in terms of the brain's **neurotransmitter** systems. Still other researchers may rely on brain-imaging techniques such as computer tomography (CT) to assess whether the functions of the brain are somehow impaired in antisocial individuals.

Defining *crime* is also a complex task. While some researchers have examined the link between biology and crime by comparing "normal" individuals to individuals who have been officially diagnosed with **antisocial personality disorder (ASPD), conduct disorder (CD),** or **psychopathy,** others have used measures of **aggression** or composite indices of **antisocial behaviour** obtained via self-report or, in the case of children, from parents or teachers. Researchers often define crime using current legal definitions and examine whether biological factors correlate or predict official criminal offending in the form of arrests or convictions. Targets of study are also varied, with some researchers focusing on males and others studying females. Researchers sometimes study children, adolescents, adults, or specific groups of offenders such as violent or sexual offenders. Thus the research methods and participant pools are vast and complex.

Genetics and Crime—Twins, Adoption, and Molecular Genetics

Twin Studies To examine the role that genetics plays in criminal conduct, it is necessary to employ methodologies that allow researchers to disentangle genetic and environmental influences. Consider the following example. A researcher asks the fathers and eldest sons from 500 nuclear families to complete self-report criminal behaviour questionnaires. The researcher then correlates the answers between fathers and sons and finds that the average correlation is .30. The question remains: Is the observed correlation due to fathers passing on "criminal genes," or is it due to fathers passing on criminal attitudes and criminal life skills through years of living together? Unfortunately, this research design does not permit a clear answer. However, the field of **behavioural genetics,** which relies heavily on the study of twins and adoptions, can help separate genetic from environmental influences, at least to some degree.

Every human being shares about 99 percent of his or her DNA sequence with the rest of the human species. The percentage of DNA that humans collectively share is fixed (not free to vary), accounting for our basic similarities (e.g., we all have two arms, two legs, one heart, one brain, two eyes, and so forth) (Plomin, DeFries, McClearn, and McGuffin 2001). Behavioural genetics focuses on the remaining 1 percent of the variance that is free to vary.

Monozygotic (MZ) or identical twins are genetically identical. They share 100 percent of their genes. Specifically, the 1 percent of DNA that is free to vary from human to human is 100 percent identical for MZ twins. In contrast, dizygotic (DZ) or fraternal twins are no more alike than non-twin siblings, sharing on average only 50 percent of that 1 percent that is free to vary. Keeping this in mind, let's discuss the research.

The earliest forms of twin studies worked as follows. A researcher would identify a sample of MZ and DZ twins, both raised by their respective biological families, and obtain some estimate of criminal behaviour via self-report or perhaps official records. Next, the researcher would record whether each twin was "criminal" or "non-criminal," indicating the number of times both members of each twin pair were classified as "criminal." This frequency would then be converted into a concordance rate that represented the percentage of both twins classified as "criminal." Concordance rates would be calculated separately for MZ and DZ twins and then compared. A concordance rate of 30 percent for the DZ twins would mean that if one of the DZ twins was "'criminal," then there was a 30 percent chance that the other DZ twin was also criminal. Similarly, a concordance rate of 70 percent for the MZ twins would mean that if one of the MZ twins was "criminal," there was 70 percent chance that the other MZ twin was also criminal. Evidence for a genetic contribution to crime is inferred if concordance rates are higher among MZ than DZ twins.

Concordance rates are typically converted into a heritability coefficient—a descriptive statistic that represents the proportion of **phenotypic** variance in a given behaviour (e.g., criminal) in a sample and/or population that can be attributed to genetic variation among individuals (Polmin et al. 2001). Recently, however, more complex statistical approaches such as biometric modelling have been used to estimate heritability coefficients (DeFries and Fulker 1985; Rhee and Waldman 2002). Some of these methods—particularly statistical modelling—permit the estimation of two types of environmental factors: (1) shared environmental factors (i.e., aspects of the environment shared by all family members, such as living in poverty); and (2) non-shared environmental factors (i.e., aspects of the environment not shared by all family members, such as exposure to different peer groups or differential treatment by parents) (Quinsey et al. 2004). Thus, contrary to popular belief, genetic studies are just as much about genes as they are about environment.

A common criticism levied against this type of twin study is that it may overestimate (or in some cases underestimate) the genetic contribution for several reasons. First, parents are arguably more likely to provide similar environments for MZ twins (the same toys, clothes, and learning opportunities) than their DZ counterparts (Anderson 2007; Raine 1993), thus artificially inflating the genetic contribution. However, some twin studies have remedied this problem by taking advantage of "natural experiments" whereby MZ twins have been separated at birth and reared independently (e.g., Grove et al. 1990). Second, heritability estimates for MZ twins may be confounded by prenatal factors that by definition aren't necessarily genetic. For example, MZ twins usually share one placenta and DZ twins usually have two separate placentas, thereby introducing a potential biological difference that is not necessarily genetic. Earlier twin studies were also criticized for using small sample sizes and for being subject to political influence (e.g., two studies were conducted in Nazi Germany in 1936) (Anderson 2007). Fortunately, adoption studies have been able to address some of these criticisms.

Adoption Studies Adoption research has taken one of two forms: 1) parent–offspring adoption studies; and 2) sibling–offspring adoption studies. In the parent–offspring paradigm, concordance rates (or correlations) between adoptive parents and adoptees' **antisocial behaviour** are compared to concordance rates (or correlations) between biological parents and adoptees. If the concordance rates/correlations are higher for the biological parents and the adopted offspring than the adoptive parents and the adopted offspring, genetic contributions to antisocial behaviour are inferred (Rhee and Waldman 2002). A related variation of this design is the cross-fostering paradigm, whereby adopted children have biological parents who were criminal or non-criminal or adoptive parents who were criminal or non-criminal (e.g., Mednick, Gabrielle, and Hutchings 1984). In the sibling–offspring paradigm, concordance rates between adoptive siblings are compared with concordance rates between biological siblings.

Mednick et al. (1984) performed a particularly strong adoption study of 14 427 non-familial adoptions in Demark between 1924 and 1947. The main results were as follows: if both the biological and adoptive parents had no criminal record, then only 13.5 percent of adopted sons had criminal records; if the adopted parent had a criminal record and the biological parent did not, this percentage increased marginally to 14.7 percent. In contrast, 20 percent of adopted sons had a criminal record if the biological but not the adopted parent also had a criminal record, but the highest level of criminality (24.5 percent) was observed if *both* sets of parents—biological and adoptive—had criminal records. Not only did the study demonstrate that genes play a role in explaining crime, it also demonstrated the importance of environmental effects.

Adoption studies are not without limitations, which include: 1) generalizability problems given that adoptees have higher rates of antisocial behaviour relative to the rest of the population; and 2) that the environments of adopted offspring tend to be more advantageous relative to the general population, thereby potentially reducing shared environmental effects due to **restricted range** (Rhee and Waldman 2002).

Since 1929, over 100 twin and adoption studies have been conducted worldwide (Moffitt 2005). Rhee and Waldman (2002) recently completed the most comprehensive meta-analytic review of these studies by aggregating the results of 10 independent adoption samples and 42 independent twin samples. In sum, across all studies (involving a staggering 55 525 pairs of participants!), the variance in antisocial behaviour could be partitioned as follows: heritability, .41; shared environment, .16; and non-shared environment, .43. Notably, the removal of potential outliers (e.g., eight studies involving psychopathy) did not alter the findings. Rhee and Waldman (2002) also examined a number of potential moderators hypothesized to impact the size of the heritability coefficient. Moderators examined included: (1) zygosity determination (self-report vs. blood typing, or both); (2) assessment method (e.g., parental ratings of antisocial behaviour vs. teacher- and self-ratings vs. official criminal records); (3) operational definition of antisocial behaviour (e.g., psychiatric diagnoses of conduct disorder and antisocial personality disorder vs. legal definitions, official criminal convictions vs. overt aggressive behaviour—e.g., gets into fights, uses a weapon frequently); (4) sex of the participants; and (5) age of the participants. The results of the moderator analysis were complex and at times inconclusive. Some of the highlights include the observation that twin studies garnered higher heritability estimates than adoption studies (.45 versus .32) and that genetic effects were slightly higher for females than males (.41 versus .38). This mild gender difference disappeared once the analysis was restricted to more rigorous studies that included samples of male and female twin pairs in the same study (.43 for males, .41 for females). Also of interest is the observation that the genetic proportion of variance increased with age, with genes exerting more influence during adulthood than childhood.

Thus, genetics and the environment both contribute to variance in antisocial behaviour. It is important to highlight that research increasingly shows that the gene–crime link is most likely not a direct conduit but rather a function of the mediational effects of inherited characteristics that *predispose* an individual to antisocial behaviour (e.g., lower intelligence, impulsivity, Attention Deficit Hyperactivity Disorder) (Lyons 1996; Taylor, Iacono, and McGue 2000). This theme recurs throughout this chapter and the rest of this book—pathways to antisocial behaviour are not usually direct, nor are they uni-dimensional. Rather, antisociality often results from a series of complex interactions between numerous factors that in and of themselves may seem benign but in combination produce devastating consequences.

One avenue in the field of behaviour genetics that has garnered considerable attention in the past decade is the role that genetics might play in either reducing or magnifying the effects of environmental risk factors (Moffitt 2005). Instead of simply studying the additive effects of "genes" plus "'environment," a new generation of behavioural geneticists are increasingly asking if there are **interactive** effects between genes and the environment: Is there a "gene" by "environment" effect?

The evidence unequivocally demonstrates that childhood maltreatment (e.g., physical abuse, emotional abuse, sexual abuse, neglect) contributes to the development of antisocial and criminal behaviour. What is less clear is why 50 percent of maltreated children do not engage in delinquency, aggressive behaviour, or criminality (Widom 1997). Jaffee et al. (2005) shed some light on this issue in a prospective follow-up study of 1116 five-year-old British twin pairs. Children were classified along a genetic risk continuum based on their co-twin's conduct disorder status and the pair's zygosity. In sum, the authors reported that the experience of maltreatment (as reported by parents) increased the probability of receiving a conduct disorder diagnosis by 1.6 percent among children deemed "lowest genetic risk"—i.e., MZ co-twin did not have CD diagnosis. However, the probability of receiving a conduct disorder diagnosis increased to 23.5 percent among children deemed "highest genetic risk"—i.e., MZ co-twin had CD diagnosis.

Molecular Genetics Research Twin and adoption studies illustrate that there is a clear link between genetics and antisocial behaviour. However, the actual functional gene(s) involved has not been identified. The main function of a gene is to produce proteins comprised of **amino acids**—the basic building blocks of life. Proteins are ultimately responsible for the phenotypic expression of our **genotype**. Faulty genes generally do one of two things—produce too much or too little of a particular protein. Human genes are stored in 46 chromosomes (23 pairs). One of these pairs is the sex chromosome—males have an X and Y chromosome while females have two X chromosomes. X-linked genes are carried on the X chromosome (Campbell, Reece, and Mitchell 1999).

Caspi and colleagues (2002) published the first groundbreaking study demonstrating an interaction between a specific gene and a well-known risk factor—childhood maltreatment. Caspi et al. (2002) were specifically interested in knowing how a low-activity version of the monoamine oxidase A (MAOA) gene may or may not intensify the effects of childhood maltreatment. The MAOA gene is located on the X chromosome; hence it is sex-linked. The MAOA gene is responsible for encoding the MAOA enzyme, which in turn is responsible for metabolizing or breaking down key brain neurotransmitters such as norepinephrine (NE), serotonin (5-Ht), and dopamine (DA), all of which have been implicated in aggression and various forms of antisocial behaviour. The two existing versions of the MAOA gene—low activity and high activity—are the result of a **polymorphism**.

Caspi et al. (2002) used a methodologically rigorous design to test the MAOA gene by environment interaction. The study was **epidemiological** in nature. They followed an entire cohort from birth until age 26 in the small New Zealand town of Dunedin. The birth cohort of 1037 children (52 percent male) was assessed regularly at ages 3, 5, 7, 9, 11, 13, 15, 18, and 21 and was virtually intact by age 26 (96 percent). The assessment process essentially involved an entire day's assessments conducted on-site at the main research facility. Researchers found evidence for a strong gene by environment interaction across all four measures of antisocial behaviour—conduct disorder, violent convictions, violent disposition, and antisocial personality disorder symptoms. As Figure 2.1 illustrates, over 80 percent of youth classified as having low MAOA activity *and* as being severely maltreated were classified as conduct disordered; however, only 40 percent with high MAOA activity plus severe maltreatment were similarly classified. While maltreatment by itself had deleterious effects, its effects were exacerbated by the presence of a low-activity MAOA gene.

Recently, Foley et al. (2004) replicated Caspi et al.'s findings in a sample of 514 male twins between the ages of 8 and 17. Specifically, children who suffered from childhood adversity and had the low-activity MAOA gene variant were significantly more likely to have conduct disorder symptoms versus children who suffered from adversity but had the high-activity MAOA variant. Similarly, Frazzetto et al. (2007) also replicated the effect, with psychiatric patients and healthy adults. They showed that a low-activity MAOA gene, when combined with early traumatic life events, exacerbates an individual's propensity toward physical aggression. The MAOA gene by environment interaction has also been observed in controlled laboratory settings. McDermott, Tingley, Cowden, Frazzetto, and Johnson (2009) showed that male participants with a low-activity MAOA gene were significantly more

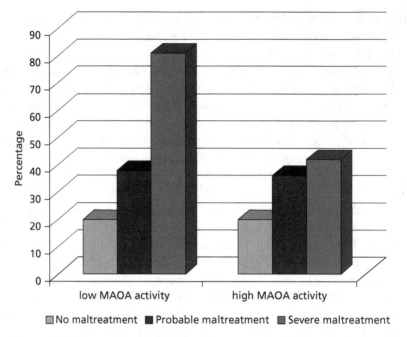

Figure 2.1 Percentage of Males Diagnosed with Conduct Disorder as a Function of MAOA Gene Functioning and Maltreatment History

Source: Adapted from Caspi et al. (2002)

likely to respond aggressively than their high-activity MAOA counterparts but only when provoked. Thus there is increasing evidence that the low-activity version of the MAOA gene, sometimes dubbed the "warrior gene," plays a significant role in the expression of anti-social behaviour, particularly aggression and violence. But, more importantly, the low-activity MAOA gene only expresses itself in the presence of certain environmental cues, such as childhood abuse or provocation.

Neurochemistry and Crime—Hormones and Neurotransmitters

Genes are largely responsible for the expression of hormones and neurotransmitters. While the endocrine system regulates hormone production and distribution, the nervous system regulates the production and function of neurotransmitters. As we shall see, a number of studies have explored whether or not certain types of hormones (e.g., testosterone) and neurotransmitters (e.g., serotonin) are linked to criminal behaviour.

Hormones and Crime The endocrine system governs more than 50 hormones in the human body. These hormones are released into our bodily fluids (typically via the bloodstream) by nine primary glands that comprise the endocrine system (e.g., hypothalamus, thyroid, and gonads—testes and ovaries). Although hormones may reach all parts of the body, only specific target cells will actually respond to a given chemical message—i.e., "deepen voice" or "produce more bodily hair" (Campbell et al. 1999). Hormones not only regulate metabolism, growth, and development, they also impact behaviour. Hormonal imbalances may be minor, resulting in mood swings (e.g., irritability experienced during a woman's menstrual cycle), or severe, resulting in serious illness or death (e.g., diabetic shock brought on by low blood-sugar levels) (Anderson 2007).

One particular hormone implicated in criminal behaviour, particularly violence and aggression, is testosterone. Testosterone is a steroidal hormone within the family of **androgens**. It is responsible for developing and maintaining male primary (e.g., growth of penis and testes and sperm) and secondary sexual characteristics (e.g., deepening of the voice, growth of facial and body hair, increased muscle mass and strength). The relationship between aggression and testosterone is well established in the animal world (Boyd 2000). However, two earlier meta-analyses (Archer 1991), including the most recent (Book, Statzyk, and Quinsey 2001), have reached the same conclusion—the relationship between testosterone and aggression in humans is positive yet weak.

Book et al. (2001) reported that the average weighted correlation between aggression and testosterone across 45 different studies (N = 9760) was .14. However, the authors also demonstrated that two factors moderated the effect: age and time of day testosterone readings were taken. Specifically, the effect was twice as strong among younger males (aged 13 to 20—weighted r = .21; aged 21 to 35—weighted r = .18) versus older males (aged 35+—weighted r = .10). Similarly, the effect size was highest when testosterone readings were taken in the afternoon (unweighted r = .45) or evening (unweighted r = .38) versus the morning (unweighted r = .20). Testosterone levels are known to fluctuate more in the morning, stabilizing in the afternoon and evening (Book et al. 2001). Gender, offender status, and method of testosterone or aggression measurement did not influence the magnitude of the findings. It is important to note that the vast majority of these studies were correlational in nature and few if any have shown that testosterone levels are either causally related to or predictive of future aggression (Boyd 2000). It is therefore plausible that aggression actually causes testosterone levels to increase or that some additional third mediating variable(s) is accounting for the effect. However, physical and chemical castration studies (physical castration removes the testes, the gland that produces testosterone; chemical castration uses anti-androgen medication to reduce the presence of testosterone) have shown that sexual re-offending is reduced in offenders who have undergone chemical and/or physical castration versus those who have not or who did not comply with anti-androgen medication (Meyer and Cole 1997; Wille and Beier 1989). These results suggest that the relationship between testosterone and sexual aggression may be more than correlational.

Given that males commit the majority of crimes, particularly violent and serious crimes (Blanchette and Brown 2006), it is not surprising that testosterone research has garnered considerable attention. However, premenstrual syndrome (PMS), a female-specific hormonal experience, has also been studied in the context of crime and aggression. Much to the chagrin of feminist advocates, PMS has been used (albeit rarely) successfully as a legal defence in Britain and the United States and as a mitigating factor in Canada (see Box 2.1).

Box 2.1

Should Premenstrual Syndrome (PMS) Be Considered a Valid Legal Defence?

Craddock was a British barmaid charged with murdering her co-worker. In 1980, a United Kingdom court found her guilty of manslaughter based on a plea of diminished responsibility because "PMS turned her into a raging animal each month and forced her to act out of character"' (Benedek 1985, as cited in Easteal 1991). Incidentally, Craddock also had an extensive record for various offences including theft, arson, and assault. Craddock is not the only case where PMS was used successfully in a court of law. Additional cases, albeit rare, have occurred in the United Kingdom, Canada, and the United States (Anderson 2007; Easteal 1991). While PMS has typically been successful in demonstrating diminished responsibility (e.g., in Canada), it has also resulted in full acquittals. In the early 1990s, an American woman was fully acquitted of drunk-driving charges on the grounds that PMS magnified the effects of alcohol (Easteal 1991).

Premenstrual syndrome (PMS) refers to a collection of physical (e.g., cramping, bloating, back pain), psychological (e.g., concentration difficulties, anxiety), and emotional (e.g., irritability, depression) symptoms related to a woman's menstrual cycle. Recently, the American Psychiatric Association included

Premenstrual Dysphoric Disorder (PMDD) in the fourth edition of the Diagnostic and Statistical Manual of Mental Disorders (DSM-IV; American Psychiatric Association 1994). The DSM-IV (p. 715) estimates that PMDD affects less than 5 percent of menstruating women and describes the symptoms as "markedly depressed mood, marked anxiety, marked affective ability, and decreased interest in activities" occurring during the last week of the menstrual cycle immediately preceding the onset of menses." However, the DSM-IV stops short of officially labelling PMDD as an official disorder.

Research suggests that the link between PMS and crime, particularly violent crime, is equivocal. Critics have noted that the stress following arrest may induce menstruation rather than menstruation preceding crime (Raine 1993). As well, menstruation impacts the body in several others ways, including reductions in blood glucose levels, which have also been linked to antisocial behaviour. While menstruation is associated with hormonal changes that cause a small group of women to be more prone to anger during menstruation, it is quite another matter to infer that PMS-induced anger is causally related to crime (Anderson 2007).

Neurotransmitters and Crime Like hormones, neurotransmitters are chemical messengers that operate in the brain. While hormones are the messengers of the endocrine system, neurotransmitters are the messengers of the nervous system. Both systems often work in concert.

Neurons or nerve cells transmit instructional signals from one part of the body to another. Neurotransmitters play a critical role in this communication process. As Figure 2.2 illustrates, there are two types of neurons—presynaptic and postsynaptic. The presynaptic cell is the sender and uses its axon's synaptic terminals to transmit the message to the receiver—the postsynaptic cell. The postsynaptic cell receives the message using its

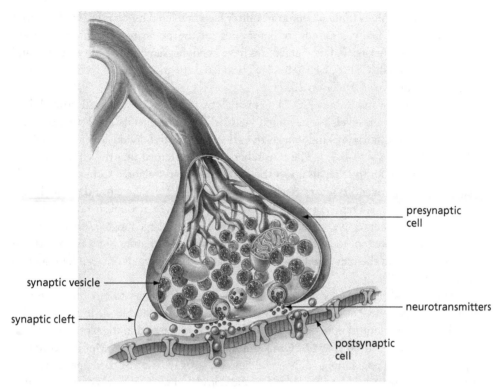

presynaptic cell

synaptic vesicle

synaptic cleft

neurotransmitters

postsynaptic cell

Figure 2.2 The Presynaptic and Postsynaptic Cell

dendrites. Narrow gaps or synapses exist between the presynaptic and postsynaptic cells. Some of these synapses are electrical and some are chemical. We are interested in the chemical synapses. An electrical impulse or signal travels along the presynaptic cell but cannot cross the synaptic cleft to the postsynaptic cell without being temporarily converted into a chemical signal. The converter or chemical messenger is the neurotransmitter (Anderson 2007; Campbell et al. 1999). Neurotransmitters are stored in synaptic vesicles. Imagine this process happening a million times in a nanosecond, just so you can scratch your nose! Although the brain is home to several neurotransmitters, we are most concerned with those that facilitate information processing, mood regulation, and communication. Three neurotransmitters in particular have been studied in relation to crime: serotonin, dopamine, and norepinephrine.

The neurotransmitter serotonin, or hydroxytryptamine (5-HT), plays an important role in behavioural inhibition and mood regulation. It is produced from an essential **amino acid**, tryptophan. Tryptophan is not produced naturally within the body but must be obtained from diet. Most notable sources include protein-based foods such as turkey and chocolate. Since 1959, research has shown that there is a link between a malfunctioning serotonin system and impulsivity, irritability, and aggression (directed at self or others). This research has operationalized malfunctioning serotonin systems in several ways, including low levels of serotonin, low levels of its precursors such as tryptophan, low levels of its metabolites (once a neurotransmitter has completed its job it breaks down into metabolites), and faulty serotonin receptor sites on the postsynaptic neuron. As well, serotonin, its precursors, and its metabolites have been measured in the blood, urine, and cerebro-spinal fluid (CSF). CSF studies are considered the most reliable method of measuring serotonin levels (Anderson 2007).

Moore, Scarpa and Raine's (2002) meta-analytic review of 16 studies illustrated that, on average, serotonin levels (as measured via CSF serotonin metabolites) were substantially lower among antisocial individuals than non-antisocial individuals (mean weighted effect size (Cohen's $d = -0.45$). The researchers also determined that the effect was even more pronounced for individuals under the age of 30 (mean weighted Cohen's $d = -1.37$) versus individuals over 30 (mean weighted Cohen's $d = -0.31$). The effect did not change as a function of gender, target of violence, history of suicide, or alcoholism. While the size of these effects is impressive, considered in the moderate to large range (Cohen 1988), it is important to note that in addition to being correlational in nature, the vast majority of studies included in the meta-analysis were based on relatively small non-random samples (e.g., less than 30).

Moffitt et al. (1998) used an epidemiological research design to test the serotonin/aggression hypothesis between serotonin levels (measured in the blood) in the Dunedin sample. It is important to note that high levels of serotonin found in the blood are indicative of low brain serotonin levels. Unlike most research in this area, Moffitt's cohort is representative of a population—of New Zealanders, anyway. The 781 participants were 21 years old when serotonin levels were taken and correlated with measures of past criminal behaviour (official criminal convictions and self-report methodology were used). The results confirmed a moderate (positive) correlation between blood serotonin levels and violent criminal behaviour for men but not women. Also of interest is that the results did not vary as a function of whether or not criminal behaviour was measured officially or via self-report.

Taken together, this research clearly suggests that there is, at the very least, a correlational link between a malfunctioning serotonin system and aggression. However, the extent to which serotonin is predictive or causally related to violence and/or aggression requires further study. Studies that artificially manipulate the level of tryptophan and then examine its impact on aggression in a laboratory setting suggest a causal link (e.g., Bjork, Dougherty, Moeller, and Swann 2000). This research is preliminary and requires replication. Similarly, other research illustrating that low levels of serotonin increase impulsivity (a known correlate of aggression) (Linnoila et al. 1983) suggests that serotonin may exert its influence indirectly on aggression through the mediator of impulsivity or perhaps negative mood. In sum, although the research remains preliminary, it is exciting given the potential treatment implications: changes in diet could reduce aggression!

The release of dopamine causes feelings of pleasure that accompany factors such as sex, love, and food. The dopamine pleasure centre can be triggered artificially with illicit drugs, alcohol, and nicotine, some of which are known to increase aggression. Unfortunately, research examining the dopamine/aggression link is relatively sparse in comparison to the serotonin literature base. The research is also somewhat mixed, with some linking both high and low levels of dopamine with aggression (Lee and Coccaro 2007). In part, this may be explained by one hypothesis that posits that individuals with low levels of dopamine require greater levels of stimulation to experience pleasure—hence they are more likely to develop addictions to illicit drugs such as cocaine that quickly increase dopamine levels and create an immediate "high" but also have the side effect of increasing aggressive tendencies. Dopamine also regulates other neurotransmitters, including serotonin and norepinephrine. It is possible that dopamine exerts its influence indirectly via these neurotransmitters (Anderson 2007). More research is needed to fully understand the role that dopamine plays in antisocial behaviour, particularly aggression.

Norepinephrine signals the body to react to short-term stress by increasing heart rate and blood pressure (Campbell et al. 1999). Limited research suggests that high levels of norepinephrine are correlated with aggression (Anderson 2007). This finding seems to be supported by the finding that certain drugs (e.g., reserpine) that reduce norepinephrine levels also reduce aggression (Anderson 2007; Raine 1993). However, further investigation is needed to determine the exact role of norepinephrine in antisocial behaviour.

Psychophysiology and Crime

A psychophysiological theory uses physiology (e.g., low resting heart rate) to explain psychological constructs (e.g., emotions, motivation, learning). Several psychophysiological theories of antisocial behaviour and related constructs (e.g., psychopathy, childhood aggression) have emerged over the years (Berkowitz 1994; Fowles 1980; 1988; Gray 1987; Gray and McNaughton 2000; Zillmann 1994). These theories try to link measures of autonomic response (e.g., heart rate, electrodermal activity/galvanic skin response/skin conductance) to various measures along the antisocial spectrum. Electrodermal activity (EDA) measures the amount of electrical current between two points on the skin. Typically, electrodes are placed on two fingers, and changes (even minor ones) in electrical activity brought on by sweating are recorded by a polygraph (Raine 1993). Increases in heart rate and EDA are related to general emotional responses such as fear, anger, or anxiety (Lange 1994).

One of the most prominent psychophysiological theories is Gray's arousal model (Fowles 1980; Gray 1987). Based largely on animal models of behaviour, Gray hypothesized that personality, learning, motivation, and emotional responses are largely governed by two underlying biological systems of autonomic arousal: the behavioural activation system (BAS) and the behavioural inhibition system (BIS). The BIS is conceptualized as an avoidance system responsible for inhibiting or stopping behaviour in the face of punishment—e.g., "Even though I may wish to hurt someone I won't because I don't want to go to prison." The BAS is an approach or reward-seeking system that responds to positive incentives/rewards—e.g., "If I punch John for flirting with my girlfriend I will feel an immediate reward—satisfaction." While the BIS is linked to anxiety, the BAS is linked to impulsivity and sensation-seeking behaviour (Gray 1987; Fowles 1980; Raine 1993).

It is hypothesized that antisocial individuals have underactive behavioural inhibition systems and consequently are more fearless, less anxious, and less responsive to aversive cues. It is further thought that this fearlessness and absence of anxiety manifests in autonomic responses such as a low resting heart rate or low EDA. It is also posited that antisocial individuals have overactive behavioural activation systems and are therefore prone to sensation-seeking and impulsive tendencies that tend to lead to antisocial behaviour (Gray 1987; Fowles 1980; Raine 1993).

Over the past 50 years, a number of methods have been used to test psychophysiological theories of antisocial behaviour in a diverse range of samples ranging from children with conduct disorder (e.g., running away from home, fighting, lying, stealing) to incarcerated offenders classified as psychopaths. These studies have typically measured heart rate (HR) or EDA in one of three paradigms—*rest*: HR/EDA is measured in the absence of a stimuli; *task*: HR/EDA is measured in the presence of a stimuli (e.g., listening to a tone, performing some form of arithmetic); or *reactivity*: HR/EDA is measured before and after a stimuli. Stimuli may also be neutral or aversive (e.g., electronic shock, burst of load noise).

Lorber (2004) conducted one of the most comprehensive reviews of this literature to date. Using a meta-analytic framework, Lorber summarized the results of 95 studies. As illustrated in Table 2.1, the findings indicate that, at most, there is a small effect for the relationship between HR or EDA and various conceptualizations of antisocial behaviour (e.g., aggression, psychopathy/**sociopathy**, conduct problems), and this small effect is most evident for psychopathy when EDA is used as the measure of autonomic arousal (regardless of whether the paradigm involved "rest," "task," or "reactivity"). The finding that psychopathy and EDA were negatively related was magnified when negative stimuli (Cohen's $d = -0.45$) versus nonnegative stimuli (Cohen's $d = -0.11$) were considered.

The Lorber (2004) review lends support to the notion that some antisocial individuals, specifically those classified as psychopathic, show deficits in their behavioural inhibition system as hypothesized by others (e.g., Fowles 1980). However, it is important to underscore that many of the studies were correlational and it is difficult to ascertain what came first: Did a faulty behavioural inhibition system (BIS) lead to psychopathic tendencies? Or did psychopathic tendencies lead to a faulty BIS?

Another meta-analysis published the same year in a different journal reported that heart-rate level is actually a medium-sized correlate of antisocial behaviour in children (Cohen d's ranged from -0.43 in the resting heart-rate paradigm to -0.76 in the reactivity heart-rate paradigm) (Ortiz and Raine 2004). In addition, Ortiz and Raine (2004) included five prospective studies illustrating that heart rate is also predictive of future antisocial behaviour. However, this finding was not replicated in a recent study that found that EDA is not predictive of abstaining from crime in a sample of youthful males (Loeber, Pardini, Stouthamer-Loeber, and Raine 2007). In sum, while measures of autonomic arousal are small or possibly moderate correlates of antisocial behaviour, the predictive and/or causal status requires more research.

Table 2.1 The Relationship Between Autonomic Arousal and Antisocial Behaviour: A Summary of Lorber's (2004) Meta-Analysis

Measure	Cohen's d[a] (95% CIs[b])	# of studies	Meaning of effect
Resting Heart Rate			
Aggression	−0.38 (−0.50, −0.26)	16	Moderate
Psychopathy/sociopathy	0.06 (−0.08, 0.21)	17	None
Conduct problems	−0.33 (−0.43, −0.23)	13	Small
Task Heart Rate			
Aggression	−0.02 (−0.15, 0.11)	14	None
Psychopathy/sociopathy	−0.16 (−0.41, 0.09)	7	None
Conduct problems	−0.04 (−0.21, 0.14)	8	None
Heart Rate Reactivity			
Aggression	0.10 (−0.03, 0.22)	14	None
Psychopathy/sociopathy	0.06 (−0.11, 0.23)	14	None
Conduct problems	0.20 (0.05, 0.36)	7	Small
Resting EDA[c]			
Aggression	0.10 (−0.14, 0.34)	not reported	None
Psychopathy/sociopathy	−0.30 (−0.46, −0.15)	18	Small
Conduct problems	−0.15 (−0.28, 0.00)	11	None
Task EDA			
Aggression	0.07 (−0.18, 0.32)	4	None
Psychopathy/sociopathy	−0.25 (−0.34, −0.15)	28	Small
Conduct problems	−0.23 (−0.35, −0.10)	14	Small
EDA Reactivity			
Aggression	−0.07 (−0.24, 0.10)	5	None
Psychopathy/sociopathy	−0.31 (−0.48, −0.13)	14	Small
Conduct problems	Na[d]	1	Na

Note: [a]Cohen's d is an effect size that represents the mean difference between the "antisocial group" and the "control group" divided by the pooled standard deviation. [b]CI = Confidence Intervals; [c]EDA = electrodermal activity; [d]an effect size was not calculated given that only one study was conducted on children.
Source: Adapted from Lorber (2004)

The Brain and Crime—Neuroimaging and Neuropsychology

In 1848, Phineas Gage was packing gunpowder into a rock with a tamping iron when it ignited prematurely. The iron shot into his left check through to the top of his skull, destroying his frontal lobe in the process. Remarkably, he survived. Although his memory and intellect remained unchanged, Gage's friends and family reported that he was "no longer Gage." Before the accident, he was reportedly kind, polite, and responsible, but after the accident he became irritable, profane, and violent. This was the first documented "natural experiment" linking the brain to personality and behaviour. Scientists have accumulated much knowledge about the brain and antisocial behaviour since Gage's unfortunate accident along two main avenues—brain imaging studies and neuropsychology (Anderson 2007).

Brain Imaging Brain imaging (or "neuroimaging") research examines the structural (e.g., reduced grey matter size, tumours, lesions) and functional characteristics of the brain (e.g., blood flow, glucose metabolism—the brain's primary energy source). Brain structure is typically studied with magnetic resonance imaging (MRI) and computed tomography (CT), while brain function is studied through positron-emission tomography (PET) and single photon emission computed tomography (SPECT) (Anderson 2007; Raine 1993).

Brain imaging studies are complex and diverse. Typically, they involve assessing a small number of "known" antisocial individuals (e.g., sex offenders, violent offenders, psychopaths) to a comparison group (e.g., non-sex offenders, non-violent offenders, non-psychopaths, or non-offenders). While earlier studies (see Raine 1993 for a review) simply compared the brain structures and/or functions of the two groups, more recent studies have compared brain function while the test subjects were engaged in some cognitive activity (such as while viewing emotionally negative pictures) (see Birbaumer et al. 2005). These studies have been reviewed by several researchers (see Anderson 2007; Henry and Moffitt 1997; Raine 1993), but a recent review by Raine and Yang (2006) is most helpful in not only summarizing the results but in providing an integrated conceptual framework.

Raine and Yang (2006) hypothesized that structural and/or functional damage to the areas of the brain posited to be responsible for moral reasoning and emotional regulation result in an "antisocial tendency." This antisocial tendency is thought to manifest in a variety of forms, ranging from violent and sexual offending to psychopathic tendencies and general criminality. Raine and Yang's (2006) summary identified structural and/or functional deficits in four areas of the brain: 1) the frontal lobe—implicated in several higher order functions such as cognitive reasoning, planning, sound judgment, patience, abstract thought, moral reasoning, violence, and aggression regulation; 2) the temporal lobe—also implicated in the production and inhibition of aggression (includes the amygdala, specifically involved in emotional and fear situations; and the hippocampus, specifically involved in memory, learning, and emotion regulation); 3) the parietal lobe—integrates sensory information related to movement and space; and 4) the cingulate gyrus—the part of the brain that partially surrounds the corpus callosum (the juncture in the brain that joins the left and right hemispheres). Importantly, several of these structures are part of the interconnected limbic system (i.e., the amygdala, hippocampus, and cingulated gyrus). In general, the limbic system is associated with emotion and the autonomic expression of emotion—faster heartbeat, faster respiration, trembling and sweating, and basic drives such as sex, hunger, thirst, and the "fight or flight" response (Anderson 2007; Raine and Yang 2006). See Figure 2.3 for an illustration.

Raine and Yang made several key conclusions. First, structural and/or functional damage to the frontal lobe, specifically the pre-frontal lobe, is the most replicated brain imaging abnormality found in offenders to date. Second, the evidence is starting to suggest that structural/functional impairments to parts of the limbic system (e.g., the amygdala and the hippocampus) and the temporal lobe are also implicated in antisocial behaviour. Third, there is no single brain structure that is ultimately necessary for the development of antisocial behaviour; rather there are multiple potential contenders and as the number of deficits increases, so does the probability of antisocial behaviour. It is also important to underscore that while this body of research is intriguing it is not flawless. It is built on small samples of incarcerated offenders (predominately sex and violent offenders) without non-criminal comparison groups. This precludes our ability to determine whether brain abnormalities cause antisocial behaviour or, alternatively, whether engaging in antisocial behaviour ultimately changes the brain's structure and/or function (Henry and Moffitt 1997).

Neuropsychology Unlike neuroimaging studies that examine the brain using direct physical means, neuropsychology studies brain function indirectly. For example, if you are

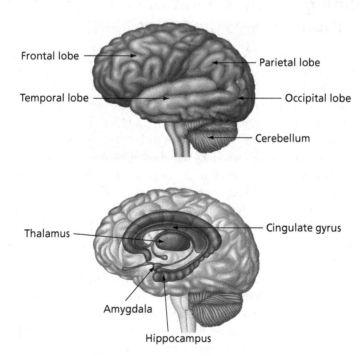

Figure 2.3 The Human Brain and the Limbic System

suspected of having brain injury following an accident, a neuropsychologist may administer a battery of paper/pencil and/or motor tests designed to diagnose what part of the brain
is malfunctioning. Experts in the field of neuropsychology have studied whether deficits
in executive functioning are related to antisocial behaviour. In brief, executive functioning refers to cognitive functioning involving future goal-oriented behaviour, purposive
attention, organizational skills, and inhibitory control (Morgan and Lilienfeld 2000).
While these functions have been associated with the frontal lobe, it is impossible to rule
out that other components of the brain such as the connector pathways also play a role in
executive functioning. Although two narrative reviews reached inconclusive results
regarding the link between executive functioning and antisocial behaviour (Kandel and
Freed 1982; Lilienfeld 1992), a recent meta-analytic study has shed new light. Morgan
and Lilienfeld (2000) meta-analytically reviewed 39 studies comparing antisocial groups
with non-antisocial or "less antisocial" groups on six measures of executive functioning
considered to have the highest validity in the field. Overall, they aggregated the results of
4589 participants. A robust effect (weighted Cohen's $d = 0.62$) was observed, indicating
that poor executive functioning is related to antisocial behaviour. However, the authors
noted that there was considerable variability from study to study, suggesting that further
research is needed to enhance our confidence in this finding. The studies were also largely correlational in nature.

[handwritten margin note: ie frontal lobe not functioning at 100%.]

Other Biological Considerations—Pregnancy, Birth Complications, Toxins, and Diet

The evidence reviewed thus far clearly suggests a link between biology and various forms of
antisocial behaviour. It should also be clear by now that the biology/environment or nature/
nurture dichotomy is false. Biology and the environment are inextricably linked. We have
shown how biology can predispose an individual to future antisocial behaviour. Now we
consider how certain environmental insults change our biology in a manner that heightens
our propensity toward antisocial behaviour. Specifically, researchers are beginning to suggest
that inadequate prenatal (during pregnancy) conditions, perinatal (during birth) complications, improper diet, and environmental toxins (e.g., lead) result in changes to our biology
that may in turn make us more likely to engage in antisocial behaviour.

There is some evidence of a link between hypoglycemia (low blood sugar—known to
result in panic, irritability, nervousness, and aggression, Raine 1993) and antisocial behaviour (Anderson 2007). Schoenthaler (1983) conducted a particularly intriguing analysis
demonstrating this effect. Using a double-blind study, Schoenthaler examined the effects of
a healthy diet (designed to regulate blood sugar levels) on a sample of incarcerated juvenile
offenders for two years. For half the sample, soft drinks and junk-food snacks were replaced
with fruit juices and nutritious snacks. High-sugar desserts and cereals were eliminated. The
other half of the sample received the usual meal plan. This study was double-blind because
neither the researcher nor the participants were told which group they belonged to.
Impressively, the program reduced antisocial behaviour by 48 percent.

Researchers have also investigated the impact of certain neurotoxins, namely lead, cadmium, and manganese, on brain development. Needleman, Riess, Tobin, Biesecker, and Greenhouse (1996) conducted a study of 212 boys in the Pittsburgh school system aged 7 to 11. During the course of the study, the researchers assessed lead concentration levels as well as antisocial behaviour in the children. While no effect was observed at age 7, there seemed to be a cumulative effect of lead so that by age 11, children with elevated lead levels exhibited significantly more antisocial behaviour than their "normal lead level" peers as rated by themselves, their parents, and their teachers, even after controlling for other factors such as socioeconomic status and parental quality. This study demonstrated that even small amounts of lead can have deleterious effects.

Manganese is known to impact serotonin and dopamine levels and to somehow alter the levels of the monoamine oxidase (MAO) enzyme. Tran et al. (2002) found that children with learning problems, attention deficits, and attention deficit hyperactivity disorder (ADHD) (all known correlates and/or predictors of antisocial behaviour) had elevated levels of manganese. Similarly, there is a growing body of diet-related research regarding the impact that vitamins, minerals, fat, fatty acids, food additives, and even food allergies can have on antisocial behaviour as well as the known precursors of antisocial behaviour—e.g., hyperactivity (Anderson 2007). It is important to stress that this research in no way asserts that poor diet or environmental toxins cause antisocial behaviour, but rather these are factors that may act in concert with other causal factors.

An equally important body of research has examined how abnormal fetal development (due to a variety of factors: maternal smoking, drinking, ultimate expression **Fetal Alcohol Spectrum Disorder**, poor nutrition, trauma experienced by the mother, and birth complications) may predispose an individual to antisocial behaviour. For example, it is well known that hypoxia or lack of oxygen to the brain at birth can have a profound impact on development, increasing the probability of learning disabilities, impaired cognitive functioning, and intelligence. Arguably, such factors would enhance one's propensity toward antisocial behaviour. However, Raine (1993) has hypothesized that there may also be a direct link between birth complications and adult violence. It is also important to note that research has shown two things. First, the environment (e.g., positive parenting) can reverse the potentially deleterious effects associated with pregnancy and birth-related insults and thus serve to protect individuals from their "biology" (Mednick and Kandel 1988). Second, the environment (e.g., poor parenting) can aggravate "biological risk," such as children born with subtle neurological impairments (perhaps due to birth complications) (Anderson 2007).

In sum, the research is clearly impressive, but it is important to underscore the complex interactions occurring not only within the biological subsystems but also between them. For example, improved diet has a multitude of effects not only on blood glucose and hormonal levels but also on serotonin levels, all of which have been linked to antisocial behaviour. Furthermore, there are complex interactions occurring at the environmental level. For example, the positive impact of "diet" on hyperactive children is magnified when accompanied by a supportive home environment (Rumsey and Rapoport 1983).

It is critical to ascertain how all these factors fit together—specifically, what are the true causal risk factors, mediators, and moderators of these effects? It is imperative that research move in a direction such that causal factors can emerge to allow for the efficient allocation of limited treatment resources.

EVOLUTIONARY THEORIES OF CRIME

So FAR WE HAVE EXPLORED BIOLOGICAL EXPLANATIONS OF ANTISOCIAL BEHAVIOUR AND CRIME that have focused on genetics, the brain, hormones, autonomic arousal, and other factors that find their triggers in the environment, such as diet and pregnancy complications. This level of explanation can be considered proximate. Proximate explanations identify which factors in a person's immediate environment cause certain behaviours. Proximate explanations also ask how the behaviour develops over an organism's lifespan, questioning causation and development at the individual level. In contrast, ultimate or more distal explanations ask questions about function and adaptation for an entire species. This level of analysis asks questions such as, "Why did humans develop the capacity for speech, emotion, or aggression?" Ultimate explanations focus on identifying the evolutionary function of behaviours that contribute to the survival of individuals (Mishra and Lalumière 2008; Quinsey et al. 2004).

Some modern biology textbooks (e.g., Campbell et al. 1999) state that "biology came of age" the day Charles Darwin published *On the Origin of Species* in 1859. Darwin made two critical points in his book: 1) species did not always exist in their current form but evolved or transformed from ancestral species; and 2) the evolutionary mechanism for this transformation was **natural selection** (Campbell et al. 1999). Even more impressive, Darwin foresaw the emergence of evolutionary psychology: "In the distant future I see open fields for more important researches. Psychology will be based on a new foundation, that of the necessary acquirement of each mental power and capacity by graduation." (Darwin 1859, as cited in Buss 2005).

Charles Darwin (1809–1882)

Evolution 101: Natural Selection, Adaptation, and Beyond

Evolutionary psychology is a relatively new yet thriving discipline that seeks to understand human psychology from a Darwinian perspective. In essence, evolutionary psychologists are trying to "map a universal human nature" (Tooby and Cosmides 2005: 5). To date, this perspective has been applied to a vast array of psychological constructs ranging from altruism, phobias, emotions, and group dynamics to the focus of this chapter—antisocial behaviour. Before we explore what evolution or, more accurately, forensic evolutionary psychology (Duntley and Shackelford 2008) has to say about antisocial behaviour, it is necessary to review a few basic principles of evolution, beginning with natural selection.

Evolutionary psychology posits that the human mind comes equipped with numerous psychological mechanisms that have been designed and maintained through selection over thousands of years of evolution. These psychological mechanisms are sometimes conceptualized as a series of mini computer programs that have been designed by one master programmer. The master programmer wasn't a person but rather the environment itself that our hunter–gatherer ancestors inhabited many years ago. Our ancestral environment was comprised of various **selection pressures** and adaptive problems—finding a mate, hunting, gathering, protecting children, avoiding predators, and finding shelter. "Hunters" and "gatherers" who successfully responded to adaptive problems and/or selection pressures not only survived, but lived long enough to reproduce children and pass these successful adaptations on to the next generation. Unsuccessful responses resulted in death or reduced capacity to reproduce. Herein lies the basic assumption of natural selection: a successful **adaptation**—be it biological or psychological—is housed in an individual's genetic makeup, so the only way adaptations can be passed on is through genetic rather than cultural transmission. A prerequisite to becoming a potential adaptation is that the "candidate" adaptation must first appear in the organism's genetic makeup by chance, for example as a genetic mutation. If the mutation enhances the organism's reproductive fitness—how good an organism is at reproducing plentifully and keeping offspring alive long enough for them to reproduce—it will be retained and passed on to the next generation, and so on. Gradually, as a result of its enhanced reproductive fitness, the adaptation works its way into the species' genome. It is important to note that this process takes, on average, a few thousand generations (although it can happen much faster), and adaptations that increase reproductive fitness by as little as 1 percent (on average) are naturally selected over other less beneficial characteristics (Shackelford and Duntley 2008; Tooby and Cosmides 2005; Campbell et al. 1999).

Given that evolution takes so long, our existing psychological mechanisms are the result of selection pressures that existed during the hunter and gatherer era rather than the industrial or even the agricultural revolutions. Our existing psychological mechanisms *were* adaptive in a typical hunter-and-gatherer environment characterized by life in small, face-to-face nomadic bands of less than 100 people, most of whom we were genetically related to. It does not necessarily follow that these evolved mechanisms will be adaptive in any sense in contemporary society (Buss 2005; Daly and Wilson 1988)! We are the way we are because existing attributes (ability to walk upright, to feel fear, to fight) were adaptations in the distant past that enhanced our reproductive fitness and consequently were naturally selected for and became part of the human genome. See Box 2.2 for a discussion of common criticisms and misconceptions about evolutionary psychology.

Box 2.2

Top Three Criticisms and Misconceptions— Evolutionary Psychology Takes the Stand

Critique: Determinism

Critics argue that evolution (and biology, for that matter) is not useful because of its determinist nature—we can't change what happened in an ancestral environment, so how can we use a theory about the past to solve current problems? If evolution's blueprint is housed in our genes, we cannot change its impact because our genes are immutable. Determinists also argue that evolution ignores environmental factors.

Defence:

Hopefully, it has become apparent that our evolved psychological mechanisms developed in response to the environment, albeit a distant one. Thus, arguably, evolution is all about the environment! The present-day environment "cues" an organism about what the future likely holds and, in turn, directs the organism to adopt a course of action most likely to enhance reproductive fitness—a path that will vary as a function of contemporary environmental cues (see Life History Theory, Risk-Taking, and Antisocial Behaviour below). The section of this chapter that addressed biology clearly demonstrated that "biology" is not destiny and that while "biology" may predispose an individual in certain ways, these predispositions will most likely not manifest in the absence of the appropriate environmental trigger. Additionally, numerous "biological" ailments are readily solved with environmental treatments that are sometimes as simple as changing one's diet. Phenylketonuria (PKU) is a biologically based disease that prevents individuals from metabolizing phenylalanine, an essential amino acid. Buildup of this amino acid results in severe brain impairment in young children. Once the biology of the disease was understood, the remedy was simple: keep phenylalanine out of an affected child's diet until age seven, at which point the buildup is no longer harmful. The solution to this biological problem was environmental.

Critique: Naturalistic fallacy

Evolutionary theory is flawed because it legitimizes aggression and violence along with myriad social injustices. For example, in reference to evolutionary explanations of female crime, Belknap (2001) states " . . . this perspective is . . . insulting to girls and women, viewing them as pathetic, needy competitors for male attention . . . " (p. 57).

Defence:

The most straightforward response to this position is that just because a scientist studies a given behaviour, good or bad—doesn't mean he/she endorses it. For example, researchers who study cancer and the evolution of viruses do not condone the spread of such diseases; quite the contrary. Because something was adaptive in an ancestral environment does not make it morally right, yesterday or today.

Misconception: Natural selection is a conscious process

Evolutionary psychology assumes that individuals consciously decide to act in a certain way, which ultimately results in our present-day adaptations.

Box 2.2   Continued

Defence:
Sometimes the principles of natural selection are misunderstood and it is erroneously concluded that our ancestors consciously made decisions to act adaptively because they wanted to. The only true progenitor of evolutionary adaptations is the gene—or, in Dawkins's terms, the Selfish Gene (1989).

RESEARCHING EVOLUTIONARY EXPLANATIONS OF CRIME

RESEARCHERS USE AN ARRAY OF METHODS TO TEST EVOLUTIONARY THEORIES AND HYPOTHESES, including historical, anthropological, and cross-cultural methods. Researchers also use methods that are routine among psychologists (e.g., paper/pencil questionnaires, interviews, computer simulation studies), with the key difference being in how evolutionary theorists frame questions and interpret results. While a social learning psychologist might interpret aggressive behaviour between two males as pathological, stemming from each individual's interpretation of the rewards outweighing the costs for such behaviour, an evolutionary psychologist would look for an ultimate explanation and explore whether the behaviour served some adaptive function in an ancestral environment such that the reward/cost ratio favours the species. If it is not an adaptation, evolutionary psychologists would test whether it is a byproduct of another adaptation or the result of a malfunctioning adaptation.

Evolution and Crime: What Do We Know?

The application of evolutionary principles to criminal behaviour is a burgeoning yet novice field. Evolutionists posit that recurring conflict (over resources, mates, or offspring, for example) drove the selection pressures that shaped evolutionary adaptations, manifesting in a wide range of antisocial behaviours including violence (rape, homicide) and non-violent offenses (sexual harassment, theft) (Shackelford and Duntley 2008). In this section, we describe how researchers have applied certain micro-level theories that exist within the grand framework of evolutionary psychology to four areas. First, life-history theory is used to explain risk-taking and antisocial behaviour among two prominent offender groups: the life-course persistent offender and the adolescent limited offender (Moffitt 1993). Second, frequency-dependence selection is used to explain psychopathy. Third, homicide is explained through the notion of male–male competition. Last, parental investment and mating effort theories are used to explain gender differences in crime.

Life History Theory, Risk-Taking, and Antisocial Behaviour

Like us, our ancestors had several competing demands on their time. Not only did they have to hunt and gather, and find and attract a mate, they also had to protect and nourish offspring. It is easy to see how these activities could enhance survival and/or reproductive fitness. The challenge, however, was in how an individual would "decide" how best to allocate his/her time toward each activity. Allotting time to one activity, such as nourishing and protecting offspring, would offer an important reproductive benefit—increasing the probability that the offspring would live long enough to mate and transfer his/her (and ultimately your) genetic material to the next generation. A cost would simultaneously be incurred, however. Protecting offspring would take time away from siring other children, or, if for females, would reduce survival or fertility (Mishra and Lalumière 2008). There was always a tradeoff between the costs and benefits associated with the various activities that defined our ancestors' lives. Life history theory argues that natural selection favours allocation strategies that, on average, optimize reproductive fitness within a given *ecological niche* (Kaplan and Gangestad 2005).

Life history theory seeks to explain how various selection pressures and/or adaptive problems faced by our ancestors shaped the development of the present-day psychological mechanisms responsible for directing allocation strategies. The theory speaks to three primary tradeoffs. The first focuses on present versus future reproduction efforts (i.e., Should I invest in life-sustaining activities now—growing, predator reduction—thereby increasing my odds of living and reproducing later, or should I allocate my energy toward reproduction, reducing my reproduction capabilities later, given that I may be dead?). The second tradeoff involves quantity versus quality of offspring. It addresses questions such as: Should I simply have as many children as I can, thereby reducing the available resources I can devote to any one child, or should I have fewer children and thus have more available resources per child? The final tradeoff involves mating effort versus parental investment. Mating effort refers to how much time and energy one devotes to acquiring and maintaining sexual partners. Parental investment refers to how much time and energy one devotes to caring for and protecting mates and offspring (Kaplan and Gangestand 2005; Lalumière, Harris, Quinsey, and Rice 2005; Mishra and Lalumière 2008).

An additional caveat to life history theory is that the optimal tradeoff strategy that an organism ultimately adopts is highly dependent on environmental cues—both present and future. Life history theory hypothesizes that psychological mechanisms have evolved to adapt to current cues regarding present or impending hardship. Thus, if the environmental cues suggest that life is likely to end "at any time" (e.g., constant food scarcity and/ or predatory threats) or that the future is bleak and unpredictable, the optimal tradeoff might be to "risk it all for love now" rather than worry about immediate health and safety. Life history theory also posits that the optimal allocation strategy will vary as a function of how many children you already have. For example, adopting a high mating effort strategy immediately following puberty will incur more reproductive fitness advantages than costs. However, as the number of offspring increases with age, the balance of rewards and costs shifts. High mating effort becomes more costly (e.g., retaliatory violence from mates' relatives, "wasted" energy on finding new mates) and less rewarding. In contrast, parental investment becomes more rewarding (ensures the survival of offspring and hence one's own genes) (Kaplan and Ganestand 2005).

In sum, life history theory posits that natural selection has created psychological mechanisms that weigh the costs and benefits associated with various resource allocation strategies. These mechanisms are designed to select the strategy that maximizes reproductive fitness. The "cost/benefit mechanism" is not static; it responds not only to present-day environmental cues but also to age and number of offspring. The theory also predicts that optimal life course strategies will not necessarily be the same for males and females.

A group of Canadian researchers (Lalumière, Mishra, Harris, Quinsey, and Rice; see Box 2.3 for a profile of Dr. Lalumière) has begun using life history theory to explain the development of two distinct offender groups: life course persistent offenders and adolescent limited offenders (Moffitt 1993; see Patterson, Reid, and Dishion 1992 and Loeber and Farrington 2000 for similar typologies).

Box 2.3

Canadian Researcher Profile: Dr. Martin Lalumière

Dr. Martin Lalumière is an internationally recognized expert on sexual aggression, crime, and risk-taking behaviour who works from an evolutionary perspective. He currently serves as Associate Professor in the Department of Psychology at the University of Lethbridge.

Before his current position, Dr. Lalumière was a research psychologist at the Centre for Addiction and Mental Health in Toronto and Associate Professor of Psychiatry and Criminology at the University of Toronto. Previously, he was a research psychologist at the Mental Health Centre Penetanguishene and a post-doctoral fellow at the Correctional Service of Canada. He obtained his Ph.D. in 1995 under Professor Vernon Quinsey. Dr. Lalumière's dissertation, titled "The sexual interests of sexual coercive men," earned him the Governor General's Academic Gold Medal for graduate work at Queen's University.

Dr. Lalumière has published extensively, including four books and over 50 book chapters and peer-reviewed journal articles. His work has appeared in a variety of influential journals, ranging from Psychological Bulletin and Psychological Assessment to Archives of Sexual Behaviour, Evolution and Human

Continued >

Behaviour and Social Science and Medicine. He is best known for his work on the phallometric assessment of rapists and the evolution of psychopathy, and for establishing a link between handedness and sexual orientation. His approach to research involves a mix of proximal (mechanistic or developmental) and ultimate (functional) questions to fully understand the hows and whys of behavioural phenomena. For example, what are the developmental and contextual factors that influence risk taking? What are the evolved functions, if any, of risk taking?

When Dr. Lalumière isn't working in his "Sex, Crime, and Evolution Lab" with students, he is busy teaching courses on criminal behaviour, psychopathology, and evolutionary psychology. What he loves most about teaching is "interacting with smart students, helping them become critical thinkers." In his spare time, Dr. Lalumière enjoys hiking with his wife, Dr. Gail Hepburn, also a faculty member in the same department at the University of Lethbridge, and fly fishing for trout in the beautiful prairie and Rocky Mountain rivers of western Canada.

What's next for Dr. Lalumière? Certainly more fishing trips, but more importantly, he will continue to have a profound impact on our understanding of sexuality and criminality.

As will be discussed in Chapter 5, life course persistent offenders begin committing various serious, antisocial acts prior to adolescence and continue well into adulthood. In contrast, adolescent limited offenders engage in milder forms of antisociality (e.g., promiscuity, vandalism, substance abuse) that start at puberty and end in late adolescence or early adulthood. The life course persistent pathway to crime is complex, resulting from a series of negative, bi-directional interactions between a high-risk child (e.g., neurological deficits, cold/callous temperament) and a high-risk environment (e.g., poor parenting—inadequate supervision, parental psychopathology). Conversely, the adolescent limited pathway stems primarily from one risk factor—a low-risk youth's association with high-risk, persistent offenders in a bid to access the fringe benefits of adulthood—status, freedom, and money (Moffitt 1993). Interestingly, the male to female ratio in the life course persistent group is 10:1, versus 1.5:1 in the adolescent limited group (Moffitt and Caspi 2001; Moffitt et al. 2001).

Traditional explanations of life course and adolescent limited behaviour have been proximate in nature, focusing on social learning at the micro level—the person in the immediate situation (see Chapter 3). These theories posit that antisocial behaviour and the correlated activity of risk-taking and impulsivity (see Mishra and Lalumière 2008) are pathological deviations from "normalcy" resulting in counterproductive and self-destructive behaviours. In contrast, Canadian evolutionary psychologists (e.g., Lalumière, Mishra, Harris, Quinsey) have taken the novel approach of interpreting this form of behaviour through an evolutionary lens, hypothesizing that some risk-taking and antisocial behaviours exist today because they were adaptive in the sense that they contributed to reproductive fitness in an ancestral environment.

First, let's explain adolescent limited behaviour within the life history framework. Recall that life history theory states that whether an individual will favour high mating effort over parental investment tactics depends largely on age—adolescents are more likely to exhibit high mating effort because in an ancestral environment, it gave them (on average) a competitive edge in the reproductive sense. In the absence of existing offspring, a mate, accumulated status, and/or resources, no costs would be incurred for engaging in strategies that would help secure as many sexual partners as possible. However, the potential benefits could be substantial. Thus natural selection would favour life history strategies (in youth) characterized by high mating effort. So what does strong mating effort actually look like? It is argued that traits such as dominance, risky behaviours such as fighting or willingness to fight, independence, strength, fearlessness, and physical prowess are expressions of high mating effort (in men, typically). From the female's point of view, it is easy to see why these characteristics would be enviable in a tough and brutish ancestral environment characterized by food scarcity and dangerous predators. Right or wrong (see Box 2.2 for a discussion of the naturalistic fallacy), this is the kind of person a female would have needed to protect and provide for her and her offspring. If she did not "select" this mate, the chances for offspring survival might have been diminished.

Reviews of the literature have shown that high mating effort is correlated with risk-taking and antisocial behaviours in both genders. For example, aggressive and antisocial behaviour are related to early sexual intercourse in boys and girls. Risk-taking is one of the best predictors of adolescent pregnancy (see Ellis and Walsh 2000; Lalumière, Harris, Quinsey, and Rice 2005). As discussed in Chapter 1, the vast majority of crimes, particularly serious crimes, are committed by young men during adolescence. This finding persists across time and culture (Ellis and Walsh 2000; Quinsey et al. 2004). In fact, Moffitt (1993) considers adolescence-limited offending behaviour to be normative in that the vast majority of youth engage in these behaviours—both male and female. In other words, high mating effort and antisocial behaviour characterize adolescence. Life course theory provides an ultimate explanation for why these behaviours co-exist during adolescence and early adulthood. The rewards associated with high mating effort tactics (some of which would be considered antisocial) outweighed the costs in an ancestral environment, and individuals who used high mating efforts more frequently would have (on average) produced more offspring and consequently passed their "adaptive psychological mechanism" on to the next generation.

Evolutionary psychologists take a somewhat different approach regarding life course persistent offenders. Recall that life history theory dictates that individuals will adopt different life course strategies depending on environmental cues. If environmental cues signal that the future is bleak and unknown, the organism will respond in kind with an early onset high mating effort that unfortunately coincides with antisocial behaviour. Evolutionary psychologists argue that this is essentially what occurs in life course persistent offenders. Recall that life course persistent offenders suffer from a number of deficits most likely acquired early in life, perhaps during pregnancy (e.g., maternal malnutrition) or childhood (e.g., parental abuse).

Thus the environment signals that the best course of action is early onset high mating effort as the chances of reproducing in the future would be uncertain (Mishra and Lalumière 2008).

These disadvantages accumulate over time and manifest as subtle neurological and/or intellectual deficits that make it difficult to maintain friendships, succeed in school, or, ultimately, obtain a high-status and/or well-paying job. In the end, such an individual is placed at a competitive disadvantage in the realm of mate acquisition and retention. Evolutionists refer to this situation as low embodied capital. Embodied capital refers to intrinsic abilities such as health, skills, strength, speed, attractiveness, and so forth, which translate into enhanced reproductive fitness. Embodied capital is operationalized both similarly and differently for men and women. While health and attractiveness would be positive indicators for both genders, strength and speed might be more salient for men. Life history theorists also argue that individuals who suffer from low embodied capital, such as life course persistent offenders, are placed at a competitive disadvantage that catalyzes early onset, high mating effort behaviour. So while age catalyzes adolescent limited behaviour, low embodied capital and negative environmental cues catalyze life course persistent behaviour (Mishra and Lalumière 2008). We now turn our attention to a third offender group—psychopaths.

Psychopathy

The construct of psychopathy has intrigued the public and the academic community for some time. In brief, psychopathy is typified by a constellation of affective, interpersonal, and behavioural characteristics, such as superficial charm, grandiosity, manipulation and lying, absence of remorse, inability to feel empathy, impulsivity, risk-taking behaviour, irresponsibility, and living a parasitic lifestyle (see Chapter 10 for an in-depth discussion).

In the previous section, evolution-based hypotheses were presented positing that life course persistent offending behaviour emerges in two circumstances. The first occurs when environmental insults (e.g., childhood abuse, malnutrition experienced as a fetus) "cue" an individual that the future is uncertain, thus directing him/her to adopt a high mating effort strategy that encompasses a host of antisocial behaviours, such as coercive sexual behaviour, fighting, aggression, and other behaviours that are not necessarily "criminal" but are known correlates and/or predictors of antisocial behaviour (e.g., impulsivity and risk taking). The second pathway argues that when individuals are competitively disadvantaged (i.e., suffer from low embodied capital) in a reproductive sense, perhaps due to environmental insults (e.g., neurological deficits, low socio-economic status) or not (e.g., not attractive), they will adopt a high mating effort strategy and consequently engage in antisocial behaviour.

The researchers behind these theories (Harris, Lalumière, Mishra, and Quinsey) have hypothesized that the pathway to psychopathy is entirely different but can still be explained using an evolutionary framework—specifically, the principle of frequency dependent selection. Before defining frequency dependent selection, it is necessary to understand polymorphisms. In biological terms, when two or more forms of a discrete character exist (e.g., eye colour—blue eyes, brown eyes, green eyes; blood types—A, B, AB, O), the contrasting forms are called morphs. One way that natural selection maintains diversity in a population is through frequency dependent selection, which states that the reproductive success of a particular morph relative to another morph (hence its ultimate survival) depends on its frequency (or, more accurately, its *phenotypic* expression) in a given population (Campbell et al. 1999). If it becomes too common, its phenotypic expression will no longer be adaptive because its success is dependent on its rarity in comparison to its sister morph(s) (see Box 2.4 for an illustrative example involving the "sneaker" salmon).

Lalumière and colleagues argue that psychopathic behaviour is a morph that has arisen as a direct result of frequency dependent selection. It is easy to see how "cheater" strategies (e.g., "have sex with me and I will protect you"; "let me have some of your food and next time I will share with you") would enhance one's reproductive success in an ancestral environment if, *and only if,* a small minority of individuals engaged in such tactics (e.g., 1 out of 100). As the number of cheaters increases, so does the probability that non-cheaters will find out and thus nullify the cheaters' success. Similarly, cheater strategies require a substantial pool of honest, trusting, cooperative individuals to manipulate in order to be successful. This life history strategy is predicted to emerge irrespective of environmental insults (Lalumière et al. 2005; Quinsey et al. 2004).

Two lines of evidence have been presented in support of psychopathy as an adaptive life history strategy. The first involves the mere existence of "psychopathic-like" behaviour in the animal world (see Box 2.4). The second line of evidence is somewhat indirect. Proponents of this perspective (see Harris, Rice, and Lalumière 2001; Quinsey et al. 2004) cite evidence illustrating that psychopaths are distinct from life course persistent offenders because they do not suffer from low embodied capital and thus are not competitively disadvantaged in a reproductive sense (Lalumière, Harris, and Rice 2001). So if there is nothing "wrong" with psychopaths in terms of embodied capital, yet they still adopt a high mating effort/risk taking/criminal lifestyle, it can be inferred that their particular life history strategy must have been adaptive, evolutionarily speaking. There is some evidence that counters the psychopathy-as-adaptation argument, however. Recall that frequency dependent selection (the hypothesized mechanism through which psychopathy is posited to have been selected for) only works with polymorphisms. And polymorphisms must be discrete not continuous—either you have blue eyes or you don't. Unfortunately, the evidence is mixed as to whether psychopathy is a continuous or discrete entity (see Chapter 10). Until it can be proven beyond a doubt that psychopathy is a taxon, it seems unlikely that a strong case can be made for the adaptionist perspective. While there is some evidence linking genetics and psychopathy, an actual "'psychopathy" genetic marker has yet to be found (see Chapter 10). Such evidence would further serve to bolster the evolutionary explanation for the origins of psychopathy.

Box 2.4

What Do a Psychopath and "Sneaker" Salmon Have in Common?

Most of us are familiar with the life of a typical Pacific male salmon. They are born, leave their birth place (a fresh-water stream), and swim into the open sea, only to return (swimming upstream) to spawn and eventually die. But the battle doesn't end there. Once the male salmon arrives home, he has to compete with other males to "convince" a female that he is a worthy candidate to fertilize her eggs.

Female salmon are extremely selective, with experimental conditions revealing that 90 percent of eggs will be fertilized by one or two males——generally the biggest and reddest ones who guard the best territory, which has better water flow/gravel conditions. Scientists have discovered that there are two pathways to fertilization. The first is exhibited by the vast majority of male salmon—the direct "look at me—I'm worthy of your eggs" approach. The second pathway is extremely rare but still manages to be effective. A type of male salmon affectionately known as a "sneaker" uses it. He lies in wait, hidden from the legitimate courtship ritual, and once the female releases her eggs and makes them available to the target male salmon—Mr. Big and Red—the sneaker sneaks in and fertilizes as many eggs as he can until Mr. Big and Red

extricates him. Unlike typical Pacific salmon, which spend about 18 months away from home, some varieties of sneaker only leave the stream for 6 months or, in some cases, not at all. While sneakers are small and would not be able to compete physically with Mr. Big and Red to win the affections of a typical female, the sneaker fertilization strategy is a successful alternative—even if he only manages to fertilize a few eggs relative to the massive fertilization efforts of Mr. Big and Red.

The obvious question is why natural selection has allowed the sneaker to live. Biologists have calculated that the total expected payoff for each strategy—personal survival multiplied by the number of fertilized eggs—is about equal for Mr. Big and Red (fertilizes a lot of eggs but has a high probability of being killed in the open sea) and the sneaker (fertilizes only a few eggs but has a much lower probability of dying because he either doesn't make it to the open sea or only remains for a short time). Thus neither strategy produces any reproductive advantage, allowing the balanced polymorphism to exist (Palumbi 2002).

So what do you think? Are psychopaths the human equivalent of sneakers in the salmon world?

Homicide

In 1988, Daly and Wilson presented one of the first seminal accounts of homicide from an evolutionary perspective. They used evolution to understand various forms of homicide—spousal, blood-relative, casual acquaintance, revenge killings, and so forth. For the purposes of illustration, we will describe Daly and Wilson's evolutionary account of homicide between male strangers or male acquaintances.

Despite media reports, most homicides occur as the result of altercations arising from arguments, insults, or rivalries between male acquaintances. Usually, the men involved are unmarried and unemployed. Daly and Wilson cite numerous examples to support this position, ranging from anecdotal accounts from contemporary hunter-and-gatherer societies to large-scale quantitative studies dating back to Wolfgang's (1958) classic treatise on homicide. In his study, Wolfgang classified a large number of homicides as "altercations of relatively trivial origin; insult, curse, jostling, etc." (p. 125, as cited in Daly and Wilson 1988). It is noteworthy that an evolutionary-focused re-analysis of Toch's (1988) classic book *Violent Men* confirms Daly and Wilson's position.

Daly and Wilson argue that a man's reputation depends largely on his ability to maintain a credible threat of violence. Evidence was based on various historical accounts (e.g., duels often led to status enhancement among prominent men in America) and anthropological accounts such as this quote from a Dani tribesman from New Guinea: "'A man without valor is kepu—a worthless man, a man-who-has-not killed'" (Matthiessen 1962, as cited in Daly and Wilson 1988: 131).

Daly and Wilson claim that the apparent "trivial" nature of homicide motives may not be trivial after all, suggesting that homicide perpetrators are actually responding to perceived reputational or status threats. The researchers argue that failure to restore one's reputation in an ancestral environment would have resulted in dire consequences from a

"Here's how it works, Freddie. Over millions of years the male brain has evolved to help us to find a mate, get a meal, and ward-off hostile takeovers."

reproductive fitness standpoint for two reasons. First, responding with violence would prevent current and future exploitations of one's resources—territory, shelter, food, and so forth. Second, it would also signal prospective mates to a strong provider for herself and her future children, thereby enhancing her reproductive fitness.

It is important to underscore that Daly and Wilson do not necessarily argue that the act of killing has been naturally selected for, but rather that the broader spectrum of violence and aggression has been selected for, which at times can "go too far" and result in death. Their argument posits that homicide is an evolutionary byproduct of the more encompassing, evolved mechanism of violence and aggression that occurs in response to environmental cues or threats to status/reputation. This position stands in stark contrast to an alternative evolutionary account of homicide that argues that natural selection has selected for the act of homicide in and of itself (see Duntley and Buss 2008). It is therefore argued that violence, aggression, and homicide exist today because in an ancestral environment they enhanced reproductive fitness, particularly among men.

Interestingly, a recent study involving Genghis Khan (Zerjal et al. 2003) provides vivid evidence in support of the hypothesis that violence, status, and power can dramatically enhance one's reproductive fitness. Genghis Khan (c. 1162–1227) and his male descendants established the largest land empire in history, spanning east and southwest Asia and parts of central Europe. Historical accounts indicate that Khan and his descendants were extremely violent (slaughtering conquered populations, raping women) but were simultaneously excellent progenitors of their genes, keeping multiple wives and concubines as a direct result of war conquests (Turnbull 2004).

Genghis Khan in the Battle of the Indo Valley

Zerjal et al. (2003) examined the Y chromosomes of 2123 men from across Asia. Interestingly, 8 percent had Y chromosomes that were virtually identical, indicating a common forefather. It is estimated that 16 million men across Asia—from the Sea of Japan to Afghanistan—possess this particular Y chromosome. Although it is impossible to conclude with 100 percent certainty that Genghis Khan was the originator of this chromosome, researchers are reasonably confident that it most likely belonged to his paternal grandfather. It is estimated that the average man who lived at the time of Genghis Khan would have 20 direct descendents alive today—a far cry from Khan's 16 million!

Female-Perpetrated Crime

There is one universally accepted fact about crime. Men commit more crime, particularly more violent and serious crime, than women, irrespective of the disciplinary orientation of the researcher, the study methodology, or the timeframe of investigation (Blanchette and Brown 2006). While a number of evolutionary theorists are beginning to understand why females are simply less criminal than males (Daly and Wilson 1988; Quinsey et al. 2004; Walsh and Beaver 2008), it is the explanations put forth by Anne Campbell (Campbell, 1995; 1999; 2002; Campbell, Muncer, and Bibel, 2001) that have been the most influential. Anne Campbell and other evolutionary theorists posit that risky behaviours were naturally selected for in the environment of evolutionary adaptation because they enhanced survival and consequently reproductive success under certain environmental pressures: specifically, resource scarcity. Campbell's perspective is succinctly described as follows:

> We argue that resource scarcity [e.g., food, money, shelter] drives both property and violent offending in women. Property offenses reflect women's attempts to provision themselves [directly] while violence reflects female–female competition for provisioning males [indirect source of resources]. Evolutionary pressure (the critical importance of maternal survival to females' reproductive success) [dependency of offspring on mother for survival] resulted in females' lower threshold for fear, relative to males, when faced with the same level of objective physical danger. This adaptation inhibits women's involvement in crime, makes them more likely to be involved in property rather than violent crimes and, when direct confrontation is inevitable, causes them to use low-risk or indirect tactics [e.g., verbal aggression]. (Campbell et al. 2001: 481)

Campbell (2002) further argues that poverty (the immediate cause of resource scarcity) is a necessary precursor to female crime. However, it is not necessarily sufficient. Individual differences in fear thresholds among women explain why some poverty-stricken females resort to crime while others do not. She recognizes the importance of a number of direct and indirect factors that mediate the relationship between poverty and crime. These factors operate at both the macro (e.g., overcrowding) and individual levels (e.g., poor parenting) and are derived from existing criminological theories such as social learning theory, social control theory, and life course perspectives (see Chapter 3).

We can also understand Campbell's thinking in the context of life history theory—particularly by examining the costs and rewards associated with mating effort versus parental investment and whether they should or do differ for men and women. In fact, the rewards and costs associated with mating effort and parental investment are different for men and women. Further, it is these very differences that evolutionists use to explain why women commit less crime, particularly less serious forms of crime, than men. These differences are captured by the term **reproductive fitness variance**. In short, women's fitness variance is restricted in comparison to men's. Over the course of her life, it is impossible for a woman to produce more offspring than a man could. In other words, the number of offspring a woman can actually produce and take care of during her lifespan is relatively small compared to her male counterparts. Not only does she carry a finite number of eggs, it also takes considerable time and resources to raise one child (e.g., nine months gestation; lengthy lactation period, particularly in ancestral times before the advent of bottle feeding). It also takes time before she is physically able to conceive another child following birth. Hence a woman's fitness potential is restricted.

In contrast, these limitations do not exist for men. In theory, men can produce significantly more children and with little effort (i.e., the time it takes to ejaculate, technically speaking, is all that is needed to produce a child). The male reproductive fitness potential is considerably wider—he may have no children or could have several hundred (recall Genghis Khan). Herein lies one reason why men commit more crime than women. In an ancestral environment, the cost/benefit ratio favoured high mating effort over parental investment (on average) for men, whereas it favoured high parental investment for women. On average, men who focused more of their energy on finding and maintaining sexual partners versus parental investment were more successful in propagating their genetic material. Conversely, women who were more selective about mates (pairing up with someone who would keep them and their children alive) and devoted more time to protecting their offspring were, on average, more successful in propagating their genetic material. Natural selection favoured evolved psychological mechanisms that supported high mating in men and high parental investment in women. For women, the costs of engaging in high mating effort and consequent risk-taking and aggressive behaviours simply weren't worth the risk of dying and not being able to ensure the survival of offspring. However, offspring survival wasn't nearly as dependent on the father's life. There is considerable evidence that men invest more energy in mating effort than women and that women are more partial to parental investment (Low 2000; Schmitt 2005). This statement is based on averages; it doesn't mean that men never invest in their children or that women never exhibit high mating effort.

Below is a list of the top 10 issues and people to consider when thinking about theories of crime and correctional practice in Canada.

Top 10 List

Advances to Come, Debates, Ethical Conundrums, and People to Watch

1 How do we advance the interdisciplinary understanding of behaviour?

2 Longitudinal studies that systemically assess and re-assess promising biological markers of antisocial behaviour to see how they interact with changes in the environment.

3 How do different biological and evolutionary pathways correspond to different "types" of antisocial behaviour—sexual, violent, risk taking?

4 Is crime simply a byproduct of other adaptive mechanisms? Or is it a genuine adaptation in its own right?

5 Is psychopathy a discrete or continuous entity? A discrete entity is a necessary prerequisite if one subscribes to the theory that psychopathy is an evolved adaptation arising specifically from frequency dependent selection.

6 Will evolutionary approaches lead to different measurement strategies for important criminological constructs such as psychopathy? Is psychopathy really a discrete entity—a "taxon"— but our existing measures (i.e., the Hare Revised Psychopathy Checklist; Hare 2003) simply aren't good enough to capture its taxonic nature?

7 As biological advancements continue to grow and it becomes increasingly clear that biological impairment plays a role in the development and maintenance of certain forms of antisocial behaviour, how should this be addressed by the courts?

8 Should at-risk children be genotyped and given a full neurological assessment? Who should have access to this information?

9 Should biological risk markers be incorporated into risk assessment devices and treatment approaches?

10 People to watch: Martin Lalumière, Vern Quinsey, Terrie Moffitt, Adraine Raine, Sandeep Mishra.

SUMMARY

1. There are multiple pathways to crime. In this chapter, we have focused on evolutionary and biological explanations. Multiple pathways also exist within each perspective, including a host of biological factors such as genetics, neurochemistry, hormones, psychophysiology, and others. Evolutionary perspectives are complex, and evolution is not a monolithic theory but is comprised of a series of micro evolutionary theories (e.g., life history theory, frequency dependent selection). We have only scratched the surface in this chapter.

2. Despite popular belief, biological and evolutionary explanations of crime underscore the importance of the environment. Environmental insults (e.g., a mother who

drinks during pregnancy) change the biological makeup of an individual such that he or she is now predisposed to a future criminal lifestyle. Evolutionary mechanisms were shaped by the environment, albeit a distant one. Evolution itself has shaped our minds such that they adapt and change to current environmental cues. The theory of evolution has more in common with environmental theories such as social learning (discussed in Chapter 3) than one might think. The only difference is that evolution focuses on the learning environment of the entire species whereas social learning theories focus on the learning environment of an individual.

3. It is a myth that evolutionary accounts of crime contradict traditional theories such as those reviewed in Chapter 3. Evolutionary perspectives simply focus on providing ultimate explanations, and traditional criminological theories focus on more proximate explanations. The perspectives tend to complement rather than contradict one another. When theories do diverge it indicates that one perspective is incorrect.

4. This chapter has shown that "the evidence for genetic influences on criminality is no longer scientifically questionable" (Ellis 2008: 249). It has also demonstrated that the path to crime is complex and that a number of biological subsystems interact with one another to increase risk of future criminality, with the environment greatly influencing whether certain biological predispositions will manifest.

5. Evolution is uncontested in scientific circles. However, evolutionary psychology, in particular evolutionary forensic psychology, is in its infancy. More research from different perspectives is required.

6. The link between evolutionary and biological explanations of crime is a natural one. In the evolution section, we focused on psychological mechanisms that have evolved in response to ancestral selection pressures. This does not negate the existence of evolved biological mechanisms such as those reviewed in the first part of the chapter.

Discussion Questions

1. Identify your favourite explanation of crime. Now put it to the test. What kind of a grade does it get with respect to the criteria reviewed at the beginning of this chapter (what makes a strong theory)? What challenges did you face while you were doing this task? What additional information would have made your task easier?

2. What are the legal implications (if any) for biological explanations of crime? If your "genes made you do it," should you be held accountable in a court of law?

3. Does society hold a more deterministic view of biological/evolutionary explanations of crime versus sociological explanations (i.e., if the cause is in your genes, we can't fix it, but if the cause is in the environment we can)? If so, how can we change current thinking?

4. What is the implication of the MAOA findings for females? Recall that the MAOA is X-linked. Does this mean that females might have built-in resiliency against aggression and crime? If so, why?

5. Evolutionary psychology argues that modern human brains are comprised of evolved psychological mechanisms that helped solved adaptative problems during the hunter-and-gatherer period. Given that it usually takes thousands of generations for an evolved adaptation to become commonplace in the population, our brains have not yet had the chance to incorporate adaptations from the industrial or agricultural revolutions. Knowing this, fast forward a few thousand generations and predict how human behaviour will change. How will the technological revolution impact our future, evolutionarily speaking?

Additional Reading

Anderson, G.S. 2007. *Biological influences on criminal behaviour*. Boca Raton: Simon Fraser University Publications, CRC Press, Taylor & Francis Group.

Daly, M. and Wilson, M. 1988. *Homicide*. New York: Aldine de Gruyter.

Duntley, J.D. and Shackelford, T.K., eds.. 2008. *Evolutionary forensic psychology: Darwinian foundations of crime and law*. New York: Oxford University Press.

Relevant Website

Human Behavior and Evolution Society
www.hbes.com

Chapter 3
Theories of Crime: Learning and Environment

Aaron was 22 years old when he was convicted of murder and sentenced to time in a federal penitentiary. Reflecting on his life, one could wonder how he got himself into the situation he was in. Like many people, Aaron was raised in a single-parent home by his mother, who had to work extra shifts to support him and his two older brothers (his father was in prison for armed robbery). Aaron's family was not poor, though, and he felt he had all he needed growing up in what he called "a typical middle-class neighbourhood." Aaron was a very bright boy and remembers enjoying school, at least initially. Problems began when Aaron was around 10 years old. During the evenings, his mother would work, and he would hang out with his brothers and their friends. The types of crimes he initially committed were fairly minor, mostly consisting of vandalism "committed just for fun" and stealing from local stores, often in response to challenges from the older boys. Unfortunately for Aaron, things progressed. Soon, he was throwing rocks off bridges at passing cars, stealing stereos from vehicles, and getting into fights with other kids at school. Throughout his teens, Aaron started spending less time at school and more time at the local arcade. His mother would frequently be called to school to discuss his truancy, fighting, and poor grades. As he got older, fights at school turned into fights on the street, and Aaron quickly gained a reputation among his friends as someone who "liked to knock one off." He also had a reputation as a partier and would frequently get into fights while under the influence of alcohol. Aaron's reputation eventually caught up with him when he started a fight one night at a local bar because someone had embarrassed his friends. Sadly, things went too far. After moving the fight outside, one of Aaron's friends passed him a knife, which he used to kill his 20–year-old opponent.

Learning Objectives

1   Describe the primary differences between psychodynamic, learning, and social learning theories of crime.

2   Identify the key principles of psychodynamic theories and explain how these principles relate to our understanding of criminal behaviour.

3 Describe the major predictors of crime from the perspective of "control" theories, such as Gottfredson and Hirschi's general theory of crime.

4 Describe the principles of classical and operant conditioning.

5 Explain the role of classical conditioning in Eysenck's biosocial theory of crime.

6 Identify the key elements of Sutherland's differential association theory and Akers's social learning theory of crime.

7 Examine the personal, interpersonal, and community-reinforcement theory of crime proposed by Andrews and Bonta.

INTRODUCTION

AS YOU SAW IN THE PREVIOUS CHAPTER, PSYCHOLOGISTS HAVE ATTEMPTED TO explain why people get involved in crime in a few different ways. In explaining Aaron's behaviour, for example, biological theories of crime—while not discounting the importance of social factors—tend to focus on the impact of physiological, biochemical, neurological, and/or genetic factors. Biological theorists might stress the fact that criminality seems to run in Aaron's family, indicating a genetic basis to his behaviour. Evolutionary theories of crime, on the other hand, focus on explanations of how crime can be thought of as adaptive behaviour, developed as a means to survive in both our ancestral and present-day environments. To an evolutionary psychologist, the murder committed by Aaron may be viewed primarily as a means for him to achieve status among male competitors, which will ultimately influence his reproductive success either because his fighting makes him more attractive to females or because murder helps defeat rival males.

In this chapter, we will continue to explore how psychologists attempt to explain criminal behaviour, focusing on theories that emphasize learning and the environment. We will look at how variables such as a lack of parental supervision, the presence of pro-criminal role models, and positive reinforcement from friends for committing antisocial acts affect the lives of people like Aaron. We will present three general perspectives on crime—psychodynamic, learning, and social learning perspectives—and discuss specific theories that fall into each of these categories. These theories include some of the most well-known and well-validated theories of crime to date, such as Hirschi's social control theory, Gottfredson and Hirschi's general theory of crime, Eysenck's biosocial theory, Akers's social learning theory, and Andrews and Bonta's personal, interpersonal, and community-reinforcement theory. In reviewing these theories, we will describe their key components, discuss how they differ from one another and how they are similar, evaluate the degree to which the theories are supported by empirical evidence, and examine some of the criticisms that are raised in relation to each theory.

PSYCHODYNAMIC THEORIES

A SUITABLE PLACE TO START OUR DISCUSSION IS WITH **PSYCHODYNAMIC** THEORIES. Most of you will likely be familiar with the psychodynamic (or psychoanalytic) approach to understanding human behaviour. No introductory psychology class is complete without a discussion of this perspective and its founding father, Sigmund Freud. Freud is well known for his theories of the unconscious mind, the defence mechanisms he proposed, and the various therapeutic techniques he endorsed, such as free association and dream interpretation (see Jones 1953; 1955; 1957 for an account of Freud's life and his many contributions to the field of psychology). Oddly, given his vast interests, Freud had relatively little to say about crime or criminal behaviour (see Freud 1901; 1938). This is not to say, however, that the psychodynamic perspective is irrelevant to our understanding of crime. Some of the most important theories of crime in recent history draw on psychodynamic principles.

Basic Psychodynamic Principles: The Id, Ego, and Superego

Before discussing some of the psychodynamic theories of crime, let us turn our attention to a few basic psychodynamic concepts that are potentially relevant for understanding why people become involved in criminal activity. From a psychodynamic perspective, humans are thought to be inherently antisocial, driven by pleasure-seeking and destructive impulses (Blackburn 1995). According to this perspective, crime generally occurs when these (often unconscious) impulses are not adequately controlled. This is thought to happen when internal psychic forces tasked with the job of regulating such impulses fail to develop as they should, typically due to traumatic childhood experiences.

As an example of how a psychoanalyst might explain the emergence of criminal behaviour, consider the work of the late David Abrahamsen, a well-known forensic psychiatrist, psychoanalyst, and author of many books, including an interesting in-depth analysis of the crimes of serial killer David Berkowitz (a.k.a. Son of Sam) (Abrahamsen 1985). Like many other psychiatrists of his time, Abrahamsen's general perspective on crime and its development was psychodynamic. Consider the following passage from his book *The Murdering Mind* (Abrahamsen 1973), a detailed account of his involvement with Tiger, the murderer of a young girl:

> Having examined hundreds of people who have killed . . . I have found that homicide usually does not originate because of a clearly defined impulse to kill, but is released by the intensity of internal conflicts . . . In examining those who have committed murder, I have found one common characteristic . . . all the murderers were intensely tormented. Deep down, they felt beset, trapped in an intense conflict growing out of the struggle between their sexual and self-preserving feelings on the one hand and their external surrounding on the other . . . It is these inner drives which shape the aggressive thrust that in a certain situation may trigger murderous impulses that result in violent acting out to the point of murder.

The conflict I refer to is due to serious traumatic situations, primarily experienced in the earliest childhood . . . When as children we feel hurt by people's rejection or criticism, we either give vent to it or push away from our mind our real resentment until we "forget" about them. They become unconscious. When we continue to repress and it becomes a pattern of behaviour, without finding any outward expression or release, these hateful emotions accumulate within us. If we are unable to curb these hostile feelings, our ego-protecting defences crumble and murderous acting-out impulses emerge. (pp. 9–10)

References to "inner drives," "traumatic situations," and "protecting defences" are commonplace in psychodynamic explanations of crime, but where exactly do psychoanalysts believe these "sexual and self-serving feelings" come from? What experiences "in the earliest childhood" are important, and what internal forces are meant to "curb" the potentially dangerous impulses that supposedly reside within us? To answer these questions, Freud and his followers relied on a set of psychic structures thought to develop throughout childhood and adolescence to form a dynamic personality system (Freud 1923).

Psychoanalysts believe that pleasure-seeking and destructive impulses originate in the **id**, part of an individual's personality that is present at birth and represents unconscious, primitive, and instinctual desires. The id is thought to be governed by the **pleasure principle**: it seeks immediate pleasure with little consideration of the undesirable consequences that may result if an impulse is acted upon. These potentially destructive forces are believed to be controlled in one of two ways (Blackburn 1995). First, psychoanalysts believe that the activity of the id is opposed by the next personality structure to develop, the ego, which attempts to mediate between one's primal needs and society's demands. The ego is guided by the **reality principle**: its development coincides with the emergence of reality-oriented thinking and it allows the id to function in socially acceptable ways by suppressing the id's impulses until appropriate situations arise (e.g., by allowing for the delay of gratification). Second, in challenging id drives, the ego is guided by the **superego**, the last of the three personality systems to develop according to psychoanalysts. The superego represents the internalization of group standards, typically conveyed to the child through parental care and discipline, and it acts as a moral regulator, tasked with the job of overseeing the choices we make. The superego is thought to consist of two sub-systems: the **conscience**, which allows an individual to distinguish between right and wrong and forces the ego to inhibit id pursuits that are out of line with one's morals, and the **ego-ideal**, which represents the socially accepted standards to which we all aspire.

Freud (1938) believed that personality development occurs across five **psychosexual stages** (see Table 3.1) and argued that difficulties resolving conflicts within any given stage can potentially result in problems with personality development, which would be apparent in one's behaviour. Much of Freud's thinking about these psychosexual stages is now incorporated into our common everyday thinking about the personalities of the people we interact with. For example, we all know people who are said to possess an "anal" personality—such people are known for their stingy, stubborn, controlling, and perfectionist ways. To Freud, this "anally retentive personality" is the result of a person's inability to resolve conflicts encountered in the anal stage of development.

Table 3.1 Freud's Psychosexual Stages of Development

Stage	Description
Oral	Begins at birth and ends around age one to one-and-a-half. The child is preoccupied with seeking gratification through sucking and feeding. The primary conflict is weaning, which deprives the child of sensory and psychological pleasures such as nursing and feeling cared for by the mother.
Anal	Begins around age one to one-and-a-half with the introduction of toilet training and lasts until about age two to three. The primary conflict is one of control, as the child has to learn to delay the pleasure associated with bodily expulsion.
Phallic	Begins around age two to three and lasts until age five to six. The primary conflict is sexual. At this stage, the child becomes interested in their genitals and begins to develop an unconscious desire for the opposite-sex parent and fear of retribution from the same-sex parent. This conflict is called the **Oedipus complex** in boys. Through fear of castration (i.e., castration anxiety) and gradual identification with the father, which allows the boy to possess his mother vicariously, the young male becomes indoctrinated into the appropriate sexual role in life and develops a superego. The same conflict is called the **Electra complex** in girls. The young female recognizes that, unlike her father, she has no penis and blames this on her mother (i.e., penis envy). By gradually identifying with the mother figure, girls begin to resolve this conflict, though Freud believed that females remain slightly fixated at the phallic stage and therefore never develop as strong a superego as boys.
Latent	Begins around age five to six and lasts until puberty (age twelve or later). A time where the sexual drive becomes de-emphasized and repressed sexual energy gets redirected to asexual pursuits such as same-sex friendships.
Genital	Begins in adolescence and lasts until adulthood. Interest in the genitals is reborn and the individual focuses on a search for intimacy with an opposite-sex adult partner. The energy that can be devoted to these pursuits depends on the extent to which the conflicts encountered in the previous stages have been successfully resolved.

Source: Adapted from Ewen (2003) and Stevenson (2001)

Problems that result in superego formation, which are generally thought to stem from a failure to identify with prosocial parental figures, are of particular interest to those attempting to develop explanations of crime. In fact, psychoanalysts have proposed three main sources of criminal behaviour, each relating to inadequate superego formation. The three sources relate to the development of a harsh, weak, or deviant superego (Blackburn 1995; see Andrews and Bonta 2006 for additional types of criminals studied by psychoanalysts).

The individual who commits crime as a result of a harsh superego is sometimes referred to as a **neurotic criminal** (Alexander 1935; Blackburn 1995; Meloy and Gacono 1997). The existence of a harsh superego is assumed to lead to pathological levels of unconscious guilt (typically over unresolved infantile desires) and criminal behaviour is meant to subconsciously invite punishment in an attempt to resolve this guilt. David, the offender described in Box 3.1, is an example of a neurotic criminal. Individuals who commit crime because of a weak superego are commonly associated with the psychopathic personality (Millon, Simonsen, and Birket-Smith 2002). Possessing a superego that fails to sufficiently regulate the primitive and instinctual needs of the id, this type of individual is typically "egocentric, impulsive, guiltless, and unempathic" (Blackburn 1995: 114). Many violent offenders, including serial killers, are often assumed to commit crimes due to a weak or underdeveloped superego. The third type of criminal commits crime as a result of a deviant superego. As Blackburn (1995) explains, for these individuals, superego standards have developed, but those standards are thought to reflect **deviant identification** (i.e., identification with a deviant role model). This could occur, for example, when criminal parents have a good relationship with their son and the son grows up to mirror his parents' criminality; in this case, the child's delinquent behaviour "reflects an absence of guilt, but not the abnormality of psychic structures" (Blackburn 1995: 115). Processes that lead to deviant identification are examined more closely in Chapter 5, where we discuss the development of juvenile offending.

Box 3.1

David: An Example of a Neurotic Criminal

Freud (1916) believed that many criminals are motivated by a sense of guilt and a need to deal with this guilt by being punished through legal sanctions. Today, psychologists generally accept that neurotic criminals of this kind are very rare, although some appear to exist. David, a patient/criminal presented by Meloy and Gacono (1997), arguably fits the bill. Meloy and Gacono's description of David may provide a glimpse inside the mind of the neurotic criminal.

David is described as a 42–year-old Caucasian male, born and raised in a Greek Roman Catholic middle-class family. David had two older brothers. His mother was a housewife and his father was a store manager until his death from a heart attack when David was 31. David's early life was one of turmoil, filled with fear, unhappiness, and confusion, and while he was never physically or sexually abused as a child, he clearly had a poor relationship with his father. Indeed, as David recalls, "I had no warm times with [my father]. He told me what a shit I am. He'd scream, holler like a madman" (Meloy and Gacono, 1997: 290). David described his mother as emotionally withdrawn, and stated that she would often justify or rationalize his father's behaviour. Despite these issues, there were no signs of

Continued >

Box 3.1   Continued

significant behavioural or medical problems in his childhood, and no history of criminality, alcoholism, or psychiatric illness in his family history.

David married while in college and subsequently had three sons. However, after seven years of marriage, he divorced his first wife and began dating another woman. It was at this time that David started gambling. Gradually, more and more of David's time was spent gambling, which he viewed as an escape from his father—an environment where he could finally make his own choices instead of following his father's. When his father died, David said he became reckless, affirming his "father's opinion that I would f— up without him here" (Meloy and Gacono, 1997: 290). While David regularly won when he gambled, he was borrowing larger and larger sums of money, and three years after he started he owed approximately $600 000 to various individuals.

David sought treatment from a psychiatrist at this time, but was not hospitalized until he was arrested and charged with conspiracy to obtain, distribute, manufacture, and possess illegal drugs. Speaking of these crimes, David says, "Most compulsive gamblers will [commit crimes] . . . The meth manufacturing was part of my self-destruction. I knew I was being surveilled by the police five weeks before I did the lab" (Meloy and Gacono, 1997: 290). In other words, despite knowing the police were on to him—even watching him—David continued to commit crimes. From a psychoanalytic perspective, this was done because the crimes David committed brought on the punishment he unconsciously felt he deserved (from disappointing his father).

David pled guilty to three non-violent crimes, including theft and tax evasion, and was sentenced to five years in prison. He was released to a halfway house after seven months and successfully completed his parole two years later.

Source: Meloy and Gacono (1997)

Psychodynamic Theories of Crime

While these general categories of criminal types—representing harsh, weak, or deviant superegos—are useful, they provide inadequate information about the actual causes of crime, other than the fact that problems with superego development may play an important role. This simplistic approach to understanding crime also fails to address key issues with respect to what we know about criminal behaviour. For example, the consistent finding that males are more likely than females to commit crime does not fit well with the psychoanalytic assumption that girls are less likely than boys to develop a strong superego (due to their inability to resolve psychosexual conflicts, especially at the phallic stage) (Blackburn 1995). In an attempt to better understand what causes crime, at least from a psychodynamic perspective, we now turn our attention to a discussion of various theories of crime that relate to this perspective. Although Freud may have had little to say about why people become involved in criminal activity, many other individuals have applied psychodynamic principles to this problem. Indeed, the influence of Freud's ideas can be seen in many common approaches to understanding crime.

Bowlby's Theory of Maternal Deprivation The theory of maternal deprivation, which was developed and tested by the British child psychiatrist John Bowlby (1907–1990), draws heavily on the psychodynamic perspective and is a popular theory for how juvenile delinquency develops. Consistent with psychodynamic thinking, Bowlby's view was that young children require consistent and continuous maternal care in order for them to develop normally (i.e., to resolve the many psychological conflicts that children encounter throughout their psychosexual development) (Bowlby 1989). According to Bowlby, disruption to the mother–child relationship will have many harmful and potentially irreversible long-term effects, especially in relation to the child's ability to establish meaningful prosocial relationships. Lacking such abilities, the child will not develop the means to control his conduct (i.e., destructive impulses) and will be more likely to exhibit antisocial patterns of behaviour (Bowlby 1989).

Bowlby had some empirical data to support his view. For example, in a study of 44 juvenile delinquents, who were matched to a control group of non-delinquents, Bowlby (1944) found a significantly higher level of maternal deprivation in the delinquent group (39 percent) compared to the non-delinquents (5 percent). However, his research has been challenged, both on methodological and empirical grounds (Feldman 1977). Methodologically, his studies have been criticized for everything from the unrepresentative nature of his delinquent sample to poor control group matching (Morgan 1975). Empirically, Bowlby's results do not appear to hold up, especially in studies where large sample sizes are relied on (e.g., Hirschi 2002; McCord and McCord 1959; Nye 1982). Even Bowlby himself didn't always find strong evidence for the role of maternal deprivation in explaining delinquency (e.g., Bowlby et al. 1956). What now seems clear is that maternal deprivation is not a critical factor to a child's healthy development (i.e., a paternal figure can provide adequate care), that any damage caused by early deprivation is not necessarily irreversible, and that the theory over-predicts juvenile delinquency given that many individuals who experience maternal deprivation do not get involved in crime (Rutter 1981; Wootton 1962).

Unravelling Juvenile Delinquency: The Work of Glueck and Glueck
Despite the criticisms of Bowlby's theory, it does seem to be the case that family discord in general (e.g., a lack of parental supervision) is associated with delinquent behaviour and this variable is included in several theories of crime that have received more support than Bowlby's theory (e.g., Andrews and Bonta 2006; Glueck and Gleuck 1950; Hirschi 1969). The work of Glueck and Glueck (1950) is one such example, though what this Harvard husband and wife team proposed was less a formal theory of crime (indeed, the Gleucks have often been described as anti-theory; Sampson and Laub 1995) and more a summary of their empirical findings. That being said, the Gleucks were heavily influenced by psychodynamic thinking (Andrews and Bonta 2006) and often spoke of such things as

"mental conflict," "tensions between repressed and forgotten emotional experiences and more recent experiences," and "divergent instinctual energy propulsions" in typical psychoanalytic fashion (Glueck and Glueck 1950: 15).

According to Sampson and Laub (1995), the primary interests of the Gluecks were discovering the causes of crime and assessing the effectiveness of correctional treatment in controlling criminal behaviour. One of the approaches they adopted to examine these issues, which is nicely described in their book *Unravelling Juvenile Delinquency*, was to conduct **cross-sectional research** comparing the lives of juvenile delinquents with non-juveniles (Glueck and Glueck 1950). The incredibly ambitious study described in this book was based on 500 delinquent boys selected from the Massachusetts correctional system and 500 non-delinquent boys from Boston public schools, matched on age, race, type of neighbourhood (i.e., underprivileged), and intelligence (the Gluecks also conducted **longitudinal research** on the delinquent boys included in this study by following them up at different points in time; see Glueck and Glueck 1968). The Gluecks took a multidisciplinary approach to examining delinquency; for each boy, a wealth of information was collected, including social, psychological, and biological information, in addition to information about the boys' family lives, school performance, and work experiences. Not only were the boys interviewed, so were their parents and teachers.

Based on their findings, the Gleucks were able to provide a portrait of the delinquent. In summarizing their findings, they describe these individuals in the following way (note the psychodynamic tone to much of their description):

> The delinquents, far more than the non-delinquents, are of the essentially mesomorphic [strong and muscular], energetic type, with tendencies to restless and uninhibited expression of instinctual-affective energy and to direct and concrete, rather than symbolic and abstract, intellectual expression. It is evidently difficult for them to develop the high degree of flexibility of adaptation, self-management, self-control, and sublimation of primitive tendencies and self-centred desires demanded by the complex and confused culture of the times. (Glueck and Glueck 1950: 278)

To a large extent, the Gluecks attributed the differences between delinquents and non-delinquents to parenting factors, the primary source for superego development. The Gluecks' findings clearly indicated a marked difference between these groups across a range of parenting variables. For example, among the parents (and grandparents and siblings) of the delinquents, there was a greater incidence of emotional disturbances, mental retardation, alcoholism, and criminality. Parents of the delinquent boys were also less educated, less likely to stay together, and less ambitious. Furthermore, the parents of the delinquents showed greater carelessness in the supervision of their children and often appeared neglectful. Finally, a greater proportion of delinquent families were found to lack cohesiveness, warmth, and respect for the integrity of family members, and fewer of the delinquents were affectionately attached to their parents, especially their fathers. Viewing these findings through a psychodynamic lens, the Gluecks stated that "the development of a mentally hygienic and properly oriented superego (conscience) must have been greatly hampered by the kind of parental ideals, attitudes, temperaments, and behavior found to play such a major role on the family stage of the delinquents" (Glueck and Glueck 1950: 281).

Drawing on these types of findings, the Gluecks proposed a "tentative causal formula" that could, in their view, be used to predict who would become engaged in juvenile delinquency. Indeed, they believed that by drawing on their physical, temperamental, attitudinal, psychological, and socio-cultural data they could make accurate predictions, from a very young age, about the likelihood of children getting involved in crime. Unsurprisingly, such claims were met with resistance, and researchers quickly proceeded to show that the claims being made by the Gluecks were exaggerated, largely because they failed to take into account the actual base rate of delinquency in the general population (which clearly did not match the 50 percent base rate that characterized their sample of delinquents and non-delinquents; Reiss 1951).

In addition, the work of the Gluecks has been challenged for other methodological and ideological reasons (see Sampson and Laub 1995 for a detailed discussion of these challenges). For example, the Gluecks have been heavily criticized for not carefully examining issues related to causal ordering (i.e., whether the factors they highlighted preceded delinquency or were the result of delinquency) as well as for a range of other methodological weaknesses in their research, including inappropriate use of statistical techniques and procedures (e.g., Hirschi and Selvin 1967; Robins and Hill 1966). From an ideological standpoint, the Gluecks' work has been criticized for not emphasizing certain explanatory variables deemed important in mainstream criminology, such as class of origin (Snodgrass 1972, cited in Sampson and Laub 1995), and for placing so much emphasis on familial (e.g., supervision) and biological (e.g., mesomorphy) factors (see Laub and Sampson 1988). While contemporary psychologists would likely not have a problem with the Gluecks' omission of social class in their explanation of crime or the inclusion of familial and biological variables, the exclusion of other variables has been considered more problematic (e.g., interactions with anti-social peers and misconduct in school; Andrews and Bonta 2006). This is especially true in light of the fact that the Gleucks' own data suggested that these variables are important to consider.

Despite the criticisms levelled against their research, the Gluecks' work is still regarded as a piece of classic research in the field of criminology; research of a scope that is unlikely to be seen again (Sampson and Laub 1995). In addition, while the research may not be well-suited for the purpose of predicting juvenile delinquency (e.g., due to base rate issues), it can be used to examine the correlates of delinquency and non-delinquency (Hirschi and Selvin 1967). In fact, much recent research, which does not suffer from the same methodological limitations, provides support for many of the important variables associated with criminal involvement that were highlighted by the Gleucks, especially variables related to peers, family, and school (e.g., Andrews and Bonta 2006; Loeber and Stouthamer-Loeber 1986; Wells and Rankin 1991). Most notable is the research by Sampson and Laub (1988; 1995), who have painstakingly re-analyzed much of the Gluecks' original data. The Gluecks' research was also instrumental in the development of other psychodynamically oriented theories of crime that have become extremely popular, such as those proposed by Travis Hirschi and his colleagues.

Hirschi's Control Theories   Although not traditionally considered psychodynamic theories, it has been argued that Hirschi's control theories contain important psychodynamic themes (Andrews and Bonta 2006). For example, like the Gluecks, Hirschi (1969; 2002) views all humans as having the potential to exhibit antisocial behaviour and he incorporated into his theories of crime ideas about superego- and ego-type mechanisms that play a central role in controlling one's antisocial impulses. Although Hirschi does not appear to rely on Freudian thinking to the same extent that the Gluecks did (Andrews and Bonta 2006), the major question that he considers when attempting to understand crime is a classic psychodynamic one: it is not why people violate the law, but rather why more people don't violate the law. According to Hirschi's original **social control theory**, or social bond theory, the reason why people don't violate the law is because of social controls, or "the bond of the individual to society" (Hirschi 2002: 16). Specifically, Hirschi presented four interrelated types of social bonds that are collectively thought to promote socialization and conformity: attachment, commitment, involvement, and belief. According to Hirschi (2002), "delinquent acts result when an individual's bond to society is weak or broken" (p. 16).

The first bond, attachment, refers to attachment and interest in others, most importantly parents, friends, and teachers. Hirschi (2002) believed that one's acceptance of and abidance with social norms and ideals depend on attachments to other human beings (particularly the depth and quality of such attachments). One does not commit crime, Hirschi suggests, partly because one does not wish to jeopardize these valued relationships. In psychodynamic terms, attachment represents the ego-ideal. The second bond, commitment, refers to the time, energy, and effort placed in conventional behaviour (e.g., "getting an education, building up a business, acquiring a reputation for virtue"; Hirschi 2002: 20). As argued by Hirschi, people who

Travis Hirschi (1935–) proposed social control theory to explain why people conform to societal rules. Later, he and Gottfredson proposed their general theory of crime.

have an investment in conventional pursuits run a heightened risk of losing that investment if they become involved in crime. Commitment serves the same theoretical value
as the ego, according to Hirschi. The third bond, **involvement**, refers to the time and
energy one spends taking part in activities that are in line with the conventional interests of society (e.g., school). Hirschi argues that heavy involvement in conventional
activities limits the time that is available to participate in criminal pursuits, for, as
Hirschi says, "[t]he person involved in conventional activities is tied to appointments,
deadlines, working hours, plans, and the like" (p. 22). Lastly, **belief** refers to one's conviction to the view that people should obey common rules. This entails a respect for a
societal value system, including a respect for the law and institutions that enforce the
law. If such beliefs are weak or totally absent, involvement in crime is assumed to be
more likely. This bond has clear parallels with the conscience part of the superego.

Following the strategy adopted by the Gluecks, Hirschi (1969) tested his social
control theory by conducting a study of delinquents and non-delinquents, using a cross-
sectional design described in great detail in his book *Causes of Delinquency*. Like the
Gluecks, Hirschi collected a wide range of data on an impressively large sample of
adolescents—4077 in all (3605 were boys), some of whom were delinquent and some
of whom were not. Hirschi's analysis largely supported the core concepts of social control
theory (and, for that matter, the major findings of the Gluecks; Andrews and Bonta
2006), and it has become the most frequently discussed and tested theory in criminology
(Akers and Sellers 2004).

That being said, recent research suggests that Hirschi's (1969; 2002) theory might
need to be re-assessed, at least to some extent (Bureind and Bartusch 2005). Several
findings are particularly important. For example, in Hirschi's theory, attachment refers
to one's relationship with his/her parents, peers, and school. In each case, stronger
attachments are thought to result in more conformity and less delinquency. With respect
to peer attachment, for instance, Hirschi believed that its presence or absence was
important, not whether the peers were involved in delinquent acts (i.e., even for youths
who were attached to delinquent peers, the stronger the attachment, the less likely
the individual was to be delinquent). This is no longer thought to be the case. Now,
attachment to peers is thought to lead to conformity only when the peers are not delinquent (Hindelang 1973). Indeed, as you will see in coming chapters, interacting with
antisocial peers is now considered to be one of the strongest predictors of criminal
involvement (Andrews and Bonta 2006). Several other recent findings also require us
to rethink Hirschi's original social control theory (Bureind and Bartusch 2005). For
example, causal ordering is important to consider, given that some research shows that
delinquent behaviour can precede weak bonds (e.g., delinquency may precede weak
attachment to school; Liska and Reed 1985; see also Matsueda's 1989 work on beliefs).
In addition, some bonds (e.g., attachment) seem to be more important than others
(Agnew 1991), different bonds appear to be more or less important at different ages
(LaGrange and White 1985), and the explanatory power of certain social bonds appears
to vary across genders (Rosenbaum and Lasley 1990).

DENNIS THE MENACE

"BY THE TIME I THINK ABOUT WHAT I'M GONNA DO...I ALREADY **DID** IT!"

According to Gottfredson and Hirschi's (1990) general theory of crime, the trouble that Dennis the Menace often finds himself in can be explained by one underlying problem: low self-control.

In 1990, Hirschi, along with his colleague Michael Gottfredson, proposed a more refined and parsimonious control theory (Gottfredson and Hirschi 1990). Instead of focusing on the indirect controlling effects of social bonds, as Hirschi's (1969) original theory did, Gottfredson and Hirschi's **general theory of crime** argues that self control, internalized early in life, is the primary determinant of crime. That being said, Gottfredson and Hirschi believed that crime is not an inevitable consequence for those who lack self-control; opportunities to commit crime are also crucially important. Thus low self-control in the presence of criminal opportunities is assumed to explain an individual's propensity to commit crimes. Still, given their view that most offences are easy to commit, requiring "little in the way of effort, planning, preparation or skill" (Gottfredson and Hirschi 1990: 16–17), and that opportunities for crime are readily available, Gottfredson and Hirschi argued that, over time, people with low self-control will inevitably become more deeply involved in a criminal lifestyle.

Gottfredson and Hirschi's (1990) theory of crime is referred to as a general theory of crime because they believe that it can account for all crime in addition to a range of other behaviours that have been deemed "analogous" to criminal behaviour (e.g., alcohol, drug, and tobacco use). According to the creators of this theory, self-control can explain "all crime, at all times, and, for that matter many forms of behaviour that are not sanctioned by the state" (Gottfredson and Hirschi 1990: 117). What is common about these crimes and other analogous behaviours? According to Gottfredson and Hirschi, they are all "short lived, immediately gratifying, easy, simple, and exciting" (p. 14), and therefore are appealing to those who are unable to resist temptations of the moment, those who are insensitive to the needs of others, and those who are unable to consider the potential long-term negative consequences of their own behaviour; in short, to people who can be characterized as low in self-control.

Interestingly, in addition to being the primary cause of crime, a low level of self-control is also thought to be at the root of a range of other social consequences, many of which constitute the causes of crime in other theories. For example, the weak social bonds that ultimately lead to crime in Hirschi's (1969) social control theory are, according to Gottfredson and Hirschi (1990), the consequences of low self-control (e.g., given their dislike of settings that require discipline, people who are low in self-control do not feel attached to school/teachers and lack the commitment to strive for a better education). Other important social consequences of low self-control that can be related to crime are thought to include (among others) a dysfunctional family background and interacting with delinquent friends (Gottfredson and Hirschi 1990).

Consistent with a psychodynamic perspective, and the work of the Gluecks, Gottfredson and Hirschi (1990) believe that the level of self-control one possesses depends on the quality of parenting in a child's early years. Specifically, their general theory of crime emphasizes effective monitoring of children's behaviour, recognition of deviant behaviour when it occurs, and consistent and proportionate punishment of rule violations. According to their theory, children whose parents care about them, monitor them, and discipline them appropriately will likely develop the self-control that is needed to behave in a prosocial manner. Such children will be "more capable of delaying gratification, more sensitive to the interests and desires of others, more independent, more willing to place restraints on his activities, and more unlikely to use force or violence to attain his ends" (Gottfredson and Hirschi 1990: 97)—all things that are important to success in life. Children without such an upbringing, the thinking goes, will tend to be "impulsive, insensitive, physical (as opposed to mental), risk-taking, short-sighted, and nonverbal" (Gottfredson and Hirschi 1990: 90); thus explaining the increased likelihood of these individuals giving in to the temptations presented by crime. While the general theory of crime does recognize other sources of socialization, such as schools, Gottfredson and Hirschi believe that the role of these other sources in influencing one's level of self-control is severely limited given that self-control is assumed to be established very early in life and remain stable throughout the lifespan.

In terms of support, Gottfredson and Hirschi (1990) present a wealth of data about the correlates of crime and delinquency, and the theory, despite being proposed relatively recently, has generated an enormous amount of interest and attention from other researchers (see Goode 2008). Most of the subsequent research provides at least partial support for the predictions put forward by Gottfredson and Hirschi. For example, there seems to be a link between low self-control and crime, and this link appears to exist across a variety of cultures (e.g., Hessing et al. 2001). In addition, meta-analytic research supports the view that there is a relationship between self-control and crime, even when self-control is defined using a broad range of behavioural and attitudinal measures and applied to a broad range of samples (e.g., community members vs. offenders, young vs. old, etc.; Pratt and Cullen 2000). However, Pratt and Cullen's meta-analysis also clearly showed that, while self-control is an important predictor of criminal behaviour, it is not the sole cause of crime, given that it only accounted for approximately 19 percent of the variance in criminal behaviour (as we discuss below, social learning variables were also found to be important predictors of crime, above and beyond self-control). In looking at the role of parenting, self-control, and delinquency, Perrone et al. (2004) also found partial support for the general theory of crime. Based on a random sample of over 15 000 youths, they found that parental efficacy (basically the mother's attachment to the child) was a significant predictor of the youth's level of self-control, which is consistent with the view of Gottfredson and Hirschi. However, self-control only partially mediated the relationship between parental efficacy and delinquency, indicating that a valid theory of crime needs to account for more than just self-control.

Despite the fact that the general theory of crime is reasonably well supported, several criticisms exist. Perhaps the most commonly raised concerns have to do with the concept of self-control. For example, Akers (1991) views the general theory of crime as tautological, based largely on circular reasoning. According to him, defining self-control as the failure to refrain from crime (or other analogous behaviours), and then proposing self-control as a cause of crime (or other analogous behaviours), makes it impossible to falsify the hypothesis that self-control is the primary determinant of crime (or other analogous behaviours). Why do people commit deviant acts, one might ask? Because they lack self-control. How do we know they lack self-control? Because they're committing deviant acts! To avoid this tautological problem, Akers argues that operational measures of self-control must be developed that are separate from measures of deviant acts or a propensity toward committing such acts. According to Akers, at least, this issue has not been adequately resolved (however, see Grasmick, Tittle, Bursik, and Arneklev 1993). In addition, Gottfredson and Hirschi's (1990) argument that self-control is fixed at a very young age, and thus stable throughout the lifespan, has been the target of much criticism. Gottfredson and Hirschi's argument is not that criminal involvement won't decline with age, which is a consistent empirical finding, but that between-individual differences in self-control will remain stable over time and be unaffected by social (or other) factors (i.e., if Person A is lower in self-control at Time 1 compared to Person B, they will be consistently lower in self-control, and thus always more likely than Person B to be involved in crime given equal opportunities; Lilly, Cullen, and Ball 2006). Yet longitudinal studies have consistently demonstrated that social bonds developed beyond childhood (e.g., a strong marriage) can "redirect offenders into a pathway to conformity" (Lilly et al. 2006: 109), leading some to conclude that the general theory of crime is overly simplistic, ignoring the reality that "change is as much a part of criminal careers as stability" (Lilly et al. 2006: 319).

In addition to potential problems with the concept of self-control, the theory has also been criticised for not dealing with important questions around opportunities for crime (Schulz 2006), which is another crucial aspect of the theory. For example, as Goode (2008) points out, we do not yet fully understand what the relationship is between self-control and criminal opportunities. Are they independent or related in some meaningful way? Is it possible that individuals with low self-control are more likely to perceive criminal opportunities where high self-control people do not (Goode 2008)? Furthermore, does the lifestyle of individuals of low self-control open up more criminal opportunities?

Answers to such questions are necessary before we can validate Gottfredson and Hirschi's (1990) general theory of crime.

Summary

Psychodynamic theories of crime have come a long way since the time of Freud. This perspective on human behaviour, which has long been a guiding force in psychiatric circles for the assessment and treatment of offenders, has been incorporated into several popular theories of crime. While each relies on different terminology, all the theories discussed in this section have certain things in common: they focus on inner drives that lead individuals to behave in an antisocial manner; they speak to psychic mechanisms that prevent people from behaving in this way; and they emphasize the role of parent–child relationships (i.e., the socialization process) in the development of these mechanisms. To be sure, some psychodynamically-oriented theories of crime have received substantially more support than others, but each has played an important role in the development of our thinking about crime and criminals. These theories have even had an influence on behaviouristic, or learning, theories of crime, despite the fact that **behaviourism** (with its emphasis on observable processes) is commonly thought to be at odds with the psychodynamic approach (with its emphasis on internal psychological mechanisms). For example, much work in the area of crime by learning theorists has been devoted to determining the exact learning processes that lead to the internalization of moral inhibitions—what we have been referring to as "socialization." This is not to say that the psychodynamic and behavioural approaches to understanding crime are the same, however. As you will see in the next section, they are drastically different in many important respects.

LEARNING THEORIES AND CRIME

AN IMPORTANT APPROACH IN PSYCHOLOGY SEES OFFENDING, LIKE ALL BEHAVIOUR, as something that is learned. Learning in this case refers to "a change in pre-existing behaviour or mental processes that occurs as a result of experience" (Cassel and Bernstein 2001: 85). This emphasis on learning is what distinguishes learning theories of crime from psychodynamic theories of crime such as the control theories proposed by Hirschi and his colleagues. For example, you will recall that control theories assume that "we would all be deviant if only we dared" (Thornberry 1996: 224). Learning theories of crime, on the other hand, assume that there is no natural, or inherent, impulse to act antisocially (Thornberry 1996). Instead, as we say above, criminal behaviour must be learned, just as we learn to exhibit non-deviant behaviour. Although not really theories of crime per se, two general forms of learning—based on classical conditioning and operant conditioning—are very important to our understanding of criminal behaviour and its potential causes. Furthermore, both forms of learning have been incorporated into more formal theories of crime, which will be discussed throughout the remainder of this chapter.

Classical Conditioning

As some of you probably know, the principles of **classical conditioning** (also known as respondent or Pavlovian conditioning) originated with the work of Ivan Pavlov (1849–1936), a Russian physiologist. In the early 1900s, Pavlov was studying the digestive system of dogs and was intrigued by his observation that dogs deprived of food began to salivate when his assistants walked into the room. Pavlov's laboratory dogs, which already salivated when presented with food, had come to associate the food with the lab assistants. When Pavlov observed the dogs, what he was seeing was a conditioned response to the people they associated with meal delivery. In classical conditioning terms, the **unconditioned stimulus** (UCS—food) elicited an **unconditioned response** (UCR—salivation). By repeatedly pairing the UCS with a lab assistant, this previously neutral stimulus (the lab assistant) became associated with the UCS and took on the power of a **conditioned stimulus** (CS). After repeated pairings, the CS, even when presented in isolation, began to elicit a response—salivation—which is termed the **conditioned response** (CR).

Through his investigations, Pavlov showed that this interpretation of his observations was correct. After repeatedly pairing the delivery of food (UCS) with a tone, Pavlov found that the dogs began to salivate (CR) when the tone (CS) was presented without the food. Interestingly, when the tone was repeatedly sounded in the absence of food, in a process of **extinction**, it gradually lost its stimulus quality; the dogs salivated initially when the tone was presented, but this eventually stopped.

The principles of classical conditioning are now well established, and it has been known for some time that they operate in both animals and humans. Introductory psychology textbooks are often filled with interesting demonstrations of classical conditioning in people. Perhaps the most commonly presented example, although it is not always presented in an accurate fashion (Harris 1979), is that of Watson and Rayner's (1920) study of 11-month-old "Little Albert," who was conditioned to fear a harmless white rat (something that Albert did not fear at the outset of the experiment). By repeatedly pairing the rat with a loud noise, a conditioned response to the rat (fear) was established and was found to generalize to other similar (e.g., furry) stimuli (a process known as **stimulus generalization**). Many more recent examples exist, and classical conditioning is now assumed to be a powerful way of shaping many aspects of human

Master Pavlov is a bit strange these days:
For some reason,
he rings a bell before serving us dinner...

The principles of classical conditioning were first established by Ivan Pavlov in experiments conducted with dogs.

behaviour (e.g., see Webb 1999 for an interesting application of classical conditioning to the field of consumer marketing, where products are often paired with popular celebrities, for example, in an attempt to influence our buying behaviour). For an illustration of how classical conditioning can be used to influence the expression of antisocial behaviour, specifically sexually deviant behaviour, see Box 3.2.

Box 3.2

Forms of Aversive Conditioning in the Treatment of Sex Offenders

Some view the development of sexually deviant fantasies/behaviours as the result, at least in part, of classical conditioning (e.g., the pairing of sexual arousal with an early deviant experience or object) (Laws and Marshall 1990; McGuire, Carlisle, and Young 1965; Storms 1981). Given this, treatment approaches have been developed for sex offenders that attempt to decrease sexual arousal to deviant objects (e.g., children) through conditioning procedures. In one common approach, aversive conditioning, the client is exposed to an unpleasant stimulus while experiencing sexual arousal, the goal being to create an aversion to the source of the arousal. In this context, several methods of aversive conditioning are available.

Using covert aversive conditioning, the goal is to have the offender pair an imagined aversive consequence with his deviant fantasies or behaviour in order to eliminate such fantasies or behaviour. A standard technique, described by Maletzky (1991), consists of having the offender listen to a story that contains the following three parts: (1) the offender's preferred deviant stimulus and a buildup of sexual arousal (e.g., a child molestation); (2) an aversive consequence that causes intense disgust,

pain, or humiliation (e.g., imagining that they are vomiting while carrying out the offence); and (3) release from the adverse consequence by reversing the activity (e.g., removing the imaginary aversive consequence and encouraging relaxation).

Overt aversive conditioning techniques have the same goal as covert techniques, but actual rather than imagined aversive stimuli are presented during or immediately after the deviant stimulus. The deviant stimulus may involve slides, videos, or movies depicting the deviant experience or object. The aversive stimuli may be electric shocks, foul odors, nausea-inducing drugs, or even shame (e.g., by having the offender act out the deviant behaviour in front of observers).

Once the deviant arousal has been eliminated, it is often necessary to create non-deviant arousal to appropriate stimuli and arousal reconditioning is used for this purpose. According to Maletzky (1991), the goal of arousal reconditioning is to weaken deviant sexual arousal and simultaneously strengthen appropriate arousal. One method is called masturbatory satiation, which might involve an offender masturbating to consenting adult pornography. Just after ejaculation, when sex drive is assumed to be lowest,

Continued >

Box 3.2   Continued

he continues masturbating but switches to pornography involving sex between a man and a child. He does this for 30 minutes. The rationale of this method is that it causes the deviant fantasy to become conditioned to low sex drive as well as to excessive masturbation—an aversive stimulus—while the "normal" fantasy becomes conditioned to the pleasure of ejaculation.

Source: Maletzky (1991)

Eysenck's Biosocial Theory of Crime   While it may seem a stretch to generalize from studies of dogs, children, and consumers to potentially violent criminals, the principles of classical conditioning are built into some very popular and arguably well-validated theories of criminal behaviour. Perhaps nowhere is this more obvious than in Eysenck's (1977) **biosocial theory of crime** (Raine 1997; see Bartol and Bartol 2008 for an excellent review of Eysenck's theory). Eysenck (1916–1997), a famous personality psychologist from Britain, argued that crime can largely be explained by individual differences in the functioning of the nervous system, which impacts the degree to which people learn from environmental stimuli such as parental discipline. Eysenck also believed that differences in nervous system functioning shape one's personality and behaviour, and he made predictions about personality differences between antisocial and prosocial individuals (we will just focus on the conditioning aspect of his theory here).

Specifically, Eysenck believed that criminals and other antisocial individuals are deficient with respect to classical conditioning, or conditionability, a process he thought was important in the socialization or conscience-building process (Eysenck 1964; 1977; Eysenck and Gudjonsson 1989). As Raine (1997) argues in his discussion of Eysenck's views on classical conditioning and crime:

> . . . the crucial mechanism that stops most of us from committing criminal and antisocial acts is the concept of conscience; a well-developed conscience is what holds many of us back from not stealing even in those situations when we are almost certain of getting away with the theft undetected. Eysenck argues that what we call "conscience" is, in effect, a set of classically-conditioned emotional responses. The greater the individual's ability to develop and form classically-conditioned emotional responses, the greater the conscience development, and the less likely will be the probability of becoming antisocial . . .
>
> Taking the scenario of a small child stealing a cookie (CS) from the kitchen, punishment by the parent (scolding or physical punishment—UCS) elicits an unconditioned response (UCR) whereby the child is upset and feels uncomfortable. After a number of similar "learning trials," the sight of the cookie (or even the thought of stealing the cookie) will elicit an uncomfortable feeling in the child (conditioned response—CR) which acts to avert the child from enacting the "theft." Similar "conditioned emotional responses" developed relatively early in life in varying situations combine, in Eysenck's view, to represent what we call "conscience".

> In this analysis, socialized individuals develop a feeling of uneasiness at even contemplating a criminal act (robbery, assault) presumably because such thoughts elicit representations or "unconscious" memories of punishment early in life for milder but related misdemeanors (theft, behaving aggressively). (pp. 123–124)

It is fair to say that there is a reasonable amount of research supporting the predictions made by Eysenck. Indeed, with respect to the prediction that antisocial individuals will condition less effectively than prosocial individuals, several reviews of the research have found that, generally speaking, this is true (e.g., Hare 1978; Passingham 1972; Raine 1997). According to Raine, most of the research conducted in this area uses skin conductance to assess conditionability. Using this technique, a UCS (e.g., an electric shock) and CS (e.g., a tone) are repeatedly paired together, and the CR (i.e., skin conductance) is then measured when the CS is presented in isolation. Research of this type shows that problems with conditionability are generally more pronounced in people with antisocial inclinations (e.g., psychopaths). What is less clear is how conditionability relates to the socialization process (Hollin 1989), though there has been some work done on the "social" aspect of the biosocial theory of crime.

For example, Raine and Venables (1981) conducted a study that examined an interesting question: Eysenck predicted that antisocial individuals will suffer from conditioning deficits and will therefore not learn what their prosocial parents attempt to teach them, but what would happen in homes where parents are not law-abiding and where antisocial behaviour patterns are displayed? In this case, Eysenck's prediction is the opposite of what's stated above; specifically, "children who are highly conditionable and who have antisocial parents will become 'socialized' into their parents' antisocial habits [what Eysenck 1977 referred to as anti-socialization], whereas children who condition poorly will, at least in this environment, paradoxically avoid becoming antisocial" (Raine 1997: 127).

To examine this possibility, Raine and Venables (1981) sampled 101 school-aged boys and assessed them on skin conductance conditioning. For each boy, they also assessed their level of antisocial behaviour by gathering teacher ratings of antisocial school behaviour and having the boys fill out an antisocial personality questionnaire. The socio-economic status of the families was used to assess the quality of the home environment, with low socio-economic class serving as a proxy for a criminogenic home environment (Raine and Venables acknowledged the potential problems with using social class for this purpose). In line with Eysenck's prediction, antisocial boys from higher-class (prosocial) homes showed relatively poor conditioning, while antisocial boys from lower-class (antisocial) homes showed relatively good conditionability (see Figure 3.1). The opposite pattern was found for the boys who were prosocial.

Despite these types of findings, there has certainly been much criticism levelled against Eysenck's theory of crime (e.g., Taylor, Walton, and Young 1973). Many of these criticisms relate to the predictions (not dealt with here) that Eysenck made regarding personality differences between antisocial and prosocial individuals, some of which are not supported by empirical research (see Hollin 1989 for a review). However, criticisms have also been brought against Eyenck's ideas about classical conditioning and crime.

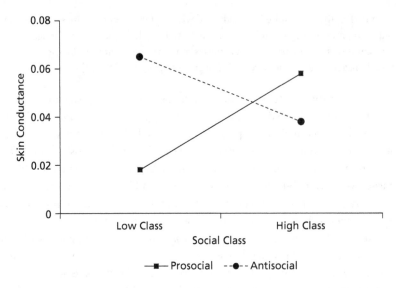

Figure 3.1 The Interaction between Socio-Economic Class (Criminogenic Home Environment) and Antisocial Behaviour in Relation to Skin Conductance (Conditionability)

Source: Raine and Venables (1981)

Many of these challenges are philosophical in nature and question the view that behaviour is as rule-governed and deterministic as Eysenck makes out, or that individuals are simple passive receptors of the conditioning process (e.g., Taylor et al. 1973). Other challenges are based on empirical grounds and relate to the fact that not all studies demonstrate conditioning deficits in antisocial individuals (Passingham 1972), and to the fact that strong evidence linking conditionability to the socialization process is currently lacking (Raine and Venables 1981).

Operant Conditioning

While Eysenck viewed the conscience as a set of conditioned fear responses, the relationship between learning and criminal behaviour can be conceptualized in other ways as well. For example, in addition to the associative learning that takes place in classical conditioning, behavioural psychologists have proposed another form of learning, one that is based on principles of **operant conditioning**, also known as instrumental or Skinnerian conditioning (Skinner 1953). While operant conditioning principles have been used to intervene with offenders for a long time, we know of few theories of crime that focus exclusively on these principles. In this section, we will discuss the underlying principles of operant conditioning given that they play a crucial role in many criminal justice interventions, and we will briefly examine how they have been incorporated into some theories of crime. This discussion will continue into the next section, where we examine accounts of criminal behaviour in social learning terms; a perspective that draws heavily on Skinner's operant conditioning principles.

Principles of Operant Conditioning   Building on the work of Edward Thorndike (1874–1949), who proposed the "law of effect," Harvard psychologist B.F. Skinner (1904–1990) is primarily credited with establishing the principles of operant conditioning (Skinner 1953). According to the law of effect, behaviour that brings about desirable effects tends to occur again, whereas behaviour that brings about undesirable effects tends not to be repeated (Thorndike 1898). Operant conditioning is based on very similar principles. Basically, this approach to understanding human behaviour, including criminal behaviour, assumes that the emergence, maintenance, and cessation of behaviour is determined largely by its environmental consequences (Skinner 1953). Most commonly, four contexts, or contingencies, of operant conditioning are discussed, as illustrated in Table 3.2.

Specifically, **positive reinforcement** occurs when a behaviour is followed by a pleasant stimulus that increases the frequency of that behaviour. **Negative reinforcement** occurs when a behaviour is followed by the removal of an aversive stimulus, thereby increasing that behaviour. **Positive punishment** occurs when a behaviour is followed by an aversive stimulus, resulting in a decrease in that behaviour. Finally, **negative punishment** occurs when a behaviour is followed by the removal of a pleasant stimulus, resulting in a decrease in that behaviour. Note that the labels "positive" and "negative" are not being used in the popular sense to mean "good" and "bad"; offenders may see nothing "good" about positive punishment. Instead, "positive" and "negative" refer to either the addition or subtraction of a stimulus from the environment following a behaviour (either naturally or through manual means). Also note that the processes of reinforcement and punishment are defined solely in terms of their behavioural outcome and can be situation and/or person specific. In other words, a stimulus is not a "reinforcer" or a "punisher" unless it increases (in the case of reinforcement) or decreases (in the case of punishment) the preceding behaviour, and what might be reinforcing or punishing for one situation (or for one person) might not be for another.

It is also important to appreciate that the effectiveness of the above strategies for either increasing or decreasing the likelihood of a behaviour depends on a wide range of

Table 3.2 Different Types of Reinforcement and Punishment (and Their Associated Behavioural Outcomes)

		Stimulus	
		Added	Subtracted
Stimulus valence	Pleasant	Positive reinforcement (behaviour increases)	Negative punishment (behaviour decreases)
	Aversive	Positive punishment (behaviour decreases)	Negative reinforcement (behaviour increases)

factors (see Andrews and Bonta 2006 for a more detailed discussion of these factors as they relate to punishment). Three factors in particular are important. First, immediacy is important in that the sooner the reinforcement (or punishment) follows the targeted behaviour, the more likely that behaviour will be to increase (or decrease) (Moffit 1983). Why is delayed reinforcement or punishment not as effective? Because delays increase the likelihood that some behaviour other than the one of interest becomes the target of the reinforcement or punishment (Skinner 1953). Second, consistency is a crucial variable to consider (Moffit 1983). Essentially, the more often the consequence follows the targeted behaviour, the more effective the consequence will be (however, in the case of reinforcement, intermittent schedules of reinforcement, where the consequence only occasionally follows the behaviour, can produce behaviours that are very resistant to extinction; Andrews and Bonta 2006). Finally, the intensity of the consequence is an important factor that partly determines how effective the consequence will be in increasing or decreasing behaviour (Moffit 1983). As a general rule, the stronger the consequence, the more effective it will be, although care must be used when employing very intense punishment so that unwanted side effects (e.g., the suppression of other desirable behaviours) do not occur (Andrews and Bonta 2006).

Application of Operant Conditioning Principles to Criminal Behaviour

Within the field of criminal justice research, the principles of operant conditioning have typically been drawn on to develop strategies for intervening with offenders. Indeed, it is a fairly easy task to think of criminal justice interventions that fall nicely into each of the cells in Table 3.2. The use of token economies in prisons or psychiatric facilities, for example, where prisoners/patients earn points for good behaviour, which can then be exchanged for desired items (e.g., cigarettes) is an obvious instance of positive reinforcement. Similarly, we are all familiar with the use of positive punishment in our criminal justice system, such as when a fine or prison sentence is handed down by a judge in an attempt to decrease undesirable behaviour. It is also common to see the factors listed above (specifically lack of immediacy, consistency, and maximum intensity) called on to explain real-world failings of criminal justice strategies, especially the ineffective use of punishment to deter crime (e.g., Andrews and Bonta 2006; McCord 1999; Moffitt 1983).

What is less common is the direct application of operant conditioning principles to an understanding of how criminal behaviour patterns emerge (versus an understanding of what to do with individuals once they are committing crimes). As we mention above, few theories of crime rely exclusively on these principles, although some come pretty close. The theory proposed by Jeffery (1965) is perhaps one of the most cited examples of a theory based largely on operant conditioning. Jeffery proposed simply that whether someone commits crime depends on whether the individual has been reinforced for similar behaviour in the past. Specifically, he believed that what matters most is whether the reinforcing stimuli associated with previous criminal behaviour (e.g., the value of stolen goods in the case of burglary) outweighs the aversive stimuli associated with that behaviour (e.g., legal sanctions). Jeffery's differential reinforcement theory states that "A criminal act occurs in an environment in which in the past the actor has been reinforced for behaving in this manner, and the aversive consequences attached to the behaviour have been of such a nature that they do not control or prevent the response" (Jeffery 1965: 295). Thus, if an offender experiences only reinforcing stimuli when committing burglaries, the criminal behaviour is likely to continue. If, on the other hand, legal sanctions (or some other negative consequence) are consistently experienced, the aversive consequence is likely to deter the act.

Operant conditioning principles are also featured in more recent theories of crime (e.g., Wilson and Hernstein 1985), and the principles play a central role in social learning theories of crime, which will be discussed next. These social learning theories were proposed in part to deal with the primary criticisms of theories based on operant and/or classical conditioning principles, which include the fact that these theories underemphasize: (1) the role of internal (i.e., cognitive) processes in the learning of criminal behaviour and (2) the important role that social context plays in the learning process, in particular learning that occurs by observing others.

Summary

While psychodynamic theories have undoubtedly contributed to our understanding of crime and have highlighted the crucial role that the childhood socialization process plays in the development of criminal behaviour, they do not adequately deal with how people learn to become criminal. Learning theories of crime, which are based heavily on the principles of classical and/or operant conditioning, fill in some of the gaps left by psychodynamic theories. Learning theories suggest that people learn to commit crime in the same way they learn any other behaviour—through processes of associative learning and/ or by experiencing the environmental consequences of their behaviour. While learning theories contribute to our understanding of criminal behaviour and form the basis of many successful intervention strategies for tackling crime, they also have several weaknesses, most notably the lack of attention they pay to the cognitive elements of learning and an under-emphasis on learning in social settings.

Social Learning Theories and Crime

As Coleman and Norris (2000) point out, "[i]t has long been a criticism within psychology that behaviouristic accounts [of human action] are deficient in that they do not give sufficient attention to internal mental processes," such as attention, memory, and understanding (p. 41). In addition, such accounts rarely speak directly to the important role of social context in learning. In psychology generally, these criticisms have led to an increased focus on the role of cognitive factors in the learning process, in particular how people process information in social contexts (e.g., Cacioppo and Bernston 2005; Fiske and Taylor 2007). A similar trend can be found in explanations of crime. While building on theories from the past, more and more theories of crime are explicitly dealing with the role of cognition in explaining the development of criminal behaviour and emphasizing the importance of social settings in this process. As a group, these new theories are referred to as social learning theories, though they are also sometimes called cognitive social learning theories to emphasize the cognitive aspect of learning in social contexts (McGuire 2004). Many of these theories are based on an important theory of crime, proposed in the mid 1900s, referred to as differential association theory.

Sutherland's Differential Association Theory Differential association **theory** was first proposed by Edwin Sutherland (1883–1950) in the 1939 edition of his book *Principles of Criminology*, although it was not until the next edition in 1947 that the final version of the theory was put forward (Sutherland 1947). Unlike many theorists before him, Sutherland discounted "internal" causes of crime, such as those suggested in psychodynamic theories such as the Gluecks', and believed instead that crime could be explained by learning in social contexts through interaction and communication (especially small informal groups, such as family and friends). In particular, Sutherland proposed that the nature of one's conduct, including the likelihood of committing crime, is influenced by the norms present in the particular groups to which one belongs; norms that can include attitudes toward the law and its violation. According to differential association theory, it is the balance between contact with prosocial attitudes on the one hand and antisocial attitudes on the other that influence behaviour.

Differential association theory can be summarised in nine testable postulates put forth by Sutherland (1947):

1. Criminal behaviour is learned.

2. Criminal behaviour is learned in interaction with other persons in a process of communication.

3. The principal part of the learning of criminal behaviour occurs within intimate personal groups.

4. When criminal behaviour is learned, the learning includes: (a) techniques of committing the crime . . . and (b) the specific direction of motives, drives, rationalizations, and attitudes.

5. The specific direction of motives and drives is learned from definitions of the legal code as favourable or unfavourable.

6. A person becomes delinquent because of an excess of definitions favourable to violations of the law over definitions unfavourable to violations of the law.

7. Differential associations vary in frequency, duration, priority, and intensity.

8. The process of learning criminal behaviour by association within criminal and anti-criminal patterns involves mechanisms that are involved in any other learning.

9. Though criminal behaviour is an expression of general needs and values, it is not explained by those general needs and values since non-criminal behaviour is an expression of the same needs and values. (pp. 6–8)

As indicated above, the heart of Sutherland's differential association theory is postulates 6 and 8, but postulate 7 is also very important. To be clear, postulate 7 says that the impact of criminal and anti-criminal definitions can be affected by: (1) how often one interacts with the group(s) exhibiting these definitions (frequency); (2) the length of exposure to particular definitions (duration); (3) how early in life one encounters the definitions (priority); and (4) the prestige or status of the group members holding the definitions (intensity) (Akers and Jensen 2006). Put simply, to the extent that these four conditions are favourable to violations of the law (i.e., high frequency of contact, for a long duration, beginning early in one's life, with high status members), the more likely it is that a person will become involved in an antisocial or criminal lifestyle.

There is no question that differential association theory has had a significant impact on the field of criminology (Gaylord and Galliher 1988) and a significant influence on other theories of crime, including the theories that will be discussed in the remainder of this chapter. It has also received a reasonable amount of empirical support (e.g., Andrews 1980; Johnson 1979; Matsueda 1982; Short 1957). Perhaps the strongest support comes from research demonstrating that some of its core concepts—the importance of antisocial attitudes and antisocial associates, in particular—are important predictors of crime (Andrews and Bonta 2006; Gendreau, Andrews, Goggin, and Chanteloupe 1992 as cited in Andrews and Bonta 2006; Simourd and Andrews 1994). These variables have emerged as two of the most powerful predictors of crime and are included in some of the most effective modern-day assessment tools for predicting re-offending (Andrews and Bonta 1995).

In terms of criticisms that have been levelled against the theory of differential association, the most common, and potentially the most serious, relates to Sutherland's concept of "definitions." Sutherland was never clear what he meant by definitions that are favourable or unfavourable to violations of the law. Even more contentious, Sutherland provided no guidelines on how to operationalize the ratio of definitions favourable to violations of the law over definitions unfavourable to law violations (Akers 1998). Some have argued that, in practice, it would be extremely difficult if not impossible to quantify these values (Glaser 1956; Newburn 2007; Short 1957), and even Sutherland (1947) himself recognized the problems inherent in this endeavour. Similar arguments can be made in reference to the measurement of factors that influence the impact of differential associations. For example, how does one measure the prestige or status of group members, or the frequency (or duration) of contact with them? Equally problematic is the fact that Sutherland neglected to specify how the learning process operates (Burgess and Akers 1968). Because Sutherland proposed that criminal behaviour is learned the same way other behaviours are learned (postulate 8), it was logical to seek insight into the learning mechanisms within behavioural psychology. This is exactly what Robert Burgess and Ronald Akers did. We briefly discuss their differential association-reinforcement theory next, but focus more thoroughly on Akers's social learning theory of crime, which was an extension of this theory.

Ron Akers (1939–) proposed the very popular and well-validated social learning theory of crime.

Akers's Social Learning Theory In an attempt to overcome some of the limitations of Sutherland's differential association theory, particularly the lack of any explicit formulation of how learning takes place, several theorists developed versions of differential association theory that emphasized the learning process. The **differential association-reinforcement theory** proposed by Burgess and Akers (1966) is one such example. Essentially, Burgess and Akers combined Skinner's (1953) ideas on operant conditioning with Sutherland's (1947) ideas of differential association, and by so doing made differential association theory more appealing and more testable. A crucial part of Burgess and Akers's work was their reformulation of Sutherland's original nine propositions in terms of reinforcement theory. The key proposition in the Burgess and Akers reformulation was that criminal behaviour is learned through a process of operant conditioning (i.e., when it is more reinforced than non-criminal behaviour). Differential association-reinforcement theory received little attention when it was first proposed and Burgess eventually turned his attention to other matters. Akers, however, re-worked the theory, and in 1973 presented his social learning theory of crime in the book *Deviant Behavior: A Social Learning Approach* (Akers 1973). Unlike differential association-reinforcement theory, Akers's theory has had a substantial impact in the field and is still a leading theory of crime.

Like Gottfredson and Hirschi's theory, Akers's **social learning theory** is a general theory of crime (i.e., it is intended to explain all crime). As such, it goes beyond a model of learning based on direct environmental consequences of behaviour. While Akers's theory includes an emphasis on the operant conditioning principles outlined by Skinner (1953), it also draws heavily on the work of social learning theorists, such as Albert Bandura (e.g., Bandura 1973; 1977; Bandura and Walters 1963). Social learning theorists, while acknowledging the obvious importance of classical and operant conditioning in shaping peoples' behaviour, drew attention to another form of learning that can influence behaviour: learning by watching others (i.e., **observational learning**) and by vicariously experiencing the consequences of other people's behaviour (i.e., **vicarious conditioning**) (Bandura 1977).

Thus, according to social learning theories, not only can criminal behaviour be learned through a history of associative learning or by being personally reinforced for criminal behaviour, it can also be learned by watching others being reinforced for their antisocial behaviour and then imitating the rewarded behaviour. The primary role models that can influence behaviour are assumed to include parents, peers, and the media. Interestingly, the mass media played absolutely no role in Sutherland's (1947) differential association theory, but its importance in shaping behaviour, including antisocial behaviour, is generally well-accepted today (see Box 3.3 for a more detailed discussion of this issue). In contrast to the learning that takes place in classical and operant conditioning, the learning that takes place through vicarious conditioning depends heavily on active cognitive processes—hence the often-used term cognitive social learning. In essence, vicarious conditioning depends on "what we think about what we see and hear" (Cassel and Bernstein 2001: 103): when a youngster hears and sees a parent being rewarded for dishonest or unlawful behaviour, they process that information, remember it, and reason that it is not only okay to mimic their parents' actions, but it is potentially beneficial to do so.

Box 3.3

The Impact of Media Violence on Antisocial Behaviour

In 1981, John Hinckley, Jr., attempted to assassinate President Ronald Reagan. Some say he was imitating the behaviour of the protagonist Travis Bickle in the movie Taxi Driver (starring Robert DeNiro), who plotted to assassinate a presidential candidate (Andersen, Wurmstedt, and Woodbury 1981). In 1993, a five-year-old boy lit his little sister on fire. The boy's mother blamed MTV's Beavis and Butthead and a psychiatrist who was consulted about the case referred to the show as "Sesame Street for psychopaths" (Torre 2009). In 1995, two attackers set fire to a token booth clerk in a Brooklyn subway station. It was generally believed that they were copying a scene from the recently released movie *Money Train*, starring Wesley Snipes and Woody Harrelson (Carlson, Mattos, and McDowell, 1995). In 1998, Oregon teenager Kip Kinkel, who was fascinated with the 1996

violent re-make of Romeo and Juliet (starring Leonardo DiCaprio) and the controversial music of Marilyn Manson (Kinkel had framed the lyrics to Manson's song The Reflecting God), killed his mother and father. He then drove to Thurston High School, where he went on a shooting rampage that left two students dead and 25 wounded (Ramsland 2009). In 1999, Eric Harris and Dylan Klebold shot 12 students

Continued >

Box 3.3 Continued

and a teacher at Columbine High School before killing themselves. Both individuals were avid players of the online game Doom, and reportedly referred to the shooting in a pre-recorded video, saying it was going to be just like Doom (Cullen 1999).

We've all read them—headlines blaming various forms of media violence for serious acts of antisocial behaviour. Based on the news stories described above and countless others we're sure you've also seen, it appears that the news media would have us believe that much of the violence in society can be attributed, at least in part, to the violent television programs, movies, music, and video games that today's children and adolescents are exposed to. Even "experts" who appear in the media passionately argue that exposure to violent media contribute in a significant way to tragedies such as the Thurston High and Columbine shootings. As budding psychologists, it is important to be skeptical of such claims and rely as much as possible on what research tells us about this issue (while also understanding that research is typically far from perfect). So what does the research say? What role does media violence play in the types of tragedies discussed above?

As is typical in much of psychology, the answer is more complicated than we would probably like. Below is a summary of what research says, as presented by leading experts in the field (Anderson et al. 2003):

■ Today's youth are exposed to an incredible amount of electronic media and the presentation of violence is common in much of this media, especially television programs and video games.

■ With respect to aggression in general, media violence seems to have a small to moderate positive effect ($r=.18$ to $r=.38$, where values approaching $r=1.00$ represent extremely strong positive effects—the more exposure, the more aggression).

■ With respect to more serious forms of violence (e.g., physical violence), media violence also seems to have a small to moderate positive effect ($r=.13$ to $r=.32$).

■ Repeated exposure to media violence can have both short-term (leading to increases in children's, adolescents', and young adults' aggressive thoughts and emotions, as well as verbal and physical aggression) and long-term effects (leading to an increased likelihood in adulthood of serious physically aggressive behaviour, such as physical assault, domestic assault, and other types of crime).

■ While research suggests that no one is exempt from the potentially deleterious effect of media violence, a number of factors appear to influence its impact on aggression (these findings relate to television violence, as sufficient research doesn't yet exist with respect to other forms of media). Specifically, the violent media-aggression effect seems to be greatest when: the viewer is younger; the viewer is already characterized as aggressive; the viewer can identify strongly with the aggressive character(s); the violent scenes are realistic; the violence is portrayed as justified; and the viewer's parents do not intervene (e.g., discussing the inappropriateness of television violence with their children).

■ A variety of factors have not been shown to have such moderating effects. These

Box 3.3 Continued

currently include the gender of the viewer, the intelligence of the viewer, the socio-economic status of the viewer, and characteristics (e.g., personality) of the parents.

- Psychologists believe that the interactive nature of videogames may lead to even greater effects on children's behaviour than television and movies.

- Psychologists believe that reducing exposure to media violence will help to reduce short- and long-term aggression and violence, but it is not yet clear what interventions will lead to a reduction in exposure.

Source: Anderson et al. (2003)

According to Akers's social learning theory, crime is learned primarily through group interactions, by way of operant and vicarious conditioning. In the words of Akers himself:

> Whether deviant or confirming behaviour is acquired and persists depends on past and present rewards or punishments for the behaviour and the rewards and punishments attached to alternative behaviours . . . In addition, people learn in interaction with significant groups in their lives evaluative definitions . . . of the behaviour as good or bad . . . The more individuals define the behaviour as good . . . or at least justified . . . rather than as undesirable . . . the more likely they are to engage in it.
>
> The reinforcers can be non-social . . . or social, but the theory posits that the principal behavioural effects come from interaction in or under the influence of those groups which control individuals' major sources of reinforcement and punishment and expose them to behavioural models and normative definitions. The most important of these groups . . . are the peer-friendship groups and the family but they also include schools, churches, and other groups. Behaviour (whether deviant or conforming) results from greater reinforcement, on balance, over punishing contingencies for the same behaviour and the reinforcing-punishing contingencies on alternative behaviour. The definitions are conducive to deviant behaviour when, on balance, the positive and neutralizing definitions of the behaviour offset the negative definitions of it. Therefore, deviant behaviour can be expected to the extent that it has been differentially reinforced over alternative behaviour (conforming or other deviant behaviour) and is defined as desirable or justified. (Akers, Krohn, Lanza-Kaduce, and Radosevish 1979: 638)

Like most of the theories we've discussed in this chapter, Akers's theory is continually being updated. For example, he has now incorporated new ideas about how social structure and social learning interact, specifically arguing that social structure (e.g., age composition, social class, structural anomie, friendship networks, etc.) provides the context in which social learning variables operate (Akers 2009). While some of these elaborations have yet to be thoroughly tested, a review of the research shows that both direct and indirect evidence exist in support of his social learning theory as it has been discussed here.

The indirect evidence largely comes from studies examining the effectiveness of rehabilitation and treatment programs that are based on social learning principles. As you will see in other chapters, compared to alternative approaches, these programs have been shown to have a significantly greater impact on reducing crime (e.g., Andrews and Bonta 2006; Cullen, Wright, Gendreau, and Andrews 2003; Pearson, Lipton, Cleland, and Yee 2002). More direct evidence in support of social learning comes from research that shows the importance of variables derived from the theory in explaining criminal (and other deviant) activity. For example, studies that have directly compared social learning theory to other theories usually show that social learning variables account for a larger proportion of the variance in dependent variables such as delinquency, crime, and other deviant behaviour (for a review, see Akers 2009). In addition, a recent meta-analysis of 140 studies showed consistent support for the theory (Pratt, Sellers, Cullen, Winfree, and Madensen 2006, cited by Lilly et al. 2006), while another meta-analysis showed that social learning variables (e.g., antisocial attitudes and peers) were at least as promising as other variables (e.g., Gottfredson and Hirschi's 1990 construct of self-control) in accounting for variations in criminal involvement (Pratt and Cullen 2000). Empirical support for this theory appears to hold across nations and cultures (e.g., Kandel and Adler 1982; Kim and Goto 2003; Lopez, Redondo, and Martin 1989).

In terms of criticisms, social learning theory has been challenged just as all of the theories that came before it have. Given the important role that antisocial peers play in this theory, it is perhaps unsurprising that this aspect of the model has come under particularly close scrutiny and many of its criticisms relate to this construct. For example, just as the issue of causal ordering was raised in relation to the work of the Gluecks, Akers's social learning theory has often been criticized for not paying enough attention to the temporal sequence of its primary variables, most notably differential peer association and crime. Specifically, rather than delinquent associations causing delinquency, some have argued that it might be the case that delinquency actually causes delinquent associations (e.g., Glueck and Glueck 1950; Gottfredson and Hirschi 1990). Akers, however, argues that research has tackled this issue, generally showing that involvement with delinquent peers predates delinquent behaviour and that delinquency can and often does lead to further association with delinquent peers (i.e., the relationship between delinquency and delinquent peers is reciprocal; Akers 1999). Another common argument is that social learning theory places too much weight on antisocial peer associations while ignoring other potentially important sources of reinforcement for antisocial behaviour. For example, Sellers and Akers (2005) state that many people view social learning theory as "just a peer influence theory" (p. 94), which isn't helped by the fact that peer association is often the only variable studied in many tests of the social learning approach. This is an unfair criticism. While antisocial peer associations are undoubtedly front and centre in Akers's theory, other sources of influence are clearly incorporated, most notably the family (Sellers and Akers 2005).

Andrews and Bonta's Personal, Interpersonal, and Community-Reinforcement Theory

The final theory that we will discuss is the personal, interpersonal, and community-reinforcement theory of crime (**PIC–R**) developed by Don

Andrews and Jim Bonta, both well-respected Canadian psychologists (see Box 3.4 for a profile of Don Andrews). Outlined in their important book *The Psychology of Criminal Conduct* (Andrews and Bonta 2006), this theory fits within a general personality and social psychological framework and is heavily influenced by a behavioural and cognitive social learning perspective. While the theory does not yet appear to have the same status as some of the others discussed in this chapter, it is the driving force behind much recent research and many offender treatment approaches being implemented worldwide (Ward, Melser, and Yates 2007).

Box 3.4

Canadian Researcher Profile: Dr. Don Andrews

As an undergraduate student at Carleton University in the early 1960s, Dr. Don Andrews recalls touring the Kingston Penitentiary and the Kingston Mental Hospital. He hated the prison and remembers saying, "I would rather be a hospital patient than a prison worker!" As fate would have it, Dr. Andrews completed a summer internship in one of the departments of the Kingston Pen in 1963. He continued to work there for two years, gaining an appreciation for the complex histories of the inmates and the primitiveness of psychological assessment tools. Dr. Andrews credits these experiences as fuelling his interest in the assessment and treatment of offenders.

After completing a Master's degree at Carleton and a Ph.D. at Queen's University, Dr. Andrews took a full-time position as a psychologist at Rideau Correctional Centre and a part-time position at Carleton University. In 1970, Dr. Andrews switched the amount of time he spent at Rideau and Carleton, becoming a full-time faculty member at Carleton University. There he started on a path of trying to understand criminal behaviour, especially how it could be predicted and how it could be changed. Much of what he learned over the past 40 years can be found in his classic book *The Psychology of Criminal Conduct* (co-authored with Dr. Jim Bonta). This text breathed new life into psychological theorizing on criminality. In it, Dr. Andrews argues convincingly for a paradigm shift in the field of criminology by demonstrating that general personality and cognitive social learning differences among individuals do a better

Continued >

Box 3.4   Continued

job of explaining criminal conduct than the more popular theories of class differences.

Dr. Andrews is a pioneer in the development of assessment instruments for offenders that identify key variables, which, when targeted in treatment, will lead to behavioural change. Two of Dr. Andrews's instruments widely in use are the Level of Service Inventory family of instruments (developed with Drs. Jim Bonta, Robert Hoge, and Stephen Wormith) and the Correctional Program Assessment Inventory (developed with Dr. Paul Gendreau). These instruments facilitate applying the principles of effective treatment that reflect the knowledge base of prediction and treatment.

Dr. Andrews's love for research is evidenced in his teaching. He wants students to experience the excitement of serious thought and systematic research. He states that his greatest moments at the university are when students defend their theses. He is thrilled to see students become active members of the community of researchers, practitioners, and scholars.

Dr. Andrews's contribution to the field of forensic psychology has been recognized with numerous awards and distinctions, including the Margaret Mead Award for Humanitarian Contributions from the International Community Corrections Association and the Career Contributions Award from the Criminal Justice Section of the Canadian Psychological Association.

The PIC–R is a truly integrated theory of criminal behaviour, using knowledge from both the biological and social sciences to explain crime. The theory emphasizes many different potential paths into crime and draws on key components from the various perspectives on crime (and its causes) discussed in this chapter (Andrews and Bonta 2006). For example, the theory incorporates ideas on the role of socialization in the development of antisocial attitudes, self-control in resisting temptations in the immediate situation, classical and operant conditioning in shaping criminal and non-criminal behaviour, and observational learning, especially in the context of peer groups, as a way of picking up on the many rewards and costs that can be associated with crime (Andrews and Bonta 2006).

True to its roots in behavioural psychology, behaviour, including criminal behaviour, is assumed to be under the control of both antecedent and consequent events in the PIC–R theory (Andrews and Bonta 2006). In other words, criminal behaviour is thought to be determined both by events (antecedents) that precede the behaviour (e.g., encouragement by peers to commit a criminal act may increase the likelihood of a crime being committed) and by events (consequences) that follow the behaviour (e.g., increased status among peers following the commission of a crime may increase the probability of crimes being committed in the future). According to the theory, antecedent and consequent events are believed to gain control over one's behaviour primarily by signalling various rewards and costs for different classes of behaviour (Andrews & Bonta, 2006). As discussed in our review of operant conditioning, these rewards and costs can be either additive or subtractive.

In line with a cognitive social learning perspective, the controlling properties of antecedent and consequent events are assumed to be acquired from multiple sources. In the PIC–R model, four sources are viewed as particularly important: the individual (i.e., personally mediated events, e.g., rewarding oneself after evaluating the impact of a criminal act); other people (i.e., interpersonally mediated events, e.g., approval from one's peer group for exhibiting antisocial behaviour); the act itself (i.e., non-mediated events, e.g., experiencing the arousal of getting away with a crime); and other aspects of the situation (Andrews and Bonta 2006).

The PIC–R theory also reserves important roles for the major predictors of crime that have been identified through empirical research, specifically antisocial attitudes, antisocial associates, a history of antisocial behaviour, and having an antisocial personality (see Andrews and Bonta 2006 for a review of the relevant research). For example, antisocial attitudes, or, more precisely, the existence of prosocial versus antisocial cognitions, are assumed to "determine the direction of personally mediated control . . . [and] determine whether personally mediated control favors criminal over non-criminal choices" (Andrews and Bonta 2006: 155–156). The construct of antisocial associates, on the other hand, is assumed to "influence the pro-criminal versus anti-criminal nature of modeling . . . as well as govern the rules by which rewards and costs are signaled and delivered" (Andrews and Bonta 2006: 156).

Socio-economic factors such as social class also play a role in the PIC–R theory, though not the same role as in traditional criminological theories of crime. Specifically, in the PIC–R theory, these factors do not directly explain individual differences in criminal conduct, a view supported by numerous meta-analytic studies (see Andrews and Bonta 2006 for a review). Instead, they act as background contextual conditions, believed to influence behaviour by establishing the fundamental reward and cost contingencies that are in effect within various social settings and communities (Andrews and Bonta 2006).

Like Akers's social learning theory, much of the support for the PIC–R theory comes indirectly, from evaluations of offender treatment (rehabilitation) programs based on principles derived from the theory (some of these are described more thoroughly in other chapters; see also Andrews 2001 for a comprehensive overview of principles of effective correctional interventions). A very impressive body of research (much meta-analytic) now exists demonstrating that these programs are among the most effective when the goal of treatment is to reduce the risk of an offender committing further crime (e.g., Andrews and Bonta 2006; Andrews, Zinger, Hoge, Bonta, Gendreau, and Cullen 1990; Dowden and Andrews 1999; 2000). Of course, because PIC–R theory is based largely on components of other theories, research evidence supporting the value of those theories can also be treated as evidence in support of PIC–R. Thus, consistent support for modern control (Gottfredson and Hirschi 1990) and social learning (Akers 2009) theories of crime clearly provide substantial backing for many aspects of PIC–R theory (e.g., the important roles of socialization, self-control, conditioning, observational learning, etc.). The very limited role of socio-economic factors in PIC–R theory is also supported by empirical research, despite what many criminological texts say about their role in predicting crime (e.g., Gendreau et al. 1992, cited in Andrews and Bonta 2006; Gendreau, Little, and Goggin 1996; Simourd and Andrews 1994; Tittle, Villimez, and Smith 1978).

However, despite signs that the PIC–R theory may provide a valuable framework, especially for guiding the construction of offender treatment programs, it, like each of the other theories, has come under fire from critics. Again, because PIC–R draws on components from other theories of crime, not only does evidence supporting those theories come into play when evaluating its validity, so do criticisms levelled against those theories. These criticisms have been discussed throughout the chapter and will not be reiterated here. Criticisms that are more specific to the PIC–R theory of crime include the views that: the link between the theory and its principles of effective correctional treatment is arguably weak; the relationship between the risk factors embedded in the theory, most notably antisocial attitudes, antisocial associates, a history of antisocial behaviour, and antisocial personality, is vague; and it is unclear how exactly these various risk factors operate and how they result in specific criminal actions (e.g., sex offences) being exhibited in specific settings (Ward et al. 2007).

CONCLUSION

LEARNING THEORIES OF CRIME FILL AN IMPORTANT GAP IN PSYCHODYNAMICALLY-oriented theories by specifying possible learning mechanisms that can result in the emergence of criminal behaviour. However, theories based on classical and operant conditioning ignore another important form of learning that can account for crime; that is, learning that takes place by watching how others behave, by observing how their behaviour is reinforced and/or punished, and by imitating their actions. This emphasis on vicarious conditioning, and the role that cognitive processes play in this form of conditioning, is what sets social learning theories apart from other learning theories of crime. Theories of crime that are based on social learning principles, such as Akers's social learning theory, are among the most well-supported theories of criminal behaviour. Social learning theories, especially those with a heavy cognitive component, are arguably the most clinically relevant as well, leading to practical (and apparently quite effective) methods for intervening with offenders in order to manage their behaviour and reduce their likelihood of reoffence. In the next chapter, we will discuss in more detail how one moves from theoretical accounts of crime to strategies for intervention at various stages of the criminal justice system.

Below is a list of the top 10 issues and people to consider when thinking about theories of crime in Canada.

Top 10 List

Advances to Come, Debates, Ethical Conundrums, and People to Watch

1 How do we best go about integrating the most promising components of the various theories of crime that currently exist, and is this a useful approach for developing better theories?

2 Is it possible to develop a general theory of crime? Or do we need different theories to explain the causes of different crime types? How do we deal with an offender who has committed different types of crimes?

3 What role do meta-analytic techniques play in testing the relative effectiveness of the various theories of crime?

4 Given the clear role that parental practices play in the development of crime, to what extent should parents be held responsible for their children's antisocial behaviour?

5 Given the importance of parental practices in juvenile delinquency, what can be done to improve parenting practices?

6 Is self-control really fixed at an early age, thus making longitudinal studies of crime largely irrelevant?

7 Should measures be put into place to reduce the exposure of young people to violent media such as violent television programs and videogames? If so, what measures would be effective?

8 How can we objectively measure the most important predictors of crime, such as antisocial associates?

9 How do we translate ideas about why people commit crime into effective, practical interventions in order to prevent and manage criminal behaviour?

10 People to watch: Ron Akers, Don Andrews, Francis Cullen, Travis Hirschi.

SUMMARY

1. In explaining the causes of crime, psychodynamic theories emphasize the inability of internal psychic forces to control antisocial impulses, learning theories emphasize the role of associative learning and stress the importance of environmental factors in shaping criminal behaviour, and social learning theories emphasize the role of vicarious conditioning in the crime acquisition process, focusing on the cognitive mechanisms that facilitate learning in social settings.

2. Psychodynamic theories of crime are based on several key principles, including the existence of internal psychic forces, such as the id, ego, or superego, that are supposed to develop through a series of psychosexual stages and control the antisocial impulses

that are assumed to be an inherent part of human nature but sometimes do not develop normally because of traumatic childhood experiences (often centring on problematic parenting practices).

3. Many psychodynamic theories of crime can be thought of as control theories in that they emphasize factors that control people's behaviour and prevent them from committing crime. Two of the most popular control theories are: (1) Hirschi's social control theory, which suggests that people don't commit crime because of the bonds they have with society, including attachments to significant others, commitment to conventional behaviour, involvement in conventional pursuits, and belief in common rule systems; and (2) Gottfredson and Hirschi's general theory of crime, which suggests that people don't commit crime because they possess a high degree of self-control, gained largely as a result of effective parenting practices.

4. Classical conditioning is a form of learning that takes place when an unconditioned stimulus (e.g., food) that produces an unconditioned response (e.g., salivation) is paired with a neutral stimulus (e.g., a tone) such that, over time, a conditioned response (e.g., salivation) is reproduced using only the previously neutral stimulus (now referred to as the conditioned stimulus). Operant conditioning, on the other hand, is a form of learning that takes place by experiencing environmental consequences caused by behaviour (e.g., reinforcement and punishment).

5. In Eysenck's biosocial theory of crime, he argues that criminals are deficient with respect to their conditionability, a process he thought was important in the socialization or conscience-building process. Eysenck argued that the "conscience" is essentially a set of classically-conditioned emotional responses that, when well-developed, decreases the likelihood that people will exhibit antisocial behaviour.

6. Sutherland's differential association theory emphasizes that criminal behaviour is learned when we interact with others, especially those who are important to us, and get exposed to a higher proportion of antisocial rather than prosocial attitudes. Akers's social learning theory builds on differential association theory by explicitly addressing the mechanisms by which we learn to commit crime. His theory emphasizes the role of operant conditioning in the crime acquisition process, whereby people learn to commit crime as a result of a personal history of being reinforced for that activity, but also the role of vicarious conditioning, whereby people learn to commit crime by observing that activity being reinforced in other people, especially intimate personal groups.

7. Andrews and Bonta's PIC–R theory of crime is influenced by a behavioural and cognitive social learning perspective. The theory emphasizes many different potential paths into crime, and crime is thought to be determined both by events that precede the behaviour and by events that follow it. These events are believed to gain control over one's behaviour primarily by signalling various rewards and costs for different classes of behaviour, which can be either additive or subtractive. The controlling properties of antecedent and consequent events are assumed to be acquired from

multiple sources, including the individual, other people, the act itself, and other aspects of the situation.

Discussion Questions

1. In this chapter, we mentioned various types of research strategies that could be used to identify the potential causes of crime—for example, cross-sectional research designs, longitudinal studies, meta-analyses, etc. What do these strategies involve? What are the advantages and disadvantages of these various approaches to conducting research? Is one approach better suited to identify the causes of crime, or is it preferable to use multiple approaches?

2. Do you think it's possible to develop a general theory of crime that not only explains the causes of all crime, but also the causes of other antisocial or deviant behaviours? Why or why not?

3. As part of your practicum at an outpatient clinic, you have been assigned to work with a psychiatrist who has a patient with a serious foot fetish. The psychiatrist is interested in using aversive conditioning in an attempt to eliminate the fetish and asks for your opinion of how the treatment should be delivered. What you would suggest?

4. We discussed some ways in which operant conditioning principles are implemented in an attempt to reduce crime (or institutional misconduct). Think of other interventions that exist in our criminal justice system. Determine whether they are examples of positive reinforcement, negative reinforcement, positive punishment, or negative punishment.

5. You are a summer intern at Correctional Service of Canada and are tasked with the job of coming up with a new treatment program for offenders based on Akers's social learning theory of crime. Describe what this program would look like (e.g., what would you target in treatment?) and explain your decisions.

Additional Reading

Akers, R.L. 1999. *Criminological theories: Introduction and evaluation.* 2nd ed. Los Angeles: Roxbury.
Andrews, D.A. and Bonta, J. 2006. *The psychology of criminal conduct.* 4th ed. Cincinnati: Anderson.
Cullen, F.T., Wright, J.P., and Blevins, K.R. 2006. *Taking stock: The status of criminological theory.* New Brunswick: Transaction Publishers.

Relevant Websites

Association for Behavior Analysis International
www.abainternational.org/

Criminology journal
www.wiley.com/bw/journal.asp?ref=0011-1384&site=1

Chapter 4

Linking Theories to Practice

Bill, age 28, is before the courts for an armed robbery charge. He robbed a convenience store late at night, threatening the lone store clerk with a knife. Bill admitted he was high on drugs and needed money for more. This is not his first involvement with the courts. He served time in secure custody as a youth and in numerous provincial jails for property crimes (theft, break and enter, drug possession) and a couple of serious assaults. He dropped out of high school prior to completing Grade 10 and has infrequently held odd jobs, although neither situation appears to cause him much concern. Presentence reports describe a fairly chaotic childhood and family situation, with both family and friends being predominantly antisocial. Perhaps not surprisingly, he also has a long history of drug and alcohol abuse and multiple brief relationships.

The Crown is asking for a 48-month sentence, noting his prior criminal history and stressing the need for deterrence. His defence attorney is trying to convince the Crown that Bill's history is the result of his poor family background and lack of stable employment. While Bill is reluctant to plead guilty, he wonders if the Crown would offer a lower sentence in a plea bargain. He recalled that the last time he was before this particular judge, he was warned not to return with new charges or he would suffer serious consequences.

What would be a reasonable sentence for Bill? Do you think a longer sentence would deter him from committing new crimes in the future? Should this be the only reason for deciding on a particular sentence?

Learning Objectives

1 Understand the role and importance of theory to inform how correctional practice works.

2 Understand the contribution of Canadian researchers to evidence-based correctional practice.

3 Review selected approaches in the areas of assessment and treatment to better understand why such approaches are popular in Canadian corrections and elsewhere.

4 Review contemporary challenges in order to understand future directions for corrections research.

INTRODUCTION

AFTER READING CHAPTERS 1 AND 3, SEVERAL CONCLUSIONS SHOULD BE APPARENT. IN CHAPTER 1, we learned that criminal justice issues are of great concern to Canadians and public opinion regarding corrections and parole is modest at best. Moreover, it has been noted that sensational media coverage invokes strong opinions regarding crime and criminals. In short, ideology typically polarizes Canadians' views regarding how to enhance public safety. There are generally two sides in the debate over what is needed to reduce crime and make Canada safer: greater rehabilitation or greater punishment. While both camps have their champions, in psychology we emphasize the importance of evidence to guide our actions. Specifically, what evidence is there that unbridled rehabilitation or punishment will yield better correctional outcomes (i.e., lower crime rates, lower recidivism)? Do all offenders respond positively to **rehabilitative programs**? Do all offenders require more severe punishment (i.e., longer sentences) in order to "get it"? In Chapter 3, we reviewed a variety of theories posited to explain criminal behaviour, noting that they have evolved over time, often integrating constructs from earlier viewpoints. While it seems there is no single and agreed upon "winner," social learning theories, especially those with a heavy cognitive component, were presented as the most clinically relevant. The purpose of this chapter is to describe how this theoretical work is reflected in contemporary correctional practice. Essentially, why do we do the things we do, and in the manner we do them? Underscoring correctional practice is the interplay between theory and evidence.

In order to more clearly illustrate the issues, challenges, and present-day approaches, we will describe contemporary practice across a range of correctional and criminal justice activities. Beginning with a review of the research on punishment models and deterrence, mainly in terms of sentencing, we will consider the evidence for its effectiveness. We will then contrast the increasing interest in utilizing restorative justice models with respect to philosophy and evidence, followed by a review of the history and evolution of correctional programming efforts in support of **offender rehabilitation**. With respect to programming, recent research regarding challenges to a risk-based model of understanding offender change will also be highlighted to reflect the current debate in this literature. Further, specific applications such as **custody classification** will be reviewed in some detail, as this is an important correctional activity often overlooked in texts. While custody classification is the method by which incarcerated offenders are assigned to security level, Canadian assessment methods typically consider treatment issues and the development of a correctional plan throughout the offender's sentence. In this manner, theory is embedded within the information considered in custody classification and the process is more broadly referred to as offender classification. Table 1.4 in Chapter 1 illustrates in a fairly simplistic manner how an assessment and understanding of criminal risk factors might inform the differential management of offenders. Offenders with different numbers and severities of criminal risk factors may warrant assignment to different security levels or custody placement and to different correctional programs in order to better manage their risk of escape, institutional adjustment problems, and reoffending. This chapter will more fully describe the central importance of initial offender assessment on numerous key decisions made throughout offender sentences. Our review of theory and practice then moves to **risk assessment** and **risk management**, although this will be covered in greater detail in Chapters 7, 9, and 10.

The goal of this chapter is to highlight Canadian contributions to best practice and illustrate how theory is embedded within such practice, even if it is refined through empirical research. Finally, we will review recent research regarding crime desistance and comment on how it might be incorporated into current practice.

CHANGING CRIMINAL BEHAVIOUR

TABLE 4.1 PRESENTS AN ILLUSTRATION OF HOW CRIMINAL AND PROSOCIAL BEHAVIOUR IS PRESUMED to be affected by changes in contingencies. The grid illustrates guidelines from Andrews and Bonta (2006) for what should be increased or decreased in order to decrease crime. Later in the chapter we will discuss the evolution in correctional programming, but for now it is worth noting that over time there had been a shift away from individualized rehabilitation programs to a greater reliance on punishment to deal with crime. A utilitarian model suggests that people engage in criminal behaviour because crime pays, and to reduce crime, its costs must increase. Andrews and Bonta (2006) and others (McGuire 2004) question if such a model applies equally to all offenders. They also refine the model and assert that criminality can be decreased when the rewards for crime are reduced and the costs for crime are increased while the rewards for prosocial behaviour are increased and the costs for prosocial behaviour are decreased. It is worth noting that for several decades, the United States has focused mainly on increasing individual costs to crime as a deterrent. More recently this emphasis has been on evidence-based practice, where empirical research is used to inform how to assess and intervene with offenders (Aos, Miller, and Drake 2006; National Institute of Corrections 2008; Taxman et al. 2004). Paradoxically, the rehabilitative approach that focuses on increasing rewards for prosocial behaviour of offenders, which was championed in Canada and later exported to the United States (Andrews and Bonta 2006), now appears to be losing ground in Canada despite empirical evidence that rehabilitation is more effective than punishment at reducing crime (French and Gendreau 2003).

From this description of the cost and benefits of crime, we can determine that multiple efforts are required to change offender behaviour and to decrease crime. It is also clear that different elements of the criminal justice system (courts, probation, prisons, and

Table 4.1 Decreasing the Chances of Crime

Behaviour	Rewards	Costs
Criminal	(A) Reduce	(B) Add
Prosocial	(C) Add	(D) Reduce

Source: Andrews and Bonta (2006)

parole) may have different foci despite an agreed-upon goal of crime reduction. Notwithstanding the role of expert witnesses, the interplay between psychology and the courts is mainly academic, whereas psychology is much more influential in directly informing clinical practice in prisons and community corrections.

Purposes of Sentencing

According to section 718 of the Canadian *Criminal Code*, the fundamental purposes of sentencing are to ensure respect for the law and the maintenance of a just, peaceful, and safe society. The expectation is that this is achieved through the imposition of sanctions. Other key purposes of sentencing are:

- To denounce unlawful conduct
- To remove offenders from society
- To assist in rehabilitation of offenders
- To provide reparation to victims
- To promote a sense of responsibility in offenders

As noted previously, the most obvious goal of sentencing is to change the criminal behaviour of individuals who come into contact with the courts. Through the means of **specific deterrence** and **general deterrence**, the expectation is that **sanctions** by the courts will reduce the criminal behaviour of both the specific individual and the general population, respectively.

Deterrence

Referring to Bill's case, a central issue relates to distinguishing between the purpose and the impact of sentencing. While the latter is perhaps of greatest concern in this book, the former is worth reviewing in order that we have an appreciation of the complex challenges facing the courts. Consider Bill's sentencing for armed robbery. If punishment and deterrence are the sole issues, then a longer sentence would be preferred. This might find favour with many Canadians, especially those intolerant of crime and criminals. A longer sentence would have more merit if it could be demonstrated that it will reduce Bill's likelihood of future crime.

Consistent with the issue of ideology, it can be proposed that there are underlying assumptions with punishment and rehabilitation extremes. The punishment extreme can be described as "hard," although some may prefer the word realistic. Underlying this approach are the views that: 1) those who commit crimes are bad; 2) criminals are unlikely to change unless compelled to do so; 3) criminals need to be dealt with more strictly (to get their attention); and 4) the costs and consequences of committing crimes need to be made as serious as possible. In contrast, the rehabilitation extreme can be described as "soft," although some may prefer the word liberal. Underlying this approach are the views that: 1) those who commit crimes are no different than others; 2) criminals have the capacity to live decent lives and reform themselves; and 3) offenders have grown up in adverse surroundings and need to be presented better opportunities (you will note that this was Bill's lawyer's assertion!). While sentencing may not be specifically informed by these viewpoints, they nonetheless influence the public's perception of the courts.

As we consider how punishment affects practice, it is worth noting that sentencing and sanctions reflect the major themes of retribution, incapacitation, and deterrence. **Retribution** asserts that society has the right, when harmed, to harm the offender. This harm or punishment should correspond with the crime (an eye for an eye). From an administration of justice perspective, retribution is not necessarily intended to address issues at the individual level. Essentially, the commission of a crime warrants social retribution. **Incapacitation** is the application of crime control by removing offenders' ability to commit crimes by incarcerating them. In terms of reducing future crimes, since the vast majority of offenders do not die in prison but return to their communities, this may have limited impact. Tarling (1993) presents data consistent with the view that incapacitation is an expensive method for reducing crime. **Deterrence** is the application of punishment to influence behaviour. Given the popularity of viewpoints emphasizing deterrence, researchers have investigated the effectiveness of its application. McGuire (2004) provides a detailed explanation of the issue, to which interested readers are referred. For instance, he notes that deterrence is measured across four dimensions: certainty (likelihood of legal punishment); celerity (the amount of time that elapses between an offence being committed and an official sanction being imposed); severity (magnitude of the punishment); and scope (the relationship between types of crime in statutes and types of punishment). More specifically, Gendreau (1996) and McGuire (2004) note that for punishment to be maximally effective, it must first be unavoidable. Second, its application should immediately follow the target behaviour. Third, it should be very severe. Even when these conditions are met, it is necessary to ensure that individuals being punished cannot meet their goals through some alternative manner. It should be readily apparent that these dimensions are rarely applied in a systematic manner within the criminal justice system, potentially diminishing the effectiveness of punishment to change behaviour. For instance, offenders often report committing crimes for which they were not caught, as confirmed by the discrepancy between police-reported crime and arrests (see "crime funnel" in Chapter 1). Further, there are often long delays between arrest and conviction, resulting in the contentious two-for-one rule (one day on remand equals a day of a sentence, if found guilty), now under review in Canada.

This brief discussion about punishment is a good introduction to examples of correctional practice (i.e., getting tougher on crime) decreasing crime. Again, the interested reader is referred to McGuire (2004) and French and Gendreau (2003) for a fuller description. To illustrate the issue, we will briefly review evidence for the effectiveness of deterrence in criminal justice applications, which comes from six areas: 1) sentencing, in terms of crime statistics; 2) the relationship between imprisonment and crime rates; 3) the effects of enhanced punishers; 4) meta-analytic reviews of outcome studies; 5) self-report surveys; and 6) research on the death penalty. Of note is that these studies are not uniquely Canadian and as such there may be debate regarding the generalizability of the findings.

Research from the United Kingdom (Kershaw 1999; Lloyd, Mair, and Hough 1994) compares two-year reconviction data by type of sentence (imprisonment, community service orders, probation orders, and probation with additional requirements) while controlling for risk level of the offender, (Note: Simple comparisons between raw rates of reconviction following different court disposals are not meaningful due to prior differences in risk levels between groups.) Using a national risk scale on a sample of approximately 130 000 cases to provide an estimate of reoffending, actual reconviction rates were compared with predicted rates, showing no difference. The conclusion was that there was no difference between immediate custody and community penalties on reconviction rates. Similar findings were reported in meta-analyses completed by Gendreau, Goggin, and Cullen (1999) and presented in Table 4.2. Compared to those who spend longer (average 30 months) versus shorter (17 months) terms in custody, those with longer sentences had 2 to 3 percent increases in recidivism (as reflected by **phi coefficients**). Mean prison time was 10.5 months for the incarceration samples (k=19).

These findings suggest that general deterrence does not reduce crime in that longer sentences and incarceration are not highly related to a lack in recidivism. Further, if specific deterrence is effective, there should be some association between the activity of the courts for targeted crimes and the amount of that crime. This does not appear to be the case. For example, Martin (1993) considered fines versus short jail sentences and noted there was no effect on rates of drinking and driving. Moreover, Weisburd and Chayet (1995) found no difference in crime rates when considering white-collar crimes (prison versus no prison with a 10-year follow-up of 742 offenders). Both these examples precede the considerable intolerance in Canada of these types of crimes, but are notable in that they suggest simply getting tougher on certain types of crime may not diminish the rates of these crimes.

Table 4.2 Meta-Analysis of Type of Sanction and Recidivism

Type of Sanction (k)	N	M^{ϕ}(SD)	CI^{ϕ}	$Z^{\pm}$	$CIZ^{\pm}$
More versus less (222)	68 248	.03(.11) .02 to .05		.03	.02 to .04
Incarceration versus community (103)	6 267 804	.07(.12) .05 to .09		.00	.00 to .00
Total (325)	336 052	.04(.12) .03 to .06		.02	.02 to .02

Note: $\underline{k}$ = number of effect sizes per type of sanction; $\underline{N}$ = total sample size per type of sanction; $\underline{M^{\phi}(SD)}$ = mean phi and standard deviation per type of sanction; $\underline{CI^{\phi}}$= confidence interval about $\underline{M^{\phi}}$; $\underline{Z^{\pm}}$= weighted estimation of $\underline{\phi}$ per type of sanction; $\underline{CIZ^{\pm}}$ = confidence interval about $\underline{Z^{\pm}}$.

Source: Gendreau, Goggin, and Cullen (1999)

It may be of note that more adult males are given Canadian federal sentences, but these sentences have generally decreased in length over the past two decades (Boe, Motiuk, and Nafekh 2004), although the median provincial sentence has slightly increased (Boe, Motiuk, and Muirhead 1998).

Another deterrence strategy has been described as punishing smarter. In this approach, enhanced punishers such as boot camps, shock incarceration, electronic surveillance, curfews, and intensive supervision are applied. Various studies have disputed the effectiveness of this brand of deterrence. MacKenzie, Wilson, and Kider (2001) reviewed 29 studies relating to boot camps in the United States, finding no effect in reducing criminal behaviour. Bonta (2002) and Petersilia and Turner (1993) have noted that intensive supervision does not reduce crime unless it includes rehabilitation programming. In an informative summary of the utility of enhanced punishers, Gendreau et al. (2001) reviewed 135 outcome studies and similarly reported a mean effect size of approximately zero. These findings are presented in Table 4.3. Note that only fines and restitution resulted in a decrease in recidivism, albeit it very slight!

The next area where we consider the effect of deterrence relates to self-report surveys of offenders. In a study of teenagers involved in shoplifting, Klemke (1982) interviewed juveniles several months apart. Experiencing an arrest had little impact on their subsequent criminal behaviour. Moreover, findings from the Denver Youth Survey (Huizinga et al. 2003), a longitudinal study of youth at risk, indicated that the majority of offenders, whatever their level of seriousness, were not arrested. Even the more serious offenders were rarely arrested for their most serious offences (remember the issue of certainty!).

Perhaps the most ultimate deterrence is the use of the death penalty. Specifically, among the 71 countries that still retain its use, "the most common political justification is that it has a unique general deterrent capacity to save further innocent lives or

Table 4.3 Effects of Sanctions on Recidivism

Type of Sanction	Sample Size	Average Effect Size
Supervision program	19 404	.00
Arrest	7779	.01
Fine	7162	−.04
Restitution	8715	−.02
Boot camp	6831	.00
Shock incarceration	1891	.07
Drug testing	419	.05
Electronic monitoring	1414	.05

Source: Gendreau et al. (2001)

Sentencing options cartoon.

significantly reduce other capital offences" (Hood 2002: 209). In his 40-year review for the United Nations, comparing countries that were abolitionist, retentionist, or users with a moratorium, there was no difference in frequency of capital crimes. Further, in comparisons between neighbouring states, with and without capital punishment, there was no difference. In Texas, arguably the state with the highest rate of capital punishment, there was no relationship between the execution rate and the murder rate; higher execution rates did not yield a lower murder rate. It would seem that commission of crimes, including capital offences, is not influenced by punishment and deterrence.

Explanations for why punishment is ineffective include perceived risk of (non)arrest (Foglia 1997) and the fact that criminal behaviour is dominated by "here and now" thinking (Andrews and Bonta 2006). Prior to committing an offence, most individuals are preoccupied with the implementation of the act, rather than deliberating on the consequences should they be caught (McGuire 2002).

The Canadian Picture

Since much of the data reviewed regarding the effect of punishment on crime rates is from other countries, it is worth providing a Canadian context for consideration. We do so at the risk of confusing the reader, who thus far should have concluded that the link between punishment and deterrence, while intuitively appealing, nonetheless lacks empirical support. Overall decreases in crime rates might be misinterpreted as indicating the effectiveness of deterrence, but it is unclear that this is the preferred explanation. Compared to other countries, Canada's crime rate is relatively low, but there is still a push for tougher sentences.

As discussed in Chapter 1, using data from the Corrections and Conditional Release Statistical Overview (Public Safety 2008), the police-reported crime rate decreased from 1981 to 2007 (except for a blip in 1990–92). Concurrently, the overall rate of juveniles and adults charged decreased, although there were slight variations for certain groups (juvenile girls are more involved in crime) and types of crime (property crime is on the rise). Moreover, Canada's incarceration rate has decreased over the past two decades. Boe (2004) compared types of crime (homicide, robbery, aggravated assault, break and enter/burglary, and motor vehicle theft) and highlighted a unique contrast between the United States, the United Kingdom, and Canada. These data are

Table 4.4 Crime Incidents per 100 000 of the Population, 2001

Country	Canada	United States	England and Wales
National population	31 110 600	284 796 887	52 939 000
Actual crimes per 100 000 of the population			
Homicide	1.8	5.6	1.4
Robbery	88	148	159
Aggravated assault	182	319	438
Break and enter/burglary	908	741	1,712
Motor vehicle theft	547	431	640

Source: Boe (2004)

presented in Table 4.4 and their rates over time and controlling for size of population are presented in Figure 4.1.

Not only are the rates higher, but when combining crime categories and tracking changes over time, there are noticeable differences, as seen in Figure 4.1.

It is apparent that Canada's situation is generally better than that in other countries in terms of rates for different types of crime. Nonetheless, recent years have seen a call in

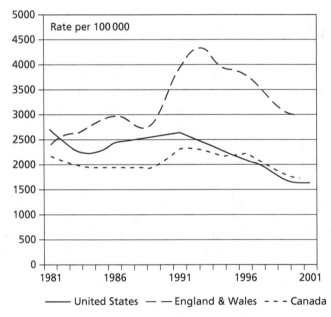

Figure 4.1 Annual Rates of Five Comparable Crimes

Source: Boe (2004)

Canada for getting tougher on crime in order to enhance public safety. This call from politicians and victims groups comes despite evidence disputing the effectiveness of such policies in decreasing crime. A question that arises is whether there are alternate sentencing approaches, less punitive in focus, that might be more effective in decreasing crime, at least for some offenders. Restorative justice is a model that fits such a niche and although it has been utilized for more than two decades, it has increased in popularity in recent years. Numerous countries have adopted restorative techniques, including Canada, England, Australia, Scotland, New Zealand, Norway, the United States, Japan, and several European countries (Hughes and Mossman 2001).

RESTORATIVE JUSTICE

ALTHOUGH A UNIVERSALLY ACCEPTED DEFINITION HAS YET TO BE ESTABLISHED, A MAJOR TENET of **restorative justice** (RJ) is that "crime is a wound, justice should be healing" (Zehr 2002) (see also Marshall 1996; Braithwaite 1999). Restorative justice responds to a criminal act by putting the emphasis on the wrong done to a person as well as the wrong done to the community. It recognizes that crime is both a violation of relationships between specific people and an offence against everyone—the state. In this manner, it is not simply that crime is a violation of law (Zehr 1990). RJ emphasizes healing the wounds of victims, offenders, and communities caused or revealed by criminal behaviour, and is seen as a viable third alternative to the traditional rehabilitation versus retribution debate (Zehr 1990). The following quote illustrates the impact of crime on the victim:

> This is crazy
> I am crying
>   screaming
> hiding my face in shame
> I am weak
> and can't rest.
> My stomach is like a stone and
> My fingers ache from clenching.
> I suffer.
> You!
> You walk calmly
> Among people, relatives.
> They don't know you
> as I do.
> You smile
> and feel no guilt
>   no shame.
> You walk away from my pain.
> This is crazy.
> I carry the weight of the sentence
>
> But you are the killer. (Janssen 1983)

Unsurprisingly, proponents of restorative justice, many with affiliations to such groups as the Mennonites, argue for a path of healing that attends to the needs of both victims and offenders. RJ is not simply an approach to "be soft on crime"; rather, it emphasizes accountability by the offender and recognition of the harm they have caused. Other research we will discuss in more detail later highlights this transformation by the offender as a critical component in their eventual desistance of criminal behaviour (Maruna 2002).

Key elements of restorative justice include:

1. Identifying and taking steps to repair harm

2. Involving all stakeholders

3. Transforming the traditional relationship between communities and their governments in responding to crime

Restorative justice programs involve the voluntary participation of the victim of a crime, the offender, and, ideally, members of the community in discussions. The goal is to "restore" the relationship, fix the damage that has been done, and prevent further crimes from occurring. Restorative justice requires wrongdoers to recognize the harm they have caused, to accept responsibility for their actions, and to be actively involved in improving the situation. Wrongdoers must make reparation to victims, themselves, and the community. It is of interest that RJ initiatives can occur at different entry points and by different agents: police at precharge; the Crown at postcharge; the courts at presentence; corrections at postsentence; and parole at prerevocation (Latimer, Dowden, and Muise 2005).

Embedded within these elements are key values that underlie the various approaches of restorative justice. These values are:

1. Encounter: Create opportunities for victims, offenders, and community members who want to do so to meet and discuss the crime and its aftermath.

2. Amends: Expect offenders to take steps to repair the harm they have caused.

3. Reintegration: Seek to restore victims and offenders to whole, contributing members of society (the goal is not to return them to their pre-crime state).

4. Inclusion: Provide opportunities for parties with a stake in a specific crime to participate in its resolution.

Types of approaches include:

1. **Victim offender mediation**: Increasingly, this is described as conferencing (Amstutz and Zehr 1998) because mediation implies parties who are on somewhat equal ground seeking a settlement. This is not the case with victims and offenders, where one party has usually wronged another. Conferencing has also been referred to as circles, consistent with Aboriginal culture (see Chapter 12), and has been used in sentencing and parole decision making.

2. **Victim assistance**: Various criminal justice departments provide victim services. A good source for information is the public safety portal, which provides sites for provincial and federal assistance (www.safecanada.ca/menu_e.asp). The courts,

correctional agencies, and parole boards provide information and services to victims. Admittedly, much of this work involves assisting victims to be aware of their legal rights regarding representation and notification, and assisting them, should they choose, to provide information to decision makers regarding their experiences.

3. **Ex-offender assistance**: In some respects, victim assistance has overshadowed a long tradition of the National Volunteers Association (www.csc-scc.gc.ca/text/benevols/vols/2-eng.shtml) and its community agencies, such as the Elizabeth Fry Society, St. Leonard's Society, and others providing support and assistance to offenders. This work often begins while the offender is incarcerated and continues, through an after-care model, to include assistance with reintegration to the community. Similar to recent work in the Unites States called offender re-entry (Travis, Solomon, and Wahl 2001), this assistance involves rehabilitative programming (e.g., addictions), support in returning to a community that may have changed markedly during the time of the offender's incarceration, and assistance with accommodation and employment.

4. **Restitution**: This involves financial compensation to the victim by the offender for loss related to their victimization. Typically, the courts assign this amount; however, in RJ models it involves discussion among all parties. The compensation can include direct or tangible (i.e., repairing a broken door) costs and indirect or intangible (i.e., suffering) costs.

5. **Community service**: Sometimes as an alternative to incarceration and perhaps as part of a probation order, the offender is required to complete some sort of community service (i.e., provide labour for community projects) to make amends.

Both federal and provincial corrections agencies provide services to victims, including notification, as does the National Parole Board. Moreover, the Correctional Service of Canada (CSC) has a restorative justice portfolio (www.csc-scc.gc.ca/text/rj/bckgrndr-eng.shtml) and an annual award in recognition of individuals who contribute to restorative issues in Canada. CSC's description is that "Restorative justice is a non-adversarial, non-retributive approach to justice that emphasizes healing in victims, meaningful accountability of offenders, and the involvement of citizens in creating healthier, safer communities . . . It strives to provide support and opportunities for voluntary participation and communication between those affected—victims, offenders, and community—to encourage accountability, reparation, and movement towards understanding, feelings of satisfaction, healing and closure" (Correctional Service of Canada 2009a) (see also Braithwaite 1999; Latimer and Kleinknecht 2000; Van Ness and Strong 1997).

Does Restorative Justice Work?

To answer this question, it is necessary to clarify what is meant by "work." The gold standard of effectiveness is the reduction of future crime, as evidenced by lowered recidivism rates for offenders who participate in RJ initiatives. As noted earlier, however, RJ is voluntary, so there may be a selection bias (i.e., only motivated or less serious offenders participate) (Latimer,

Dowden, and Muise 2005). Moreover, not all RJ approaches are comparable and most of the evaluation research has been restricted to victim offender mediation approaches. One wonders how realistic it may be for a pre-trial intervention to reduce reoffending post-release if the RJ approach has not been reinforced over the time of the offender's incarceration or period of community supervision. Fortunately, RJ evaluation research (Latimer, Dowden, and Muise 2005) typically incorporates multiple indices of success, including:

- Victim satisfaction
- Offender satisfaction
- Restitution compliance
- Recidivism

There are two predominant approaches to evaluating research in restorative justice. One involves assessing a specific program (Bonta, Wallace-Capretta, and Rooney 1998; Rugge, Bonta, and Wallace-Capretta 2005) or a few distinct programs, as in a study from the United Kingdom (Shapland et al. 2008). Another preferred strategy is to aggregate across all identified studies using meta-analysis (described in Chapter 1), such as by Latimer, Dowden, and Muise (2005). In the study by Bonta, Wallace-Capretta, and Rooney (1998), despite lower recidivism rates for offenders who had completed the restorative program, only 10.3 percent of victims agreed to meet the offender, although 78.6 percent submitted victim impact statements. Restitution was ordered by the courts in just over half the cases. In a later study by Rugge, Bonta, and Wallace-Capretta (2005), the major finding was that client satisfaction increased for those who had participated in the Collaborative Justice Project. As well, there was a small reduction in recidivism over a three-year follow-up. The United Kingdom study compared indirect mediation (information is passed by a mediator between victim and offender), direct mediation (a meeting between victim and offender with a mediator present), and conferencing (a meeting with critic/third party and offender present). Based on a two-year follow-up, summed over all three restorative justice schemes, offenders who had participated in restorative justice projects committed statistically fewer offences compared to a control group. Some qualitative analyses from this work with adults suggested the extent to which the offenders felt the conference had enhanced their active involvement: it made them realize the harm done and reoffending was diminished. The authors made an attempt at determining the cost benefits of mediation-type RJ programs, implying that they are cost-effective.

Although some meta-analytic reviews are available within an overall evaluation of offender programming (Aos, Miller, and Drake 2006), the meta-analysis completed by Latimer, Dowden, and Muise (2005) is the most comprehensive on the topic of the effectiveness of RJ models. It evaluated 22 unique studies for 35 individual programs (8 conferencing, 27 victim offender mediation), generating 66 effect sizes. The programs generally target young (74 percent), male (94 percent) offenders. Their conclusions are presented in Table 4.5.

It would appear that restorative justice programs show positive effects across a range of dependent measures. The greatest effect relates to restitution compliance and the weakest

Table 4.5 Effectiveness of Restorative Justice Programs

Dependent Measure	Mean Effect Size (Standard Deviation)	95% Confidence Interval
Victim satisfaction	.19 (.18)	.08 to .30
Offender satisfaction	.17* (.13)	N/A
Restitution compliance	.33 (.24)	−.02 to .63
Recidivism	.07 (.13)	.02 to 12

Note: * outlier removed

Source: Latimer, Dowden, and Muise (2005)

effect relates to recidivism. The findings are encouraging and suggest that in some cases, RJ approaches may be an effective alternative to incarceration. Latimer, Dowden, and Muise (2005) conclude that RJ programs may complement rehabilitation programs and when utilized in conjunction may further reduce reoffending. The next section considers the evolution of rehabilitative (i.e., correctional) programs and the evidence regarding their effectiveness.

OFFENDER REHABILITATION

CORRECTIONAL PROGRAMMING HAS EXPERIENCED A MARKED EVOLUTION OVER THE PAST THREE decades. This evolution has moved researchers from views of pessimism regarding the efficacy of direct intervention with offenders with the aim of reducing their future reoffending to one of modest optimism. Perhaps the seminal work in this area was completed by Don Andrews and his colleagues. Andrews et al. (1990) provided the first evidence regarding what became the "What Works" model. A goal of this chapter is to describe what appears to work with offenders to reduce reoffending. Other chapters will provide more specific information regarding programming for specific types of offenders (e.g., violent, women, Aboriginal, sexual, and juvenile offenders). This newest iteration to offender rehabilitation is described as evidence-based practice (Serin 2005). However, it is important to realize that despite increased evidence regarding the effectiveness of these correctional programs (Aos, Miller, and Drake 2006; Smith, Gendreau, and Swartz 2009), social and political confidence in offender rehabilitation in Canada remains modest (Latimer and Desjardins 2007).

Most authors in the area of offender rehabilitation refer to Martinson's (1974) pessimistic review of the extant outcome data noting the ineffectiveness of rehabilitation as a "watershed event" (McGuire 2004). Martinson (1974) stated the results "give us very little reason to hope that we have in fact found a sure way of reducing recidivism through rehabilitation." He concluded, "Education at its best, or psychotherapy at its best, cannot overcome, or even appreciably reduce, the powerful tendency for offenders to continue in criminal behavior" (p. 47). Rebuttals from prominent scholars (e.g., Palmer 1975), in addition to

Martinson's (1979) re-analysis of his data and Gendreau and Ross's (1979) compilation of more favourable studies, were unsuccessful in stemming the anti-rehabilitation (i.e., punishment) wave. It is perhaps not surprising, then, that advocates of offender treatment refer to this period as the "dark ages" in offender rehabilitation. Martinson (1979) later recanted, stating that some interventions were beneficial, others were not, and some were downright harmful. The balance of this section will describe beneficial interventions, coined "appropriate human service delivery" by Andrews and Bonta (2006).

It is important to have an historical context in order to appreciate how offender programming has changed due to empirical evidence. Three decades ago, initial efforts at counselling were mainly conducted by psychologists (the numbers were relatively few compared to current standards!; 1–2 per 400 offenders versus current rates of 1–2 per 200 offenders), although chaplains also offered counselling. Perhaps because correctional and forensic psychology was in its infancy, the treatment targets in the 1970s were often related to attenuating psychological symptoms (e.g., anxiety, self-esteem, depression) because they were consistent with psychologists' training. It was expected that improved psychological functioning would yield reduced reoffending. (Nowadays this is often described as making a happy criminal, not a prosocial individual!) Recently, counselling in the CSC utilizes para-professionals (parole and program staff with B.A. degrees and specialized training), although psychologists often provide oversight for certain types of criminals (e.g., sex offender, domestic violence) or higher intensity programs. In some respects, psychologists have seen a dilution of their role in treatment as they spend increasing amounts of time completing risk assessments (see Chapter 13). Provincial corrections and other countries are reviewing similar considerations to determine the preferred role for psychologists. This comes at a time of increasing operational challenges (it is hard to recruit and retain psychologists; the number of clinical training programs is few in Canada) and fiscal realities (psychologists' salaries are higher than those of social workers and parole officers).

It is becoming increasing popular to utilize para-professionals to provide structured, skills-based correctional programming to offenders. As well, in community corrections, with the exception of specialized counselling by psychologists, most rehabilitation programming and aftercare is provided by para-professionals. Encouragingly, a majority of these programs, whether prison-based or in the community, strive to deliver services consistent with an evidence-based model. That is, these services address criminogenic needs. There nonetheless remains considerable variability regarding staff skills, program intensity, and degree of oversight. As we will see later in the chapter, these factors greatly influence the effectiveness of correctional programming.

Self-help groups and therapeutic communities are becoming less popular given the improved efficacy of skills-based programs that focus on risk factors for criminality (Motiuk and Serin 1991; Taxman et al. 2004). Off-the-shelf skills-based programs are increasingly becoming available (Multi-Health Systems 2005; National Institute of Corrections 2005) for a variety of treatment targets (i.e., anger, problem solving, and substance abuse) and populations (i.e., juveniles, adults, women). Essentially, the current approach to correctional programming is to target and reduce criminogenic needs using a cognitive-behavioural model that assists offenders to understand high-risk situations and increases skills to become prosocial. Substantial published research across multiple countries and correctional agencies has demonstrated that such correctional programming reduces reoffending (Andrews et al. 1990; French and Gendreau 2003; Lösel 1995; McGuire 1995; 2002; Smith, Gendreau, and Swartz, 2009). Arguably, rehabilitation programs are a critical strategy utilized by correctional agencies to reduce recidivism, thereby enhancing public safety. This is particularly important in federal corrections, where offenders are convicted for more serious crimes and receive longer sentences, thereby raising concern regarding their safe return to the community at the end of their sentence.

What Does an Effective Program Look Like?

Risk   Based on the research by Andrews and others, the preferred contemporary approach to correctional programming has the primary principles typically referred to as **risk, need,** and responsivity (Andrews and Bonta 2003). Risk refers to the requirement to provide higher intensity programming to higher risk offenders. The need to increase program dosage can be addressed by more frequent sessions (i.e., every day versus once weekly), a longer program (i.e., three months versus six weeks), or some combination to meet an acceptable level of intervention. There are two aspects of risk that are important to consider. First, providing programming to lower risk offenders may actually increase their risk of reoffending (Andrews and Bonta 2003). It appears that lower risk offenders with presumably less antisocial characteristics adopt some of the less preferred attitudes when associating with higher risk offenders (e.g., lower motivation, denial, rationalization, antisocial views). Second, some minimum dosage is required in order for change to occur. At present, high-intensity programs in CSC are typically 250 hours, while some programs in New Zealand are almost 300 hours. Of particular note is a study by Bourgon and Armstrong (2005) demonstrating that about 200 hours of correctional programming yields improved effect sizes (i.e., higher effect size equates to decreases in recidivism). An effective program must be of sufficient intensity and must target higher risk cases. At one point, it was assumed that program intensity was linearly related to risk such that the highest risk cases warranted to greatest programming. Recently, there has been recognition that there may be a small group of very high risk offenders who may not fully benefit from programming (or that programming is insufficient to reduce risk). Certain sensational serial sex offender and murder cases would likely qualify. Figure 4.2 presents data regarding the effectiveness of risk reduction when targeting higher versus lower risk offenders.

Criminogenic Need   As noted earlier, from the mid 1970s the issue of treatment targets evolved from a focus on psychological symptoms to a focus on factors related to crime. Table 4.6 summarizes correlational data regarding these factors, illustrating why

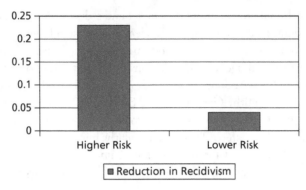

Figure 4.2 Higher Risk versus Lower Risk Offenders: Results from Meta-Analyses of Behavioural Programs

Source: Adapted from Bonta, Wallace-Capretta, and Rooney (2000)

criminogenic needs have become a mainstay of offender assessment by correctional staff (parole officers and psychologists). All Canadian correctional agencies apply assessment procedures when an offender is admitted (see "Offender Classification" later in this chapter) to determine the presence and severity of criminogenic needs. Further, Figure 4.3 presents evidence that targeting criminogenic need yields greater reduction in recidivism. It is also important to note in Figure 4.3 that targeting non-criminogenic need actually increases recidivism. The figure also illustrates that targeting multiple criminogenic needs is important, since most offenders have more than a single factor to change in order to improve success upon release.

Responsivity The responsivity principle states that the mode and style of treatment must be matched to the learning style and abilities of the offender. There are two types of responsivity: general and specific. The former relates to the issue of matching offenders to

Table 4.6 Types of Need and their Relationship to Criminal Behaviour

Criminogenic (*r*)	Non-Criminogenic (*r*)
Procriminal attitudes (.21)	Self-esteem (−.02)
Criminal associates (.21)	Vague emotional feelings (.08)
Antisocial personality (.22)	Physical training (.08)
Family/marital concerns (.18)	Fear of punishment (−.05)
School/employment concerns (.15)	Conventional ambition (.08)
Substance use (.11)	

Source: Andrews and Bonta (2006)

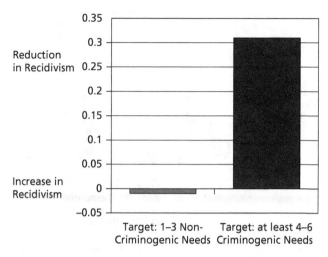

Figure 4.3 Targeting Criminogenic Need: Results from Meta-Analyses

Source: Gendreau, French, and Taylor (2002)

programming that is cognitive-behavioural and based on adult learning. While meta-analyses of treatment indicate that type of treatment is perhaps less important than the therapeutic relationship or certain client factors (Lambert 1992), offenders are adult learners and respond best to program models that are cognitive-behavioural (see Chapter 3) and skills-based. This is reflected in Figure 4.4, where interventions that are non-behavioural (e.g., insight oriented) yield much lower reductions in recidivism. This supports the principle of **general responsivity**. The issue of **specific responsivity** contends that offenders differ significantly in their motivation and potential readiness for intervention. As well, other factors such as intelligence, age, gender, ethnicity/race, and language are seen to be potential barriers to successful participation in programming. Further, therapists have specific styles that may not universally apply to all offenders. Specific

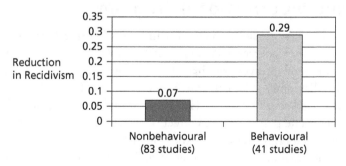

Figure 4.4 Type of Program and Effect on Recidivism

Source: Andrews (1994)

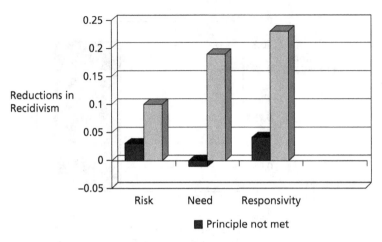

Figure 4.5 Empirical Evidence for Risk, Need, and Responsivity Principles

Source: Andrews and Bonta (2006)

responsivity is the understanding of the need to match therapist style to the offender's circumstance.

Taken together, the principles of risk, need, and responsivity reflect a model for offender programming. When these principles are applied consistently, researchers demonstrate the greatest reductions in reoffending, as illustrated in Figure 4.5. The most recent meta-analysis with respect to offender programming indicates that when all these principles are adhered to, there is an overall reduction of 28 percent in recidivism (Smith, Gendreau, and Swartz 2009). It is also worth noting that program effects appear to vary slightly by type of program. That is, some program domains (e.g., substance abuse) yield greater effects than others (e.g., domestic violence) (Drake, Aos, and Miller 2009).

Describing a Correctional Program

Information on CSC's website provides a definition of **correctional program** that is consistent with other sources (McGuire 2001). CSC states that "a Correctional Program is a structured intervention that addresses the factors directly linked to offenders' criminal behaviour." (Correctional Service of Canada 2009b). Moreover, the *Corrections and Conditions Release Act* (1992) specifies the legal framework for rehabilitative programs: "The purpose of the correctional system is to assist the rehabilitation of offenders and their reintegration into the community as law-abiding citizens through the provision of programs in penitentiaries and in the community" (Correctional Service of Canada 2009b). CSC describes the components and principles of such programs.

Correctional programs must:

be based on theory and supporting research (empirically-based model of change);
target criminogenic factors;
address the diverse needs of women, Aboriginal, and other groups of offenders with special requirements;
be skills oriented;
take into account the particular characteristics of offenders to help ensure that they derive maximum benefit (responsivity);
address the particular risk and need profiles of offenders through the scope, intensity, duration, and type of group setting (program intensity);
ensure a continuum of care between institutions and the community (continuity of care);
include a detailed program description;
include a plan for monitoring and evaluation; and
be delivered:
using proven treatment methods
in the least restrictive environment possible consistent with staff, offender, and public safety
according to approved standards

It should be apparent that correctional programs are very specific activities clearly described in standardized manuals and in the training of staff such that criminal risk is potentially reduced and managed.

A Sample of Program Content

While programming for sexual and violent offenders is described in Chapters 7 and 9, initial offender rehabilitation programming focused on problem-solving and criminal attitudes, since they seem to be primary reasons for engaging in criminal behaviour. The initial cognitive-based program was called Cognitive Skills or Reasoning and Rehabilitation, depending on the country where it was delivered (Tong and Farrington 2006; Robinson and Porporino 2001). While this type of program is still in use in some jurisdictions, more recent versions are multidimensional and target multiple criminogenic needs. One such example is the program Counter-Point. Counter-Point has recently been revised, but its purpose and goals remain relevant and are illustrative of how theory informs the practice of correctional programming.

According to Yessine and Kroner (2004), the primary goal of Counter-Point is to reduce reoffending by providing participants with the skills necessary to identify, challenge, and enhance their willingness to alter antisocial attitudes and develop more prosocial ones. Additional objectives include promoting access to prosocial people and activities, identifying high-risk situations, and developing the necessary resources to prevent future criminal activity. To do so, offenders participate in 25 sessions, which are divided into three processes: the intake process; the intervention process; and the closure process. Utilizing **motivational interviewing** techniques, the intake process consists of three individual sessions that entail orientation, assessment, and goal setting. The intervention process contains six modules that are introduced sequentially over 20 two-hour group sessions, which can be delivered from one to three times a week. The modules are

- Setting the context for change (two sessions)
- Identifying support for change (two sessions)
- Identifying pro-criminal attitudes, values, and beliefs (seven sessions)
- Altering pro-criminal sentiments (three sessions)
- Prosocial problem-solving (two sessions)
- Maintaining change (four sessions)

The closure process is comprised of two individual sessions used to review the progress report and, together with a **parole officer** (PO), the relapse prevention plan of each participant. To facilitate attitudinal and behavioural change and increase participants' personal responsibility and accountability, Counter-Point is based on a social learning perspective and applies cognitive-behavioural principles and methods. For example, the program teaches self-monitoring, self-management, perspective-taking, and generic problem-solving skills, and features interactive presentation and practice, sequential and structured learning, prosocial modelling, role play, rehearsal, and effective reinforcement and disapproval. Program integrity is maintained through ongoing process evaluations and standardized manuals. Further, program entry and participation guidelines are clearly outlined, and **correctional program officers** (CPOs) who are experienced in working with correctional clients have access to clinical support and guidance and receive training in the principles of effective intervention and professional conduct.

Results show that, compared to program non-completers and non-participants, offenders who complete Counter-Point programs have significant reductions in three correctional outcome measures. Statistically, controlling for criminogenic need, risk, and prior program participation, offenders who complete Counter-Point have a 24 percent reduction in the risk of having been suspended, a 38 percent reduction in the risk of having been revoked, and a 33 percent reduction in the risk of having committed a new offence when compared to offenders who fail to complete the intervention or are not exposed in any way to the program's content.

To summarize, programs are mandated by CSC mission and the **Corrections and Conditions Release Act** (1992). Their major goal is to manage risk and reduce recidivism, but they also help with population management (offenders who participate in programs are more likely to receive earlier release). Programs assist in institutional management in that offenders who participate are less likely to be involved in institutional misconducts (French and Gendreau 2003). Moreover, they provide the opportunity to better understand individual offenders' case-specific risk factors, thereby enhancing risk management upon release to the community.

Program Evaluation and Accreditation

Increasingly, correctional jurisdictions are interested in and obliged to evaluate their programs to ensure that: 1) the programs are delivered in a manner consistent with policy; 2) the programs reflect a contemporary community standard; and 3) the programs yield reductions in reoffending. These criteria are reflected in program evaluation, which is often conducted by internal researchers. Occasionally this is done collaboratively with academic colleagues. CSC has also adopted the requirement for external experts to review programs as part of an accreditation process. From CSC's website,

> Programs are presented to review panels that consist of internationally-recognized experts in the field who assess the program in relation to specific criteria. Those programs that are rated as fulfilling the required criteria are then recommended by the panel to the Commissioner for **program accreditation**. In turn, the quality of the delivery of accredited programs in the field (institutions and community) is then assessed through a process of site accreditation. The Performance Assurance Sector is primarily responsible for coordinating the overall accreditation process, however, the Reintegration Programs Division assists in the process of identifying suitable programs for review. (Correctional Service of Canada 2009c)

Essentially, if a program fails to meet accreditation and/or fails to reduce reoffending, its chances of survival are slight. Further, reintegration (correctional) program staff constantly review programs and consider revisions to enhance such goals as offender engagement, offender retention, responsivity concerns, improved release rates, and improved release outcomes.

In an effort to more systematically consider the issue of program integrity, Don Andrews and Paul Gendreau developed the Correctional Program Assessment Inventory (CPAI–2000). Higher scores on the CPAI–2000 (meaning higher quality programs) are related to higher program effectiveness in terms of lower recidivism. In fact, the CPAI–2000 rivals standard risk assessments and indices of general responsivity with respect to its relationship to recidivism (Andrews and Bonta 2006).

OFFENDER CLASSIFICATION

How Are Offenders Referred to Programs?

As discussed previously, all Canadian correctional agencies complete some form of risk and needs assessment when an individual is admitted following sentencing. (Note: This assessment does not occur for individuals prior to sentencing, including those held on

Box 4.1

Canadian Researcher Profile:
Dr. Paul Gendreau

Dr. Paul Gendreau was appointed to the Order of Canada in 2007 in recognition that he

> has made seminal contributions to correctional theory and practice that have had an impact on criminal justice systems around the world. A psychologist and professor emeritus at the University of New Brunswick, he has used evidence-based research to develop rehabilitation programs for offenders. A highly sought-after consultant and advisor, he has shared his broad knowledge with government agencies, private sector organizations and universities across North America and in England, Australasia and Jamaica. He has also earned accolades as an educator who has influenced a generation of criminology and psychology students and inspired them to become leaders in their field. (Governor General of Canada 2007)

Dr. Gendreau has had a profound influence on correctional research and practice both in Canada and internationally.

Graduating from the University of Ottawa and Queen's University (where he claimed he majored in golf and basketball, respectively!), Dr. Gendreau remains an influential and engaging pioneer in the area of corrections research and practice. A colourful speaker who is not shy about expressing his opinion, he has influenced practitioners and administrators alike regarding correctional policy. Less well-known facts about Dr. Gendreau are that he was a food critique for *Where to Eat in Canada* for 16 years, is an ardent musician but a compulsive golfer, and that he went to high school with Paul Anka and university with Alex Trebek.

Dr. Gendreau remains an active researcher, focusing on the prediction and treatment of criminal behaviour, the effects of prison life, alternatives to null hypothesis testing for data analysis, and assessing the quality of offender treatment programs with the CPAI-2000. He and his students continue his tradition of research excellence, most recently through meta-analysis to clarify and refine our understanding of effective corrections while challenging what Dr. Gendreau refers to as "correctional quackery." Most importantly, underlying his more than three decades of research is the goal to help people. He believes (as do we!) that when the criminal justice system functions in a more humane fashion, the client and public are better served.

remand.) The assessment process includes initial determinations for custody placement and eventual considerations for correctional programming. In all jurisdictions, it yields a **correctional treatment plan** or roadmap for the offender for the duration of his or her sentence. This process is known as offender classification.

The initial part of **offender classification** is an intake assessment. Typically, the initial screening is completed by correctional staff, who follow a standardized set of questions regarding current mental state, outstanding charges, incompatibles (i.e., Are there other offenders with whom the newly admitted offender may have problems?), and prior incarcerations. What follows is an orientation of the rules and regulations of the jail or prison, how to access information, and the availability of resources such as parole officers, social workers, psychologists, chaplains, and elders. Most correctional agencies distribute an offender handbook. Newly admitted offenders are also seen by health care providers to determine if there are any ongoing health concerns. If mental health concerns are noted, the offender may be seen by a forensic nurse, psychologist, or psychiatrist, depending on the setting. All correctional settings screen for suicide risk at intake, given that it is a time of increased risk (Wichmann, Serin, and Motiuk 2000). A typical screening involves

- May be suicidal/has suicidal thoughts
- Has plan for suicide
- Has previous suicide attempt(s) in the past five years
- Has had recent psychiatric/psychological intervention/hospitalization
- Recent loss of relationship, death of a close relative/friend
- Excessively worried about problems
- Influence of alcohol or drugs, signs of withdrawal
- Shows signs of depression/hopelessness

Canadian corrections agencies are world leaders in the area of offender classification. The applied and theoretical work of Don Andrews and his colleagues Jim Bonta and Steve Wormith in the development of the Level of Service Inventory (LSI) and its various derivatives has been internationally lauded. This research forms the core of offender classification in many countries, especially the United States, and is incorporated into all provincial corrections. Work by Austin and his colleagues over several decades defined the issues and challenges regarding offender classification in the United States (Austin and McGinnis 2004; Brennan 2004).

CSC uses the Offender Intake Assessment (OIA), which was validated on the federal offender population and is similar in construction but more expansive than the original LSI (Motiuk 1994). The OIA has undergone revisions since its inception in 1994, with CSC refining items so that they are more dynamic, conducting consultations with staff, and completing statistical analyses to confirm predictive validity (Brown and Motiuk 2005). It is important to note that concerns by such groups as the Office of the Correctional Investigator have challenged CSC to develop classification scales that can be dynamic over the duration of an offender's sentence (i.e., Security Reclassification Scale) and responsive to gender (i.e., Security Reclassification Scale for Women). Essentially, offender classification is a risk–and-need assessment where the outcomes of interest are specific to prisons (i.e., risk of escape, institutional adjustment, risk to the community if the offender escapes) and not recidivism per se.

These classification risk factors are articulated in the following guidelines for offender classification:

a. the seriousness of the offence

b. any outstanding charges against the offender

c. the offender's performance and behaviour while under sentence

d. the offender's social, criminal, and, where available, young offender history

e. any physical or mental illness or disorder

f. the offender's potential for violent behaviour

g. the offender's continued involvement in criminal activities

According to CSC policy, offender classification has specific goals:

1. To protect public safety by ensuring offenders are placed in an institution with the appropriate level of security throughout their sentence

2. To assign to each offender a minimum, medium, or maximum security classification based on the application of the Security Reclassification Scale or Security Reclassification Scale for Women and assessment of other relevant factors to ensure ongoing review and reclassification as required.

There is also a requirement for assessments to be responsive to ethnicity. The concern regarding overrepresentation of Aboriginal offenders has led to a reinforcement of the **Gladue decision** in considering security classification (see Chapter 1). CSC policy notes:

> In determining the security classification of Aboriginal offenders, staff will be sensitive to the spirit and intent of the Gladue decision and will take into consideration the following factors:
>
>> history of dislocation such as residential school experience or family history of residential school experience;
>> unemployment due to a lack of opportunity or options;
>> lack or irrelevance of education;
>> history of substance abuse;
>> history of systemic and direct discrimination;
>> history of previous experience involving restorative/community based sanctions;

history of participation in Aboriginal traditional teachings, ceremonies and activities;

history of living on or off reserves. (Correctional Service of Canada 2009d)

Assessment Domains in Offender Classification

CSC has perhaps the most standardized index of offender classification, which uses the Custody Rating Scale (Luciani 2001). As noted earlier, the three main factors considered for custody placement are institutional adjustment, escape risk, and public safety rating. These are combined to yield an overall custody placement of minimum, medium, or maximum security. The initial rating performed at intake is revised following 12 months of incarceration. At that time, the index (i.e., current) crime is weighted less and factors such as program completion are included. Lower scores may be sufficient to meet the threshold for recommendation to transfer to reduced security. As in most classification schemes, there is provision for **professional override**, whereby the parole officer can choose to recommend something disparate from the empirically validated scoring. Some evidence suggests that overrides diminish the accuracy of the assessment procedure (Motiuk, Luciani, Serin, and Vuong, 2001).

According to CSC policy,

An inmate will be classified as maximum security where the inmate is assessed by the Service as:

presenting a high probability of escape and a high risk to the safety of the public in the event of escape; or,

requiring a high degree of supervision and control within the penitentiary;

medium security where the inmate is assessed by the Service as:

presenting a low to moderate probability of escape and a moderate risk to the safety of the public in the event of escape; or,

requiring a moderate degree of supervision and control within the penitentiary;

minimum security where the inmate is assessed by the Service as:

presenting a low probability of escape and a low risk to the safety of the public in the event of escape; and,

requiring a low degree of supervision and control within the penitentiary. (Correctional Service of Canada 2009d)

In order to appreciate the variations in ratings for the three domains, Table 4.7 presents each along with a representative rating (low, moderate, high).

Impact of Offender Classification

The Custody Rating Scale (CRS) was developed and first implemented in 1992. By tracking the escape rate, concordance between clinical judgments by staff and instrument

Table 4.7 Sample Offender Classification Ratings

Domain	Rating	Description
Institutional adjustment	Low	A pattern of satisfactory institutional adjustment; no special management intervention is required.
		The ability and motivation to interact effectively and responsibly with others, individually and in groups, with little or no supervision.
		Motivation toward self-improvement by actively participating in a correctional plan designed to meet dynamic factors, particularly those relating to facilitating his or her reintegration into the community.
Escape risk	Moderate	Has a recent history of escape and/or attempted escapes OR there are current indicator(s) of escape potential.
		Is unlikely to make active efforts to escape but may do so if the opportunity presents itself.
		Presents a definite potential to escape from an institution that has no enclosure.
Public safety risk	High	Criminal history involves violence and the inmate has not demonstrated any progress in addressing those dynamic factors that contributed to the violent behaviour or a willingness to attempt to address them.
		There are current indicators of high risk/concern.

Source: Correctional Service of Canada (2009e)

ratings, and the distribution of cases sent directly to minimum security, it is possible to evaluate the merits of the scale. Bear in mind that the CRS is a statistical risk instrument; hence the expectation is that its use would enhance practice compared to unstructured clinical judgment. These data are presented in Table 4.8. Of note, concordance increased over the eight-year study period, as did the proportion of offenders placed directly in minimum security, yet escape rates decreased. Table 4.8 shows that as staff ratings (the ultimate classification decision) followed instrument ratings over time (increased concordance rates), minimum security placements increased and escape rates decreased. This indicates that before staff followed CRS, more offenders could have been safely placed in minimum security. The results have had significant cost savings in that it costs less to incarcerate someone in minimum security relative to other security levels (community supervision is even more cost effective!) and it

Table 4.8 CRS Placement Concordance and Escape from Minimum Security

Concordance	1992 (%)	1993 (%)	1994 (%)	1995 (%)	1996 (%)	1997 (%)	1998 (%)	1999 (%)
Concordance (%):								
Overall	63.0	59.0	56.6	57.1	57.4	71.5	79.4	76.7
With minimum rated	75.7	73.1	73.5	73.5	75.2	75.6	80.4	80.7
Distribution to minimum	12.0	24.4	27.3	27.0	25.1	26.6	32.7	37.5
Minimum security escape rate	131	102	104	53	28	24	30	45

Source: Luciani (2001)

meets the *Corrections and Conditional Release Act* requirement of least restrictive level of custody.

It is worth noting that similar findings show that staff tend to overclassify security level compared to unstructured clinical judgment. For this reason, the LSI-R has been a mainstay of offender classification for more than two decades in Canadian provincial corrections and state corrections in the United States. Moreover, general principles and lessons learned are available to enhance the practice of offender classification and are in fact important in the application of theory to practice. Offender assessment and classification involve more than simply completing a risk instrument (Bonta, Bogue, Crowley, and Motiuk 2001). Box 4.2 presents a case study and a series of questions regarding custody classification.

Box 4.2

Case Study

Bill Smith, age 28, is convicted of armed robbery (three counts) and receives a five-year sentence. This is his first federal sentence, but he has more than 10 prior property offences relating to substance use and two fail to appears. He also has had two serious assault charges. He has no outstanding charges and reports being motivated for treatment. Bill is married with a young son and expects visits from his family while incarcerated. He feels it is time for him to change his life. He plans to begin his own roofing business upon release. Bill is asking to go to minimum security to be closer to his family.

Continued >

There was a knife involved in the robberies, but Bill states that he is non-violent and that the robberies were to get money to provide for his new family, although presentence report suggests money for drugs may also have been a motive. He noted that he had a fight in the county jail while on remand when others hassled him. Nonetheless, he reports he can be in regular population. He has never been seen by a mental health professional.

- What are Bill's major criminogenic needs?
- What is his escape risk?
- What is his institutional adjustment risk?
- What is Bill's public safety risk?
- What security level would you recommend?

CONTEMPORARY CHALLENGES

THIS SECTION WILL HIGHLIGHT SOME RECENT TRENDS AND CONTEMPORARY CHALLENGES in correctional practice. Areas of increasing interest to researchers and clinicians who struggle with bridging theory and practice are:

- Offender change in correctional programming
- Crime desistance
- Risk management

Offender Change

Offender change refers to the acquisition of prosocial attitudes and new skills to avoid future criminal behaviour, usually through completion of structured programming. With respect to rehabilitative programming, the challenge continues to be how to enhance effectiveness. As discussed earlier, program integrity appears to be important, in addition to the principles of risk/need/responsivity. Recently, efforts to enhance program effectiveness have focused on the additional areas of treatment readiness, staff skills and competencies, and offender change. The expectation is that addressing offender motivation, recognizing the characteristics of effective staff, and better understanding the process of offender change would lead to further gains in program effectiveness. Several new measures and conceptual models for understanding **treatment readiness** have been proposed and empirical investigations are underway (Serin, Mailloux, and Kennedy 2008; Ward, Day, Howell and Birgden 2004). These approaches are offender-specific and may prove more valid than generic models such as the Stages of Change (Prochaska, DiClemente, and Norcross 1992). Encouragingly, a brief but structured motivational interviewing intervention appears to reduce reoffending (Antiss and Polaschek, in press), giving credence to the focus on offender motivation and treatment readiness.

With respect to the importance of staff, meta-analytic findings confirm that it influences offender outcome (Dowden and Andrews, 2004). Staff who adopt the maxim of fair but firm are more effective in correctional practice than staff who are overly authoritative or rehabilitative (Skeem and Manchak 2008). Skilled staff are becoming an important foundation for effective offender programming (Marshall and Serran 2004; Marshall et al. 2003; Serin and Shturman 2007) and community supervision (Skeem, Eno Louden, Polasheck, and Cap 2007) beyond the issue of following risk/need principles. Various authors have summarized the characteristics of effective staff:

- Empathic (reflects awareness and concern for others)
- Directive (active, leads discussions, sets goals)
- Fair (balances the rights of all parties)
- Respectful (doesn't talk down to offenders)
- Reinforcing (supports and encourages positive efforts and accomplishments)
- Communication skills (has good interpersonal and verbal skills)

Broadly, staff who reflect these skills will have improved outcomes (Dowden and Andrews 2004; Liebling 2006; Marshall et al. 2003; Skeem, Louden, Polasheck, and Cap 2007). Such outcomes include more disclosure in interviews, improved engagement in programs, acceptance of responsibility for criminal behaviour, improved program participation and completion, better adherence to group rules, fewer prison misconducts, favourable response to supervision, and reduced reoffending

Finally, while programming results in offender change, the process by which it occurs is unclear. Despite the encouraging effect sizes, there is little empirical evidence to indicate that clinicians are able to identify specific offenders who benefit most from programming and whose likelihood of reoffending is diminished. In particular, change scores on pre/post test batteries have had little to no predictive validity. Further, while researchers argue that the internal mechanisms driving the desistance process are of key importance (Maruna 2001), the psychological mechanisms hypothesized to underlie observable changes in life circumstance and reductions in criminal activity have not been adequately explored (Serin and Lloyd 2009). That is, certain events (i.e., getting a good job, abstaining from drugs and alcohol, maintaining a stable relationship) signal a change from an antisocial lifestyle but do not specifically identify the propensities or psychological constructs that underlie them.

Crime Desistance

Crime desistance refers to the cessation of crime. A consistent finding of criminal behaviour research is that the aggregate level of crime peaks in the late teens and early twenties and rapidly declines thereafter. That is, research shows that criminal behaviour is largely an attribute of youth. Rates of criminal activity drop sharply around age

30 and decline to close to insignificant numbers later in the life course (Farrington and West 1993; Hoffman and Beck 1984). It appears, then, that offenders, given time, will eventually desist from criminal activity (Sampson and Laub 2005). Most researchers uphold that desistance is best understood as a process (for specific discussion, see Maruna 2001; McNeill 2004). So, while desistance is often defined dichotomously as the absence of criminal activity, current theory recognizes that richer, more detailed data arises from conceptualizing it as an active, ongoing process of change and growth rather than a distinct instantaneous event (Burnett and McNeill 2005; Maruna 2001). Recently, a transition model of offender change has been proposed (Serin and Lloyd 2009) that asserts that psychological mechanisms (i.e., propensities) moderate the change from an individual's self-perception of being an offender to being a citizen. These propensities could be a belief that one can change, an expectation that change requires effort, and so on. As well, a commitment to change one's goals, beliefs, and expectations is considered a prerequisite to eventual crime desistance (Ward and Marshall 2007). Such change drives crime desistance. Other factors, such as getting older, becoming involved in a stable relationship, maintaining stable employment, and securing prosocial friends, combine such that the costs of crime increase (see Table 4.1). Andrews and Bonta (2006) assert that this change in contingencies underlies crime desistance. That is, the rewards for prosocial behaviour increase and are greater than the rewards for criminal behaviour.

It appears that crime desistance is not solely a function of age, although aging is an important component. So, too, is substance abuse. Figure 4.6 illustrates how substance abuse increases crime risk in terms of earlier onset and delayed desistance; youth who are actively involved in substance use are more likely to initiate crime earlier, and adult offenders who have substance abuse problems are more likely to delay the cessation of

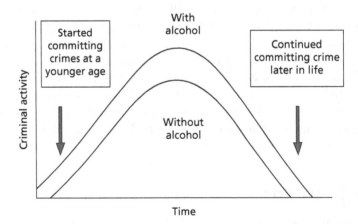

Figure 4.6 Age–Crime Curve and Effect of Substance Abuse

Source: Lloyd (2009)

their criminal involvement. For this reason, substance abuse treatment programs remain an important component of correctional programs in all jurisdictions. The example of the National Substance Abuse Program is provided in Chapter 6.

In summary, the assessment and targeting of criminogenic needs is fundamental to effective programming. There is renewed interest in identifying and measuring intra-individual factors of offender change and desistance, thereby enhancing correctional programming efforts. In addition to programming, there has been much focus on risk assessment in corrections over the past 30 years. Approaches to risk assessment are described more fully in Chapters 7 and 9, and concerns regarding issues of gender and ethnicity in risk assessment are presented in Chapters 11 and 12, respectively. Nonetheless, the application of risk assessment to offender supervision (i.e., risk management) is generating considerable attention (Douglas 2009).

Risk Management

Theory and practice nicely dovetail regarding the enterprise of risk assessment. Evidence-based practice would argue that all criminal justice assessments must consider the issue of criminal risk. The application of this assessment relates to risk management. With exponential increase in risk assessment approaches, this has led to a virtual shopping list of risk assessment scales for clinical application in the areas of juvenile offenders, violent offenders, sexual offenders, domestic violent offenders, and mentally disordered offenders. In general, it is recommended that assessment approaches match the nature of the case (i.e., use sex offender scales for sex offenders). The issue of the accuracy of different risk assessment instruments continues to be a preoccupation, but the field is moving to discussions about relative and absolute indices of risk (Hanson and Morton-Bourgon 2009) as well as improved considerations regarding risk communication (Babchishin and Hanson 2009). For instance, what does "low risk" really mean? Another challenge is the difference between group and individual estimates of risk. Group estimates (i.e., **nomothetic**) assign risk according to a large group of offenders. For example, the statement that Mr. X has a 35 percent probability of recidivism within three years is relevant only to the degree that Mr. X is representative of the group on which the scale was validated. Often, estimates are derived from the completion of statistical scales. Further, the factors reflected on these scales are often historical (i.e., static) and need not reflect theory about criminal behaviour. Rather, if the factor predicts recidivism, it would be included in the risk scale regardless whether it informs theory about criminal behaviour.

Psychology, however, is interested in individual differences and understanding the individual (i.e., **idiographic**). Unfortunately, sometimes relying on the uniqueness of cases (i.e., unstructured clinical judgment) leads to inaccuracy in decision-making (Grove, Zald, Lebow, Snitz, and Nelson 2000). One effort to better understand risk is to consider the issue of **dynamic risk**, which gives a more accurate approximation of when Mr. X is at risk (i.e., when drinking, when fantasizing about young children, or when angry). The notion of dynamic risk has become a key component to understanding risk management

(Douglas and Skeem 2005; Quinsey, Jones, Book, and Barr 2006) (see Chapter 9 for a discussion of dynamic risk assessment with sex offenders). Structured professional judgment approaches to risk assessment (see Chapters 7 and 9) are becoming more popular in that they are more individualized and also more reliable and structured than clinical judgments (Campbell, French, and Gendreau, in press; Hanson and Morton-Bourgon 2009). It remains to be determined which risk assessment method (statistical or structured professional judgment) will prove popular as practitioners continue to struggle with risk management of offenders in the community. Further, the field continues to debate the relative strengths of actuarial (Quinsey, Harris, Rice, and Cormier, 2006; Hanson and Morton-Bourgon 2009) versus case formulation (Hart 2008) approaches to risk assessment.

Below is a list of top 10 issues and people to consider when thinking about correctional practice in Canada.

Top 10 List

Advances to Come, Debates, Ethical Conundrums, and People to Watch

1. You are working at a correctional agency and asked to complete an assessment that fails to consider criminogenic needs. What do you do?

2. You use a risk scale that does not distinguish between male and female offenders. Is this a problem?

3. You are a new employee working with a senior colleague who has developed her "own" treatment program. It focuses on shame and uses storytelling as a method of sharing information. Does this meet evidence-based practice? If not, what should you do?

4. Should low- and high-risk offenders be in the same correctional program?

5. Based on the information covered in this chapter, how likely is it that correctional programs must address multiple criminogenic needs?

6. A convicted child molester (stranger victim) wants to engage in a restorative justice model. What are the potential issues and pitfalls?

7. You apply a classification scale at intake and it indicates the offender should be assigned to maximum security (high escape risk, high public safety concerns). What factors might change this rating when reclassification is done at the 12-month review?

8. Given that crime decreases with age, why shouldn't all older offenders be released early on parole?

9. Which is more important in order to address the issue of staff skills: good selection or appropriate training?

10. Names to watch: Don Andrews, Jim Bonta, Guy Bourgon, Paul Gendreau, Paula Smith, and Steve Wormith.

SUMMARY

From this brief review it should be apparent that theory continues to inform practice and that challenges from practice continue to advance theory in a kind of symbiotic relationship. This notion of using research to inform practice underpins the scientist–practitioner model (Douglas, Cox, and Webster 1999). Specifically, it asserts that practice must be informed by the empirical literature and that clinicians must constantly strive to inform and improve practice. Delivery of effective practice is an ethical requirement of professional psychology (Canadian Psychological Association 2009).

Increasingly, correctional practitioners are encouraged and required to ground their work in evidence, hence the phrase evidence-based practice. Despite slight variations across the provincial and federal systems, correctional agencies must account for their methods in terms of efficacy and best-practice models. Partly this is driven by cost issues. Wasting tax dollars on inefficient or ineffective services is problematic. However, it is also driven by a long tradition of Canadian social scientists being world leaders in corrections theory and practice. Canadian researchers in academia and government continue to make important contributions to correctional issues with a commitment to balancing rehabilitation with public safety.

Specifically:

1. Effective correctional practice must be informed by theory and evidence.

2. Punishment and deterrence leads to increases in crime and incarceration, not decreases.

3. Offender change and crime desistance is influenced by an increase in rewards for prosocial behaviour. The factors that inform crime desistance may be different than those that inform crime acquisition.

4. For some offenders, restorative justice approaches are a viable alternative to getting tough on crime.

5. Using standardized classification measures yields lower levels of custody and lower rates of escape but the application of risk assessment must consider ethnicity and gender.

6. Provincial and federal corrections utilize standardized assessment approaches at intake and throughout an offender's sentence and supervision to target criminogenic needs and develop a correctional plan.

7. Correctional programming that is cognitive-behavioural and skills-based is most likely to result in decreases in reoffending.

8. Effective correctional programming reflects the principles of risk, need, and responsivity.

9. Staff skills are fundamental to effective corrections.

10. Research regarding dynamic risk is increasingly utilized to inform risk management of offenders.

Discussion Questions

1. What is the legislative backdrop to custody classification? What are some challenges to current approaches to custody classification?

2. If punishment seems to yield the least reduction in reoffending, why is it so popular?

3. Under what circumstances would restorative justice be appropriate? Inappropriate?

4. Which principle of correctional programming (risk, need, responsivity) seems most critical?

5. What are the implications of having callous and authoritarian staff delivering programs to offenders?

6. Age is related to crime desistance. Does this mean young offenders cannot change?

Additional Reading

Andrews, D.A. and Bonta, J. 2006. *The psychology of criminal conduct*. 4th ed. Cincinnati: Anderson.

Motiuk, L.L. and Serin, R.C. 2001. *Compendium 2000 on effective correctional programming*. Ottawa: Correctional Service Canada.

McMurran, M. 2004. *Motivating offenders to change: A guide to enhancing engagement in therapy*. Chichester: Wiley.

Chapter 5

Developmental Issues:

Juvenile Offending

Billy was transferred to four different schools as a result of bad behaviour. His kindergarten teacher used to call Billy's mom, Mrs. Smith, on a weekly basis. If Billy wasn't punching other boys for their toys, he was damaging school property or throwing temper tantrums when he didn't get his way. His behaviour didn't change when he entered elementary school—in fact, it accelerated, and by the time he was 12, he was being truant from school, playing with fire, and bullying both boys and girls. At 14, Billy brought weapons to high school and sexually coerced females. The police were called several times throughout his childhood, unfortunately to no avail in changing his behaviour. Not knowing how best to keep Billy and other students safe, he was referred to a psychologist for assessment.

After interviews with Billy, his parents, and his teachers, as well as some direct observation of interactions between Billy and his friends, Billy was diagnosed with conduct disorder, a precursor to antisocial personality disorder often found in adult offenders. However, not all youths diagnosed with conduct disorder go on to be adult offenders. Will Billy?

Learning Objectives

1 Describe the history of juvenile justice in Canada.

2 Differentiate between the theories to explain juvenile offending.

3 Define and list the risk and protective factors associated with juvenile offending.

4 Identify the psychiatric diagnoses and their trajectories relevant to juvenile offenders.

5 Describe the tools used to assess juvenile offenders.

6 Distinguish between primary, secondary, and tertiary interventions for children, youth, and juvenile offenders.

INTRODUCTION

YOUTH CRIME IS OFTEN CONTROVERSIAL AND RAISES A NUMBER OF QUESTIONS FOR THE criminal justice system and the larger community. You may assume that "anyone" who commits an act that is found in the Canadian *Criminal Code* will be charged and prosecuted. This is not the case, however. Children under the age of 12 are not charged, even when they commit violent acts such as murder. Professionals such as social workers, psychologists, and even police officers may intervene but the goal is to provide appropriate intervention or treatment so that these acts do not continue. In order to be processed through Canada's criminal justice system, an offender must be a minimum of 12. Prior to this age, children's behaviour is governed by the *Child and Family Services Act*. Box 5.1 describes a Canadian case involving a seven-year-old, his younger brother, and a death over a toy.

Once a child is 12, they are assumed to be in sufficient control of their behaviour such that acts committed against the Canadian *Criminal Code* will be pursued by the justice system. However, Canada does recognize that youth between the ages of 12 and 18 are developmentally different than adults (over 18) and outlines provisions for younger aged "offenders" in the *Youth Criminal Justice Act*, which provides direction on how youth committing *Criminal Code* offences should be "processed." This chapter will examine the history of juvenile justice in Canada; the development of juvenile offending; and prevention, intervention, and treatment strategies for juvenile offenders.

Box 5.1

When Siblings Fight

Many siblings disagree, argue, and fight. The interaction typically ends with one sibling crying and another pleased to have gotten their way. Unfortunately, the following case ended in death. During the holiday season in a quiet Edmonton neighbourhood, two young brothers, ages seven and five, fought over a toy. The five-year-old allegedly stabbed his older brother, who died shortly thereafter. Edmonton police declared the stabbing a "non-culpable homicide" with the child deemed too young to be responsible for his actions. The five-year-old will not be processed in the criminal justice system given that he does not meet the minimum age requirement to be held criminally responsible for one's actions in Canada. Instead, the Victims' Services Unit (part of the police department) and Child and Family Services will work with the family to provide counselling and other services as deemed necessary to ensure adequate parenting, supervision, and support for the child and family.

Source: Canwest News Service (2008)

THE HISTORY OF JUVENILE JUSTICE IN CANADA

PRIOR TO THE NINETEENTH CENTURY IN CANADA, CHILDREN AND YOUTH WHO committed criminal acts were treated similarly to adult offenders. No provisions or accommodations for age or developmental stage were made when it came to charging, sentencing, or incarceration. Youth were not even exempted from the death penalty.

In 1908, Canada enacted the *Juvenile Delinquents Act* (JDA) to recognize the special circumstances inherent with juvenile offenders. This legislation applied to individuals between the ages of 7 and 16 (although in some jurisdictions the upper limit was 18). These juveniles were termed "delinquents" rather than offenders and were seen to commit acts of delinquency (e.g., truancy) rather than criminal offences. A separate court was designed for delinquents, with parents encouraged to take part in the proceedings, which were more informal than was customary in adult court. Sanctions included adjournment without penalty, fines, probation, mandatory attendance in an industrial school to learn a skill or trade, and foster care. Delinquents who committed serious and violent acts could be transferred to adult court. Although the enactment of the JDA was a positive first step in juvenile justice, criticisms included the informality of youth court denying youth their rights, such as the right to legal representation and the right to appeal; that judges could impose open-ended sentences; and the broad definition of delinquency that included acts that were *not* illegal for adults.

In 1984, the *Young Offenders Act* (YOA) replaced the JDA. Juvenile offenders were recognized as cognitively different than adults and consequently their level of accountability and the sanctions for their behaviour should be more commensurate with their developmental stage. There was also a recognition that the community had a right to be protected from juvenile offenders while granting these juveniles their rights as stated in the *Canadian Charter of Rights and Freedoms* (R.S.C. 1985: c. Y-1, s. 3).

With the YOA came an increase in the minimum age at which an individual could be charged with a criminal offence, from 7 years old to 12 (and up to 18). Child and Family Services would intervene with anyone under 12 who engaged in behaviour that violated the Canadian *Criminal Code*. Youth court judgments, with the possibility of a transfer to adult court, continued. However, in order to be transferred, a youth had to be at least 14 (R.S.C 1985: c. Y-1, s. 16).

The YOA also allowed youth cases to be diverted. **Diversion** is a decision not to prosecute a young offender but rather have them undergo an educational or community service program. A young offender would have to plead guilty for diversion to be possible (R.S.C 1985: c. Y-1, s. 4). Other dispositions available for young offenders included absolute discharge (i.e., the young offender received no sentence other than a guilty verdict), a fine, compensation for loss or damaged property, restitution to the victim, a prohibition order (i.e., no weapons), community service, probation, and custody. Custody could be open (placing the youth in a community residential facility, group home, or childcare facility) or secure (incarceration in a prison facility) (R.S.C 1985: c. Y-1, s. 20).

The YOA was amended a number of times. In 1986, Bill C-106 section 16 was introduced to combat the problem of juveniles pleading guilty to avoid transfer to adult court. Youth court would be required to consider whether the Crown or defence would like to make an application to transfer. In 1995, Bill C-37 changed section 16 once again. Charged with murder, manslaughter, or aggravated sexual assault, 16- and 17-year-olds would automatically be tried in adult court. However, on application, these cases could stay in youth court if the youth court felt the objectives of rehabilitation and public protection could be reconciled. Also under Bill C-37, youth sentencing changed: for first-degree murder, a ten-year maximum with a six-year maximum to be served incarcerated was available. For second-degree murder, a seven-year maximum with a four-year maximum to be served incarcerated was available.

As can be seen by the number of amendments regarding transfers to adult court, the perception was that juvenile offenders received relatively short or light sentences even if committing seriously violent crimes. Moreover, the way the YOA was written allowed for discrepancies in the factors leading to transfer to adult court and how cases were handled. There was also issue with the overuse of incarceration. Canada has the highest incarceration rate for youth in the Western world, including the United States.

On April 1, 2003, the *Youth Criminal Justice Act* (YCJA) replaced the YOA. Part of the intent of the YCJA is to keep juvenile offenders out of court and out of custody. The three main objectives of the YCJA are

1. To prevent youth crime
2. To provide meaningful consequences and encourage responsibility of behaviour
3. To improve rehabilitation and reintegration of youth into the community

As a first step when coming into contact with antisocial youth, police are to consider community options and less serious alternatives before bringing juveniles to the attention of youth court (*Youth Criminal Justice Act* 2002: s. 7). These alternatives are called **extrajudicial measures** and include giving a warning or making a referral for treatment (with the consent of the juvenile) (*Youth Criminal Justice Act* 2002: s. 10). Once a juvenile is charged, however, they can no longer be transferred to adult court under the YCJA. Rather, if a juvenile defendant is found guilty the judge can impose an adult sentence as long as the defendant is at least 14 years old (may be set at 15 or 16 depending on jurisdiction). An adult sentence cannot be applied unless the Crown notifies the youth court that it will be seeking an adult sentence (*Youth Criminal Justice Act* 2002: s. 61). A key issue in determining sentencing is that the sentence must be proportionate to the seriousness of the offence (*Youth Criminal Justice Act* 2002: s. 38(2)(c)).

Expanded sentencing options are also provided for under the YCJA. Judges can give a reprimand (i.e., lecture or warning to the juvenile), an intensive support and supervision order, an attendance order (i.e., juvenile must attend a specific program), a deferred custody

Table 5.1 Overview of Key Changes to Canada's Juvenile Offending Legislation

Prior to JDA	JDA	YOA	YCJA
No legislation for youth	Minimum age set to seven years	Minimum age set to 12 years	Less serious and less violent crime kept out of court
Youth treated as adults	Separate court for children/youth	Youth not as accountable as adults	Increased extrajudicial measures
Adult sentences imposed	Parents encouraged to participate	Young offenders have rights	Greater focus on prevention and reintegration into the community
Sentences served with adults	Increased sanctions	Public has the right to be protected	No transfers to adult court
	Judicial discretion		Judge can impose adult sentences
			Victims are recognized

and supervision order (i.e., juvenile can serve sentence in community as long as imposed conditions are met), and an intensive rehabilitative custody and supervision order (i.e., juvenile in custody receive intensive services and supervision) (*Youth Criminal Justice Act* 2002: s. 42).

The YCJA also considers the victims of juvenile offenders. Victims are to be informed of court proceedings and given an opportunity to participate. They also have the right to access youth court records and participate in community-based dispositions (*Youth Criminal Justice Act* 2002: s. 3). Table 5.1 provides an overview of the historical changes in juvenile justice in Canada.

Youth Crime Rates

Canadian police services reported an approximate 3 percent increase in the overall crime rate for juveniles from 2005 to 2006. Table 5.2 presents the total cases heard in youth court by offence category and year. From 2006 to 2007, Canadian youth courts processed 56 463 cases involving 179 873 charges—a 26 percent decrease from 2002–2003, the year prior to the introduction of the YCJA. Note that legislation may not decrease the number of actual crimes committed by youth but rather may affect the reporting/recording of crimes. Figure 5.1 presents youth crime rates before and after the introduction of the YCJA. Following its implementation, there was a decrease in property crime, though violent crime remained fairly stable.

Table 5.2 Cases Heard in Youth Courts in Canada, 2002–2003 to 2006–2007

Offence Category	2002–03	2003–04	2004–05	2005–06	2006–07
Total cases	76 153	64 002	57 588	56 271	56 463
Crimes against person	18 446	16 716	15 127	15 166	15 126
Crimes against property	31 359	25 532	22 722	21 522	21 279
Administration of justice	5924	5186	4904	4793	4945
Other criminal code offences	4686	4457	4200	4348	4471
Traffic	1329	1216	1136	1049	1086
Other federal offences	14 409	10 895	9499	9393	9556

Source: Statistics Canada (2008)

Youth Sentences

As noted previously, the YCJA seeks to keep juvenile offenders out of the court system and out of custody. Following the YCJA, in 2006 to 2007, about 17 percent (5640) of guilty offenders received custodial sentences. In contrast, in 2002 to 2003, 27 percent

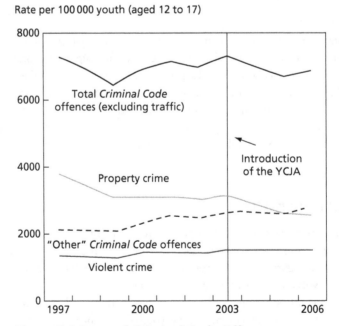

Rate per 100 000 youth (aged 12 to 17)

Figure 5.1 Rates of *Criminal Code* Offences Committed by Juveniles

Source: Statistics Canada (2008)

(13 246) of cases received custodial sentences. Custodial sentences are typically reserved for serious violent crimes against a person. For example, in 2006 to 2007, 15 of the 21 guilty murder cases and 5 of the 6 attempted murder cases resulted in custodial sentences. The most common sentence for juveniles was probation, awarded to 59 percent of guilty juveniles. Of the new sentences available under the YCJA, deferred custody and supervision orders were used in 3 percent of cases in 2006 to 2007. Also in that period, 2 percent of guilty juveniles were given reprimands, 1 percent were ordered into intensive support and supervision programs, and less than 1 percent were ordered to attend a non-residential program. In total, in about 7 percent of guilty cases the new sentencing options found under the YCJA were imposed (The Juristat 2006: 85-002-XIE). Box 5.2 presents a case involving a 12-year-old girl receiving a custodial sentence and the sentence of her adult boyfriend.

Box 5.2

Youth Is No Excuse for Murder

She was a 12-year-old girl dating a 23-year-old man named Jeremy Allan Steinke. Even more striking than the age difference, the couple was found guilty of murdering her parents and eight-year-old brother. Police found the bodies at the family's home in Medicine Hat, Alberta, on April 23, 2006. Under the YCJA, the girl's name cannot be released.

Jurors and community members were shocked and confused. Why would a child kill her own parents? Courtroom testimony revealed that the girl's parents did not approve of their daughter's relationship. At her trial, the girl testified that she was angry with them. She had talked about killing them and wanting them dead but said she never meant any of it. According to the girl, she was "just saying it." The defence argued that the girl's boyfriend took matters into his own hands and ultimately killed the family. Following deliberation, the jury sided with the Crown and found the girl guilty of first-degree murder on three counts. As a juvenile, the girl received the maximum sentence for her crime—a 10-year maximum sentence with no more than six years spent in custody in an Edmonton psychiatric hospital. She is the youngest person in Canada to have been convicted of multiple homicide.

During Steinke's trial, the Crown described him as an unemployed high-school dropout who planned to marry his young girlfriend in a Gothic wedding and move to Germany. The defence painted a different picture, arguing that he had been abused as a child by his alcoholic mother's ex-partners and bullied by classmates. At 13, it was claimed that Steinke was diagnosed with depression and hyperactivity and later attempted suicide. However, the jury sided with the Crown and found Steinke guilty of three counts of first-degree murder. For an adult offender, first-degree murder receives an automatic life sentence with no eligibility for parole for 25 years, a sentence Steinke received in December 2008.

Source: CBC News (2008); Zickefoose (2008); Stevenson (2007)

Trajectories of Juvenile Offenders

There are two types of juvenile offenders: child-onset, life-course persistent and adolescent-onset, adolescent limited (Moffitt 1993). The histories of these types differ. For **child-onset juvenile offenders,** behavioural problems start very early in childhood. These juveniles often have histories that include behavioural problems dating back to daycare and preschool. As babies, they were difficult to soothe with problematic temperaments and were aggressive with other children, physically hitting and throwing temper tantrums. In contrast, **adolescent-onset juvenile offenders** begin to show behavioural problems in their teen years. These youth may engage in antisocial acts such as truancy, theft, and vandalism. Often the adage of "boys will be boys" is used to describe this group.

When examining the trajectory to adult offending, age of onset is a critical factor. A clear pattern has been found linking early onset of antisocial behaviour to more serious and persistent antisocial behaviour later in life (e.g., Fergusson and Woodward 2000; Loeber and Farrington 2000). In addition, those with a childhood onset also may have a number of other challenges, including attention-deficit hyperactivity disorder, learning disabilities, and academic difficulties (Hinshaw, Lahey, and Hart 1993). The childhood-onset trajectory is a less frequent occurrence, affecting about 3 to 5 percent of the general population (Moffitt 1993). It is important to remember that most young children with behavioural difficulties do not go on to become adult offenders.

The adolescent-onset pattern occurs in about 70 percent of the general population (Moffitt 1993). Many youth rebel against authority and engage in antisocial acts during adolescence, but these behaviours are few and limited. Although it is more common for adolescent-onset youth to desist antisocial behaviour in early adulthood than for those with a childhood onset, some continue to engage in antisocial acts in adulthood (Moffitt, Caspi, Harrington, and Milne 2002).

Brame, Nagin, and Tremblay (2001) followed a group of boys with high levels of aggression in Montreal from the time they entered kindergarten through to their late teens. The researchers found that the overall level of aggression decreased as the boys got older, regardless of how high it was when the participants were youngsters. For a small proportion of the boys, their levels of aggression continued into the teens. However, for a much larger proportion, little or no aggression was reported in the teens. Thus, for a small group of youngsters with high levels of aggression, these levels will continue into later years.

THEORIES TO EXPLAIN JUVENILE OFFENDING

A NUMBER OF THEORIES HAVE BEEN PROPOSED TO EXPLAIN WHY SOME JUVENILES OFFEND. BELOW are descriptions of some common theories in the current literature on juvenile offending.

Biological Theories A number of genetic and physiological differences exist between youth who engage in antisocial behaviour and those who do not. Genetic studies have found that fathers who engage in antisocial behaviour are more likely to have children (a stronger link for sons than daughters) who also engage in antisocial behaviour (Frick et al. 1992). Twin and adoption studies further support this conclusion. Specifically, children who have an antisocial biological father are more likely to engage in antisocial behaviour, even when raised apart from the father, suggesting that environment is not the only influence (Cadoret and Cain 1980; Jarey and Stewart 1985). Wadsworth (1976) found that antisocial youth have slower heart rates than non-antisocial youth, suggesting a higher threshold for excitability and emotionality.

Along this line, researchers have investigated the brain region responsible for planning and inhibiting behaviour—the frontal lobe—to explain why some youth engage in antisocial acts. Moffitt and Henry (1989) found that antisocial youth have less frontal lobe inhibition than youth who do not engage in antisocial behaviour. Thus the likelihood that these youth will act impulsively is increased, making it more likely that they will make poor behavioural choices.

Cognitive Theories Kenneth Dodge and his colleagues proposed a model of conduct-disordered behaviour that focuses on the thought processes that occur in social interactions (Crick and Dodge 1994; Dodge 2000). The model begins with thought processes, which start when individuals pay attention to and interpret social and emotional cues in their environment. The next step is to consider alternate responses to the cues. Finally, a response is chosen and performed. Conduct-disordered youth demonstrate cognitive deficits and distortions (Fontaine, Burks, and Dodge 2002), often attending to fewer cues and mis-attributing hostile intent to ambiguous situations. Moreover, conduct-disordered youth demonstrate limited problem-solving skills, producing few solutions to problems, often solutions that are usually aggressive in nature. Cognitive deficits are likely to be present in early childhood and may contribute to child-onset conduct disorder (Coy et al. 2001).

Dodge and his colleagues also distinguished between two types of aggressive behaviour—reactive aggression and proactive aggression (Dodge 1991; Schwartz et al 1998). **Reactive aggression** is described as an emotionally aggressive response to a perceived threat or frustration. In contrast, **proactive aggression** is aggression directed at achieving a goal or receiving positive reinforcers (e.g., money, goods). Referring to Dodge's model, deficiencies in the process occur at different points for reactive and proactive aggression. Reactively aggressive youth are likely to demonstrate deficiencies early in the cognitive process, such as focusing on only a few social cues and misattributing hostile intent to ambiguous situations. Proactive aggressive youth are likely to have deficiencies in generating alternate responses and often choose an aggressive response. Furthermore, reactive and proactive aggressors tend to have different trajectories: reactive aggressors tend to have an earlier onset of problems (Dodge et al. 1997).

Social Theories Bandura's (1965) social learning theory suggests that children learn their behaviour from observing others. Children are more likely to imitate behaviour that receives positive reinforcement than behaviour that receives negative reinforcement or punishment. As children develop, numerous models are available to imitate, including parents, siblings, peers, and media personalities. Studies have found that children who are highly aggressive and engage in antisocial behaviour have often witnessed parents, siblings, or grandparents engage in similar behaviour (Farrington 1995; Waschbusch 2002). This is a pattern of intergenerational aggression, in which one aggressive generation produces the next (Glueck and Glueck 1968; Huesmann et al. 1984).

Consistent with this view is Patterson's (1982) coercive family process model, where aggressive behaviour among youth develops from imitation of parents and reinforcement. Other aspects of Patterson's model include the role of inadequate parental supervision and inconsistent disciplining of children. The combination of these factors increases the likelihood of youth behaving in antisocial ways (also Huizinga, Esbensen, and Weiher 1991). Dr. Marlene Moretti, a researcher at Simon Fraser University, and colleagues found that adolescents who witness interparental violence are at risk for aggression (Moretti, Obsuth, Odgers, and Reebye 2006). Their study assessed males and females between the ages of 13 and 18. Females who had witnessed their mothers' aggressive behaviour toward partners were significantly more aggressive toward friends. This pattern was also found for males who had witnessed their fathers being aggressive toward their partners: they were more likely to be aggressive toward friends. Both females and males who had witnessed parental violence were more likely to be aggressive with their romantic partners. See Box 5.3 for more about Dr. Moretti's research.

Box 5.3

Canadian Researcher Profile: Dr. Marlene Moretti

While a graduate student at Simon Fraser University, Dr. Marlene Moretti developed an interest in self-development, self-regulation, and interpersonal relationships. She has continued to pursue this theme through the lens of developmental psychopathology, cutting across various mental health problems such as depression, aggression, and antisocial behaviour. Dr. Moretti completed her undergraduate degree at Brock University and went on to complete graduate degrees at Simon Fraser University. She is now a professor there and holds a Canadian Institutes of Research senior research chair. When talking about her research, Dr. Moretti states that "even though the 'self' has been a long-standing interest in psychology and philosophy, we are only beginning to understand the complex relationships between social contexts, interpersonal relationships, and development. It is clear that these factors have impacts at the cognitive, affective,

Box 5.3   Continued

behavioural, and biological level—how systems unfold over time is largely unknown. We also have a limited understanding of how some individuals are able to turn adversity into opportunity, or at the very least, minimize the impact of risk exposure" (quote from personal correspondence with the author).

Dr. Moretti uses a number of methodologies for her research, relying on both quantitative and qualitative methods. She takes a strong developmental perspective on criminal behaviour. Within this developmental framework, she is interested in how relationships and attachment shape the emergence of self-regulation, which in turn is related to risk for aggression and antisocial behaviour.

From an applied perspective, Dr. Moretti is interested in promoting prevention and risk reduction to prevent youth from reaching or sinking deeper into the criminal justice system. As a teacher and student supervisor, she is committed to the training of future researchers and believes it is critical that students be exposed to working in multidisciplinary teams and learn how to navigate complex networks. She feels that students need to acquire skills in how to build partnerships with community agencies and learn how to facilitate the transfer of knowledge from the lab to the real world. Dr. Moretti enjoys teaching courses on ethics and professional practice and developmental psychopathology.

Watching extremely violent television and movies in which actors are rewarded for aggression also increases children's likelihood of acting aggressively (Bushman and Anderson 2001). Aggressive videogames present a forum for youth to be reinforced for their aggression, which may increase their likelihood of acting aggressively in real life (Anderson and Dill 2000). Moreover, some data indicate a link between violent video exposure and aggressive behaviour to brain processes believed to be associated with desensitization to real-world violence (Bartholow, Bushman, and Sestir 2006).

RISK FACTORS FOR JUVENILE OFFENDING

THE TERM **risk factor** REFERS TO A VARIABLE THAT, IF PRESENT, POSES AN INCREASED likelihood of an undesirable outcome such as delinquency or antisocial behaviour (Kazdin, Kraemer, Kessler, Kupfer, and Offord 1997). The presence of several criminological risk factors increases a youth's likelihood of offending (Hawkins et al. 1998). Rarely will one risk factor be sufficient to lead to offending, nor does the presence of numerous risk factors guarantee a youth will become a juvenile offender. When several risk factors are present, however, they may interact and have a multiplicative influence, thereby compounding the likelihood of offending. For example, Herrenkohl et al. (2000) found that a 10-year-old who is exposed to six or more risk factors is 10 times more likely to commit a violent act by age 18 as a 10-year-old exposed to only one risk factor. Risk factors occur across various domains: individual, familial, school, peer, and community, described in more detail below.

Individual A number of prenatal complications can predispose a fetus to behavioural problems in childhood and potential juvenile offending. Mednick and Kandel (1988) suggest that offenders are more likely to have had delivery/birth complications compared to non-offenders. However, even before delivery, a mother's use of drugs, alcohol, and cigarette smoking during pregnancy increases the fetus's risk for later behavioural difficulties (Cohen et al. 2002).

Once a child is born, their own temperament can present a risk factor for later delinquency. For example, Farrington (1995) found that children who are difficult to soothe can be at risk for later behavioural difficulties. Hyperactivity, attention problems, impulsivity, and risk-taking have been associated with later juvenile offending (Hawkins et al. 1998). Substance abuse, especially starting at a young age (before the teen years), has received substantial support as a risk factor for juvenile offending (Elliott, Huizinga, and Ageton 1985). Low verbal intelligence and delayed language development also have been associated with behavioural problems (Seguin, Pihl, Harden, Tremblay, and Boulrice 1995). Perhaps the strongest predictor of juvenile offending is the presence of aggressive behaviour before the age of 13.

Familial A number of parental factors are risk factors for later antisocial behaviour. Researchers have found that poor parental supervision, low parental involvement, parental conflict, and parental aggression are related to later antisocial behaviour (Dekovic 1999; Carson and Butcher 1992; Farrington 1995; Hoge, Andrews, and Leschied 1996; Kumpfer and Alvarado 2003; Monahan et al. 2001; Melton et al. 1997; National Crime Prevention Council 1995; 1997; Patterson, Reid, and Dishion 1998; Rutter 1990). Child abuse, neglect, and maltreatment are also risk factors for behavioural difficulties. Abuse factors may pose a greater risk to boys, who may respond by acting aggressively and later engaging in spousal abuse (Fergusson and Lynskey 1997; Health Canada 2003; Loos and Alexander 1997). (See Chapter 11 for more on gender differences.) Widom (1989) found that abused or neglected children were 38 percent more likely to be arrested for a violent offence than children who had not been abused or neglected.

Children who do not attach securely to their parents, parental loss, and divorce are risk factors for later behavioural problems (Amato and Keith 1991; Cummings, Davies, and Campbell 2000; Fagot and Kavanagh 1990). Other risk factors for delinquency include low socioeconomic status, large family size, and parental mental health problems (Frick 1994; Patterson, Reid, and Dishion 1998; Waschbusch 2002). Parents who are heavy drinkers increase the likelihood that their children will act in antisocial ways, possibly because when parents drink, they are unable to provide adequate parenting and supervision (Lahey, Waldman, and McBurnett 1989).

School A number of school-related risk factors, such as poor academic performance, particularly in elementary school; low commitment to school; and low educational aspirations have been found to be associated with delinquent behaviour (Blum, Ireland, and Blum 2003; Hinshaw 1992). Truancy or not attending school is also a risk factor. For example, Farrington (1989) found that high truancy rates between the ages of 12 and 14 are related to juvenile offending that extends into adulthood. How academic difficulties are handled can be a risk factor as well. For example, suspension and expulsion may not reduce delinquent behaviour.

Peer Risk factors related to peers are perhaps the most important during adolescence, when the peer group reigns paramount over family influences. A consistent relationship exists between associating with delinquent peers and engaging in delinquent behaviour. This association is true even at a very young age. Young children who play with aggressive peers at an early age are at risk for behavioural problems (Fergusson and Horwood 1998; Laird et al. 2001). Lipsey and Derzon (1998) found that 12- to 14-year-olds who associate with delinquent peers are more likely to engage in delinquency. McCord et al. (2001) found that peer approval of delinquent behaviour, allegiance to delinquent peers, time spent with delinquent peers, and peer pressure for delinquency are also associated with juvenile antisocial behaviour (also Moffitt 1993). Taking this risk factor one step further, gang membership is more predictive of antisocial behaviour than associating with delinquent peers (Hill, Howell, Hawkins, and Battin-Pearson 1999) (see Box 5.4). Peer influence may compound when parents are uninvolved with their children. Farrington (1989) found that the presence of delinquent siblings acts much like the presence of delinquent peers in that it is predictive of violent juvenile offending.

Social disapproval and being rejected are likely to occur with aggressive children and adolescents (Coie, Belding, and Underwood 1988; Ebata et al. 1990; Rutter 1990), and rejected, aggressive children are at risk for behavioural problems (Parker and Asher 1987; Rudolph and Asher 2000). Juveniles who are socially isolated or withdrawn (e.g., low involvement in traditional, structured social activities) are at an increased risk for engaging in antisocial behaviour.

Community Where one is raised can be a risk factor for juvenile offending. Just as parental income (i.e., lower socio-economic status) is a familial risk factor, so is living in a low-income neighbourhood (e.g., Farrington 1989; Henry, Avshalom, Moffitt, and Silva 1996). Assault when committing a felony or robbery are twice as common among juveniles raised in low-income/subsidized neighbourhoods than juveniles raised in middle-class areas (Hawkins et al. 2000).

Lower-income neighbourhoods also give rise to the opportunity to witness violence. Farrell and Bruce (1997) found that exposure to community violence is related to juvenile offending. Thus disadvantaged neighbourhoods provide an opportunity to learn delinquent behaviour, associate with delinquent peers, and possibly have delinquent behaviour reinforced. Brewer et al. (1995) found that having access to weapons also increases the risk for violence.

Running Around with the Wrong Crowd: A Look at Gangs

The National Crime Prevention Centre (NCPC) of Public Safety Canada is the federal organization responsible for providing direction on how to deal with the problem of youth gangs in Canada. There are three key elements to a youth gang:

1. The individuals involved must identify themselves as a group (they may have a group name, group colours, etc.).
2. Other people see the members as a distinct group.

3. Group members commit "delinquent" acts, often imposing on the rights of others in the community.

Although anyone can be a gang member, gangs are often comprised of individuals from lower socioeconomic backgrounds who belong to a minority ethnic group. In Canada, the largest proportion of youth gang members are African-Canadian, at 25 percent, then First Nations at 21 percent, and Caucasian at 18 percent. An overwhelming proportion of gang members are male (approximately

Table 5.3 Youth Gang Numbers in Canada

Province	No. of Youth Gangs	No. of Gang Members	Youth Gang Members Per 1000
British Columbia	102	1027	.26
Alberta	42	668	.22
Saskatchewan	28	1315	1.34
Manitoba	15	171	.15
Ontario	216	3320	.29
Quebec*	25	533	.07
Nova Scotia	6	37	.04
Prince Edward Island	0	0	0
Newfoundland and Labrador	0	0	0
Yukon	0	0	0
Northwest Territories	0	0	0
Nunavut	0	0	0

Note: *Data were obtained from only four police agencies and should be interpreted cautiously; may not be representative of the province.

Source: Astwood (2002)

Box 5.4   Continued

94 percent). However, there is an increasing trend for female Aboriginal gang membership in Western Canada. In addition, it is not uncommon for gang members to have a pre-existing substance abuse problem and to have engaged in violent juvenile offending prior to joining. Often the motivation to join a gang involves a desire to gain prestige, status, protection, and an opportunity to make money.

A Canadian police survey conducted in 2002 estimated that there are approximately 434 youth gangs in Canada with a total membership slightly over 7000. The top three provinces with absolute number of gangs and gang membership (not taking population into account) are Ontario, Saskatchewan, and British Columbia. Table 5.3 illustrates youth gang numbers and membership as a function of province/territory.

Erickson and Butters (2006) examined the relationship between gangs, guns, and drugs in Toronto and Montreal. A total of 904 male high school students, school dropouts, and young offenders were interviewed. The researchers found that as gang presence in schools increased, so did the number of guns and amount of drugs. Almost 19 percent of boys aged 14 to 17 in Toronto and 15 percent in Montreal brought a gun to school. Dropouts who sell drugs are more likely to be engaged in gun violence than dropouts who do not sell drugs.

What Do Canadian Youth Report?

The Department of Justice Canada conducted a study to examine the factors related to self-reported delinquency between the ages of 12 and 15 using data from the National Longitudinal Survey of Children and Youth (Latimer, Kleinknecht, Hung, and Gabor 2003). Slightly less than 40 percent of youth reported engaging in at least one antisocial act in the 12-month period prior to the survey. This percentage translated into more than 540 000 youth across Canada reporting having committed at least one delinquent act in the previous year. It is important to note that the majority of these acts would be considered minor offences. The five main correlates of delinquency for male and female youth were: 1) inconsistent and inadequate parenting; 2) history of victimization; 3) antisocial peer involvement; 4) negative school attachment; and 5) aggression. These correlates are consistent with the risk factors described above.

PROTECTIVE FACTORS

ALTHOUGH CHILDREN MAY EXPERIENCE SIMILAR ENVIRONMENTS AND SETS OF RISK factors, their responses and outcomes vary, with some children prevailing and prospering and others encountering a number of difficulties and negative outcomes. The child who has multiple risk factors but who can overcome them and prevail has been termed **resilient.** Resilience is described as the ability to overcome stress and adversity (Winfield 1994).

It has been suggested that resilient children may have "protective" factors that allow them to persevere in the face of adversity. The notion of protective factors was introduced in the early 1980s (Garmezy 1985). Garmezy (1991) identified a number of areas where protectiveness can be present: genetic variables, personality dispositions, supportive family environments, and community supports. There is some debate over the definition of protective factors and how they work. Many agree, however, that they help improve or sustain some part of an individual's life (Leadbeater et al. 1999). We define **protective factors** as variables or factors that, if present, decrease the likelihood of a negative outcome such as antisocial behaviour and juvenile offending or increase the likelihood of a positive outcome (DeMatteo and Marczyk 2005). Rutter (1990) identifies four ways that protective factors are effective:

1. They reduce negative outcomes by changing the level of the child's exposure to a risk factor.

2. They change the negative chain reaction following exposure to risk.

3. They help develop and maintain self-esteem and self-efficacy.

4. They avail opportunities to children they would not otherwise have.

As with risk factors, protective factors occur across various domains: individual, familial, school, peer, and community, described in more detail below.

Individual Factors that reside within an individual can serve to protect against acting in antisocial ways. For example, Carson and Butcher (1992) found that intelligence and a commitment to education serve as protective factors for juveniles at risk for antisocial behaviour (also, Hoge and Andrews 1996; Kandel et al. 1988). By focusing on schoolwork, there is less time available to engage in antisocial behaviour.

Vance (2001) found that exceptional social skills, child competencies, confident perceptions, values, attitudes, and beliefs can serve to protect a child from engaging in juvenile offending. Research from twin studies suggests that social support may have a heritable component that is influenced by personality. For example, likeable children may respond to good role models in a positive manner, thus promoting a positive and continuing relationship.

Perhaps one of the strongest protective individual factors is having an intolerant attitude toward antisocial behaviour (Department of Health and Human Services 2001). This may also reflect a commitment to social norms and a rejection of antisocial behaviour. An intolerant attitude may decrease the likelihood that a youth would associate with antisocial peers, hence further reducing the likelihood of antisocial behaviour.

Being female and a perception that peers disapprove of antisocial behaviour have also been identified as protective factors by the U.S. Department of Health and Human Services (2001).

Other protective factors include sociability, positive temperament, the ability to seek social support, and acting in a reflective (not impulsive) manner. Resilient adolescents typically utilize flexible coping strategies. Having a sense of control over one's environment may be associated with a decreased risk for antisocial behaviour. The acquisition of various skill sets such as problem solving, conflict resolution, anger management, and critical thinking also are seen as protective factors. The presence of certain internalizing disorders, such as nervousness and anxiety, may have a modest negative correlation with juvenile offending (Hawkins et al. 2000; Mitchell and Rosa 1979).

Familial Factors Protective familial factors are the positive qualities of parents and home environment (Carson and Butcher 1992; Kumpfer and Alvarado 2003; Melton et al. 1997; Thornberry et al. 1995). For example, a child having a supportive relationship with an adult protects against the child engaging in antisocial behaviour (Werner 2000). This protective factor is generally effective regardless of whether the adult caregiver is a parent, teacher, or volunteer in a mentoring program such as Big Brothers Big Sisters (see Box 5.5). High levels of parental supervision and secure parent–child attachment are also protective factors. Providing clear and consistent norms for behaviour can reduce the likelihood that youth will engage in antisocial behaviour.

School Commitment to school and achieving academically is a protective factor for children at risk for juvenile offending (e.g., Carson and Butcher 1992; Department of Health and Human Services 2001; Hoge and Andrews 1996; Kandel et al. 1988). Children who are committed to school may be less likely to commit antisocial acts for fear of reducing their academic potential (Jessor, Van Den Bos, Vanderryn,

Box 5.5

Turning to Big Brothers and Big Sisters for a Little Help

Over the years, many have argued that providing at-risk youth with adult mentoring reduces the likelihood that they will engage in antisocial behaviour. Perhaps one of the oldest and most far-reaching programs in many countries is the Big Brothers Big Sisters (BBBS) program.

In general, most BBBS programs follow the same protocol. Adult volunteers are screened to be paired with a child/youth.

Adults are matched based on background, preferences of the youth, preferences of the adult volunteers, and geographic proximity. The adult and child/youth will meet three to four hours about three times a month for at least a year.

An impact study of BBBS branches in 11 cities across the United States was conducted in 1995 by Tierney, Grossman, and Resch. Youth sampled were between 10 and 16 years old.

Continued >

Almost all were living in single-parent, low-income homes with prior histories of either family violence or substance abuse. Participants were randomly assigned to participate in BBBS or put on an 18-month waitlist for the program.

In total, 959 youth remained in contact to participate in the follow-up interview that took place 18 months from the time of placement or being put on the waitlist. The results indicated that youth paired with a Big Brother or Big Sister were less likely to use drugs or alcohol than youth on the waitlist. This effect was even larger for minority youth. Youth with a Big Brother or Big Sister were less likely to be physically aggressive and had better relationships with family and peers. Overall, BBBS can have a positive influence on youth at least in the short term. Approximately 50 percent of the matches do not continue to form ongoing relationships. It is estimated that the cost per match is approximately $1000 (for screenings, supervision, activities, etc.).

Source: Tierney, Grossman, and Resch (1995)

Costa, and Turbin 1995). Participating in structured extracurricular activities, such as team sports and academic clubs, protects against juvenile offending (Jessor et al. 1995). Extracurricular activities allow less time for antisocial acts and may instil a sense of achievement for children.

Peer Vance (2001) reported that peer groups can have a strong effect on child outcomes. Associating with deviant peers is a risk factor for antisocial behaviour. The converse is a protective factor; that is, associating with prosocial children protects against antisocial behaviour (Fergusson and Horwood 1996). Some researchers have found that associating with peers who disapprove of antisocial behaviour is protective against performing antisocial acts (Hawkins et al. 2000).

Community There is little research in the area of "community" protective factors. A strong community infrastructure that may provide opportunities for adolescents to engage in organized activities helps to reduce the likelihood that children will engage in antisocial behaviour. Social cohesion is associated with lower levels of violence among juveniles (Sampson, Raudenbush, and Earls 1997).

GENDER SIMILARITIES AND DIFFERENCES IN RISK AND PROTECTION

A RECENT STUDY BY FAGAN, LEE VAN HORN, HAWKINS, AND ARTHUR (2007) examined gender similarities and differences for risk and protective factors. Twenty-two risk and protective factors were assessed using self-report information from 7829 Grade 10 students. Overall, the risk factors examined were linked to increased involvement in serious offending, while the protective factors were linked to decreased involvement. There was a stronger association to serious offending for males than females across 12 of the factors. More specifically, of those 12 factors, the risk factors had a stronger positive association for males than females for serious offending, while the protective factors had a stronger negative association for males than females. For the 10 remaining factors, there were no significant gender differences between the factors and serious offending. Overall, these data suggest that males may be involved in more serious juvenile offending than females because of greater exposure to risk factors and lower exposure to protective factors. Table 5.4 presents a list of the risk factors and protective factors examined across gender. Dr. Moretti and colleagues (2005) note that there may be differences in the risk and protective factors between boys and girls; however, the work on female risk and

Table 5.4 Sex Differences for Risk and Protective Factors

Risk (R) and Protective (P) Factors	Sex Difference
Family	
Prosocial opportunities (P)	No
Attachment to mother (P)	No
Attachment to father (P)	Yes
Rewards for behaviour (P)	No
Family conflict (R)	No
Pro-delinquency (R)	Yes
Pro-substance use (R)	Yes
Poor family management (R)	No
School	
Prosocial opportunities (P)	Yes
Rewards for behaviour (P)	No
Academic failure (R)	No
Low commitment (R)	No
Individual/Peer	
Moral beliefs (P)	Yes
Social skills (P)	Yes
Pro-delinquency (R)	Yes
Pro-substance use (R)	Yes
Drug use not risky (R)	No
Rebelliousness (R)	Yes
Sensation seeking (R)	No
Peer drug use (R)	Yes
Peer delinquency (R)	Yes
Rewards for delinquency (R)	Yes

Source: Fagan et al. (2007)

protection is still in its infancy. (See Chapter 11 for a further discussion of gender differences in theory, crime trends, etc.)

When developing prevention, intervention, and treatment programs, it may be important to consider both risk and protective factors across stages of development and gender such that targeted programs may be more efficient and cost-effective. An assessment is often the start of identifying the needs and appropriate programs for children and adolescents.

ASSESSMENT

Assessing the Under-12-Year-Old For children under 12, behavioural problems are usually first identified at school, where the child's disruptive behaviour is a challenge to the teacher. Often parents are notified that the school is unable to manage their child's behaviour, which may include arguing, fighting, bullying, excessive talking, and possibly poor school performance. A psychological assessment may be recommended by the school and/or parents. Prior to the assessment, a clinician (e.g., psychologist, psychiatrist) must obtain two levels of consent: that of parents or guardians, and that of the child or adolescent him- or herself. It is not uncommon to interview the child and parent individually and together. Teachers may be asked to provide information on school performance and behaviour. To get a more complete picture of the issues, the clinician may want to observe the child at home and/or at school. Tools used to assess the child include standardized tests such as intelligence tests and academic achievement tests, checklists to identify symptomology, play sessions, and structured interviews to assess for psychiatric diagnoses.

Broadly, children's emotional and behavioural difficulties can be categorized as **internalizing** or **externalizing problems** (Rutter 1990). Internalizing problems are emotional difficulties such as anxiety, depression, and obsessions. Externalizing problems are behavioural difficulties such as delinquency, fighting, bullying, lying, and destructive behaviour. It is the externalizing problems that can develop into more persistent and serious antisocial acts and receive the attention of parents, teachers, and the criminal justice system. Externalizing problems have been considered more difficult to treat and more likely to have long-term persistence (Ebata, Peterson, and Conger 1990; Robins 1986). Externalizing disorders have been known to be quite stable, though symptoms often peak in teenage years and decrease in the late 20s (Rutter 1995). Males are more likely to have externalizing difficulties than females, with a ratio of about 10:1 (Barkley 1997; Rutter 1990).

To assess externalizing problems, multiple informants are necessary because the child or youth may not be aware of their behaviour or the influence it has on others (McMahon 1994). As mentioned above, parents, teachers, and peers may be interviewed or asked to rate the child or adolescent. It is also important that behaviour be viewed within a developmental context. For example, rebelling against rules set by parents may be normative for adolescents but worrisome if younger children are oppositional and continually refuse to comply with parents' requests. The duration, severity, and frequency of troublesome behaviours should be measured.

Three childhood psychiatric diagnoses that occur with some frequency in juvenile offenders are **attention-deficit hyperactivity disorder** (ADHD), **oppositional defiant disorder** (ODD), and **conduct disorder** (CD). ADHD is described as an inattention and restlessness (APA 1994). Some examples of features associated with ADHD include: does not appear to listen when spoken to; has difficulty in organization; loses items; fidgets; and talks excessively. To qualify for an ADHD diagnosis, a number of symptoms must be present, occur in two or more settings, and persist for at least six months. When making an ADHD diagnosis, it is important to consider the age of the child. In young children, many of the symptoms of ADHD are part of normal development and behaviour. Many children with ADHD also receive diagnoses of ODD or CD (Barkley 1991).

ODD is defined as a "pattern of negativistic, hostile, and defiant behaviour" (APA 1994: 93). Some examples of features associated with ODD include: loses temper; deliberately annoys others; and is vindictive. Approximately 40 percent of children with ODD develop CD (Loeber et al. 1993). CD is a repetitive and persistent pattern of behaviour in children and youth whereby the rights of others or basic social rules are violated. These behaviour patterns are usually displayed at home, school, and in social situations. If a child with ODD qualifies for a CD diagnosis, an ODD diagnosis is not used. Some examples of features associated with CD include: initiates physical fights; is physically cruel to animals; sets fires; lies for gain; and is truant before 13 years of age. Approximately 50 percent of children who meet the criteria for CD go on to receive diagnoses of antisocial personality disorder in adulthood (APA 1994; Loeber and Farrington 2000).

A child answers questions as part of an assessment.

Rates of Behaviour Disorders in Children

Approximately 5 to 15 percent of children display severe behavioural problems (Rutter 1990). This estimate may be too low, however. In the Ontario Child Health Study in 1987, approximately 18 percent of children between the ages of 4 and 16 were found to experience conduct disorder, hyperactivity, emotional disturbance, or a combination of these (Offord et al. 1987). Researchers have found that behavioural disorders commonly co-occur. For example, 20 to 50 percent of children with ADHD also have symptoms consistent with CD or ODD (Offord, Lipman, and Duku 2001). Internalizing problems such as depression may be more severe in children with CD (Marriage, Fine, Moretti, and Haley 1986).

Assessing the Adolescent Once an adolescent's antisocial behaviour receives the attention of the courts, a court-ordered assessment may be issued. In such cases, the adolescent need not provide consent/assent. The issue for the courts to determine is the risk a particular juvenile poses to reoffending. In other words, does having a juvenile in the community pose a risk for others? Does the juvenile have the potential to change in a positive manner? Juveniles are assessed so that resources can be used effectively and the risk to the community is reduced.

The instruments used to assess a juvenile offender's risk generally include a "checklist" where items are scored on a scale, the points are summed, and a cut-off value is set for either detaining or releasing the juvenile. Risk assessment instruments collect information about a set of factors, both static (i.e., factors that cannot change, such as age of first arrest) and dynamic (i.e., factors that can change, such as antisocial attitudes). Interviews with the juvenile as well as case files and histories may be used to complete a risk assessment. A total risk score is then obtained. Generally, the notion is that the more relevant risk factors are present, the more likely it is that the juvenile will reoffend. Any number of professionals (front-line staff in institutions, probation staff, credentialed professionals) may be responsible for conducting the risk assessment.

The task of identifying risk factors for juvenile offenders who will reoffend is different than for adults (Mulvey 2005). For example, history of behaviour often is considered in the risk assessment of adult offenders. This may be limited for and ambiguous for juvenile offenders. They simply do not have the years behind them that can be examined. Child and adolescent behaviour may be more influenced by context than enduring character. Children and adolescents may display behaviour that is adaptive to the environment they are in rather than the behaviour being a demonstration of their character across all situations (Masten and Coatsworth 1998). A child who is disruptive in one school may not be disruptive in another, so interpreting a behaviour problem may be inaccurate. Children and adolescents experience more change developmentally and in character than adults. It is a challenge to separate developmental issues from persistent personality and character for the prediction of future offending. Some researchers argue further that risk assessment may differ between adolescent boys and girls (Odgers, Moretti, and Reppucci 2005). Box 5.6 presents a list of risk assessment tools used with juvenile offenders in Canada.

Box 5.6

Risk Assessment Tools Used with Juvenile Offenders in Canada

Adolescent Chemical Dependency Inventory (ACDI)—Corrections Version II

This instrument is designed for 14- to 17-year-olds to screen for substance (alcohol and other drugs) use and abuse, overall adjustment, and issues for troubled youth. Juvenile offenders respond to 140 items that break down into seven scales: truthfulness; violence; adjustment; distress; alcohol; drugs; and stress and coping abilities.

Criminal Sentiments Scale (CSS)

This 41-item self-report questionnaire uses five-point scales to assess key dimensions of criminal sentiments, such as antisocial attitudes, values, and beliefs that may play a role in the maintenance of antisocial behaviour. The offender reports on attitudes toward the law, courts, police, tolerance for law violations, and identification with other criminals.

HCR-20

The HCR-20 takes its name from the three scales it assesses—historical, clinical, and risk management—and from the number of items. It examines risk and violence broadly, including risk factors from the past, present, and future. The scale consists of ten historical factors, five clinical items to reflect current factors related to violence, and five risk-management items that focus attention on situational post-assessment factors that may aggravate or mitigate risk.

Level of Service Inventory—Ontario Revised (LSI-OR)

The LSI-OR is a standardized instrument used by the Ontario Ministry of the Solicitor General and Correctional Services with offenders aged 16 and older. It is used to assess risk of recidivism, need for correctional programs to reduce recidivism, and factors related to the likelihood the offender will respond to treatment.

Offender Risk Assessment and Management System (ORAMS)

ORAMS is a set of tools developed by Manitoba Corrections to assess the different risks offenders pose. Two scales can be used with juvenile offenders: Inmate Security Assessment and Primary Risk Assessment.

Inmate Security Assessment (ISA)—Young Offenders

The objective of the ISA is to obtain information to assess a juvenile offender's threat to him- or herself and others in an institution. Dangerous behaviour includes suicide, assaults on other inmates or staff, and escape risk. This scale is completed once an offender has been admitted into an institution for security reasons and also assists decisions relating to institutional placement or transfer.

Primary Risk Assessment (PRA)—Young Offenders

This scale is a modified version of the Youthful Offender—Level of Service Inventory (YO-LSI) described below. It is used to predict a juvenile offender's risk to reoffend in any type

Continued >

Box 5.6 Continued

of offence (as opposed to specific types of offences such as sexual assault). This information is then used to determine the degree and type of supervision needed and to assist in the formulation of a case plan.

Pride in Delinquency Scale (PID)

The PID is a 10-item self-report scale used to assess a juvenile offender's comfort level (i.e., pride versus shame) in getting involved in specific criminal behaviour. It is used to complement the CSS measure.

Structured Assessment of Violence Risk in Youth (SAVRY) (Borum, Bartel, and Forth 2002)

The SAVRY is used to make assessments and recommendations about the nature and degree of risk that a juvenile may pose for future violence. Twenty-four risk factors and six protective factors are considered.

Youth Level of Service/Case Management Inventory (YLS/CMI) (Hoge and Andrews 2002)

This is a standardized instrument including a 42-item checklist for use by professional workers in assessing risk of future violence, need for correctional programs to reduce future violence, and responsivity factors that impact on case plan goals. A detailed survey of youth risk and needs factors is produced that can be used to create a case plan. The instrument contains seven sections: 1) assessment of risk and need; 2) summary of risk/need factors; 3) assessment of other needs/special considerations; 4) assessment of the client's general risk/need level; 5) contact level; 6) case management plan; and 7) case management review.

Youthful Offender—Level of Service Inventory (YO-LSI)

The YO-LSI is a risk/needs assessment instrument used to classify and assess a juvenile offender's overall risk level and to identify and target areas of criminogenic need. The YO-LSI consists of 82 static and dynamic predictors of criminal risk/needs that are grouped into the following seven categories: criminal history; substance abuse; educational/employment problems; family problems; peer relation problems; accommodation problems; and psychological factors.

Source: Hannah-Moffat and Maurutto (2003)

PREVENTION, INTERVENTION, AND TREATMENT OF JUVENILE OFFENDING

PREVENTION, INTERVENTION, AND TREATMENT OF JUVENILE OFFENDING CAN BE conceptualized as occurring at three levels: primary, secondary, and tertiary (DeMatteo and Marczyk 2005; Flannery and Williams 1999; Mulvey et al. 1993). **Primary intervention strategies** are implemented prior to any violence occurring with the goal of decreasing the likelihood that violence will occur later on. **Secondary intervention strategies** attempt to reduce the frequency of violence. **Tertiary intervention strategies** attempt to prevent violence from reoccurring.

Primary Intervention Strategies

At the primary level of intervention, the goal is to identify groups (of children) that have numerous risk factors for engaging in antisocial behaviour later on. The belief is that if the needs of these children are addressed early, before violence has occurred, then the likelihood that they will go on to become juvenile offenders is reduced. Because "groups" (rather than specific individuals) are targeted, often these intervention strategies occur at broad levels such as in the family, at school, and in the community (Mulvey et al. 1993). Examples of primary intervention approaches include family-oriented strategies, school-oriented strategies, and community-wide strategies.

Family-Oriented Strategies Targeting the family may be an effective means of preventing juvenile offending, given that family poses a number of risk factors (Kumpfer and Alvarado 2003). According to Mulvey et al. (1993), family-based intervention efforts can generally be classified as either parent-focused or family-supportive. **Parent-focused interventions** are directed at assisting parents to recognize warning signs for later juvenile violence and/or training parents to effectively manage any behavioural problems that arise. **Family-supportive interventions** connect at-risk families to various support services (e.g., child care, counselling, medical assistance) that may be available in their community.

An example of a family-oriented strategy is a popular parent-education program known as "The Incredible Years Parenting Program," a 12-week training program that starts with building a strong emotional bond between parent(s) and child, then teaches parents how to set behavioural expectations for their children, monitor children's behaviour, reinforce positive behaviour, provide consequences for inappropriate behaviour, and develop and use effective communication skills (Webster-Stratton 1992). Videos are used to demonstrate parenting techniques and enhance parent learning. Although parent-focused approaches have shown some success in the shorter term, the most common research finding is that parents of high-risk children tend to discontinue the training at rates that may exceed 50 percent (Mulvey et al. 1993). With such high attrition rates, particularly among families with the greatest need for these services, it is unlikely that parent-focused approaches are a reliable mechanism for preventing youth violence. Parenting programs usually are not "stand alone" and are part of more comprehensive programs that may involve a child component, school component, and/or community program.

School-Oriented Strategies Given the amount of time children spend in school and the number of difficulties that can arise there, school is a common environment for primary prevention strategies. School-based prevention programs include preschool programs (e.g., Project Head Start, which incorporates The Incredible Years Parenting Program); social skills training for children, which may include cognitive behavioural therapy; and broad-based social interventions designed to alter the school environment (Mulvey et al. 1993; Loeber and Farrington 1998a). Box 5.7 describes a school-based program intended to scare students into *not* offending.

Can You Scare Children Not to Commit Crime?

Scared Straight was developed in the United States in the 1970s to "scare" at-risk children from choosing a life of crime. The premise involves actual inmates making aggressive presentations about life behind bars. Discussions of sexual assault are included as is a visit to a prison (Finckenauer 1982). The theory is one of deterrence: children and youth will be so scared of what will happen to them in prison that they will not offend in the first place. In 1979, a documentary on the Scared Straight program reported that 94 percent of 16- and 17-year-olds who took part were law-abiding for three months following participation (Finckenauer 1982). Not all data support this conclusion, however.

The Scared Straight program has gone through several changes and has become less aggressive and more educational. The program is fairly inexpensive to conduct (estimated at about $1 a participant) and provides an opportunity for offenders to contribute productively to society (Finckenauer 1982). A number of countries have implemented Scared Straight and other "kids visit prison" programs: "Day in Prison" in Australia (O'Malley, Coventry, and Walters 1993) and "Day Visits" in the United Kingdom (Lloyd 1995), for example. The program has also been tried in Canada (O'Malley, Coventry, and Walters 1993). In a systematic review by Petrosino (2000), Scared Straight–type programs produced a 1 to 28 percent increase in crime (also Petrosino, Turpin-Petrosino, and Buehler 2003). Despite the evidence of their inefficacy, Scared Straight–type programs remain in use.

Project Head Start is designed for children from low socio-economic backgrounds. A number of social services are provided to these children and families (e.g., nutrition, structured activities, academic tutoring, and medical services) to reduce disadvantages that may interfere with learning. Preschool programs can produce some positive outcomes in the short term; however, the positive effects at reducing antisocial behaviour over the long term are questionable (Mulvey et al. 1993; Loeber and Farrington 1998a).

It is not uncommon to recommend a social skills program to children showing some early signs of interpersonal and behavioural difficulties. Social skills training may involve a structured program with a limited number of sessions (e.g., 12), teaching alternative methods for conflict resolution, adjusting social perceptions (recall that a cognitive theory approach suggests that aggressive children may interpret ambiguous situations aggressively; e.g., Lochman, Whidby, and FitzGerald 2000), managing anger, and developing empathy. Cognitive behavioural therapy usually is a component of social skills programs. The cognitive behavioural component focuses on children's thought processes and social interactions. Concrete strategies for handling interpersonal conflict are outlined, which children practise through role-playing and modelling with others in the class. Program evaluations have suggested that social skills training with cognitive behaviour therapy can be beneficial in the short term, although long-term follow-up suggests that the effects on reducing antisocial behaviour may be small (e.g., Denham and Almeida 1987). Larger effects may be obtained if social skills programs are combined with others such as parent education (Webster-Stratton and Hammond 1997).

"Social process intervention" is another school-based approach that alters the school environment (Gauce, Comer, and Schwartz 1987; Mulvey et al. 1993). Changes include increasing the connection among students with learning problems, assisting the transition from elementary school to high school, improving the perception of safety in school, and providing students with experiences in the community (Mulvey et al. 1993). Although these efforts may improve academic success, their influence on reducing the likelihood of juvenile offending is unclear.

Community-Wide Strategies Community approaches include providing structured community activities for children's participation and increasing a community's cohesion. Few community-based programs exist for children under 12 who are at risk for future juvenile offending. One such program developed in Canada in 1985 is known as the SNAP Under 12 Outreach Project (ORP).

The ORP is a standardized 12-week outpatient program with five key components:

1. The SNAP Children's Club—a structured group that teaches children a cognitive-behavioural self-control and problem-solving technique called SNAP (Stop Now And Plan) (Earlscourt Child and Family Centre 2001a)

2. A concurrent SNAP parenting group that teaches parents effective child management strategies (Earlscourt Child and Family Centre 2001b)

3. One-on-one family counselling based on SNAP Parenting

4. Individual befriending for children who are not connected with positive structured activities in their community and require additional support

5. Academic tutoring to assist children who are not performing at an age-appropriate grade level

Recently, the ORP's effectiveness was assessed in Toronto by Augimeri, Farrington, Koegl, and Day (2007). Sixteen pairs of children were matched on age, sex, and severity of delinquency (e.g., theft, fighting, severe defiance at home, vandalism, assault, arson, trespassing, and public mischief) and then randomly assigned to the ORP or to a control program that received a less-intensive version of ORP (i.e., arts and crafts and cooperative game activities). Data were collected at five intervals: Time 1 (pretreatment); Time 2 (post-treatment—at least three months after Time 1); Time 3 (three months after Time 2); Time 4 (six months after Time 3); and Time 5 (six months after Time 4). A national criminal record search was conducted between each participant's twelfth and eighteenth birthday. Results indicated a significant decrease in externalizing behaviours for children in the ORP group compared to those in the control program. These gains were sustained over the one-year follow-up period. Although children in the ORP group had fewer official contacts with the criminal justice system between the ages of 12 and 18 than the control group, this difference was not significant. Multifaceted interventions with cognitive behavioural skills training along with parent training may have produced positive effects for children under 12 displaying antisocial behaviours.

Secondary Intervention Strategies

Secondary intervention strategies are directed at juveniles who have either had contact with the police or criminal justice system or have demonstrated behavioural problems at school. The goal of these strategies is to provide social and clinical services so that juveniles do not go on to commit serious violence. Many of the same approaches used in primary intervention strategies are used here. One of the main differences is the "target" (i.e., which children are involved in the program) rather than the content of the intervention. Common secondary intervention strategies include diversion programs, alternative and vocational education, family therapy, and skills training (see Mulvey et al. 1993).

Diversion programs "divert" youth offenders from the juvenile justice system into community- or school-based treatment programs. The belief is that the justice system may cause more harm than good in reducing offending. Intervention and treatment in the community may be more successful at reducing the likelihood that the juvenile will escalate their offending. Alternative and vocational education programs offer the option of mainstream schooling. Family therapy and skills-training programs incorporate the juvenile and family. Diversion and certain school-, family-, and community-based interventions have shown some success at reducing antisocial behaviour in youth (e.g., Davidson and Redner 1988; Kazdin 1996).

One particular secondary intervention program that has undergone considerable evaluation is Multisystemic Therapy (MST). MST examines a child across the contexts or "systems" in which they live—family, peers, school, neighbourhood, and community (Henggeler and Borduin 1990; Henggeler, Melton, and Smith 1992; Henggeler, Schoenwald, and Pickrel 1995; Henggeler et al. 1998). MST has been implemented in various parts of Canada and the United States. To evaluate its effectiveness, a four-year randomized study was conducted across four Ontario communities: London, Mississauga, Simcoe County, and Ottawa (Leschied and Cunningham 2002). Approximately 200 families received MST from 1997 to 2001. During the same time period, another 200 families (acting as the comparison group) were asked to access the services that were available through their local youth justice and social service organizations. These services included probation and specialized programs. All families underwent psychological testing at the start of the study and then again at the end.

The psychological testing included measures to assess family functioning, caregiver depression, the youths' social skills, pro-criminal attitudes, and behavioural problems. Based on this assessment, the youth and families in the MST group were provided services and had access to a case manager 24 hours a day, 7 days a week. Areas that may be targeted in MST treatment include family communication, parent management, and cognitive-behavioural issues. All youth were followed for three years following the end of treatment (until 2004). Overall, MST was not found to be more effective than the typical services available in Ontario. For example, after the three-year follow-up, 68 percent of the participants in the MST group had at least one conviction, compared to 67 percent of those in the "comparison" group. The average number of days to reconviction for the MST group was about 283, compared to 310 for the control group (this difference was not statistically significant). It is important to note, however, that MST may have benefitted youths and their families on factors that were not measured. Interestingly, some studies evaluating MST in the United States have found it more effective than incarceration, individual counselling, and probation (Henggeler et al. 1986; 1992; 1995). Perhaps the quantity and quality of programs available in various parts of the United States differ from those in Canada—accounting for some of the differing results between the two countries.

Tertiary Intervention Strategies

Tertiary intervention strategies are aimed at juveniles who have engaged in criminal acts and who may have already been processed through formal court proceedings (Flannery and Williams, 1999). As such, these intervention efforts are actually more "treatment" rather than prevention, and the recipients are often chronic and serious juvenile offenders. The goal of tertiary intervention strategies is to minimize the impact of existing risk factors and foster the development of protective factors, which may reduce the likelihood that the at-risk adolescent will engage in future offending.

Tertiary intervention strategies include inpatient treatment (i.e., institutional, residential) and community-based treatment (Mulvey et al. 1993). The approach can be one of retribution or rehabilitation. For those who favor retribution, they believe that juveniles should be held accountable for their actions, punished accordingly, and separated from society. Treatment for these juveniles should be provided in an institutional setting (e.g., juvenile detention centre) By contrast, those who favour rehabilitation believe that treatment based in the community is a more effective way to reduce the likelihood of reoffending. Box 5.8 examines the effectiveness of boot camps, an alternative to traditional custodial institutions, for juvenile offenders. One meta-analysis reported that shorter stays (rather than longer stays) in institutional settings and greater involvement with community services are more effective for violent juveniles (Wooldredge 1988).

Box 5.8

Getting Back to Basics: Are Boot Camps Effective?

"Boot camps" for young offenders are not a new idea. They have been operating in various jurisdictions for over 20 years. Some of the first boot camps took place in Oklahoma and Georgia in the early 1980s. As an alternative to traditional custodial facilities such as detention centres and prisons, boot camps use a military-style environment to rehabilitate juvenile offenders. The day typically starts at 6:00 A.M. and includes literacy training, life skills, physical fitness, personal-hygiene classes, substance-abuse counselling, and job training (Hendley 2000). The day ends around 10:00 P.M. Youthful offenders wear military-style uniforms and learn marching steps.

The Ontario government applied the principles of a military-style camp to young offenders with the goal of deterring their engagement in future offending. In part, boot camps were a response to a desire from the public for harsher sentences for young offenders. The underlying principles of boot camps are: 1) to deter future crime by increasing the degree of punishment; 2) to promote self-discipline; and 3) to develop accountability by focusing on structure and hard work. On the surface, these principles are appealing. The Ontario government's boot camp, known as Project Turnaround, was located near Barrie and opened in 1997. Directed at 16- and 17-year-old offenders, the facility provided room for 32 inmates, with 54 staff supervising. But was Project Turnaround effective at reducing recidivism?

In an evaluation of Project Turnaround, it was reported that approximately 33 percent of young offenders reoffended after completing their stay (Agrell 2003). In contrast, approximately 50 percent of youthful offenders in traditional custodial facilities reoffend after release. These rates were not statistically significant, and Ontario's premier, Dalton McGuinty, decided to close Project Turnaround in 2004.

Interestingly, young offenders attending boot camps have a more positive perception of the facilities than young offenders attending traditional custodial facilities. In a survey by Styve, MacKenzie, Gover, and Mitchell (2000), young offenders who had completed a boot camp (in the United States) perceived it as a more controlled, active, and structured environment with less potential for harm by other residents compared with young offenders in more traditional correctional facilities. Boot camps were also perceived as providing more therapeutic and transitional programming than traditional facilities. Although these perceptions may be positive, they do not seem to significantly influence recidivism rates.

Source: Agrell (2003); Hendley (2000); Styve et al. (2000)

GUIDING PRINCIPLES AND RECOMMENDATIONS FOR REDUCING ANTISOCIAL BEHAVIOUR

MOST WOULD AGREE THAT THE SOONER THE PREVENTION OR INTERVENTION, THE GREATER the likelihood of success. Programs that target both the family and child in the context of school and community are most likely to have positive effects, reducing offending in the short and long term. Although these comprehensive, multipronged programs are most promising, they pose a number of challenges given the availability of services, the coordination of those services, and the commitment of participants and service providers. Also important to take into account are the two types of juvenile offenders, life-course persistent and adolescent limited. Different interventions are needed for each. More comprehensive and extensive programs should be directed toward life-course persistent juveniles. School-based prevention programs are more successful for adolescent limited juveniles. Risk and protective factors should be considered for each child when deciding on appropriate programs. Overall, reducing antisocial behaviour in the long term requires an extensive approach.

Below is a list of the top 10 issues and people to consider when thinking about juvenile offending in Canada.

Top 10 List
Advances to Come, Debates, Ethical Conundrums, and People to Watch

1. Should prenatal intervention for reducing delinquency be mandated or legislated?

2. Should youth (or even younger children) be labelled as criminal?

3. Should youth be given adult sentences for violent crime?

4. Do we need harsher sentences for juvenile offenders?

5. Should under-12s be charged and processed through the criminal justice system? Is there a minimum age limit?

6. Is police diversion of juvenile offenders working to reduce crime?

7. Should parents be held responsible for a youth's behaviour?

8. How do we reduce the number of guns in the hands of Canadian youth?

9. Do protective and risk factors for juvenile offenders differ as a function of ethnicity?

10. Names to watch: Scott Henggeler, Rolf Loeber, and Terrie Moffitt.

SUMMARY

1. The first Canadian legislation to address juvenile offending was the *Juvenile Delinquents Act* (JDA) in 1908. In 1984, the *Young Offender's Act* (YOA) replaced the JDA with several major changes to juvenile justice. Although the YOA underwent several amendments, it was finally replaced in 2003 with the *Youth Criminal Justice Act* (YCJA).

2. Biological theories focus on genetic and physiological differences between juvenile offenders and those who do not behave antisocially. Cognitive theories propose a model of antisocial behaviour that focuses on thought processes that occur in social interactions. Social theories are based in social learning theory, which proposes that children learn behaviour from observing others and through reinforcement contingencies.

3. A risk factor is a variable or factor that, if present, increases the likelihood of an undesirable outcome such as antisocial behaviour. Risk factors occur across various domains that include individual (e.g., difficult temperament), familial (e.g., low parental involvement), school (e.g., low commitment to school), peer (e.g., associating with antisocial peers), and community (e.g., low-income neighbourhood). A protective factor is a variable or factor that, if present, decreases the likelihood of an undesirable outcome such as antisocial behaviour. Protective factors occur across various domains that include individual (e.g., intelligence), familial (e.g., supportive relationship with parent), school (e.g., commitment to school), peer (e.g., associating with peers who disapprove of antisocial behaviour), and community (e.g., strong community infrastructure).

4. There are three common disorders diagnosed in juvenile offenders: attention-deficit hyperactivity disorder (ADHD), oppositional defiant disorder (ODD), and conduct disorder (CD). Children/youth diagnosed with CD are at greatest risk for juvenile offending. CD is a precurser to adult antisocial personality disorder.

5. The instruments used to assess a juvenile offender's risk generally involve a "checklist" where items are scored on a scale, the points are summed, and a cutoff value is set for either detaining or releasing the juvenile. These instruments collect information about a set of factors, both static and dynamic, related to reoffending, such as number of prior arrests, use of a weapon, and presence of a drug problem.

6. Primary intervention strategies are implemented prior to any violence occurring with the goal of decreasing the likelihood that violence will occur later on. Secondary intervention strategies attempt to reduce the frequency of violence. Tertiary intervention strategies attempt to prevent violence from reoccurring.

Discussion Questions

1. Johnny Blanco had behavioural problems in daycare. His behaviour seemed to get worse as he got older. By the time he was 14, he was skipping school and starting fires. Describe the two types of trajectories to juvenile offending. Which does Johnny fit?

2. Your neighbour, Mrs. Brown, asks if you can babysit her five-year-old son Billy. You have known Billy since he was born—most neighbours know Billy because of his "lively" behaviour. While you are babysitting, you notice that Billy has a number of risk factors for juvenile offending. Make a list of protective factors that Mrs. Brown may be able to implement to reduce the likelihood that Billy will engage in antisocial behaviour when he is older.

3. You want to become an elementary school teacher focusing on children who display externalizing disorders. Describe the three most common psychiatric diagnoses for children displaying disruptive behaviours. What are the core features of each? Which diagnoses co-occur?

4. Describe three risk assessment tools for juvenile offenders.

5. As part of your summer vacation, you decide to volunteer at the local Boys and Girls Club, which offers at-risk children a number of programs to reduce the likelihood that they will behave antisocially. You have been tasked with developing a social-skills program for 8-to 12-year-olds. Outline an eight-week program.

6. Design a study that will allow you to examine the effectiveness of the program you developed in question five. Test whether your program reduces antisocial behaviour in the short and long terms.

Additional Reading

Chettleburgh, M. 2007. *Young thugs*. Toronto: HarperCollins Canada.

Hollin, C.R., Browne, D., and Palmer, E. 2002. *Delinquency and young offenders*. Chichester: John Wiley and Sons.

Relevant Websites

The Canadian Safe School Network
www.canadiansafeschools.com

Boys and Girls Clubs of Canada
www.bgccan.com/index.asp

Chapter 6
Economic Crime

DVDs, iPods, clothes—there wasn't anything Sam "Sticky Fingers" couldn't get at a substantially marked-down price. Sam would enlist a friend and they'd make their way to the mall, each armed with a cell phone. Once Sam found the store he wanted, he would go in as any other "customer," with his "friend" serving as the lookout via cell phone. Sam would "browse" while his friend stood outside the store watching the employees, relaying information to Sam via phone. Sam wouldn't be bothered by store employees when they saw he was on the phone. The friend would inform Sam when the workers weren't watching and Sam would pick up whatever he needed. Sam wore larger clothes with big pockets and even sometimes a knapsack for "storage." Once he had his cache, he would casually walk out of the store.

Sam was committing the theft of shoplifting. Although his target was not personal and he did not use violence to commit his crime, his behaviour was a criminal offence. Economic offending is associated with a large financial cost on society and the criminal justice system. Should the justice system treat economic offenders differently than other types of offenders?

Learning Objectives

1   Distinguish the various types of white-collar crime.

2   Differentiate between theft and fraud.

3   Contrast characteristics of prostitutes versus their clients.

4   Describe characteristics of organized crime groups.

5   List the illegal activities engaged in by organized crime.

6   Discuss the connection between substance abuse and economic crime.

7   Identify the core features of drug treatment courts.

INTRODUCTION

A NUMBER OF CRIMES ARE COMMITTED WITH THE PURPOSE OF ECONOMIC GAIN. ALTHOUGH Canada may have a "getting tough on crime" position, which is evidenced in higher incarceration rates compared to other countries, this notion seems to apply to violent offending rather than economic offending. In fact, on an international scale, Canada is viewed as "soft" on white-collar crime, with few prosecutions and even fewer convictions. Following a four-year span where a group of dedicated Royal Canadian Mounted Police were tasked with investigating white-collar crime in Canada, there were only two convictions—both against the same person.

This chapter will focus on crimes that occur with a primary goal of financial profit. We will examine various types of economic crime and their offenders. Violence may or may not occur during the commission of these crimes, although most often, if violence does occur, it is when the financial gain is in jeopardy. We will also discuss the role of substance abuse both in the context of a commodity to be sold for financial gain as well as the role it plays in other types of offending.

Definition

Although there are many definitions of economic crime, for the purposes of this chapter we define **economic crime** as criminal offences where the primary motivation is for economic gain (e.g., Freeman 1996). Often to combat economic crime, a partnership must be formed across various levels of government, law enforcement, business, and private sectors. The Reporting Economic Crime Online (RECOL) group is just that: the Royal Canadian Mounted Police (RCMP), along with the Ontario Provincial Police (OPP) and the Internet Fraud Complaint Centre (IFCC), joined together to provide a mechanism to report economic crime that deals with corporate/occupational/white-collar crime and fraud. Learn more about RECOL later in the chapter. For other types of economic crime, such as prostitution and drug trafficking, the RCMP and/or provincial police and international agencies may be involved.

TYPES OF ECONOMIC CRIME

White-Collar Crime

Often white-collar crime is partitioned into occupational crime versus corporate crime. **Occupational crimes** are offences committed against businesses and government by perpetrators with a "higher" social status. These offences include expense account fraud and tax evasion. **Corporate crimes** are offences committed by organizations to advance their own interests. Corporate crime offences include **price fixing** (i.e., companies that all sell the same product decide on a price, preventing price variability for the consumer) and the payment of kickbacks to manufacturers or retailers (who use the organization's product). The distinction between occupational and corporate crime can be thought of as crime focused on individuals versus crime focused on organizations (Holtfreter 2005).

White-collar criminals tend to work for the institution they are stealing from. This theft may be ongoing due to lack of detection, or the organization may prefer not to report it to avoid publicity. White-collar criminals may be fired and/or requested to pay back the equivalent of what they stole. Federal, provincial, and municipal laws prohibit various corporate crimes.

Typically, government inspectors are responsible for the enforcement of corporate offences and tend to have less authority to investigate than police. Corporate crime can cause far greater financial harm and personal injury (sometimes leading to death) than traditional crimes such as assault. Box 6.1 profiles two high-profile white-criminals: Conrad Black and Bernie Madoff.

Profiling the Typical Offender of White-Collar Crime

Historically, white-collar criminals were viewed as high status and respectable (Sutherland 1949), often male, highly educated, and in an upper management position. Following the work of Sutherland in the 1940s, a further distinction was made to recognize corporate crime that occurs with the support of an organization and occupational crime committed by an individual offender (Clinard and Quinney 1967). Occupational fraudsters were thought to be primarily middle class (Weisburd, Wheeler, Waring, and Bode 1991).

Box 6.1

From Penthouses to Jail Cells

Born in Montreal, Conrad Black became one of the most powerful men in newspaper publishing. A media baron, he controlled Hollinger International Incorporated, the publisher of many newspapers including the *National Post* and the *Chicago Sun Times*. A number of complaints from investors started to surface in 2003 alleging company misconduct. After some pressure, Black resigned; however, his resignation did not protect him from being charged with various counts of fraud (e.g., prosecutors alleged in court that Black and his co-conspirators participated in fraud and obstruction of justice worth US$32.15 million. Although he was born in Canada, Black was charged in Illinois and convicted of three counts of fraud and one count of obstruction. He was sentenced to six-and-a-half years in jail, fined $120 000, and forced to forfeit $6.1 million.

White-collar crime isn't just an issue for publishing giants. Bernard Madoff was thought to have the "golden touch" when it came to investing. An investment manager based in New York, Madoff had a number of high-profile clients, including celebrities, and also invested for average citizens. He was running a Ponzi scheme (i.e., a pyramid investment scheme where no legitimate investment occurs and the money from later investors is used to pay earlier investors). A number of individuals and organizations trusted their fortunes to Madoff. The Wilpon family, owners of the New York Mets baseball team, made a $300-million investment with Madoff. Another family invested $100 million and yet another sunk $10 million. Some early investors received a double-digit return, while other investors received nothing. Madoff pleaded guilty to 11 criminal charges including fraud, money laundering, and perjury on March 12, 2009. U.S. prosecutors estimated client losses of almost $65 billion. In June Madoff was sentenced to the maxium of 150 years in prison.

Source: Esposito, Harper and Sauer (2009); Lenzner (2008); Westhead (2007).

Holtfreter (2005) provides the following review of the literature examining some of the common characteristics of offenders of "white-collar" crime:

Age, Race and Gender: Unlike "traditional" offenders, the common white-collar offender is a White, male, approximately 40-years-old (Wheeler, Weisburd, Waring, & Bode, 1988). In contrast, the common street offender is described as a Black, male, approximately 30-years-old (U.S. statistics). Male offenders seem to outnumber female offenders when it comes to white-collar crime. Historically, women tended to occupy lower level positions such as clerical positions compared to males who tended to have higher level positions making it more likely that males would be in a position to commit white-collar or economic crime.

Education: White-collar criminals tend to have greater educational attainment compared to other types of offenders (Benson & Moore, 1992). Once again, higher level corporate positions require a particular level of education whereas, more traditional offenders may have histories of low academic achievement and be high school dropouts for example.

Position: Often white-collar criminals will have knowledge and be involved in the financial aspects of the organization that would facilitate occupational crime such as embezzlement. An individual's position in the organization facilitates the types of white-collar crimes possible to commit. Those in managerial or executive positions may have greater opportunities to commit white-collar crime. (pp. 355–356)

It should be noted that for most crime, including white-collar crime, male offenders outnumber female offenders; an exception being prostitution as described later in this chapter.

Common characteristics of victims of organizational crime are also outlined (Holtfreter 2005):

Organizational Type: A study by Smigel (1956) found that there was a positive association between the size and level of bureaucracy of the organization and the willingness to approve of stealing from that organization. Corporations with large bureaucracies can receive little sympathy from the public, often perceived as making large profits (Smigel and Ross 1970).

Organizational Size: Very generally, larger organizations are associated with greater crime than smaller organizations (Gricar, 1983). A number of factors have been found to interact with organizational size however, including decentralization and level of control (Hill, Kelley, Agle, Hitt, and Hoskisson 1992).

Internal Controls: Organizations that have greater internal controls such as audits and anonymous reporting systems, are less likely to be victimized. Furthermore, if these controls then result in the dismissal of guilty employees less victimization will occur (Trevino and Victor 1992)." (pp. 356–367)

In a recent study, Holtfreter (2005) examined 1142 occupational fraud cases to differentiate between individual offender characteristics and organizational victim characteristics.

Three types of occupational fraud were assessed: asset misappropriation, corruption, and fraudulent statements. The results found that individuals who made fraudulent statements tended to be "high status." In comparison, those involved in asset misappropriation or corruption were considered "middle-class" offenders. The organizations that were victimized for corruption were large profit-generating corporations. Asset misappropriation was committed in smaller organizations compared to larger organizations. Fraudulent statements were primarily made in smaller organizations.

Blickle, Schlegel, Fassbender, and Klein (2006) surveyed 76 prisoners convicted of white-collar crime in Germany, in addition to 150 managers working in various companies. Some significant differences were found: white-collar criminals were more hedonistic (i.e., more supportive of the pursuit of pleasure and life enjoyment) and had a greater likelihood of giving into temptation where they had the opportunity to make money illegally. The criminals also had stronger narcissistic tendencies and less behavioural self-control than the managers. Somewhat surprisingly, white-collar criminals were more conscientious. The researchers speculated that the criminals were high-level executives who would require conscientiousness to obtain the education and training necessary to achieve their level of employment. Collins and Schmidt (1993) found that white-collar criminal have lower integrity than non-criminals. Other differences included irresponsibility, lack of dependability, and a disregard of rules and social norms on the part of white-collar criminals.

According to a 2007 survey by PricewaterhouseCoopers, approximately 52 percent of Canadian companies surveyed stated they had been victims of economic crime. This rate is a 3 percent decrease from data obtained in 2005, but a 6 percent increase from 2003. The estimated average loss was US$3.7 million. A similar survey was conducted among companies in various countries around the world. Approximately 43 percent reported being victims of economic crime, losing an average of US$2.4 million.

Rosoff, Pontell, and Tillman (2004) state that white-collar crime results in a loss of approximately $250 billion per year in the U.S., compared to an approximate $17.6 billion for losses due to personal and household crimes. Although the loss is greater, the U.S. Department of Justice (2005) reports that white-collar crime is a low priority compared to violent crime and issues regarding national security. This lower priority also is reflected in the degree to which researchers and the criminal justice system investigate personal violence crime versus white-collar crime (Cullen, Link, and Polanzi 1982).

Punishing White-Collar Criminals

In a national telephone survey to assess the public's view on white-collar crime versus street crime, Holtfreter, Van Slyke, Bratton, and Gertz (2008) examined responses from 402 U.S. citizens. A large proportion of respondents wanted white-collar criminals punished as harshly or more harshly than violent criminals. This finding is contradictory to earlier research, possibly due to the recent media attention on a number of high-profile white-collar crime cases (see Box 6.1). Respondents also wanted greater government resources allocated to combat white-collar crime. Along similar lines, Schoepfer,

Table 6.1 Acts that Prohibit Types of White-Collar Crime

Competition Act (1986): Advertising sales when prices have not been lowered, claiming a product can do something it cannot, and selling used cars as new cars

Food and Drugs Act (1985): Selling contaminated food and/or drugs

Hazardous Products Act (1985): Selling dangerous items

Immigration Act (2008): Bribing an immigration officer

Income Tax Act (2007): Not paying tax owed

Carmichael, and Piquero (2007) found that U.S. citizens perceived street criminals as more likely to be apprehended and sentenced more severely than white-collar criminals. These researchers also found that the public felt that those who commit robbery should be punished similarly to those who commit fraud.

In 2003, the National White-Collar Crime Centre of Canada (NW4C) was incorporated under the *Canada Corporations Act* in order to prevent and respond to economic crime by linking national and international systems through the Reporting Economic Crime Online centre (RECOL) and Phonebusters National Call Centre (PNCC) for private- and public-sector regulatory and law-enforcement organizations concerned with preventing, investigating, and prosecuting economic crime.

There are a number of acts dealing with various forms of economic crime, as outlined in Table 6.1.

Theft

Economic crime generally is synonymous with the notion of "stealing"; that is, taking something that belongs to someone else. The *Criminal Code of Canada* (section 322) states that "every one commits theft who fraudulently and without colour of right takes, or fraudulently and without colour of right converts to his use or to the use of another person, anything, whether animate or inanimate, with intent." There is a demarcation at $5000 when deciding on the punishment for a crime. Theft over $5000 is an indictable offence with a maximum punishment of 10 years imprisonment. Theft under $5000 is considered a hybrid offence, meaning it can be treated either as an indictable offence or a less serious summary conviction. This decision is made by the Crown's office prosecuting the case. If theft under $5000 is prosecuted as an indictable offence, the maximum penalty is imprisonment for not more than two years. As a summary conviction, the maximum penalty is six months imprisonment, a fine of $2000, or both.

A common type of theft, as described in the opening vignette, is shoplifting. It is not a specific criminal offence, but simply a theft categorized by the value of the merchandise stolen under the Canadian *Criminal Code*. It incorporates both low-value and high-value items. Box 6.2 describes the theft of a high-value item—a car—and the role it plays in Canada.

The World Capital of Car Theft: Canada

A car is stolen approximately every three minutes in Canada, making it the leading country in the world in car theft (Statistics Canada 2007). Consequently, motor vehicle theft is a frequently reported offence to Canadian police, following theft under $5000, mischief, break and enter, and common assault in occurrence. Winnipeg boasts the highest rate of car theft per 100 000 population, with 1932 thefts reported in 2007 (Statistics Canada 2007). Abbotsford (1155 thefts), Edmonton (1076), Regina (1008), and Vancouver (745) round out the top five.

The top five cars stolen in Canada in 2008 were the Honda Civic, Subaru Impreza, Dodge/Plymouth Grand Caravan/Voyager, and Acura RSX (Insurance Bureau of Canada 2008). The list may seem surprising at first, but perhaps not once you consider what happens to cars once they've been stolen. Lower-end cars are often targeted for the sale of their parts, their use in other crimes, and transportation. Luxury cars are more likely to be stolen for export by organized crime groups.

The following cars are least likely to be stolen in Canada: the Cadillac Deville, Lincoln Continental, Lincoln Town Car, Chevrolet Impala, Toyota Avalon, and Toyota Tacoma. Although these cars may not be "sporty," you're likely to find them where you last parked them. In 2007, auto theft cost Canadian insurers $542 million—an average of $35 per auto insurance policy.

Fraud

Under section 380 of the *Criminal Code of Canada*, fraud is divided into two categories: fraud under $5000 and fraud over $5000. Fraud occurs when deceit or fraudulent means are used to deprive someone of property, money, valuable security, or services. Many thefts can also be fraud, and it is sometimes up to the police to decide whether to lay a fraud charge or a theft charge against an offender. Consider the scenario in which a person switches price tags at a store, attaching the price tag of a lower-priced good to a more expensive item. This is really an example of theft, but police may choose to lay a fraud charge because the person technically paid for something. In other words, the price paid was illegitimate, so the fraud is the difference between the actual value and the price paid. A critical element in fraud is that the offender uses deception to take something that does not belong to them.

Two young women shoplift

Identity theft refers to the collection, possession, and trafficking of personal information. It typically takes place independent of, or in preparation for, the commission of identity fraud. **Identity fraud** refers to the use of another's personal information without their knowledge or consent to commit various crimes such as fraud, theft, or forgery.

The *Criminal Code* lists as offences the misuse of another person's identity information, including impersonation and forgery. However, the collection, possession, and trafficking of identity information is not against the law. The Canadian government is working on legislation to amend this area of the code. The new legislation will provide law enforcement and the legal community with tools to deal with the these offences. Box 6.3 describes identity theft in greater detail.

Box 6.3

Will the Real Jane Smith Please Stand Up

You apply for a credit card and receive a rejection. You're not quite certain how this is possible. You have a stable job with a good income, no debt, and have never been late on your rent. You think that maybe if you bought a house and paid a mortgage, it would further demonstrate that you're a "good risk" client. You make an appointment with your bank's manager to find out how much of a mortgage you can have. Much to your surprise, your bank manager looks up your credit rating and discovers that your identity has been stolen. Someone is registering for credit cards in your name, maxing them out, and not paying them on their due date. No wonder you've been rejected for credit cards. Since you've been a client at the same bank since you were a child, the manager knows you're the real Jane Smith and not the one with the "bad credit." How did this happen? According to the Strategic Counsel for the Competition Bureau of Canada (2007), 4.2 million people have been the victims of identity theft, either directly or within their household. That's approximately one out of every six Canadians.

Thieves can use social insurance numbers, driver's license numbers, credit card and banking information, bank cards, calling cards, birth certificates, and passports to steal your identity. But how do they get your information? It can be as easy as going out for dinner. If a restaurant takes your credit card, that information can be used in ways that have nothing to do with you paying for your dinner. It may take days, months, or even years to realize you have been a victim of identity theft and fraud.

Commonly targeted information includes:

- Name

- Home address

- Phone numbers

- Work address

- Date of birth

- Social Insurance number

- Driver's license

- Bank and credit card numbers (and PINs)

- Tax returns

- Passport

Continued >

Box 6.3 Continued

This information can be obtained by:

1. Going through your mail; having your mail redirected to another address

2. Going through your garbage (note that the court recently declared that once you place your garbage on the curb for pickup, it is no longer your private property)

3. Posing as a creditor, landlord, employer, or some other "official" to get your personal information

4. Stealing your wallet, or information in your vehicle, websites you visit, or e-mails you send

5. Tampering with automated banking machines and credit card terminals to read your information and PIN

6. Searching public sources such as newspapers (obituaries), telephone books, and records open to the public (professional certificates)

7. Bribing an employee where personal and/or financial information is stored

Other Types of Fraud

In addition to identity fraud, a number of other types of fraud are possible. These include (www.recol.ca/fraudprevention.aspx):

1. Advance fee fraud: Fraud that requires a payment before delivery of service

2. Online auction fraud: Fraud that occurs through online purchasing (e.g., non-delivery of goods and services, non-payment for goods delivered)

3. Investment fraud: Fraud that occurs with investments impacting a person or company (e.g., insider trading)

4. Counterfeit: Fraud associated with counterfeit currency or payment cards (e.g., currency counterfeiting)

5. Home renovation fraud: Fraud associated with home and property renovation services or sale (e.g., real estate fraud)

6. Health fraud: Fraud associated with health care or services, including insurance

7. Fraudulent bankruptcy: Fraud associated with personal or corporate bankruptcy claims (e.g., concealment of assets)

8. Corruption/bribery: Any misuse of power and position by a public or non-government official (e.g., bribery of a public official)

PROSTITUTION

PROVIDING SEXUAL SERVICES IN EXCHANGE FOR MONEY IS BROADLY KNOWN AS **prostitution**. This "exchange" requires a buyer and a seller, who may be heterosexual or homosexual. Female sellers and male buyers constitute the most common form of prostitution, with male homosexual exchanges occurring less frequently. Very little information exists regarding lesbian prostitution.

In Canada, there is no prostitution law per se in the *Criminal Code*, but the activities associated with prostitution are illegal. Arranging to buy sex in a public place is illegal; living off of the monies someone obtained from prostitution (i.e., pimping) is also illegal, and can carry maximum sentence of 14 years imprisonment. So although prostitution itself may not be against the law, the unlawful activities surrounding it make the act virtually illegal.

There are currently four activities related to prostitution that are against the law, according to the *Criminal Code*:

1. Procuring or living on the avails of prostitution
2. Owning, operating, or occupying a bawdy house (i.e., brothel)
3. All forms of public communication for the purpose of prostitution
4. Knowingly transporting another to a bawdy house

Prostitution can occur in brothels (i.e., a place where people pay to have sexual relations with prostitutes—brothels can sometimes be disguised as massage parlours) or on the street. Some model and escort services are actually covers for prostitution. Street prostitution in Canada is the smallest proportion of the sex trade, comprising about 10 to 33 percent.

Brothels were the prominent environment for prostitution through the 1800s in Canada. These houses were often grouped together near taverns and poorer parts of town. It was not uncommon to find alcohol and gambling in these brothels, as well. Following the late 1800s, it became more difficult to legally operate brothels and prostitution moved to the streets. It represented a means for some women to make money. When greater opportunities existed for employment following World War II, the number of women involved in prostitution declined.

It is important to note that the prostitute/seller and the buyer are both engaging in illegal acts. Prostitution is one crime where women are more likely to be penalized than men. While male buyers accounted for approximately 56 percent of prostitution-related offences in the mid 1990s, they were less likely to receive incarceration than women convicted of prostitution-related offences (3 percent versus 39 percent) (Duchesne 1997).

The Male "Client"

Xantidis and McCabe (2000) examined the characteristics and motivations of men seeking the services of female sex workers. Sixty-six clients and 60 non-clients completed a questionnaire assessing sex roles, social-sexual effectiveness, and sensation-seeking behaviour. In terms of demographics, the clients and non-clients were similar in age, education, marital status, and occupation. Clients were significantly less likely to subscribe to a feminine sex-role orientation, they had lower social-sexual effectiveness, and had higher sensation-seeking behaviours. In terms of motivation to visit sex workers, the client group appeared to partition into two separate groups: one group had low social-sexual effectiveness and seemed motivated to visit sex workers because they desired interpersonal intimacy, and the other had a high level of sensation seeking and seemed motivated to visit sex workers because they wanted novelty and variety in sexual encounters.

A Profile of the Adolescent Prostitute

Many children and adolescents who run away from home end up using prostitution as a means for survival (Mathews 1987). (See Chapter 11 for a discussion of feminist pathways that focuses on the link between abuse at home and later criminal behaviour for runaway girls.) Research on youth prostitution suggests that many were abused sexually (Bagley and Young 1987) and physically (Silbert 1982). Their homes were often plagued with poor family relations (Mathews 1987), inter-parental violence (Silbert 1982), parental alcohol abuse (Silbert1982), adolescent alcohol and/or drug use (Silbert 1980; 1982), and low self-esteem (Bracey 1979). Much of the research did not include comparison groups, however. Nadon, Koverola, and Schludermann (1998) sought to compare youth prostitutes with youth non-prostitutes. They found that compared to non-prostitute youth, the adolescent prostitutes were classified as runaways more frequently and used a wider variety of drugs, whereas the non-prostitute youth had experienced more childhood physical abuse. The characteristics reported in previous research, although present in adolescent prostitutes, did not differ significantly from adolescent non-prostitutes.

Human Trafficking

Human trafficking is the recruitment, transportation, or harbouring of persons by means of threat, use of force, or other forms of coercion; abduction, fraud, or deception for the purpose of exploitation. Trafficked females are often sexually exploited and frequently lured by individuals known to them or their families with promises of jobs as waitresses, nannies, or cleaners, then forced into sex work or exploited while working. Women risk abuse and exploitation as prostitutes for up to 18 hours a day, 7 days a week, until they repay so-called travel debts to regain their passports from their captors/employers. The trafficking of women and adolescents is increasingly recognized as one of the world's fastest-growing crimes and a significant violation of human rights. The RCMP estimates that 800 persons are trafficked into Canada each year. Using data from non-governmental agencies, however, this figure is closer to 16 000 persons. On an international scale, some sources suggest that there are approximately 4 million girls and women sold for prostitution, slavery, or forced marriage every year.

Bill C-49 (section 279.01—279.04) created three new indictable criminal offences to specifically address trafficking in persons:

Section 279.01 prohibits anyone from recruiting, transporting, transferring, receiving, holding, concealing, or harbouring a person, or exercising control or influence over the movements of a person for the purpose of exploiting or facilitating the exploitation of that person. The maximum penalty for trafficking involving the kidnapping, aggravated assault, aggravated sexual assault, or death of an individual is life in prison.

Section 279.02 prohibits anyone from receiving a financial or other material benefit for the purpose of committing or facilitating the trafficking of a person, with a maximum penalty of 10 years.

Section 279.03 prohibits the withholding or destruction of documents such as a victim's travel documents or documents establishing their identity for the purpose of committing or facilitating the trafficking of that person (maximum penalty: five years).

Under the new federal legislation, charges were laid against an acupuncture centre in 2005. The defendant was charged with bringing women into Canada under false pretences and forcing them into prostitution (Treasury Board of Canada 2006).

The changes to the *Criminal Code* also allow for charges against Canadians who go to other countries to seek child prostitution (known as **sex tourism**). The first such charge occurred in 2004 against a British Columbia man who travelled to Cambodia for child prostitution. A married father, he filmed himself having sex with young children (the oldest was a 12-year-old girl). He was charged with sexual interference, sexual touching, and soliciting the services of a girl under the age of 18 (The Associated Press 2005). Law-enforcement agencies also can charge tour operators or travel agents who arrange for such services (Criminal Intelligence Service of Canada 2002). The B.C. man pled not guilty, arguing that Canada could not lawfully prosecute citizens for behaviour they engaged in in other countries. In 2005, he changed his plea to guilty of 10 counts of sexual assault and received a 10-year prison sentence.

Organized crime groups are involved in prostitution, human trafficking, and the drug trade. We will discuss organized crime in greater detail later in the chapter.

The Effects on Human Trafficked Women
Zimmerman et al. 2008 surveyed 192 women ranging in age from 15 to 45 years who were entering services following their trafficking. All had been sexually exploited. Almost all (95 percent) reported being sexually and/or physically abused while being trafficked, and 59 percent had been abused prior to being trafficked. Twelve percent had a forced or coerced sexual experience before 15 years of age. Three-quarters of the females reported having had personal freedoms restricted and had not been able to do what or go where they wished. The respondents were asked about 26 physical symptoms experienced in the previous two weeks, rating the intensity of each symptom. The most common were:

- Headaches (82 percent)
- Feeling easily tired (81 percent)
- Dizzy spells (70 percent)
- Back pain (69 percent)

- Memory problems (62 percent)
- Stomach pain (61 percent)
- Pelvic pain (59 percent)
- Gynaecological infections (58 percent)

Depression was often reported, with 39 percent reporting suicidal thoughts within the previous seven days.

Treatment/Support for Sex-Trade Workers

Women working in the sex trade may experience violence, substance abuse, physical and mental health issues, and homelessness. In order to address these issues, a group of Victoria, B.C., sex-trade workers formed the PEERS program (Prostitutes Empowerment Education and Resource Society) in 1995 (Rabinovitch and Strega 2004). PEERS is based on four principles:

1. Choice: PEERs supports both women who want to get out of the sex trade and those who want to continue working within it. PEERS focuses on providing sex-trade workers with concrete, practical, and accessible help without judgment.

2. Capacity building: Recognizing the strengths of sex workers (e.g., communication and interpersonal skills, adaptability, ability to work under pressure, experience with difficult clients, and the ability to negotiate). Capacity building includes employee therapy, counselling, and chemical dependency treatment.

3. Harm reduction: Provides a variety of programs for people who are actively in addiction and working regularly in the trade.

4. Trust: Peer-led services. Sex-trade workers design and deliver their own services.

Through PEERS, sex-trade workers may become empowered to make choices in their best interests. Some workers will choose to remain in the profession and others may choose to leave and enter mainstream employment.

THE DRUG TRADE

GENERALLY OPERATED BY ORGANIZED CRIME GROUPS, THE DRUG TRADE GENERATES GREATER profits than any other trafficked commodity. Requests to deliver drugs, however, occur at an individual level (Vale and Kennedy 2004). Drugs may hidden in luggage, in personal belongings, or swallowed or stuffed into body cavities. Harper and Murphy (2000) undertook an analysis of 1715 adult drug traffickers caught smuggling drugs into Heathrow airport between 1991 and 1997. They found that the majority were male (72 percent), and the most common method of smuggling was in luggage (32 percent).

Street value is used when estimating the revenue potential of drugs seized by law-enforcement agencies. In 2006, drug seizures in Canada were estimated at $2.3 billion. Table 6.2 illustrates the amount of drugs seized by Canadian law-enforcement agencies that year and their potential proceeds at street level. The lowest street prices were used for calculations. Box 6.4 describes the legalization of an illegal drug—marijuana.

Money generated from drug sales is typically laundered. **Money laundering** is the process whereby money received through illegal activity is disguised to mask where it came from. Money from drug deals can be laundered by wiring it in small amounts to off-shore accounts or using legitimate businesses (such as restaurants) that produce large amounts of cash to combine legitimate and illegitimate funds.

Table 6.2 Potential Drug Proceeds from Seized Drugs in 2006

Drug Type	Units	Price/unit (CAN$)	Proceeds
Cannabis plant	1 749 057 plants	$1000	$1 749 057 000
Cannabis herb	13 154 057 grams	$10	$131 540 750
Hashish	27 730 066 grams	$10	$277 300 660
Hashish oil	1 060 511 grams	$10	$10 605 110
Opium	124 683 grams	$30	$3 740 490
Heroin	93 246 grams	$180	$16 784 280
Cocaine	2 676 000 grams	$40	$107 040 000
MDMA/Ecstasy	65 505 grams	$200	$13 101 000
	3 000 347 units	$5	$15 001 735
Methamphetamine	58 506 grams	$70	$4 095 420
Khat (Catha Edulis)	13 917 012 grams	$0.50	$6 958 506
	1262 bundle	$25	$31 550
Total			$2 335 256 501

Source: RCMP (2006)

Box 6.4

When Marijuana Isn't Illegal

Marijuana plant

Although cannabis (marijuana) has been used for medicinal purposes for over 4000 years in some cultures, its medicinal use in Canada has been legal for less than 10. Health Canada provides access to marijuana for sufferers of serious and debilitating illnesses, including cancer, HIV/AIDS, multiple sclerosis, arthritis, epilepsy, and glaucoma. Its medical use is regulated by the Marihuana Medical Access Regulations (MMAR). It is estimated that 400 000 Canadian adults use marijuana for medicinal purposes (Ogborne, Smart, and Adlaf 2000).

The history of the legalization of medicinal marijuana in Canada occurred according to the following timeline:

- June 1999: The health minster tables a plan for the use of marijuana medicinally.

- December 2000: A plant in Saskatoon receives a five-year $5.75-million contract to grow marijuana for medicinal purposes.

- July 2001: Health Canada implements the Marihuana Medical Access Regulations

Continued >

(MMAR), making Canada the first country in the world to allow citizens to legally access marijuana for medicinal purposes.

- September 2002: Recommendations are put forth to amend the MMAR to establish new rules regarding eligibility, production, and distribution of medicinal marijuana.

- August 2003: Health Canada distributes the first batch of medicinal marijuana. Consumers are unsatisfied with the quality.

- December 2003: Amendments are made to MMAR.

- May 2004: The second batch of medicinal marijuana is distributed.

- November 2004: The third batch is released, with more changes.

- February 2005: The *Income Tax Act* allows medicinal marijuana expenses as an eligible medical tax credit.

- March 2005: The fourth batch of medicinal marijuana, with greater potency, is distributed.

- April 2005: Sativex, a new drug with many of the same properties as marijuana, is approved for relief of neuro-pathic pain. Canada is the first country to approve it.

- September 2005: A pilot project for pharmacies to distribute medicinal marijuana is introduced. Canada is the second country, after the Netherlands, with this access. (Medical Marijuana Information Resource Centre 2009)

Because medicinal marijuana is authorized, does this mean you can smoke it anywhere? The federal government must clarify the rules regarding the possession and consumption of medical marijuana in order to avoid human rights complaints. Federal medical marijuana regulations conflict with Ontario's liquor laws. Recent legal cases involve complaints from medical users who allege discrimination after being forbidden from smoking marijuana outside pubs and restaurants. In February 2009, Ted Kindros, owner of Ted's Tap and Grill in Burlington, faced a human rights complaint for asking a medical marijuana smoker not to light up outside his business. Kindros feared losing his liquor licence given that the rules for both conflict. The federal government is now considering its next steps. Should authorized marijuana smokers be allowed to smoke with cigarette smokers in designated areas?

ORGANIZED CRIME

A "CRIMINAL ORGANIZATION" IS DEFINED IN SECTION 467.1 OF THE *CRIMINAL CODE* as a group "that 1) is composed of three or more persons in or outside Canada; and 2) has as one of its main purposes or activities the facilitation or commission of one or more serious offences that, if committed, would likely result in the direct or indirect receipt of material benefit, including financial benefit, by the group or by any of the persons who constitute the group." This definition does not include a group of individuals who come together randomly to commit a single offence.

The Criminal Intelligence Service of Canada (CISC) estimates that there were approximately 900 organized crime groups in Canada in 2008. A number of groups exist with varying presence, including:

- Outlaw motorcycle gangs
- Asian-based groups
- Italian-based (or traditional) groups
- Aboriginal-based groups
- Eastern European-based groups
- Street gangs
- Columbian groups
- Latino groups
- Haitian groups
- Lebanese groups
- South American groups
- Japanese (Yakuza) organizations
- Quebecois groups
- Indo-Canadian groups
- Nigerian groups
- Jamaican groups
- Somali organizations

CISC (2008) identified the following as cornerstones to organized crime in Canada:

1. The British Columbia lower mainland, southern Ontario, and greater Montreal contain both the largest concentrations of criminal groups and the most active criminal markets. The illegal drug trade remains the largest criminal market in terms of extent, scope, and the degree of involvement by most organized crime networks.

2. Any impact that law enforcement has in disbanding organized crime networks is short-lived. These organizations can quickly regroup in response to consumer demand.

3. Most organized crime networks have international affiliations, ensuring that the supply and distribution chains for several commodities remain strong. In addition, strategically located areas on the Canada/United States border provide significant opportunities for the movement of illegal commodities and/or people without requiring large or sophisticated operations.

4. Organized crime groups infiltrate and exploit legitimate businesses, laundering money, facilitating criminal activity (i.e., through import and export companies), co-mingling licit and illicit goods, and further protecting organized crime networks from legal action.

Organized Crime Operations

How do organized crime networks work? How do they remain strong and stable? A number of methods are used to increase profitability, expand power bases, and protect against criminal charges. Some crime groups have a hierarchy and a core membership, but more often these groups are fluid, working competitively or collaboratively among various networks. The following methods are used to gain a competitive advantage in the criminal marketplace (CISC 2008):

Violence and Intimidation   Violence and intimidation are used both externally against criminal rivals and internally to maintain discipline. Lower-level criminal groups may pose a more immediate and direct public safety threat through acts of violence that are often carried out in public places. These groups are largely but not entirely composed of street gangs, some of which have committed assaults or shootings in public places across the country. In some instances, intimidation is used against individuals and their communities to silence witnesses to crimes.

Critical Skills   Organized crime groups use and manipulate individuals or organizations with critical skills that are necessary to facilitate certain crimes (i.e., securities fraud, counterfeiting, mortgage fraud, etc.). Skilled outsiders are either recruited or coerced into provision of these services. For instance, organized crime groups often exploit financial professionals such as accountants, bank representatives, and lawyers to facilitate fraud or the movement of money through different stages of the money-laundering process.

Money Laundering   Lower-level criminal groups conduct simpler money-laundering processes, including the use of cash-intensive businesses (e.g., restaurants), casinos, currency exchanges, and the purchase of luxury goods. Higher-level criminal groups insulate themselves through more complex methods such as real estate ventures and off-shore investment opportunities, which exploit weaknesses in the global financial regulatory and reporting systems. Criminal groups also use both legitimate and shell companies to launder money, which allows for the co-mingling of funds, provides the appearance of legitimacy, and insulates groups from detection.

Organized Crime and Fraud

Organized crime groups engage in a number of fraud activities.

Mass Marketing Fraud   Organized crime groups in Canada target Canadians and consumers in other countries, including the United States and Australia. Top mass-marketing fraud schemes include prize/sweepstakes/lottery and gift schemes, Internet auctions, and vacation giveaways. Canadian mass-marketing fraud grosses over $500 million annually. Canadians are also targeted by foreign fraudsters from approximately 105 countries.

Mortgage Fraud   Organized crime groups operate a number of schemes involving fraudulent mortgage applications that contain false information about the prospective buyer or property through the use of false appraisals and employment records. Organized groups may recruit family members to submit fraudulent mortgage applications to avoid detection.

Payment Card Fraud   Information is transferred from point-of-sale terminals to vehicles nearby and almost instantly transferred to "card factories" (locations where payment cards are manufactured illegally), which can be located anywhere in the world. This presents a lucrative market for organized crime.

Contraband Tobacco Illegal cigarettes are primarily supplied by organized crime groups based in Ontario and Quebec. It is estimated that approximately 22 percent of the cigarettes smoked in Canada are illegal. Of these, some are legitimately manufactured, smuggled, and illicitly sold through Aboriginal reserves.

Intellectual Property Rights Crime Ever been tempted to buy a fake designer bag or watch? Organized crime groups are involved in the illegal import of counterfeit goods into Canada, mainly from China. Sometimes these fakes are difficult to detect and make their way into the legitimate market without the supplier or customer knowing. Counterfeit goods are sold on the Internet and through classified ad sites.

Vehicle-Related Crime Primarily in Toronto and Montreal, organized crime groups are involved in the theft of vehicles, changing VIN numbers once obtained. These cars can be exported or disassembled and the parts resold. Few vehicles are exported internationally. Some organized crime groups are involved in staging collisions for insurance fraud.

Identity Theft and Fraud This area is a highly profitable endeavour for organized crime groups with low potential for detection. Not all identity theft and fraud is committed by organized groups, however; some fraud occurs independently.

Lower-level criminal groups are usually involved in activities related to identity theft, and mid- to higher-level groups are generally involved in identity fraud.

Organized Crime and the Sex Trade

A number of the organized crime networks have been involved in the sex trade for decades. Involvement has evolved from street-level pimping (characteristic of the mid 1990s) to more organized networks that operate out of strip bars, massage parlours, hotel/motels, the Internet, and private residences. The majority of street gang networks are found in Ontario, Quebec, Nova Scotia, and New Brunswick. Organized crime groups traffic Canadian-born women and underage girls within provinces, across provinces, and to the United States (for the sex trade).

Middle-class females between the ages of 12 and 25 are typically recruited by males of the same age who are members of street gangs and promise affection to lure victims. They may have been specifically recruited by organized crime networks for this job. Females already under the organized crime network's control can also play a role in the recruitment and grooming of young females for prostitution. Recruitment strategies are constantly changing, and girls may be lured overseas by false modelling opportunities that result in their exploitation in the sex trade. Trafficked females are controlled by the use of direct force (abduction, rape, forcible confinement, assault) and indirect forms of coercion, such as controlling where they live, work, and with whom they associate, and the threatening of family members. In addition, the women may have nightly quotas to meet and a set fee to pay if they wish to leave the trade. Their personal items and documents may be confiscated. Women are often provided with false identification, allowing underaged girls to work in strip bars (and making detection of adolescent missing persons and runaways difficult). Victims can be traded or sold between criminal groups and may be used to contact customers for additional criminal activities, such as cocaine trafficking. The frequent movement of prostitutes by organized crime networks is designed to isolate females, facilitate the creation and adherence to new loyalties (typically replacing the traditional family), and enable pimps to meet the customer demand for new faces.

The national range for profits derived from prostitution ranges from $300–$1500 daily per prostitute, with an average of $900. Based on average daily revenues and number of prostitutes, Table 6.3 illustrates projected daily, weekly, and annual profits earned by organized crime networks from prostitution in Canada (CISC 2008). The women involved receive clothing, food, and lodging, and are often moved from street level to strip bars and escort agencies that generate higher revenues and reduce visibility, minimizing public complaints. Prostitution may take place in private residences or motels.

Organized Crime and the Drug Trade

The most trafficked illegal drug in Canada is marijuana, with extensive organized crime involvement at all levels of production, distribution, and exportation. Canada is a source country for marijuana, meeting significant domestic and U.S. cross-border demand. British Columbia, Ontario, and Quebec are the primary locations for the production and distribution to domestic and U.S. markets.

Cocaine also constitutes a major drug market and is imported by organized crime groups directly from source countries, particularly Peru, or through transit countries such as the Dominican Republic, Guyana, Jamaica, and Mexico. Inter-provincial distribution of cocaine is coordinated from British Columbia, Ontario, and Quebec, where it is sold at

Table 6.3 Projected Daily, Weekly, and Annual Revenue for Organized Crime Networks from Prostitution

No. of Prostitutes	Daily Profit	Weekly Profit	Profit Annually
1	$900	$5400	$280 800
5	$4500	$31 500	$1 638 000
10	$9000	$63 000	$3 276 000
15	$13 500	$94 500	$4 914 000
20	$18 000	$126 000	$6 552 000
25	$22 500	$157 500	$8 190 000
30	$27 000	$189 000	$8 282 000
35	$31 500	$220 500	$11 466 000
40	$36 000	$252 000	$13 104 000

Source: Criminal Intelligence Service Canada (2008)

the wholesale level to criminal groups that subsequently sell it to retail distributors. Crack, a derivative of cocaine, is concentrated in urban centres across Canada. Because the drug effects are short-lived, users often engage in low-level property crimes, robbery, and crimes against persons to pay for the drug. The majority of the criminal groups involved in crack cocaine are street gangs, who distribute primarily from street corners, crack houses, and "dial-a-dope" (a system used to sell illicit drugs by responding to requests placed to a series of disposable cell phones).

Consumer demand for heroin is relatively low in Canada. As such, a limited number of organized crime groups, mainly in British Columbia and Ontario, are involved in the heroin market, importing heroin primarily from Southwest Asia and Latin America. Organized crime groups in Canada are also involved in the Ecstasy market, methamphetamine production, and opium. Canadians are among the heaviest consumers of pharmaceutical opiates in the world. In fact, in some communities, heroin use is being replaced with prescription drugs such as Oxycodone (e.g., OxyContin) and Hydromorphone (e.g., Dilaudid). Several organized crime groups, particularly in Atlantic Canada, distribute prescription opiate drugs.

The Role of Street Gangs in Organized Crime

Organized crime groups may seek street gangs to carry out various criminal acts (e.g., drug running). Those committing the acts provide a buffer between the organized crime group and law enforcement. Members of street gangs may also be recruited to join organized crime groups. If particular street gang members are successful at the "jobs" handed down from organized crime groups, then they may be recruited or "promoted." Not all street gangs are linked to organized crime, however. A common characteristic of street gang members is that they live in one geographic area, contained within a few blocks of each other. Street gangs may commit violence against rival gangs and be territorial when competing for drug revenues. In contrast, a group of youth who join together occasionally would not be considered a true street gang with organized crime group affiliations.

Many organized crime groups are involved in the drug trade. The individuals involved may or may not have drug abuse problems. It is not uncommon for substance abusers to engage in economic crimes, such as theft and prostitution, to "feed" their drug habits.

SUBSTANCE ABUSE

Substance Abuse among Offenders

Offenders fall under the governance of the Correctional Service of Canada (CSC). CSC provides standardized assessments of offenders to ensure that the same measures are used across the country. These assessments facilitate decision making for the best programming and treatment for each offender. The Computerized Assessment of Substance Abuse (CASA) was implemented in 2002 to assess its utility with offenders. Nine hundred and seven male offenders admitted into federal custody between 2002 and 2004 pilot-tested the CASA (Kunic and Grant 2006). Seven components of substance abuse are measured: 1) alcohol; 2) drug abuse severity; 3) patterns of use; 4) links to criminal behaviour; 5) parental substance abuse; 6) previous participation in programs; and 7) treatment readiness. Severity of substance abuse is also assessed using the Alcohol Dependence Scale (ADS), the Drug Abuse Screening Test (DAST), and the Problems Related to Drinking Scale (PRD).

The pilot program results indicated that 5 percent of the offenders had a severe substance abuse problem, 16 percent had a substantial problem, 15 percent had a moderate problem, 32 percent had a low-level problem, and 31 percent had no substance abuse problems. The most commonly used drugs during the 12 months prior to the offenders' arrests were cannabinoids (e.g., marijuana) (52 percent), cocaine (26 percent), and opioids (13 percent). The CASA was found to accurately differentiate between levels of abuse among offenders. Dr. John Weekes is a psychologist who has studied substance abuse problems with offenders and is an advocate for measures used by CSC; namely, CASA, ADS, and DAST. Box 6.5 discusses Dr. Weekes and his research.

Compared to offenders with lower severity levels, offenders with higher severity levels on the ADS and DAST were strongly associated with substance use and impairment at the time they committed the offence. Increased aggression at the time of offence was related to alcohol impairment but not drug impairment. Property offences were more closely related to drug impairment than alcohol impairment.

Box 6.5

Canadian Researcher Profile: Dr. John Weekes

Dr. John Weekes is a leading researcher in substance abuse issues, having worked almost exclusively in this area since 1993. His research has explored the nature and dynamics of offenders' use of alcohol and other drugs as well as the relationship between substance abuse and criminal behaviour. Dr. Weekes gets excited when he hears about issues that can be resolved by research. Fortunately for the criminal justice system, he feels driven to find answers.

Dr. Weekes subscribes to social psychological explanations for criminal conduct, not surprising given his training as a cognitive-social psychologist. Over the years, he has undertaken much research using the Alcohol Dependence Scale and the Drug Abuse Screening Test. These instruments are an integral part of the Computerized Assessment of Substance Abuse instrument used by CSC. Dr. Weekes states that he is continually impressed by the accuracy of these instruments in measuring offender alcohol and drug use. "They are brief, behaviourally oriented measures that really capture problematic substance use." Recently, he switched gears, moving from researcher to administrator. "I never thought that I'd like managing researchers and their activities as opposed to doing the research myself. But I do really like the new role." In terms of training future researchers interested in forensic psychology and criminal behaviour, Dr. Weekes believes Canada has been at the cutting edge of criminal justice research since the late 1980s and thinks that expanding the number of related academic programs in

Box 6.5 Continued

Canada will benefit future generations of forensic researchers and practitioners. He enjoys teaching introductory psychology classes, where he imparts his enthusiasm and excitement about forensic psychology to new students. He is committed to teaching and actively encourages students' questions, comments, and class participation.

Dr. Weekes relaxes with his favourite pastime, aviation. He received his private pilot's license at age 17. When not working, he can be found in his workshop, building or repairing model airplanes. He lives with his wife and children in Ottawa.

Women Who Abuse Drugs

A recent study examined the life histories of 28 drug-abusing women from low-income neighbourhoods in New York City (Miller and Neaigus 2002). The women were 18 years or older and were users of heroin (79 percent), crack (43 percent), or cocaine (21 percent). Of interest to the researchers was how the women financed their drug use. Most reported engaging in illegal activities to acquire money and/or drugs. Seventy-five percent reported working in the drug trade, 68 percent stole, and 68 percent worked in the street-based prostitution. In addition, 79 percent of the women had sex partners who would provide financial compensation and/or other benefits (i.e., drug supply). Eighty-nine percent of women had been arrested for drug offences. Overall, the vast majority of the respondents financed their illegal drug use by illegal means.

Substance Abuse Programs

CSC is responsible for drug treatment programming for offenders. With 70 percent of offenders experiencing some level of substance abuse, CSC provides national substance abuse programs that constitute a component of a larger drug strategy to combat abuse and related difficulties. The National Substance Abuse Program (NSAP) is designed to help offenders alter their substance problems and criminal behaviour. The techniques employed in the program are directed at helping offenders better manage the situations that may trigger a relapse into crime and/or substance abuse.

NSAP is based on an integrated theoretical model, where substance abuse problems occur for many reasons but can be explained by the principles of learning to some degree. It is believed that substance abuse is poor coping for ongoing challenges in life. Behaviour is begun and maintained by previous learning experiences, including peer modelling, reinforcement, cognitive expectations or beliefs, and biological factors. Using this model, substance abuse is treated as a learned behaviour that can be changed to behaviour that is more positive and provides offenders with better coping mechanisms to daily stressors. Programs are offered at a range of intensity levels: low, moderate, and high. In addition, specialized programs are available for women and Aboriginal offenders with substance problems.

Using an offender's CASA information, in addition to their ADS and DAST scores, offenders are referred to the appropriate level of intensity of NSAP. It is important to note that in order for an offender to be referred to NSAP, their substance abuse must have been directly involved in their current offence. Offenders scoring within the substantial to severe range using CASA are referred to the "high" level NSAP. Offenders scoring in the moderate to substantial range using CASA are referred to the "moderate" NSAP, and those scoring in the low range are deemed not to require any substance abuse programming. Chapter 4 includes a greater discussion of the risk-need principle. Figure 6.1 illustrates the need level of offenders as a function of CASA and its relation to NSAP.

Each year, approximately 3000 offenders participate in NSAP. CSC reports that recidivism rates decrease up to 50 percent for offenders who complete the substance abuse program (CSC 2006).

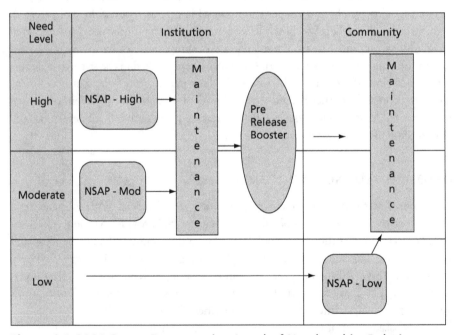

Figure 6.1 CASA Scores Representing Level of Need and its Relation to NSAP Intensity

Source: Correctional Service of Canada (2009)

Drug Treatment Courts

Drug courts provide defendants who have not committed a violent offence with an alternative to traditional courts and jail sentences. Drug courts are used for various charges where drugs are involved either because of addiction (e.g., drug possession, possession for the purposes of trafficking) or because being under the influence of a drug led to the commitment of the offence. For example, a drug addict may commit theft in order to use the money generated to purchase drugs to feed his or her habit. In most drug courts, the defendant must plead guilty before entering the program.

Drug courts have the following objectives:

1. Reduce crime committed as a result of drug dependency through court-monitored treatment and community service support for offenders.
2. Reduce the cost of substance abuse on the Canadian economy (estimated at $9 billion for law enforcement, prosecution, and incarceration)

Drug courts have the following characteristics:

1. Offenders participate in a structured outpatient program where they attend both individual and group counselling sessions, receive appropriate medical attention (such as methadone treatment), and are tested randomly for drugs.
2. Offenders make regular court appearances, where a judge reviews their progress and can either impose sanctions (ranging from verbal reprimands to expulsion from the program) or provide rewards (ranging from verbal praise to fewer court appearances).
3. Staff associated with drug courts coordinate with community partners to address offenders' needs, such as housing and employment. Once an offender has conquered their addiction, criminal charges are either stayed (i.e., suspended or postponed) or the offender receives a non-custodial sentence (i.e., house arrest). If unsuccessful, an offender will be sentenced as part of the regular court process.

In 1998, Toronto was the first city in Canada to enact a drug court. In 2001, an additional court was established in Vancouver. Four other cities have since followed suit: Edmonton, Winnipeg, Ottawa, and Regina. Approximately $3.4 million is spent on drug courts in Canada annually.

Do Drug Treatment Courts Work? The drug courts in Vancouver and Toronto have been evaluated for effectiveness (Devlin et al. 2006). In Vancouver, only 14 percent of offenders completed the program, another 65 percent withdrew from the program voluntarily, and approximately 20 percent were asked to leave. More than half of all participants (52 percent) incurred new charges within six months of participating. Thirty percent of participants who completed the program tested positive for cocaine or heroin within six months of completion. Unfortunately, there were no significant reductions in new charges and convictions between program participants and the comparison group. When comparing participants who had completed the program with participants who had been asked to withdraw or left voluntarily, program completers had significantly fewer new charges and convictions compared to non-completers (10 percent versus 35 percent, after six months). In terms of cost analysis, it was estimated that for offenders who had completed the program, participating in the drug court was more cost efficient ($22 248) than the processing of the comparison group through traditional courts ($26 737).

The results from the Toronto evaluation were more encouraging. Approximately 16 percent of offenders completed the drug treatment court. Graduates failed to make about 25 percent of required court appearances, in contrast to 50 percent for participants who had left the program and 90 percent of participants who had been asked to leave. On a very positive note, less than 15 percent of graduates reoffended, compared to 90 percent of comparison clients. Overall, drug courts appear to face the challenge of low graduation rates. For participants that succeed, the courts show promise at reducing recidivism.

Below is a list of top 10 issues and people to consider when thinking about economic crime in Canada.

Top 10 List

Advances to Come, Debates, Ethical Conundrums, and People to Watch

1. Marijuana is legal in Canada for medicinal purposes. Should approved users be allowed to smoke marijuana alongside cigarette smokers in designated public places?

2. Sex-trade workers may experience abuse at the hands of those who profit from their trade. Would the legalization of prostitution reduce abuse against sex-trade workers?

3. White-collar criminals often pose a greater cost to the community than street criminals. Should they serve the same sentences in the same facilities as street criminals?

4. Many offenders have substance abuse problems. If substance abuse is managed, would we see a reduction in the national crime rate?

5. Some of the data on drug courts is only modestly encouraging. Should the justice system continue with their use?

6. Organized crime networks have a stronghold on many illicit activities, including the drug trade. Would the legalization of drugs eliminate or reduce the number of organized crime networks in Canada?

7. Many women are trafficked into Canada. Should they be allowed to stay and become Canadian citizens?

8. In a recent case, a Canadian male argued that he should not be prosecuted in Canada for engaging in the sexual exploitation of young girls in another country. Should the Canadian government have the power to prosecute Canadians who commit crimes in other countries?

9. We often throw out our garbage with discarded mail containing vital

information that can be used for identity theft. Should going through someone's garbage be illegal? (Currently it is not.)

10 Names to watch: John Weekes has participated in a number of reports regarding the assessment and treatment of offenders addicted to various illegal substances. His work provides insight into the state of substance abuse programs for offenders in Canada.

SUMMARY

1. White-collar crime is partitioned into occupational crime versus corporate crime. Occupational crimes are offences committed against businesses and government by those with a "higher" social status. Examples include expense account fraud and tax evasion. In contrast, corporate crimes are committed by organizations to advance their own interests. Corporate crime offences include price fixing. The distinction between occupational and corporate crime can be thought of as occupational crime being focused on individuals and corporate crime being focused on organizations.

2. Theft is the notion of "stealing"; that is, taking something that belongs to someone else. Theft is covered in section 322 of the Canadian *Criminal Code*. There is a demarcation line at $5000 when deciding on punishment for theft. Fraud occurs when deceit or fraudulent means are used to deprive someone of property, money, valuable security, or services. The *Criminal Code* defines fraud in section 380. There are two categories that are similar to theft: fraud under $5000 and fraud over $5000. Many thefts also can be frauds and it is sometimes up to the police to decide whether to charge an offender with fraud or theft.

3. Compared to non-prostitute youth, adolescent prostitutes are classified as runaways more frequently and use a wider variety of drugs, whereas the non-prostitute youth experience more childhood physical abuse. The characteristics reported in previous research, although present in adolescent prostitutes, do not differ significantly from adolescent non-prostitutes. Although adolescent prostitutes have a number of issues (e.g., abuse and poor family relations, low self-esteem), these variables are also present in the adolescent non-prostitutes. Clients are significantly less likely to subscribe to a feminine sex role orientation, have lower social-sexual effectiveness, and have higher sensation seeking tendencies.

4. A "criminal organization" is defined in section 467.1 of the *Criminal Code* as a group that is: 1) composed of three or more persons in or outside of Canada; and 2) has as one of its main purposes or activities the facilitation or commission of one or more serious offences that, if committed, would likely result in the direct or indirect receipt

of material benefit, including financial benefit, by the group or by any of the persons who constitute the group.

5. Organized crime groups engage in fraud, including mass-marketing fraud and intellectual property rights crime, the sex trade (including prostitution and human trafficking), and the drug trade, including the importation and distribution of a variety of drugs such a marijuana and cocaine.

6. The drug trade often involves organized crime groups. Individuals in the drug trade may or may not have drug abuse problems. Those with substance abuse problems may engage in economic crimes such as theft and prostitution to support their drug habits.

7. The core features of drug treatment courts include: 1) they reduce crime committed as a result of drug dependency through court-monitored treatment and community-service support for offenders; 2) they reduce the cost of substance abuse on the Canadian economy; 3) offenders participate in a structured outpatient program where they attend both individual and group counselling sessions, receive appropriate medical attention (such as methadone treatment), and are tested randomly for drugs; 4) offenders make regular court appearances, where a judge reviews their progress and can then either impose sanctions (ranging from verbal reprimands to expulsion from the program) or provide rewards (ranging from verbal praise to fewer court appearances); and 5) staff associated with drug courts coordinate with community partners to address offender needs, such as housing and employment. Once an offender has conquered his or her addiction, criminal charges are either stayed (i.e., suspended or postponed) or the offender receives a non-custodial sentence (i.e., house arrest). If unsuccessful, an offender will be sentenced as part of the regular court process.

Discussion Questions

1. During the summer, you work for a large manufacturing company. You notice that the supply cabinet has many of the supplies (e.g., paper, pens, Post-it notes, binders, etc.) you will need when you go back to school in September. You decide to start taking a few things each week, believing that such a large corporation won't notice the items missing. Debate whether your actions constitute white-collar crime or theft.

2. You volunteer at an after-school drop-in program for teens aged 13 to 16. Many of the teens have difficult home lives. List factors that should be targeted to reduce the likelihood that these teens will run away and become prostitutes.

3. Debate whether the legalization of drugs would reduce drug trafficking.

4. You recently applied for a credit card but were denied. You decide to contact the bank to better understand why your application was rejected. After speaking with the manager, it becomes clear that someone has stolen your identity and applied for numerous credit cards in your name, only to exceed the limit on the cards and then default on payment. What are some strategies to prevent this from happening to others?

5. The current government is uncertain about whether to continue funding for drug treatment courts. Discuss the pros and cons of these courts.

Additional Reading

Babiak, P. and Hare, R. 2007. *Snakes in suits: When psychopaths go to work.* Toronto: HarperCollins Publishers.

Dorais, M. 2008. *Gangs and girls: Understanding juvenile prostitution.* Toronto: McGill-Queen's University Press.

Relevant Websites

Canadian Centre on Substance Abuse
www.ccsa.ca

Street Kids International
www.streetkids.org

Chapter 7
Violent Offending: General Violence and Homicide

Robert: A Persistently Violent Offender

Robert Smith is a 36-year-old fourth-time federal offender currently serving a three-year sentence at Kingston Penitentiary in Ontario. Shortly after his release from his last term of incarceration, he decided to go on "a spree" in which he threatened to kill a man who refused to lend him money; used counterfeit money at a convenience store; broke a window at his ex-girlfriend's house by throwing rocks at it and was found to be in possession of a knife and a toy gun at the time; and threatened to kill a woman. Once taken into custody for these offences, he threatened and assaulted several correctional officers and offenders at various prisons. Robert has a long history of criminal behaviour, including violence. Not counting the offences noted above, he has 32 previous adult and 4 youth convictions. The most serious of these were assaults, weapons offences, armed robbery, and break and enters. Also on his record are numerous thefts, escapes from custody, failures to comply with release conditions (e.g., bail, probation), and failures to appear in court. His past prison sentences were also marked by threats and assaults on correctional officers and inmates; not surprisingly, he has spent a great deal of time in segregation (isolated from other offenders).

Robert grew up in a small town in Ontario. His biological father, who also has a criminal history, left his mother before he was born. He was raised by his biological mother and alcohol-abusing stepfather, who threw Robert out of the family home when he was 11 years old because of his stealing and other disruptive behaviour. He was subsequently placed in a series of group and foster homes, but was removed from each of them as a result of his unmanageable behaviour. At age 16, he robbed two variety stores at knifepoint.

Robert has spent most of his adult life incarcerated and has little in the way of educational or vocational skills or experience. He is impulsive, easily frustrated, and has difficulty focusing his attention. He has worked a total of six months and one week in his entire life. Most of his jobs lasted for only a short time and ended with him being fired (e.g., for sleeping on the job). When not in prison, Robert lives on the street, relies on social assistance, or is taken in for brief periods of time by various women. However, he has never been married and never lived with the same woman for more than a few months. All his friends and associates are involved in crime. Robert's financial situation is chronically poor. He has a history of abusing alcohol and drugs; he is often drunk or high during his criminal offences. Robert holds deeply entrenched antisocial attitudes. Although he says he wants to stop being violent, he perceives it to be rewarding for him in many ways. He says that being aggressive gets him women and money, and generally facilitates his needs. "If I'm going to be a nice guy, people will start egging me on and saying I'm scared and I gotta prove myself."

Learning Objectives

1   Review the prevalence and characteristics of violent offending as well as consequences for victims.

2   Cover some of the major theories of aggression.

3   Introduce some of the key assessment instruments used to estimate risk of violent recidivism and examine their predictive accuracy.

4   Examine the effectiveness of treatment in reducing violent recidivism.

5   Review the prevalence and characteristics of homicide and describe different types of multiple murder.

INTRODUCTION

MUCH OF THE THEORY AND RESEARCH PRESENTED IN PREVIOUS CHAPTERS APPLIES TO violent behaviour. In the opening vignette, Robert's violent behaviour may be explained by his biology (e.g., genes from his criminal father), adverse childhood environment, social disadvantage (e.g., low education and poor employment skills), direct and vicarious learning experiences, beliefs about the costs and benefits of violence relative to prosocial alternatives, antisocial associates, impulsivity, hostility, poor problem-solving ability, or substance abuse. In this chapter we will review the prevalence and characteristics of violence in Canada. We will also present some theories of violent behaviour, the major approaches to risk assessment, some of the more established risk assessment instruments, and research on the predictive accuracy of these instruments. Research on the effectiveness of treatment programs for violent offenders will also be reviewed. Finally, homicide, the most extreme form of violence, will be examined.

DEFINING AGGRESSION AND VIOLENCE

AGGRESSION RESEARCHERS HAVE PROVIDED USEFUL DEFINITIONS OF AGGRESSION AND violence. The terms have a considerable degree of overlap, but they are not synonymous. Human aggression has been defined as "any behavior directed towards another individual that is carried out with the proximate (immediate) intent to cause harm. In addition, the perpetrator must believe that the behavior will harm the target, and that the target is motivated to avoid the behavior" (Anderson and Bushman 2002: 28). Violence has been defined as "aggression that has extreme harm as its goal (e.g., death)" (Anderson and Bushman 2002: 29).

Prevalence of Violence

Violent crime accounts for approximately one in eight criminal incidents in Canada (Dauvergne 2008). The rate of violent crime reported to the police (**Uniform Crime Reporting Survey**) in 2007 was 930 per 100 000 people. As illustrated in Figure 7.1, this rate has decreased since the early 1990s. Interestingly, in 2007, the lowest rate was in Ontario (5228 per 100 000 people) and the highest was in Saskatchewan (13 225 per 100 000 people) (Dauvergne 2008).

Robbery is often considered a violent offence because it involves at the very least an implied threat of violence. The robbery rate for Canada in 2007 was 90 per 100 000 people. In 2007, 11 percent of all robberies involved a firearm, whereas 60 percent involved no weapon. Of all Canadian provinces, PEI had the lowest rate of robbery in 2007 (11 per 100 000 people) and Manitoba had the highest (179 per 100 000 people). Robbery rates have decreased since the early 1990s, as shown in Figure 7.2. This is the case for armed robbery involving a firearm or some other weapon. However, robbery without a weapon has increased slightly.

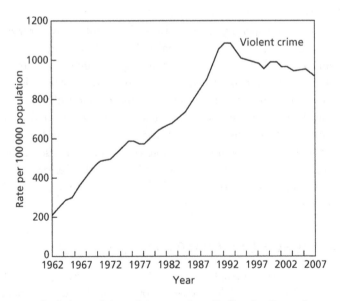

Figure 7.1 Rate of Violent Crime Reported to Police in Canada

Source: Dauvergne (2008)

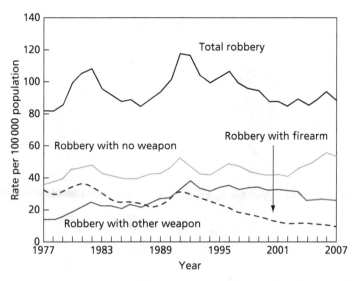

Figure 7.2 Rates of Robbery Reported to Police in Canada

Source: Dauvergne (2008)

In contrast to decreases observed in other types of crime, violent crime by youth (aged 12 to 17) has increased fairly steadily over the past 20 years, as shown in Figure 7.3. The rate of violent crime reported by youth in 2007 was 6811 per 100 000 people.

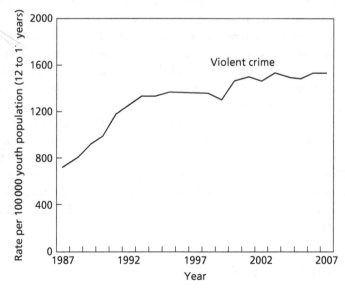

Figure 7.3 Rate of Violent Crime by Youth Reported to Police in Canada

Source: Dauvergne (2008)

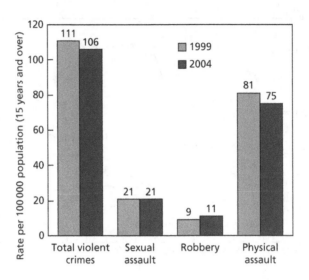

Figure 7.4 Self-Reported Rates of Violent Victimization in Canada
Source: Gannon and Mihorean (2005)

Crime reported to the police is an underestimate of the actual number of violent incidents. For a variety of reasons, some violent incidents do not come to the attention of the authorities. The **General Social Survey (GSS) on Victimization** reflects reports from the Canadian population aged 15 and older on their criminal victimization. According to the most recent GSS, which was administered in 2004, only 33 percent of violent incidents were reported to the police (Gannon and Mihorean 2005). The reporting rates were highest for robbery (46 percent), followed by physical assaults (39 percent) and sexual assaults (8 percent). There are a number of reasons why victims may or may not report violent crimes. Reporting to the police was more likely in incidents involving physical injury (47 percent) compared to no physical injury (28 percent), and for incidents involving weapons (53 percent) compared to no weapons (25 percent). The most common reasons given for not reporting crimes were that the victim dealt with the incident in another way (60 percent), it was not important enough (53 percent), did not want police involved (42 percent), felt it was a personal matter (39 percent), did not think police involvement could help (29 percent), or for fear of retaliation from perpetrator (11 percent).

The rates of violent victimization did not change dramatically from the preceding GSS, administered in 1999, to the most current, as illustrated in Figure 7.4 (Gannon and Mihorean, 2005).

Victim Characteristics

The rates of violent victimization were quite similar for men and women: 111 per 1000 men versus 102 per 1000 women in 2004 (Gannon and Mihorean 2005). However, differences between men's and women's victimization become apparent when the type of

between hostile and instrumental aggression that helps smooth out some difficulties in categorizing different types of aggression. Specifically, they conceptualize both hostile and instrumental aggression as characterized by the intention to harm at the proximate level, and differing in their goals primarily at the ultimate level. So in the example above, the man assaulting his wife's lover would still be defined as an instance of hostile aggression. However, a hired assassin who murders someone for money would more easily be classified as a case of instrumental aggression: his proximate goal is clearly to harm the victim, but the ultimate goal of his aggression is to receive payment.

Operationally defining hostile and instrumental aggression can be challenging. Some acts of aggression may have elements of both types. Consider some recent school shootings, in which the primary goal was clearly to harm victims, but there was considerable planning and preparation, and the specific victims may not have provoked the attack and may not have known the shooter well, if at all. Is this type of violence instrumental or hostile? Vitacco, Neumann, Caldwell, Leistico, and Van Rybroek (2006) developed the Instrumental Aggression Rating Measure to assess the extent to which violence is instrumental versus hostile. The five items below are coded from file information (p. 77):

1. Planning or preparation before the aggression
2. Goal directed—the act helped obtain a specific and identifiable goal (e.g., money)
3. The aggressive behaviour was unprovoked by the victim
4. Lack of anger during the aggression
5. The victim of the aggression was a stranger

Higher ratings on these items would be associated with instrumental aggression. Thus hostile and instrumental aggression may be best viewed as opposite ends of a continuum along which acts of aggression can fall. Violence may be completely hostile, completely instrumental, or fall somewhere in between.

EXPLAINING VIOLENCE

Social Learning Theory

Social learning theory (Bandura 1973) holds, as the name suggests, that aggression is learned (see Chapter 3 for more details). The main tenet is quite simple and parsimonious: aggression is more likely to occur when it is expected to be more rewarding than non-aggressive alternatives. As Bandura (1973: 2) noted:

> Concern over the adverse consequences of aggression obscures the fact that such behaviour often has functional value for the user. Indeed, there is a property unique to aggression that generally creates conditions fostering its occurrence. Unlike other social behaviors that cannot be effective without some reciprocity acceptable to the participants, aggression does not require willing responsiveness from others for its success. One can injure and destroy to self-advantage regardless of whether the victim

likes it or not. By aggressive behaviour, or dominance through physical and verbal force, individuals can obtain valued resources, change rules to fit their own wishes, gain control over and extract subservience from others, eliminate conditions that adversely affect their well-being, and remove barriers that block or delay attainment of desired goals. Thus, behaviour that is punishing for the victim can, at least on a short-term basis, be rewarding for the aggressor.

How is aggression learned? As stated above, expected outcomes influence the likelihood and extent of aggressive behaviour. In operant conditioning, behaviour is shaped by its consequences; that is, reinforcement or punishment. Reinforcement increases the likelihood that a given behaviour will occur, whereas punishment decreases the likelihood of its occurrence. For example, a young child wants another child's toy, but the other child does not want to share it. The child pushes the other child out of the way and takes the toy. Aggression is rewarded by obtaining the toy (positive reinforcement). Alternately, instead of getting the toy, the child's aggression may result in a scolding from their mother (positive punishment). Consider the child who is being made fun of by other children, but is able to silence them by punching one of them. In this case, aggression is rewarded by the removal of some aversive state (negative reinforcement). Alternately, instead of silencing his harassers, the child's aggression may earn him or her exclusion from that day's fun field trip by a teacher who observed the child's behaviour (negative punishment).

Adding to the familiar concept of operant conditioning, Bandura (1973) argued that people learn not only from direct experience, but also from observing the behaviour of others and the outcomes of others' behaviour. Observing others receiving various rewards for their aggression would increase the likelihood that one would engage in similar forms of aggression. In contrast, observing others receiving punishment for their aggression would decrease the likelihood that one would engage in similar forms of aggression. The self is also an important source of reinforcement. Self-reinforcement refers to the influence of self-administered rewards or punishments for aggression. If self-evaluation following aggression is positive, aggression would be more likely than if self-evaluation is negative. For example, following aggression, one person may feel powerful, assertive, and generally quite pleased, whereas another person may be racked with guilt and self-contempt. These reinforcement influences on aggressive behaviour are mediated by cognition, such as one's attention, perception, memory, and resulting expectancies regarding reinforcement.

General Aggression Model (GAM)

The General Aggression Model (GAM) (Anderson and Bushman 2002) is an integration of a number of smaller, more specific theories of aggressive behaviour. Shown in Figure 7.6, the GAM describes the processes involved in any one episode among an ongoing series of episodes of a social encounter. The main components are inputs from the person and situation, the routes (cognitive, affective, and arousal states) that mediate the influence of inputs, and the appraisal and decision processes that lead to a particular action in the episode. The outcome influences the social encounter, which then provides inputs in the

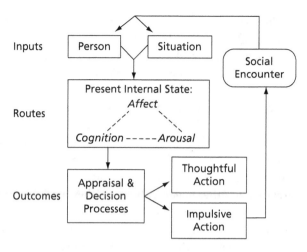

Figure 7.6 The General Aggression Model

Source: Anderson and Bushman (2002)

next episode. Person inputs, such as traits, gender, beliefs, attitudes, values, long-term goals, and behavioural scripts, refer to relatively stable characteristics that individuals bring to any given situation and can predispose one toward or against aggression. Situational inputs can also influence aggression in a given episode. Such factors include aggressive cues, provocation, frustration, pain and discomfort, drugs, and incentives. The routes through which person and situation inputs influence aggression are cognitive, affective, and arousal states. Cognitive states include hostile thoughts and behavioural scripts. Affective states include mood and emotion as well as expressive motor responses. Arousal can influence aggression in a number of ways. For example, high levels of physiological arousal preceding a provocation can be mislabelled as anger, thereby increasing aggressive behaviour. Note that cognition, affect, and arousal are all interconnected in the GAM and each may influence the other. For example, hostile thoughts (cognition) may increase feelings of anger (affect). Some of the variables may seem to overlap between inputs and routes; for example, scripts are listed as both a person factor and a cognitive state. However, scripts as a person factor refer to a relatively stable characteristic (i.e., the presence and level of activation of such a script typical of a given person), whereas scripts as a cognitive state refer to the degree to which a particular behavioural script is activated in a particular situation.

Evolutionary Psychological Perspective

An evolutionary perspective on criminal violence has been championed for quite some time by Dr. Vern Quinsey, who is profiled in Box 7.1. As you will recall from Chapter 2, in our ancestral environments certain physiological, psychological, and behavioural characteristics were associated with increased reproductive success (i.e., having a relatively high number of children who in turn have a relatively high number of children, and so on) (Lalumière, Harris, Quinsey, and Rice 2005). To the extent that such characteristics are heritable, the genes responsible for them would be passed on to subsequent generations more so than genes that are responsible for characteristics associated with reproductive failure.

Building on research and theory on general antisocial behaviour (e.g., Harrris, Rice, and Lalumière 2001; Moffitt 1993; Quinsey, Skilling, Lalumière, and Craig 2004), Lalumière et al. (2005) propose that most violent people fall in one of three groups: young men, competitively disadvantaged men, or psychopaths. Adolescent and young men typically have relatively few resources and low status, which puts them at a competitive disadvantage relative to other males with whom they are competing for resources and mates. Through violence and general risk taking, these young men may be able to increase their status, resources, and/or access to more and better mates. However, as they move into adulthood and begin to acquire legitimately gained resources and status, the costs of violence begin to outweigh the benefits, so they switch from short-term high-risk strategies to more long-term lower-risk strategies. So the violent behaviour of this group is limited to adolescence and young adulthood. This is the most common type of violent offender.

This desistance with adulthood, however, does not occur for the competitively disadvantaged men. Their violent behaviour is life-course persistent. The ability to compete for resources and status in prosocial ways is impaired by early neurodevelopmental insults, such as obstetrical complications and low IQ. Because men in this group do not have the skills or abilities to achieve status and resources in prosocial ways, they maintain their high-risk approach into adulthood. The final group, psychopaths, are also life-course-persistent. In contrast to the competitively disadvantaged men, psychopaths are not competitively disadvantaged but select short-term high-risk strategies as an alternate approach. Competitively disadvantaged men and psychopaths are thought to make up a relatively small proportion of violent individuals.

Box 7.1

Canadian Researcher Profile: Dr. Vern Quinsey

Dr. Vern Quinsey is a professor of psychology, biology, and psychiatry at Queen's University in Kingston. He was born in Flin Flon, Manitoba, and completed his B.Sc. with a major in psychology and a minor in zoology at the University of North Dakota at Grand Forks. He then completed his M.Sc. and Ph.D. (just one year after completing his M.Sc.!) in biopsychology at the University of Massachusetts at Amherst. Dr. Quinsey's Ph.D. research examined classical conditioning in rats. After a Killam Postdoctoral Fellowship at Dalhousie University, he took a position as a psychologist at Oak Ridge, a maximum security psychiatric unit of the Penetanguishene Mental Health Centre in

Box 7.1 Continued

Penetanguishene, Ontario, where he later founded the research department and became its Director. In 1988, Dr. Quinsey joined Queen's University as a Queen's National Scholar and professor of psychology. His favourite course to teach is human behaviour and evolution. He is a prolific researcher, with several books, over 100 papers in refereed journals, and numerous chapters in edited books. Dr. Quinsey's research interests include the prediction, modification, and management of antisocial and violent behaviour, applied decision making, program development and evaluation, sexual deviance, and evolutionary explanations of sexual and aggressive behaviours. He is a co-author of two risk-assessment instruments discussed in this book: the Violence Risk Appraisal Guide (VRAG) and the Sex Offender Risk Appraisal Guide (SORAG). Numerous awards and honours have been given to Dr. Quinsey, such as the Significant Achievement Award from the Association for the Treatment of Sexual Abusers in 1994, the Career Contribution Award from the Criminal Justice Section of the Canadian Psychological Association in 2005, and the Hebb Award from the Canadian Psychological Association for contributions to psychology as a science in 2008. Dr. Quinsey believes that, "The foreseeable future belongs to theories, usually termed evo-devo theories, that combine ultimate and proximal causation."

He says his interest in serious sexual and violent offenders began with an interest in institutional violence, particularly committed by psychotic or developmentally handicapped men. He had worked as a psychiatric hospital attendant and has always loved institutions. Once he began working in a maximum security setting, he became interested in all of the issues and offenders involved. Dr. Quinsey is a strong advocate for evidence-based practice. He and his colleagues (e.g., Marnie Rice and Grant Harris) have been a sometimes provocative voice, challenging the status quo and raising the standard for what constitutes acceptable scientific evidence in risk assessment, correctional programs, and management of offenders.

Among the vast amount of research he has conducted, one of Dr. Quinsey's favourite studies (Quinsey and Ambtman 1979) shows that forensic psychiatrists and high school English teachers make the same predictions of future violent behaviour and mock release decisions. They also use the same sorts of information to arrive at their decisions. He likes this study mainly because audiences invariably find it amusing when he describes it in lectures.

Dr. Quinsey feels that improvements to the criminal justice system "depend on minimizing ideology and wishful thinking and maximizing evaluative outcome work upon which to base policy. Operational research is relatively easy to conduct and can have an immediate impact upon policy and procedures. Broader questions concerning policy (i.e., those that transcend particular jurisdictions) are much more difficult. With respect to interventions, for example, a sharp distinction needs to be made between developmental and evaluative

Continued >

Box 7.1　Continued

research. With respect to the latter, poorly controlled correlational research arguably does more harm than good. Proper scientific hygiene involves trying to disprove that a particular intervention works—hard to do, given the difficulty in developing the intervention in the first place."

When asked about training of future researchers in the psychology of criminal behaviour, Dr. Quinsey says, "Increasingly, cutting-edge research requires multidisciplinary teams and psychologists have a lot to offer in this new context. Nevertheless, psychology students tend to specialize too early as undergraduates and then tend to stay specialized in graduate school. Knowing only

psychology at an advanced level can make one's research program parochial. In terms of theory, consilience with the more advanced sciences is the goal (we want a theory of everything) and its benefits lie primarily in abstract habits of thought rather than in techniques. In applied areas, psychologists need more mathematical training (I don't mean just statistics) and more exposure to evaluation research in economics and health" (quotes taken from personal correspondence with Dr. Quinsey).

Although he will be retiring soon, Dr. Quinsey will continue his research on sexual conflict. He is involved with the Kingston Field Naturalists.

RISK ASSESSMENT

Recidivism Rates

Compared to general criminal recidivism, violent recidivism is less frequent. For example, in a meta-analysis of recidivism of mentally disordered offenders, Bonta, Law, and Hanson (1998) found an average violent recidivism rate of 24.5 percent and a general recidivism rate of 45.8 percent over a mean follow-up period of 4.8 years. A similar rate of violent recidivism was reported for non-mentally disordered offenders in a meta-analysis by Campbell, French, and Gendreau (2009), with 21.73 percent over a follow-up period of approximately 2 to 5 years. Although most violent offenders do not violently recidivate, it is possible to identify subgroups with relatively high rates of violent recidivism.

Approaches

Approaches to risk assessment can be categorized in a number of ways. Four key categories are described here: unstructured clinical judgment; empirical actuarial; mechanical; and structured professional judgment (Hanson and Morton-Bourgon 2009). Unstructured clinical judgment involves arriving at an estimate of risk based on the assessor's own idiosyncratic decisions about what factors to consider and how to combine those factors. In contrast, the empirical actuarial and mechanical instruments both follow explicit rules about what factors to consider and how to combine those factors to arrive at a final estimate of risk. However, two characteristics distinguish empirical actuarial from mechanical. For **empirical actuarial instruments**, (1) the selection and combination of items are derived from their observed statistical relationship with recidivism; and (2) tables linking scores to expected recidivism rates are provided. For **mechanical instruments**, the selection and combination of items are derived from theory or reviews of the empirical literature and no tables are provided. **Structured professional judgment** incorporates features of both unstructured clinical judgment and the actuarial approach; there are explicit guidelines for which factors to consider (although additional factors may also be considered), but the combination of those factors is left up to the discretion of the assessor.

Instruments

Violence Risk Appraisal Guide (VRAG)
The Violence Risk Appraisal Guide (VRAG) (Harris, Rice, and Quinsey 1993) is an empirical actuarial risk-assessment instrument designed to estimate risk for violent recidivism. It was developed with a sample of 618 patients at Oak Ridge, a maximum-security forensic psychiatric institution in Penetanguishene, Ontario. Approximately half of these 618 patients were admitted to Oak Ridge and received treatment there ($n = 332$), and the other half were only briefly at Oak Ridge for a pre-trial psychiatric assessment ($n = 286$). Violent recidivism was operationally defined as a new charge for violent offence, which included homicide, attempted homicide, kidnapping, forcible confinement, wounding, assault, armed robbery, and contact sex offences (e.g., rape, child molestation). This group was initially followed up after an average of seven years (81.5 months) of opportunity to reoffend (e.g., released to the community or a halfway house). The observed rate of violent recidivism was 31 percent (191 of the 618). The VRAG consists of 12 static items that were selected from an initial pool of approximately 50 variables. The final 12 items are those that made the strongest independent statistical contribution to predicting violent recidivism. The correlation between each VRAG item and violent recidivism is shown in Table 7.1.

Scores on the VRAG can range from –26 to +38, with higher scores indicating greater risk of violent recidivism. Scores are grouped into nine risk categories (or bins), each containing seven points. The inter-rater reliability of the VRAG is very high ($r = .90$) (Harris et al. 1993). Figure 7.7 shows the observed violent recidivism rates as a function of VRAG risk category over the average seven-year follow-up period for the 618 Oak Ridge patients. As you can see, violent recidivism rates steadily increased as VRAG risk category increased. Focusing on the extremes, none of the patients who scored in the lowest VRAG risk category violently recidivated, whereas all the patients who scored in the highest risk category violently recidivated.

HCR-20 Violence Risk Assessment Scheme
The HCR-20 (Webster, Douglas, Eaves, and Hart 1997) is a structured professional judgment instrument designed to assess

Table 7.1 VRAG Items and Their Correlations with Violent Recidivism

VRAG Item	r
1. Separation from either biological parent by age 16 (except for death of parent)	.25
2. Elementary school maladjustment score	.31
3. Alcohol problems	.13
4. Never married	.18
5. Criminal history score for nonviolent offences (using the Cormier-Lang system)	.20
6. Failure on prior conditional release	.24
7. Age at index offence	−.26
8. Victim injury	−.16
9. Female victim	−.11
10. Meets DSM-III criteria for any personality disorder	.26
11. Meets DSM-III criteria for schizophrenia	−.17
12. Revised psychopathy checklist score	.34

Source: Adapted from Quinsey et al. (2006)

risk for violence. It consists of ten historical items, five clinical items, and five risk management items. The historical items, which are static and reflect the past, include previous violence, young age at first violent incident, relationship instability, employment problems, major mental illness, psychopathy, early maladjustment, personality disorder, and prior supervision failure. The clinical items, which are dynamic and reflect current functioning, include lack of insight, negative attitudes, active symptoms of major mental illness, impulsivity, and unresponsive to treatment. The risk management items, which concern future circumstances that may be encountered in the institution or community that could increase or decrease risk, include feasibility of plans, exposure to destabilizers, lack of personal support, noncompliance with remediation attempts, and stress. The HCR-20 items were selected based on a review of factors related to violence in the empirical literature and based on clinical experience. Each item is scored on a three-point scale: zero indicates that the particular factor is not present, two indicates the factor may be present, and three indicates the factor is present. Although subscale and total scores are computed by summing the appropriate items, Webster and colleagues (1997) recommend that evaluators use their professional judgment to arrive at a final risk estimate of low, moderate, or high. Unlike the VRAG, then, risk level would be determined primarily by consideration of the salience and relevance of each of the 20 items for the individual being assessed as well as any other information thought to be relevant. Subscale and total scores (i.e., summing the items) has yielded high levels of inter-rater reliability. For example, Douglas, Yeomans, and Boer (2005) found intraclass correlations between raters of .90 for the historical scale, .81 for the clinical scale, .91 for the risk

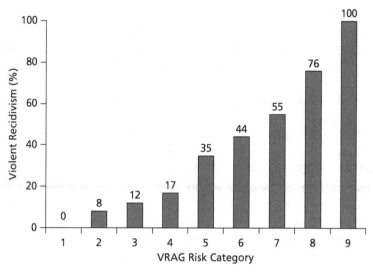

Figure 7.7 Violent Recidivism Rate by VRAG Risk Category over Seven Years of Opportunity to Reoffend

Source: Adapted from Harris, Rice, and Quinsey (1993)

management scale, and .93 for the total score. However, when structured professional judgment was used to arrive at a final risk estimate (i.e., not necessarily simply summing the scores across the 20 items), the inter-rater agreement was not as impressive: intraclass correlation = .41.

Self-Appraisal Questionnaire (SAQ)   The Self-Appraisal Questionnaire (SAQ) (Loza 2005) is a self-report empirical actuarial risk-assessment instrument developed to estimate risk of violent and non-violent recidivism (Loza, Dhaliwal, Kroner, and Loza-Fanous 2000). Initially, the SAQ consisted of 67 self-report items designed to tap a variety of factors theoretically and empirically linked to recidivism. From an initial pool of 100 items, 67 were retained through consultation with correctional staff and examination of correlations between items within each subscale and frequency of responses to each item. These items were grouped into six subscales: (1) Criminal Tendencies (CT; 27 items; sample item: "I have carefully planned a crime before"), which assesses antisocial attitudes, beliefs, behaviours, and feelings; (2) Antisocial Personality Problems (AP; 5 items; sample item: "Since the age of 15, I have been described by others as manipulative"), which assesses antisocial personality characteristics; (3) Conduct Problems (CP; 18 items; sample item: "I have spent time at a group home, a juvenile facility/training school/reformatory"), which assesses childhood behavioural problems; (4) Criminal History (CH; 6 items; sample item: "My criminal involvement has been getting worse"), which assesses past criminal behaviour; (5) Alcohol/Drug Abuse (AD; 8 items; sample item: "I would not have served time if it was not for my alcohol or drug habit"), which assesses substance abuse; and (6) Antisocial Associates (AS; 3 items; sample item: "One reason for my involvement with crime is my friends or acquaintances"), which assesses association with antisocial peers. Subscale scores are calculated by summing the appropriate items and a total score is calculated by summing all items in the six subscales noted above. Higher subscale and total scores indicate higher risk for violent and non-violent recidivism.

The SAQ demonstrated good test-retest reliability over one week: $r = .95$ for the total score, .69 for CT, .71 for AP, .95 for CP, .78 for CH, .93 for AD, and .85 for AS subscales. Most of the subscale scores showed adequate internal consistency, as measured by Cronbach's alpha: $\alpha = .78$ for CT, .58 for AP, .87 for CP, .68 for CH, .76 for AD, and .42 for AS. The SAQ subscales demonstrated expected correlations with similar constructs assessed by other measures. For example, self-reported Antisocial Personality Problems (AP) was correlated with the PCL-R ($r = .36$). In addition, the SAQ was significantly correlated with number of past violent offences ($r = .32$). The SAQ was also correlated with validated risk assessment instruments and the PCL-R, which are scored by an assessor and require file reviews, interviews, or both—see Table 7.2.

Subsequently, two new subscales were added, for a total of 72 true/false items. These new subscales, Anger and Validity, do not contribute to the total score. Instead, the Anger subscale is used to assess the degree to which anger is present and anger management treatment may be appropriate. The Validity subscale is used to evaluate the degree to which responses can be trusted. The SAQ was designed to be an efficient and informative risk assessment instrument. It is efficient because offenders complete it themselves. Most offenders can complete it in 15 to 20 minutes. It does not require assessors to conduct extensive file reviews or interviews like most other risk-assessment instruments do.

Table 7.2 Correlations between SAQ and Other Risk Studies

Measure	SIR	LSI-R	PCL-R	VRAG
SAQ total	−.61	.70	.54	.67
SAQ subscales				
Criminal tendencies	−.31	.31	.25	.34
Antisocial personality problems	−.42	.42	.36	.46
Conduct problems	−.56	.65	.54	.68
Criminal history	−.66	.62	.53	.57
Alcohol/drugs	−.31	.53	.27	.23
Associates	−.24	.40	.31	.45

Note: All correlations are statistically significant ($p < .05$). SIR = Statistical Information on Recidivism (lower scores reflect higher risk); LSI-R = Level of Service Inventory Revised; PCL-R = Psychopathy Checklist Revised; VRAG = Violence Risk Appraisal Guide.

Source: Adapted from Loza et al. (2000)

It is informative in that it addresses theoretically relevant domains and over half the items are potentially dynamic. Thus, not only does the SAQ indicate risk of recidivism, it may also provide information relevant to the planning of treatment and supervision because it suggests areas of criminogenic need that could potentially be treated or otherwise managed.

Would you use self-report measures to estimate risk for violent recidivism? Many people would probably say no. Why? Usually this has to do with skepticism about the accuracy of offenders' self-reports. Offenders are often considered unreliable sources of information, especially when the information they provide will be used to make decisions that impact them, such as whether to grant conditional release or to move them to lower security facilities. So one major concern is whether they will respond deceptively to make themselves appear lower risk or just better in general. Inaccurate reports could also stem from lack of insight; that is, misrepresentation of themselves due to lack of awareness rather than intentional deceptiveness. Despite these concerns, the available evidence suggests that the SAQ can predict violent recidivism as well as more typical risk-assessment instruments.

Accuracy

The primary concern with violent risk assessment instruments is the extent to which they are accurate. Obviously, it is important that such instruments are relatively accurate at predicting violent recidivism if they are to be used to make decisions about release and other offender management issues. Assessors and assessment instruments typically provide an estimate of risk for violent recidivism rather than a dichotomous prediction about whether an offender will or will not violently recidivate. However, these estimates are often used by parole boards or other bodies to make dichotomous decisions, such as whether to grant conditional release to the community. Essentially, two predictions can be made for a given offender: either the offender will violently recidivate or the offender will not violently recidivate. Each of these predictions can be correct or incorrect. Thus there are four possibilities: true positives, true negatives, false positives, or false negatives. As illustrated in Table 7.3, a **true positive** occurs when it is predicted that an offender will violently recidivate and he/she in fact does so. A **true negative** occurs when it is predicted that an offender will not violently recidivate and he/she in fact does not recidivate. A **false positive** occurs when it is predicted that an offender will violently recidivate but

Table 7.3 Predictive Accuracy: True Positives, True Negatives, False Positives, and False Negatives

	OUTCOME	
PREDICTION	**Violently recidivates**	**Does not violently recidivate**
Will violently recidivate	True positive	False positive
Will not violently recidivate	False negative	True negative

he/she actually does not. A false negative occurs when it is predicted that an offender will not violently recidivate and he/she actually does. So true positive and true negatives are correct predictions, and false positives and false negatives are incorrect predictions.

Unfortunately, predictive errors happen and some degree of error is inevitable. Thus there is a tradeoff between false negatives and false positives because both cannot be completely avoided simultaneously. In other words, as false positives decrease, false negatives increase and vice versa. Similarly, as true positives decrease, true negatives increase and vice versa. For example, imagine you are a parole board member and you have made recommendations at the hearings of 100 violent offenders eligible for parole. Playing it safe, you predicted that every offender would violently recidivate and accordingly recommended denying parole for all of them. Much to your annoyance, however, your fellow board members completely ignored your recommendations and decided to grant parole to all 100 offenders. You decide to make the best of the situation and check out the accuracy of your predictions. A few years later, you check the criminal records of the 100 offenders that were released and find that 30 of them did eventually violently recidivate (30 percent base rate of violent recidivism). You achieved a 100 percent true positive rate because you correctly predicted violent recidivism for all 30 offenders who actually violently recidivated (30/30). Nice work! However, your false positive rate is also 100 percent, because you incorrectly predicted violent recidivism for all 70 offenders who did not actually violently recidivate (70/70). Your true negative rate is 0 percent because you did not predict non-recidivism for any of the 70 offenders who did not actually violently recidivate (0/70). On the upside, your false negative rate is also 0 percent because you did not predict non-recidivism for the 30 offenders who did actually violently recidivate (0/30). So your colleagues were right to ignore your recommendations! But they did not do any better than you. Your colleagues who predicted that nobody would violently recidivate had a 0 percent true positive rate (0/30), 0 percent false positive rate (0/70), 100 percent true negative rate (70/70), and 100 percent false negative rate (30/30).

Different predictive errors have different consequences. False positives result in unnecessarily restricting offenders' liberty and wasting scarce resources, and false negatives result in harm to those who are victimized by the offender. So if the board had followed your recommendations and not released any of the offenders, the harm done by those 30 violent recidivists would have been prevented. However, the 70 offenders who did not violently recidivate would have been incarcerated for much longer than necessary. These examples are obviously at the extreme ends of the continuum, but they demonstrate the balance that must be struck between too many false positives and too many false negatives. The optimal balance will vary depending on the relative costs and benefits of each outcome. For example, the cost of a false negative would be lower and the benefits of true negatives would be higher with some manifestations of violent recidivism (e.g., simple assault) than others (e.g., murder).

So which risk-assessment instrument best predicts violent recidivism? A number of researchers have examined the accuracy of various instruments. In a recent meta-analysis, Campbell, French, and Gendreau (2009) summarized the findings from these studies.

Table 7.4 Average Correlation (Weighted by Sample Size) between Risk-Assessment Measures and Violent Recidivism

Measure	k	N	r	95% CI
SAQ	8	1094	.37	.31 to .43
VRAG	14	2082	.32	.28 to .36
LSI/LSI-R	19	4361	.28	.25 to .31
PCL/PCL-R	24	4757	.27	.24 to .30
SIR	17	5618	.22	.19 to .25
HCR-20	11	1395	.22	.17 to .27

Note: k = number of effect sizes; N = number of subjects; CI = confidence interval around the average correlation.

Source: Adapted from Campbell, French, and Gendreau (2009)

Measures examined included those designed specifically to estimate the risk of violent recidivism, such as the VRAG and HCR-20, as well as measures designed to estimate risk of general recidivism (i.e., violent or non-violent), such as the Level of Service Inventory-Revised (LSI-R) (Andrews and Bonta 1995) and the Statistical Information on Recidivism scale (SIR) (Nuffield 1982). In addition, the PCL-R was examined. Although the PCL-R was not designed to estimate risk of recidivism, it is an important predictor of violent recidivism and is addressed in many risk assessments. The effect size used by the researchers was the average correlation coefficient weighted by sample size. As shown in Table 7.4, the SAQ and VRAG were among the best predictors of violent recidivism. The SAQ performed significantly better than the LSI, PCL, SIR, and HCR-20. The VRAG performed significantly better than the SIR and HCR-20.

Although Campbell et al. (2009) did not examine the accuracy of unstructured clinical judgment, it has been found to be less accurate at predicting violent recidivism than actuarial approaches in a number of meta-analyses (Bonta et al. 1998; Hanson and Morton-Bourgon 2009; Mossman 1994).

Mental Disorder

It is worth taking a closer look at mental disorder as a predictor of violence because it is a contentious issue that is often debated. The difference of opinion is apparent in the risk scales considered above. On the HCR-20, the presence of major mental illness and active symptoms of major mental illness are both risk factors for future violence. In contrast, on the VRAG, a diagnosis of schizophrenia, which is considered a major mental illness, reduces risk of violent recidivism. So is mental illness a risk factor for violence or not? The answer seems to be yes and no, depending on whether the focus is on the entire population or exclusively on offenders. When the focus is on the entire population, the answer seems to be yes: people with major mental disorders are more likely to be violent than those without mental disorders. Monahan (1997) reviewed the literature to address this issue. In a representative sample of residents in certain U.S. cities, people meeting the criteria for an Axis I psychiatric diagnosis, such as schizophrenia, major depression, or mania/bipolar disorder, had higher rates of violence within the past year (11 to 13 percent) than people who did not meet diagnostic criteria (2 percent) (Swanson, Holzer, Ganju, and Jono 1990). Converging findings with a different methodology and population that come from a longitudinal study of over 15 000 people in Sweden (Hodgins 1992). Hodgins found that people with schizophrenia or major affective disorder were more likely to be convicted of a violent offence than those with no major mental disorder or intellectual disability. Interestingly, other evidence suggests that the association between major mental disorder and violence may be best accounted for by the presence of active psychotic symptoms, such as hallucinations and delusions (Link, Andrews, and Cullen 1992). In particular, elevated violence is associated with "**threat/control-override**" psychotic symptoms, in which one feels that their self-control is overridden by outside forces, or feels they will be harmed by others (Link and Stueve 1994; Swanson, Borum, Swartz, and Monahan 1996). For example, if a person is experiencing powerful delusional beliefs that family members are imposters sent to murder them, the person may make a preemptive violent strike against them. However, symptoms that do not lead one to feel threatened by others or to feel driven to violence by forces beyond one's control would not generally increase one's likelihood of violence, all else being equal. Although elevated rates of violence are observed among the groups described above, it is important to keep in mind that the vast majority of people with major mental disorders and even those with active threat/control-override symptoms are not violent (Monahan 1997).

However, when focusing on offenders or forensic psychiatric patients, researchers have found that psychiatric diagnoses and symptoms do not predict violent recidivism (Bonta et al. 1998; Quinsey, Coleman, Jones, and Altrows 1997) or they are predictive of reduced violent recidivism (Harris et al. 1993; Monahan et al. 2001). As Quinsey et al. (2006: 106) suggest, the most likely explanation of this apparent discrepancy (i.e., positive relationship between mental illness and violence versus negative or no relationship) between studies

has to do with the composition of the seriously mentally ill and comparison groups. Studies that have found higher rates among mentally ill participants have not selected mentally disordered offenders as the mentally ill population and have used the general population as their comparison group. However, we (and others who have found similar findings) have compared offenders experiencing major mental disorders, or schizophrenia specifically, with other offenders. The comparison offenders were more likely than the seriously mentally ill offenders to have a diagnosis of antisocial or some other personality disorder. Thus, the difference between the findings of the two types of study maybe accounted for by the way the two groups were formed.

TREATMENT AND MANAGEMENT

A NUMBER OF TREATMENT PROGRAMS HAVE BEEN DEVELOPED TO REDUCE VIOLENT RECIDIVISM. Some of these programs are designed to develop effective management of emotions, such as anger, that may play a role in violence. Others are more general in focus, such as the Correctional Service of Canada's Violence Prevention Program, which is described in more detail in Box 7.2.

Box 7.2

Correctional Service of Canada's Violence Prevention Program (VPP)

The Violence Prevention Program is an intensive cognitive-behavioural reintegration program for incarcerated federal offenders. It is grounded in contemporary theory and research, and delivered by a mental health professional and a program officer.

Target Group

The Violence Prevention Program is intended to help offenders who have already committed at least two violent offences or who are considered at high risk to commit violent crimes (based on the Statistical Information on Recidivism scale [SIR]).

Philosophy

Aggression and violent behavioural problems are multidimensional. Because the targets of change are usually complex and multiple, the Violence Prevention Program integrates a variety of rehabilitative approaches. The conceptual model integrates theories of social learning and social information processing. The program focuses on violent criminal activity and interpersonal aggression that are not exclusively based on anger or emotional control problems. The primary intervention approach is cognitive behavioural and skills-based, with an emphasis on violence (relapse) prevention. These intervention techniques are reinforced by a consistent strategy emphasizing self-control, social problem-solving, education, self-management, role playing, and homework assignments. The goal of the program is to improve the skills of the participants and subsequently reduce the risk of future violence.

Methodology

The Violence Prevention Program consists of 120 two-hour sessions and at least three individual sessions that vary according to the needs of the participants, plus two testing sessions. The program (excluding assessment sessions) is delivered in four months. Group sessions are two hours in length. Each group is formed of a maximum of 12 participants.

The principal interventions (modules) include:

1. Making Change: Orientation and the process of change

2. Violence Awareness: Examining the personal origins of violence

3. Anger Control: Basic skills of anger and stress management

4. Solving Problems: Social problem-solving and information-processing skills

Continued >

Box 7.2   Continued

5. Social Attitudes: Examining and refor-
   mulating the beliefs supporting
   violence

6. Positive Relationships: Reducing victimization and intimate violence

7. Resolving Conflicts: Communication
   and negotiation skills

8. Positive Lifestyles: Restructuring the
   lifestyle triggers of violence

9. Self Control: Developing short-term
   and long-term direction

10. Violence Prevention: Developing a com-
    prehensive violence prevention plan

Continuum of Service

A primary objective of the violence prevention
program is for each participant to develop,
articulate, and manage a comprehensive
violence (relapse) prevention plan. This plan is
based on an understanding of prior expressions of aggression, and recognition of high-
risk circumstances that may result in further
aggression. Institutional and community prevention programs assist participants to apply
their violence prevention plan to their environment and circumstances. This is accom-
plished by brief group and individual sessions
that focus on adapting and modifying relapse
prevention efforts. Although new skills
may be required, the purpose of these
sessions is not to re-introduce program content, but rather to assist participants in applying program content to their changing
circumstances.

Source: Correctional Service of Canada (2009)

Effectiveness

There are a number of ways to address questions about the effectiveness of treatment for violent offenders. However, the most important issue regarding effectiveness is the extent to
which treatment reduces violent recidivism. Studies addressing this issue typically compare the
recidivism rates of offenders who receive the treatment to those who do not. There have been
surprisingly few well controlled evaluations of the effectiveness of these programs (Jolliffe and
Farrington 2007; Polaschek and Collie 2004). Dowden and Andrews (2000) conducted a
meta-analysis of studies on treatment and violent recidivism, which included 52 comparisons
from a total of 35 studies of any programs (broadly defined to include treatment as well as sanctions) for male offenders, most of whom were adults. The effect size used in their meta-
analysis was the phi coefficient (a correlation coefficient for the relationship between two
dichotomous variables; in this case, treatment versus comparison group and violent recidivism
versus non-violent recidivism). By convention, a phi of around .10 is considered small, .30 is
considered medium, and .50 is considered large (Cohen 1988). The average correlation for any
treatment was .12 ($p < .05$), which reflects violent recidivism rates about 12 percentage points
lower among treated groups than comparison groups. This was significantly higher than the
correlation between sanctions (e.g., prison) and violent recidivism (−.01). Thus treatment was
associated with significant reductions in violent recidivism, whereas sanctions were not.

Programs can vary widely in terms of who is treated, what is treated, and how treatment
is delivered. Here we are referring to the principles of effective correctional treatment: the

risk, need, and responsivity principles discussed in Chapter 4 (Andrews, Bonta, and Hoge 1990). Dowden and Andrews (2000) also examined whether reductions in violent recidivism for treated versus comparison groups would be greater when programs adhered to these principles than when they did not. Their findings were generally supportive of the importance of these principles for maximizing the effectiveness of treatment. Concerning the risk principle, effects were larger (though not significantly so) for programs directed at higher risk offenders ($r = .09$) than programs directed at low-risk offenders ($r = .04$). With regard to the need principle, effects were significantly larger for programs focusing primarily on criminogenic needs ($r = .20$) than those focusing primarily on non-criminogenic needs ($r = .00$). For the responsivity principle, effects were significantly larger for behavioural or cognitive-behavioural programs ($r = .19$) than other approaches to treatment ($r = .01$). In addition, the greater number of principles to which programs adhered, the greater the observed reductions in violent recidivism. Specifically, for sanctions and treatment that adhered to none of the three principles, the average effect was .01; for treatment following only one of the three principles the average effect was .07; for treatment following any two of the three principles the average effect was .15; and for treatment following all three of the principles the average effect was .20. Thus, just as with general offending, treatments that follow the principles of effective corrections are associated with larger reductions in violent recidivism than treatments that do not follow these principles.

Although the outcome examined by Dowden and Andrews (2000) was violent recidivism, their meta-analysis included studies not only on violent offenders in programs designed to reduce non-sexual violence, but also on other offenders (e.g., sex offenders, mixed groups of offenders) and programs (e.g., sex offender, family violence, general crime). It is very encouraging that these programs reduced violent recidivism despite the breadth of participants and focus, but how well do programs with the explicit aim of reducing violent recidivism perform with general violent offenders? Jolliffe and Farrington (2007) addressed this issue in a recent meta-analysis on the effectiveness of general violence programs with generally violent offenders. They only included studies (a) on generally violent (e.g., not primarily family violence or sex offending) adult male offenders, (b) with relatively strong methodology (e.g., random assignment to treatment and comparison condition; matching of treatment and comparison subjects on a risk-relevant variable), (c) with at least 25 offenders in both the treated and comparison groups, and (d) published between 1975 and 2007. Jolliffe and Farrington (2007) found eight studies that met their criteria and that included the outcome of violent recidivism. The effect they used in their meta-analysis is Cohen's d. By convention, a d of around 0.20 is considered small, 0.50 is considered medium, and 0.80 is considered large (Cohen 1988). In this meta-analysis, a d of 0.00 would indicate no difference between treated and comparison groups in their rates of violent recidivism. A d greater than zero would reflect lower rates of violent recidivism in the treated groups than in the comparison groups, whereas a d less than zero would reflect higher rates of violent recidivism in the treated groups than in the comparison groups.

The effect sizes, both for the individual studies and the average of these studies, are shown in Figure 7.8. Looking at the effects for the individual studies in the meta-analysis, you can see that most found lower rates of violent recidivism in the treated group than in the comparison group; six of the eight effects are above zero. However, these individual effects reached statistical significance ($p < .05$) in only two studies. Overall a small significant average effect size was found; mean d between 0.13 and 0.16 depending on whether the effects were calculated using a fixed effect or random effect model. Thus, treatment for violent offenders is associated, on average, with lower rates of violent recidivism.

Jolliffe and Farrington (2007) also examined some potential moderators of treatment effectiveness, such as the features of the treatments and research designs. With regard to treatment features, they determined whether a given program included each of the following elements: (a) addressed offenders' anger (anger control); (b) included cognitive-behavioural skills training (cognitive skills); (c) included training about morals (moral training); (d) used role-playing for training (role play); (e) addressed empathy (empathy); (f) included relapse prevention planning (relapse prevention); and (g) included rehearsal of skills or training between treatment sessions (homework). As illustrated in Table 7.5, some of these features were associated with observed reductions in violent recidivism. More specifically, the violent recidivism rate for treatments that included anger control was significantly lower than the rate for comparison groups ($d = 0.14$). However, the violent recidivism rate for treatments that did not include anger control was not significantly lower than for comparison groups ($d = 0.08$). Similarly, treatments that included cognitive skills, role play, relapse prevention, or homework were associated with significant reductions in violent recidivism, whereas treatments that did not include these elements were not significantly associated with reductions in violent recidivism. In contrast, some features seemed to detract from treatment effectiveness. Treatments that included moral training or empathy training were not significantly associated with reductions in violent recidivism, whereas treatments that did not include these features were significantly associated with reductions in violent recidivism. Surprisingly, treatments delivered by a rehabilitation professional such

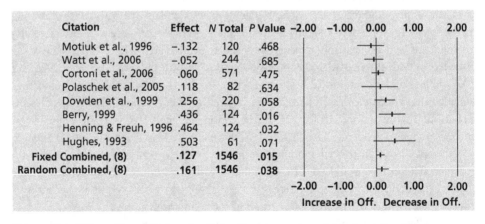

Figure 7.8 Effect Sizes (Cohen's *d*) for Treatment and Violent Recidivism

Source: Jolliffe and Farrington (2007)

as a psychologist were not significantly associated with reductions in violent recidivism, whereas treatments delivered by correctional or probation officers were significantly associated with reductions in violent recidivism!

Note, however, that just because one effect reached statistical significance and the other did not, it does not necessarily mean that the two effects are significantly different from each other. For example, the effect for treatments including cognitive skills ($d = 0.16$) was not significantly higher than the effect for treatments not including cognitive skills ($d = -0.05$). Similarly, effects did not significantly differ as a function of the presence or absence of anger control, moral training, and relapse prevention. Nor did they differ between programs delivered by rehabilitation professionals or correctional/probation officers. However, the difference between effect sizes was statistically significant for role play, empathy training, and homework.

You may now be ready to conclude that these treatments generally do reduce violent recidivism. Violent recidivism rates are on average lower among treated offenders than comparison groups. These differences may be small, but they are significant, and better treatments (e.g., those adhering to principles of effective treatment, those including role play to practice and develop new skills) show larger differences between the treated and comparison groups. What else do you need to know? There are some important methodological issues to take into consideration before drawing any conclusions from the available findings. Although Jolliffe and Farrington (2007) included only studies that met a minimal standard of methodological rigour, there was still variability in the quality of these studies. Two key issues in these sorts of studies are random assignment and attrition. The most rigorous tests of causal relationships are true experiments, which, in this case,

Table 7.5 Effect Sizes for Violent Recidivism by Program or Study Features

Feature	k	Mean d	Feature	k	Mean d
Anger control	6	0.14*	No anger control	2	0.08
Cognitive skills	7	0.16*	No cognitive skills	1	-0.05
Moral training	3	0.06	No moral training	5	0.15*
Role play	6	0.19*	No role play	2	-0.08
Empathy training	3	-0.05	No empathy training	5	0.20*
Relapse prevention	5	0.18*	No relapse prevention	3	-0.01
Offender homework	3	0.37*	No offender homework	5	0.07
Rehabilitation professional	5	0.10	Correctional officer	3	0.15*
High quality studies	5	0.08	Low quality studies	3	0.37*
Intention to treat	3	0.07	Completers	5	0.22*

Note: k = number of studies; * $p < .05$.

Source: Adapted from Jolliffe and Farrington (2007)

would involve randomly assigning violent offenders to a treatment group or a comparison group (e.g., no-treatment control group or treatment as usual). Offenders would then be followed up after a few years in the community to determine whether they had violently reoffended. One could be fairly confident that any observed difference in violent recidivism between treated and comparison groups was caused by the treatment.

But what should be done with offenders who were assigned to the treatment group but did not complete it? Attrition presents a real challenge to researchers and non-completion rates can be fairly high among violence programs (over 30 percent in some studies; e.g., Cortoni, Nunes, and Latendresse 2006). On one hand, it seems reasonable to exclude non-completers from the treatment group and compare the recidivism rate for the completers against the rate for the untreated offenders. Exclusion of the non-completers can introduce bias, however. Non-completion of treatment is associated with increased violent recidivism (Cortoni et al. 2006) and non-completers are generally more antisocial than completers (Nunes and Cortoni 2006; Nunes, Cortoni, and Serin, in press). Although it is easy to identify and exclude non-completers in the treated group, it is not possible to identify those in the untreated group who would not have completed treatment had it been offered. Thus we would expect lower rates of violent recidivism among treatment completers compared to untreated offenders even if treatment had no effect at all. The most conservative way to deal with attrition, then, is to retain all offenders who had been assigned to treatment (whether they actually completed it or not) in analytic comparisons with the untreated group. This approach is sometimes referred to as "intention to treat."

Jolliffe and Farrington (2007) found that studies of higher methodological quality generally yielded smaller effect sizes than studies of lower quality ($r = -.64$). Ratings of methodological quality generally reflected the degree to which a study was a relatively accurate and unbiased test of the effectiveness of treatment. Among other things, these ratings considered the issues mentioned above: assignment to groups, non-equivalence of treated and comparison groups, and attrition. As shown in the last two columns of Table 7.5, treatment was not associated with significant reductions in violent recidivism in studies of high methodological quality or studies that did intention-to-treat analyses. However, treatment was associated with significant reductions in violent recidivism in studies of lower methodological quality or studies that only compared completers to comparison groups. The difference between these effect sizes was statistically significant for methodological quality (0.08 vs. 0.37, $p < .05$), but not for intention to treat (0.07 versus 0.22, non-significant).

As Jolliffe and Farrington (2007) point out, the finding that methodological quality is negatively correlated with effect size makes it "difficult to ascertain the extent to which the interventions with large effect sizes are effective because of their superior type or method of treatment or because their effects were artificially increased by biased methods" (p. 10). To address this issue, Jolliffe and Farrington (2007) re-analyzed the program features presented in Table 7.5, but this time statistically controlled for the study feature of methodological quality. In these multivariate analyses, none of the program features emerged as significant moderators of treatment effectiveness. That is, program features such as role play and homework that were associated with greater effectiveness in the univariate analyses described above were no longer significantly related to observed reductions in violent recidivism after methodological quality was taken into account. Given the small number of studies in this meta-analysis, it would be premature to draw any strong conclusions. Based on the available evidence, it remains unclear whether the lower rates of violent recidivism associated with treatment actually demonstrate that treatment is effective or are more parsimoniously attributed to methodological shortcomings (Dowden and Andrews 2000; Jolliffe and Farrington 2007; Quinsey et al. 2006).

EXTREME FORMS OF VIOLENCE: HOMICIDE

AS NOTED PREVIOUSLY, CRIMINAL VIOLENCE IS RELATIVELY RARE IN CANADA, AND HOMICIDE—thankfully—is exceptionally rare. In 2007, 594 homicides were reported to the police in Canada; the rate was 1.80 per 100 000 people. As shown in Figure 7.9, Canada has a low rate of homicide relative to many other countries.

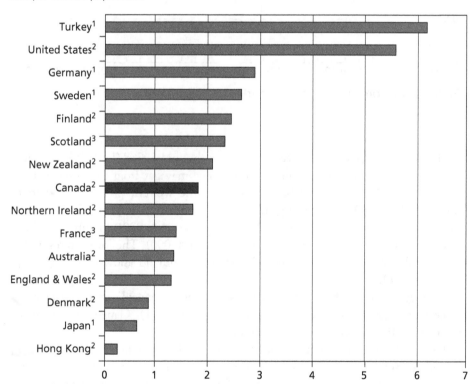

1. Figures reflect 2005 data.
2. Figures reflect 2007 data.
3. Figures reflect 2006 data.

Figure 7.9 Homicide Rates for Selected Countries

Source: Li (2008), Interpol Ottawa, and national statistical office websites

Rate per 100 000 population

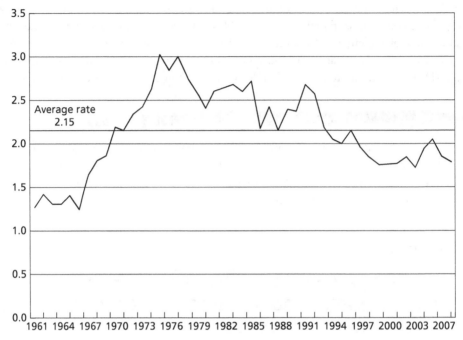

Figure 7.10 Homicide Rate in Canada

Source: Li (2008)

Homicide rates have been decreasing since the mid 1970s (Li 2008) (see Figure 7.10), which is contrary to the impression people may get from the popular media. Homicide rates have typically been highest in the western provinces and in the territories (Li 2008). Specifically, the highest homicide rates in 2007 were in Nunavut (22.50 per 100 000 people), Yukon (6.45 per 100 000), Manitoba (5.22 per 100 000), and the Northwest Territories (4.69 per 100 000). The lowest rates in 2007 were in PEI (0.00 per 100 000 people) and Newfoundland and Labrador (0.59 per 100 000 people).

Although homicides have decreased, the proportion of homicides that are gang-related has been increasing over the past decade (see Figure 7.11). Gang-related homicides accounted for 19.7 percent of all homicides in 2007.

Like most other violent crimes, males are more likely to commit and be victims of homicide than females (Li 2008). Males were more likely to be perpetrators (89.9 versus 10.1 percent for females) and victims (72.7 versus 27.3 percent for females) in homicide charges in 2007. Victims are most likely to be killed by someone they know (Li 2008). Most homicides in 2007 were committed by an acquaintance (e.g., friend, boyfriend, casual acquaintance; 36.5 percent) or family member (e.g., spouse, parent, sibling; 32.9 percent). Less common were homicides committed by strangers (15.9 percent)

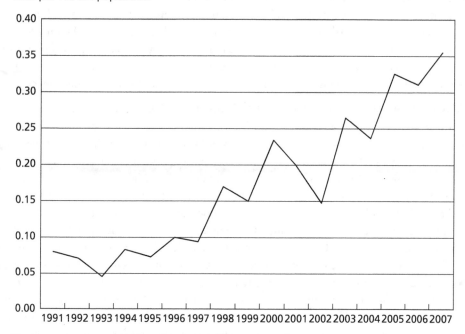

Rate per 100 000 population

Figure 7.11 Gang-Related Homicide

Source: Li (2008)

and homicides linked to other illegal activities (e.g., drug trade, prostitution, loan sharks, gang members; 14.5 percent). The most common methods used in homicides in 2007 were shooting (31.6 percent), stabbing (32.0 percent), and beating (19.5 percent) (Li 2008). Some less common methods were strangulation or suffocation (8.4 percent), vehicle (2.7 percent), fire (smoke inhalation or burns; 0.7 percent), and shaken baby syndrome (0.5 percent).

Types of Homicide

Four types of homicide are identified in the Canadian *Criminal Code*: **first-degree murder**, second-degree murder, infanticide, and manslaughter. Murder is first degree when it is planned and deliberate. However, even when not planned and deliberate, murder is also first degree if (a) the victim is a peace officer (e.g., police officer) or a prison employee (e.g., correctional officer, institutional parole officer) or (b) the victim's death is caused while committing or attempting to commit hijacking of an aircraft, sexual assault, kidnapping, hostage taking, criminal harassment, terrorist activity, use of explosives in association with a criminal organization, or intimidation. Second-degree murder is defined as murder that is not first degree. Infanticide is defined in section 233 of the *Criminal Code* as such: "A female person commits infanticide when by a willful act or omission she causes the death of her newly-born child, if at the time of the act or omission she is not fully recovered from the effects of giving birth to the child and by reason thereof or of the effect of lactation consequent on the birth of the child her mind is then disturbed." Homicide that would otherwise be considered murder can be reduced to manslaughter if it was committed during the heat of passion or caused by sudden provocation that would overwhelm one's self-control. Homicide is also manslaughter if death results from criminal negligence.

Multiple Murder: Definitions and Characteristics Multiple murder is usually defined as killing three or more victims. Multiple murders can be divided into mass murder, spree murder, and serial murder. **Mass murder** occurs in a single location with no "cooling-off period" between murders. The cooling-off period refers to the time between murders. Some well-known Canadian mass murderers are Mark Lepine, who killed 14 women and then killed himself at Montreal's École Polytechnique in 1989; Valery Fabrikant, who killed four fellow professors at Concordia University in 1992 (see Box 7.3); and Pierre Lebrun, who in 1999 killed four employees and subsequently killed himself at the head office of Ottawa-Carleton Transpo, where he had formerly worked. **Spree murder** is also characterized by no cooling-off period between murders, but the murders occur at two or more locations. Spree murder often occurs in the context of another crime. For example, a person may kill one or more of his associates in an apartment over an illegal drug deal gone bad. While fleeing the scene he is confronted on the street by an associate of the people in the apartment. He kills this person as well and runs off. Police patrolling the area see him, give chase, and eventually corner him. He shoots and kills one of the police officers before being apprehended by the other officers.

Box 7.3

Concordia University Massacre

On the afternoon of 24 August, 1992, Dr. Valery Fabrikant, a member of faculty in the Department of Mechanical Engineering of Concordia University, Montreal, entered the campus armed with several revolvers and shot five persons, four members of faculty and a secretary. All four faculty died, two at once, the others later in hospital. Arrested at the scene, Dr. Fabrikant was charged with murder.

After a trial lasting five months, including a month devoted to deciding whether he was mentally fit to stand trial, in April 1993 Dr. Fabrikant was convicted and given the maximum sentence—life imprisonment without possibility of parole for 25 years. The essential evidence against him was never in question, but the defendant pleaded Not

Box 7.3 Continued

Guilty and used the trial, at which for the most part he acted as his own counsel, to argue that he was a peaceful, reasonable person provoked to act because of the unjust treatment he had suffered at Concordia University.

This multiple tragedy grew out of a series of grievances, real and imagined, extending over a period of years. The grievances were against academic colleagues in the Faculty of Engineering and Computer Science, principally the chairman of his department, the chairman's brother who was the director of CONCAVE—a research centre associated with the department—the dean of the faculty, and other senior officers of the university. Ironically, none of the victims had been a major figure in the disputes that led up to the murderous rampage.

This account of the Concordia Massacre is taken directly from an article on the case of Valery Fabrikant (Monahan 1995: 129)

Like mass and spree murders, **serial murder** involves three or more victims but differs from other multiple murders in that there is a cooling-off period between murders and the murders usually occur in different locations. Some high-profile Canadian serial killers are Clifford Olson, who murdered eight girls and three boys aged 9 to 18 in the early 1980s in British Columbia; Paul Bernardo and Karla Homolka, who killed three teenage girls in the early 1990s in St. Catharines, Ontario; and, most recently, Robert Pickton, who murdered several women in Port Coquitlam, British Columbia (see Box 7.4). Hickey (2006) examined the characteristics of serial killers in the United States between 1825 and 1995. As with homicide and other violence, most serial murderers are male (83 percent), commit their murders alone (i.e., without an accomplice), are white (73 percent), and usually victimize young female strangers.

Box 7.4

Robert Pickton

Robert William Pickton was born on October 26, 1949, and lived and worked on his pig farm in Port Coquitlam, British Columbia. He has been charged with the murders of 26 women, most of whom were prostitutes. Pickton picked up the women from Vancouver's Downtown Eastside, about a half-hour drive from the farm, and brought them back to the trailer in which he lived. The women were killed on the farm, and the remains of some of their bodies and personal effects were later found there by police. His first trial dealt with six murder charges, for which he was eventually convicted of six counts of second-degree murder and sentenced to life with eligibility for parole after 25 years. An appeal of the verdicts was dismissed by the British Columbia Court of Appeal in June 2009. Pickton's lawyers will appeal to the Supreme Court of Canada.

Continued >

Box 7.4   Continued

Below are some key dates in the case:

Sept. 1998: Vancouver police set up team that reviews files of women missing from city's Downtown Eastside as far back as 1971.

Feb. 5, 2002: RCMP officers, accompanied by members of the missing women joint task force, enter property in suburban Port Coquitlam on firearms warrant.

Feb. 6, 2002: Task force officers use their own warrant to begin searching pig farm for clues in missing women case.

Feb. 22, 2002: Robert Pickton, who owns the property with his brother and sister, is charged with two counts of first-degree murder—Sereena Abotsway and Mona Wilson.

April 2, 2002: Crown announces three more first-degree murder charges against Pickton—Diane Rock, Jacqueline McDonell, and Heather Bottomley.

April 9, 2002: Sixth murder charge laid against Pickton—Andrea Joesbury.

May 22, 2002: Pickton charged with first-degree murder of Brenda Wolfe.

June 6, 2002: Police begin excavating Pickton properties with help of archeologists.

Sept. 19, 2002: Pickton charged with four more murders—Georgina Papin, Helen Hallmark, Patricia Johnson, and Jennifer Furminger.

Oct. 2, 2002: Pickton charged with murders of Heather Chinnock, Tanya Holyk, Sherry Irving, and Inga Hall.

Jan. 13, 2003: Preliminary hearing begins in provincial court in Port Coquitlam.

July 23, 2003: Judge David Stone commits Pickton for trial on 15 counts of first-degree murder.

Nov. 18, 2003: Investigators wrap up mass excavation and search of Pickton farm.

Feb. 20, 2004: B.C. government reports investigation costs will likely run up to $70 million and that the money has been set aside in the provincial budget.

May 2005: Crown lays 12 more first-degree murder charges.

June 2005: Pre-trial hearings begin in B.C. Supreme Court in New Westminster under a publication ban.

October 2005: Pre-trial hearings end.

Jan. 30, 2006: Voir dire portion of Pickton trial begins in B.C. Supreme Court.

March 2006: Judge quashes murder count involving unidentified woman.

Aug. 9, 2006: Judge decides to sever charges to prevent unreasonable burden on jury.

Sept. 8, 2006: Crown decides to proceed on six counts first, with other 20 counts to be tried at a later date.

Dec. 9, 2006: Jury selection begins.

Dec. 12, 2006: Jury selected.

Jan. 22, 2007: Crown opens case against Pickton on six charges of first-degree murder.

Aug. 13, 2007: Crown closes case after calling 98 witnesses.

Oct. 16, 2007: Defence closes case after calling 30 witnesses.

Nov. 19, 2007: Final arguments begin.

Nov. 30, 2007: Jury begins deliberations.

Dec. 9, 2007: Jury finds Pickton guilty of six counts of second-degree murder.

Source: December 9, 2007 © The Canadian Press

Typologies of Serial Murderers

One popular typology of serial murderers was developed by Holmes and colleagues (Holmes and DeBurger 1988; Holmes and Holmes 1998). They identified four major types of serial murderers: visionary, mission-oriented, hedonistic, and power/control. Holmes and Holmes (1998: 43–44) describe each type as follows:

> The first type of killer is the **visionary**. Truly, this serial murderer is psychotic and suffers from a severe break with reality. An inner voice or an apparition commands that he or she kill.
>
> The second type is the **mission-oriented serial murderer.** This person, who is not psychotic, takes upon himself the task of ridding the world or the community of a group of people that he considers to be undesirable. The undesirable may be any group—homosexuals, prostitutes, blacks, Catholics, and so on. There are two subtypes of mission-oriented killers, *demon-mandated* and *God-mandated*.
>
> The third type of serial killer is the **hedonistic** serialist. There are three subtypes: *lust*, *thrill*, and *comfort*. The first two types are similar in that both have made an integral connection between personal violence and sexual gratification. However, with the lust killer, gross acts of necrophilia may accompany the process-kill. With the thrill killer, however, the victim must be alive so that the killer can feed off the terror that the victim is experiencing. The third subtype is the *comfort* type. This killer murders because of anticipated gains that are materialistic: money, business, or other financial considerations.
>
> The fourth type of serial murderer is the **power/control** killer. This murderer desires the total capture of the victim and wants to hold the fate of the victim in his hands.

Below is a list of the top 10 issues and people to consider when thinking about violent offending in Canada.

Top 10 List

Advances to Come, Debates, Ethical Conundrums, and People to Watch

1 What explains the recent drop in violent crime rates?

2 Why is violence more prevalent in the Canadian west and north?

3 How will proximal causal theories of aggression be integrated with ultimate causal (evolutionary) theories of aggression?

4 If major mental illness is not associated with increased violent recidivism, should it be included as a risk factor in instruments like the HCR-20?

5 Given that static factors are such robust predictors of long-term violent recidivism, is incapacitation a more realistic goal than rehabilitation with very high-risk offenders?

6 Evidence indicates that the SAQ, a self-report risk-assessment instrument, can

predict violent recidivism as accurately as instruments based on extensive file reviews, such as the VRAG. Should correctional agencies and assessors start using the SAQ instead of other more resource-demanding instruments?

7   Although studies of poorer methodological quality have found that treatment is associated with significant reductions in violent recidivism, studies of better methodological quality have not. How should these findings be interpreted?

8   Is it justifiable to deny treatment to some violent offenders in randomized control studies to more conclusively determine whether treatment actually does reduce violent recidivism?

9   Given that serial killers are so rare, can research yield reliable and useful information about them?

10 People to watch: Kevin Douglas, Grant Harris, Stephen Hart, Daryl Kroner, Wagdy Loza, Jeremy Mills, David Nussbaum, Vern Quinsey, Marnie Rice, Chris Webster, and Stephen Wong.

SUMMARY

1. Violence is relatively rare in Canada. The rate of violent crime has generally decreased since the early 1990s. Only about one-third of violent incidents are reported to the police. Being young, being single, often going out in the evening, and living in cities are associated with higher rates of violent victimization.

2. Hostile aggression is an impulsive reaction to some real or perceived provocation or threat, whereas instrumental aggression is premeditated and ultimately aimed at achieving some secondary goal. Hostile and instrumental aggression may be best viewed as opposite ends of a continuum along which acts of aggression can fall.

3. Four key approaches to risk assessment are unstructured clinical judgment, empirical actuarial, mechanical, and structured professional judgment. Actuarial risk-assessment instruments (e.g., VRAG, SAQ) are generally more accurate at predicting violent recidivism than structured professional judgment instruments and unstructured clinical judgment.

4. In violence risk assessment, different predictive errors have different consequences. False positives result in unnecessarily restricting offenders' liberty and wasting scarce resources, whereas false negatives result in harm to those who are victimized by the offender. The optimal balance between the two types of errors will vary depending on the relative costs and benefits of each outcome.

5. Researchers generally find lower violent recidivism rates among treated compared to untreated offenders, and programs that follow the general principles of effective corrections appear to be more effective than programs that do not. Although these

findings are very encouraging, debate continues about whether the lower rates of violent recidivism associated with treatment actually demonstrate that it is effective because the research methodology used in most studies leaves the results open to alternate interpretations.

6. Homicide rates are quite low in Canada compared to many other countries. Perpetrators and victims are more likely to be male than female. Victims are most likely to be killed by someone they know. Multiple murders, such as mass murder, spree murder, and serial murder, are exceedingly rare.

Discussion Questions

1. Considering the risk-assessment items presented in this chapter, how likely do you think it is that Robert Smith (from the vignette at the beginning of the chapter) will violently recidivate upon release from Kingston Penitentiary?

2. Imagine you are a forensic psychologist doing a risk assessment of a violent offender for his upcoming parole hearing. What approach to risk assessment would you use? Which risk-assessment instrument would you use? If challenged, how would you justify your decisions about approaches and instruments?

3. What is the relationship between major mental illness and violent recidivism?

4. Do you think treatment reduces violent recidivism? Why or why not?

5. Imagine you have been asked to conduct a high-quality evaluation of the effectiveness of a new violence program at CSC. How would you do it?

6. In terms of Holmes and DeBurger's (1988) serial killer typology, how would you classify Robert Pickton? Why?

Additional Reading

Bonta, J., Law, M., and Hanson, R.K. 1998. "The prediction of criminal and violent recidivism among mentally disordered offenders: A meta-analysis." *Psychological Bulletin, 123*, 123–142.

Quinsey, V.L., Harris, G.T., Rice, M.E., and Cormier, C.A. 2006. *Violent offenders: Appraising and managing risk*. Washington, DC: American Psychological Association.

Stoff, D.M., Breiling, J., and Maser, J.D. 1997. *Handbook of antisocial behavior*. New York: John Wiley.

Relevant Websites

Correctional Service of Canada
www.csc-scc.gc.ca

Public Safety Canada
www.publicsafety.gc.ca

Mental Health Centre Penetanguishene Research Department
www.mhcp.on.ca/Site_Published/internet/ResearchActivities.aspx

Chapter 8

Behind Closed Doors:

Family Violence

Susan was 21 when she married her college sweetheart, Matthew, an officer in the Canadian Armed Forces. Prior to his deployment to Afghanistan, Matthew occasionally yelled at Susan about her excessive spending and her failure to keep the children quiet. When they first married, he called her names and threatened to use violence, which escalated to slapping her several times and once shoving her down the front steps of the house. Despite the verbal and physical abuse, Susan never called the police or told her family or friends due to her fear of what would happen to her, her husband, and children. Shortly after Matthew returned from overseas, the military transferred him, Susan, and their two children Michael (ten) and Natalie (seven), from their on-base home in Petawawa to off-base in Alberta. Susan hoped that moving to a new location would bring a fresh start. However, the verbal and physical abuse resumed once the family had settled into their new home. While in Alberta, Matthew continued to limit the amount of money Susan was allowed to spend. One evening Mathew and Susan again argued about money but this time it escalated to Mathew punching Susan in the face, throwing her on the ground, and choking her. The next morning she went to a medical clinic to get treatment for a fractured wrist. The physician who examined Susan suspected domestic abuse but she denied the allegation. Susan felt partly to blame and believed that if she could change her behaviour Matthew would be happier and stop the abuse.

Learning Objectives

1   Distinguish between the different types of family violence.

2   Explain the ecological model of family violence.

3   Outline how social learning theory has been used to explain intimate violence.

4   Describe the effectiveness of treatment programs for intimate violence.

5   Identify the short- and long-term consequences of child abuse.

6   Identify the victim and perpetrator risk factors for elder abuse.

INTRODUCTION

IDEALLY, A FAMILY IS A PLACE WHERE SOMEONE CAN FEEL LOVED, SECURE, AND SAFE. However, within some families, there is abuse, fear, and a lack of emotional bonds that can lead to violence. The occurrence and aftermath of this violence can have devastating short- and long-term effects. In some cases, children who experience abuse become abusers themselves and the cycle passes from generation to generation. As in the opening vignette, it is not unusual that victims of abuse initially blame themselves. Victims will often attempt to change their behaviour in order not to trigger an abusive episode, but the abuse usually continues and even escalates.

Why study family violence? First, it is the most prevalent form of violence in society. Second, it is distinct from other types of violence since the victims and perpetrators know each other and there is often an ongoing relationship prior to, during, and after the violent episode. Finally, in contrast to other forms of violence, some forms of family violence are sanctioned (e.g., physical punishment of children) or considered normal (e.g., fighting among siblings) and therefore not considered criminal.

This chapter is divided into three parts. The first covers abuse within intimate relationships; the second, child abuse; and the third discusses elder abuse. Major themes in each are the prevalence of the abuse, its causes, and interventions. Estimates of the magnitude of family violence vary depending on the sample, type, and severity of violence and the method of data collection. What is clear, however, is that family violence is likely the most common form of criminal activity.

VIOLENCE WITHIN THE FAMILY: BACKGROUND ISSUES

FAMILY VIOLENCE IS ANY VIOLENCE OCCURRING BETWEEN MEMBERS OF A FAMILY. FOR MUCH OF history, family violence had a quasi-legitimacy, due primarily to cultural and religious attitudes that effectively placed women and children in subservient roles within the family. Only in the recent past have attitudes toward the issue changed. The women's liberation movement and the growth of feminism led women to question the long-standing acceptance of family violence. Not until the 1980s did major changes take place in Canadian law dealing with family violence. In approximately the same time period, it also become a major research area.

Defining family violence is controversial. Should all abuse in the context of a family be included or only more serious forms of abuse? How family violence is defined has a considerable impact on the reported rates. Unfortunately, no consensus exists for a definition, although most current definitions of family violence include non-violent abuse (such as emotional or financial abuse). Differential rates of abuse can be the result of differences in who is sampled and what is counted. For example, some child abuse studies record the number of cases reported and others only include allegations substantiated by investigation.

When examining the frequency of violence, it is important to clarify the distinction between prevalence and incidence. **Prevalence** refers to the *total* number of people who have experienced violence in a specified time period, whereas **incidence** is the number of *new* cases identified or reported at a given point in time, usually one year. When reporting on the estimates of family violence, many factors will influence the prevalence and incidence figures.

Most researchers have focused on one specific type of family violence, but there is evidence of considerable overlap in the risk factors and causes of different forms. Research is needed to integrate different theories, understand the impact of multiple forms of violence on the victims, and focus on prevention of all forms of violence.

Types of Violence

The types of abuse that can occur within families are described in Table 8.1. Some forms of abuse are more common than others. For example, neglect is the most common form

Table 8.1 Types of Family Violence

Types of Abuse	Characteristics	Examples
Psychological/ emotional	The infliction of mental distress	Insulting, swearing, yelling, threatening, mocking, ignoring, isolating, or excluding the person from meaningful activities
Physical	The infliction of pain or injury	Beating, punching, burning, pushing, kicking, hitting with hand or object, stabbing, choking, force-feeding, or restraint
Financial/ material	The illegal or improper exploitation and/or use of funds or resources	Misusing power of attorney, tricking or threatening a person out of assets, cashing cheques without authorization, restricting access to bank accounts, or using a person's money for something it was not intended to be used for
Sexual	Any kind of sexual behaviour directed toward a child or unwanted sexual behaviour directed toward an adult	Showing of pornography, exposure of genitals, sexual harassment, exploitation through prostitution, or sexual assault
Neglect	Intentional or unintentional refusal or failure of caregiver to provide adequate care	Inadequate nutrition, clothing, personal care, or clean safe living environment; lack of access to medical care; poor supervision; or abandonment
Exposure to parental violence	Seeing or knowing about parental violence	Any form of psychological or physical violence occurring between parents

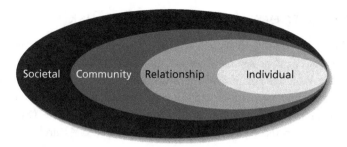

Figure 8.1 Ecological Model of Family Violence

Source: Dahlberg and Krug (2002)

of abuse in both children and the elderly. Psychological abuse is often described by individuals as one of the most hurtful types of abuse. Financial abuse is most often studied in the context of elder abuse but can also occur within intimate relationships.

Ecological Model of Family Violence

The **ecological model** of family violence (Dahlberg and Krug 2002) provides a useful way to conceptualize the interaction among factors related to violence in intimate relationships, child abuse, and elder abuse. As illustrated in Figure 8.1, the model focuses on the relationship between multiple levels of influence in understanding family violence, including individual, relationship, community, and societal factors. At the individual level, biological, and personal history characteristics of the abuser and victim need to be considered. Such factors often include age, substance use, and history of abuse.

At the relationship level, a person's closest social circle of peers, partners, and family members may contribute to an increased risk. Important factors may include level of stress or exposure to violence. The community level incorporates places such as schools and neighbourhoods that are associated with becoming a victim or perpetrator of family violence, as well as factors such as poverty, social isolation, and community disorganization. The societal level includes broad societal factors in which violence is supported or discouraged, including social norms, cultural beliefs, and police and government policies.

INTIMATE PARTNER VIOLENCE

INTIMATE PARTNER VIOLENCE (ALSO CALLED SPOUSAL VIOLENCE) OCCURS BETWEEN INTIMATE partners who are living together or separated. Varying in type and severity, it includes physical (e.g., hitting, punching, stabbing, burning), sexual, financial (e.g., restricting access to personal funds, forcing complete financial responsibility, theft of paycheques), and emotional abuse (e.g., verbal attacks, degradation, threats to hurt pets or family members, isolation from family members, unwarranted accusations about infidelity).

Intimate Partners: A Potential for Risk

How often do couples engage in violence? Fifty-one percent of women reported at least one incident of physical or sexual violence since the age of 16 according to a 1993 Statistics Canada Violence Against Women survey of 12 500 women (Johnson 1996).

A 2004 survey by Statistics Canada provides additional information on intimate partner assault. A modified version of the Conflict Tactics Scale (Straus 1979; see Box 8.1) was administered to a large sample of men (10 604) and women (13 162)

In 1979, Murray Straus was interested in studying conflict in intimate relationships but needed some way to quantify the different forms of conflict resolution techniques. He developed the **Conflict Tactics Scale** (CTS) to assess how a person and their partner resolve conflict. The CTS consists of 18 items ranging from constructive problem-solving (e.g., discussing the issues calmly) to verbal aggression (e.g., swearing or threatening to hit) and physical aggression (e.g., slapping or using a knife). Respondents indicate how often they have used different methods and how often they have experienced these acts. The CTS has been used in hundreds of studies in over 25 countries to measure intimate violence. Having a common measurement tool enables researchers to compare findings across studies. However, a number of limitations have been identified (see Archer 1999 and Dobash, Dobash, Wilson, and Daly 1992 for reviews). These limitations include a failure to assess for the context and purpose of violent acts (offense versus defensive responses), few items measuring psychological aggression, no assessment of sexual aggression, and no assessment of

the consequences of aggression (what types of injury occur). In response to these concerns, Straus, Hamby, Boney-McCoy, and Sugerman (1996) developed a more comprehensive version—the CTS-2. The following changes were made:

1. The physical aggression scale was expanded to include more acts (e.g., burned or scalded partner on purpose, slammed partner against wall).

2. The verbal aggression scale was renamed psychological aggression and additional items were added (e.g., did something to spite partner).

3. The reasoning scale was renamed negotiation and additional items added (e.g., explained side of argument).

4. New scales were added to measure sexual aggression (e.g., I used threats to make my partner have sex) and physical injury (e.g., I had a broken bone from a fight with my partner).

5. A better description was developed of minor versus more serious forms of acts.

6. Items from each scale were interspersed to minimize response sets.

Box 8.1   Continued

The CTS-2 contains 78 items and has become the dominant instrument for assessing violence among dating and cohabiting partners. Researchers have also begun to investigate whether couples agree with each other. Simpson and Christensen (2005) had 273 treatment-seeking couples complete the CTS-2. There were low to moderate levels of agreement, with both men and women reporting that their partner had committed more aggressive acts than they had committed. There was better agreement on specific objective acts (e.g., I slapped my partner) as compared to more general items (e.g., I did something to spite my partner). Some researchers have started to develop alternative methods to assess intimate violence, such as interviews or diary methods where participants record violent acts as they occur (Fals-Stewart, Birchler, and Kelley 2003).

across Canada. The scale was designed to measure psychological, physical, and sexual violence in intimate relationships, including threats and sexual assault over both the past 12 months and the past five years. Respondents reported that in the year preceding the survey, 2 percent of men and women had experienced physical and/or sexual assault. In the five years preceding the survey (1999 to 2004), 7 percent of female and 6 percent of male respondents reported having experienced physical and/or sexual assault. Although both men and women experienced violence, women reported experiencing more severe forms of violence (i.e., being choked, sexually assaulted, or threatened by a partner using a knife or gun). Violence against women was more likely to be reported to the police (36 percent) than was violence against men (17 percent), a finding echoed in research discussed later in the chapter.

Although abuse against women occurs at all socio-demographic levels, a recent study by DeKeseredy, Schwartz, and Alvi (2008) found much higher rates of abuse in women living in Ontario public housing compared to rates reported in the 2004 national survey. DeKeseredy et al. found that 19 percent of women reported have been physical assaulted in the past year, over eight times the average reported in the national survey.

The World Health Organization has studied the lifetime and past-year prevalence of physical and sexual violence in intimate relationships across 10 countries (WHO 2005). Wide variations of prevalence rates were found. Lifetime rates of physical violence ranged from 13 percent in Japan to 61 percent in Peru and sexual violence from 6 percent in Japan and Serbia to 59 percent in Ethiopia. Physical and sexual violence were experienced more often by women in rural as compared to urban settings.

The International Dating Violence Study (Chan et al. 2008) used the Conflict Tactics Scale–2 (see Box 8.1) to examine the prevalence of dating violence in 14 252 university students across 32 countries. Table 8.2 presents victimization reports of any physical aggression including minor violence (e.g., threw something to hurt partner, slapped, twisted my partner's arm) to severe violence (e.g., choked partner, beat up my partner, used a knife or gun

Table 8.2 Victimization Rates of Physical Assault and Sexual Coercion in Dating Relationships in University Students over a 12-Month Period

Country	Any Assaults (%)	Severe Assaults (%)	Sexual Coercion (%)
Asia and Middle East			
China	27.2	7.8	15.4
India	35.5	13.7	18.6
Israel	13.9	4.9	21.4
Australia and New Zealand			
Australia	22.3	5.8	22.6
New Zealand	27.0	5.6	26.4
Europe			
Belgium	25.4	4.5	11.3
Germany	30.4	8.3	41.6
Greece	34.4	14.0	46.2
Netherlands	28.0	2.3	9.1
Portugal	14.4	2.8	24.4
Russia	27.3	7.1	25.6
Sweden	15.1	2.7	16.4
United Kingdom	32.1	7.5	24.2
Latin America			
Brazil	19.3	5.4	37.0
Mexico	39.1	10.2	21.4
North America			
Canada	22.2	7.3	28.4
United States	28.3	9.3	31.8

Source: Adapted from Chan et al. (2008)

on my partner) over the previous 12 months in selected countries. Rates of being a victim of sexual coercion in selected countries were also reported. Sexual coercion included both minor acts (e.g., made my partner have sex without a condom, insisted on sex when my partner did not want to) to more severe acts (e.g., used force to make my partner have oral or anal sex, used threats to make my partner have sex). Although there were substantial variations across nations, it is important to note that even in the country with the lowest rate, Israel, 14 percent of students had been physically assaulted by a dating partner within the previous 12 months. In comparison to other countries, Canadian dating violence rates were in the lower half of the nations surveyed; however, about one in five Canadian university students reported have experienced physical assault by their dating partners in the previous 12 months. In contrast, the United States and Canada had relatively high rates of sexual coercion as compared to other countries.

Recently, Statistics Canada (Ogrodnik 2008) provided information on the number of police-reported spousal violence incidents across Canada. A total of 38 000 incidents were reported in 2006 (15 percent of all violence reported to police). The data likely reflect an underestimate of the amount of violent offences, since most victims do not call the police. In addition, police data only include forms of spousal abuse that are chargeable under the Canadian *Criminal Code* (most forms of psychological and financial abuse are excluded). As a proportion to other violent incidents, spousal violence is most common in Nunavut, PEI, Quebec, and Alberta, with the lowest rates in B.C., New Brunswick, and Nova Scotia. These differences may be due to the differing number of risk factors across the provinces and territories: social isolation, younger couples, higher levels of unemployment, higher rates of alcohol consumption, more common-law marriages, and the proportion of Aboriginals (Ogrodnik 2008). Females are the most likely victims of police-reported spousal violence across all provinces and territories, with 83 percent of the victims being female. Charges were laid in 77 percent of the incidents against female victims. Whether a charge is laid depends on the province, with police charges most prevalent in Manitoba (92 percent) and Ontario (90 percent) and least prevalent in Newfoundland (56 percent) and New Brunswick (57 percent). It is not clear why differences exist across provinces for police charges in response to spousal violence. Some positive news can be found in the midst of these findings: there was a steady decline in police-reported spousal violence between 1998 and 2006.

Police forces recognize that spousal abuse is a continuing problem that requires a serious response. Unfortunately, the majority of women who are abused by their partner do not call the police. A recent study by Akers and Kaukinen (2009), using data from the Canadian General Social Survey from 1999, examined which demographic and incidence-related variables were related to police-reporting decisions. Married women were less likely to report violence to the police. This finding may be due to the stronger financial and emotional ties a married woman has toward her spouse. In contrast, women with children living at home who witness their abuse were more likely to contact the police. Minority women were more likely than Caucasian women to report spousal violence. The likelihood of reporting increases with age, but in older samples this effect is reduced. Women were also more likely to call the police if they were injured or if a weapon was involved. If the abuser was drinking during the incident or if he also destroyed property, the victim was more likely to report the abuse. Police officers responding to calls of domestic violence need to be aware of who is likely to contact them (and, potentially, who is not likely to contact them, despite the presence of abuse). Knowing this information, they can respond with sensitivity and care.

Triggers for Violence

What triggers a man to engage in physical violence? (The question is framed in terms of male violence against a female partner because much of the research has focused on male-initiated violence.) When battered women are asked about what triggers violent incidents, their answers have included:

- Not obeying or arguing with the man
- Not having food ready on time
- Not caring adequately for the children or home
- Questioning the man about money or girlfriends
- Going somewhere without the man's permission
- The man suspecting the woman of infidelity
- Refusing the man sex

Certainly none of the above are acceptable reasons for anyone to use violence. Nonetheless, it is important to understand what constitutes a trigger in order to challenge these beliefs in treatment programs. In some countries, men perceive themselves as "owners" of their wives and children and feel that it is justified to use force in certain circumstances. For example, in Egypt, 57 percent of urban women and 81 percent of rural women agree that a man is justified in beating his wife if she refuses to have sex with him. In New Zealand, the majority of men believe that under no circumstances should you physically abuse a women, although 5 percent agree that physical force would be justified if the man came home and found his wife in bed with another man. The World Health Organization (2005) study cited earlier asked women under which circumstances a man would be justified in beating his wife. The reasons most commonly given were not completing housework, refusing to have sex, disobeying her husband, or being unfaithful. Across all countries, the most widely accepted justification for violence was female infidelity, ranging from 6 percent in Serbia to 80 percent in Ethiopia. Woman were also asked if they believe a woman has the right to refuse sex if she is ill, if her husband is drunk, if her husband is mistreating her, or if she does not want to have sex. The most acceptable reason to refuse sex was illness, and the least acceptable reason was if she did not want to have sex. In some countries, such as Ethiopia and Tanzania, about 20 percent of women felt they did not have the right to refuse sex under any conditions. In a large survey of 5238 adults in the United States, Simon et al. (2001) found that 98 percent of men did not think it was "ok to hit your wife to keep her in line" (p. 118). In addition, participants were more accepting of women hitting men as compared to men hitting women. To date there have been no published studies measuring Canadian beliefs about intimate partner violence. (See Box 8.2 for how intimate violence has been studied in the laboratory.)

Studying Intimate Violence in the Lab

How do you study intimate violence in a laboratory? Dutton and Browning (1988) conducted one of the first analogue lab studies to examine the influence of abandonment themes in groups of violent men. They presented video or audio clips of a woman telling her husband she was joining a women's consciousness-raising group and was spending the weekend with a group of women in another city. They had tested three groups of men: men who had engaged in intimate partner violence, generally violent men, and non-violent men. Men who had engaged in intimate partner violence reported much higher rates of anxiety and anger to the clips.

In another analogue study, Costa and Babcock (2008) used an anger induction task to measure articulated cognitive thoughts of intimately violent and non-violent men. In this study, the men were asked to imagine two scenarios. First they overheard their female partner flirting with another man. Then they were asked to imagine their female partner criticizing them (e.g., about job performance, performance in bed, their friends and family, and intelligence) to a female friend. After each scenario, the subjects were asked to verbalize how it made them feel. The researchers found no group differences in men's verbalizations after the first scenario but found that intimately violent men were more likely to express anger during the criticism scenario and non-violent men were more likely to express sadness.

Theories of Intimate Violence

Several theories have been proposed to account for intimate violence. This section focuses on two of these theories: patriarchal theory and social learning theory. Patriarchal theory assumes a long-standing set of cultural beliefs and values that support the idea that the male dominance of women contributes to the domestic assault of women by men (e.g., Dobash and Dobash 1979; Ellis 1989; Straus 1977). Often associated with sociology and feminism, the theory was first described in the 1970s. Dobash and Dobash (1979) state: "the seeds of wife beating lie in the subordination of females and in their subjection to male authority and control" (p. 33). **Patriarchal theory** is somewhat challenging to evaluate directly because it is hard to show a causal link between patriarchal attitudes and intimate violence. A correlational study by Yllo and Straus (1990) showed that degree of patriarchal attitude was positively correlated with rate of intimate violence. Yllo and Straus compared spousal abuse rates in the United States by identifying the degree to which each state was characterized by patriarchal structure. States with higher levels of patriarchal attitudes (as measured by male-dominant norms) had much higher rates of spousal assault than states with less patriarchal attitudes. (See Box 8.3 for a profile of Dr. Donald Dutton.)

Patriarchal theory has been criticized because it provides an incomplete explanation of intimate violence and cannot predict which individuals will engage in it. Dutton (1995) argues that additional variables are necessary to account for intimate violence, including community (e.g., work, peers), family (e.g., communication level between couple), and individual characteristics (e.g., coping skills, empathy). Thus if two men grow up to have the same cultural values, comparable social support, and similar levels of conflict with their partners, one man may respond with violence and the other may not. Dutton and Corvo (2007) provide a cogent review of the lack of scientific evidence for patriarchy being a key factor in explaining intimate violence.

An alternative account of intimate violence is **social learning theory** (see Chapter 3). The theory was originally proposed by Bandura (1973) to explain aggression and was extended by Dutton (1995) to account for intimate violence. It has three major elements related to aggression: origins, instigators, and regulators. A key feature of social learning theory is how individuals acquire new behaviours, especially aggression. A prominent mechanism for learning new behaviours is observational learning, in which an individual models a behaviour that they observe. Bandura (1973) proposed that observational learning could occur in three contexts: family of origin, the subculture in which a person lives, and the media. Consistent with social learning theory, men who engage in intimate violence are more likely to have witnessed parental violence than men who do not engage in intimate violence (Kalmuss 1984; Straus, Gelles, and Steinmetz 1980). It is important to note that not all behaviour that is observed will be repeated by the observer. Bandura (1973) argues that for a behaviour to be acquired, it must have functional value for the observer. Like operant conditioning, behaviour that is rewarded increases the likelihood that it will be repeated, whereas behaviour that is punished decreases its likelihood of being repeated.

Social learning also states that acquired behaviours are only manifested if an appropriate event in the environment, called an **instigator**, acts as a stimulus. Dutton (1995) proposed three categories of instigators in intimate violence: aversive instigators, incentive instigators, and delusional instigators. Aversive instigators are stimuli that the individual attempts to avoid. They produce emotional arousal, and how a person labels that emotional arousal will affect how they react. Male batterers have a predisposition to interpret a wide variety of emotional states as anger. Gondolf (1985) describes this tendency as the "emotional funnel system" (p. 41). Incentive instigators are stimuli that are perceived as rewards for engaging in aggression. When individuals believe they can satisfy their needs by using aggression, they may decide to be violent. Delusional instigators are associated with bizarre belief systems, such as delusional jealousy, in which an individual erroneously believes their partner to be unfaithful, potentially resulting in aggression.

An additional concept in social learning theory includes the assumption that behaviour is regulated by the outcomes it generates (similar to the concept of reinforcement that underlies operant conditioning). **Regulators** include external punishment and self-punishment. External punishments are exogenous forms of punishment, such as when a person is arrested for engaging in violence. Self-punishment is an internal reaction to the

Box 8.3

Canadian Researcher Profile:
Dr. Donald Dutton

The work of Donald Dutton is a consummate blend of basic and applied research. He has contributed greatly to the issue of understanding why men engage in domestic violence while showing how to apply this knowledge to real-world situations. Dr. Dutton completed his degrees at the University of Toronto, focusing on social psychology. Currently he is a professor in the Department of Psychology at the University of British Columbia, where he conducts research on domestic violence, spousal homicide, and other forms of extreme violence such as genocide.

In a recent review of his more than 30 years of research on domestic violence, Dutton (2008) describes how he became interested in the topic:

> I started by riding on police patrol and asking the police what part of their job they felt the least equipped to handle. The answer was 'domestic disturbances.' I developed a police training manual and was then asked to assist with police intervention (p. 1).

Dutton recognized early on in his career that in order to protect victims from future violence, a treatment program for batterers was needed. He and his colleagues developed a court-mandated cognitive-behavioural treatment (CBT) program in the early 1980s. This program and subsequent CBT programs have been found to be the most effective type of treatment for reducing future spousal assaults.

In response to a question about what keeps him interested in research, Dr. Dutton replied, "[c]uriosity." He is intrigued with the question of why someone would kill someone they love or how "ordinary men" become cruel and sadistic in war situations. He uses a range of methodologies in his work, from laboratory studies to field research and, more recently, forensic ethology. Forensic ethology is a perspective that examines the details of real-world events to understand the motivation of individual perpetrators.

Dr. Dutton's favourite research topic is also the title of his book, *The Abusive Personality*, first published in 2003. In it he describes abusive personalities as a constellation of traits that lead people to become easily threatened and jealous, and to mask these feelings with anger and control behaviours. In the second edition of his book in 2007, Dr. Dutton extended the concept to explain women's use of violence in intimate relationships. He encourages students interested in domestic violence to become familiar with the considerable amount of research conducted on the psychology of domestic violence. He is frustrated by the focus of policy makers and treatment providers on attempting to explain domestic violence by focusing on male dominance and acceptance of violence. He believes that the causes of

Continued >

Box 8.3 Continued

intimate violence are complex, that both men and women engage in this form of violence, and that a multifaceted treatment approach is needed.

Dr. Dutton was called to testify at one of the most high-profile criminal trials in U.S. history—the O. J. Simpson murder trial. His expertise in the areas of spousal violence and homicide were particularly relevant to the case.

Dr. Dutton enjoys teaching forensic psychology, social psychology, and a graduate course titled "Nested Ecology of Violence." He recently published a book, *The Psychology of Genocide, Massacres, and Extreme Violence: Why "Normal" People Commit Atrocities,* which he dedicated to his dog. When asked why, Dr. Dutton explained, "[d]ogs are inherently nicer than humans"— a theory many dog-lovers would agree with.

consequences of one's behaviour that is akin to "having a conscience," such as when a person feels remorse for engaging in violent behaviour. According to social learning theory, the likelihood of intimate violence should be reduced if the consequences for violence are exceeded by incentives for engaging in non-violent behaviour and if alternatives are provided to attenuate the effect of any instigators.

Male Victims of Intimate Violence

Historically, domestic violence has been conceptualized as male violence against female partners, and this form of violence has been the focus of research and public policy. However, intimate violence is not solely the province of men acting against women. Women also initiate violence and, according to some studies, engage in more minor violence than men (Archer 2002). In a large study, Williams and Frieze (2005) analyzed the occurrence of violence in 3519 couples and found that the most frequently occurring type of violence was mutual and mild violence followed by mutual severe violence. This pattern indicates that, at least for some forms of intimate violence, the long-held belief that males are the primary instigators is false (Carney, Buttell, and Dutton 2007). Recent evidence indicates that it is possible to identify personality and behavioural features in 15-year-old girls that will predict their use of violence in dating relationships at age 21 regardless of whether their male partner uses violence (Moffitt, Caspi, Rutter, and Silva 2001). Mutuality of violence is also found in dating relationships. In a large international study of dating violence among university students in 32 countries, Straus (2008) reported that a slightly higher percentage of women engage in minor violence (e.g., slapping, throwing something at a partner that could hurt) and that equal rates of serious violence occur for men and women.

Gender biases in which men are disadvantaged exist in several other contexts. A long-standing belief associated with intimate violence is that due to differences in physical size and strength, women are most likely to suffer serious injuries compared to men. However, several studies (e.g., Carney, Buttel, and Dutton 2007; Felson and Cares 2005) have shown that while it is true that women are more likely to be injured than men as a consequence of intimate violence, the incidence of men being injured by women is surprisingly high. A gender bias is also present in police responses to domestic violence. Brown (2004) found that when the female partner was injured, the male was charged in 91 percent of the cases; however, when the male was injured, the female was charged only 60 percent of the time. When no injury occurred, the female was charged in 13 percent of cases as compared to 52 percent of the time for males. The way courts treat men and women charged with domestic violence also differs. Charges against women are more likely to be dropped by prosecutors and, if charged, women are less likely to be found guilty. Brown (2004) reported that in severe injury cases, 71 percent of men and 22 percent of women defendants were found guilty. A major factor for why such a low percentage of women are found guilty was that the male victim was not willing to testify.

Follingstad, Helff, Binford, Runge, and White (2004) found that the gender bias even extends to psychologists. They presented two scenarios to a large sample of clinicians (N = 449, 56 percent male, median age 52). The scenarios provided a context and description of psychologically abusive behaviours. Critically, Follingstad et al. reversed the gender of the protagonists in the scenarios. Results showed that the same behaviour was rated more abusive and severe when it was carried out by a male than when carried out by a female. Moreover, this bias was not affected by the context of the scenario (i.e., frequency, intent, perception of recipient) nor by the gender of the psychologist. Specific items rated more abusive if performed by a man included "made to account for whereabouts at all times," "would not allow to look at members of same sex," "threatened to have committed to an institution," and "made derogatory comments."

Almost all prevention and intervention programs target men who abuse their partners. It is essential that violence by women be recognized and that robust efforts are implemented to end assaults by women.

Typologies of Male Batterers

In order to better understand the motivations and characteristics of men who engage in intimate violence and to develop more targeted interventions, researchers have developed typologies or categories of male batterers. The typology that has received the most attention was developed by Holtzworth-Munroe and Stuart (1994), who identified three types of male batterers based on the severity and frequency of violence, generality of violence, and psychopathological features.

The **family-only batterer** type displays the following characteristics:

- Engages in the lowest levels of intimate violence
- Is infrequently violent outside the home and rarely engages in other criminal acts
- Does not show much psychopathology

- Has few risk factors (i.e., witnessing violence as a child, poor relationship skills)
- Aggression is triggered by stress

The **generally violent/antisocial batterer** type has the following features:

- Engages in moderate to high levels of intimate violence
- Is frequently violent outside the home and engages in other criminal acts
- Has antisocial and psychopathic personality features
- Has substance abuse problems
- Has problems with impulsivity and many violence-supportive beliefs
- Attachment style best described as dismissive

The **dysphoric-borderline batterer** type is characterized by:

- Engages in moderate to severe levels of intimate violence
- Usually focuses violence on female partners
- High rates of mood disorders
- Has borderline personality features such as instability, jealously, and fear of rejection
- Experienced childhood abuse
- Attachment style best described as preoccupied

Holtzworth-Munroe and Stuart's typology has been replicated by several studies (Holtzworth-Munroe et al. 2003; White and Gondolf 2000). Dixon and Browne (2003) reported, on average, that offenders were classified as 50 percent family-only type, 30 percent generally violent/antisocial type, and 20 percent dysphoric-borderline type.

Several other typologies of male batterers have been proposed that focus on behavioural, psychological, or physiological characteristics. Most of these alternative typologies classify batterers into two or three groups. For example, Gondolf (1988), using data from 6000 battered women, created a three-tier typology based on the severity and generalizability of violence. The Type I or sociopath (accounting for about 10 percent of batterers) engages in the most severe levels of violence in and outside the home. Type II or antisocial (accounting for about 30 to 40 percent of batterers) is primarily violent within the home and is less likely to have a criminal record. The Type III or typical (accounting for 50 to 60 percent of batterers) engages in less severe violence, engages in violence within the home, and is least likely to have a criminal record. Using a psychological perspective, Hamberger and Hastings (1994) identified three types of male batterers: the low-risk non-pathological, who engages in family-only violence; the passive aggressive–dependent type with attachment and psychopathological problems; and the antisocial type, who engages in high levels of violence in and outside the home.

Working from a physiological perspective, Gottman and colleagues (1995) used the heart rate of male batterers at rest and during conflict to categorize batterers into groups. Type 1 abusers or the "cobra group" (accounting for 20 percent of the sample) showed a decreased heart rate as they became verbally abusive. Type 1 abusers engaged in high rates of severe violence in and outside the home. Type II or the "pitbull group" (accounting for 80 percent of the sample) showed an increased heart rate as they became verbally abusive. Type II abusers were more insecure and emotionally dependent, and primarily engaged in violence inside the home. In a study of 201 male batterers, Chiffriller and Hennessy (2007) found evidence for five types of batterers: pathological batterers, sexually violent batterers, generally violent batterers, psychologically violent batterers, and family-only batterers. The plethora of typologies has led to criticism of the methodology used in this area. In a recent critique of the male batterer literature, Chiffriller, Hennessy, and Zappone (2006) point out the methodological deficits of the existing research, including a lack of control groups, inconsistent terminology, and poor measurement of constructs.

Further research is needed to determine how different types of male batterers respond to different types of treatment, what risk factors are associated with each type, and whether different causal mechanisms exist for each type.

Victims' Response to Abuse

The options available to a person determine how they respond to an abusive event. One person might leave immediately, whereas another might stay in an abusive relationship. While one person will tell others about the abuse, another will remain silent. In most cases, leaving an abusive relationship is an extended process, with many women leaving then returning several times before deciding to permanently end the relationship (Shurman and Rodriguez 2006). In addition, victims often seek help from a variety of sources—both legal and extralegal—in their effort to address the violence in their lives (Cattaneo, Stuewig, Goodman, Kaltman, and Dutton 2007). Researchers have found that the following factors can keep an abused women in a relationship:

- Fear of retribution
- Lack of economic support
- Concern for the children
- Emotional dependence
- Lack of support from friends and family
- Hope that the man will change
- Fear of being socially ostracized (in developing countries)

Abuse does not necessarily end when the abusive relationship ends. Ending a relationship may subsequently initiate unwanted behaviour by the ex-partner, such as stalking, in a bid to re-start the relationship using intimidation. This type of behaviour can lead to tragic consequences. A significant portion of intimate partner homicides occur when the woman makes the decision to leave her abusive mate. Between 1997 and 2006 in Canada, there were 766 spousal homicides, with 616 being female and 150 being men (Li 2008). Sixteen percent of the female homicides occurred when the woman was separated from her partner.

What types of support do survivors of abuse find most helpful? What barriers do women encounter when seeking help? Most clinicians and researchers agree that seeking help will lessen the long-term impact of battering (Coker et al. 2002). Most battered women seek help first from friends and family and some may then seek help from more formal supports (e.g., police, domestic violence shelters). In a study assessing the help-seeking behaviour of women who had experienced violence (92 percent had experienced intimate partner violence), Postmus, Severson, Berry, and Yoo (2009) found that the options women used were not necessarily what they considered the most helpful. The top five resources used were emotional support from friends or family (75 percent, ranked helpfulness = 12), professional counselling (64 percent, ranked helpfulness = 13), medication for emotional problems (54 percent, ranked helpfulness = 15), welfare (51 percent, ranked helpfulness = 4), and support group or self-help (50 percent, ranked helpfulness = 16). However, only welfare was rated as one of the top five in terms of helpfulness: subsidized day care (ranked 1), religious or spiritual counselling (2), subsidized housing (3), welfare (4), and educational support (5). Women also indicated the barriers to using resources, categorizing the top five as: "I wanted to handle the problem myself" (82 percent), "I thought the problem would go away" (70 percent), "I was unsure about where to go or whom to see" (59 percent), "I didn't think treatment would work" (54 percent), and "I was concerned about how much money it would cost" (48 percent). This study suggests that although battered women need emotional support, they also need more tangible support (e.g., housing, financial, child care) that will provide them with the resources necessary to obtain self-sufficiency.

Typologies of Female Victims

Little research has been done to develop typologies of battered women. Recently, however, Roberts and Roberts (2005) developed a typology that classified victims into five types based on duration and severity of abuse using interviews with 501 battered women.

The features of the Level 1 or short-term group include

- Mild to moderate intensity violence
- One to three violent incidents
- Less than one year in the dating relationship
- Leaving the relationship shortly after the onset of violence
- Middle class with secondary or higher education
- Presence of caring support system

The features of the Level 2 or intermediate group include

- Moderate to severe intensity violence
- Three to fifteen incidents

- Cohabitating or recently married for several months to two years
- Leaves when the violence escalates
- Middle class
- Presence of caring support system

The features of the Level 3 or intermittent long-term group include

- Severe intensity violence with long periods without violence
- Four to thirty incidents
- Married with children
- Leaves when children are grown up
- Middle to upper class, reliant on husband's resources
- No alternative support systems

The features of the Level 4 or chronic and predictable include

- Severe and frequent violence including use of weapons, forced sexual acts, and death threats; serious injuries sustained
- Several hundred violent acts
- Married with children
- Violence precipitated by substance abuse
- Abuse continues until husband is arrested, hospitalized, or dies
- Lower to middle class

The features of the Level 5 or homicidal group include

- Severe and frequent violence
- Hundreds of severe violent acts
- Long-term marriage or separated
- Lower class with limited education
- Abuse ends when woman kills her partner
- Suffers from depression, suicidal ideation, post-traumatic stress disorder, and battered woman's syndrome

Roberts and Roberts's typology provides an initial step toward understanding types of battered women. However, additional research is needed to replicate this typology. Categorizing women this way serves more than an academic purpose. Roberts (2007) has proposed that intervention be geared toward different types of battered women based on typology. For example, Level 1 or Level 2 women may benefit from crisis intervention, brief psychotherapy, support groups, and restraining orders. In contrast, Level 3 and Level 4 types who have experienced more severe violence over longer periods will likely need more intensive psychotherapy.

Intimate Violence: What are the Risk Factors?

Like all violence, a combination of individual, situational, social, and community factors cause intimate violence. Table 8.3 summarizes the range of risk factors that have been identified. Much research has focused on the individual characteristics of men who abuse.

Young age and low income have consistently been found to be associated with an increased likelihood of a man committing physical violence against a partner (Kantor, Jasinski, and Aldarondo 1994). Exposure to parental violence as a child is a historical risk factor that has been related to domestic violence. For example, Mitchell and Finkelhor (2001) found a more than 100 percent increase in the risk for spousal violence if the perpetrator had been exposed to violence as a child. There are also psychological, relationship, community, and societal risk factors that have been found to contribute to the perpetration of intimate violence.

RISK ASSESSMENT

DIFFERENT METHODS OF RISK ASSESSMENT ARE DESCRIBED IN CHAPTER 7. MANY OF THE RISK factors described in in Table 8.3 are included in risk-assessment measures. There is empirical support for both actuarial and structured professional judgment methods in the prediction of future intimate violence. An actuarial instrument developed in Ontario to predict future intimate violence is the **Domestic Violence Risk Appraisal Guide** (DVRAG) (Hilton et al. 2008). The DVRAG is an empirically derived 14-item measure designed to predict spousal assault recidivism in male spousal assault offenders. It consists

Table 8.3 Risk Factors for Intimate Violence

Individual	Relationship	Community	Society
Young age	Relationship conflict	Weak sanctions	Traditional gender norms
Alcohol use problems	Dominance imbalance	Poverty	Social norms supportive of violence
Personality disorders	Economic stress	Low social capital	
Depression			
Fear of rejection			
Childhood exposure to violence			
Anger and hostility			

of individually weighted items from the Ontario Domestic Assault Risk Assessment (ODARA) (Hilton et al. 2004), a scale designed to be used by frontline police officers, and scores on the Hare Psychopathy Checklist-Revised (PCL-R) (Hare 2003). Scores on the DVRAG can range from –10 to +41, and are divided into seven risk categories or bins. Each risk bin has a probability of spousal assault recidivism within five years ranging from 14 percent (bin 1) to 100 percent (bin 7). Only 3 percent of the scale development sample was included in bin 7. Whether or not the recidivism rates linked to each bin will replicate in other samples remains to be studied. The items in the DVRAG include:

- Number of prior domestic incidents
- Number of prior non-domestic incidents
- Prior correctional sentence (30 days or more)
- Failure on prior conditional release
- Threat to harm or kill at the index incident
- Confinement at the index incident
- Victim concern
- Number of children
- Victim's number of biological children from previous partner
- Violence against others
- Substance abuse score
- Assault on victim when pregnant
- Number of barriers to victim support
- Hare PCL-R score

The **Spousal Assault Risk Assessment** (SARA) (Kropp, Hart, Webster, and Eaves 1999) was designed to assess the risk for spousal assault in male offenders. The SARA uses the structured professional judgment approach to risk assessment and was developed by a group of researchers in British Columbia. The evaluator conducts a comprehensive assessment and refers to a list of risk factors, each having a specific coding criteria and a demonstrated relationship with spousal assault recidivism based on the existing professional and empirical literature. The SARA consists of 20 risk factors: 10 general violence risk factors and 10 spousal violence risk factors. Users code each of the items on a three-point scale, indicating the presence of any case-specific risk factors, designating any "critical" risk factors (those that are particularly salient to the degree of risk), and making a summary risk judgment of low, moderate, or high risk for future spousal violence. Some researchers have summed the risk factors together to create a total risk score. The items included in the SARA include:

- Past assault of family members
- Past assault of strangers or acquaintances
- Past violation of conditional release

- Recent relationship problems
- Recent employment problems
- Victim of or witness to family violence as a youth
- Recent substance abuse problems
- Recent suicidal or homicidal ideation
- Recent psychopathic or manic symptoms
- Personality disorder with anger, impulsivity, or behavioural instability
- Past physical assault
- Past sexual assault/sexual jealousy
- Past use of weapons and/or credible threats of death
- Recent escalation in frequency or severity of spousal assault
- Past violation of "no contact" orders
- Extreme minimization or denial of spousal assault history
- Attitudes supportive of spousal assault
- Severe and/or sexual assault during index offence
- Use of weapons and/or credible threats of death during index offence
- Violation of "no contact" order during index offence

In a meta-analysis of 18 studies, Hanson, Helmus, and Bourgon (2007) investigated the effectiveness of different approaches and measures used to assess the risk of recidivism in male spousal assault offenders. The researchers compared measures that were designed specifically to predict spousal assault (average weighted d of .40), measures designed to predict general or violent recidivism (average weighted d of .54), and general assessments of risk provided by the female victims (average weighted d of .36). The results for the SARA, DVRAG, and ODARA are presented in Table 8.4. Although only based on a

Table 8.4 Averaged Weighted Effect Size for Spousal Assault Recidivism across Measures

Measure	Cohen's d	Number of Studies	Sample Size
SARA—total score	0.43	5	1768
SARA—risk judgment	0.35	2	531
ODARA	0.60	2	446
DVRAG	0.74	1	367
VRAG	0.65	2	736

Source: Adapted from Hanson, Helmus, Bourgon (2007)

limited number of studies, the DVRAG and the VRAG are the most accurate. Additional research will need to be conducted to determine if spousal-specific risk measures are more accurate than other risk measures designed to assess for violence in general.

Treatment: What Works

Many intervention programs have been developed to target men who engage in intimate violence. One of the most widely used originated in 1981 in Duluth, Minnesota, called the Duluth Domestic Abuse Intervention Project (DAIP), often referred to as the "**Duluth model**." The goal of this program, like other treatments, is to prevent future violence. However, in contrast to more multifaceted treatment programs, it focuses on men's use of power and control. The Duluth model focuses on changing patriarchal beliefs; some programs are judgmental and use shaming to accomplish this change. A very high drop-out rate (75 percent) has been observed in some programs using the Duluth model.

Despite its widespread adoption, the Duluth model has been criticized on several grounds. For example, Dutton and Corvo argue that "the Duluth model, and its underlying ideological assumptions, is incompatible with progressive social theory and policy" (Dutton and Corvo 2007: 477). There is an ongoing debate in the literature concerning its effectiveness. Dutton and Corvo (2006) summarize the literature evaluating this model as having "negligible success in reducing or eliminating violence among perpetrators" (p. 462).

The other most common type of treatment program for male batterers is based on social learning models of violence and uses cognitive-behavioural techniques. These programs are multifaceted, targeting a range of different risk factors with the goal of helping participants understand their motivations for engaging in violence and focus on alternative skills and behaviours to form non-abusive positive relationships. These programs often include both individual and group counselling. One example of such a program is the Correctional Service of Canada's Family Violence Prevention Program. Consistent with the risk principle of effective correctional programming (see Chapter 4), there is a shorter program targeting moderate risk offenders (Moderate Intensity) and a longer, high-intensity program (High Intensity) designed to target offenders who are at high risk to engage in future intimate violence. Approximately 40 percent of male federal offenders and 15 percent of female federal offenders have a history of violence against their intimate partners (Gabora, Stewart, Lilley, and Allegri 2007; Robinson and Taylor 1995). This program targets a range of factors, including:

- Motivation for change
- Attitudes and beliefs that condone the use of violence
- Management of emotion skills relating to jealously, anger, and fear of relationship loss
- Development of communication skills
- Coping strategies to deal with criticism

- Relapse prevention plans to avoid and manage high-risk situations
- Identification of social support networks to assist in maintaining healthy relationships

Stewart, Gabora, Kropp, and Lee (2008) recently evaluated the effectiveness of these programs in a sample of 572 male Canadian federal offenders who participated in either the moderate- or high-intensity program. In contrast to community-based programs, the attrition rate was relatively low with only 18 percent of offenders dropping out of the high-intensity program and 14 percent of offenders dropping out of the moderate-intensity program. Comparing pre- and post-treatment characteristics, offenders had lower levels of jealously, fewer negative attitudes about relationships, better relapse prevention skills, and increased empathy. A sample of 160 treated offenders was compared to a combined sample of 86 drop-out/untreated offenders using a six-month follow-up. Only 4 percent of treated offenders were charged with a spousal-related offence compared to 13 percent of the untreated group. Whether the program effects continue with longer follow-up periods or using partner reports remains to be evaluated.

The largest evaluation of treatment effectiveness done to date was by Dunfond (2000), who compared a cognitive-behavioural group, a couples therapy group, and a non-treatment control group in a sample of U.S. Navy personnel. Based on victims' reports, neither the cognitive behavioural treatment nor the couples therapy had a significant impact on spousal assault recidivism in a one year follow-up. What was unusual about this sample was the atypically low rates of recidivism, even in the untreated group (4 percent). The participants in this study were all employed and had a high stake in conformity. Thus any intervention, including arrest and identification by the authorities, may have been sufficient to deter these men from committing future violence.

To date, one meta-analysis has been conducted to compare outcomes for different types of treatment for male batterers. Babcock, Green, and Robie (2004) examined 22 studies to test the relative effectiveness of the Duluth model, cognitive-behavioural therapy, and other types of interventions on police- and victim-reported recidivism. There were no differences in the effectiveness of the different types of treatment, and overall treatment had "a minimal impact on reducing recidivism beyond the effect of being arrested" (p. 1023).

CHILD ABUSE

"FAMILIES, DEFINED WIDELY, HOLD THE GREATEST POTENTIAL FOR PROTECTING CHILDREN from all forms of violence" (United Nations 2004: 47). However, families are also dangerous places for some children, since a substantial proportion are emotionally and/or physically hurt by the people closest to them.

It is very difficult to estimate the prevalence of **child abuse** since children are often reluctant to disclose abuse and parents are motivated to hide it. Thus much of the prevalent data is based on official reports of abuse, which are likely only the tip of the iceberg. There are many reasons child abuse remains hidden. Depending on the age of the child, they may not be able to communicate what has happened to them or they may not be believed. Some children fear punishment if they tell or that they may be taken away from their parents. The abusers might bribe, manipulate, or threaten the child not to talk. In addition, there may be a lack of awareness of what constitutes child abuse and some people may not wish to become involved in private family matters. In Canada, children are most likely to be physically and sexually assaulted by someone they know (Statistics Canada 2008).

There have been two national surveys of child abuse in Canada, one completed in 1998 and the other in 2003 (Trocmé et al. 2005). Both surveys collected data from child protection workers' reports across Canada. Reports were divided into three types: substantiated, in which the balance of evidence indicated that abuse or neglect has occurred; suspected, in which it was not certain if the abuse or neglect occurred; and unsubstantiated, where the balance of evidence indicated the abuse or neglect did not occur. Table 8.5 presents results from the 1998 and 2003 surveys of substantiated cases. The following can be concluded from the table.

1. A substantial increase in the substantiated rates of child abuse occurred between 1998 and 2003. Across the country, the rate of child abuse investigations increased 78 percent, from a rate of 21.5 per 1000 children to 38.3 per 1000 children.

2. In both time periods, the most common type of abuse was neglect.

3. A dramatic increase in the rate of two types of substantiated abuse occurred: exposure to domestic violence and emotional maltreatment. The only decrease in rates was for sexual abuse.

Table 8.5 Substantiated Child Maltreatment Investigations in Canada (excluding Quebec) in 1998 and 2003

Abuse Category	1998			2003		
	Number	per 1000	%	Number	per 1000	%
Physical abuse	12 353	2.56	27	25 257	5.31	24
Sexual abuse	4322	0.89	9	2935	0.62	3
Neglect	17 292	3.58	37	30 366	6.38	29
Emotional abuse	4137	0.86	9	15 369	3.23	15
Exposure to domestic violence	8284	1.72	18	29 370	6.17	28
Total	46 388	9.60	100	103 297	21.71	100

Source: Adapted from Trocmé et al. (2005)

What accounts for the increase in investigations of child abuse? There are four possible explanations: 1) an actual increase in the rates of child maltreatment; 2) changes in legislation or child welfare policies; 3) differences in study methodologies; or 4) changes in reporting by professionals and public. It appears that in 2003, child protection workers classified a greater percentage of cases as substantiated as compared to 1998 (24 percent of cases were classified as suspected in 1998 versus 13 percent in 2003). It is likely that the increase in rates of reported exposure to domestic violence and emotional maltreatment reflect a change in awareness on the part of both professionals and the public of the serious impact of these forms of maltreatment.

Data were also collected on who perpetrated the abuse, plus the age and gender of the child. The rates of abuse were approximately the same across boys and girls for all forms of abuse (21.6 per 1000 males; 21.7 per 1000 females) except for sexual abuse (girls, 63 percent; boys, 37 percent). Some age by sex differences were found, with no sex difference from birth to age 7, males being victimized more often among 8- to 11-year-olds, and females being victimized more often among 12- to 15-year-olds. Table 8.6 provides information on who committed the abuse. In contrast to all other forms of abuse, sexual abuse was most often committed either by a non-parental relative (e.g., grandparents, uncle/aunt, or sibling) or by someone outside the family (15 percent of the time, the sexual abuse was perpetrated by the child's friend). The overrepresentation of mothers in the neglect category is partly due to the 42 percent of substantiated neglect cases involving single female-parent families.

A police investigation occurred in 19 percent of substantiated child abuse cases, with criminal charges being laid in 5 percent of cases. Police investigations varied dramatically across the different types of abuse, with sexual abuse and physical abuse prompting the largest number of police investigations (sexual abuse, 63 percent; physical abuse, 29 percent; neglect, 17 percent; emotional

Table 8.6 Identified Perpetrator across Substantiated Abuse Categories in Canada (excluding Quebec) in 2003

	Biological/ Stepfather	Biological/ Stepmother	Other Relatives	Non-Relatives
Physical abuse	50%	53%	10%	2%
Sexual abuse	22%	5%	35%	38%
Neglect	45%	84%	6%	2%
Emotional abuse	56%	66%	13%	1%
Exposure to violence	88%	28%	2%	4%

Note: The rows do not add up to 100 percent since sometimes there is more than one perpetrator.

Source: Adapted from Trocmé et al. (2005)

abuse, 14 percent; exposure to domestic violence, 37 percent). In some cases, in order to protect the child, he or she was removed from the home and either placed with other family members or taken into child welfare care. Children are most likely to be removed from the home if they are neglected (23 percent removed), as compared to the 15 percent who are removed for experiencing physical abuse and 4 percent who are removed if they witness domestic violence.

Statistics Canada (2008) provides information on the incidence of children and youth (under age 18) who were subjected to physical and sexual violence that was reported to police. In 2006, for every 100 000 children and youth, 187 were victims of family violence. The most common perpetrator of this violence was the child's parent, with physical assault more frequent then sexual assault.

Child abuse and witnessing domestic violence often co-occur (Appel and Holden 1998; Renner and Slack 2006). Findings from the National Survey of Adolescents in United States found that among youth between the ages of 12 to 17 who reported exposure to violence, over 40 percent reported multiple forms of exposure (Saunders 2003). Correlations between the frequency of childhood physical abuse and domestic violence range from .28 to .56 (Appel and Holden 1998). In a longitudinal study done in New Zealand, Moffitt and colleagues (2004) found that the risk for abuse was up to nine times higher in homes in which parents physically fought as compared to homes where there was no domestic violence. The "double whammy" effect (Hughes, Parkinson, and Vargo 1989) has been used to describe the worse outcomes for children who experience both abuse and exposure to domestic violence. Future research should examine the developmental outcomes for children who experience multiple forms of abuse. This research should focus on the compounding effects of child abuse, witnessing abuse, and other adverse factors such as exposure to community violence.

To Tell or Not to Tell: Disclosing Childhood Sexual Abuse

A large number of abused children never report abuse or delay the disclosure of their abuse. Consequently, childhood abuse is significantly underreported. The lack of disclosure or **delayed disclosure** is particularly salient for childhood sexual abuse. For example, in a study of 228 adult female victims of childhood incest, Roesler and Weissman-Wind (1994) found that the average age of abuse onset was six years of age, but only a third of the sample disclosed the abuse prior to age 18 and the average age of disclosure was 26. A survey by Smith and colleagues (2000) investigated the length of time women who were raped prior to age 18 delayed disclosing their rape. Delayed disclosure was very common, with approximately half of the children who had been raped waiting more than five years before disclosing the abuse, and in 28 percent of the cases, child rape victims never told anyone until asked by the researcher.

What Factors Contribute to Child Abuse?

There is not a single, definitive cause of child abuse, and any child—regardless of age, sex, ethnicity, socioeconomic status, or living arrangements—may be vulnerable to abuse. In a recent review, Herrenkohl, Sousa, Tajima, Herrenkohl, and Moylan (2008) identified two main types of risk factors: family factors and environmental or community factors. Family factors that are related to child abuse and exposure to violence include parental problems such as unemployment, substance abuse, mental illness, crime, stress, poor health, and lower education. Parental substance abuse is a risk factor seen across many studies (Hartley 2002; Tajima 2004; Young, Boles, and Otero 2007). Environmental factors include poverty, community disadvantage, and being exposed to violence outside the home. The strongest environmental factor that has been related to child abuse is poverty (Gewirtz and Edleson 2007; Lee, Kotch, and Cox 2004).

Table 8.7 provides a summary of the risk factors for abuse. In addition to family and community factors, child and societal risk factors also exist. For example, an infant is at higher risk of abuse due to physical frailty and the state of dependency on their mother or caregiver. Infants are at highest risk immediately after birth and are at increased vulnerability (especially for neglect) up to age four. Although physical abuse is equally directed against boys and girls, girls are at higher risk for sexual abuse. In addition, in societies where sons are preferred, girls are more likely to be neglected. Children with disabilities are a heightened risk for abuse due to cultural prejudices or the increased social, economic, physical, and psychological demands the disability may place on the family. Characteristics of the child that hinder parent–child attachment, such as severe behavioural problems, can also increase the risk for abuse (Leventhal 1996). At the societal level, some countries have laws that condone violence against children. For example, some countries still permit parents to use physical force to discipline their children

Table 8.7 Risk Factors for Child Abuse

Type of Abuse	Child	Parental/Family	Social
Physical abuse	• Young age • Male • Aboriginal • Disabilities	• Single parent • Young maternal age • Low education • History of childhood physical abuse • Intimate partner violence • Unplanned pregnancy or negative attitude toward pregnancy • Social isolation or lack of social support • Substance abuse problems	• Poverty • Large family size • Recent life stressors • Lack of legal sanctions
Sexual abuse	• Female • Aboriginal	• No biological parent in family • Poor relationship between parents • Presence of stepfather • Poor child–parent relations	
Neglect	• Young age	• Single parent • Young maternal age • Parental psychopathology • Poor relationship between parents • Substance use problems • Lack of parental attachment • Early separation from mother	• Poverty • Large family size
Psychological abuse		• History of childhood abuse • Intimate partner violence • Separation or divorce of parents • Substance abuse problems • Blended family	• Poverty
Exposure to family violence		• History of witnessing parental violence • Separation or divorce of parents • Substance abuse problems • Blended family	

Box 8.4

Corporal Punishment: Discipline or Abuse?

"The basic argument is that children are people, and hitting people is wrong."

Peter Newell, 1989: 4 (Leading expert on corporal punishment)

Although the level of acceptance for corporal punishment is decreasing in Canada and the United States, a majority of parents continue to support the use of slapping, spanking, or roughly grabbing their children to enforce discipline, and current laws permit the use of corporal punishment at home. Corporal punishment is defined by the United Nations as "any punishment in which physical force is used and intended to cause some degree of pain or discomfort, however light" (Committee on the Rights of the Child 2006). In the United States, two large national surveys found that 43 percent of American parents use corporal punishment to discipline their 13-year-old children (Straus and Stewart 1999), and 55 percent of caregivers use corporal punishment to discipline their 15-year-old children (Molnar, Buka, Brennan, Holton, and Earls 2003). Bernstein (2006) cites a national 2003 survey that reported that 51 percent of Canadians believe corporal punishment should be banned, and 69 percent believe teachers should not be allowed to physically discipline children.

The Canadian Paediatric Society strongly recommends that physicians discourage the use of corporal punishment by parents (Canadian Paediatric Society 2004). The use of parental corporal discipline has been outlawed in 24 countries, beginning with Sweden in 1979. The United Nations has set a target of 2009 for its worldwide prohibition.

In Canada, section 43 of the *Criminal Code* justifies the use of corporal punishment, stating: "Every schoolteacher, parent or person standing in the place of a parent is justified in using force by way of correction toward a pupil or child, as the case may be, who is under his care, if the force does not exceed what is reasonable under the circumstances." The Supreme Court of Canada, in a 6:3 split decision in 2004, upheld the constitutionality of section 43 of the *Criminal Code* (*Canadian Foundation for Children, Youth and the Law v. Canada* 2004).

The summary of the decision is as such:

■ Parents may use reasonable physical force solely for purposes of correction

■ Teachers may no longer use corporal punishment but can use physical force to remove a child from classroom or to obtain compliance with their instructions

■ Parents may not use corporal punishment to children under the age of 2 or over the age 13 years

■ Parents cannot use corporal punishment on children of any age if they are unable to learn from it due to some form of disability

■ Parents cannot discipline with use of objects, blows, or slaps to the head

■ Parents may only use corporal punishment to discipline a child, not out of anger, frustration, or an abusive personality

The Supreme Court's decision is out of step with what is known about the harmful

Box 8.4   Continued

effects of corporal punishment of children. A meta-analysis of 88 studies by Gershoff (2002) found that children who were physically punished had more mental health problems, less positive relationships with their parents, lower levels of moral internalization, increased levels of aggression, and increased

delinquency and antisocial behaviour. As stated by Bernstein (2006), "Although Canada has taken a progressive stance on numerous social and human rights issues, it is seriously lagging behind on the issue of respecting the fundamental dignity and human rights of children and youth" (p. 115).

(see Box 8.4) or do not have laws against harmful traditional practices (see Box 8.5). Being a member of an indigenous group also increases the risk for childhood violence (see Chapter 12). Aboriginal children in Canada are much more likely to experience abuse. This heightened risk is likely due to a confluence of other risk factors, such as high rates of poverty, unemployment, alcohol abuse, and household crowding. After summarizing the risk factors, it is important to realize that they only represent a potential for abuse; many individuals associated with these risk factors *do not* abuse their children. See Box 8.6 for a description of whether or not polygamy should be considered child abuse.

Box 8.5

Traditional Practice or Child Abuse?

In some cultures, children are subjected to painful practices such as mutilation, scarring, branding, and tattooing. One harmful traditional practice that has received widespread attention is female genital mutilation (FGM), known as "cutting" in areas where it is practiced. It is estimated that about 100 million girls in the world have undergone some form of genital mutilation. Girls vary in age but some as young as four undergo varying forms of genital mutilation. This type of procedure is often done to protect virginity or as a beautification process,

and is considered an important precondition to marriage. In the most extreme cases, the internal minora and external labia majora are cut and the edges are sutured together, leaving the vagina almost sealed. Following the procedure, the victim's legs are bound together to encourage scar tissue to form. Women who experience this procedure often have difficulty in sexual relationships and during childbirth.

It is difficult to know the prevalence of FGM, but it is estimated that about 3 million girls a year undergo some form of this

Continued >

Box 8.5 Continued

procedure. The highest prevalence is found in Somalia, Ethiopia, Eritrea, and Djibouti, followed by Guinea, Egypt, Sudan, and East and West Africa. Within countries, the prevalence varies by geography and culture. For example, in Kenya, nearly every Somali and Masai girl is "cut," but only 32 percent undergo the procedure in the country as a whole.

There are also cases of girls who live in Western countries being sent back to their country of origin to experience this procedure. In England, it is estimated that 500 British girls a year are circumcised, with some procedures happening in England itself (*The Times,* 2009). FGM is illegal in Canada. Section 273.3 of the Canadian *Criminal Code* protects children who are citizens or landed immigrants from being removed from the country and subjected to FGM.

The Consequences of Child Abuse

The consequences of child abuse depend on the type, duration, and severity of the abuse. Abuse can have devastating consequences, some of which occur immediately and others surface only in adolescence or adulthood. In rare cases, the consequences are fatal, such as when the abuse escalates to a parent killing their child. In 2006, 6 in 10 homicides of Canadian children (less than age 18) were committed by family members (90 percent of the time by a parent and most often a father).

Being abused or witnessing domestic violence results in a range of emotional, psychological, and behavioural issues. Child victims report feelings of fear, guilt, and shame (Widom 2000). Some children blame themselves for the abuse or think their parents are fighting because of them. Psychological effects such as post-traumatic stress disorder, depression, and anxiety occur frequently (Mcleer et al. 1998). In adolescence, abused children are more likely to become pregnant (Herrenkohl, Herrenkohl, Egolf, and Russo 1998), drop out of school (Widom 2000), suffer from depression and attempt suicide (Fergusson, Horwood, and Lynsky 1996; Widom 2000), and engage in substance use and delinquency (McCabe, Lucchini, Hough, Yeh, and Hazen 2005; Smith and Thornberry 1995; Widom 2000). The adverse effects of abuse can be long-lasting. In adulthood, victims of childhood physical or sexual abuse are less securely attached to their partners, have poorer conflict resolution skills, and are more likely to be depressed or have eating disorders, abuse drugs and alcohol, engage in crime, and are more vulnerable to future victimization (Cunningham 2003; Felitti et al. 1998; Widom 2000).

Do the effects of abuse and exposure to domestic violence differ between boys and girls? There have been few studies investigating the differential impact and the results of these studies have been inconsistent. Some studies have found that boys who experience abuse are more prone to externalizing behaviours such as aggression or delinquency, whereas girls are more likely to exhibit internalizing behaviours such as anxiety or depression (Widom 1998). In contrast, other studies have not found gender differences (Magdol, Moffitt, Caspi, and Silva 1998; McCloskey and Licther 2003).

Why do some children who experience abuse emerge with no significant or long-term impairments? **Resilience** is defined as the capacity for children to experience adverse events and yet not experience negative outcomes. There is a growing body of research attempting to identify protective factors including characteristics of the child, parenting characteristics, and community factors that are associated with resilience. Child protective characteristics include internal locus of control, high intelligence, positive self-image, strong commitment to school, and a belief that they want to be different from their parents (Cicchetti and Rogosch 1997; Herrenkohl et al. 2008). Family characteristics include having a least one stable, non-abusive caregiver, positive perception of one's mother, positive parenting characteristics, and not experiencing chronic abuse (Toth, Cicchetti, and Kim 2002). Community features include having a positive relationship with a caring, non-abusive adult, having prosocial and supportive peers, and involvement with a religious community (Herrenkohl, Tajima, Whitney, and Huang 2005). In the Herrenkohl and colleagues (2005) study, the greater the number of protective factors, the lower the risk for future delinquency and violence in abused children.

Religion or Child Abuse: The Polygamy Debate

On March 29, 2008, a local distress centre took a call from a woman named "Sarah" claiming to be 16 years old and a child bride who had been forced to marry a much older man who repeatedly raped her at the Yearning for Zion Ranch. The ranch is located in Eldorado, Texas, and is owned by the Fundamentalist Church of Jesus Christ of the Latter Day Saints. The phone call triggered a response by Children's Protection Services (CPS) and law enforcement, who eventually removed 462 children from the ranch and put them in protective custody by the State of Texas. The children were removed because CPS thought they were being abused or were at immediate risk for abuse. The children and mothers were initially housed at Fort Concho, but were moved to the San Angelo Coliseum after complaining about the inadequate facilities. On April 18, a judge ordered all children to be placed in protective custody and that DNA testing be done to establish maternal and paternal relationships. On May 22, an appeals court ruled that there was not sufficient evidence that the children had been abused or were at risk for abuse and ordered the children to be returned to their families within 10 days. On May 29, the Texas Supreme Court (2008: 4) ruled also that the CPS must return all children since "[O]n the record before us, removal of the children was not warranted."

Who made the call to the distress line? CPS was not able to identify Sarah, the alleged victim, but police traced the calls to Rozita

Continued >

Box 8.6 Continued

Swinton, a 33-year-old woman who is alleged to have made the call. Ms. Swinton had previously been found guilty of making false reports and is suspected of being "Sarah."

The leader of the FLDS is Warren Jeffs, a bigamist who is currently serving a 10-years-to-life sentence in the Utah State Prison for sexual assault on a minor. He also faces sexual charges in Arizona stemming from the arranged marriages of three teenage girls to older men. Warren Jeffs became the leader of the FLDS when his father died in 2002. Jeffs's official title in the church was "President and Prophet, Seer and Revelator." In his role as leader, he would assign wives to husbands and could discipline male believers by reassigning their wives to other men. He believes in plural marriage and has preached that the more wives a man has, the closer he is to heaven. It is alleged that Jeffs has between 40 and 70 wives. When Jeffs's father died, he married 12 of his father's wives.

The Canadian chapter of the FLDS, located in Bountiful, British Columbia, was led by Winston Blackmore. Blackmore was ex-communicated from the FLDS in 2002 by Jeffs, following a power struggle. About 800 to 1000 people live in Bountiful, and are either members of the FLDS community led by James Oler (appointed by Jeffs) or of an off-shoot sect led by Blackmore. On January 6, 2009, both Blackmore and Oler were charged under section 293 of the Canadian *Criminal Code*, which bans polygamy. Blackmore is alleged to have 19 wives and up to 80 children. Oler is believed to have three wives. Both men are planning to plead not guilty and claim they are being persecuted for their religious beliefs.

For more about Warren Jeffs, read *When Men Become Gods: Mormon Polygamist Warren Jeffs, His Cult of Fear, and the Women Who Fought Back* by S. Singular (2008).

Protecting Our Children?

In the 1960s, Canada introduced child welfare laws that required all suspected cases of child abuse to be investigated. In order to increase the reporting of child abuse, there are mandatory laws that require Canadian citizens to report suspected cases. However, even with **mandatory reporting** laws, a person who witnesses abuse or suspects that a child is being abused may still not report it because they:

- Do not want to get involved
- Believe the abuse is not serious enough to warrant reporting
- Believe that reporting the abuse would not be in the child's best interest or will not solve the problem
- Do not understand their responsibility to report abuse or do not know to whom they should report the abuse
- Do not know that there are no legal consequences unless the report is known to be false and is made with malicious intent

ELDER MALTREATMENT: THE INVISIBLE VICTIMS

WHILE INTIMATE VIOLENCE AND CHILD ABUSE HAVE BEEN THE SUBJECT OF MUCH STUDY BY professionals and researchers, relatively little attention has been paid to **elder maltreatment**. Elder maltreatment has been called the "forgotten area of family violence" (Harris 1996: 2). The first reference to elder abuse was made in a British scientific journal in 1975, where it was called "granny battering." The World Health Organization defines elder abuse as "a single or repeated act, or lack of appropriate action, occurring within any relationship where there is an expectation of trust which causes harm or distress to an older person" (WHO 2002, as cited on the Ontario Network for the Prevention of Elder Abuse website). Definitions of elder abuse need to consider cultural influences. For example, in some traditional societies, an older widow may be subject to losing property, forced marriage, or ejection from her home. Elder abuse has a range of negative consequences to the victims, including poor quality of life, psychological distress, loss of property, multiple health problems, and increased mortality. Elder abuse occurs across all countries and all levels of society. Some researchers suggest that the lack of attention to elder abuse is partly due to ageist attitudes that permeate many societies and place older people at risk for discrimination and abuse. The focus on domestic violence emerged from the feminist movement, whereas the concern for elder abuse emerged from the professional concerns of health and social service workers.

Elder abuse is an ongoing problem, as demonstrated by cases such as

- A recently married 79-year-old Edmonton man who was left financially stranded after having his life savings drained by his new 50-year-old wife
- A mentally exhausted 53-year-old caregiver in Nova Scotia physically assaulted his 98-year-old mother, stating that he had "cracked" from the stress of looking after her
- A 53-year-old room cleaner at a Quebec retirement home is facing several theft and fraud-related charges after stealing a bank card from a room she was cleaning and robbing the resident of her life savings
- An investigation team was called to inspect a long-term care centre in Alberta after an 89-year-old woman was deliberately given improper medication and hospitalized for dehydration

Concern over the abuse of older people is heightened by the dramatic increase in the number of older people globally. In 2005, the number of people aged 60 years or older was 672 million, a number that is expected to triple to 1.9 billion by 2050 (United Nations 2005). In 2001, one in eight Canadians was older than 65, and by 2021, one in five will be older than 65. In other words, by 2021, 20 percent of Canada's population will be aged 65 years or older. A starting point for considering the problem of elder abuse is to determine its prevalence. Unfortunately, we simply don't know. In 1990, Podnieks, Pillemer, Nicholson, Shillington, and Frizzel conducted a phone survey of 2000 older Canadian adults living in private residences. They reported that 4 percent of respondents had experienced abuse or neglect. The most common form of abuse was financial, followed by chronic verbal abuse and physical abuse (by spouse). This study may have underestimated the rates of neglect, however, since those who suffer this form of abuse may not have been allowed to speak to the researchers. A more recent study of family violence in Canada by Health Canada found that 7 percent of older Canadians had experienced some form of psychological abuse, 1 percent had faced financial abuse, and 1 percent had been the victim of physical or sexual abuse by their children, caregivers, or partners in the previous five years (Health Canada 2000).

Similar estimates have been reported in United States, where between 2 and 10 percent of residents aged 65 or older have been abused (Lachs and Pillemer 2004). It has been estimated that for every case of elder abuse or neglect that is reported to the authorities, about five go unreported (National Elder Abuse Incidence Study 1998).

Statistics Canada (Orgrodnik 2008) reports that seniors (aged 65 or older) were the least likely age group to experience family violence, with 43 incidents for every 100 000 older people being reported to the police. Senior victims were most likely to be victimized by an adult child or current spouse.

Who Are the Perpetrators?

The stereotype of elder maltreatment is institutional caregiver abuse. (See Box 8.7 for a description of elder abuse that occurs in institutions.) In fact, most abuse is perpetrated by the children of the elder or their spouse (Statistics Canada 2008). The next largest

Box 8.7

Elder Abuse in Institutions: The Hidden Crime

Older people who live in institutions are vulnerable to abuse due to insufficient institutional resources and a lack of support systems. In some cases, there is not enough staff to provide for the older persons' needs, or the staff may not have received adequate training in how to care for older people. In addition, some older people suffer from diseases or disabilities, such as Alzheimer's, which makes them act in ways that some staff or other residents find frustrating or threatening. Because of their illnesses, some older people may not be able to tell anyone they have been abused. How widespread is the problem of institutional elder abuse? Two surveys of nursing home staff have been conducted. The Ontario College of Nurses (1993) surveyed 804 nurses and 804 nursing assistants and found:

- 20 percent reported witnessing abuse of patients
- 31 percent reported witnessing rough handling of patients

- 28 percent reported witnessing yelling and swearing at patients
- 10 percent reported witnessing other staff hitting or shoving patients

Equally disturbing rates have been reported in United States. Pillemer and Moore (1989) surveyed 577 nurses and nursing aides in 31 different nursing homes in New Hampshire. The staff reported that in the year prior to the survey:

- 36 percent reported witnessing physical abuse
- 21 percent reported witnessing excessive use of restraints
- 15 percent witnessed slapping or hitting of patients
- 81 percent witnessed psychological abuse including yelling, swearing, insulting, or isolating the resident inappropriately

group of elder abusers is spouses who have a lengthy history of spousal abuse. This involves the perpetuation of intimate violence from youth to old age ("Spouses who batter are not likely to stop when they turn sixty," Baron and Welty 1996: 33).

Screening for Elder Abuse

The elderly suffering from abuse cannot be helped until the abuse is detected. Screening refers to the process by which professionals detect an abused individual (screen in) while excluding (screen out) a non-abused individual. Screening tests of all types have been called "a double-edged sword, sometimes used clumsily by the well-intended" (Grimes and Schultz 2002: 881) In any screening test for elder abuse, the benefits should outweigh the risks of the test. In some cases, a false negative (screening out an elder who is being abused) will discourage professionals from gathering more information and will leave the elder at risk for continued abuse. On the other hand, a false positive error (screening in for abuse when no abuse has occurred) can lead to numerous negative outcomes, such as psychological distress, family tensions, loss of residence, or loss of autonomy for the elder. A range of screening tools has been developed, although there is limited research on their validity. Table 8.8 describes some of these scales. In some cases, screening measures ask questions directly of the older person, others are completed by practitioners, and some are directed at caregivers.

Because elders visit physicians relatively frequently, primary care physicians are in a unique position to identify maltreatment and to intervene. Unfortunately, in a

Table 8.8 Examples of Elder Abuse Screening Tools

Screening Tool	Features	Validation Setting
Indicators of Abuse Screen (IOA) (Reis and Nahmiash 1998)	48 items Trained practitioner as respondent Identifies abuse among health and social services clients	Home assessment of 341 health and social services clients aged 55 and older
Caregiver Abuse Screen (CASE) (Reis and Nahmiash 1995)	8 items Caregiver as respondent Identifies potentially abusive caregivers	44 known abusive caregivers and 45 nonabusive caregivers receiving care from social services agency
Brief Abuse Screen for the Elderly (BASE) (Reis and Nahmiash 1998)	5 items Trained practitioner as respondent Assesses likelihood of abuse with caregiver's elder	Home assessment of health and social services agency cases
Elder Assessment Instrument-Revised (EAI-R) (Fulmer 2000)	44 items Trained nurses as respondent Identifies elders at high risk for abuse or neglect	Acute care
Elder Abuse Suspicion Index (EASI) (Yaffe 2004)	6 items Older person as respondent Assesses likelihood of abuse	Home assessment of 663 respondents by social workers

Source: Adapted from Perel-Levin (2008)

recent study of mandatory reporting, Rodriguez and colleagues (2006) found that physicians were often reluctant to report suspected elder maltreatment. The potential benefit of reporting, which is the protection of the elderly person, is often weighed against the potential disadvantages, including putting the patient at an increased risk, reducing the patient's autonomy, and disrupting the patient's trust and rapport with their physicians. As one physician reported, "Once I step across the line, saying 'I'm going to report you,' I lose all rapport with that family, my relationship with the patient is going to be altered forever, I will not continue to be maintained as their physician" (Rodriguez et al.; 205). This makes it clear that prior to an elderly person disclosing abuse, there must be trust and good communication between them and the health practitioner. In addition, the practitioner must believe they have resources available to help their patients.

Risk Factors for Elder Abuse

As seen in other types of family violence, a combination of psychological, social, and economic factors are associated with the victim and the perpetrator that contribute to the occurrence of elder maltreatment. Research has identified the following risk factors (Baker 2007; Dyer, Pavlik, Murphy, and Hyman 2000; Hansberry, Chen, and Gabien 2005; Lachs, Williams, O'Brien, Hurst, and Horwitz 1997; Phillips, de Ardon, and Briones 2000):

- Caregiver stress
- Social isolation of the victim
- Frailty of the victim, functional disability, and cognitive impairment
- Pathology of the abuser, such as alcohol or substance abuse, mental-health problems, prior history of domestic violence
- Dependence of the victim on the abuser (e.g., caregiver is the abuser) or dependence of abuser on the victim (e.g., adult child who is financially dependent on parent)

Consequences of Elder Abuse

As with victims of other abuse, the consequences to elderly victims include psychological and physical harm and, in some cases, death. In a nine-year study conducted in Connecticut, a sample of 2812 older people were classified as being physically abused or neglected or not abused (Lachs et al. 1998). Mortality rates for the two groups were compared 13 years after the study began, with 40 percent of the not abused or neglected still alive, compared to 9 percent of those who had been physically abused or neglected. Even after controlling for such factors as age, income, functional and cognitive problems, diagnosis, and degree of social support, researchers concluded that mistreatment was related to mortality.

Laws that Protect Elders from Abuse

There are four types of laws used in Canada to protect older adults from abuse and neglect. These include family violence laws (similar to what was discussed earlier for intimate violence), criminal laws, adult protection laws, and adult guardianship laws. Adult protection laws are designed to help cases of abuse or neglect that come to the attention of the authorities. The legislation varies as to whether mandatory reporting is required. The aim of these laws is not to punish the abuser but to help the elderly with health, social, or other services. As of 2008, only Nova Scotia, New Brunswick, Newfoundland, PEI, British Columbia, and the Yukon had adult protection laws. Adult guardianship laws are designed to provide protection to adults who are mentally incapable of protecting or providing for themselves. These laws can be used whether or not abuse or neglect is occurring. Often a relative is provided temporary guardianship to make decisions for the elderly person. If there is no relative, a trustee can be appointed to make decisions. It is not clear how effective these laws are at protecting elderly victims of abuse and neglect. Research is needed to determine their rates of deterrence and whether in some cases they create other harms to the victim (e.g., restrict the autonomy of the elder to make decisions).

Below is a list of top 10 issues and people to consider when thinking about family violence in Canada.

Top 10 List

Advances to Come, Debates, Ethical Conundrums, and People to Watch

1. Intimate violence is still common in Canadian society. Should men and women who are abusive toward their intimate partners be forced to participate in psychological treatment?

2. When a homicide occurs, the media pays attention. What role can the media play to educate the public about family violence?

3. Prevention of family violence is the key, rather than dealing with the aftermath.

What can schools do to help prevent all forms of violence?

4. People from many countries immigrate to Canada. What might be deemed acceptable in an immigrant's country of origin may not be acceptable in Canada. Should social services agencies, the police, or the courts take cultural issues into consideration when dealing with family violence?

---

5 It is not against the law to physically discipline your children. Should physical punishment be considered appropriate discipline or physical abuse?

6 In Canada it is illegal to be married to more than one person at the same time. Are there any situations in which polygamy would be permissible?

7 Child abuse in Canada is a widespread, serious, and hidden problem. Additional research is needed to understand the impact of multiple forms of abuse on children and what can be done to provide the most effective support and interventions for these children.

8 With the increasing number of older people in Canada, there will be increased numbers of elderly victims of abuse. How can we detect this abuse and what can we do to support the victims?

9 There is mandatory reporting of child abuse for everyone in society. Elderly people are a vulnerable segment of our communities. Should the government develop legislation requiring all citizens to report suspected elder abuse?

10 Names to watch: Donald Dutton, David Finkelhor, Todd Herrenkohl, Karl Pillemar, Randy Kropp, Murray Straus, and Zoe Hilton.

SUMMARY

1. Family violence can be classified into the following types: physical abuse, sexual abuse, neglect, financial abuse, and emotional abuse. The prevalence rates of family violence are difficult to estimate accurately since the abuse often occurs in private. In addition, researchers do not agree on what should be included in the definition of family violence. Researchers often study the prevalence and effects of specific types of abuse.

2. The ecological model of family violence focuses on the relationship between multiple levels of influence in understanding family violence, including individual, relationship, community, and societal factors. Risk factors associated with each of these levels have been identified for intimate violence, child abuse, and elder abuse.

3. The two prominent theories of intimate violence place emphasis on society versus the individual. Patriarchal theory focuses on long-standing cultural beliefs and values that support the male dominance of women. In contrast, social learning theory focuses on the observational learning of new behaviours, different types of instigators, and the regulators that increase or decrease the probability of intimate violence.

4. Typologies of male batterers have been proposed, with most identifying three main types: family-only, generally violent/antisocial, and dysphoric/borderline. The two

most common treatments for male batterers are the Duluth model, which focuses on power and control, and cognitive-behavioural treatments. Meta-analysis of male batterer treatment programs have found no differences in the effectiveness across treatment types and relatively small treatment effects.

5. The most common form of child abuse is neglect, although many children experience multiple forms of abuse. Being abused or witnessing domestic violence results in a range of short-term and long-term emotional, psychological, and behavioural consequences, including an increased likelihood of the child abusing his or her own children.

6. Clinicians and researchers have paid relatively little attention to elder maltreatment. With the increasing number of older people in Canada, there are concerns about the prevalence of the abuse of older people. The most common perpetrators of elder abuse are the victim's spouse or adult children. Because elders visit physicians relatively frequently, primary care physicians are in a unique position to identify maltreatment and to intervene. However, some physicians are reluctant to report suspected elder maltreatment. Several screening instruments have been designed to help professionals detect potential abuse.

Discussion Questions

1. Both men and women engage in dating violence. Do they do so for the same reasons? What are the motives for engaging in dating violence, and do you think there are any gender-specific motivations?

2. A new battered women's shelter has opened up in your city. What are the factors that might encourage or discourage abused women from using this resource?

3. You are interested in conducting a study to determine if the typologies that have been identified in male batterers are the same as for female batterers. Describe the methodology you would use and what variables you would measure.

4. The Children's Aid Society has proposed a new treatment program for abusive parents. You have been hired to develop an evaluation of the program to see whether it is effective. Describe how you plan to evaluate this program.

5. Your friend works in a local dog shelter. He believes that there is a strong association between animal abuse and child abuse. You are not sure if this is true. Describe how a researcher might go about testing the association between animal abuse and child abuse.

6. You have been hired by the World Health Organization to identify the risk factors for elder abuse across different countries. Describe the study you would propose, focusing on what risk factors you would measure.

Additional Reading

Dutton, D. 2006. *Rethinking domestic violence*. Vancouver: UBC Press.

Hilton, N.Z., Harris, G.T., and Rice, M.E. 2009. *Risk assessment for domestically violent men*. Washington: American Psychological Association.

Crosson-Tower, C. 2008. *Understanding child abuse and neglect* (7th edition). Toronto: Allyn & Bacon.

Bonnie, R.J. and Wallace, R.B. 2003. *Elder mistreatment: Abuse, neglect, and exploitation in an aging America.* Washington: National Research Council.

Relevant Websites

The National Clearinghouse on Family Violence (NCFV)
www.phac-aspc.gc.ca/ncfv-cnivf/index-eng.php

Canadian Society for the Investigation of Child Abuse
www.csicainfo.com

The Canadian Network for the Prevention of Elder Abuse
www.cnpea.ca

Chapter 9

Sexual Offenders

A Pedophilic Child Molester

Arnold is a 24-year-old man currently serving a four-year sentence at Warkworth Institution, a medium-security federal penitentiary in Ontario, for sex offences against two children who lived in his neighbourhood. The first victim was an eight-year-old boy who often rode his bicycle around the streets of the suburban neighbourhood on summer days. Arnold spent hours in his garage with the door open so that he could see and talk to the boy when he rode by. The boy sometimes had trouble with his bicycle, and Arnold would fix it for him in his garage. The first time he simply fixed the bicycle, but eventually he began sexually abusing the boy. The abuses occurred on two separate occasions roughly one month apart. The first time he touched the boy's genitals. The second time, he and the boy touched each other's genitals. The boy did not return to Arnold's house after that. The second victim was an 11-year-old girl who delivered the newspaper to Arnold's house. Arnold would usually be in his garage when the girl came. He routinely spoke with her and invited her in for a drink and snack. Eventually, Arnold began sexually abusing the girl. The abuse occurred on four separate occasions and escalated from touching to oral sex. Arnold gained compliance from his victims through psychological manipulation (e.g., befriending them, bribes) rather than physical coercion or threats of violence. The younger victim told his mother about the abuse, the police were notified, and Arnold was arrested. Upon news of his arrest, the other victim came forward and Arnold was also charged for offending against her.

Arnold has four prior sexual offence convictions. The first two were for sexual offences committed on numerous occasions when he was 16 against a five-year-old boy in the foster home in which he lived. He was sentenced to probation for these offences. When Arnold was 18, he exposed himself to an eight-year-old boy in the restroom of a local park. He asked the boy to come into one of the bathroom stalls with him. The boy ran away and told a group of adults. Arnold pleaded guilty to this offence and was sentenced to three months in prison. At 20, he sexually abused a six-year-old girl in the restroom of her elementary school. He exposed himself and fondled the girl. He pleaded guilty and was sentenced to a year in prison.

Arnold's childhood was difficult. His father left his mother when he was two years old and was not involved in raising him. Arnold was put into foster care at age four because of extreme neglect and physical abuse by his mother. He was repeatedly sexually abused while in foster care. Arnold left high school at age 17 and began working for minimum wage on an assembly line in a factory. He has never been married, lived with a romantic partner, or had a long-term romantic relationship. He has no adult friends and likes to spend most of his free time with children. He has a sexual preference for prepubescent boys, as indicated by his self-report and physiological testing (penile plethysmography (PPG)). Compared to other offenders in the prison, he possesses relatively few psychopathic traits and does not have any major mental disorders (e.g., schizophrenia). By all accounts, Arnold is a model inmate. He is respectful of staff and cooperative with supervision, assessment, and treatment. He has been very motivated regarding treatment. In addition to other programs, he participated in a pre-treatment program for sex offenders when he began his sentence and subsequently participated in a moderate-intensity sex offender program and a maintenance sex offender program. He successfully completed all programs. He is very remorseful and takes full responsibility for his offences.

Learning Objectives

1   Review the scope of sex offending and consequences for victims.

2   Introduce the paraphilias and their diagnostic criteria.

3   Cover some of the major theories explaining the initiation of sex offending.

4   Examine some typologies of sex offenders.

5   Review key research on factors associated with the initiation of sex offending.

6   Examine observed rates of sexual recidivism and predictors of sexual recidivism.

7   Introduce some of the key assessment instruments used to estimate risk of recidivism among sex offenders.

8   Consider various approaches to the treatment and management of sex offenders and the extent to which these approaches are effective in reducing sexual recidivism.

INTRODUCTION

READING THE OPENING VIGNETTE AND CONSIDERING SEX OFFENCES PRESENTED IN THE MEDIA raises a number of intriguing questions. How common is this sort of behaviour? What are the causes of sexual offending? What are the prototypical characteristics of sex offenders? After being caught, do sex offenders typically persist with sex offending? What can be done to identify the most persistent sex offenders and reduce their risk of sexual recidivism? We will address these and other questions in this chapter. Specifically, we will consider the scope and characteristics of sexual offending in Canada. A number of psychiatric disorders called paraphilias relevant to sexual offending will be discussed. We will also review a number of key theories that attempt to explain why some people sexually offend. Research examining the association between sex offending and some of the factors identified in theory will also be reviewed. We will then present research findings on predictors of sexual recidivism, a number of key sex offender risk assessment instruments, and the research on the predictive accuracy of these instruments. Finally, some of the major approaches to treatment for sex offenders will be presented and research on the effectiveness of treatment will be reviewed.

Scope of Sexual Offending

Before examining sex offenders themselves, it is important to consider the scope of sex offending. How many sex offences are committed and how many people are victimized? Although these questions seem very simple, they are extremely difficult to answer accurately. Estimates are typically derived from two main sources: surveys of the public and police reports. Every five or six years since 1988, Statistics Canada has surveyed the population about their victimization experiences in the General Social Survey (GSS) on Victimization. In 2004, a representative sample (territories excluded) of people over the age of 14 in 24 000 Canadian households was telephoned (random digit dialing). The sexual offences examined in the GSS were restricted to sexual touching and sexual attacks against victims at least 14 years or older. The questions the respondents were asked were as follows (Brennan and Taylor-Butts 2008: 7):

> Sexual attack: During the past 12 months, has anyone forced you or attempted to force you into any unwanted sexual activity, by threatening you, holding you down or hurting you in some way?
>
> Unwanted sexual touching: During the past 12 months, has anyone ever touched you against your will in any sexual way? By this I mean anything from unwanted touching or grabbing, to kissing or fondling.

Considering both types of sexual assault (i.e., sexual attacks and unwanted sexual touching), approximately 512 200 people in Canada reported having been sexually assaulted in the past 12 months on the 2004 GSS at a rate of 1977 incidents of sexual assault per 100 000 people (Brennan and Taylor-Butts 2008). Few of these offences were reported to the police. Responses on the GSS indicate that less than 10 percent of sexual assaults were reported. The reporting rate was slightly higher (22 percent) when only more violent forms of sexual assault (i.e., sexual attacks) were considered. However, for all forms of sexual assault, the rate of reporting to police was considerably lower than for other violent offences (robbery, 47 percent; physical assault, 40 percent). Victims' reasons for not reporting sexual assault incidents to the police most commonly included: "felt it was not important enough" (58 percent), "incident was dealt with in another way" (54 percent), "felt it was a personal matter" (47 percent), or "did not want to get involved with the police" (41 percent).

Another valuable source of information about the scope of sex offending in Canada is the Uniform Crime Reporting (UCR) Survey. The UCR Survey reports on the incidence of crimes reported to police in a given year and some of the characteristics of those crimes. In contrast to the GSS on Victimization, the UCR Survey includes offences against victims of all ages and includes the territories as well as the provinces. On the UCR Survey, sexual offences include sexual assaults of varying severity (i.e., Levels 1, 2, and 3) and other sexual offences, many of which are against children (e.g., sexual interference and invitation to sexual touching). In 2007, 73 sexual offences were reported per 100 000 people in Canada. The UCR Survey also tracks clearance rates. Clearance refers to laying charges or otherwise resolving reported offences (e.g., complainant asks that charges not be laid, accused is deceased, or police discretion). Clearance rates were lower for sexual offences than other violent offences in 2007. Over one-third (37 percent) of sexual offences were not cleared by police, whereas only 26 percent of other violent offences were not cleared. In terms of sentencing, convictions for sexual offences (54 percent) were more likely to result in custodial sentences (e.g., prison rather than probation only) than other violent offences (30 percent) for adult offenders in 2006–2007 (Brennan and Taylor-Butts 2008).

Contrary to what people might hear in the popular media, there is no evidence that sexual offending is on the rise. Neither self-reported (GSS) nor police-reported (UCR Survey) data show an increase in victimization over the past five to ten years. The UCR incidence rates are shown in Figure 9.1. Although any amount of sex offending is a serious concern, its frequency does not appear to be increasing. Thankfully, more serious types of sexual offences are relatively rare. The minority of sexual assaults reported in the 2004 GSS were sexual attacks (19 percent); most were incidents of unwanted sexual touching (81 percent). Similarly, 14 percent of sexual offences reported to the police in 2007 were for Level 2 or 3 sexual assaults and other sexual offences; most were for Level 1 sexual assault (86 percent). This is not meant to minimize the seriousness of unwanted sexual touching or Level 1 sexual assault; rather, this information is provided to indicate that only the minority of cases fit the sensational sexual offences often portrayed in the media.

The GSS and UCR Survey indicate that women and girls are more likely to be victims of sexual offences than men and boys. Young people are at greater risk for sexual victimization. Most sexual offences reported on the GSS were against victims aged 15 to 24 and the rates dropped off steeply as victim age increased (recall that the GSS does not include anyone under 15). Similarly, the UCR Survey indicates that the majority of sexual offences are committed against victims under the age of 18 (25 percent below age 12). UCR Survey data indicate that men are more often the offenders in sexual crimes (97 percent) than in other violent offences (78 percent). Sexual offences reported to the police in 2007 were committed considerably more often by young people (rates for youth aged 12–17 were 90 per 100 000 people) than even slightly older people (e.g., rates for 18–34-year-olds were 55 per 100 000). Both GSS and UCR Survey data indicate that the offender and victim often know each other (e.g., acquaintances, friends, family members) prior to the sexual offence in the majority of incidents. Children are most often victimized by family members, whereas adolescents and adults are most often victimized by acquaintances or friends.

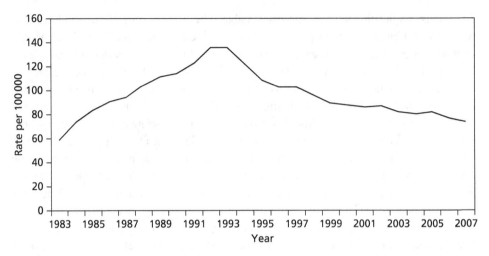

Figure 9.1 Incidence of Sexual Offences Reported to Police per 100 000 People Since 1983 from the Uniform Crime Reporting (UCR) Survey

Source: Brennan and Taylor-Butts (2008)

Consequences for Victims

Physical injury to victims occurs in relatively few sexual offences (7 percent on the GSS and 23 percent on the UCR Survey). On the GSS, victims reported a number of negative emotional reactions following the sexual assault: anger (24 percent); confusion and frustration (20 percent); shock and disbelief (16 percent); annoyance (16 percent); and fear (15 percent). More generally, sexual assault and child sexual abuse are associated with a number of negative outcomes, such as concerns about sexually transmitted diseases and pregnancy, post-traumatic stress disorder (PTSD), depression, and sexual disturbances (Beitchman et al. 1992; Browne and Finkelhor 1986; Paolucci, Genuis, and Violato 2001; Resick 1993).

Paraphilias

Paraphilias, as defined in the *Diagnostic and Statistical Manual of Mental Disorders* (DSM-IV-TR) (American Psychiatric Association 2000), "are recurrent, intense sexually arousing fantasies, sexual urges, or behaviors generally involving 1) nonhuman objects, 2) the suffering or humiliation of oneself or one's partner, or 3) children or other nonconsenting persons that occur over a period of at least 6 months" (p. 566). Not all paraphilias involve illegal behaviour (e.g., fetishism), but many can manifest as sexual offending; specifically, pedophilia, sexual sadism, frotteurism, exhibitionism, and voyeurism.

    Pedophilia comes from the Greek words pedeiktos (young children) and philia (love) and generally refers to a sexual preference for children who have not yet begun puberty (Seto 2008).

The specific diagnostic criteria for pedophilia in the DSM-IV-TR (American Psychiatric Association 2000: 572) are:

(A) Over a period of at least 6 months, recurrent, intense sexually arousing fantasies, sexual urges, or behaviors involving sexual activity with a prepubescent child or children (generally age 13 years or younger).

(B) The person has acted on these sexual urges, or the sexual urges or fantasies cause marked distress or interpersonal difficulty.

(C) The person is at least age 16 years and at least 5 years older than the child or children in Criterion A.

Although the terms pedophile and child molester are often used interchangeably, they are not synonymous. Some adults who sexually abuse prepubescent children are not pedophiles and some pedophiles do not sexually abuse children. As we will discuss later, child sexual abuse can be motivated by a number of factors besides a sexual preference for prepubescent children. **Sexual sadism** refers to being sexually aroused by inflicting humiliation or pain on others. Even among sex offenders, sexual sadism is relatively rare, but because of the extreme victim injury often associated with sexual sadism, it is a concern with both rapists and child molesters. **Frotteurism** is an interest in touching and rubbing against a nonconsenting person. These acts often occur in crowded places (e.g., full subway car) where the frotteur can more easily access victims and avoid detection. **Exhibitionism** refers to an interest in exposing one's genitals to an unsuspecting stranger. **Voyeurism** involves an interest in observing unsuspecting people naked or engaging in sexual activity.

EXPLAINING SEX OFFENDING

WHY DO SOME PEOPLE SEXUALLY OFFEND AGAINST ADULTS AND CHILDREN? A NUMBER OF theories have attempted to address this question and explain the initiation of sex offending.

Finkelhor's Model   Finkelhor (1984) attempted to organize existing explanations of child sexual abuse into a multifactor framework, which reflects four underlying factors he identified in the literature. The first is **emotional congruence** and refers to a perceived "'fit' between the adult's emotional needs and the child's characteristics" (Finkelhor 1984: 38). An individual may find sexual contact with a child emotionally gratifying because he or she is psychologically immature and views him or herself as a child. In addition, some individuals may feel emotionally gratified by sexually abusing a child because they feel powerful and competent when doing so; for example, they may generally feel inadequate (e.g., low self-esteem, low social self-efficacy). Emotional congruence alone would not necessarily lead to sexual abuse of children. What is also needed is some degree of sexual arousal to the prospect of sexual contact with a child, which is the second factor in this model. This need not be as extreme as pedophilia, but there must be at least some arousal to children. **Blockage** is the third factor and refers to the idea that some people may be blocked from meeting their sexual and emotional needs in prosocial ways (e.g., consenting sexual contact with adults). Blockage may occur because of social anxiety, social skills deficits, problems in a current romantic relationship, or repressive beliefs about sexual norms (e.g., against masturbation and extramarital affairs). The final factor, **disinhibition**, refers to the fact that inhibitions against child sexual abuse are either circumvented or are absent to allow one to act on his or her sexual interest in children. Disinhibition may occur because of personality (e.g., impulse control deficits, lack of empathy), situational (e.g., intoxication, extreme stress), or cultural factors.

Finkelhor suggests that not all four factors are necessary for a person to sexually abuse a child, but they likely work as complementary processes, possibly having additive or interactive effects. Finkelhor (1984) wisely argued that "many people have important pre-requisite components to engaging in child molesting, but never do. Theories from only one level of the model will never accurately discriminate between those who engage and do not engage in such behavior. Sex abusers will always show up as having some of these characteristics, such as arousal to children, shyness, impulsivity, or need for dominance, but there will also be large numbers of nonabusers in the population at large who have these characteristics too" (p. 47).

Integrated Theory of the Etiology of Sexual Offending Marshall and Barbaree (1990) proposed a biopsychosocial explanation of sexual offending against adults or children. They argued that biological, developmental, socio-cultural, and transitory situational factors can create a proclivity to sexually offend. Concerning the biological contribution, Marshall and Barbaree argue that the default position for men is the fusion of sex and aggression. If a boy's childhood experiences and culture do not teach him to inhibit aggression in the context of sexuality, sexual offending may be likely once he reaches puberty. Although this is the default biological position, the researchers argue that environmental factors are the primary determinants of whether one becomes a sexual offender. Negative childhood experiences, such as abuse and neglect from caregivers, lead to insecure childhood attachment and provide models of aggressive and self-centred antisocial behaviour. Consequently, the child enters puberty without the social skills and self-confidence required to establish relationships with peer-aged partners. Inability to secure intimate relationships with peer-aged partners may then lead a young man to turn his sexual attention to children, who are viewed as less rejecting and intimidating than peers, or to sexually aggress against peers. This may occur first in his masturbation-accompanied fantasies, which would condition arousal to children or violence, and then occur in actual sexual offending.

Marshall and Barbaree (1990) argue that socio-cultural messages and situational factors may interact with a vulnerable predisposition to increase or decrease the likelihood of sexual offending against children or peers. For example, media messages promoting male dominance may be more readily accepted by an inadequate young man because they bolster his fragile sense of masculinity. Such messages may justify or otherwise facilitate sexual offending, making it more likely. Transitory situational factors also interact with pre-dispositions and can either inhibit or facilitate sexual aggression. For example, a person who is sexually interested in children or who is incapable of obtaining appropriate sexual partners may choose to sexually abuse a child only when he is sufficiently disinhibited due to intoxication or when he is experiencing negative affect (e.g., stress, anxiety). The biological, childhood, socio-cultural, and transitory situational factors are thought to interact with one another to produce varying levels of propensity for sexual offending.

Quadripartite Model of Sexual Aggression against Adults

Hall and Hirschman (1991) proposed a quadripartite model to explain why some men sexually assault women. The four factors are physiological sexual arousal, cognitions that justify sexual aggression, affective dyscontrol, and personality problems. Sexual arousal to rape or generally high levels of sexual arousal are thought to increase the likelihood of rape. A variety of cognitions may also increase the likelihood of rape. For example, rape may be more likely for men who hold relatively positive beliefs about rape and its potential consequences; hostility toward women; beliefs that women are complicit, desirous, or deserving of rape; or misperceptions of or disregard for victims' refusal and distress. Affective dyscontrol refers to anger and hostility as motivating sexual assault. Sexual assault may also be motivated by personality problems, particularly antisocial personality features, which may be rooted in adverse developmental experiences such as parental divorce, criminality among family members, neglect, physical abuse, or sexual abuse. Not all four factors are necessary for sexual assault to occur, but Hall and Hirschman argue that it generally becomes more likely as the number of factors present increases. The relative strength of influence among these four factors varies across offenders to create subtypes; for example, for some offenders sexual arousal may be the dominant factor leading to sexual offending, whereas for others the primary motivational precursor may be cognitions that justify sexual offending.

Quadripartite Model of Sexual Aggression against Children

Hall and Hirschman (1992) also applied their quadripartite model to explain sexual offending against children. The first factor is physiological sexual arousal to children. The second factor, cognitions that justify sexual abuse of children, refers to beliefs such as that sexual contact with children is not harmful or wrong and is enjoyable for victims. Such beliefs are often called cognitive distortions. Child sexual abuse may also result from negative affective states. It may be an attempt to cope with negative affective states (i.e., depression), or, less commonly, an expression of anger and hostility. The final factor, personality problems, refers to developmentally related personality problems or disorders, which can manifest as emotional difficulties, poor social skills, or impulsivity. One of these four factors or various combinations of these factors can lead to child sexual offending. The relative strength of influence among the factors varies across offenders to create subtypes; e.g., for some offenders sexual arousal to children may be the dominant factor leading to sexual offending against a child.

Hierarchical-Mediational Confluence Model (HMC)

Malamuth (2003) formulated an etiological model of sexual aggression against women derived from his extensive research (e.g., Dean and Malamuth 1997; Malamuth 1986; Malamuth, Sockloskie, Koss, and Tanaka 1991). The model is an ongoing process and has been revised over the years, incorporating new research findings. The major components of Malamuth's Hierarchical-Mediational Confluence Model (HMC) are shown in Figure 9.2. According

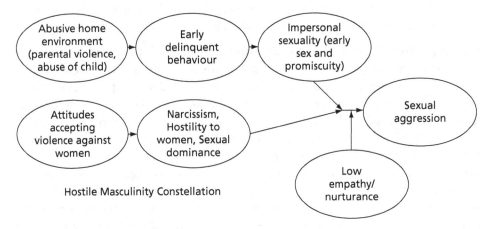

Figure 9.2 Malamuth's Hierarchical Confluence Model (HCM) of Sexual Aggression

Source: Malamuth (2003)

to the model, there are two major paths that lead to sexual aggression: the antisocial and impersonal sex path and the hostile masculinity path. In the **antisocial path**, abusive home environments (e.g., physical violence between parents and childhood physical or sexual abuse) lead to early delinquent behaviour (e.g., delinquent peers, running away), which leads to impersonal sexuality (e.g., young age at first intercourse and many sexual partners), which in turn leads to sexual aggression. In the **hostile masculinity path**, attitudes accepting violence toward women (e.g., rape myth acceptance and acceptance of interpersonal violence) lead to narcissism, hostility toward women, and sexual dominance, which in turn lead to sexual aggression. In addition to an independent influence on sexual aggression, these constellations also interact with each other, such that an increasing number of risk factors greatly increases the risk of sexual aggression.

As illustrated in the figure, empathy and nurturing personality characteristics moderate the influence of the risk factors listed above. Specifically, for men who are low in empathy and nurturance (egotistical and self-oriented), the risk factors listed are strongly associated with sexual aggression. However, for men who are high in empathy and nurturance (empathic and other-oriented), the risk factors are only weakly related to sexual aggression (Dean and Malamuth 1997).

Evolutionary Explanation of Rape

Evolutionary psychology was described in detail in Chapter 2, but briefly the idea is that in our ancestral environments, certain physiological, psychological, and behavioural characteristics were associated with increased reproductive success (i.e., having a relatively high number of children who in turn have a relatively high number of children, and so on). To the extent that such characteristics are heritable, the genes responsible for them would be passed on to subsequent generations more so than genes that are responsible for characteristics associated with reproductive failure. Today, we generally think and do what led to reproductive success in ancestral environments. A very important thing to keep in mind when thinking about evolutionary psychology is the distinction between proximal and ultimate causes. *Proximal causes* are immediate influences that motivate or otherwise drive behaviour, whereas *ultimate causes* refer to the reproductive fitness selection pressures of ancestral environments. To illustrate, consider this example from Quinsey (2002). Why do most people have sex with people of the opposite sex and not with trees? One obvious proximal cause is sexual preference; that is, people have sex with whom or what they find attractive. Most people find people of the opposite sex most attractive and trees not at all sexually attractive. The ultimate cause, however, would be natural selection; that is, sexual intercourse with the opposite sex will often result in reproduction, whereas sexual contact with trees will not. So the genes of people having a preference for sexual contact with the opposite sex would be much more likely to be passed on to subsequent generations than the genes of people having a preference for sexual contact exclusively with trees. As Quinsey (2002) notes, you can be certain that a person who only had sex with trees is not your ancestor. So in this case a sexual preference for the opposite sex would be adaptive because it led to greater reproductive success in ancestral environments.

People are driven by proximal influences, but these influences may have been shaped by ultimate causes. That is, most people do not consciously choose to have sex with the opposite sex instead of trees because they want to maximize their reproductive fitness. Instead, most people are simply driven by their attraction to the opposite sex. Another important thing to note is that "adaptive" does not necessarily equal "good" in a moral sense. As we are about to see, some of the behaviours people view as immoral and wrong may have been adaptive in our ancestral environments. Conversely, some acceptable behaviours (e.g., homosexuality, celibacy) would not have been adaptive in our ancestral environments. It is important to keep in mind that the evolutionary psychological perspective neither condones nor condemns any characteristics or behaviours, but rather seeks to explain their origins. It is an important perspective to consider because it may provide a fuller understanding of why such behaviours occur and how to deal with them.

A final distinction to make is between mating effort and parental investment. Both are reproductive strategies at opposite ends of a continuum. Mating effort refers to a short-term, low-investment approach to mating in which the focus is partner variety and casual sex. Parental investment, in contrast, refers to a long-term investment in ensuring the health and well-being of one's offspring. Although the most successful strategy would usually have been a blend of both approaches, high mating effort may have been a reproductively successful strategy depending on the individual and the conditions. For most mammals, including humans, the minimal parental investment is much lower for males than females. The man's minimal investment is limited to the time and sperm it takes to impregnate a woman, whereas the woman's minimal investment goes well beyond sexual intercourse to include carrying the fetus and giving birth along with all the physical demands and health risks of pregnancy and labour. Although many men willingly choose to invest in their partner and offspring, they have the option of choosing not to do so. This discrepancy in minimal parental investment resulted in different selection pressures for men and women in ancestral environments. For example, because sexual intercourse was more costly for women than men in terms of minimal parental investment, women who were more selective about mates both in terms of attractiveness and status were more likely to have successful offspring than women who mated indiscriminately. In addition, because of the difference in minimal parental investment, there was (and is) less variability across women in the number of offspring they would produce compared to men. For example, a woman could produce a maximum of approximately one child per year during most of her adult life (excluding twins, triplets, etc.). However, a man could, at least theoretically, impregnate hundreds if not thousands of women every year of his adult life; the main limits would be opportunity and stamina.

Lalumière et al. (2005) have attempted to explain sexual assault from an evolutionary perspective. Specifically, Lalumière et al. argue "that rape is part of a general antisocial, aggressive, and risk-tolerant lifestyle and that very few rapists specialize in rape" (p. 184). Building on research and theory on general antisocial behaviour (e.g., Harrris, Rice, and Lalumière 2001; Moffitt 1993; Quinsey, Skilling, Lalumière, and Craig 2004), Lalumière et al. propose that most rapists fall into one of three groups: young men, competitively disadvantaged men, or psychopaths. Adolescent and young men typically have relatively few resources and low status, which puts them at a competitive disadvantage relative to other males with whom they are competing for mates. Through violence (including sexual coercion) and general risk taking, these young men may be able to increase their status, resources, and/or access to more and better mates. However, as they move into adulthood and begin to acquire legitimately gained resources and status, they switch from high mating effort to high parental investment. So the sexual assaults and other antisocial behaviour of this group are limited to adolescence and young adulthood. This is the most common type of rapist.

This desistance with adulthood, however, does not occur for the competitively disadvantaged men. Their sexual coercion and other antisocial behaviour is life-course persistent. The ability to compete for resources and status in prosocial ways is impaired by early neurodevelopmental insults, such as obstetrical complications and low IQ. Because men in this group do not have the skills or abilities to achieve status and resources in prosocial ways, they maintain their high mating effort and antisocial approach into adulthood. The final group, psychopaths, are also life-course persistent. In contrast to the competitively disadvantaged men, psychopaths are not competitively disadvantaged but select high mating effort over parental investment as an alternate strategy. The competitively disadvantaged and psychopaths are thought to make up a small proportion of rapists. This quote from Lalumière and colleagues (2005) sums it up nicely: "Young men are involved in intense competition, competitively disadvantaged offenders are trying to make the best of a bad deal, and psychopaths are pursuing a finely tuned alternative strategy of defection and aggression" (p. 124).

Seto's Developmental Theory of Child Sexual Offending

Seto (2008) recently put forth a comprehensive model of the etiology of child sexual abuse. This model draws from a very broad literature of theory and research. It is somewhat similar to the model above in that there is an adolescence-limited path, a pedophilia path, and an antisociality path, which includes the sub-paths of competitive disadvantage and psychopathy. Basically, adolescence-limited child molesters are those who may be blocked from romantic relationships with peers because of lack of resources (e.g., unattractive, poor, weak) or poor social skills. These boys may occasionally sexually abuse a child. Some adolescence-limited offenders may also be pedophiles, motivated by their sexual interest in children. Two more persistent paths are presented in Figure 9.3. As proposed above for rape, persistent offending may be a manifestation of antisociality, stemming from enduring competitive disadvantage or psychopathy. Sexual attraction to

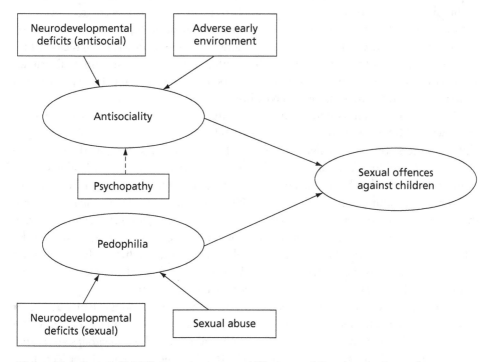

Figure 9.3 Seto's (2008) Developmental Theory of Persistent Sexual Offending Against Children

Source: Seto (2008)

prepubescent children (pedophilia) would be another cause of child molestation. Offending against children would be especially likely when both antisociality and pedophilia are present.

TYPOLOGIES

Massachusetts Treatment Centre: Child Molester Typology, Version 3 (MTC:CM3)
Knight and colleagues (Knight, Carter, and Prentky 1989) developed a typology to reflect the heterogeneity of child molesters: the **Massachusetts Treatment Centre: Child Molester Typology, Version 3 (MTC:CM3)**. The MTC:CM3 was developed with 177 extrafamilial child molesters (only contact sex offences; at least one victim outside the family; victims under 16 years old) civilly committed (from one day to life) for their sex offences and evaluated at the MTC between 1959 and 1981. The MTC:CM3 is shown in Figure 9.4. There are two orthogonal (or distinct) axes on which child molesters can be differentiated. On the first axis, child molesters are differentiated by their level of *fixation*, which refers to the extent of their pedophilic interests. For example, child molesters who think and fantasize about sexual contact and interpersonal relationships primarily with children would be high on fixation. Each of these groups can be further differentiated by their degree of *social competence*, which reflects their degree of achievement with regards to adult responsibilities and relationships. For example, someone with an unstable employment history, no long-term live-together sexual relationships with adults, no involvement in any adult-oriented organizations, and no adult friends would be considered extremely low in social competence. Axis I defines four types of child molesters differing in their degree of pedophilic and social competence.

On Axis II, child molesters are first differentiated by the amount of time they have spent with children in both sexual offence and non-sexual situations. For example, child molesters who are involved in work or leisure activities that put them in close proximity to children, such as a school teacher or coach of a children's sports team, would be considered *high contact*. The high-contact child molesters are further differentiated by the meaning of their contact with children: *interpersonal* versus *narcissistic*. For the interpersonal type, the goal is to establish interpersonal relationships with children, whereas for the narcissistic type, the motivation for contact is exclusively sexual. So the interpersonal type (Type 1) views the sexual abuse as a mutually satisfying romantic relationship, whereas the narcissistic type (Type 2) is self-focused and views the sexual abuse primarily as a means to achieve his own sexual gratification.

Like the high-contact child molesters, low-contact child molesters can also be further differentiated. First, they are distinguished by the degree of physical injury they inflict on their victims: low physical injury versus high physical injury. These subgroups are further differentiated by their degree of sadism. Type 3 (Exploitative, Nonsadistic) inflicts little physical injury on victims. If any aggression is used, it is instrumental (i.e., aggression may be used to gain compliance from victims and the amount of aggression does not exceed what is required to gain compliance), and this aggression is not sexually arousing for the

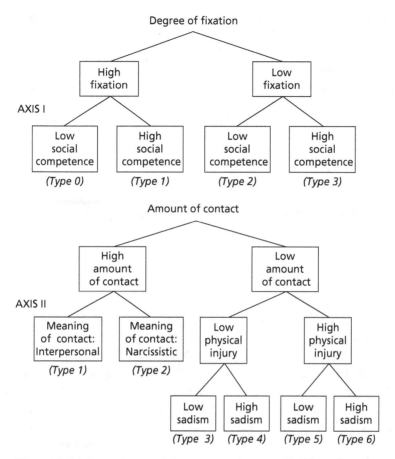

Figure 9.4 Massachusetts Treatment Centre: Child Molester Typology, Version 3 (MTC:CM3)

Source: Knight, Carter, and Prentky (1989)

offender. Type 4 (Muted Sadistic) has sadistic sexual interests and fantasies (i.e., is aroused by the pain, fear, and humiliation of victims) but does not act on them enough to cause physical injury to victims. Type 5 (Nonsadistic, Aggressive) uses violence causing physical injury to victims, which is either accidental or motivated by anger, but in neither case is it sexually arousing for the offender. Type 6 (Sadistic) inflicts injury on victims and is sexually aroused by their pain, fear, and humiliation.

Massachusetts Treatment Centre: Rapist Typology, Versions 3 (MTC:R3) and 4 (MTC:R4)

Knight and Prentky (1990) have also developed a typology of rapists. The most familiar and commonly referred to version of their rapist typology is the **Massachusetts Treatment Centre: Rapist Typology, Version 3 (MTC:R3)**, which is shown in Figure 9.5. In the MTC:R3, rapists are distinguished by

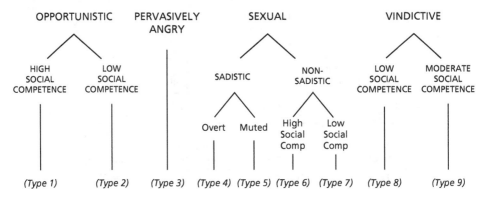

Figure 9.5 Massachusetts Treatment Centre: Rapist Typology, Version 3 (MTC:R3)

Source: Adapted from Knight (2010)

four primary motivations: opportunity, generalized anger, sexual gratification, and misogynistic anger. *Opportunistic rapists* (Types 1 and 2) are generally antisocial and impulsive men who commit sexual assault when the opportunity to do so presents itself (i.e., a potential victim in the right context). For example, these rapists may commit sexual assault during the course of burglary if a woman happens to be present in the home. They are more influenced by situational factors than driven by enduring sexual fantasies or preference for rape. In contrast to some of the other rapist types, there is little offence planning and any non-sexual aggression is primarily instrumental. As a result, physical injury to victims is relatively low. Opportunistic rapists are further distinguished by their level of social competence. Social competence here refers to "the presence and durability of interpersonal relationships and the stability of the offender's employment and wage-earning history" (Prentky and Knight 1991: 650). Type 1 rapists are higher in social competence and their impulsivity emerged in adulthood, whereas Type 2 rapists are lower in social competence and their impulsivity became apparent during adolescence.

Pervasively angry rapists (Type 3) are characterized by global anger, which manifests as sexual assault against women as well as non-sexual aggression against men and women. These rapists have long histories of aggressive behaviour and engage in relatively little offence planning. In contrast to some other types (e.g., opportunistic), they use expressive aggression in their sexual assaults that results in higher levels of physical injury.

Rapists motivated by sexual gratification are characterized by enduring sexual or sadistic fantasy or preoccupation. Compared to the other types, these rapists engage in more offence planning. They can be divided into two groups based on the presence or absence of sadistic fantasies. Sadistic rapists are further divided into two groups based on the extent to which they act on their sadistic fantasies. Specifically, *overt sadistic rapists* (Type 4) act on their sadistic fantasies, evidenced by sadistic acts and resulting in a high degree of physical injury. *Muted sadistic rapists* (Type 5) engage in acts intended to scare and humiliate the victim (driven by their sadistic fantasies), but inflict relatively little physical injury. Non-sadistic offenders are also divided into two groups based on their level of social competence: Type 6 is characterized by higher social competence and Type 7 is characterized by lower social competence.

Vindictive rapists are motivated primarily by misogynistic anger. In contrast to pervasively angry rapists (Type 3), vindictive rapists' anger is not global but rather is focused exclusively on women. Their intent is to degrade, humiliate, and physically harm their victims. There is relatively little offence planning. As would be expected, these rapists use expressive aggression, which results in high physical injury. These rapists are divided based on their social competence: Type 8 is lower in social competence, whereas Type 9 is moderate.

Since the initial development of Version 3, new evidence suggests some structural problems exist with the MTC:R3 (Knight, in press). Knight has incorporated these new findings and revised the typology to create Version 4 of the Massachusetts Treatment Centre: Rapist Typology (MTC:R4). The main changes are that the *muted sadistic type* (Type 5) has been dropped, some of the types have been repositioned, and the linear structure has been reconfigured as circular (see Figure 9.6). Knight (2010) convincingly argues that the MTC:R4 better fits with current empirical evidence.

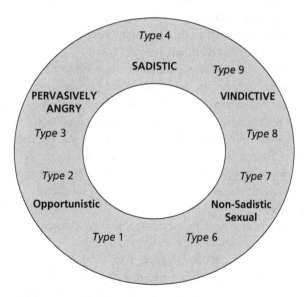

Figure 9.6 Massachusetts Treatment Centre: Rapist Typology, Version 4 (MTC:R4) Circumplex Model

Source: Adapted from Knight (2010)

RESEARCHING INITIATION FACTORS

HOW WOULD YOU TEST THE ASSERTIONS OF THE THEORIES AND MODELS WE HAVE JUST described? Empirically demonstrating that a given factor plays a causal role in the initiation of sex offending is more difficult than you might think. To illustrate the methodology typical of this research, consider a hypothetical study designed to examine the relationship between sex offending and beliefs about sex offending. Researchers would typically identify a group of people who had been convicted of a sexual offence and another group with no known history of sex offending (i.e., non-sex offenders or non-offenders). A questionnaire would be administered to all participants asking them to indicate the degree to which they endorse a variety of beliefs that justify, excuse, or otherwise support sex offending. The sex offenders and non-sex offenders would then be compared on their questionnaire scores. Note that this would be an observational study rather than a true experiment. Unlike true experiments, the variable of interest is not manipulated in observational research. Although this diminishes control and the ability to infer causation, it is difficult, if not impossible, to do anything other than observational studies on factors associated with the initiation of sex offending. Studies like the one described above often find that sex offenders endorse more beliefs supportive of sex offending than do non-sex offenders. What can we conclude from such findings? Do they indicate that such beliefs cause sex offending? Not necessarily. Because of the lack of control and cross-sectional design in this kind of research, the results are open to alternate explanations. For example, it is possible that convicted sex offenders may endorse more offence-supportive beliefs than non-sex offenders as a *result* of their sex offending. Prior to their offending, sex offenders may not have endorsed such beliefs, but after committing their first sex offence they may increasingly endorse them in an attempt to justify and excuse their offending to themselves and others.

Obviously it would be unethical and undesirable to conduct a true experiment to examine the effects of such beliefs on the initiation of sex offending. A true experiment here would involve randomly assigning some participants to a condition designed to increase beliefs supportive of sex offending and the rest to a control condition (i.e., designed to have no impact on their offence-related beliefs). The researchers would monitor the participants for a given period of time and observe whether they commit sex offences. If more of the participants in the offence-supportive beliefs condition committed sex offences than participants in the control condition, researchers could be fairly confident that the beliefs played a causal role in sex offending. This is clearly not an option because no researcher would want to do anything that might lead to someone being sexually victimized by a participant—and, of course, no ethics review board would permit such a study.

Focusing on observational studies that compare sex offenders to people who have not committed sex offences, different comparison groups can address different questions. Comparing sex offenders to non-sex offenders (i.e., people who have committed exclusively non-sexual crimes) examines the factors that may lead specifically to sex offending versus other criminal behaviour. Comparing sex offenders to non-offenders (i.e., people who are not known to have committed any crimes, sexual or otherwise) addresses the factors that may lead to sex offending versus not engaging in any criminal behaviour. And finally, comparing different types of sex offenders (e.g., child molester versus rapists) examines the factors that may lead to specific forms of sex offending versus others. All these comparisons provide useful complementary information about potential causes of sex offending. Although these studies would not demonstrate a causal relationship, finding a difference between groups would suggest plausible causal factors that could be further examined in more rigorous and resource-demanding designs (e.g., longitudinal studies) (Seto and Lalumière 2009; Whitaker et al. 2008).

Two recent meta-analyses provide much needed summaries of existing studies comparing sex offenders to non-sex offenders. Seto and Lalumière (2009) meta-analyzed studies comparing adolescent male offenders who had committed sex offences to those who had not. Whitaker et al. (2008) meta-analyzed studies comparing men who had committed sex offences against children to men who had committed sex offences against adults (rapists), offenders who had committed non-sexual offences (non-sex offenders), and men who had not committed any offences (non-offenders). A third meta-analysis (Jespersen, Lalumière, and Seto 2009) focused exclusively on differences in childhood abuse and neglect between sex offenders and various comparison groups.

Childhood Sexual Abuse

Many of the theories we have mentioned posit that sexual victimization in childhood plays an important role in later sexual offending. Studies generally find a strong association between childhood sexual abuse and sexual offending. Adolescent sex offenders have been found to have experienced significantly more childhood sexual abuse than adolescent non-sex offenders (Seto and Lalumière 2009). Similarly, adult sex offenders have experienced higher rates of childhood sexual victimization than adult non-sex offenders and non-offenders (Jespersen, Lalumière, and Seto, in press; Whitaker et al. 2008). Interestingly, even when information beyond self-reports was used to document childhood sexual victimization, sex offenders were still found to have significantly higher rates of victimization than non-sex offenders (Jespersen et al. 2009; Seto and Lalumière 2009). These analyses compared reports of abuse based solely on self-report with information gained in part by other sources of information (in combination with self-report), such as reports from parents or exclusively from files from child protection agencies. Thus the higher rates cannot be accounted for simply by potential biases associated with self-report. For example, we might expect some sex offenders to falsely report childhood sexual abuse after being caught for their offences in an attempt to gain sympathy or to excuse their offending (Hilton 1993). Sex offenders against children have significantly higher rates of childhood sexual victimization than sex offenders against adults. This is the case for adolescent sex offenders (Seto and Lalumière 2009) and adult sex offenders (Jespersen et al. 2009; Whitaker et al. 2008). These differences also remained significant and in the same direction whether abuse was determined exclusively through self-report or other sources of information (Jespersen et al. 2009).

Childhood Physical Abuse

Higher rates of physical abuse in childhood have also been found among sex offenders compared to non-sex offenders and non-offenders, but the differences between groups are not as dramatic as for childhood sexual abuse. Significantly higher rates of physical abuse have been found among adolescent sex offenders than adolescent non-sex offenders (Seto and Lalumière 2009). A similar significant difference was found for studies on adolescents based on self-report only, but virtually no difference was found for other sources (Seto and Lalumière 2009). Significantly higher rates of physical abuse have also been observed among adult sex offenders than among non-sex offenders and non-offenders in one meta-analysis (Whitaker et al. 2008), but the higher physical abuse rates among sex offenders compared to non-sex offenders did not reach statistical significance in another meta-analysis that included a larger number of studies (Jespersen et al. 2009). And when based on self-report, adult sex offenders had non-significantly higher rates of childhood physical abuse than non-sex offenders, but non-significant differences in the opposite direction were found with sources beyond self-report (Jespersen et al. 2009). In contrast to the findings for childhood sexual abuse, sex offenders against children were less likely to have been physically abused in childhood than sex offenders against adults. This is the case (significant) for adult sex offenders and held whether the comparisons were based only on self-report or other information (Jespersen et al. 2009). However, non-significant differences in the opposite direction were found with adolescent sex offenders (Seto and Lalumière 2009); that is, adolescent sex offenders against younger children had slightly higher rates of childhood physical abuse than adolescent sex offenders against peers or adults.

Neglect and Emotional Abuse

Rates of neglect or emotional abuse were also significantly higher among adolescent sex offenders than non-sex offenders (Seto and Lalumière 2009). The size and the direction of the difference were similar for self-report and other sources, but were only significant for self-report (Seto and Lalumière 2009). Among adult offenders, however, neglect and abuse were non-significantly less common among sex offenders than non-sex offenders (Jespersen et al. 2009). Sex offenders against children had slightly (but non-significantly) higher rates of neglect and emotional abuse in childhood than did sex offenders against adults (Jespersen et al. 2009).

Attachment and Family Functioning

Despite the higher rates of abuse among sex offenders, it is somewhat surprising to find that problems with attachment and family functioning do not differ between child molesters, rapists, and non-sex offenders (Seto and Lalumière 2009; Whitaker et al. 2008). However, when compared to non-offenders, child molesters do have more problems with attachment and family functioning (Whitaker et al. 2008).

Deviant Sexual Interests

Perhaps not surprisingly, sex offenders generally have more deviant sexual interests than non-sex offenders and non-offenders. Adolescent sex offenders also have more deviant sexual interests than adolescent non-sex offenders (Seto and Lalumière, 2009) (e.g., behaviour, fantasies, and interest in sexual contact with children or sexual assault). Adult child molesters have significantly more deviant sexual interests than adult non-sex offenders and non-offenders but do not differ from rapists (Whitaker et al. 2008). Considering sexual interest in children, in particular, child molesters showed much more interest in children than non-sex offenders, but this difference did not reach significance in the meta-analysis (Whitaker et al. 2008). However, when this finding is considered along with a number of earlier studies not included in the meta-analysis, there is little question that the average child molester is more sexually interested in children than the average man who does not molest children (e.g., Harris, Rice, Quinsey, and Chaplin 1996).

Meta-analytic reviews indicate that, on average, rapists show greater sexual arousal to rape than non-rapists (e.g., Lalumière and Quinsey 1994; Lalumière, Quinsey, Harris, Rice, and Trautrimas 2003). Arousal to non-sexual violence, however, does not appear to distinguish most rapists from non-rapists (e.g., Quinsey, Chaplin, and Varney 1981) but it does distinguish rapists who have seriously physically injured their victims from those who have done less serious physical damage (Quinsey and Chaplin 1982). It is generally assumed that the greater arousal to rape observed among rapists compared to non-rapists is most often the result of reduced inhibition of sexual arousal in the presence of violence rather than a sexual preference for rape over consenting sex (e.g., Barbaree and Marshall 1991). Although there are certainly some rapists who prefer rape and are sexually aroused by the violence and suffering of the victim (e.g., sexual sadism), most rapists do not seem to differ from non-rapists in the extent to which they find consenting sex arousing. What differentiates most rapists is that their sexual arousal is relatively less diminished when sexual activity is accompanied by violence and victim suffering. This is consistent with the results shown in Figure 9.7 from a study comparing the penile arousal of rapists and non-rapists (Lalumière et al. 2003). Note that the data in Figure 9.7 were transformed to z-scores to control for individual differences in overall arousal. Higher z-scores indicate greater arousal.

Deviant sexual interests have most commonly been measured with **penile plethysmography (PPG)**, which involves the physiological measurement of penile tumescence (erection) during the presentation of various stimuli, such as descriptions of sexual activity. Sexual attraction is usually inferred from the amount of arousal in response to deviant stimuli (e.g., stories about sexual abuse of a child, rape) relative to non-deviant stimuli (e.g., stories about consenting sex between adults). As measures of sexual interest go, PPG has received much research attention and is among one of the best measures currently available (Kalmus and Beech 2005; Lalumière et al. 2005; Seto 2008). Other measures of sexual interest include self-report (e.g., Laws, Hanson, Osborn, and Greenbaum

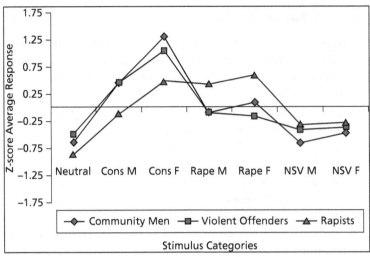

Figure 9.7 Penile Arousal of Rapists, Non-Sexually Violent Offenders, and Community Men in Response to Stories Told from the Man's Perspective (M) or the Woman's Perspective (F) Describing Consenting Sex (Cons), Rape, and Non-Sexual Violence (NSV)

Source: Lalumière et al. (2003)

2000), viewing time (e.g., Harris et al. 1996), and, more recently, a number of promising cognitive approaches (e.g., Thornton and Laws, 2009).

Although on average differences in sexual arousal to rape have been found between rapists and non-rapists, there is considerable variability from study to study. Different interpretations of the source of this variability have led to different conclusions about the role that sexual interests may play in rape. Some researchers have attributed the variability to the samples examined, whereas others have attributed it to the stimuli and procedures employed. With regard to the samples, some researchers (e.g., Marshall and Fernandez 2000) have argued that elevated sexual arousal to rape is only found in groups of rapists with high proportions of sadistic rapists. Thus, they argue that sexual arousal to rape is only characteristic of a small number of rapists who are sadistic, but not the majority of rapists. In contrast, other researchers (e.g., Lalumière and Quinsey 1994; Lalumière et al. 2003; Rice, Chaplin, Harris, and Coutts 1994) argue that rapists can be differentiated from non-rapists when appropriate stimuli and procedures are used.

General Antisociality

On average, sex offenders do not appear to be higher on general antisociality than non-sex offenders. They are, however, more antisocial than non-offenders. Specifically, child molesters generally are more angry and hostile than non-offenders, but slightly less angry and hostile than non-sex offenders and significantly less angry and hostile than rapists (Whitaker et al. 2008). Child molesters were significantly lower on lifestyle instability/impulsivity and antisocial personality disorder than non-sex offenders but did not differ from rapists on antisocial personality disorder (comparisons were not done for lifestyle instability/impulsivity because there were too few studies) (Whitaker et al. 2008). In contrast, child molesters were higher than non-offenders on lifestyle instability/impulsivity (non-significant) and antisocial personality disorder (significant) (Whitaker et al. 2008).

Seto and Lalumière (2009) found that adolescent sex offenders were generally less antisocial than adolescent non-sex offenders in a number of areas (e.g., fewer prior involvements with the criminal justice system, lower general antisocial beliefs, fewer antisocial associations). However, adolescent sex offenders did not differ from adolescent non-sex offenders on antisocial personality traits (Seto and Lalumière 2009). Seto and Lalumière (2009) found adolescent sex offenders against children were less generally antisocial (e.g., antisocial personality, substance abuse, antisocial attitudes, antisocial associations, etc.) than adolescent sex offenders against peers or adults.

Substance Abuse

Sex offenders appear to be somewhat less likely or similar to non-sex offenders in terms of substance abuse. However, substance abuse is more common among sex offenders than non-offenders. And within sex offenders, rapists are more likely to have substance abuse issues than child molesters. Whitaker et al. (2008) found that child molesters were similar to non-sex offenders in terms of substance abuse, but were less likely than rapists to abuse substances and more likely to do so than non-offenders. Among adolescent offenders, however, sex offenders were considerably less likely to abuse substances than non-sex offenders (Seto and Lalumière 2009).

Social Skills, Social Anxiety, and Self-Esteem

Child molesters had significantly more anxiety and lower self-esteem than rapists, non-sex offenders, and non-offenders (Whitaker et al. 2008). Child molesters also had significantly more problems with social skills, were lonelier, and had more difficulty with intimate relationships than non-sex offenders and non-offenders, but did not differ significantly from rapists (Whitaker et al. 2008). In another meta-analysis, Dreznick (2003) found similar results for heterosocial competence. **Heterosocial competence** refers to "the ability to competently interact with members of the other sex" (Dreznick 2003: 170). Child molesters were less heterosocially competent than rapists, non-sex offenders, and non-offenders. Rapists, however, did not differ from non-sex offenders but did have significantly lower levels of heterosocial competence than non-offenders.

Among adolescents, sex offenders had non-significantly more problems with heterosocial skills than non-sex offenders (Seto and Lalumière 2009). Adolescent sex offenders had significantly lower quality social relationships, were more socially isolated, and were more introverted than adolescent non-sex offenders (Seto and Lalumière 2009). Seto and Lalumière (2009) also found that adolescent sex offenders had more social anxiety and lower self-esteem than non-sex offenders.

Beliefs about Children, Women, and Sex Offending

Sex offenders against children generally endorse more beliefs supportive of sexual offending against children than non-sex offenders, rapists, and non-offenders. Specifically, more so than non-sex offenders, rapists, and non-offenders, child molesters endorse beliefs that children are interested in and receptive to sexual contact with adults, are able to consent to such contact, and are unharmed by such contact (Bumby 1996; Hanson, Gizzarelli, and Scott 1994; Mann, Wakeling, Webster, and Marshall 2007; Whitaker et al. 2008). These are often referred to as **cognitive distortions**, but a more precise term is beliefs supportive of child sexual abuse.

Similarly, rapists generally endorse more beliefs supportive of rape than non-sex offenders (e.g., Bumby 1996). Specifically, more so than non-rapists, rapists endorse beliefs that some women enjoy and deserve to be raped. These are often referred to as **rape myths**, but again a more precise term is beliefs supportive of rape. Rapists also generally have more negative and stereotypical beliefs about women than non-rapists. A meta-analysis of beliefs about women found that self-reported past sexual coercion or likelihood to rape was significantly associated with more acceptance of interpersonal violence (i.e., belief that violence is appropriate in sexual and non-sexual situations), more adversarial sexual beliefs (belief that romantic relationships are mutually exploitive and adversarial), more stereotypical beliefs about women (beliefs about women's rights and roles in society relative to men), dominance/power over women (importance of dominance in sex and, more generally, in romantic relationships), hostility toward women (belief that women are untrustworthy, manipulative, and malicious), hypermasculinity (macho), and rape myth acceptance (Murnen, Wright, and Kaluzny, 2002). However, adolescent sex offenders do not appear to differ from adolescent non-sex offenders in their beliefs about sex offending or women (Seto and Lalumière 2009). Cognitions like the ones just described have most commonly been assessed with self-report measures, but researchers are beginning to use innovative social-cognitive methods (e.g., reaction time measures) in an attempt to better understand the role of various cognitions in sex offending (e.g., Gannon 2009).

Neurodevelopmental Perturbation

There is growing evidence that pedophilia, in particular, is associated with neurodevelopmental perturbation, which refers to problems in brain functioning. Compared to non-pedophilic men, pedophilic men have been found to have lower intelligence, have poorer memory, be shorter, be less likely to be right handed, and have less cerebral white matter (Cantor et al. 2006; Cantor et al. 2008). These features are manifestations of early perturbations of brain development. The same perturbations that cause these features are thought to also cause pedophilia (Cantor et al. 2006). Thus the relationship between these features and pedophilia is not thought to be causal (e.g., lower intelligence does not lead to pedophilia); rather, the same perturbations that cause lower intelligence are thought to cause pedophilia (Blanchard et al. 2002).

RECIDIVISM

CONTRARY TO WHAT MOST PEOPLE IN THE GENERAL PUBLIC BELIEVE (E.G., LEVENSON, BRANNON, Fortney, and Baker 2007), arrest or conviction for a new sexual offence following an initial sex offence conviction is relatively rare. A large-scale meta-analysis indicates that over an average follow-up period of five to six years, the observed recidivism rates are 13.7 percent for sexual recidivism, 14.0 percent for non-sexual violent recidivism, 25.0 percent for any violent recidivism (sexual or non-sexual violent recidivism), and 36.9 percent for any recidivism (sexual, non-sexual violent, or non-violent recidivism) (Hanson and Morton-Bourgon 2004). These rates surely underestimate the actual rates of sexual reoffending given that many sex offences are not reported to the police (Brennan and Taylor-Butts 2008). Nevertheless, they have important implications for managing sex offenders. For example, if the majority of sex offenders do not persist in sex offending, then it is only the persistent minority that require extreme measures such as intensive treatment and supervision or long-term incarceration to prevent their potential recidivism. But how can you know in advance who will persist and who will desist? Luckily, there has been a lot of research on predictors of sexual recidivism to help identify offenders who pose the greatest risk.

Box 9.1

Offender Profile: Peter Whitmore

In July 2007, Peter Whitmore pleaded guilty in Regina to charges for the abduction and sexual assault of two boys aged 10 and 14. The 36-year-old was sentenced to life in prison without eligibility for parole for seven years. Whitmore arrived at this point following a troubled childhood and a string of sex offences spanning more than 10 years. When he was born, his father left him and his developmentally disabled mother. Whitmore spent most of his childhood in foster care, was sexually and physically abused, and was living on the street at age 16. Details of some of the major events in Whitmore's criminal history are presented on the next page.

Continued >

Box 9.1 Continued

■ 1993: Peter Whitmore is convicted of abduction and five sexual offences involving four young boys in Toronto. He is sentenced to a year and four months in custody.

■ 1995: Whitmore, who posed as a professional babysitter, is sentenced to five years in jail for sexual offences including the abduction and confinement of an eight-year-old girl from Guelph, Ont., and sexual interference with a boy, 9, from outside Toronto. He is banned from being close to children under age 14 for the rest of his life.

■ 2000: Less than a month after his release, Whitmore is found in a downtown Toronto motel with a 13-year-old boy. He is sentenced to one year in jail for breaching a court order.

■ 2002: A Toronto judge sentences Whitmore to three years in jail for probation violations because he fled to British Columbia after being found in the company of a five-year-old boy.

■ March 2004: A National Parole Board report notes clinicians believe Whitmore has a "100 percent probability of recidivism."

■ June 16, 2005: Whitmore is released after serving his entire three-year sentence and takes up residence in Chilliwack, B.C.

■ June 2, 2006: RCMP issue a news release saying Whitmore will be visiting the area of Morinville, Alta., for a few days.

■ June 15, 2006: After returning to British Columbia for a brief time, Whitmore comes back to Morinville. He willingly tells police he's back. RCMP set a court date so Whitmore can legally extend his stay, but he never shows up.

■ July 22, 2006: Whitmore resurfaces in Winnipeg, where he is alleged to have befriended a 14-year-old boy. He takes him to Brandon to buy a truck and does not bring him back as promised. The boy's parents file a missing person's report.

■ July 30, 2006: RCMP issue an Amber Alert for a 10-year-old Saskatchewan boy believed to have been abducted by Whitmore.

■ July 31, 2006: A Canada-wide warrant is issued for Whitmore, charging him with abduction.

■ Aug. 1, 2006: A vehicle matching the description of the one Whitmore was driving is spotted near Kipling, Sask., by a local farmer. When RCMP arrive, the 10-year-old boy runs out of some brush on the property. Whitmore surrenders after a 10-hour standoff with police, and the 14-year-old boy is taken into police protection.

■ Aug. 3, 2006: Whitmore appears in provincial court in Regina and is charged with abducting and sexually assaulting two boys. He faces five counts, including sexual assault causing bodily harm to both children, who can't be named under a publication ban.

■ July 23, 2007: Whitmore pleads guilty and is sentenced to life in prison without eligibility for parole for seven years.

Source: August 4, 2006 © The Canadian Press

Predictors of Sexual Recidivism

Hanson and Bussière (1998) and Hanson and Morton-Bourgon (2004) have conducted important meta-analyses that organized and summarized a large number of studies on predictors of recidivism among sex offenders. As shown in Table 9.1 from Hanson and Morton-Bourgon (2004), among the variables that have received empirical attention, the best predictors of sexual recidivism are sexual deviancy (Cohen's d = 0.30) and antisocial orientation (d = 0.23). **Sexual deviancy** indicators took a variety of forms: any deviant sexual interests (assessed with PPG or other measures), sexual interest in children (assessed with PPG or other measures), any paraphilic interests, sexual preoccupation, and sex as coping. All were significant predictors of sexual recidivism. PPG-assessed sexual interest in rape and violence, however, was not a significant predictor of sexual recidivism. The alternate interpretations of PPG findings also apply to research examining the extent to which sexual arousal to rape and violence predicts sexual reoffending (Hanson and Morton-Bourgon 2004; Lalumière et al. 2005).

Indicators of **antisocial orientation** include antisocial personality (e.g., antisocial personality disorder and psychopathy), antisocial traits (e.g., self-regulation problems, impulsivity, hostility, and employment instability), and history of rule violation (e.g., childhood behaviour problems, any prior criminal history, history of non-sexual crime, and violation of conditional release). Almost all of these aspects of antisocial orientation significantly predicted sexual recidivism.

Beliefs supportive of sex offending, included under the broader category of sexual attitudes, were found to significantly predict sexual recidivism. However, this effect was

Table 9.1 The Predictive Accuracy of the Main Categories of Risk Factors

	Type of Recidivism			
Category	Sexual	Violent Non-sexual	Violent	Any
Sexual Deviancy	.30 ±.08	−.05 ±.17	.19 ±.08	.04 ±.08
Antisocial Orientation	.23 ±.04	.51 ±.07	.54 ±.05	.52 ±.04
Sexual Attitudes	.16 ±.12	.17 ±.22	.14 ±.11	.24 ±.10
Intimacy Deficits	.15 ±.11	.12 ±.21	.12 ±.12	.10 ±.10
Adverse Childhood Environment	.09 ±.08	−.02 ±.17	.14 ±.08	.11 ±.07
General Psychological Problems	.02 ±.10	.21 ±.14	.00 ±.10	−.04 ±.11
Clinical Presentation	−.02 ±.09	.16 ±.20	.09 ±.09	.12 ±.08

Source: Hanson and Morton-Bourgon (2004)

relatively small. Interestingly, beliefs supportive of sex offending in general were significant predictors, but beliefs specific to child molestation were not significantly predictive of sexual recidivism, although the effect was in the expected direction. A more recent prospective study of nearly 1000 sex offenders (discussed below) conducted by Hanson, Harris, Scott, and Helmus (2007) also found that beliefs supportive of sex offending were poor predictors of sexual recidivism. Specifically, neither beliefs supportive of rape nor beliefs supportive of child molestation distinguished sex offenders who sexually recidivated from those who did not; this was the case even when rapists and child molesters were examined separately. As Hanson and colleagues (2007) have suggested, it is possible that the poor performance of such attitudes reflects measurement limitations. Further research is needed to clarify whether such beliefs play a role in sexual recidivism.

Among the constructs that made up intimacy deficits, neither social skills deficits ($d = -0.07$), loneliness ($d = 0.03$), nor negative social influences ($d = 0.22$) significantly predicted sexual recidivism; however, the effect for negative social influences was in the expected direction and was larger than for social skills and loneliness. Conflicts in intimate relationships and emotional identification with children were both significant predictors of sexual recidivism.

Many people are surprised to learn that adverse childhood environments, general psychological problems, clinical presentation, and seriousness of the sex offence have not been found to be very good predictors of sexual recidivism. Adverse childhood environments include separation from parents; sexual, physical, or emotional abuse or neglect; and negative relationship with father or mother. Other than a small effect for separation from parents, none of these negative experiences significantly predicted sexual recidivism. Sex offenders who had been separated from one or both parents at a young age were significantly more likely to sexually recidivate than those who had not been separated ($d = 0.16$).

General psychological problems such as anxiety, depression, and low self-esteem were also poor predictors of sexual recidivism. However, a more recent study not included in this meta-analysis found large effects for self-esteem, with higher rates of sexual recidivism among sex offenders with lower self-esteem compared to those with higher self-esteem (Thornton et al. 2004). Thus the relationship between self-esteem and sexual recidivism warrants further investigation.

In terms of clinical presentation variables, lack of victim empathy, denial of the sex offence, minimization of responsibility, low motivation for treatment at intake, and poor progress in treatment were not significant predictors of sexual recidivism. Recent research suggests that the relationship between denial and sexual recidivism may differ for different types of sex offenders. For example, Nunes, Hanson, Firestone, Moulden, Greenberg, and Bradford (2007) found that denial was associated with increased sexual recidivism among low-risk sex offenders such as incest offenders but associated (non-significantly) with decreased sexual recidivism in higher-risk sex offenders. Risk in this study was measured with an actuarial risk-assessment instrument called the Rapid Risk Assessment for Sexual Offense Recidivism (RRASOR) (Hanson 1997).

A seemingly counterintuitive finding is that greater intrusiveness (e.g., penetration) in sex offences was significantly associated with lower rates of sexual recidivism. That is, offenders who had engaged in more intrusive sex offences were less likely to sexually recidivate. In addition, offenders who had committed any non-contact sexual offences (whether or not they had also committed contact sex offences) were significantly more likely to sexually recidivate.

There is convincing evidence that sexual deviancy and psychopathy interact in predicting sexual recidivism (e.g., Harris et al. 2003; Olver and Wong 2006; Rice and Harris 1997). So although sexual deviance and psychopathy are generally associated with increased sexual recidivism on their own, sex offenders with both characteristics are much more likely to sexually recidivate than sex offenders with only one. In addition to the updated 2004 meta-analysis, Hanson and Bussière's initial meta-analysis (1998) examined a number of offender, offence, and victim characteristics that have become established predictors of sexual recidivism. These include young age, never married, prior sex offences, unrelated victims, stranger victims, and male victims.

RISK ASSESSMENT

THERE ARE MANY INSTRUMENTS USED TO ASSESS RISK OF SEXUAL RECIDIVISM; FOR EXAMPLE, STATIC-99 (Hanson and Thornton 1999; 2000), RRASOR (Hanson 1997), Sex Offender Risk Appraisal Guide (SORAG) (Quinsey, Harris, Rice, and Cormier 1998), Risk Matrix-2000-Sexual (Thornton et al. 2003), Sexual Violence Risk-20 (SVR-20) (Boer, Hart, Kropp, and Webster 1997), Violence Risk Scale: Sex Offender version (VRS:SO) (Wong, Olver, Nicholaichuk, and Gordon 2003), Stable-2007 (Hansonet al. 2007), and Acute-2007 (Hanson et al. 2007). Approaches to risk assessment can be categorized in a number of ways. Four key categories are described here: unstructured clinical judgment, empirical actuarial, mechanical, and structured professional judgment (Hanson and Morton-Bourgon 2009). **Unstructured clinical judgment** involves arriving at an estimate of risk based on the assessor's own idiosyncratic decisions about what factors to consider and how to combine those factors. In contrast, the empirical actuarial and mechanical instruments both follow explicit rules about what factors to consider and how to combine those factors to arrive at a final estimate of risk. However, two characteristics distinguish empirical actuarial from mechanical. For **empirical actuarial** instruments, 1) the selection and combination of items are derived from their observed statistical relationship with recidivism; and 2) tables linking scores to expected recidivism rates are provided. For **mechanical** instruments, the selection and combination of items are derived from theory or reviews of the empirical literature and no recidivism tables are provided. **Structured professional judgment** incorporates features of both unstructured clinical judgment and the actuarial approach; there are explicit guidelines for which factors to consider (although additional factors may also be considered), but the combination of those factors is left up to the discretion of the assessor. Hanson and Morton-Bourgon's (2009) meta-analysis revealed that, on average, all approaches are significantly accurate in predicting sexual recidivism.

However, unstructured clinical judgment is the least accurate and empirical actuarial and mechanical instruments are the most accurate. The predictive accuracy of structured professional judgment fell between actuarial and unstructured clinical judgment.

Static-99   The Static-99 (Hanson and Thornton 2000) is an empirical actuarial risk-assessment instrument designed to estimate risk of sexual recidivism among adult sex offenders. It consists of 10 static items. *Static* refers to items that cannot potentially be changed through intervention. The items include: young age at the time of the assessment, absence of long-term cohabitation (two years or longer) with a romantic partner, current and prior convictions for non-sexual violent offences, prior sex offences, prior sentencing dates (i.e., number of separate occasions on which an offender has been sentenced for one or more offences of any kind), presence of convictions for non-contact sex offences (e.g., indecent exposure), any unrelated victims versus exclusively related victims, any stranger victims (i.e., offender did not know victim for at least 24 hours prior to offence) versus exclusively known victims, and any male victims versus exclusively female victims. Examples of victims that would be considered related are daughters, sons, spouses, siblings, nieces, and nephews. In addition, step-relations are counted as related if the step-relationship started at least two years prior to the offence. Scores for the 10 items are summed to calculate a total score, which can range from 0 to 12. Higher scores indicate higher risk of recidivism.

Given that these characteristics were found to predict sexual recidivism in the meta-analysis discussed earlier (Hanson and Bussière 1998; Hanson and Morton-Bourgon 2004), you may not be surprised to learn that the Static-99 has repeatedly demonstrated good predictive validity; that is, research indicates that it is a good predictor of sexual recidivism. The Static-99 is the most widely used sex offender risk-assessment instrument and has received by far the most research attention. A meta-analysis by Hanson and Morton-Bourgon (2009) examined the predictive accuracy of various sex offender risk-assessment instruments. On average, across 63 studies and over 20 000 sex offenders, the Static-99 is one of the most accurate tools available for estimating risk of sexual recidivism.

Box 9.2

Canadian Researcher Profile: Dr. Karl Hanson

Dr. R. Karl Hanson is Senior Research Scientist at Public Safety Canada (in Ottawa) and Adjunct Professor in the psychology department at Carleton University. Dr. Hanson is a leading researcher in the field of sexual offender risk assessment and treatment. He has published more than 100 articles, including several highly influential meta-analytic reviews, and has developed the most widely used risk-assessment tools for sexual offenders: Static-99, Stable-2007, and Acute-2007. He is a Fellow of the Canadian Psychological Association, and in 2002 was awarded the Significant Achievement Award from the Association for the Treatment of Sexual Abusers.

Box 9.2 Continued

When asked about his education and training, Dr. Hanson recounted that "after several false starts (e.g., physics, music therapy), I was inspired to pursue psychology after attending a lecture by Anand Paranjpe on the psychology of yoga. I was fortunate to have the opportunity to work closely with Dr. Paranjpe at Simon Fraser University, completing my B.A. thesis on meditation." He then completed his Ph.D. in clinical psychology at the University of Waterloo; Donald Meichenbaum (one of the founders of cognitive-behavioural therapy) was his dissertation supervisor. His Ph.D. research was on personality assessment from the perspective of cognitive schema. Dr. Hanson says that "after graduating I was marginally employed until I found focus working with offenders."

Dr. Hanson became interested in his current areas of research when he was conducting clinical work in general mental health settings. He says, "[i]t soon became apparent that most of the individuals I saw had had difficult lives. Many had been abused, physically and sexually. I began to ask questions about why people victimized others, and the answers I got were unsatisfying (e.g., 'they are bad'). I thought I might be able to do better." When asked what keeps him interested in these research topics, Dr. Hanson says, "I like doing intellectual work on applied topics. It is gratifying to see my work influence how we address the major social problems of sexual and physical victimization. These problems will never go away. Even if we learn to better manage identified offenders, most abusers are never detected, and each new generation provides a new generation of potential offenders."

His work has been highly influential to practitioners and policy-makers because it strikes a balance between methodological rigour and the realities of the field. One of the many ways in which Dr. Hanson has contributed to knowledge in this area is through meta-analyses. He believes that "every student should conduct a meta-analysis as part of their basic training in statistics." Of the many studies he has done, his favourite is his first meta-analysis on recidivism predictors for sexual offenders (Hanson and Bussière 1998). "After completing that project, I felt that we had made a significant step forward. It was as if we had drawn a line, and everything would have to begin again from here." Dr. Hanson also enjoys the travel opportunities afforded by being an international expert: "How else would I get invited to discuss deviant sexuality in the private inner chambers of the Vatican, or play rock 'n' roll with patients in the forensic hospital in Utrecht?" (quotes taken from personal correspondence with Dr. Hanson).

Sex Offender Risk Appraisal Guide (SORAG)   The Sex Offender Risk Appraisal Guide (SORAG) (Quinsey et al. 1998) is an empirical actuarial risk-assessment instrument designed to estimate risk of violent recidivism among adult sex offenders. It consists of 14 static items. The items include: separation from one or both biological parents before age 16, elementary school maladjustment, history of alcohol problems, never married, non-violent criminal history, violent criminal history, prior sex offences, exclusively female victims under the age of 14, failure on prior conditional release, age at index offence, personality disorder, schizophrenia, deviant PPG results, and PCL-R score. Note that exclusively offending against girls under the age of 14 and having a diagnosis of schizophrenia are associated with lower risk of violent recidivism on the SORAG. The SORAG is a good predictor of sexual recidivism and a strong predictor of violent recidivism (Hanson and Morton-Bourgon 2009).

What about Dynamic Factors?

Although the Static-99 and the SORAG are invaluable for estimating the likelihood of serious recidivism, they do not provide any information about how to reduce or manage offenders' risk. This is clear from looking at the items. They are all static factors. A sex offender's score on the Static-99 can decrease if he gets older or lives with a romantic partner for two years or more. The scores for almost all the remaining items, however, will stay the same or worsen; for example, if he commits additional offences. So as a treatment provider, the Static-99 does not tell you what areas to address in treatment to reduce the offender's risk of sexual recidivism. Similarly, assessors cannot determine with the Static-99 if offenders' risk has decreased over time; for example, from the start of their prison sentence to the time they become eligible for conditional release. This is where dynamic risk factors come in.

In contrast to static risk factors that are not changeable with intervention (e.g., number of prior sex offences), dynamic risk factors vary over time and may be changeable through intervention. Research on dynamic risk factors has lagged behind work on static risk factors. It is much easier to extract static factors from archival data for groups of sex offenders that have already spent considerable time in the community than to prospectively assess potential dynamic risk factors and follow up groups of sex offenders. Given the low base rate of detected sexual recidivism and large numbers of offenders, long follow-up periods (around five years) are required to adequately test the relationship between a potential dynamic risk factor and sexual recidivism. In addition, demonstrating that a given variable is truly a dynamic risk factor for sexual recidivism requires more evidence than static risk factors. Specifically, to demonstrate that a variable is truly a dynamic risk factor, it must not only be able to change, but changes on that variable must be related to changes in risk (Douglas and Skeem 2005). The putative dynamic variable must also add incrementally to the predictive accuracy achieved with static risk factors (Seto 2008). Thus the mere possibility that a variable can change does not necessarily make it a dynamic risk factor. Despite these enormous challenges, assessment instruments that include potential dynamic risk factors for sexual recidivism have been developed. A few are described below.

Sexual Violence Risk—20 (SVR-20) The Sexual Violence Risk—20 (SVR-20) (Boer, Hart, Kropp, and Webster 1997) is a structured professional judgment instrument designed to assess risk for sexual offending. It includes static factors as well as putatively dynamic factors. It consists of a total of 20 items subdivided into three major sections: psychosocial adjustment (11 items), sexual offences (7 items), and future plans (2 items). The psychosocial adjustment items are sexual deviation, victim of child abuse, psychopathy, major mental illness, substance use problems, suicidal/homicidal ideation, relationship problems, employment problems, past non-sexual violent offences, past non-violent offences, and past supervision failure. The sexual offences items are high density of sex offences, multiple sex offence types, physical harm to victim(s) in sex offences, use of weapons or threats of death in sex offences, escalation in frequency or severity of sex offences, extreme minimization or denial of sex offences, and attitudes that support or condone sex offences. The future plans items are lacks realistic plans and negative attitude toward intervention. Each item is rated on a three-point scale: zero indicates that the particular factor is not present, one indicates the factor may be present, and two indicates the factor is present. Although subscale and total scores can be calculated by summing the appropriate items, Boer et al. (1997) recommend that evaluators use their professional judgment to arrive at a final risk estimate of low, moderate, or high. Unlike the Static-99 and SORAG, risk level would be determined primarily by consideration of the salience and relevance of each of the 20 items for the person being assessed as well as any other information thought to be relevant. Although the predictive accuracy of the SVR-20 has not been examined as often as the Satic-99, the available evidence suggests that it is also a good predictor of sexual recidivism (Hanson and Morton-Bourgon 2009). Interestingly, the SVR-20 was significantly more accurate when risk estimates were based on structured professional judgment than on simply adding the item scores (i.e., treating it like a mechanical instrument). However, it should be noted that this effect for structured professional judgment ratings of the SVR-20 was based on only three studies.

Violence Risk Scale—Sexual Offender version (VRS-SO) The Violence Risk Scale—Sexual Offender Version (VRS-SO) (Wong et al. 2003) is an actuarial instrument consisting of 7 static items and 17 dynamic risk items and is designed to estimate risk of sexual recidivism, identify treatment targets, and assess change on the dynamic factors. The static items are similar to those in the Static-99. The dynamic items are: 1) sexually deviant lifestyle (hobbies, interests, work, or relationships involving sexually deviant behaviours); 2) sexual compulsivity (high sex drive and frequent sexual behaviours and thoughts); 3) premeditation and victim-grooming in sex offence; 4) interpersonal and emotional antisocial personality features; 5) cognitive distortions; 6) interpersonal physical or verbal aggression; 7) over- or under-control of emotions related to sex offending; 8) poor understanding of factors causing sex offending and unwillingness to talk or think about his or her sex offending; 9) substance abuse; 10) lack or rejection of positive supports, services, and plans in the community; 11) released to high-risk situations; 12) presence of a pre-offence cycle of interpersonal, situational, and personal factors; 13) impulsivity; 14) negative attitude or poor compliance with community supervision; 15) negative attitude or poor compliance with sex offender treatment; 16) deviant sexual interests; and 17) intimacy deficits. For dynamic items that are rated as problematic for a particular offender, the extent to which the offender has accepted and attempted to remediate those problems is assessed prior to treatment and again after treatment (or at other key points, such as when being considered for conditional release). Offenders' scores on the dynamic factors can increase or decrease depending on the amount and direction of change in their acceptance and remediation efforts for each factor.

Although the VRS-SO has not yet received as much research attention as the Static-99, SORAG, and SVR-20, the available evidence is very encouraging. Olver, Wong, Nicholaichuk, and Gordon (2007) found that the static and dynamic scores predicted sexual recidivism. The dynamic items predicted sexual recidivism even after controlling for the static items. Importantly, change on the dynamic items predicted sexual recidivism even after controlling for pre-treatment scores on static and dynamic risk. Taken together, the results indicate that the static, pre-treatment dynamic scores, and change in dynamic risk all provided independent information about sexual recidivism, which means that considering static risk, dynamic risk, and change yields more accurate estimates of risk than considering any one of them alone. This suggests that the VRS-SO is a valid instrument not only for estimating risk of sexual recidivism, but also for identifying important treatment targets and monitoring change on those dynamic factors.

Stable-2007 and Acute-2007 The Stable-2007 and Acute-2007 are empirical actuarial instruments developed by Hanson et al. (2007) to assess dynamic predictors of sexual recidivism. Dynamic risk factors can be divided into stable and acute. **Stable dynamic risk factors** are slowly changing (e.g., sexual preoccupation), whereas **acute dynamic risk factors** are quickly changing (e.g., negative mood). Stable-2007 consists of the following 13 stable dynamic risk factors: 1) proportion of negative social influences relative to positive social influences; 2) ever married and quality of current romantic relationship; 3) emotional identification with children; 4) hostility toward women; 5) general social rejection; 6) lack of concern for others; 7) impulsivity; 8) poor problem-solving skills; 9) negative emotionality; 10) high sex drive and sexual preoccupation; 11) use of sex as coping; 12) deviant sexual interests; and 13) lack of cooperation with supervision. A Stable-2007 assessment would typically be conducted once every six months to a year for an offender.

The Acute-2007 consists of seven acute dynamic items: 1) victim access; 2) hostility; 3) sexual preoccupation; 4) rejection of supervision; 5) emotional collapse; 6) collapse of social supports; and 7) substance abuse. Four of these items are specifically related to sexual and non-sexual violent recidivism (victim access, hostility, sexual preoccupation, and rejection of supervision), whereas all seven items are related to general recidivism. An Acute-2007 assessment would typically be conducted at each meeting with an offender.

How do static, stable, and acute risk factors fit together? All three provide important information that can inform different levels of decision-making about supervision and treatment (Hanson et al. 2007). Static risk factors indicate a baseline of risk and an estimate of the likelihood of sexual reoffending over the long term. Stable dynamic factors indicate potential treatment targets and permit measurement of improvement or deterioration over time (e.g., prior to treatment versus after treatment). Acute dynamic factors indicate the imminence of sexual recidivism (i.e., is he likely to offend now?).

The Stable-2007 and Acute-2007 (Hanson et al. 2007) were developed and evaluated in the only truly prospective study of dynamic risk factors for sex offenders. Assessments on the Static-99 and the stable and acute dynamic items were conducted by 156 supervision officers (e.g., probation officers, parole officers) on a total of 997 sex offenders beginning community supervision in all Canadian provinces and territories, as well as the states of Alaska and Iowa. Consistent with past research, the Static-99 was a good predictor of sexual recidivism. The Stable-2007 and the Acute-2007 also significantly predicted sexual recidivism. Importantly, the Stable-2007 added independent information to the prediction of sexual recidivism above the Static-99. Similarly, the Acute-2007 significantly predicted short-term sexual recidivism (within 45 days of Acute-2007 rating) after controlling for Static-99 and Stable-2007 scores. So all three instruments together provided more comprehensive information and thus more accurate predictions of sexual recidivism than each one alone.

However, change on the Stable-2007 or Acute-2007 was not significantly related to sexual recidivism. This may have been due to the relatively short time frame examined for the Stable-2007 (approximately six months between the first and second assessment). Hanson and colleagues (2007) speculate that perhaps if the timeframe had been longer, more meaningful changes would have occurred that would be related to changes in sexual recidivism. With the current findings, however, it remains to be determined whether these variables are truly dynamic risk factors. In the absence of evidence that change is related to recidivism, the alternate, more parsimonious, explanation that these putative dynamic factors are simply manifestations of underlying static characteristics cannot be ruled out.

TREATMENT AND MANAGEMENT

WE HAVE SEEN THAT SEXUAL RECIDIVISM RATES ARE GENERALLY QUITE LOW, BUT SOME characteristics are associated with increased rates of sexual recidivism, and by combining these characteristics into risk-assessment instruments it is possible to distinguish sex offenders at the highest risk to sexually recidivate from those who are at lower risk. The community is especially concerned about the management of risk posed by sex offenders. Horrific but infrequent sex offences, often involving the abduction, sexual assault, and murder of children, understandably elicit fear and outrage from the public and demands for harsher penalties and closer monitoring of sex offenders in the community (e.g., Levenson, Brannon, Fortney, and Baker 2007). The response from the criminal justice system is often to enact increasingly extreme measures, such as community notification and sex offender registries. **Community notification** involves informing the public that a sex offender is being released to a particular city or neighbourhood. These notifications increasingly utilize the Internet to disseminate information about released sex offenders. Although such notifications in Canada are reserved for offenders judged to be high risk and the information is limited to the offender's name, photograph, and offence description, some states in the United States provide home addresses, telephone numbers, employment locations, and other specific information on all released sex offenders, regardless of their level of risk. **Sex offender registries** require sex offenders to register with the police upon release and to maintain current information about their address. In Canada, this information is accessible only by the police, but in some states, personal details about offenders are accessible by the public.

Despite much public support of extreme (and expensive) measures for sex offenders (e.g., Levenson et al. 2007), the available evidence generally does not indicate that they achieve their intended effect of reducing recidivism (e.g., Sandler, Freeman, and Socia 2008; Zevitz 2006). In fact, public registries and community notification may have unintended negative effects on sex offenders that may hinder their safe reintegration into the community, such as losing employment, being threatened or harassed by neighbours, having their property damaged, being forced to move from their residences, and being physically assaulted or injured (Levenson, D'Amora, and Hern 2007).

Harsher prison sentencing is another common demand from the public (Levenson et al. 2007). Although incarcerating sex offenders obviously limits opportunity for sexual offending while incarcerated, indefinite incarceration of all sex offenders is not a realistic option. As discussed earlier, the majority of sex offenders do not return to the criminal justice system for another sexual offence. Thus incarcerating all sex offenders in the name of preventing sexual recidivism would be an unacceptable use of scarce resources and unfairly restrict the liberty of the majority of sex offenders. Currently, most sex offenders do not receive indefinite sentences and are released to the community at some point. A more important question is whether incarceration deters sex offenders from recidivating once they have been released. An intuitive expectation is that receiving a prison sentence, especially a long sentence, would deter an offender from sexually recidivating once released back into the community. Prisons are generally not the greatest places for sex offenders and you would think the threat of returning to that environment would be enough to curb any behaviour. However, as with general criminal behaviour (Gendreau, Goggin, and Cullen 1999; Smith, Goggin, and Gendreau 2002) (see Chapter 4 for a full discussion), the available evidence does not support the effectiveness of prison as a deterrent of post-release sexual recidivism (Hanson and Bussière 1998).

In a recent study, the relationship between incarceration and recidivism among sex offenders was more thoroughly examined in a sample of 627 men who had been assessed at the Royal Ottawa Hospital because of a sexual offence they had committed (Nunes, Firestone, Wexler, Jensen, and Bradford 2007). The sample consisted of intra-familial child molesters, extra-familial child molesters, rapists, and a mixed group (with more than one type of sex offence). Most subjects were assessed around the time of sentencing for their index sexual offences. The index offence is the one for which offenders had been initially assessed at the Royal Ottawa Hospital. Almost two-thirds were sentenced to a period of incarceration (64 percent) and the rest received some form of community supervision (e.g., probation). For those sentenced to time in prison, the average sentence was 21.24 months ($SD= 19.91$); the shortest sentence was 1 month and the longest was 10 years. Average time with opportunity to reoffend in the community was 8.11 years ($SD= 4.86$). Recidivism was defined as any new charge following the index offence. The rate of sexual recidivism was 12.8 percent and the rate of any violent recidivism (including sexual) was 20.6 percent.

Incarceration for the index offence was unrelated to sexual or violent recidivism. This was the case whether incarceration was examined as a dichotomous variable (incarceration versus community sentence) or as a continuous variable (length of incarceration). The recidivists were not significantly more or less likely to have been incarcerated than the offenders who did not recidivate (respectively, 68 versus 63 percent for sexual recidivism and 67 versus 63 percent for violent recidivism). Among those who had received a prison sentence, average sentence length did not differ significantly between recidivists and non-recidivists for sexual recidivism (23 months versus 21 months, respectively) or violent recidivism (23 versus 21 months, respectively). No significant association between incarceration and recidivism was found even after taking into account variables such as time at risk and offenders' estimated risk for sexual recidivism (as measured by the RRASOR). Sentencing sexual offenders to terms of incarceration appears to have little, if any, impact on sexual and violent recidivism following release. Although incarceration does not seem to achieve the goal of specific deterrence, it is a good way to incapacitate high-risk sex offenders.

So if incarceration and other punitive measures do not reduce reoffending among sex offenders, what else can be done? Treatment designed to target putative dynamic risk factors is an obvious option. Treatment of sex offenders varies widely and can take a number of different approaches; some of the main ones are discussed on pp. 317–319.

Box 9.3

Canadian Researcher/Practitioner Profile: Dr. William Marshall

Dr. William Marshall is Director of Rockwood Psychological Services, Co-Director of the Sexual Offenders Unit at the St. Lawrence Valley Corrections and Treatment Centre in Brockville, and Emeritus Professor of Psychology at Queen's University. He was born in Perth, Australia, completed his undergraduate degree in psychology at the University of Western Australia, his M.Sc. at the University of London, England, and his Ph.D. at Queen's University under the supervision of Professor Andrew McGhie. His Ph.D. research was on thought disorder in schizophrenia. His favourite course to teach was Abnormal Psychology.

Continued >

Box 9.3 Continued

Dr. Marshall is a well-respected leader in the area of sex-offender treatment and a prolific author. For over 30 years, he has been treating and researching sex offenders, as well as developing treatment programs and training clinicians. He has over 300 publications, including 16 books. He regularly consults with clinicians in places like Australia, New Zealand, South Africa, the Netherlands, Japan, Hong Kong, England, Scotland, Austria, and Poland, to name a few. Dr. Marshall was the 1999 recipient of the Santiago Grisolia Prize for his worldwide contributions to the reduction of violence and in 2000 he was elected a Fellow of the Royal Society of Canada. Dr. Marshall was the President of the Association for the Treatment of Sexual Abusers from 2000 to 2001. In 2006, he was named an Officer of the Order of Canada for transforming the way prison systems around the world rehabilitate sex offenders.

He became interested in working in this area while in a part-time position at Kingston Penitentiary during his Ph.D. studies at Queen's. He says that the "fascinating and complex, and sometimes dangerous, cases" he sees keep him interested in research and clinical work with sex offenders. His primary approach to treatment is a positive/strength-based version of cognitive-behavioural therapy. Although Dr. Marshall has enjoyed all his research endeavours, two studies that stand out for him examined the relationship between characteristics of therapists and the gains made by offenders in treatment (Marshall et al. 2002; Marshall et al. 2003). "Our two studies on therapist characteristics were the most interesting as no one had done anything on this before

with sexual offenders. These studies were among the most elegant done on therapist features in any area of clinical psychology because of the fact that we were able to study videos of therapy in action over 20 settings where the therapists rigorously followed the same manual and all clients were assessed pre- and post-treatment on the same measures."

When asked about his favourite case, Dr. Marshall says, "I liked them all. That is the job of therapists working with sexual offenders (maybe all offenders), to unlock the good person behind the offending. If I had to pick one it would be 'John' who had molested 420 boys over a 26-year period. He was one of the most gentle and loving men I have ever met. He knew he would likely never be released but he was determined to overcome his attraction to boys in order to make up for what he had done. John was a fascinatingly complex character and was one of my early clients in a prison setting." In terms of future directions, Dr. Marshall plans to "continue the development of our program toward a more positive emphasis and building better lives rather than the old relapse prevention approach." He continues to argue for changes to the criminal justice system's management of sex offenders, but feels that "Canada has got it mostly right. When I visit other countries I realize what a wonderful system Canada has when it comes to crime. I would like Correctional Service Canada to allow offenders with indeterminate sentences to gradually move down through the security levels as their first steps toward release if they are to be released instead of being discharged from maximum security."

Box 9.3 Continued

When asked about training for future researchers and clinicians in the psychology of criminal behaviour, Dr. Marshall says, "[m]ost Canadian universities do a good job training graduate students but we need more forensic programs. They need to integrate clinical and research rather better, particularly having those who intend to be researchers do clinical training. Nothing irritates me more than researchers who have never done clinical work designing programs and assessments. Personally I adhere to Barbara McClintock's edict: 'In order to do good research you have to have a feel for the organism.' McClintock was a Nobel Laureate in biology who studied 'jumping genes' in corn. My guess is that when it comes to human subjects a sensitivity for the organism is likely more important. McClintock, throughout her whole career, spent time in the fields growing corn so she could better understand it." Dr. Marshall says that most of all, he enjoys spending time with this wife, son, daughter-in-law, and two grandsons. He also enjoys reading novels: "[t]hey tell us things about human nature that psychology can't. I just finished re-reading Dante's Divine Comedy—bloody amazing" (quotes taken from personal correspondence with Dr. Marshall).

APPROACHES TO TREATMENT OF SEX OFFENDERS

Pharmacological Treatment Pharmacological treatments generally reduce sex drive (e.g., desire, arousal). This is an obvious target given the sexual nature of offending and evidence that places sexual deviancy among the top predictors of sexual recidivism. A number of drugs have been used in this sort of treatment (Seto 2008). The most common are antiandrogens, selective serotonin reuptake inhibitors (SSRIs), and gonadotropin releasing hormone (GnRH) agonists. Antiandrogens like cyproterone acetate (CPA) and medroxyprogesterone acetate (MPA) reduce circulating testosterone. GnRH agonists like leuprolide acetate also reduce testosterone. SSRIs like buspirone, fluoxetine, and sertraline inhibit the binding of serotonin to receptors. A side effect of SSRIs is decreased sex drive, which makes them potentially useful for sex offenders. Unfortunately, some of these medications have a number of unpleasant and sometimes serious side effects. For example, antiandrogens are associated with the development of breasts and osteoporosis in men.

Behavioural Treatment Behavioural treatments attempt to reduce deviant sexual interests and, sometimes, to increase appropriate sexual interests. Some examples are aversion, covert sensitization, and masturbatory satiation. Aversion involves pairing deviant sexual stimuli or thoughts with aversive stimuli, such as unpleasant odours or pain (Laws, Meyer, and Holmen 1978; Marshall 1971; Quinsey et al. 1976). For example, a person may be presented with deviant stimuli such as pictures of children or stories about sexual offending, while an unpleasant odour or ammonia is inhaled. The goal is to decrease deviant interests by developing an association between deviant stimuli and unpleasant stimuli. Covert sensitization (Callahan and Leitenberg 1973) pairs negative thoughts (e.g., potential consequences of sex offending, such as prison, loss of family and friends, etc.) with deviant stimuli. In masturbatory satiation (Marshall and Lippens 1977), the person masturbates to an appropriate fantasy (i.e., consenting sex with adult partners) until orgasm. A short time after orgasm, the person resumes masturbating but this time to a deviant fantasy (e.g., sexual abuse of children). During the refractory period following orgasm, genital stimulation is generally not arousing and boring or unpleasant for most men. The goal here is to increase appropriate interests by pairing pleasant stimulation and orgasm with appropriate fantasies and to reduce deviant interests by pairing unpleasant stimulation with deviant fantasies.

Cognitive-Behavioural Therapy As the name suggests, **cognitive-behavioural therapy (CBT)** combines elements of cognitive and behavioural treatments to address psychological problems and abnormal behaviour. Some of the main targets in many cognitive-behavioural sex-offender programs include attitudes supportive of sex offending, victim empathy, social skills, and self-management. The dominant approach in CBT programs for sex offenders for many years was **relapse prevention (RP).** In this case, relapse would be a new sex offence (i.e., recidivism). Generally, the focus in RP is on addressing putative dynamic risk factors, identifying situational risk factors (e.g., high-risk situation), and developing ways to avoid or otherwise cope with these situational risk factors, with the ultimate goal being to avoid recidivating (Pithers 1990; Pithers Marques, Gibat, and Marlatt 1983). After two decades, support for the RP model began to waiver in the late 1990s. A number of limitations of RP have been identified, such as the poor fit of the RP model for many sex offenders and the negative tone. The RP model focuses on facilitating the avoidance of sex offending, but what about sex offenders who do not want to avoid offending? Some offenders do follow the RP offence pathway, where they initially want to avoid offending but their resolve weakens and eventually they offend. Many other offenders, however, want to offend from the onset, make no attempt to avoid it, and may even carefully plan and execute their offences (Ward and Hudson 1998). The RP model does not readily accommodate sex offenders of the latter type.

In terms of the negative tone, the RP model emphasizes the removal of risk factors and avoidance of risky situations. Marshall and Ward have argued that although reducing sexual recidivism should clearly remain the ultimate goal of treatment, this alone does not fully address important issues and leaves offenders with little to motivate them to change (Marshall et al. 2005; Ward and Gannon 2006). Their argument is captured very nicely in this quote from Marshall et al. (2005):

> Traditional relapse prevention has taken the form of specifying a list of 'don'ts.' Typically, relapse prevention plans consist of a list of people, places, and activities to be avoided. Although it makes intuitive sense to direct child molesters to avoid places where access to children is likely and to proscribe alcohol use for a rapist whose offending was facilitated by intoxication, it might be more effective to assist these offenders in designing an enjoyable and productive lifestyle that is exclusive of drunkenness or contacts with children. If child molesters are simply required to avoid children, then all we have done is

take away their only pathway to the goals they were achieving by sexual offending without providing them with alternative prosocial pathways for meeting their needs. (p. 1106)

Current treatment models are more positive and collaborative than RP. The most recent version is called the **Good Lives Model—Comprehensive** (Ward and Gannon 2006). In addition to focusing on the usual risk-management issues, the goal is to help offenders identify and achieve healthy goals that promote psychological well-being. As noted above, this is expected to increase the motivation of offenders to participate and engage in treatment, as well as reducing their likelihood of reoffending because they learn how to achieve fundamental human needs through prosocial means rather than through offending.

Box 9.4

Correctional Service Canada's National Moderate Intensity Sex Offender Program

The National Sex Offender Program is a cognitive-behavioural intervention that is designed to be a therapeutic, rather than solely a didactic or psychoeducational, program. It is based on empirical research and best practice in the provision of services to sex offenders, and on the principles of social learning, adult learning, group processes, therapeutic rapport and alliance, motivational enhancement, overlearning, and skills development.

The National Sex Offender Program targets criminogenic needs and known risk factors for sexual offending. Its format uses a "menu" approach based on criminogenic needs and known risk factors associated with individual offenders' patterns of sexual offending behaviour. The client is regarded as the "expert" on his own behaviour, and as such the role of the service provider is to assist the client to develop, through guided learning, an awareness of the dynamics and motivations of his sexual offending behaviour and to develop a self-management plan to avoid re-offending. The National Sex Offender Program also incorporates both group and individual work and recognizes learning that occurs outside the formal treatment venue.

Referral Criteria

The National Sex Offender Program is intended for all federal offenders who:

- Have been convicted of a sex offence, or

- Have been convicted of a sexually motivated crime, or

- Have admitted to a sex offence for which they have not been convicted.

AND

- Have a moderate risk to re-offend relative to other sex offenders, as assessed using a sex offender–specific actuarial assessment instrument such as the Static-99.

- Have moderate to high criminogenic needs as assessed using a sex offender specific measure of dynamic risk factors such as the Stable-2007 (moderate to high need levels refer to the number, type, and extent of entrenchment of dynamic risk factors).

Continued >

Box 9.4 Continued

Selection Criteria

The moderate intensity program is designed for offenders assessed as moderate risk to offend sexually and with need levels that are either moderate or high. Moderate to high need levels may be based on evidence that the offender has multiple criminogenic needs associated with sexual offending behaviour. For example, an offender whose sexual offending is associated with several domains, such as attitudes supportive of sexual aggression, deficits in social competence or skills, impulsivity, and empathy deficits, may be assessed as having moderate to high need levels and should receive treatment designed to address these criminogenic needs. Alternatively, offenders may be assessed as moderate to high need as a result of deficits in fewer domains, which are particularly well entrenched or influential on behaviour. For example, offenders whose sexual aggression is associated with well-entrenched attitudes supportive of deviant sexual behaviour and with frequent deviant sexual fantasy may also be assessed as moderate to high need.

The Moderate Intensity National Sex Offender Program is structured to require approximately four to five months to complete. There is a minimum requirement of 10 hours of group work per week, with a maximum of 14. Additionally, service providers conduct a minimum of two individual sessions with each offender during the course of the program. The program is conducted with two service providers.

Source: Correctional Service of Canada (2009)

Continuum of Service/ Maintenance Programming

The final phase of the moderate intensity program is maintenance programming. This component is designed as a follow-up to treatment intervention and is to be offered to all sex offenders completing the moderate intensity program. Maintenance is conceptualized as a component of treatment rather than a separate program to emphasize the importance of follow-up and continuity of service to sex offenders as well as the importance of continuity of care between the institution and the community. In maintenance, clients review and reinforce their self-management plans (and release plans, if applicable) to entrench these plans and strategies and to revise them in light of changes in circumstances.

Maintenance in the institution is designed to assist offenders in maintaining treatment gains and to revise their self-management plans. In the community, maintenance also performs these functions, but also continually reassesses risk and dynamic risk factors to assist in supervision. In the community, sex offenders should have a comprehensive self-management plan that outlines their high-risk situations, triggers to sex offending, and behaviours that parole officers and program officers would observe in the community if an offender's risk was increasing. These should be clearly delineated in the self-management/release plans and should be reassessed on a continual basis.

Effectiveness

Does sex offender treatment work? The question is deceptively complex and can be addressed in a number of ways. However, the most important issue regarding effectiveness is the extent to which treatment reduces sexual recidivism. Studies addressing this issue typically involve comparing the recidivism rates of offenders who received the treatment to those who did not. Although this sounds very straightforward, there are a number of major challenges. First, as you already know, sexual recidivism rates are quite low. If you were running a treatment program, you would need to follow up a large number of participants for about five years. A bigger problem is finding an adequate comparison group. Ideally, a true experimental design would be used and offenders would be randomly assigned to the treatment group or a no-treatment control group. Then when you compare the rates of recidivism, you could be reasonably confident that any observed difference between treated and untreated groups was caused by the treatment. Whether treatment works or not, the general public would probably be outraged if treatment was purposely withheld from a group of sex offenders so that researchers could determine if they are more likely to sexually reoffend than a group of treated sex offenders. Very few, if any, correctional agencies would be willing to conduct such an experiment. However, some researchers have argued that withholding treatment from some sex offenders to permit a strong test of a treatment's effects on recidivism is not unethical because there is not yet convincing evidence that treatment actually reduces sexual recidivism (e.g., Seto et al. 2008).

So, random assignment to a treatment and no-treatment group is not realistic in most cases. What about just comparing treated offenders to those who refused treatment, did not complete treatment, or for whom treatment was not available? Currently, most convicted sex offenders do participate in treatment and are actively encouraged to do so (although participation is ultimately voluntary). Thus it is difficult to find a sufficient number of untreated sex offenders. Even if such a group could be found, it is likely that they would differ prior to treatment on important variables related to treatment success and recidivism. For example, some researchers have compared treatment completers to treatment dropouts. Why is this a problem? Dropping out of treatment is associated with increased sexual recidivism (Hanson et al. 2002) and dropouts are more antisocial than completers (Nunes and Cortoni 2008). Given that dropouts are higher risk than completers to begin with, we would expect higher rates of sexual recidivism among the dropouts than completers even if treatment had no effect at all. Some researchers have compared treated offenders to offenders from an earlier time period when treatment was not offered. Although this is a large improvement over comparing completers with dropouts, it is still vulnerable to the possibility that the recidivism rates may differ between cohorts for reasons other than treatment, such as changes in reporting and arrest rates for sex offences over time (Hanson, Broom, and Stephenson 2004). In addition, the treatment group typically contains only those offenders who agreed to participate, whereas the untreated cohort contains offenders who would have agreed to treatment had it been offered as well as those who would have refused or dropped out; this is yet another potentially important source of non-equivalence between groups (Rice and Harris 2003).

These challenges leave the findings open to different interpretations, which is why knowledgeable experts considering the same studies disagree about whether treatment works and what constitutes credible evidence of treatment effectiveness (Hanson et al. 2002; Marshall and Marshall 2007; 2008; Rice and Harris 2003; Seto et al. 2008).

Nevertheless, when the findings from studies of varying credibility are combined in meta-analyses, significantly lower rates of sexual recidivism are found for the treated group compared to the untreated group (Hanson et al. 2002; Lösel and Schmucker 2005). In the most comprehensive meta-analysis of sex offender treatment outcome studies to date, Lösel and Schmucker reviewed 69 treatment studies (N = 22,181) and found significantly lower rates of sexual (11.1 percent for treated versus 17.5 percent for comparison group), violent (6.6 percent for treated versus 11.8 percent for comparison group), and general (22.4 percent for treated versus 32.5 percent for comparison group) recidivism among treated sex offenders compared to untreated sex offenders. Hanson, Bourgon, Helmus, and Hodgson (2009) recently examined whether sex offender treatment programs adhering to the principles of risk, need, and responsivity (Andrews, Bonta, and Hoge, 1990; see Chapter 4) would perform better than those not following these principles of effective correctional treatment. Hanson et al.'s (2009) meta-analysis revealed findings consistent with the general offender treatment literature. Specifically, greater reductions in sexual recidivism were found for programs that adhered to a greater number of the principles. Despite these encouraging findings, debate continues about whether the lower rates of recidivism associated with sex offender treatment actually demonstrate that treatment is effective or are more parsimoniously attributed to alternate explanations.

Below is a list of the top 10 issues and people to consider when thinking about sexual offending in Canada.

Top 10 List

Advances to Come, Debates, Ethical Conundrums, and People to Watch

1 Is pedophilia a choice or an innate sexual orientation, like being heterosexual or gay/lesbian?

2 Is rape motivated primarily by sex or power?

3 Given that static factors are such robust predictors of long-term sexual recidivism, is incapacitation a more realistic goal than rehabilitation with high-risk sex offenders?

4 Is it justifiable to deny treatment to some sex offenders in randomized control studies to more conclusively determine whether treatment actually does reduce sexual recidivism?

5 In light of the equivocal evidence for the effectiveness of existing sex offender treatment programs, could the effectiveness of new programs be measured against the existing programs (i.e., treatment as usual) in randomized control trials?

6 If incarceration does not reduce post-release sexual recidivism, should low-risk sex offenders serve their sentences in the community instead of inside prisons?

7 Does childhood sexual victimization play a causal role in sex offending? If so, how?

8 Will researchers eventually be able to identify truly dynamic risk factors that,

Top 10 List   Continued

when changed, influence long-term risk of sexual recidivism?

9 Some of the constructs identified as important in theory (e.g., beliefs supportive of child molestation, poor social skills, low empathy, motivation for treatment) have failed to emerge as useful predictors of sexual recidivism. Is this because they are irrelevant or because they have been inadequately measured in recidivism studies?

10 People to watch: Eric Beauregard, Ray Blanchard, James Cantor, Karl Hanson, Grant Harris, Martin Lalumière, Calvin Langton, Patrick Lussier, Bill Marshall, Mark Olver, Jean Proulx, Vern Quinsey, Marnie Rice, and Michael Seto.

SUMMARY

1. A significant minority of the population are victims of sexual offences. The majority of sex offences are not reported to the police, and sex offences are less likely to be reported than other violent crimes. Of the sex offences that are reported, approximately one-third are not cleared. Of the sex offences that are cleared and result in a conviction, approximately half result in a sentence of incarceration.

2. The vast majority of sex offences are committed by male offenders. Both sexual offending and victimization are more common among younger people. Offenders and victims know each other (e.g., acquaintances, friends, family members) prior to the sexual offence in the majority of incidents. Sexual victimization is associated with a number of negative emotional reactions as well as physical and psychological problems. Contrary to public opinion, there is no evidence that sex offences are on the rise in Canada.

3. Sex offenders are heterogeneous. Their characteristics, motivation, and behaviour vary considerably across and even within offence type.

4. Some paraphilias can manifest as sexual offending; specifically, pedophilia, sexual sadism, frotteurism, exhibitionism, and voyeurism. However, it is important to remember that paraphilia and sex offending are not synonymous. For example, one can be a pedophile but never commit a sex offence against a child and one can commit a sex offence against a child but not be a pedophile.

5. There is considerable overlap and convergence in most theories and models of the initiation of sexual offending. A number of factors likely combine and interact to cause sex offending. It is generally difficult to research the causal factors, but numerous observational studies suggest the following are associated with the initiation of sex offending against adults or children: childhood sexual victimization, deviant

sexual interests, general antisociality, low self-esteem, intimacy deficits, poor social skills, beliefs supportive of sex offending, and neurodevelopmental perturbations.

6. Sexual recidivism rates are generally low; relatively few sex offenders are charged with new sex offences after their initial conviction. The best predictors of sexual recidivism are sexual deviance and general antisociality. Risk factors can be static, stable dynamic, or acute dynamic. Static risk factors indicate a baseline of risk and an estimate of the likelihood of sexual reoffending over the long term. Stable dynamic factors indicate potential treatment targets and permit measurement of improvement or deterioration over time. Acute dynamic factors indicate the imminence of sexual recidivism.

7. Subgroups of sex offenders who have higher rates of recidivism can be identified and managed by assessing static and dynamic risk factors with risk-assessment instruments. The accuracy with which sexual recidivism is predicted is highest for empirical actuarial and mechanical instruments and lowest for unstructured clinical judgment. The predictive accuracy of structured professional judgment approaches falls between actuarial and unstructured clinical judgment.

8. Researchers generally find lower recidivism rates among treated compared to untreated sex offenders. And programs that follow the general principles of effective corrections appear to be more effective than programs that do not. Although these findings are very encouraging, debate continues about whether the lower rates of recidivism associated with sex offender treatment actually demonstrate that it is effective because the research methodology used in most studies leaves the results open to alternate interpretations. More creative and innovative research will move us closer to resolving these and other important questions about sex offenders.

Discussion Questions

1. Why do you think sex offences are so rarely reported to the police? Most research on sex offenders is conducted with those who have come to the attention of the criminal justice system (e.g., serving a prison sentence for a sex offence). What impact could this have on research on initiation and recidivism?

2. Consider the research reviewed on factors associated with the initiation of sex offending against adults or children. Is it consistent with the theories and models discussed? What is the nature of the relationship between these variables and sex offending? Do you think these factors play a causal role in sex offending or are they just correlates or even consequences of it? If causal, do you think their influence is direct or indirect? If indirect, what intervening variables might be involved and how?

3. Imagine you are doing a summer internship at the National Crime Prevention Centre and you are put in charge of developing a strategy to prevent sex offending. Based on the theories and research on the initiation of sex offending, what would you do?

4. What criteria must a variable meet to be a truly dynamic risk factor for sexual recidivism? If you were conducting research in this area, how would you go about demonstrating that a given variable is in fact a dynamic risk factor?

5. Imagine you are a forensic psychologist doing a risk assessment of a sex offender for his upcoming parole hearing. If you had to consider only two factors in your assessment, what would they be? What approach to risk assessment would you use? Which risk-assessment instrument would you use? If challenged, how would you justify your decisions about risk factors, approaches, and instruments?

6. If incarceration does not reduce post-release sexual recidivism, what does sentencing sex offenders to prison time accomplish? Which principles of sentencing do you think are most important when the courts are dealing with sex offenders? Why?

7. Do you think sex offender treatment reduces sexual recidivism? Why or why not?

8. Imagine you are involved in program development and research at CSC. Your current assignment is to design a new sex offender treatment program and evaluate its effectiveness. Given the research reviewed in this chapter, what would your program look like? What would you target in treatment? How would you evaluate whether the program was effective?

Additional Readings

Lalumière, M.L., Harris, G.T., Quinsey, V.L., and Rice, M.E. 2005. *The causes of rape: Understanding individual differences in male propensity for sexual aggression.* Washington, DC: American Psychological Association.

Marshall, W.L., Marshall, L.E., Serran, G.A., and Fernandez, Y.M. 2006. Treating sexual offenders: An integrated approach. New York: Routledge.

Seto, M.C. 2008. *Pedophilia and sexual offending against children: Theory, assessment, and intervention.* Washington, DC: American Psychological Association.

Relevant Websites

Association for the Treatment of Sexual Abusers
www.atsa.com

Correctional Service of Canada
www.csc-scc.gc.ca

Public Safety Canada
www.publicsafety.gc.ca

Mental Health Centre Penetanguishene Research Department
www.mhcp.on.ca/Site_Published/internet/ResearchActivities.aspx

Centre for Sex Offender Management
www.csom.org

Circles of Support and Accountability
www.stjohnsottawa.ca/pages/cosa.html

Stop It Now!
www.stopitnow.com

Chapter 10
Mentally Disordered Offenders

Twenty-six-year-old Jonathan Cogan is currently under care at the Royal Ottawa Hospital after being found unfit to stand trial for charges of threatening to kill his mother. In his late teens, Cogan began to withdraw from his family and would often refuse to leave his room. He had to drop out of college because he thought college security staff were following him around and putting listening devices in his dorm room. He threatened to punch a security officer if he did not remove the devices. In lieu of not pressing charges, Jonathan agreed to leave the college and moved back in with his parents. He landed a job working as a landscaper, and everything seemed fine until he started accusing his mother of spying on him at work. He also developed an unusual interest in knives and had a collection of 20, which were laid out on his desk and were off-limits to anyone else. He was charged with threatening to kill his mother after he held her down with a knife to her throat. Jonathan alleged that his mother had tried to poison him at dinner. He was diagnosed as having a delusional disorder and was placed on psychotropic medication.

Learning Objectives

1   Identify the most prevalent types of mental disorders in offenders.

2   Outline the differences in assessments for fitness and NCRMD evaluations.

3   Describe public and police attitudes toward mentally disordered offenders.

4   Describe the effectiveness of treatment programs for mentally disordered offenders.

5   Define psychopathy and the assessment for psychopathic traits across ages.

6   Explain the main theories of psychopathy and the recent genetic and biological research.

INTRODUCTION

SHOULD SOMEONE BE HELD RESPONSIBLE FOR THEIR ACTIONS IF THEY ARE MENTALLY ILL AT THE time they commit a crime? Should it depend on the type of mental illness or the type of crime committed? What about psychopaths who know that what they are doing is legally wrong but may not have the capacity to understand it is "morally" wrong? This chapter will discuss the range of mental disorders found in offenders, describe the role mental illness plays in the criminal justice system, and identify treatment programs for mentally disordered offenders. One particular type of personality disordered offender—the psychopath—will be discussed. Psychopaths commit a disproportionate amount of violence both in institutions and in the community, are more likely to reoffend then other offenders, and are resistant to treatment strategies.

MENTAL DISORDERS AND THE DSM

THE CONCEPT OF MENTAL DISORDERS PRESUPPOSES THAT IT IS POSSIBLE TO DISCRIMINATE between normal and abnormal behaviour. In North America, the primary tool used to diagnose mental disorders is the *Diagnostic and Statistical Manual of Mental Disorders* (DSM). (Outside North America, the World Health Organization's *International Statistical Classification of Diseases* is used to classify mental disorders.) The DSM was first published by the American Psychiatric Association (APA) in 1952 in order to facilitate the diagnosis of mental disorders and collect statistical information about the prevalence of different types of disorders. The original edition of the manual was 130 pages long and listed 106 mental disorders. The manual was revised in 1968 (to 134 pages, with 182 disorders), again in 1980 as the DSM-III (to 494 pages, with 265 disorders), and, most recently, in 1994, as the DSM-IV (886 pages with 297 listed disorders). The DSM-V is scheduled for publication in 2012. In 1980, the DSM introduced a multi-axial system designed to provide a more comprehensive description of the individual being assessed. The DSM organizes diagnoses into five levels (axes) relating to different aspects of disorders:

- Axis I: Clinical disorders, including mood disorders, anxiety disorders, phobias, schizophrenia, bipolar disorder, dissociative disorders, gender identity disorders, eating disorders, substance-related disorders, and developmental and learning disorders

- Axis II: Mental retardation and personality disorders, including avoidant, dependent, obsessive-compulsive, histrionic, antisocial, borderline, narcissistic, paranoid, schizoid, and schizotypal disorders

- Axis III: General medical conditions that may be related to the mental disorder or that might influence the choice of medications for treating the disorder

- Axis IV: Psychosocial or environmental factors that contribute to disorders, including family problems, educational problems, economic problems, or problems with the legal system

- Axis V: Assessment of the patient's general level of functioning

There have been a number of criticisms of the DSM, including construct validity and reliability of the diagnostic categories and symptoms (Baca-Garcia et al. 2007; Kendell and Jablensky 2003). It is not clear why certain disorders are included and how the symptoms for each disorder were selected. Critics have argued that the DSM lacks a strong empirical basis. Moreover, as it has evolved, it has been argued that the DSM places an undue emphasis on the existence of symptoms, which in turn leads to a proliferation of disorders. Between DSM-I and DSM-IV there was a 280 percent increase in the number of disorders listed. Even David Kupler, the most recent chairperson of the DSM-V planning committee, stated: "One of the raps against psychiatry is that you and I are the only two people in the U.S. without a psychiatric diagnosis" (Grossman 2008). The DSM's symptomatological bias also promotes an atheoretical stance that de-emphasizes etiological or causative information about a disorder. In defence of the APA, there is not consensus in the empirical literature about the etiological mechanisms underlying most mental disorders. In addition, the DSM has been criticized for having a reductionist bias, with claims that its system of making categorical distinctions between disorders and between normal and abnormal is unjustified (Helzer, Kraemer, and Krueger 2007; Wakefield 2006). Some clinicians believe the DSM should use a dimensional approach and should include a level of impairment since the impact of a symptom will vary across individuals. Despite these criticisms, the DSM continues to be the default tool for diagnosing mental disorders in North America.

MENTALLY DISORDERED OFFENDERS

A SIGNIFICANT PROPORTION OF THE MILLIONS OF INDIVIDUALS INCARCERATED worldwide experience serious mental disorders. Several factors have been proposed to account for this. With the advent of new psychotropic medications, a movement to deinsitutionalize psychiatric patients began in the 1960s. Many civil psychiatric facilities were closed and patients were moved into the community. Unfortunately, there was not a proportional increase in community facilities to help care for the released patients. In addition, the civil commitment process became more restrictive. In the United States, the "war on drugs" and mandatory sentences for drug offences resulted in more offenders with mental disorders related to substance abuse being jailed.

In 1973, Dr. Dorothy Speed estimated the prevalence of mental disorders within prison populations to be "10 percent mad, 15 percent bad, and 75 percent sad" (cited in Rotter, Way, Steinbacher, Sawyer, and Smith 2002: 338). There is certainly an overrepresentation of serious mental disorders in prisons, with many prisoners suffering from anxiety and depressive disorders. In a meta-analysis of 62 studies from 12 Western countries, Fazel and Danesh (2002) reported the prevalence rates of psychotic illness, major depression, personality disorder, and antisocial personality disorder (ASPD) in offender samples. Prevalence rates for male (n = 18,530) and female (n = 4,260) offenders were, respectively, 3.7 percent and 4.0 percent for psychotic illness, 10 percent and 12 percent for major depression, and 47 percent and 21 percent for ASPD.

A comprehensive study of mental illness in Australia by Butler et al. (2006) compared a consecutive sample of 916 prisoners to a community sample of 8168. The 12-month prevalence rate of mental illness was 80 percent in the prison sample and 31 percent in the community sample. Table 10.1 presents the results of the study (the community sample was weighted to equate for age and sex differences). Prisoners had substantially higher rates of

Table 10.1 Prevalence Rates of Major Mental Disorders in Offender and Community Samples and Odds Ratio of Prisoners Having a Disorder Compared with a Community Sample

Disorder	Offender (%)	Community (%)	Odds Ratio
Psychoses	7.0	0.7	11.5
Anxiety			
Panic disorder	9.1	1.9	5.4
Generalized anxiety disorder	15.1	4.7	3.5
Post-traumatic stress disorder	25.6	3.6	10.2
Any anxiety disorder	37.9	11.4	5.1
Affective			
Depression	17.5	7.3	2.6
Bipolar	3.5	0.8	7.0
Any affective disorder	23.2	8.5	3.3
Substances			
Alcohol use	21	13.9	2.0
Opioid use	39.5	0.4	220.4
Sedative use	14.7	0.5	41.3
Stimulant use	34.3	1.4	135.2
Any substance disorder	65.7	18.0	11.4

Source: Adapted from Butler et al. (2006)

prevalence for all disorders examined. The odds ratio, comparing the odds of prisoners having a psychiatric disorder with the community sample, indicated that prisoners were more than 10 times as likely to have a psychotic disorder, post-traumatic stress disorder, opioid use disorder, sedative use disorder, or stimulant use disorder compared to the community sample.

Motiuk and Porporino (1991) estimated the prevalence of mental disorders in Canadian offenders by selecting a random sample of 3224 male offenders from institutions across the country. The response rate was 69 percent (meaning that 31 percent of the offenders refused to participate), resulting in a final sample of 2185 male federal offenders. The lifetime prevalence of the following groups of diagnoses (as measured using the DSM-III) were obtained: organic brain syndrome (0.1 percent), psychotic (schizophrenia, manic, 7.7 percent), depressive (major depression, dysthymic, bipolar, 21 percent), anxiety (phobia, generalized anxiety, panic, 44 percent), antisocial personality disorder (57 percent), alcohol abuse/dependence (47 percent), and drug use/ dependence (41 percent). These high prevalence rates make it necessary that any correctional facility have staff trained to provide adequate support and intervention for offenders with mental health issues.

Prevalence of Personality Disorders

The rates of personality disorders in prison populations are substantially higher compared to community populations. **Personality disorders** are maladaptive patterns of relating, perceiving, and thinking that are relatively inflexible and serious enough to cause distress or impaired functioning. They play an important role in how many individuals end up in the criminal justice system.

There are 10 specific personality disorders listed in the DSM-IV grouped into three clusters: cluster A personality disorders involve odd or bizarre behaviour (includes paranoid, schizoid, and schizotypal); cluster B disorders involve dramatic or erratic behaviour (antisocial, histrionic, narcissistic, and borderline); and cluster C disorders involve anxious or inhibited behaviour (depending, avoidant, and obsessive-compulsive).

Recently, Sirdifield, Gojkovic, Brooker, and Ferriter (2009) conducted a review of 11 studies measuring the prevalence of personality disorders in offenders. Reported rates of any personality disorder ranged from a low of 14 percent of prisoners convicted of attempted homicide in Sweden (Fazel and Grann 2004) to 88 percent of young male offenders (aged 16 to 20 years) in England (Lader, Singleton, and Meltzer 2003). The most common type of personality disorders found in male prison populations are antisocial and paranoid personality disorders. In female prison populations, the most common are antisocial and borderline personality disorders.

In a study of 1396 male violent offenders in England, Roberts, Yang, Zhang, and Coid (2008) found a prevalence rate of 73 percent for any personality disorder. Table 10.2 illustrates the prevalence of personality disorders, with antisocial personality and paranoid disorders being the most prevalent and dependent and histrionic disorders the least common. Prisoners with personality disorder were more likely to report childhood

Table 10.2 Prevalence Rates of Personality Disorders in Male and Female Offenders

Personality Disorder	Male Offenders (%)	Female Offenders (%)
Paranoid	22	27
Schizoid	7	5
Schizotypal	4	4
Antisocial	65	43
Borderline	18	24
Histrionic	1	4
Narcissistic	10	10
Avoidant	9	14
Dependent	1	4
Obsessive-compulsive	7	15

Source: Adapted from Roberts et al. (2008) and Warren et al. (2002)

conduct problems, adverse childhood experiences, and victimizations than those with no personality disorder. For comparison, a sample of 261 maximum security U.S. female offenders from Warren et al. (2002) is presented, with a prevalence rate of 67 percent for any personality disorder. The most common personality disorders in female offenders are antisocial, paranoid, and borderline. The least common diagnoses are schizoid, schizotypal, and dependent disorders.

ROLE OF MENTAL ILLNESS IN THE COURTS
Unfit to Stand Trial

If you refuse to speak in court because you think a judge is trying to poison you or that your lawyer works for the devil, is it fair to go forward with a trial? In Canada, if an accused is not able to participate in their own defence on account of a mental disorder, it is deemed unfair to try this person. According to Section 2 of the Canadian *Criminal Code*, an accused is **unfit to stand trial** (UST) if he or she is:

> . . . unable on account of a mental disorder to conduce a defence at any stage of the proceedings before a verdict is rendered or to instruct counsel to do so, and in particular on account of mental disorder to:
>
> (a) understand the nature or object of the proceedings;
> (b) understand the possible consequences of the proceedings; or
> (c) communicate with counsel.

When the court finds an accused UST, the review board must give the accused a conditional release or detention order within 45 days (they cannot order an absolute discharge). Review boards must have at least three members (a judge or lawyer, a psychiatrist, and a third person). The Ontario Review Board appoints five members. When deciding on the type of disposition, the board must consider:

- The protection of the public
- The accused's mental state
- The reintegration of the accused into society
- The accused's other needs

Until a person is found UST, they remain under the authority of the board until they are deemed fit to stand trial or the charges are stayed or withdrawn. The board must review the case yearly, and the courts must review it every two years to determine if there is sufficient evidence for the accused to stand trial if fitness is restored. If there is not sufficient evidence, then the court should acquit the accused.

As a result of Supreme Court case *R. v. Demers* (2004), provisions of the *Criminal Code* that applied to an accused who was not dangerous but due to his mental condition was seen as permanently unfit to stand trial were deemed unconstitutional. Demers had been charged with sexual assault but was found UST due to mental retardation. After spending three months in a hospital, the review board gave him a conditional discharge. Because of his permanent mental disability, Demers would never be fit to stand trial and thus faced indefinite appearances before the board. The Supreme Court's decision meant that Demers did not have to re-appear. The federal government passed Bill C-10 in 2006, which gave the courts the authority to order a stay of proceedings for an accused found UST if the accused is unlikely to become fit to stand trial and does not post a significant threat to public safety.

Mental State at the Time of an Offence

In order to find a person guilty of a crime, *mens rea* or criminal intent must be established. In other words, if there is no criminal intent, there is no crime. The assumption is that if you know what you are doing and choose to do it, you are culpable. However, if you are mentally disordered and do not understand the consequences of your actions, you should not be culpable. See Table 10.3 for a summary of key cases and legislation relating to Canada's insanity defence.

On January 20, 1843, Daniel M'Naughton claimed the voice of God ordered him to kill the prime minister of Great Britain, Robert Peel. Although unsuccessful in his efforts, M'Naughton's trial led to precedent-setting rules about determining criminal responsibility in cases where the defendant was subject to a mental disorder that would affect their judgment. As a result of the trial, the House of Lords developed the so-called M'Naughton rules (also known as the M'Naughton standard): "[i]n order for a verdict of not guilty by reason of insanity (NGRI) to be returned, it must be shown that, at the time of the commission of the offense, the defendant was labouring under such a defect of reason, from disease of the mind, as not to know the nature and quality of the act he was doing; or, if he did know it, that he did not know he was doing what was wrong" (R v. M'Naughton 1843). The M'Naughton rules were widely adopted in Canada and United States. Several states in have expanded the definition to include volitional considerations. Some people may be aware of the nature and quality of their criminal act and know that it is wrong, but may not be able to control their behaviour. This standard assumes that mental disorders can affect both the cognitive and volitional aspects of behaviour. For example, Jeffrey Dahmer, charged with 15 murders in Milwaukee, Wisconsin, in 1991, pleaded not guilty by reason of insanity. His defence lawyers argued that Dahmer knew what he was doing when he lured young men to his apartment, drugged them, and killed them. However, defence experts also argued that Dahmer could not stop killing because of his mental disorder and therefore should be found NGRI. The jury disagreed and convicted Dahmer for the murders and sentenced him to 15 life sentences (Dahmer was murdered while in maximum security prison by another inmate in 1994).

The trial of Louis Riel provides an early example of a case in which the M'Naughton rules were employed in the Canadian legal system. Riel was the leader of the Métis rebellion

Table 10.3 Relevant Court Cases and Changes in Legislation for NCRMD

Case/Legislation	Details
Rex v. Hadfield (1800)	• James Hadfield fired a shot at King George III and was charged with attempted murder and treason.
	• The court found him under the influence of insanity at the time he committed the offence and only had the options of releasing him or sending him to prison. He was sent to prison.
	• British Parliament passed the *Criminal Lunatics Act*, which gave courts the option of committing people found not guilty by reason of insanity to strict custody in a place the court deemed appropriate.
R v. M'Naughton (1843)	• British case in which Daniel M'Naughton attempted to kill Prime Minister Sir Robert Peel but mistakenly killed his secretary, Edward Drummond.
	• M'Naughton was found not guilty by reason of insanity.
	• House of Lords asked judges to clarify the insanity defence and their answers became known as the M'Naughton Rules.
	• Canada adopted these rules at Confederation.
Canadian *Criminal Code* (1893)	• Legislation enacting the criminal code in Canada
	• Modified the M'Naughton Rules to include term "appreciation" of the nature and quality of the act
R. v. Swain (1992)	• Peter Swain was charged with aggravated assault against his spouse while mentally disordered. While awaiting trial he received treatment for the mental disorder; at his trial he was found NGRI and was sent to a secure forensic psychiatric facility.
	• Automatic detention of individuals found NGRI was in conflict with the *Charter of Rights and Freedoms*
Bill C-30 (1992)	• Term changed from "not guilty by reason of insanity" to "not criminally responsible on account of mental disorder"
	• Wording "disease of the mind" changed to "mental disorder"
	• Review boards were created to determine the disposition of those found NCRMD
Winko v. British Columbia (1999)	• If the NCRMD accused does not pose a significant threat to the public, the court or review board must order an absolute discharge.

in Saskatchewan in the early months of 1885 and in March 1885 was charged with treason. The defence of insanity was put forth at his trial, but Riel refused to admit he was mentally ill. Although medical witnesses testified that he was suffering from delusions of grandeur and religious persecution, the jury did not agree and found Riel guilty. Riel was executed on November 16, 1885.

From the 1800s to present day, a fundamental principle of the Canadian criminal system has been that an individual must possess the capacity to understand that his or her behaviour was wrong in order to be found guilty of an offence. If, due to a mental disorder, a person cannot understand what they have done, then it is inappropriate to punish that person. Instead, the person needs treatment. But simply having a mental disorder does not mean that you are exempt from criminal responsibility. Many people who have a mental disorder are tried and convicted by the criminal courts. According to section 16 of the *Criminal Code*, a person should be found **not criminally responsible on account of a mental disorder** (NCRMD):

> No person is criminally responsible for an act committed or an omission made while suffering from a mental disorder that rendered the person incapable of appreciating the nature and quality of the act or omission or of knowing that it was wrong.

Thus the mental disorder must be a direct cause of the person's inability to appreciate that their behaviour is wrong. If the person has a mental disorder but it does not affect their inability to appreciate that the behaviour is wrong, then the presence of the disorder is irrelevant to the person's responsibility.

Three issues must be considered in order to find a person NCRMD. First, the defendant must suffer from a mental disorder. A mental disorder is defined in the *Criminal Code* as a disease of the mind. Second, the defendant must fail to appreciate the nature or quality of their act. For example, if I cut your arm believing I was actually cutting a carrot, then I would not appreciate the nature of the act. Third, the person may understand what they are doing but might not believe it is wrong. For example, if, because of a delusion, I believed I was in imminent danger of death because I thought you were trying to physically harm me, I would likely believe that I would be entitled to some form of lethal response (see Box 10.1).

Similar to UST, the majority of NCRMD cases are sent to a review board to determine the disposition of the person (in rare cases, the judge will order the disposition). Members of a review board typically include a lawyer and a psychiatrist, with the number of members varying from province to province. In Ontario, the review board is chaired by a judge or lawyer and comprises four other members, one of which must be a psychiatrist. In provinces such as British Columbia, the board is comprised of three members. The dual goals of the board are to give a disposition to the individual that protects the public and to safeguard the rights and freedoms of mentally disordered persons. The board or the court can give an absolute discharge, a conditional discharge, or order detention in a hospital. The disposition must be the least onerous and least

Box 10.1

A Mother's Worst Nightmare

On the evening of July 30, 2008, 22-year-old Tim McLean was asleep on a Greyhound bus travelling on the Trans Canada Highway, heading home to Winnipeg. En route, Vincent Li, aged 40, boarded the bus and sat beside the sleeping McLean. After an hour and a half, Li repeatedly stabbed McLean. As the other 34 passengers fled from the vehicle, Li was observed cutting off the victim's head. He also removed several of the victim's organs, ate them, and placed parts of the victim's body in his pants pockets. The police arrived, and after a four-hour standoff, Li was arrested. According to witnesses, Li appeared calm and acted like a robot during the attack. At an August 5 court appearance, the only words he said to the judge were "Please kill me."

Li immigrated to Canada in 2001 with his wife and became a Canadian citizen in 2005. He worked numerous jobs and did not appear to have any problems. Four weeks prior to the killing, he was fired from Walmart following a disagreement with other employees.

Li was charged with second-degree murder, and on March 3, 2009, his two-day trial commenced with Li pleading not criminally responsible on account of mental disorder. Crown and defence psychiatrists diagnosed Li with paranoid schizophrenia. According to their testimony, Li was prompted to commit the murder by God's voice telling him that McLean was a force of evil and that McLean was going to execute him. Supposedly, Li felt that McLean could come back to life, so he continued to attack him. The Crown prosecutor, the defence, and the judge agreed that Li was mentally disordered at the time he killed McLean and should be found NCRMD. Vincent Li was sent to a secure mental health treatment facility, where he remains today. Every year, the Manitoba Review Board will hear testimony from mental health professionals about whether or not he is well enough and is no longer a risk to the public. McLean's mother, Carol DeDelley, is asking the Canadian government to change the *Criminal Code* so that people who are found NCRMD serve their time in jail.

restrictive for the accused. If given a conditional discharge, the most common conditions imposed include:

- Must abstain from illegal drugs and/or alcohol
- Must reside in a particular place (e.g., group home)
- Must submit to urinalysis testing for prohibited substances
- Must abide by a specified treatment plan
- Must report to a designated person (e.g., psychiatrist or psychologist) on a scheduled basis
- Must refrain from possessing weapons

The Public's Belief in the Insanity Defence

The public tends to have a negatively skewed view of the insanity defence. Misconceptions surrounding the not criminally responsible on account of mental disorder defence are common. The public often focus on high-profile defendants, such as John Hinckley Jr., Jeffrey Dahmer, or Kenneth Bianchi. Bianchi, the "Hillside Strangler" who raped and killed 13 young women, unsuccessfully malingered multiple personality disorder (which corresponds to the current dissociative identity disorder) in hopes that he would be found NGRI and avoid the death penalty. A common misconception about the insanity defence is the view that it is used as a way to avoid legal penalties, as in the Bianchi example. (See Box 10.2 for a Canadian case in which the person was found NCRMD.) Another misconception is that individuals who use NCRMD are usually successful. The public also believes that NCRMD defendants use the defence as a way to obtain release into the community much sooner than if they had gone to prison. The public also believes NCRMD defendants are at a higher risk to reoffend than other offenders. These misconceptions are listed below, with evidence challenging them. (Note that much of the research on perceptions of the insanity defence was conducted in the U.S. and therefore may not accurately reflect Canadian perceptions.)

1. The NCRMD/NGRI defence is commonly used: In the United States, the public believes that 37 percent of defendants use the NGRI defence (Silver, Cirincione, and Steadman 1994), although it is actually used in only 1 percent of cases. In Canada, the defence is used in only 2 cases per 1000 adult criminal cases (Latimer and Lawrence 2006).

2. Most NCRMD/NGRI defences are successful: The American public believes the success rate is 44 percent, as compared to the actual rate of 26 percent (Silver et al. 1994).

3. Most NCRMD/NGRI acquittees commit murder: In Canada, about 15 percent of individuals found NCRMD are charged with murder or attempted murder (Latimer and Lawrence 2006).

4. The NCRMD/NGRI is a loophole: The American public believes that 51 percent of insanity acquittees are sent to a mental hospital and 26 percent are set free, whereas in actuality 51 percent are sent to hospital and 15 percent are set free (Silver et al. 1994). In Canada, 13 percent are given an absolute discharge, 35 percent are given a conditional discharge, and 52 percent are sent to a secure psychiatric hospital (Latimer and Lawrence 2006).

5. NCRMD/NGRI defendants are not confined very long: In the U.S., the public's perception of confinement is 22 months, as compared to the reality of 33 months. In Canada, Harris, Rice, and Cormier (1991) found that insanity acquittees spend more time in confinement then persons found guilty of similar crimes.

Box 10.2

Sexsomnia: I Did It But I Was Sleeping

Should individuals who are asleep and sexually assault someone be held responsible for their actions? The case of Jan Luedecke, who used sexomnia as an explanation for sexual assault, illustrates the difficulty in establishing boundaries for the concept of criminal responsibility.

- July 3, 2003—Luedecke went to a party, got drunk, and went to sleep on an L-shaped couch. The victim, L.O., slept at the other end. She woke to find Luedecke on top of her, trying to have intercourse. She pushed him off and noticed that her underwear had been removed. She then called police to report that she had been raped. Luedecke was wearing a condom at the time of the attempted rape. He was charged with sexual assault.

- November 30, 2005—Ontario judge Russell Otter acquitted 33-year-old Luedecke of sexual assault on the basis the attack was involuntary. The defence presented expert testimony from Dr. Colin Shapiro, a sleep disorders expert, who claimed Luedecke was sleeping at the time of the attack and that it was not voluntary.

- February 7, 2008—The Ontario Court of Appeals quashed the 2005 acquittal,

replacing it with a verdict of not criminally responsible on account of mental disorder. Luedecke appeared in front of the Ontario Review Board on July 10, 2009 to determine the conditions for his release. The Board will perform a full and complete risk assessment before any decision is made.

Parasomnias are undesirable behavioural events that occur during sleep, such as sleepwalking. Sexsomnia, first described in 1996 by University of Toronto psychiatrist Colin Shapiro (Shapiro, Fedoroff, and Trajanovic 1996), is defined as engaging in sexual acts while asleep. In a more recent study, Shaprio, Trajanovic, and Federoff (2003) described 11 patients, both male and female, who engaged in sexual behaviour while asleep, and observed the following:

- More common in men than women: 2 of the 11 patients were women
- Often a family history of parasomnias exist: 7 of the 11 patients
- Nearly all had prior history of parasomnias: 9 of the 11 patients
- Sexual behaviour while sleeping varied: 5 with partner/spouse; 2 masturbating; 3 assaulting young girls; and 1 with an adult family relative

6. NCRMD/NGRI defendants are dangerous: The failure rate for released insanity patients in U.S. and Canada ranges from 30 to 60 percent (Golding, Eaves, and Kowaz 1989; Hodgins 1987; Vitacco et al. 2008). However, most of these failures relate to breaking the rules of the conditional release, not for engaging in violence. For example, Vitacco et al. (2008) found that only 4 percent of their sample had committed a violent offence.

Characteristics of People found NCRMD and UST

Latimer and Lawrence (2006) describe the demographics, criminal histories, diagnoses, and dispositions of 6802 NCRMD and 1877 UST cases between 1992 and 2004 from five provinces (PEI, Quebec, B.C., Ontario, Alberta) and two territories (Yukon and Nunavut). A substantial increase occurred in the number of individuals found NCRMD/ UST between 1992 and 2004. As seen in Table 10.4, the majority of accused were male, similar to what is observed in the overall adult criminal justice system. The UST and NCRMD were slightly older than the average age involved in the criminal justice system (median age = 31). There was not an overrepresentation of Aboriginal accused, as has been

Table 10.4 Characteristics of Accused Found NCRMD and UST

Variables	NCRMD	UST
Male	84%	83%
Median age	35 years	37 years
Aboriginal	4%	5%
No prior convictions	42%	44%
No prior NCRMD/UST findings	90%	98%
Index offence		
Homicide/attempted	14%	5%
Major assault (level 1 and 2)	22%	14%
Assault (level 1)	20%	30%
Sexual assaults	4%	8%
Other violent offences	21%	12%
Non-violent offences	19%	31%
Diagnoses		
Schizophrenia	52%	56%
Affective disorders	27%	13%
Delusional disorders	5%	4%
Mental retardation	3%	9%
Personality disorders	4%	2%
Organic brain disorders	2%	7%
Substance abuse disorder	2%	1%
Other/none on file	5%	7%

Note: Affective disorders include major depression, bipolar disorder, schizoaffective disorder.

Source: Latimer and Lawrence (2006)

reported in the criminal justice system (see Chapter 11). However, this may be due to the lack of samples from provinces that have a high proportion of Aboriginal people (i.e., Manitoba and Saskatchewan). About half of the NCRMD/UST individuals had a prior criminal conviction. Only 10 percent of individuals found NCRMD had a prior NCRMD finding. Almost none (2 percent) of people found UST had a prior UST finding. Most accused found NCRMD were charged with a violent offence (77 percent), with the most common type of offence being assault. In contrast, accused found UST were more likely to charged with a sexual offence (11 percent UST versus 4 percent NCRMD) or a non-violent offence (31 percent UST versus 19 percent NCRMD) and less likely to be charged with a violent offence (59 percent UST versus 77 percent NCRMD). About half (52 percent) of the accused were diagnosed with a single disorder, although 18 percent had three or more co-occurring disorders. The most common diagnosis was schizophrenia, followed by affective disorders. However, a small percentage of individuals found NCRMD were diagnosed with a personality disorder. When comparing NCRMD and UST cases, NCRMD accused were more likely to be diagnosed with an affective disorder and personality disorders, whereas UST accused were more likely to have been diagnosed with mental retardation or organic brain disorders. There were differences in type of index offence across the diagnoses. Individuals diagnosed with organic brain disorder or mental retardation were more likely to be charged with a sexual offence. Individuals diagnosed with a delusional disorder or substance abuse disorder were more likely to be charged with a violent offence. Those diagnosed with an affective disorder were more likely to be charged with a non-violent offence.

Latimer and Lawrence (2006) also tallied the dispositions given by review boards for NCRMD accused. The dispositions were broken down as follows: absolute discharge (13 percent), conditional discharge (35 percent), and detention (52 percent). Accused charged with non-violent offences were more likely to be given an absolute discharge as compared to those charged with violent or sexual offences. Individuals charged with violent offences were more likely to receive detention as compared to sexual or non-violent accused.

LINK BETWEEN MENTAL ILLNESS AND CRIME AND VIOLENCE

WHENEVER THERE IS A MASS SHOOTING OR A PARTICULARLY HORRIFIC HOMICIDE, the media often report that the perpetrator has received treatment for psychiatric care. In the minds of the public, a link is made between mental illness and violence, and often whether mental health professionals should have been able to foresee and prevent the violence. (See Box 10.3 for a description of a psychiatrist trying to help a mentally disordered young adult.) The association between mental illness and criminality/violence has been studied for over 20 years with mixed results. Some researchers have found a link between mental disorder and criminality/violence, and others report that use of alcohol and drugs is responsible for the elevated base rates of criminality and violence in individuals with mental disorder. Further research is needed to elucidate whether there is a causal link between mental disorder and criminality/violence in order to properly inform the public and "to avoid potentially unwarranted stigmatization of people with mental illnesses" (Elbogen and Johnson 2009:153).

Denmark is one of the few countries in the world with the ability to keep and access records that permit tracking of the entire population to determine the prevalence of criminality. Hodgins, Mednick, Brennan, Schulsinger, and Engberg (1996) did a follow-up study of all Danes born between 1944 and 1947—a total of 358 180 individuals. They were tracked to determine if they had ever been diagnosed with a mental disorder and then checked against their criminal records. Table 10.5 presents Hodgins et al.'s findings across different types of mental disorders for any conviction and for violent convictions. In both men and women, the presence of a mental disorder substantially increased the risk for criminality and violence. As concluded by Hodgins et al. (1996: 495) "It would be destructive for societies to allow the findings on the criminality of the mentally disordered and mentally retarded to be used to further stigmatize these individuals. Rather, these data can be used constructively to provide more adequate, appropriate, and humane care to individuals who, through no fault of their own, suffer from devastating disorders and at the same time to protect society." See the profile of Dr. Sheilagh Hodgins in Box 10.4 for further discussion of her research.

Choe, Teplin, and Abram (2008) reviewed the empirical literature on the perpetration of violence and the violent victimization among people with severe mental illness.

Box 10.3

Top Psychiatrist Killed by Teenage Patient

Dr. Wayne Fenton was a 53-year-old psychiatrist working for the National Institute of Mental Health in Washington developing programs to help schizophrenics adjust to community living. In the evenings and on weekends, he treated severely mentally ill patients at a private clinic. Dr. Fenton was treating 19-year-old Vitali Davydov for schizophrenia and bipolar illness. He agreed to see Davydov on Sunday, September 3, 2005, in order to persuade him to take his medication. During that appointment, Davydov attacked the psychiatrist, beating him to death. When Davydov's father came to pick him up and noticed the blood on his son's hands, he called the police. On April 3, 2007, Davydov was found not criminally responsible due to mental illness for the first-degree murder. Expert witnesses testified that Davydov believed Dr. Fenton had been raped and had asked Davydov to kill him in order to free his soul.

Dr. Fenton was a psychiatrist who devoted his career to help the most severely mentally ill. He realized the tremendous toll psychosis has on the patient and their families and would do his upmost to help. In an obituary for Dr. Fenton, the *Washington Post* (2006) quoted a 2002 interview with Dr. Fenton, who stated: "All one has to do is walk through a downtown area to appreciate that the availability of adequate treatment for patients with schizophrenia and other mental illnesses is a serious problem in this country. We wouldn't let our 80-year-old mother with Alzheimer's live on a grate. Why is it all right for a 30-year-old daughter with schizophrenia?"

Table 10.5 Percentage of People Convicted of Any Crime or Violent Crime across Different Types of Mental Disorder

	Convicted of Any Crime		Convicted of Violent Crime	
	Male (%)	Female (%)	Male (%)	Female (%)
Mental Disorder				
No mental disorder	6.1	2.1	1.5	0.1
Major mental disorder	23.0	9.5	6.7	0.9
Mental retardation	42.4	11.6	1.3	1.4
Drug abuse	46.2	23.7	13.0	1.6
Alcohol abuse	35.8	18.7	10.0	1.6
Antisocial personality disorder	32.4	13.6	10.8	1.3

Source: Hodgins et al. (1996)

They found different rates depending on the samples, time frame, and definitions of violence. For example, the rates of violent perpetration for psychiatric inpatients (17 to 50 percent) were higher than for outpatients (12 to 22 percent). The rate of violent victimization was between 20 and 35 percent in outpatients.

What can we conclude from the current literature on serious mental disorders and violence?

1. The majority of people with serious mental disorders do not engage in violence.
2. The likelihood of committing violence is greater for people with a serious mental disorder than for those with no mental disorder.
3. People with serious mental disorders are more likely to be a victim of violence than those with no mental disorder.
4. People with co-occurring mental disorders and substance abuse are at an elevated risk for violence.
5. The causal mechanisms that are responsible for the link between mental disorder and violence are not clearly understood. It may not be that factors unique to the mental illness lead to criminal behaviour, but rather factors associated with mental illness, such as poverty, substance use, unemployment, and homelessness (Junginger, Claypoole, Laygo, and Crisanti 2006).

Risk Assessment of Mentally Disordered Offenders

Are mentally disordered offenders more likely to reoffend once released? The answer depends on the type of mental disorder. Psychopaths, offenders with substance abuse problems, and people with specific types of psychotic disorders are at a higher risk.

Box 10.4

Canadian Researcher Profile:
Dr. Sheilagh Hodgins

Dr. Sheilagh Hodgins first became interested in psychology when she observed children in school who had problems and wondered why no one helped them, especially children with conduct problems. Her early childhood curiosity led to a lifelong interest in youth and adults with conduct problems and mental illness that has been the focus of her clinical and research endeavours.

Dr. Hodgins completed her Ph.D. at McGill University. Her dissertation was on measuring the psychophysiological response of psychopathic offenders in anticipation of an electric shock. Her first job was in the school of social work at the Université de Montréal. Currently, she is a professor at the Institute of Psychiatry at King's College in London, England.

During the 1980s, Canadian psychiatric hospitals were being shut down. Institutional care for the individuals with mental illness was to be replaced by intervention in the community. The public viewed this release with alarm because mentally ill patients were considered to be a dangerous group, a group that included individuals capable of criminal acts. Dr. Hodgins realized that no large-scale research had been done to measure the criminality of the mentally ill, and conducted the first large-scale epidemiological study. She evaluated 15 000 people in Sweden and found that there was an increased risk for violence in the mentally ill. Wanting to determine whether there was a specific mental illness associated with the increased violence, Dr. Hodgins conducted another study of a birth cohort that included 358 000 Danes. She found that people with schizophrenia were at an elevated risk for violence.

Dr. Hodgins uses a variety of methodologies in her research. She recognizes the necessity of conducting longitudinal prospective studies in order to gain an understanding of the development of aggressive and antisocial behaviours. She studies clinical samples of adults with schizophrenia to identify both distal and proximal factors associated with violent behaviour. A goal of this research is to find treatments that prevent violence while humanely treating people with schizophrenia.

In addition, Dr. Hodgins continues to do research on offenders with psychopathy and with antisocial personality disorder in an effort to understand their differences in etiology and treatment responsiveness in contrast with sufferers with schizophrenia. For example, with a Ph.D. student and several colleagues, she recently published a study showing that in middle childhood, boys with conduct problems and callous, unemotional traits display differences in brain structures linked to their personality and behavioural traits.

Over the next few years, Dr. Hodgins intends to focus on two areas. First, she plans to study children and adults who engage in antisocial and aggressive behaviour in order to identify both biological and non-biological factors that act at different times during development to initiate and to maintain these patterns of behaviour. Second, she plans to develop intervention programs for children who show the precursors of schizophrenia.

Dr. Hodgins attributes much of her success to fruitful collaborations with scientists in many different countries, including the United Kingdom, Canada, Sweden, Denmark, Finland, and Germany, who work in varied disciplines (e.g., clinical psychiatry and psychology, neuroscience, genetics, epidemiology, statistics), and to many bright, insightful students who push her to clarify existing knowledge. When asked what keeps her interested in research, Dr. Hodgins says, "I see enormous progress in our understanding of antisocial behaviour. I find it fascinating to advance knowledge— really discover new things. But what is most gratifying is to see results used to helped people."

Baillargeon, Binswanger, Penn, Williams, and Murray (2009) investigated prisoners in Texas to determine whether those with a major mental disorder would have a history of incarceration at a higher rate than prisoners with no major mental disorders. Prisoners with a bipolar mental disorder were 3.3 times more likely to have four or more incarcerations over a six-year period then were other non-mentally disordered offenders. (See Chapter 7 for a discussion of the VRAG and HCR-20 risk-assessment measures used to predict violent recidivism in mentally and personality disordered offenders. See Box 10.5 for a description of a new court designed to handle mentally disordered offenders.)

When doing risk assessment with a mentally disorder offender, Conroy and Murrie (2007: 172–174) suggest that the following five questions be considered:

(1) How does the mental disorder relate to the violent behaviour?
(2) What is the pattern of mental illness in the person?
(3) What are the contextual factors relating to when problematic behaviour happens?
(4) Has the mentally disordered offender responded to treatment?
(5) What is the mentally disordered offender's pattern of violent behaviour?

Police Attitudes Toward the Mentally Ill

Many people with mental illness who used to be housed in institutions are now trying to function in our communities. Police officers are becoming the frontline contact for many of these people, who are both victims of crime and offenders. As a result, some researchers

Box 10.5

Courtroom 102: The First Mental Health Court in Canada

In May 1998, a "mental health court" opened in Courtroom 102 in Toronto, the first in Canada and one of the first in the world (the United States had two mental health courts in 1997). The court was specifically designed to deal with pre-trial issues such as fitness to stand trial and to slow the "revolving door" of mentally ill people moving between homelessness and the criminal justice system. Mentally ill people living on the street often fail to take their medication, which leads to an escalation of symptoms and conflict with police. The court had specially trained workers to help accused offenders with a mental illness to establish a community plan that included a place to stay, social assistance, and contacts for psychiatric follow-up.

Nova Scotia, Manitoba, Newfoundland and Labrador, and, most recently, Quebec have followed Toronto's lead and established mental health courts.

Canada's mental health courts have not been evaluated. However, in the United States, McNeil and Binder (2007) compared 170 mentally ill people who entered the mental health court with 8067 mentally ill people who did not. Controlling for demographics, clinical diagnoses, and criminal histories, the researchers found that successful completion of the mental health court program was associated with reduced recidivism and violence.

The jury is still out on the effectiveness of mental health courts. Some people argue that they stigmatize the mentally ill, and others view them as a way to reduce the criminalization of the mentally ill.

have labelled the police as "street corner psychiatrists" (Teplin 1984) or "amateur social workers" (Cumming, Cumnning, and Edell 1965). Police have considerable discretion in deciding how to manage a crisis and whether to arrest a person. When dealing with a mentally ill person, they may decide to informally resolve the problem, arrest the person, or take the person to a hospital for evaluation. In an observation study of police encounters with mentally ill people, Teplin (1984) reported that 72 percent were handled informally, 12 percent were sent to a hospital, and 16 percent were arrested.

Cotton (2004) conducted a study of police officers in Ontario to examine police attitudes toward mental illness. A sample of 138 male and female police officers completed the Community Attitudes Toward Mental Illness scale (Taylor and Dear 1981). This instrument assesses attitudes across four scales: authoritarianism (belief that the mentally ill should be institutionalized or controlled), social restrictiveness (belief in the dangerousness of the mentally ill), social benevolence (feelings of responsibility for the mentally ill), and orientation (beliefs supportive of community integration of the mentally ill). The average scores indicated that Canadian police officers did not endorse negative attitudes toward the mentally ill (low scores on authoritarianism and social restrictiveness); rather, they felt that society should be more tolerant and should not isolate the mentally ill. Police officers were also asked about their role in managing the mentally ill and endorsed the following statements:

- Dealing with the mentally ill should be an integral part of community policing (75 percent agreed).

- If mental health services were adequate, police would not have to deal with the mentally ill (38 percent agreed).

- Nowadays, police officers need to have specialized training to deal with the mentally ill (89 percent agreed).

- The mentally ill take up more than their fair share of police time (48 percent agreed).

Although the above study indicated a generally positive attitude toward the mentally ill, a number of methodological issues may limit the validity and reliability of the findings. First, there was a relatively low response rate (34 percent) and thus it is possible that officers with more negative attitudes chose not to participate. Second, most of the police officers were from small to moderately sized cities (the largest was Kingston, Ontario), and whether or not the same attitudes are found in larger cities remains to be investigated. Finally, although self-report surveys are a useful method of collecting information on attitudes, in some cases attitudes do not necessarily predict actual behaviour.

A police officer questioning a mentally ill person.

Mental Illness and Stigma

Stigma is defined as a combination of stereotypes (cognitive labels used to describe a person), prejudices (negative emotions toward individuals), and discrimination (curtailing the rights and opportunities of individuals) toward a specific group. The term originates from ancient Greece, denoting a physical brand applied to social outcasts (e.g., slaves, traitors) to indicate their devalued status in society (Goffman 1963). Stigmatization against the mentally ill has a long history. The Greeks saw mentally ill people as being evil and believed they were being punished by the gods for some transgression. People who showed signs of mental illness in Christian countries during the Middle Ages were believed to be possessed by the devil. These discriminatory attitudes persist today (Hinshaw and Stier 2008). In a study comparing the responses of the U.S. public from 1950 to 1996, Phelan, Link, Stueve, and Pescosolido (2000) found that perceptions of the mentally ill as being frightening or violent increased. The primary source of public information is the mass media, which perpetuates negative perceptions (Diefenbach 1997; Signorelli 1989; Wahl 1995). The mentally ill are presented in television shows and newspapers as being violent. Although there is an increased risk for violent behaviour in some forms of mental disorder, the majority of the mentally ill are not violent and are more likely to be victims than perpetrators of violence (Choe et al. 2008). The media generally fail to accurately represent these facts.

As stated by Phelan et al. (2000), "Research is required to identify the precise source of these unfortunate stereotypes, and advocacy is required to change them. In the absence of these efforts, the lives of people with the most serious mental illnesses will continue to be complicated by the injurious effects of stigma and rejection" (p. 203).

The Link Between Mental Disorder and Violence

Recently, Elbogen and Johnson (2009) examined the relationship between mental disorder and violence in a longitudinal study. In phase 1 of the study, 34 653 Americans were interviewed and assessed for serious mental disorders. Participants were interviewed again about three years later and asked if they had engaged in any of the following behaviours in that time: used a stick, knife, or gun in a fight; started a fire on purpose to destroy someone's property; hit someone so hard that they were injured or had to see a doctor; or forced someone to have sex with them against their will. Figure 10.1 presents the percentage of people with mental disorders only and those with co-occurring substance dependence who had engaged in any violent act during the follow-up period. The rates of violence for people with serious mental illness were relatively low. However, individuals with substance dependence and those with co-occurring severe mental illness and substance dependence had the highest rates of violence. It is important to note the vast majority of people with serious and co-occurring mental illness did not commit any violence.

Elbogen and Johnson (2009) also examined which risk factors were most strongly related to the prediction of violence in this population. The following were ordered in terms of their strength of relationship with violence: young age; history of any violent act;

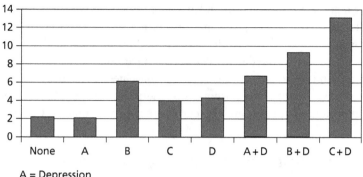

A = Depression
B = Schizophrenia
C = Bipolar Disorder
D = Substance Dependence Disorder

Figure 10.1 Prevalence Rates of Violence in Community Samples with Major Mental Disorders and Co-Occurring Mental Disorders

Source: Adapted from Elbogen and Johnson (2009)

male; history of juvenile detention, divorce, or separation in the past year; history of physical abuse; parental criminal history; unemployment for the past year; co-occurring severe mental illness and substance use; and victimization in the past year. These findings indicate that severe mental illness alone is not a major risk factor for violence. Elbogen and Johnson conclude that "The data show it is simplistic as well as inaccurate to say the cause of violence among mentally ill individuals is the mental illness itself; instead, the current study finds that mental illness is clearly relevant to violence risk but that its causal roles are complex, indirect, and embedded in a web of other (and arguably more) important individual and situational cofactors to consider." (p. 159).

Several studies have examined the risk factors for violence within samples of schizophrenics. Swanson and colleagues (2006) reported that minor violence (i.e., assault with no injury or weapon use) was related to co-occurring substance abuse and acute psychotic symptoms. Serious violence (i.e., assault with injury or with a lethal weapon, sexual assault) was related to acute positive psychotic symptoms (i.e., delusions and hallucinations), depressive symptoms, childhood conduct problems, and being victimized, while having negative psychotic symptoms (i.e., social withdrawal, blunted affect) was related to lower risk.

More recently, Swanson et al. (2008) found evidence for two pathways to the commission of violence in subgroups of schizophrenics. One group had evidence of two or more childhood conduct problems (n = 488) and the other had one or fewer (n = 956). Schizophrenics with a history of childhood conduct problems engaged in more violence (28 versus 14 percent) as compared to those without this history. The following four risk factors were associated with greater violence in both groups: younger age, lack of substantial vocational activity, living with family or relatives, and recent contact with police. For schizophrenics without a childhood history of conduct problems, acute psychotic symptoms were related to violence (see discussion below). For schizophrenics with childhood onset conduct problems, any current substance misuse—and not acute psychotic symptoms—predicted violence. The authors speculated that "antipsychotic medication may do little to reduce violence risk in patients whose violence is caused by factors other than psychosis . . . violence risk management for schizophrenia must focus on the whole person, with keen attention to the interaction of disease characteristics with developmental life history and the current social environment" (p. 238).

Risk Factors Specific to Mental Disorder

Boxes 10.1 and 10.3 describe cases in which delusions provided the primary motivation to commit a violent crime. The case of Vincent Li, who heard God telling him to kill another person and who obeyed this command hallucination, is discussed in Box 10.1. In Box 10.3, the case of Vitali Davydov, who killed his psychiatrist as a result of experiencing a delusional belief that the psychiatrist had been raped and had asked to be killed, is described. Delusions are one factor that increases the risk of violence in people with schizophrenia. Schizophrenics who experience what have been called threat/control override delusions or command hallu-cinations are at an elevated risk. The other factor that increases the risk of violence in people with schizophrenia, discussed in an earlier section, is the combination of psychotic symptoms and substance abuse/dependence (see Elbogen and Johnson 2009 for review). (See Box 10.6 for a description of the role delusions play in people who target public figures.)

According to the DSM-IV, **delusions** are "erroneous beliefs that usually involve a misinterpretation of perceptions or experiences" (p. 275). Delusions can be categorized as either bizarre (e.g., aliens are controlling your thoughts) or non-bizarre (e.g., you think the police are constantly watching you). They have been classified into several types: delusions of control (e.g., a false belief that another person or external forces are control-ling one's thoughts, feelings, or behaviours), persecutory delusions (e.g., a false belief that you are being followed, harassed, poisoned, conspired against, or spied on), delusions of grandeur (e.g., a false belief that you have special powers, talents, or abilities or that you are a famous person or character), delusional jealousy (e.g., a false belief that your partner is having an affair), and delusions of reference (e.g., a false belief that irrelevant, unre-lated, or innocuous events in the world have direct personal significance).

Link and Stueve (1994) identified a specific type of delusional symptom that is more strongly related to violence than other delusions, labelled as "**threat/control override**" **(TCO) symptoms**. The researchers defined TCO symptoms as "psychotic symptoms that cause a person to feel threatened or involve the intrusion of thoughts that can override self-controls" (p. 155). In their study, they compared three TCO symptoms (e.g., "How often have you felt that your mind was dominated by forces beyond your control?" "How often have you felt that thoughts were put into your head that were not your own?" "How often have you felt that there were people who wished to do you harm?") to 10 other psychotic symp-toms (e.g., "How often have you felt you had special powers?" "How often have you thought felt your thoughts were taken away from you by some external force?" "How often have you felt you were possessed by a spirit or a devil?"). In both a community and a psychiatric sample, only the three TCO symptoms were related to violence. In the majority of studies by Link and his colleagues (Link, Monahan, Stueve, and Cullen 1999; Link, Stueve, and Phelan 1998) and others (Hodgins, Hicocke, and Freese 2003; Swanson, Borum, Swartz, and Monahan 2000; Swanson et al. 1997), TCO symptoms were strongly related to violence. For example, Swanson et al. (1997) found that patients who endorsed TCO symptoms were twice as likely to become violent during a one-year follow-up period than those who did not.

However, other studies have failed to find a relationship between TCO symptoms and violence (Appelbaum, Robbins, and Monahan 2002; Skeem et al. 2006; Stompe, Ortwein-Svobodat, and Schanda 2004). In a prospective study, Skeem et al. (2006) found that hostility, not TCO symptoms, predicted violence in a community sample of patients.

One potential explanation for the discrepant findings has been proposed by Teasdale, Silver, and Monahan (2006). These authors found that men and women respond to TCO symptoms differently. Although the rates of threat delusions (17 versus 11 percent) and control override delusions (18 versus 16 percent) were similar in men and women, it was only in men that threat delusions were related to violence (in this study, control override symptoms were not related to violence in men). In the Appelbaum et al. (2002) and Skeem et al. (2006) studies, between 40 and 50 percent of the samples were female.

Many people with schizophrenia and delusional disorders experience auditory and visual hallucinations, but they vary in content. For example, command hallucinations are auditory hallucinations. Between 30 and 50 percent of psychiatric inpatients report experiencing command hallucinations (Hersh and Borum 1998; Rogers, Gillis, Turner, and Frise-Smith 1990). Some of these hallucinations were non-violent, others were related to self-injurious behaviour, and others still directed violence. For example, Lee, Chong, Chan, and Sathyadevan (2004) examined the content of auditory hallucinations in 100 patients with command hallucinations that were classified as either violent or non-violent. The prevalence rate of command hallucinations was 53 percent, 29 percent of which had a violent content. When asked if they had complied with the command hallucination, 62 percent indicated that they had, with most having complied to a non-violent command. However, 18 percent had complied to a self-harm command and 15 percent to a "harm others" command. Thus patients are more likely to comply with non-violent than violent commands. Junginger (1995) examined the rates of compliance to command hallucinations and found that compliance was related to less dangerous commands and voice recognition. Why do some patients obey command hallucinations but most do not? Recently, Barrowcliff and Haddock (2006) summarized 16 studies assessing the link between command hallucinations and compliance and found that both content and belief factors are related to compliance. Some of the variables they identified were:

- Type of command hallucinations: Non-violent and self-harm command hallucinations were more likely to be obeyed.

- Beliefs about the command: If the patient believed the command to be justified or if voices were from a more powerful or higher status figure, they were more likely to obey.

■ Perception of the level of malevolence or benevolence: Benevolent voices were more likely to be obeyed (e.g., God's voice versus Satan's voice).

■ Consequences: If the patient believed that something bad would happen to them or someone else, they typically would not obey.

When assessing for risk of violence in mentally disordered people, the following combination of risk factors should be considered to elevate the risk:

1. Active psychotic symptoms with a substance abuse disorder and a history of violence or current attitudes supportive of violence. For example, a person is having paranoid delusions, is intoxicated, and has a history of assaulting police officers. When the police are called to a bar and ask the person to show identification, the person assaults them.

2. The presence of a delusional belief about significant others and specific personal targets, especially if the person believes the significant other has been replaced by an

Box 10.6

Dangerous Fixations: Public Figures and Attacks

Attacks on public figures are rare. When such an event occurs, however, there is intense media coverage and speculation about the motivation. Several studies have found a link between delusional disorder and these attacks.

Attacks on the British royal family (James et al. 2008):

■ Between 1778 and 1994, there were 23 attacks on monarchs or immediate family

■ 20 (83 percent) were male and seven (20 percent) were adolescents

■ 10 (43 percent) gave prior warning of attack by sending threatening letters or communications or telling someone

■ 10 percent had a prior conviction for a violent offence

■ 57 percent used a gun (half the time the gun was not loaded!)

■ 11 (48 percent) were having delusions or hallucinations at the time of the attack

Attacks on European politicians (James et al. 2007):

■ Between 1990 and 2004, there were 24 attacks on European politicians

■ 18 (78 percent) of the attackers were men

■ 11 (46 percent) gave some type of warning (lawsuits, letters, newspaper ads, posters)

■ 38 percent had a prior violent criminal history

■ 20 (83 percent) used some type of weapon (gun, letter bomb, samurai sword)

■ 10 (42 percent) were psychotic at the time of the attack

■ Being psychotic, socially isolated, and having no political motive were related to death or serious injury imposter. For example, if the person thinks their spouse is Hitler and in order to prevent the Holocaust they kill their partner.

3. Command hallucinations to commit violence especially when the voice is identified or if the command makes reference to self-harm. For example, the person hears God telling them to kill him- or herself.

Treatment of Offenders with Mental Disorders

When a person with mental illness is put into a secure psychiatric facility or prison, their problems may by exacerbated. These facilities are stressful environments and the individual is separated from established social support systems. Moreover, some mentally ill people are subject to victimization in prison by other inmates who are willing to target vulnerable people. Blitz, Wolff, and Shi (2008) compared the rates of physical victimization of 7221 men and 564 women prisoners with and without mental disorders. Rates of physical victimization for male offenders with a mental disorder were 1.6 times higher (1.7 times higher for females) than for offenders without a mental disorder.

Hodgins et al. (2007) have identified five components of community treatment programs that are related to success with mentally ill offenders: (a) multifaceted, intense, and highly structured; (b) treating clinician accepts the dual role of treating the mental disorder and preventing violence; (c) treating clinician takes responsibility for ensuring that the patient follows the treatment program; (d) treating clinician should re-hospitalize the patient if it is needed to stabilize acute symptoms or if there is an elevation in risk for violence; and (e) obtain court orders, if necessary, to ensure patients comply with their treatment program.

A considerable amount of research on intervention with offenders with mental disorders indicates that cognitive behavioural approaches are the most effective (Bourgon and Armstrong 2005; Dowden and Andrews 2003; Lipsey and Wilson 1993; Pearson, Lipton, Cleland, and Yee 2002). Less is known about the effectiveness of structured programs with mentally disordered offenders. Duncan, Nicol, Ager, and Dalgeish (2006) reviewed 20 studies using structured group intervention, which provided a range of treatments to mentally disordered offenders including problem-solving skills, anger/aggression management, self-harm interventions, and others (e.g., moral reasoning, family relationships, social skills training). In general, the effect sizes were moderate to large for the interventions. Duncan et al. list several limitations with the empirical literature:

- Need for standardized outcome measures
- Include behavioural measures of outcomes
- Methodological problems include small samples, convenient sampling methods, lack of random assignment, and a lack of comparison groups
- Ethical approval should be obtained

PSYCHOPATHY: A PERSONALITY DISORDER WITH A BIG IMPACT IN THE CRIMINAL JUSTICE SYSTEM

THE CONSTRUCT OF **PSYCHOPATHY** HAS EXISTED FOR WELL OVER A CENTURY. PSYCHOPATHY was one of the first personality disorders to be recognized by psychiatry (see Millon, Simonsen, Birket-Smith, and Davis 1998). It was first established by French psychiatrist John Pinel, who in 1801 used the term *manie sans delire* (translated to mean mania without insanity) to describe patients who engaged in impulsive violent acts. In Britain, psychiatrist James Prichard (1883) coined the term "moral insanity" to describe patients who committed illegal and immoral acts, who knew what they were doing but did not care. (In contrast, the term sociopath has been used to describe individuals who commit antisocial acts because of family or environmental factors). The terms sociopath and psychopath are sometimes used synonymously but refer to separate groups of individuals based on the etiology of their symptoms.

In 1941, Hervey Cleckley, an American psychiatrist, described a subgroup of patients as appearing normal yet lacking in remorse and empathy, who were impulsive, deceptive, and grandiose. Their normal appearance coupled with the presence of these aberrant behaviours led Cleckley to characterize such patients as having a "mask of sanity." Psychopathy—the modern name applied to Cleckley's list of characteristics—has been the object of intense scrutiny by researchers. Since Cleckley's time, a substantial amount of research has focused on understanding how to evaluate the presence of psychopathy and to delineate its features and underlying causes. Following Cleckley's early work, psychopathy is defined by a constellation of interpersonal, affective, behavioural, and antisocial features. Psychopaths may be a small group of offenders, but they exert an influence within the criminal justice system that is disproportionate to their numbers. Approximately 10 to 25 percent of offenders are psychopaths (Hare 2003) but less than 1 percent of the general community scores high on psychopathy measures (Coid, Yang, Ullrich, Roberts, and Hare 2009).

Assessing Psychopathy: Rater- and Self-Report Methods

Over the past two decades, a variety of methods have been developed to assess for psychopathic traits in adults and youth. In rater-based assessments, either parents or teachers are asked to assess children for psychopathic features. Alternatively, clinicians can use information from interviews and related files to assess youth or adults for psychopathic traits. The other common method is self-report, in which an individual is given a questionnaire containing questions or statements that are linked to psychopathic characteristics.

Using self-report to assess for psychopathic features has been criticized by some researchers (Lilienfeld and Fowler 2006). First, psychopaths are often dishonest. Not only do they lie to obtain some tangible benefit, they also engage in what has been called "duping delight" (i.e., lying for the sheer fun of it). For example, if the psychopath is placed in a situation in which creating a positive impression is desirable (e.g., applying for early release from prison), they may attempt to make themselves look good (e.g., pretend they are remorseful when they are not). In contrast, psychopaths may find themselves in a situation in which creating a negative impression is desirable (e.g., being evaluated for insanity), where they may attempt to make themselves look bad (e.g., pretend they are delusional when they are not). Second, psychopaths may not have sufficient insight to accurately assess their traits. They may not see themselves as others see them and might not be able to report on the impact of their behaviour on others. For example, they might not consider themselves as arrogant or grandiose whereas observers might. Finally, asking a person who has never experienced a specific emotion to report on its presence is prob-lematic. Psychopaths may not understand the meaning of remorse (i.e., feeling negative emotions for the suffering caused to others) and may equate this with regret (i.e., feeling sorry for getting caught and the consequences for being caught).

Despite these concerns, self-report measures have several advantages. They are able to measure emotions or beliefs that are not easily observable by others (e.g., feelings of anger or hostile attributional style). In addition, self-reports are easy to administer, tend to be relatively quick, and are inexpensive. Many self-report scales include measures of response styles in order to detect invalid responding. Since individuals themselves com-plete the scale, concern about inter-rater reliability is eliminated. Two self-report scales that have been used with adults are the Psychopathic Personality Inventory–Revised (PPI–R) (Lilienfeld and Andrews 2005) and the Self-Report Psychopathy Scale (SRP-III) (Paulhus, Hemphill, and Hare, in press). (See Box 10.7 for a description of research using self-report psychopath scales.) Each is briefly described next.

Psychopathic Personality Inventory–Revised (Lilienfeld and Andrews 2005)

- 154-item self-report measure using a four-point rating format
- Designed to assess psychopathic traits in offender and community samples
- Validated for use in men and women aged 18 to 86 years
- Consists of eight content scales, two validity scales, and three factors of psychopathy (self-centered impulsivity, fearless dominance, cold-heartedness)

Self-Report Psychopathy Scale (Paulhus et al., in press)

- 40-item self-report measure using a five-point rating format
- Designed to assess psychopathic traits in community samples
- Validated for use in men and women aged 18 years or over
- Measures four factors of psychopathy (interpersonal manipulation, callous affect, erratic lifestyle, criminal tendencies)

Rater-based instruments for assessing psychopathy require more resources to admin-ister than self-report instruments. As formerly noted, an interview is required, plus eval-uation of collateral information (e.g., police records). In addition, the reliability of the person doing the rating should be established in order to ensure consistent application of

The Dark Triad: Narcissism, Machiavellianism, and Psychopathy

The dark triad of personalities is narcissism, machiavellianism, and subclinical psychopathy. People scoring high on narcissism have a sense of entitlement and superiority over others, are arrogant, and are self-centered. People scoring high on machiavellianism are cynical and manipulative, using others to satisfy their own self-interests. People scoring high on subclinical psychopathy are unemotional, manipulative, impulsive, risk-taking, and engage in illegal acts with no remorse or empathy.

Delroy Paulhus and his colleagues at the University of British Columbia have conducted several studies with university students to determine which of these personalities are related to various inappropriate behaviours.

Defrauding a Lottery (Paulhus, Williams, and Nathanson 2002)

Scenario: A student participates in a study and has the chance of winning $100. After the study has been completed, all study participants are sent an e-mail in which the experimenter states that they have lost the information about who was given the five $100 prizes. Participants were asked to e-mail the experimenter to let him know if they had previously been the winner.

Results: Students scoring high on subclinical psychopathy were more likely to try to defraud the experimenter and claim they were the "true" winners.

Cheating on Exams (Nathanson, Paulhus, and Williams 2006)

Scenario: The experimenter obtained computerized multiple-choice answers and seating plans from the instructors of several large introductory psychology classes. The experimenter wanted to determine which personalities would be most likely to cheat.

Results: 4 percent of the students were identified as cheating pairs, in which one student would copy answers from an adjacent student. Scoring high on subclinical psychopathy was the strongest predictor of cheating.

the instrument (i.e., inter-rater reliability). Rater-based instruments tend to be used most in forensic settings, where life-altering decisions about sentencing and risk of reoffending are required. The two most popular rater-based instruments for the assessment for psychopathy in adults are the Hare Psychopathy Checklist–Revised (PCL–R) (Hare 1991; 2003) and the Hare Psychopathy Checklist: Screening Version (PCL:SV) (Hart, Cox, and Hare 1995). The Hare PCL–R has been considered by some as the "gold standard" for assessing psychopathy (Fulero 1995) and has been adopted worldwide as the most reliable and valid measure.

Hare Psychopathy Checklist–Revised (Hare 1991; 2003)

■ 20-item symptom rating measure using a three-point scale

■ Designed to assess psychopathic traits in correctional and forensic psychiatric samples

- Validated for men and women aged 18 years and older
- Measures four factors of psychopathy (interpersonal, affective, behavioural, and antisocial)

Hare Psychopathy Checklist: Screening Version (Hart et al. 1995)

- 12-item symptom rating measure using a three-point scale
- Designed to assess psychopathic traits in the community and screen for psychopathic traits in forensic samples
- Validated for men and women aged 16 years and older
- Measures four factors of psychopathy (interpersonal, affective, behavioural, and antisocial)

Assessing Psychopathy in Youth

Until about a decade ago, relatively little attention was focused on the possibility of psychopathic traits being present in children or youth. Recently, however, a growing number of studies have been designed to understand the origins of psychopathy during development. Similar to adult assessment, there are both self-report and rater-based assessments for use with children and adolescents. Measures of psychopathic traits in children and youth are described below. All the scales were modelled after the PCL–R used with adults.

Youth Psychopathic Traits Inventory (YPI) (Andershed, Kerr, Stattin, and Levander 2002)

- 50-item self-report measure using a four-point scale
- Designed to assess psychopathic traits in community adolescents
- Valid for boys and girls aged 12 to 18 years
- Three factors measured (grandiose/manipulative, callous/unemotional, impulsive/irresponsibile)

Antisocial Process Screening Device (APSD) (Frick and Hare 2001)

- 20-item symptom rating measure using a three-point scale
- Designed to assess psychopathic-like traits in children using a parent or teacher as informant
- Valid for boys and girls aged 6 to 12 years
- Measures three factors (narcissism, impulsivity, callous/unemotional)

Hare Psychopathy Checklist: Youth Version (PCL:YV) (Forth, Kosson, and Hare 2003)

- 20-item symptom rating measure using a three-point scale
- Designed to assess psychopathic traits in juvenile justice samples
- Validated for boys and girls aged 12 to 18 years
- Measures four factors of psychopathy (interpersonal, affective, behavioural, and antisocial)

Psychopathy: Associations with Crime, Violence, and Recidivism

Research has established a strong link between psychopathic traits and criminal and aggressive behaviour in adults, adolescents, and children. Psychopathic traits identify a distinct subgroup of people who begin their criminal careers at an early age (Hare 2003), persist in violence across the lifespan (Porter, Birt, and Boer 2001), engage in high-density offences (Brown and Forth 1996), and engage in predatory/instrumental aggression (Flight and Forth 2007; Vitacco, Neumann, Caldwell, Leistico, and Van Rybroek 2006).

Table 10.6 presents the results of two meta-analyses that compared the association between psychopathy and criminal behaviour in adolescents and adults. Edens, Campbell, and Weir (2007) conducted a meta-analysis of 13 studies of adolescents as measured by the PCL:YV or a modified version of the PCL–R and the total number of incidents, a combined verbal and physical aggression category, and a category limited to physical aggression only. Guy, Edens, Anthony, and Douglas (2005) conducted a meta-analysis of 38 adult samples using the PCL–R or PCL:SV. The weighted mean effect sizes for the relation between the PCL:YV and the total number of incidents and number of aggressive incidents were similar to the effect sizes obtained for adult samples using the PCL–R or PCL:SV.

Table 10.6 Weighted Mean Effect Sizes for Hare PCL Scales and Institutional Misconduct in Youth and Adults from Two Meta-Analyses

Outcome & Score	Guy et al. (2005) Adults		Edens and Campbell (2007) Youth	
	ks & ns	$r_w s$	ks & ns	$r_w s$
Total				
Total Score	38 (5381)	.29	15 (1310)	.24
Factor 1 Score	25 (3219)	.21	– (1002)	.21
Factor 2 Score	25 (3219)	.27	– (1002)	.28
Aggression				
Total Score	31 (4483)	.23	14 (1188)	.25
Factor 1 Score	22 (2786)	.15	– (880)	.22
Factor 2 Score	22 (2786)	.20	– (880)	.34
Physical Violence				
Total Score	22 (3502)	.17	10 (1001)	.28
Factor 1 Score	16 (2129)	.14	– (775)	.24
Factor 2 Score	16 (2129)	.15	– (775)	.37

Source: Guy et al. (2005)

A weighted mean effect size of .28 demonstrates a significant association between PCL:YV and institutional physical violence and is much stronger than that reported by Guy et al. (2005) with adult samples (.17). In adults, association between psychopathy and institutional misconduct was strongest for a total number of incidents and weakest for physical violence, whereas for adolescents the opposite pattern was obtained. Thus youth with psychopathic traits are more likely to engage in overt aggression compared to their adult counterparts. For both adolescents and adults, Factor 2 (behavioural and antisocial features) consistently had greater predictive value than Factor 1 (interpersonal and affective features) across each of the three categories of institutional incidents.

What is the association between psychopathy and recidivism? Table 10.7 presents the effect sizes of three meta-analytic studies with primarily adult samples and one meta-analytic study focusing on youth. Leistico, Salekin, DeCoster, and Rogers (2008) found that age was not a significant moderator, indicating that the "relations between psychopathy and future antisocial conduct were consistent across differences in the average age of the samples" (p. 33). The results of these studies suggest that increased psychopathy scores in adults and youth are associated with increased general and violent recidivism but not sexual recidivism.

Why is there a link between psychopathy and crime/violence? Given the features of psychopathy, it is perhaps not surprising that a strong link exists. The features listed below illustrate why psychopaths engage in higher rates of criminal and violent behaviour.

Table 10.7 Weighted Mean Effect Sizes for Hare PCL Scales and Recidivism in Youth and Adults from Three Meta-Analyses

Recidivism and Score	Walters (2003ab) Primarily Adults		Leistico et al. (2008) Primarily Adults		Edens et al. (2007) Youth	
	ks & ns	$r_w s$	ks & ns	$d_w s$	ks & ns	$r_w s$
General Recidivism						
Total Score	33 (4870)	.26	62 (11 140)	.50	20 (2787)	.24
Factor 1 Score	26 (4360)	.15	29 (5439)	.37	15 (2157)	.18
Factor 2 Score	26 (4360)	.32	29 (5439)	.64	15 (2157)	.29
Violent Recidivism						
Total Score					14 (2067)	.25
Factor 1 Score	27 (6365)	.18			12 (1776)	.19
Factor 2 Score	27 (6356)	.26			12 (1776)	.26
Sexual Recidivism						
Total Score					4 (654)	.07
Factor 1 Score	5 (726)	.05			3 (437)	.03
Factor 2 Score	5 (726)	.08			3 (437)	.08

Source: Leistico et al. (2008) and Edens et al. (2007)

- Psychopaths are sensation-seekers and risk takers. They put themselves in high-risk situations.

- Psychopaths are impulsive. They fail to consider alternatives or consequences of crime or violence.

- Psychopaths are unemotional. They do not have the ability to appreciate the consequences of crime or violence.

- Psychopaths are suspicious. They perceive hostile intent in others.

- Psychopaths are selfish and arrogant. The want to have power and control over others.

Assessing Psychopathic Traits in Youth: Concerns

> Juveniles who are branded as psychopaths are more likely to be viewed as incorrigible, less likely to receive rehabilitative dispositions, and more likely to be transferred to the criminal justice system to be tried as adults and face the possibility of adult sanctions. (Steinberg 2002: 36)

This quote lists several negative outcomes that could result from youth being labelled as psychopathic. Ethical, professional, and practical concerns about the use (or misuse) of measures designed to assess psychopathy in youth have been raised by various authors (Edens, Skeem, Curise, and Cauffman 2001; Hart, Watt, and Vincent 2002; Seagrave and Grisson 2002; Zinger and Forth 1998). Their concerns have focused on three main issues:

1. Negative consequences (e.g., transfer to adult court, harsher sentences, denial of access to treatment) of labelling a youth a psychopath

2. The possibility that psychopathic traits are common features of normally developing youth

3. The stability of psychopathic traits from childhood to adolescence and on to adulthood

To address the labelling concern, several studies have investigated the effects of different labels (e.g., psychopath, conduct disorder, non-disorder) or different traits (e.g., psychopathic versus no psychopathic traits) on mock juror decision making (see Table 10.8). These studies typically provided participants with a written description of a defendant and the violent crime committed. All participants receive the same information, with the exception of the clinical assessment, which varies across participants. Studies have used a variety of samples ranging from university students to juvenile justice judges. In general, the following conclusions can be made. First, both the labels of psychopathy and conduct disorder are equally associated with higher risk. Second, describing underlying traits has a stronger impact on decision making than the label. The strongest influence on decision makers is having a history of antisocial behaviour. Third, the effect of psychopathy on treatment decisions is mixed. In some studies (Murrie et al. 2005; 2007; Boccaccini et al. 2008), participants recommended treatment more often for

Table 10.8 Studies Examining the Effects of the Psychopathy and Conduct Disorder (CD) Labels and Traits in Adolescents

Study	Sample	Manipulation	Higher Risk	Harsher Sanction	Less Treatment
Edens et al. (2003)	Students	P traits versus positive traits	Yes	Yes	Yes
Murrie et al. (2005)	Juvenile probation officers	P versus CD versus no disorder	No	No	No
Murrie et al. (2007)	Judges	P versus CD versus no disorder	No	No	No
Rockett et al. (2007)	Clinicians	P versus CD versus no disorder	Yes	--	No
Vidal and Skeem (2007)	Juvenile probation officers	Is a psychopath versus not a psychopath	Yes	Yes	Yes
Jones and Cauffman (2008)	Judges	Is a psychopath versus not a psychopath	Yes	Yes	Yes
Boccaccini et al. (2008)	Community	Is a psychopath versus P versus CD versus no disorder	Yes	Yes	No

Source: Adapted from Boccaccini et al. (2008)

youth described as psychopathic than for other youth. Finally, wording matters. If the description is worded, "Michael meets the diagnostic criteria for psychopathy," there is little impact. However, if it is worded, "Michael is a psychopath," there is a stronger negative impact.

Edens et al. (2001) raises another concern that "scores on measures of psychopathy arguably may be inflated by general characteristics of adolescence" (p. 59). Edens et al.'s argument is that during the normal course of development, many adolescents may engage in activities that could be classified as bordering on criminal, thus leading researchers to overestimate the level of psychopathic traits in adolescent samples. However, this argument is not supported by any data: high ratings of psychopathic traits are rare in community youth (80 percent of community males score very low on the PCL:YV; Forth et al. 2003).

A final concern has been the stability of psychopathic traits from childhood to adulthood. Adolescence is a period of substantial change in the biological, psychological, and social systems. There have been several studies measuring the stability of psychopathic traits. Frick, Kimonis, Dandreaux, and Farell (2003) assessed the stability of the APSD from age 10 to 14 years. Parental ratings of psychopathic traits were highly stable ($r = .80$); however, when change occurred it was rare for those children with few psychopathic traits to develop them as adolescents. More recently, Muñoz and Frick (2007) assessed the stability of the APSD from age 13 to 16 years. Parental ratings were highly stable (r = .77). In a longer follow-up study, Lynam, Loeber, and Stouthamer-Loeber et al. (2008) examined the stability of psychopathic traits between the ages 13 and 24 years. At age 13, youth were assessed on a parental rating psychopathic scale (Childhood Psychopathy Scale) (Lynam 1997) and then assessed again between the ages of 23 and 25 on the PCL:SV. The correlation between the two measures was .31. Several other studies have also found moderate stability across different age periods on measures of psychopathy (Blonigen et al. 2006; Forsman et al. 2008).

Theories of Psychopathy

Cleckley (1941) believed that the core deficit in psychopathy relates to a poverty of emotions, ". . . probably in the core of the psychopath's essential abnormality—perhaps in a lack of emotional components essential to real understanding." (p. 173). Several theories have been proposed relating to the notion of an affective deficit. Lykken (1995) proposed the low-fear hypothesis to explain psychopathy, while others (Hare 2003) have put forth more generalized affective deficits to explain the range of clinical features of psychopathy.

Certainly, developmental psychologists have emphasized the importance of emotion in the development of conscience (Kochanska 1994; Blair, Jones, Clark, and Smith 1997). Figure 10.2 illustrates the importance of emotion in the development of conscience, as well as the key role of parents. Parents make salient the connection between misbehaviour and sanctions, elicit moral emotions such as empathy and guilt, and provide incentives for engaging in prosocial behaviour. For most children, when they engage in some transgression (e.g., hitting their younger sister), the victim elicits distress and the parents disapprove, causing negative emotions in the offender that lead to guilt and empathy. These feelings then result in the inhibition of future transgressions (the dashed line in the figure).

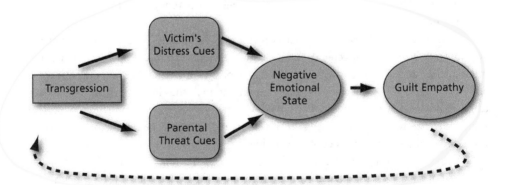

Figure 10.2 The Role of Emotions in the Development of Conscience

Source: Adapted from Kochanska (1993)

From an early age (as young as 30 months) (Kochanska, Murray, and Coy 1997), healthy children learn to inhibit behaviours that have negative consequences to others. A key component of socialization is developing the appropriate emotional response to distress in others based on cues from victims and parents. Research has shown that children and adults with psychopathic traits show reduced autonomic responses to the distress of others and reduced recognition of sad and fearful expressions (see Blair 2007 for a review). Therefore, without this emotional response, psychopaths will not learn to inhibit their behaviours.

Children with psychopathic traits, and callous/unemotional traits in particular, are less responsive to parental socialization practices (Oxford, Cavell, and Hughes 2003; Wootton, Frick, Shelton, and Silverthorn 1997), display less distress over actions that hurt others (Blair et al. 1997; Pardini et al. 2003), and have a reduced emotional response to emotional stimuli (Blair, Colledge, Murray, and Mitchell 2001; Kimonis, Frick, Fazekas, and Loney 2006; Loney, Frick, Clements, Ellis, and Kerlin 2003) compared to children with other conduct problems. Frick and Marsee (2006) proposed two developmental models, one for the development of callous/unemotional traits and the other for impulsive conduct problems. The developmental model of callous/unemotional traits posits that youth are born with a predisposition to fearlessness or low behavioural inhibition that leads them to be insensitive to parental and social sanctions, show little arousal to the misfortune of others, and ignore the harmful effects of their behaviours. Over the course of development, this leads to a callous/unemotional interpersonal style, which ultimately leads them to engage in antisocial behaviours—in particular, instrumental aggression. The developmental model for impulse conduct problems involves inadequate socializing environments, low intelligence, and poor response inhibition, leading to a lack of planning and being susceptible to angry arousal. In turn, this leads the child to engage in unplanned antisocial acts, especially reactive aggression.

Another prominent theory of psychopathy developed in research with adult offenders focuses more on cognitive as opposed to emotional processes. Newman and his colleagues proposed that psychopaths have a response modulation deficit (Newman and Wallace 1993; for review, see Newman, Brinkley, Lorenz, Hiatt, and McCoon 2007). According to this theory, once psychopaths have focused their attention, they will fail to use information to modify their response. This deficit can help explain why psychopaths fail to learn to inhibit their behaviour (e.g., show poor passive avoidance conditioning).

Genetics of Psychopathy

To examine the role of genetics in psychopathy, several researchers have focused on comparing monozygotic (MZ; identical) twins to dizygotic (DZ; fraternal) twins. The rationale is that MZ twins share all their genes, whereas DZ twins share 50 percent (see Chapter 2 for a discussion of twin studies). Twin studies have consistently found a large and significant heritable component to psychopathic traits in children (Viding, Blair, Moffitt, and Plomin 2005), adolescents (Blonigen, Hicks, Krueger, Patrick, and Iacono 2005; Larsson,

Table 10.9 Heritability Estimates for Psychopathic Traits

Study	Sample (N, sex/age)	Callous/ Unemotional	Impulsive/ Antisocial
Viding et al. (2005)	3687 males and females, 7 years	67%	
Blonigen et al. (2005)	626 males and females, 17 years	45%	49%
Blonigen et al. (2006)	626 males and females, 24 years	42%	49%
Taylor et al. (2003)	398 males and females, 16 to 18 years	40%	40%
Larsson et al. (2006)	1100 males and females, 16 years	43%	56%

Andershed, and Lichtensetin 2006; Taylor, Loney, Bobadilla, Iacono, and McGue 2003), and adults (Blonigen, Hicks, Krueger, Patrick, and Iacono 2006). These studies indicate that for all aspects of psychopathic traits, there is moderate to strong genetic influence (see Table 10.9). For studies comparing males and females (Blonigen et al. 2006; Larsson et al. 2006), there was no evidence for sex differences. But a strong genetic contribution to psychopathic traits does not imply immutability; rather, it suggests that any interventions to attenuate negative developmental trajectories must be applied as early as possible.

Biological Basis for Psychopathy

Are the brains of psychopaths different from others? Recently, neuroimaging techniques have been used to investigate if psychopaths have any structural or functional brain differences compared to non-psychopaths. A literature review by Weber, Habel, Amunts, and Schneider (2008) concluded that psychopaths have a reduction in prefrontal grey matter, less grey matter in the right superior temporal gyrus, less hippocampal volume, less amygdala volume, and an increase in callosal white matter. They argue that "psychopathy cannot be explained by one particular neurobiological theory or by one neurobiological substrate. Rather, the various brain abnormalities seem to involved a network, including prefrontal regions as well as temporo-limbic areas" (p. 23). Table 10.10 summarizes the brain areas found to be related to psychopathy by structural and functional neuroimaging studies.

Functional neuroimaging studies have reported reduced activation of the amygdala and anterior cingulate/ventromedial prefrontal cortex with psychopaths in emotional memory paradigms (Kiehl et al. 2001), aversive conditioning (Birbaumer et al. 2005), and emotional photos (Muller et al. 2003). In addition, some studies have implicated other areas in psychopathy, such as the superior temporal cortex and the dorsal anterior

Table 10.10 Brain Areas Implicated in Psychopathy

Brain Region	Function	Outcome
Ventro-medial prefrontal cortex	• Decision making • Emotion regulation • Empathy • Moral judgment	• Poor planning/impulsivity • Poor anger control • Callous disregard for others • Antisocial behaviours
Corpus callosum	• Connectivity between hemispheres • Asymmetries of function	• Reduced lateralization of functions
Superior temporal gyrus	• Social judgment • Perspective-taking and moral judgment	• Misattribution of others' motives • Antisocial behaviours
Hippocampus	• Fear conditioning	• Failure to desist from punished behaviour
Amygdala	• Social-emotion judgments • Moral emotions	• Misperception of others' feelings • Antisocial behaviours
Anterior cingulate	• Inhibition	• Failure to control behaviour

Source: Adapted from Raine (2008) and Weber et al. (2008)

cingulated cortex (Kiehl 2006). Kiehl (2006) proposed a paralimbic model to explain the emotional processing deficits seen in psychopaths.

Although neuroimaging studies have provided insight into the areas of the brain implicated in psychopathy in addition to providing tentative functional models of psychopathy, caution is required when interpreting such findings. Recently, Poldrack (2009) summarized several critical limitations of neuroimaging procedures when attempting to understand mental disorders. First, he warns that increased or decreased activation of particular brain regions should not be automatically equated with "better" or "abnormal" functioning. Second, researchers should not assume that because they see activation in an individual brain area, this area is solely responsible for a specific mental function. Poldrack provides an example to illustrate this point that is particularly relevant to accounts of psychopathy and the function of the amygdala: "The fact that the amygdala, for example, responds to threat does not mean that activity in this area signifies that a person is feeling threatened. That would be true only if threat were the only thing that activates the amygdala, and we know this is not the case."

If a psychopath suffers from brain impairments that predispose him to commit impulsive violence, should we hold him fully accountable for his behaviour? Some may argue that psychopathy should be considered a mitigating factor, while others have gone as far as to suggest psychopaths should not be found legally responsible (i.e., they should be found NCRMD). Morse (2008) reviews the literature on criminal responsibility and psychopathy and concludes that "severe psychopathy should be a basis for non-responsibility in appropriate cases because psychopathy deprives people of rational capacities that are fundamental for fair ascriptions of blame and punishment" (p. 212).

Brain differences alone are not sufficient to explain the emergence of psychopathy. Researchers are now looking for specific genes that may result in these brain abnormalities, which in turn lead to antisocial and violent behaviour. However, environment and socialization can influence gene expression. Thus any explanation of the etiology of psychopathy will need to examine the interactions between genetic predispositions, neurobiological functioning, and developmental experiences.

Treatment of Psychopaths

Until recently, psychopathy was assumed to be largely untreatable. This perspective can be traced to Cleckley's book on psychopathy, where he stated, "Over a period of many years I have remained discouraged about the effect of treatment on the psychopathy . . . I have seen some patients treated for years . . . The psychopaths continued to behave as they had behaved in the past" (1976: 454).

Most of the relatively few studies that have evaluated the effectiveness of treatment for psychopaths suggest that Cleckley's initial assessment was correct: psychopathic offenders respond poorly to treatment, display poor motivation, show little improvement, and have high drop-out rates (Barbaree 2005; Hare et al. 2000; Hobson, Shine, and Roberts 2000; Langton, Barbaree, Harkins, and Peacock 2006). Rice, Harris, and Cormier (1991) found that some treated psychopaths not only did not improve with treatment but engaged in more offending. However, more promising treatment outcomes have been observed in some recent studies. Olver and Wong (2009) examined the treatment responses of psychopathic sex offenders and found that those who dropped out of treatment were more likely to violently reoffend, whereas those who stayed in treatment showed positive treatment gains and had a reduced risk for both sexual and violent recidivism. Encouraging evidence also comes from a treatment program for high-risk violent adolescent offenders. Caldwell, Skeem, Salekin, and Van Rybroek (2006) treated violent youth with many psychopathic traits (mean PCL:YV score of 33) at the Mendota Juvenile Treatment Center. The treated group was compared to juveniles referred for assessment who returned to the juvenile correctional system without treatment (mean PCL:YV score of 32). In a two-year follow-up, the treated group's rate of violent recidivism was 21 percent, compared to the non-treated group's rate of 49 percent. The study illustrates that using cognitive-behavioural treatment can be effective for youth with psychopathic traits as long as it is sufficiently intense and sustained.

Several proposals have been made about the treatment of psychopathy. Wallace and Newman (2004) suggest that an effective treatment program should include targeting deficits in response modulation. Blair (2006) has proposed that since psychopathy is associated with reduced activity in the amygdala and associated structures, treatment could include giving pharmacological agents that increase activity within the amygdala. Blair acknowledges that "Although pharmacological agents are likely to be necessary for the successful treatment of psychopathy, they are unlikely to be sufficient . . . such agents will need to be coupled with cognitive behaviour-based treatments designed to associate actions that hurt others with an emotional response to the victim's distress" (Blair 2006: 391).

Based on the research discussed, treatment of psychopaths should have the following characteristics:

1. Psychopaths should not be considered untreatable. Treatment should target potentially changeable factors linked to the psychopathic offenders' criminal behaviour.

2. Treatment program should be high-intensity, cognitive-behavioural, incorporating relapse prevention and targeting substance abuse, anger arousal, antisocial thinking, and cognitive distortions (Wong and Hare 2005).

3. Treatment providers should be familiar with the cognitive and emotional processing deficits.

4. Intervention programs should be provided as early as possible in the person's development.

5. Treatment programs need to target treatment-interfering behaviours and develop methods to enhance psychopaths' motivations for treatment.

Psychopathy continues to gain prominence as a critical construct in accounting for a substantial portion of criminal and aggressive behaviour. Like many other mental disorders, it is complex in terms of its etiology and treatment. Research over the past 30 years has led to many advances in how to measure psychopathy, determine its biological and environmental origins, and treat it. Within the next several years, new research will provide further insights in the development and treatment of this construct.

Below is a list of top 10 issues and people to consider when thinking about mentally disordered offenders and psychopathy in Canada.

Top 10 List

Advances to Come, Debates, Ethical Conundrums, and People to Watch

1. The American Psychiatric Association continues to add mental disorders to the DSM. What concerns, if any, do you have with this proliferation of disorders?

2. The media continue to link mental illness and violence. What should organizations like the Canadian Mental Health Association do to challenge this portrayal?

3 Forty years ago, a major concern in the area of public health was the deinstitutionalization of the mentally ill. Currently, a major concern is the criminalization of the mentally ill. What can be done to reverse this trend?

4 Some of the data on mental health courts is only modestly encouraging. Should the justice system continue to use these courts?

5 The public is not very supportive of the insanity defence, especially in murder cases. Should Canada develop a new legislation titled "guilty but mentally ill" to handle such cases?

6 The mentally ill are at higher risk to engage in violence. However, researchers disagree on the reasons for this finding. Future research is needed to explain why the mentally ill are at an elevated risk.

7 Differences exist in the brains of psychopaths compared to other offenders, especially in parts of the brain related to moral decision-making. Should psychopaths be found responsible for their actions?

8 Self-report measures of psychopathy are quick and inexpensive. What are the concerns with using this method for assessing psychopathy?

9 Measures have been developed to assess psychopathic traits in children. What are the potential negative consequences for children assessed as having many psychopathic traits?

10 Names to watch: Dorothy Cotton, Colin Shapiro, Jeffrey Swanson, Delroy Paulhus, Sheilagh Hodgins, Kent Kiehl, James Blair, and Joseph Newman.

SUMMARY

1. Prevalence rates for mental disorders in offenders are much higher than for the general population. Both male and female offenders are more likely to be diagnosed with psychosis, depression, and substance abuse then are non-offenders. Antisocial personality disorder is the most common personality disorder present in male and female offenders. A number of explanations have been suggested for these high rates, including the criminalization of the mentally ill.

2. In Canada, if an accused is not able to participate in his or her defence on account of a mental disorder, it is deemed unfair to try this person. Such a person would be found unfit to stand trial (UST). The federal government passed Bill C-10 in 2006, which gives the courts the authority to order a stay of proceedings for an accused found UST if the accused is unlikely to become fit to stand trial and does not pose a significant threat to public safety.

3. In Canada, the insanity defence is called not criminally responsible on account of a mental disorder (NCRMD). If you commit a crime while suffering from a mental

disorder, it might make you incapable of appreciating the nature and quality of the crime or of knowing that it was wrong, and you could be found NCRMD. The public has many misperceptions about this defence, including the belief that it is frequently used, it is often successful, and that accused are often quickly released into the community.

4. The two strongest risk factors that increase the likelihood of violence in people with major mental disorders are co-occurring substance abuse problems and specific types of delusions. Schizophrenics who experience what have been called threat/control override delusions or command hallucinations are at an elevated risk.

5. Psychopathy is a personality disorder defined by a cluster of interpersonal, affective, and behavioural features. A variety of assessment measures have been developed to assess for psychopathic traits in children, adolescents, and adults. A number of concerns have been raised about the measurement of psychopathic traits in youth. These include the issue of labelling a youth a psychopath, how stable psychopathic traits are from childhood to adulthood, and whether psychopathic traits are normal in healthy adolescents.

6. Developmental, biological, and cognitive theories have been used to explain the etiology of psychopathy. Recent neuroimaging studies have identified two areas of the brain in those with psychopathic characteristics that are of specific interest: the amygdala and the ventromedial prefrontal cortex. Although psychopaths are resistant to treatment, recent research has reported some positive outcomes, especially for youth with psychopathic traits.

Discussion Questions

1. A federal male offender commits suicide in his cell. The Office of the Correctional Investigator concludes that the Correctional Service of Canada (CSC) is not doing enough to provide mental health services to incarcerated offenders. If you were a warden, what would you do to try and reduce the suicide rate in your prison?

2. The police in your community have been accused of being biased against the mentally ill. You have been hired by the town council to write a report on what the police should know about the association between mental illness and crime. What do you include in your report?

3. You are having a discussion with friends about the Vincent Li case (see Box 10.1), and one of them states that anyone who engages in murder should "do the time for the crime" and is adamant that being found not criminally responsible on account of a mental disorder will result in Vincent Li being released back into the community to kill again. What counterarguments would you use to respond to your friend's belief?

4. The CSC has proposed a new treatment program for personality disordered violent offenders. You have been hired to develop an evaluation of the program to see whether it is effective. Describe how you plan to make your evaluation.

5. You are interested in conducting a study on how the media portrays crimes committed by the mentally ill. Develop two hypotheses and describe the methodology you would use and what variables you would measure to test these hypotheses.

6. You have been hired by the World Health Organization to identify the prevalence of psychopathy across different countries. Describe the study you would propose, focusing on how you would measure psychopathy.

Additional Reading

Monahan, J., and Steadman, H.J. 1994. *Violence and mental disorder: Developments in risk assessment.* Chicago: University of Chicago Press.

Hinshaw, S.P. 2007. *The mark of shame: Stigma of mental illness and agenda for change.* New York: Oxford University Press.

Patrick, C.J. 2006. *Handbook of psychopathy.* New York: Guilford Press.

Relevant Websites

Society for the Scientific Study of Psychopathy
www.psychopathysociety.org

Department of Justice Canada
www.justice.gc.ca

Canadian Mental Health Association
www.cmha.ca

Chapter 11
Female Offenders

Sally and the Sex Trade

After years of living with a crack-addicted mother and an abusive stepfather, Sally Johnson left home in search of a better life on the eve of her thirteenth birthday. Alone in a coffee shop one week later with less than $10 in her pocket, a man named Sam bought her a warm meal. He drove an expensive car, wore nice clothes, and showed Sally warmth and kindness. Within a few months, she was working for Sam, selling her body for sex. The lifestyle was not her choice, but she knew it would only anger Sam if she openly discussed her reluctance. She also knew she would be severely beaten if she did not comply. With a sense of helplessness, Sally wondered if it might be easier to simply end her own life. Sam bought her nice clothes, flowers, and expensive dinners, especially after their fights, which often ended with blackened eyes and cracked ribs. The drugs he provided made her numb—a real benefit while she was working, but she had reached a point of needing the drugs to survive. Her official criminal record included break and enters, robberies, and drug trafficking. She made no apologies and was even proud of her survival strategies, believing it was okay to steal to survive or physically hurt another person if it meant getting money. After fifteen years of bouncing in and out of youth custody facilities and provincial jails, Sally eventually landed in the federal correctional system. She is now serving a life sentence for armed robbery and second degree murder. At age 28, she is ready to change. She knows the road ahead will be difficult given her profile—an abusive and unstable family background, grade eight education, no formal job training, drug addiction, and unhealthy relationship choices. But for the first time in her life, she is optimistic and has found her "voice." She honestly believes she can learn new skills, beat her drug addiction, and—most importantly—that she is worth the investment.

Learning Objectives

1   Explore the nature and types of crime committed by girls and women.

2   Highlight similarities and differences between female and male offenders and between girl and woman offenders in the domains of theory, assessment, and treatment.

3   Compare and contrast the strengths and weaknesses associated with gender neutral and gender-informed risk-assessment approaches.

4 Describe what gender-informed treatment programs look like and determine whether these programs achieve their desired effects.

5 Describe criticisms levied by feminist scholars against the existing correctional literature as it relates to female offenders.

INTRODUCTION

AS EVIDENCED THROUGHOUT THIS CHAPTER, SALLY TYPIFIES THE KIND OF FEMALE who has come into contact with the law. However, there are many pathways to the criminal justice system and "one size" definitely does not fit all. While there are young women (as well as young men) who initially turn to crime as a result of a traumatic family upbringing, there are also girls and women (and boys and men) who end up in the criminal justice system as a result of other non-familial factors such as substance abuse, antisocial personality, and negative peer association. The factors that place an individual (male or female, youth or adult) on a criminal trajectory are multifaceted and operate conjointly with one another across multiple spheres. These spheres include: 1) individual personality factors—impulsivity; 2) interpersonal factors—poor relationship choices, family factors (e.g., poor supervision, lack of warmth); 3) community factors—living in a high-crime neighbourhood; and 4) structural factors (e.g., poverty, racism). There are still many unanswered questions in the realm of female criminal conduct.

In this chapter, we examine the criminal behaviour of girls and women. We begin by reviewing why scholars and correctional agencies have historically paid little attention to female offenders. Next, we explore the nature and types of crimes that females commit and explore whether the female violent crime rate has been increasing in recent years. We also discuss the similarities and differences between female and male offenders from both theoretical and practical perspectives. Gender-neutral and gender-informed risk-assessment approaches for girls and women will be presented as well as existing challenges and controversies surrounding their use. We review the need for gender-informed treatment, describe what some of these programs look like, and attempt to determine whether they achieve their desired outcomes. Throughout the chapter, similarities and differences between youthful female and adult female offenders and male and female offenders are highlighted.

BACKGROUND
Historical Context

Cesare Lombroso (1835–1909), an Italian physician and psychiatrist, was the first individual to study criminal behaviour using traditional scientific methods. Lombroso's

L'uomo Delinquente (Criminal Man) was published in 1876 (Volume 1). Volumes 2 through 5 followed almost 20 years later but were not translated into English until 1911. Lombroso also wrote about female criminal behaviour. He published *La Donna Delinquente (The Female Offender)* in Italian in 1893 with his research assistant, Guglielmo Ferrero. It was first translated into English in 1895, but its most recent and most accurate translation was published by Rafter and Gibson in 2004.

Lombroso's account of female criminal conduct was unequivocally sexist and overly focused on biology and sexuality relative to his explanation of male criminal conduct. Nonetheless, he was the first individual to systematically study female offending using positivist methods. Although a few post-Lombrosian researchers (e.g., Thomas 1923; Pollack 1950) continued to write about female criminality, like their predecessor, their explanations were inherently sexist—females committed crime because of faulty internal mechanisms of a biological and/or sexual nature. In stark contrast, the rest of the criminological world was focused on explaining male criminality. Moreover, criminological explanations of male crime emphasized external or environmental causes, including lower social class origins and structural inequality such as Merton's theory of social structure and anomie (1938). Typically, these theories either explicitly ignored female offenders (e.g., Hirschi 1969) or implicitly assumed through omission that they would generalize to girls and women.

It wasn't until 1975 that researchers again turned their attention to female offenders. But unlike their predecessors, these scholars—Rita Simon (author of *Women and Crime*, 1975) and Freda Alder (author of *Sisters in Crime*, 1975) were female. They sought to understand female criminality through the lens of **feminism**. Since the writings of Adler and Simon, scholarly interest in female criminal conduct has flourished, largely due to vocal feminist advocates who continually pose the question, "What about girls and women?" The criminal justice system has witnessed a substantial increase in the number of females officially arrested and/or charged and subsequently imprisoned—an increase that has outpaced that of their male counterparts.

Prevalence and Nature of Female-Perpetrated Crime

There is one universal fact about crime: girls and women commit substantially less of it, and particularly less violent and less serious crime as compared to boys and men. This fact holds true regardless of researcher, or research methodology (Blanchette and Brown 2006). In 2005, approximately 20 percent of people accused of a *Criminal Code* offence in Canada were female (Kong and AuCoin 2008). Similar findings have been reported in the United States (Federal Bureau of Investigation 2002), England and Wales (Murray and Fiti 2004), and Australia (Taylor and Bareja 2002). In terms of violent offending, women account for only 16 percent of all charges filed against adult offenders in Canada. However, they do account for a relatively higher proportion (23 percent) of property charges (Canadian Centre for Justice Statistics 2004).

In 2007, 527 individuals were accused of homicide in Canada. Ninety percent were male ($n = 474$), the majority of whom were adult males—87 percent ($n = 405$). Female-perpetrated homicide is rare. Only eight girls (aged 12–17) were accused of homicide in Canada in 2007 (Statistics Canada 2007), which translates into a rate of 0 per 100 000 due to rounding error. The official statistics also reveal a staggering gender disparity in the domain of another serious form of violent offending—sexual assault. In 2003–2004, the ratio of male youth to female youth convicted of sexual assault was 79 to 1 (551 youthful males convicted versus 7 youthful females) (Kong and AuCoin 2008).

Males also outnumber females in all forms of non-violent crime, with one exception—prostitution. In 2003–2004, 622 females (predominately women) were convicted of prostitution versus 393 males (predominately men). In this instance, females surpassed males by a ratio of 1.58 to 1. While males still outpace females in theft convictions by a ratio of 3 to 1, this gender disparity is markedly smaller relative to all other forms of non-violent and violent crimes (Kong and Aucoin 2008). Official crime statistics reveal that not only do males account for the lion's share of officially reported crime, they also account for the vast majority of violent crime.

Unofficial data mirrors the official crime rate in some but not all respects. A self-report study of youth delinquency in Toronto revealed boys were twice as likely to report engaging in violent behaviour over their lifetime (30 percent) than girls (15 percent). However, the gender gap narrowed considerably when youth were asked about non-violent crimes against property (30 percent for boys versus 26 percent for girls) (Savoie 2007). A methodologically rigorous study conducted in New Zealand found similar trends. Terrie Moffitt and colleagues (e.g., Moffitt and Caspi 2001; Moffitt, Caspi, Rutter, and Silva 2001) examined the criminal trajectories of children ($N = 1037$, 52 percent male, 48 percent female) born in Dunedin, New Zealand, using a prospective cohort design. The study collected multiple sources of data at multiple time intervals from 91 percent of all children born between April 1972 and March 1973 in Dunedin (the study is ongoing). In sum, Moffitt and Caspi reported that the male-to-female ratio for individuals classified as adolescent-limited (i.e., criminal conduct begins during adolescence and is relatively minor and short-lived; see Chapter 5) was only 1.5:1. In contrast, the male-to-female ratio for individuals described as "life-course persistent" (i.e., antisocial conduct begins during childhood and is serious, diverse, and persistent) was considerably higher—10:1. Notably, the results of the Savoie and Moffitt et al. studies have been replicated in the United States (e.g., Canter 1982; Cernkovich and Giordano 1979). In sum, official and unofficial reports confirm that males commit more crime than females and that the gender gap is particularly more pronounced in the realm of serious and violent offending.

Despite this evidence, a number of highly sensationalized cases have left the general public with the impression that female violence is out of control. Canada is no exception. On November 14, 1997, near Victoria, British Columbia, seven teenage girls (including Kelly Ellard, the primary offender who was 15 at the time) and one teenage boy swarmed, severely beat, and eventually drowned 14-year-old Reena Virk. On April 15, 2006, in Medicine Hat, Alberta, a 12-year-old girl and her 23-year-old boyfriend were charged (and eventually convicted) with murdering the girl's parents and her eight-year-old brother. The motivation for the crime allegedly stemmed from her parents' insistence that she end the relationship with her boyfriend. On March 20, 2009, a 17-year-old girl from Toronto was convicted of first-degree murder in the death of a 14-year-old girl. Prosecutors argued that she had counselled her teenage boyfriend to commit the homicide via instant text messaging; the alleged motivation was jealousy. She was 15 at the time.

Females can and do commit acts of extreme violence. However, as discussed, these events are rare. Some examples of crimes that are more typical of female offenders are provided in Box 11.1. We explore the question of whether females are becoming more violent in Box 11.2.

Not only do females commit less crime and less serious forms of crime than males, there is a long-standing hypothesis that the "offence gestalt"—the motivations, circumstances, and context of their crimes—differ markedly from that of their male counterparts (Steffensmeier and Allan 1996). Greenfeld and Snell (1999) examined the characteristics of all homicide offences that occurred between 1976 and 1997 in the United States—60 000 committed by females and 400 000 committed by males. Females were markedly more likely to have murdered an intimate partner or family member (60 percent) relative to their male counterparts (20 percent). In contrast, females were less likely to have murdered a stranger (1 in 14) versus males (1 in 4), but when females do commit non-familial homicide, there is some evidence that their motivations mirror that of males—vindication and/or an attempt to restore personal integrity (Campbell 1984; Daly and Wilson 1988; Kruttschnitt 2001). When females murder an intimate partner, they often appear to do so in response to domestic violence, whereas males appear to be acting out of jealousy, infidelity, desertion, and control (Belknap 2001; Daly and Wilson 1988; Owen 2001).

Kelly Ellard was convicted of the 1997 murder of Reena Virk. She is now serving her sentence in an adult federal prison.

Sample Crimes Committed by Females—from Shoplifting to Homicide

Shoplifting

Barbara Jones, a 46-year-old divorced mother of three, has shoplifted off and on since she was 12. Initially, she started doing it in order to be accepted into a popular group of girls at school. However, as she got older her motivations changed. She reported to police that she simply couldn't get through the day without stealing and that sometimes she even took money from friends. Her most recent arrest stems from taking lipstick and face powder from a drugstore. She reported feeling depressed at the time. She received six months probation.

Fraud

Lisa Barker, a 20-year-old university student, was charged with welfare fraud after collecting both social assistance and student loans to help cover the costs of attending four years of university. Barker has no official criminal record, but has several friends who were also arrested for similar fraud-related offences. She was convicted of defrauding the government of $20 000 in benefits. She received eight months of house arrest.

Drug Trafficking

Martha Johnson had been dating Harrison Frank for 10 months when he convinced her to conceal two kilograms of cocaine in her luggage on a flight home from Jamaica. Martha had no prior criminal history before meeting Harrison. She told police that he had threatened to hurt her children if she did not comply. Martha Johnson was sentenced to three years in custody.

Familial Assault

Sarah Smith's involvement with the police commenced when she was 15. After a dispute with her mother, Sarah suddenly struck her on the side of the head with a book and then punched her in the chest. Later that day, she threatened to kill her mother in her sleep. Two days later, she attempted to steal money from her mother's wallet to buy marijuana. When her mother did not comply, Sarah removed a knife from the kitchen and began sharpening it. She then locked herself in the bathroom, and her mother notified police. Sarah was charged with assault, two counts of uttering threats, and attempted theft. She received six months closed custody and 18 months probation.

Domestic Homicide

Donna Brant was married to Harold Brant for 15 years. He repeatedly beat her and controlled every aspect of her life from where she worked to who she could socialize with. The police had been called to their home on several occasions as the neighbours frequently complained of excessive noise due to verbal and physical altercations between the couple. Neighbours also reported hearing Harold threatening to kill Donna on several occasions. One night, Donna went to her basement, unlocked her husband's gun case, and shot him to death while he slept. She told police her life had been in imminent danger and that the only way to ensure her survival was to kill her husband. She was convicted of second-degree murder with parole eligibility set at seven years.

Infanticide

Laura Jackson, age 19, was unwed when she gave birth to her first child. She suffered from a severe form of post-partum depression

Box 11.1   Continued

accompanied by hallucinations directing her to suffocate her newborn in order to cleanse his soul. She was convicted of infanticide after having intentionally placed a pillow over her son's mouth while he slept. Her family had tried to get her the help she needed, but to no avail. She received a sentence of two years less a day.

Box 11.2

Girls, Crime, and Violence: No Longer Sugar and Spice?

Teen [15-year-old girl] guilty of first-degree murder in death of Stefanie Rengel, 14 (CBC News 2009)

Medicine Hat man plotted with girlfriend [12 years old] to kill family: (CBC News 2008)

Girl violence increasing in 'lethality', experts say (Proudfoot 2009)

See Jane Hit: Why girls are growing more violent and what we can do about it (Gabarino 2006)

Headlines and book titles such as these suggest that girls are becoming more violent and that the nature of their violence is becoming increasingly lethal. But is this really the case? Let's take a closer look at the evidence and determine if girl violence is on the rise.

In 2008, the Canadian Centre for Justice Statistics (CCJS) published a report entitled "Female Offenders in Canada," authored by Rebecca Kong and Kathy AuCoin. The report highlighted that "[W]hile still quite low compared to male youth, the rate of serious violent crime among female youth has more than doubled since 1986 growing from 60 per 100,000 to 132 per 100,000 in 2005" (Kong and AuCoin 2008). Kong and AuCoin's definition of serious violent crime was restricted to serious violence—manslaughter, attempted murder, sexual assault, major assault, or unlawfully causing bodily harm; discharging a firearm with intent; abduction of a person under 14; and robbery. On the surface, the results suggest that the serious violent crime rate (as measured by the number of individuals per 100 000 charged by police) increased for both genders, but that the increase for youthful females—120 percent from 1986 to 2005—outpaced that for youthful males (84 percent from 1986 to 2005). Similar yet more pronounced findings have been reported in the United States (Synder and Sickmund 2006).

Kong and Aucoin's findings are reproduced below using two graphical illustrations. Figure 11.1 presents the serious violent charge rate for youthful females and Figure 11.2 presents the corresponding serious violent charge rate for youthful males.

Three findings are immediately apparent. First, the "surge" in violent crime occurred primarily during the late 1980s and early 1990s. Specifically, from 1986 to 1993, the serious violent charge rate for females went from 60 per 100 000 people to 134

Continued >

Box 11.2   Continued

per 100 000, representing a 123 percent increase. Similarly, the corresponding male rate went from 352 per 100 000 people to 709 per 100 000, representing a smaller but still substantial increase of 101 percent. Second, with the exception of a few "blips," the serious violent crime rate for both genders has essentially stayed the same since 1993 and has actually declined since 2002. Lastly, regardless of the year, males were always charged with committing substantially more violent crime than females (e.g., 132 per 100 000 females charged in 2005 versus 649 per 100 000 males). So are girls becoming more violent? It depends on the start point (e.g., 1986 versus 1993).

The observed increase in (female-perpetrated) serious violent crime evidenced in official police data does not emerge when unofficial crime statistics are examined. American researchers (i.e., Steffensmeier, Schwartz, Zhong, and Ackerman 2005) conducted a sophisticated analytic comparison of official police arrest data obtained from the Uniform Crime Reports (UCR), with unofficial crime data from the National Crime Victimization Survey (NCVS) from 1980 to 2003. As an aside, the NCVS is conducted annually and involves polling a large representative sample of American households about their experiences as victims of crime during the previous year, regardless of whether they had reported their experiences to the police. Steffensmeirer and colleagues reported that both the UCR and NCVS data revealed no increase in two of the most serious forms of violence—homicide and sexual assault. However, the UCR data did show a sharp increase in female-to-male arrests for criminal

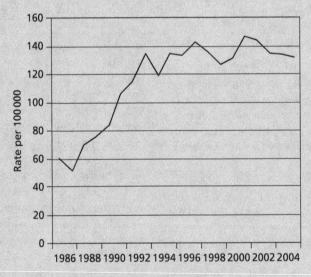

Figure 11.1 Serious Violent Offence Charge Rate for Female Youth Aged 12-17

Source: Adapted from Kong & AuCoin (2008)

Box 11.2 Continued

assault whereas the NCVS data did not. The authors argue that net-widening policy shifts such as zero tolerance policies in public schools and mandatory arrests for domestic violence have artificially increased the likelihood of females being arrested for criminal assault. Thus it is argued that females are now being arrested for crimes that they weren't arrested for in the past and that these crimes involve physical attacks and/or threats of a marginal nature—a situation more characteristic of female- than male-perpetrated assault. In sum, Steffenesmeier et al. and various other prominent researchers (e.g., Chesney-Lind and Irwin 2008; Chesney-Lind and Paramore 2001; Doob and Sprott 1998; Gaarder and Belknap 2004; Holsinger, Belknap, and Sutherland 1999) have convincingly argued that girls are not becoming more violent, but that changes in criminal justice practices and policies have artificially inflated the statistics.

Some researchers (e.g., Barron and Lacombe 2005; Luke 2008) have proposed the "moral panic hypothesis" as a means of explaining why society is seemingly so willing to believe that girls are becoming more violent. In brief, the hypothesis posits that rare yet highly sensationalized incidents of girl-perpetrated violence create panic or anxiety among the general populace. This panic leads to the belief that girls are "out of control" and need to be restrained using informal (e.g., suspensions for hurtful gossip at school) and formal mechanisms (e.g., more official policing). The moral panic hypothesis also argues that the underlying reason for mass societal anxiety is not because girls have become more violent, but because of the emergence of feminism: feminism has not only lead to greater equality in the workplace and increased "girl power," it has also eroded patriarchal norms and gender conformity, which in turn has allowed for the emergence of the "nasty girl."

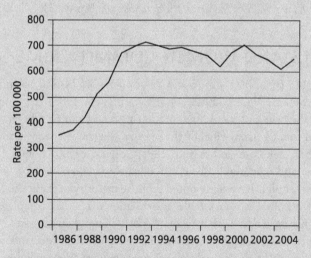

Figure 11.2 Serious Violent Offence Charge for Male Youth Aged 12-17

Source: Adapted from Kong & AuCoin (2008)

Researchers have also tried to understand if there are different reasons for the commission of non-violent crimes by males and females. In short, this body of literature suggests that women commit property crime out of economic necessity (e.g., to feed and clothe children) (Belknap 2001; Campbell 2002; Carlen 1988; Chesney-Lind 1986; Gilfus 1992; Hunnicutt and Broidy 2004), and men commit property crime as a means of adventure and status enhancement (Campbell 2002). In sum, it would seem that there are both similarities and differences between males and females in the realm of offence gestalts and that women's violence appears to be more relational—directed against intimate partners.

RESEARCHING FEMALE OFFENDERS
To Quantify or Qualify?

How do researchers study female offenders? In brief, there are two approaches: qualitative, which involves the analysis of words; and quantitative, which involves the analysis of numbers. For example, feminist pathways researchers often use qualitative interview techniques with incarcerated girls/women or self-identified prostitutes to understand female criminality. In doing so, they allow girls and women to tell their stories in their own voices. Conversely, applied correctional feminist researchers have relied on quantitative techniques such as meta-analyses and recidivism studies that do not necessarily involve interviews with girls and/or women. Historically, these approaches have yielded different results. Contemporary thinking asserts that researchers should incorporate elements of both research strategies, an approach used by Dr. Kelley Blanchette, a prominent researcher in the field of women's corrections (see Box 11.3).

WHY GIRLS AND WOMEN COMMIT CRIME

FEMINIST CRITIQUES (E.G., BELKNAP 2001; COVINGTON AND BLOOM 2003; FEINMAN 1986; Leonard 1982; Morris 1987; Naffine 1987; Smart 1976; 1982) have underscored two crucial flaws in the criminological literature. First, some feminist scholars have criticized early theoretical paradigms, specifically the pre-sociological era of criminological thought (e.g., Freud 1953; Lombroso and Ferrero 1895; Pollack 1950; Thomas 1923), for their inherent sexism and immutable focus on female sexuality, biology, and psychology. Second, feminist scholars have aptly noted that the majority of traditional criminological explanations of criminal conduct have either ignored females completely or assumed generalizability across gender without female-specific empirical support.

As a result, female-centred theories have emerged in which gender is afforded preeminent status. Moreover, most female-centred theories posit that the onset, maintenance, and eventual desistence of female criminal conduct are different from that of their male counterparts (Steffensmeier and Allan 1996).

Box 11.3

Canadian Researcher Profile: Dr. Kelley Blanchette

Dr. Kelley Blanchette is an internationally recognized expert in the study of women offenders. She received her Ph.D. in applied forensic psychology from Carleton University in Ottawa in January 2005. Interestingly, Dr. Blanchette's supervisor was Dr. Ralph Serin—the first author of this textbook. Her dissertation involved the development and field testing of a gender-informed security classification scale for women offenders. The Correctional Service of Canada (CSC) implemented this tool—the Security Reclassification Scale for Women (SRSW)—in 2005, and it has been employed ever since to help staff decide whether a woman should be moved up or down a security classification level (e.g., from medium to minimum security).

Before commencing her career with CSC in 1993, Dr. Blanchette worked in the community for six years at the Ottawa

Detoxification Centre. She supervised the assessment and treatment referral process for men and women with alcohol and drug addictions. Dr. Blanchette began her career at CSC in 1993 as a research assistant and gradually worked her way up to Director of Women Offender Research in 2000. One of her most recent and notable contributions was the development of the Women's Violence Prevention Program in 2007.

Dr. Blanchette has published extensively in peer-reviewed and government journals. Her research has addressed a multitude of areas germane to women offenders, spanning the fields of risk assessment, security classification, and program development and evaluation. In 2007, she was the co-winner of the Significant Contribution Award, awarded by the Criminal Justice Section of the Canadian Psychological Association, for her book *The Assessment and Treatment of Women Offenders: An Integrative Perspective*.

During her career, Dr. Blanchette was married and had two boys (ages seven and ten). She somehow finds time to teach courses at Carleton such as Introduction to Forensic Psychology, train for and run half marathons, attend book club meetings with friends, and captain a recreational volleyball team.

Recently, Dr. Blanchette's career has taken a directional shift. She is currently Director General of the Women Offender Sector at CSC. For the moment, Dr. Blanchette has moved from researcher to correctional administrator, where she provides advice and leadership in regards to the development

Continued >

Box 11.3 Continued

and implementation of policy and program- ming for the approximately 1000 women offenders currently under CSC's jurisdiction. Dr. Blanchette will continue to have a profound effect on how Canada deals with federally sentenced women.

Feminist Pathways Research

A body of research collectively known as *feminist pathways research* (Belknap 2007) emerged in the 1970s to explain female crime. Feminist pathways researchers use one-time qualitative interview techniques with incarcerated girls/women or self-identified prostitutes to ascertain pathways to delinquency. To date, 20 or more feminist pathways studies have concluded that aversive family environments (e.g., abuse) propel girls from homes and schools into the streets. This in turn leads to further victimization in the form of prostitution and poor coping strategies such as drug use and "criminalized" survival strategies, including robbery, fraud, and drug trafficking (Bloom, Owen, Rosenbaum, and Deschenes 2003; Chesney-Lind and Rodriguez 1983; Daly 1992; 1994; Gilfus 1992; Kruttschnitt 1996; Miller 1986; Owen 1998; Richie 1996; Silbert and Pines 1981; Simkins and Katz 2002). While this research underscores the role of childhood abuse/ trauma, some feminist pathways researchers also highlight factors such as poor parental supervision, parental psychopathology (e.g., parental criminality, substance abuse), and economic marginalization (e.g., Arnold 1990; James and Meyerding 1977).

Although feminist pathways researchers have discovered much about female criminality, our understanding remains incomplete. Notwithstanding one British study (Carlen 1988) and a few Canadian studies (Fox and Sugar 1990; Shaw 1991), most feminist pathways research has been conducted on American samples and has used qualitative techniques. Researchers have not disaggregated data by age (girls versus women), thereby potentially masking potential developmental differences. Male comparison groups have also been noticeably absent, a methodological prerequisite in the quest for **gender specificity**. As others have noted (Blanchette and Brown 2006; Moretti, Odgers, and Jackson 2004; Odgers et al. 2007), a final limitation of the research is its emphasis of a unidimensional pathway to crime—the criminalized survivor pathway (see Daly 1992; Miller 1986 for exceptions)— that denies female heterogeneity in the form of multiple female offender pathways.

Integrated Liberation and Economic Marginalization Theory

Hunnicutt and Broidy (2004) assert that changing gender roles initially brought on by the women's liberation movement have unintentionally increased the "economically marginal roles" of women by pushing them farther into the economic margins of society. Specifically, the women's movement has perpetuated the belief that women are better off financially, a situation that has caused society to overlook evidence to the contrary. Moreover, the authors argue that divorce, a consequence of liberation, has increased the economic instability of women because there are now more single female–headed households with dependent children. The women's movement has also increased female expectations in regards to status and wealth such that women may be more likely to adopt illegitimate means to achieve wealth and power.

Hunnicutt and Broidy directly tested the theory using aggregate data pooled across 10 countries. Based on a time series analysis that employed aggregate level independent variables (e.g., the number of divorces per 100 000 married persons) and an aggregate level dependent variable (crime rate per 100 000), they concluded that "liberation does indeed stimulate crime among women, to the extent that changing roles and expectations of gender equality further marginalize women" (2004: 150). However, the extent to which this finding may be explained by other individual level factors remains unknown. Future research questions must ask why all divorced mothers living in poverty don't resort to crime. Such studies are particularly important because they may reveal naturally occurring factors that protect women from a life of crime, which could be used to inform women-centred intervention strategies.

Personal, Interpersonal, and Community-Reinforcement (PIC–R) Theory

Recall from Chapter 3 that the PIC–R theory (Andrews and Bonta 2006) is a multidisciplinary perspective that integrates biological, sociological, cultural, familial, interpersonal, personal, and situational variables. Grounded heavily in social learning and self-control theory, PIC–R posits that individuals commit crime when the rewards for doing so exceed the costs. Various factors influence the balance of rewards and costs, ranging from highly proximal factors located in the immediate situation (e.g., opportunity) to more distally orientated factors (e.g., political/economic/cultural influences). The theory categorizes these factors along four dimensions: situational, personal, interpersonal, and community. Situational factors include opportunities/temptations, stressors (e.g., negative affect), facilitators (e.g., psychotic state), and disinhibitors (e.g., substance abuse), and personal factors include antisocial cognitions, history of antisocial behaviour, antisocial personality, and biological factors. Interpersonal factors include variables such as antisocial associates and family, and the community dimension encompasses factors such as neighbourhood. Although each category differs as a function of temporal proximity to the immediate situation, each influences the probability that an individual will find him- or herself in a situation conducive to committing crime. Additionally, each category also determines whether an individual will develop an internal dialogue consistent with definitions favourable of criminal conduct (e.g., rewards exceed the costs) and consequently commit the criminal act.

PIC–R concurs with sociological perspectives that suggest that broad-based societal/ structural factors are important, but only to the extent that they control the distribution of rewards and costs within a social system. Further, the theory is primarily concerned with explaining individual differences in criminal conduct. With this in mind, Andrews and Bonta (2006) identified which risk factors (derived from the empirical evidence) account for the greatest individual variation in criminal conduct.

Each risk factor has been assigned to one of three predictive accuracy levels. These **risk factors** were introduced in Chapter 1. The first and most powerful set includes: 1) antisocial cognitions (attitudes, beliefs, values that support criminal conduct); 2) antisocial associates; 3) a history of antisocial behaviour; and 4) antisocial personality (including indicators such as restless energy, adventuresomeness, impulsiveness, poor problem-solving skills, hostility, and callousness). Risk factors in the middle range include: 1) substance abuse; 2) marital/family factors; 3) poor school/employment achievement; and 4) inadequate leisure/recreation. Risk factors in the low range of predictive validity include: 1) lower-class origins; 2) low verbal intelligence; and 3) personal distress.

PIC–R is presented as a general theory that can account for individual differences in criminal conduct irrespective of gender, class, or ethnic origin. While gender is classified as a distal, personal variable that shapes both the person and the immediate situation, it is not central to the model.

FACTORS ASSOCIATED WITH FEMALE OFFENDING

SO FAR WE HAVE DESCRIBED THE PREVALENCE AND NATURE OF FEMALE CRIMINAL CONDUCT and highlighted contemporary theories used to explain this behaviour. In this section, we focus more specifically on the various risk factors that have been proposed as particularly salient to female criminal conduct. In essence, we explore the empirical evidence associated with many of the factors linked to the various theories.

Intrapersonal Factors

Criminal History Criminal history is one of the strongest predictors of future criminal behaviour. Moreover, research indicates that individuals who 1) demonstrate general behavioural problems from an early age (e.g., truancy/expulsion from school, aggressive behaviour at home and/or school, stealing from parents), 2) commit crime frequently, and 3) evidence criminal versatility (i.e., commit a range of different crimes) are substantially more likely to commit future crime (Andrews and Bonta 2006; Gendreau, Goggin, and Smith 2002; Moffitt 1993).

Until recently, few researchers asked whether criminal history was an equally important predictor for female offenders. We know that female offenders are on average lower risk than their male counterparts (e.g., they have less extensive criminal histories, are less likely to criminally reoffend) (Brown and Motiuk 2005; Kong and Aucoin 2008; Public Safety Canada 2007). However, this does not mean that criminal history is not predictive for females. The limited evidence suggests that criminal history variables predict equally well for both genders (Hubbard and Pratt 2002; Green and Campbell 2006). More research is needed, particularly to address feminist concerns that a *"high risk"* female offender should not be equated with a "*high risk*" male offender, in part because females are less likely to reoffend violently.

Antisocial Personality and Impulsivity   The construct of antisocial personality and impulsivity is multifaceted and complex. Some researchers equate it with psychopathy as measured by the Hare Psychopathy Checklist–Revised (PCL–R; Hare 2003). Others argue that the construct should be operationalized more broadly (e.g., Andrews and Bonta 2006). Regardless, it is clear that psychopathy as measured by the PCL–R is a robust predictor of both general and violent recidivism among male offenders. In general, the research to date is mixed regarding construct validity and its ability to predict recidivism among female offenders (Blanchette and Brown 2006). However, a recent study did find that the PCL–R was predictive of violent recidivism in women offenders (Coid et al. 2009). If we adopt Gottfredson and Hirschi's (1990) definition of antisocial personality— low self-control: the tendency to pursue short-term, immediate gratification while ignoring long-term consequences—then the evidence suggests that antisociality is predictive of crime in both genders (Pratt and Cullen 2000). Despite evidence in favour of self-control theory, feminist scholars criticize it for failing to assign a pre-eminent role to gender (e.g., Miller and Burack 1993).

Criminal Attitudes   Criminal attitudes and/or antisocial cognitions are considered to be one of the "Central Eight" (Andrews and Bonta 2006) predictors of crime. However, this conclusion is based primarily on male or predominantly male samples. Research suggests that adult male offenders are more likely than their female counterparts to be identified as having a need in this domain (30 percent versus 14 percent) (Boe, Nafekh, Vuong, Sinclair, and Cousineau 2003). While some studies propose that the global construct of criminal attitudes predicts crime equally well in both genders (Brown and Motiuk 2005; Green and Campbell 2006), recent research suggests that criminal attitudes may not be as strong a predictor of criminal recidivism among females (Greiner, Brown, and Jones 2009). This area needs further investigation.

Correctional programs that target criminal attitudes and cognitions in samples of female offenders have been associated with moderate reductions in criminal recidivism (Dowdens and Andrews 1999). When Brown and Motiuk disaggregated the global construct of criminal attitudes, several gender differences emerged. Women who indicated that "marital/family holds no value" were more likely to recidivate than women who believed that marriage and family do have value. This indicator evidenced no relationship with recidivism for men. Research that continues to dissect the construct of criminal attitudes may find important gender differences.

Poor Self-Efficacy/Poor Self-Esteem/Dis-Empowerment   The vast majority of applied correctional feminists have argued that low self-esteem and/or the related construct of self-efficacy—belief in one's own ability to accomplish a specific objective (e.g., gain new employment skills)—is an important risk and/or need factor to consider when working with girls and women (Bloom, Owen, and Covington 2003; Koons, Burrow, Morash, and Bynum 1997). In contrast, self-esteem is not risk deemed a risk factor for males, or for offenders in general (Andrews and Bonta 2006). However, the related construct of targeted self-efficacy (e.g., increasing an offender's belief that they can acquire new prosocial skills through positive reinforcement and behavioural rehearsal) is a risk factor (Gendreau, French, and Gionet 2004). Quantitative research suggests that interventions that target self-esteem or those that are purely empowerment-based have no impact on reductions in recidivism (Dowden and Andrews 1999; Dowden 2005). Qualitative evaluations also suggest, however, that programs that enhance empowerment and/or self-esteem are important treatment targets for women (Leeder 2004). Clearly, more research is needed in this area.

Poor Mental Health While most researchers agree that mental health issues impact male and female offenders, there is some debate about how they should be addressed. Additionally, it is clear that girls and women are not only more likely to experience certain types of mental health problems (e.g., depression, self-injurious behaviour, suicide attempts, borderline personality), they are more likely to experience co-morbid mental health problems (e.g., depression and borderline personality disorder) than their male counterparts (Blanchette and Brown 2006; Bloom et al. 2003; Johnson 2006).

Traditionally, mental health variables have been conceptualized as responsivity factors—factors that can impede treatment rather than as risk factors and/or criminogenic needs (Andrews and Bonta 2006). However, Van Voorhis, Salisbury, Wright, and Bauman (2008) found that depression and anxiety are predictive of crime in women, and Green and Campbell (2006) reported that mental health was a weak predictor of recidivism in both youthful males and females. Again, more research is needed to clarify how mental health factors impact female offending.

Substance Abuse Most researchers agree that substance abuse is a risk factor for all offenders—men, women, girls, and boys. Approximately 40 to 60 percent of women offenders have significant substance abuse problems (Boe et al. 2003; Brown and Motiuk 2005). Moreover, two meta-analyses have concluded that substance abuse predicts crime in both males and females (Dowden and Brown 2002; Green and Campbell 2006). Dowden and Brown's (2002) meta-analytic review revealed that, on average, a range of substance abuse risk factors (e.g., alcohol or drug problems, parental substance abuse) predicted future crime to the same degree in male (Mz^+—the average weighted effect size was .14, total $N = 81,795$) and female offenders (Mz^+—the average weighted effect size was .10, total $N = 2,783$). Notably, the confidence intervals corresponding to each effect size did not overlap; we can conclude that the observed effect of .14 was no different (statistically) from the effect of .10.

Although substance abuse is relevant for both genders, irrespective of age, some gender differences have been noted. Dowden and Brown observed that the predictive strength of having a parent who abused substances was stronger for females ($Mz^+ = .20$) than males ($Mz+ = .09$). Similarly, research suggests that women maintain their drug use as a coping mechanism, whereas men do so because of peer pressure or pleasure (Inciardi,

Lockwood, and Pottieger 1993). There is also some evidence that a woman's pathway to substance abuse differs from that of a man. Specifically, her substance abuse is likely to have already started before she commits any crime. In contrast, men are more likely to already be actively engaged in a criminal lifestyle before developing substance abuse problems (Johnson 2006).

Interpersonal Factors

Dysfunctional Family History Researchers agree that an array of negative family background factors play a significant role in the onset and maintenance of crime in both genders. These factors include poor parental supervision, inconsistent or inappropriate use of discipline, parental substance abuse, and parental criminality (Piquero 2008; Thornberry and Krohn 2003). However, some individuals speculate that girls may be more sensitive to these factors in the sense that perhaps only one or two negative family factors would place a youthful female at risk for future crime whereas at least three or four negative family factors would be needed to place a youthful male at the same risk level (Hipwell and Loeber 2006). This idea is elaborated further below in the section titled "Criticisms of Gender-Neutral Instruments." Dowden and Andrew's (1999) meta-analytic review of treatment programs targeting female offenders revealed that programs targeting family process variables yielded the largest reductions in recidivism (as did programs that targeted antisocial cognition). It is clear that family functioning is an important risk factor for youthful females.

Traumatic Life Experiences Research clearly indicates that girls and women are substantially more likely than men to have experienced some form of childhood or adulthood trauma in the form of physical, sexual, or emotional abuse (23 to 85 percent for females; 6 to 14 percent for males) (Bloom et al. 2003; Harlow 1999; Task Force Report 1990). Childhood abuse may be a **female-salient predictor** of future adolescent delinquency (Green and Campbell 2006; Hubbard and Pratt 2002) and prison misbehaviour among women (Van Voorhis et al. 2008). However, other studies (e.g., Andrews, Bonta, Wormith, Guzzo, and Brews 2008; Daigle, Cullen, and Wright 2007; Lowenkamp, Holsinger, and Latessa 2001) have shown that abuse is neither a female-specific nor female-salient risk factor and, more importantly, that childhood abuse may not actually exert its predictive effect until adulthood (Cernkovich, Lanctôt, and Giordano 2008). Although the exact relationship between trauma and crime remains largely unknown, it is clear that girls and women are more likely to have been traumatized, and, at a minimum, trauma should be considered as a responsivity factor for female offenders.

Negative Relationships with Friends and Acquaintances Although few studies have directly assessed the predictive strength of criminal peers in girls and women, existing research suggests it is an equally important predictor in both genders irrespective of age (Brown and Motiuk 2008; Hubbard and Pratt 2002) and that criminal peers are an important treatment target for female offenders (Dowden and Andrews 1999). Moreover, women offenders are almost as likely to be identified as having a need in this area (26 to 52 percent) as men offenders (35 to 61 percent) (Brown and Motiuk 2005).

Negative Relationships with Intimate Partners A number of researchers have identified dysfunctional and negative relationships with intimate partners as problematic for women and girls. Several theorists argue that unhealthy attachments are particularly salient for girls and women (Bloom et al. 2003). Although further empirical validation is required, Benda's (2005) longitudinal study that examined a large number of boot-camp graduates in the United States revealed that women were differentially more negatively impacted by negative romantic partners than their male counterparts.

Community-Wide/Structural Factors

Poor School Performance/Employment Difficulties Applied correctional feminists and gender neutral correctional researchers agree that inadequate schooling and employment difficulties are risk factors for both genders (Andrews and Bonta 2006; Bloom et al. 2003). Moreover, both genders appear to be lacking in education (52.6 percent of men offenders and 42.4 percent of women offenders have not completed Grade 10), and both genders evidence employment instability to the same degree (62.3 percent of men offenders; 54.5 percent of women offenders) (Brown and Motiuk 2005). There is some evidence that employment training opportunities are particularly beneficial to women offenders. Brown and Motiuk (2008) reported that while having participated in employment training programs in the past was a strong protective factor for women offenders upon release from prison, it had no protective influence for male offenders.

Poor Community Functioning Community functioning is a multidimensional construct that encompasses accommodation instability, criminogenic neighbourhoods, and poor use of leisure time. Several correctional feminist scholars have identified poor and unsafe housing as another risk factor for women (Bloom et al. 2003). Brown and Motiuk (2005) reported that 54 percent of women identified as having a considerable need in this domain were re-admitted to prison over a one-year period versus only 17 percent of women who were identified as having an asset in this domain. However, similar readmission rates were also reported for their male offenders (23.8 percent rated "asset" returned to custody versus 55.9 percent rated "considerable need for improvement"). It would appear that community functioning is equally important for both genders; however, for women, the importance of unsafe housing merits inclusion.

Economic Marginalization and Patriarchy There is evidence that economic hardship may be a genuine female salient risk factor (Andrews et al. 2008; Brown and

Motiuk 2008; Farrington and Painter 2004; Holtfreter, Reisig and Morash 2004; Hunnicutt and Broidy 2004). A recent quantitative analysis conducted at the individual level demonstrated that poverty was related to self-reported re-arrest rates in a sample of female offenders (n = 134) in the State of Oregon (Holtfreter et al. 2004). Using a methodologically rigorous design, Farrington and Painter (2004) reported that poverty indicators (e.g., low social class, low family income, poor housing) evidenced stronger predictive associations with criminal behaviour among a sample of sisters (n = 519) compared to their brothers (n= 494).

Assessing whether patriarchy—a social structure that values males over females and ultimately results in the oppression of girls and women—is directly related to crime is difficult. While some theorists argue that females internalize feelings of powerlessness and oppression that then lead to crime, others believe the general economic marginalization and oppression of females—via childhood abuse, domestic violence, and general inequality—are what force women and girls into crime (see Blanchette and Brown 2006 for a review).

Summary

Narrative (Blanchette and Brown 2006; Bryne and Howells 2002; Hollin and Palmer 2006; Hubbard and Matthews 2008; Immarigeon 2006; Sorbello, Eccleston, Ward, and Jones 2002) and meta-analytic reviews have concluded that the correlates and/or predictors of female juvenile delinquency (Green and Campbell 2006; Hubbard and Pratt 2002; Simourd and Andrews 1994) and adult female crime (Andrews et al. 2008; Lowenkamp, Smith, Latessa, and Cullen 2009) are similar across gender. However, notable differences are beginning to emerge, now that we are looking for them!

CLASSIFICATION AND RISK ASSESSMENT
Approaches

Predictions are made every day about whether someone will succeed in university, recover from depression, excel at work, violate rules while incarcerated, or commit a new crime upon release from prison. Three broad approaches have been used to make predictions about future crime committed inside or outside prison: 1) professional/clinical judgment; 2) structured professional judgment (SPJ); and 3) mathematical or statistically-based approaches (also discussed in Chapters 4 and 7).

Decision makers who use professional judgment rely on their clinical expertise and professional discretion rather than an instrument to render decisions. Structured professional judgment methods tell decision makers which factors should be considered but still allow them to decide how those various factors should be combined and weighted to render a final classification decision (e.g., low, medium, or high risk). Mathematical and statistical approaches involve the use of instruments that not only predict exactly which risk factors a decision maker must use, but also how these factors should be weighted and combined. Sometimes these approaches are called mechanical or actuarial methods. Each of the approaches results in a classification decision such as a prison security level or an estimate of likelihood of recidivism.

Gender-Neutral Risk-Assessment Instruments

We use the term **gender-neutral** to describe risk-assessment devices (including those that use math or statistics to generate recidivism probabilities and those that rely on structured professional judgment to generate indices of recidivism likelihood) that were originally crafted using samples comprised predominantly of male offenders and based on gender-neutral theories of crime but that are used on female offenders. Critics argue that "gender neutral" means "inherently male" and is hence biased against females. Defenders respond that gender neutral means "it happens to work well with males and females." We will review what the critics have to say momentarily.

Two of the most well-known and most researched risk-assessment tools are the Level of Service/Case Management Inventory (LS/CMI) (Andrews, Bonta, and Wormith 2004), used to assess adult offenders, and the Youth Level of Service/Case Management Inventory (YLS/CMI) (Hoge and Andrews 2003), used to assess youthful offenders. The LS/CMI and YS/LCI are risk/need-assessment protocols that measure eight risk factor domains: offence history, family circumstances or parenting, education or employment, peer relationships, substance abuse, leisure or recreation, personality or behaviour, and responsivity.

Table 11.1 illustrates the results of two recent meta-analytic reviews that examined the predictive ability of the Level of Service Inventory and its predecessors for males and females separately. Schwalbe (2008) focused specifically on the youth version, and Lowenkamp, Smith, Latessa, and Cullen (2009) focused on the adult version. Using the data presented in the first row (i.e., Schwalbe—girls), the results can be interpreted as follows. Four different correlation coefficients (i.e., see the column labelled "Number of Effect Sizes") were combined based on a total sample of 572 youthful female participants (i.e., see column labelled "Number of Participants") that yielded an average effect size of .35 (i.e., see column labelled "r with General Recidivism"). In this example, the 95 percent confidence interval ranged from .21 to .49. A 95 percent confidence interval simply means that we can be 95 percent sure (or confident) that the true average r value (or average effect size) ranges from .21 and .49. Because the confidence interval does not contain zero, we can safely conclude that the average r of .35 is statistically significant at the .05 level.

There are two important conclusions to take away from Table 11.1. First, although female-centred research is growing, there haven't been many studies devoted exclusively to female offenders, especially youthful females. In the case of girls, while four effect sizes may seem like a lot, it is important to realize that an earlier meta-analysis examining the predictive validity of the LS/CMI and its various predecessors (e.g., the Level of

Table 11.1 Level of Service (LS) and Youth Level of Service (YLS)/Case Management Inventory (CMI): The Predictive Meta-Analytic Evidence for Males and Females

Meta-Analysis	No. of Effect Sizes	No. of Participants	Average *r* with General Recidivism	95% Confidence Intervals
Schwalbe (2008)				
Girls	4	572	.35	.21–.49
Boys	5	2010	.31	Not reported
Lowenkamp, Smith, Latessa, and Cullen (2009)				
All women	27	14 737	.35	.34–.37
Men versus women[a]				
Men	16	9250	.27	.25–.29
Women	16	33 616	.26	.24–.26

Note: [a]Lowenkamp et al. also calculated the average *r* for a subset of studies that specifically collected data on both genders within the same study. It is argued that these approaches are methodologically more rigorous than studies based exclusively on one gender or the other.
Source: Schwalbe (2008) and Smith, Culllen, and Latessa (2009)

Supervision Inventory–Revised; Andrews and Bonta 1995) for male offenders included 30 effect sizes based on 5846 offenders (Gendreau, Goggin, and Smith 2002). Second, the average effect sizes for both girls and women are comparable to what has been obtained for males, as evidenced in these meta-analyses and also as reported by Gendreau et al., who determined an unweighted effect size of .37 for general recidivism for male offenders. If we use predictive accuracy as our benchmark for considering whether inherently gender-neutral tools such as the LS/CMI can be used with females, the answer appears to be yes.

Criticisms of Gender-Neutral Instruments

One specific area that requires more attention is the extent to which the gendered pathway to crime impacts the validity of risk-assessment devices. Critics assert that tools such as the Level of Supervision Inventory–Revised (LSI–R, Andrews and Bonta 1995; the predecessor to the LS/CMI) are invalid for females primarily because they fail to take the hypothesized gendered pathway to crime into account (Covington 2003; Holtfreter and Morash 2003; see Hannah-Moffat 2004; Hardyman and Van Voorhis 2004; Holtfreter and Cupp 2007; Kendall 2004; and Maidment 2006 for additional criticisms). Reisig, Holtfreter and Morash (2006) directly tested this concern by examining the predictive validity of the LSI–R in a sample of 235 American women offenders whom the researchers qualitatively classified into three groups: economically-motivated/male typical, gendered pathway, and unclassifiable. In sum, the LSI-R predicted recidivism for the "economically motivated" and "unclassifiable" group but not for the "gendered pathways" group.

It has also been argued that certain risk factors, while relevant to both genders, may be more important for females. There is ample evidence that family dysfunction measured in a variety of ways such as poor parental supervision, inappropriate and inconsistent use of discipline, and abuse contribute to criminal conduct in both genders (Green and Campbell 2006; Hubbard and Pratt 2002), but some researchers contend that girls have a lower risk threshold in that they are more vulnerable to family dysfunction. For example, let's assume we have a scale that measures family dysfunction, where a score of 1 represents no dysfunction and 10 represents extreme dysfunction. Now consider two youths—one female and one male—who both receive a score of 4 on this measure. Now, if the risk threshold hypothesis is correct, the female youth (scored 4) would be considered at risk for future delinquency whereas her male counterpart (who also scored 4) would not. The male youth might hypothetically need to reach a higher threshold (such as a score of 6) before negative family dysfunction would elevate his risk level. The evidence for this hypothesis is sparse and requires further validation (Hipwell and Loeber 2006). A reverse effect has been proposed in regards to criminal associates. It is hypothesized that the threshold is considerably less for boys than girls because girls have an internal protective mechanism (Mears, Ploeger, and Warr 1998).

Brown and Motiuk (2008) found that close to 45 percent of the yes/no risk indicators (e.g., drinks alcohol to excess, has impulsivity problems) that are part of the Correctional Service of Canada's standardized intake assessment protocol were identified as either female-specific (predicted for women but not men) or female-salient (predicted for men and women but the magnitude of prediction was stronger for women). A number of male-specific and male-salient risk factors have also been identified. Benda (2005) also found evidence for gender specificity and salience. He reported that while being married was protective for men in that it reduced their chances of future reoffending, it was a risk factor for women. Thus there is some evidence to support the critics' claims.

Gender-Informed Risk Instrument

In response to criticisms, risk-assessment tools built from the ground up for girls and/or women are slowly starting to emerge. Van Voorhis and colleagues (2008) developed a combined interview and self-report survey specifically for use with women in prisons or in the community. To date, the results are promising, with the scale evidencing acceptable predictive accuracy rates (e.g., Area under the Curve (AUC) = .72). Canadian researchers have developed two risk/need measures: one for girls—the Youth Assessment Screening Inventory for Girls (YASI-G) (Orbis Partners 2007a), and one for women—the Service Planning Inventory for Women (SPIN) (Orbis Partners

2007b). However, predictive validity indices have yet to be published for these instruments.

Blanchette and Taylor (2007) developed a gender-informed security reclassification tool specifically for **federally sentenced women** in Canada. This measure, the Security Reclassification Scale for Women (SRSW), is an actuarial tool designed to identify the most appropriate classification level for women that ensures placement in the least restrictive level of custody. This tool was designed with an initial pool of variables that were hypothesized to be salient for women, including child custody issues, family factors, self-injurious behaviour, and mental health factors. Additional variables included historical risk factors, program progress, motivation, and recent institutional behaviour.

The resultant SRSW has a range of 30, with higher scores suggesting higher security levels. It consists of nine items with reasonable reliability (alpha = .69) (see Table 11.2). Part of the validation process involved comparing the SRSW to clinical judgment (i.e., what security level correctional workers would place a woman at based on structured professional judgment). The SRSW placed fewer women in maximum security and more women in minimum security than the professional judgment method. These findings demonstrate that this actuarial tool does not "over-classify" women relative to clinical judgment (i.e., it does not place more women at a higher security level than the professional judgment method). In fact, the SRSW does just the opposite—it "under-classifies" women by putting more in lower security settings when compared to the clinical judgment method.

Predictive accuracy rates for the raw SRSW score were high (AUC = .75) for the prediction of any institutional misconduct versus the clinical judgment method (AUC = .69). Upon revalidation, the tool demonstrates an acceptable AUC (.69) for

Table 11.2 Security Reclassification Scale for Women

Security Reclassification Items

1. Correctional plan progress/motivation
2. Serious disciplinary convictions
3. Recorded incidents during review
4. Unlawfully at large from an unescorted temporary absence/work release or community supervision
5. Custody rating scale incident history
6. Pay grade
7. Segregation: danger to other during review
8. Number of successful ETAs during review
9. Regular prosocial family contact

Source: Blanchette and Taylor (2007)

the prediction of any institutional misconduct. The revalidation study again illustrated that professional decision making actually works against women via over-classification (Gobèil and Blanchette 2007). See Box 11.4 for further detail.

TREATMENT AND MANAGEMENT

Approaches

While females constitute a small proportion of the incarcerated population (less than 6 percent) relative to males, evidence indicates that this proportion is growing and, in some countries, growing at a faster pace than that for males (Kong and AuCoin

---

Box 11.4

Legal, Professional, and Ethical Issues: Are Women Being Over-Classified?

Classification instruments serve multiple functions. Not only do they assist correctional decision makers in making security-level placements, they also assign offenders to risk probability levels. The outcome of these decisions can profoundly impact a person in terms of freedom of movement while in prison and when they are released. A number of feminist researchers have argued that classification and/or risk tools routinely applied to girls and women are inherently biased against females because they were originally developed on males (Brennan 1998; Farr 2000; Hardyman 2001; Hardyman and Van Voorhis 2004). The primary argument against these tools is that they over-classify for two primary reasons: 1) a high-risk female has a lower probability of recidivating (in general) compared to her high-risk male counterpart; and 2) a high-risk female is not the same as a high-risk male because she is substantially less likely to commit serious violent recidivism.

Evidence examining the over-classification hypothesis is inconclusive. Some research suggests that actuarial tools actually generate more liberal decisions in the sense that they are more favourable toward the offender (Austin 1983; Blanchette and Taylor 2006). However, given that we know girls and women rarely commit violence, the second component of the over-classification argument holds merit. More research is needed and developers of tools such as the LS/CMI are diligently investigating the issue (Andrews, personal communication, 2009). While it may appear that the solution is simple—adjust the cut-off scores such that a woman would require a much higher score than a man to be considered "high risk"—there may be serious ramifications that negatively impact subgroups of females such as Aboriginal women. Aboriginal offenders demonstrate higher rates of violence and recidivism relative to their non-Aboriginal counterparts (see Chapter 12). While the critics have raised important issues, potential solutions will require careful thought prior to implementation.

2008; Lemgruber 2001). In Canada between 1981 and 2002, the incarceration rate for federally sentenced women increased at a faster pace relative to the federal male incarceration rate: 27.2 percent, from 2.2 per 100 000 to 2.8 per 100 000. Although the male incarceration rate also increased during this time (96 per 100 000 to 110 per 100 000), the relative increase was markedly less (14.5 percent) (Sinclair and Boe 2002). Growth in the incarcerated female population coupled with feminist advocacy has necessitated the development of **gender-responsive** services or, at the very least, closer scrutiny of existing services.

Until recently, most correctional treatment approaches for girls and women essentially mirrored male services or conversely promoted gender-stereotypes (e.g., hairdressing school) (Hannah-Moffat 2004). This has changed dramatically in both Canada and the United States (see Bloom, Owen, and Covington 2003 for the American approach). In 1990, a Canadian Task Force Report titled "Creating Choices: Report on the Task Force on Federally Sentenced Women" generated five basic principles that should guide programming for women: empowerment, meaningful and responsible choices, respect and dignity, supportive environment, and shared responsibility (see Box 11.5 for a detailed description). These principles remain in effect and continue to guide CSC. However, it is important to note that Canada's approach to corrections has not always been progressive and that we have advanced considerably since the first federal prison for women opened its doors in 1934 (see Box 11.6).

Box 11.5

Correctional Service of Canada's Approach to Women Offenders: Key Principles

Empowerment refers to the process of enhancing women's self-esteem and internal locus of control (the belief that they have the power and control to direct their own lives) such that they are able to gain insight into their personal situations and identify their strengths. In addition, they are supported and challenged to take positive action to gain greater control of their lives. This principle emerged from the recognition that women in society—particularly incarcerated women—have been dis-empowered as a consequence of several factors such as poverty, family violence, and racism.

Meaningful and responsible choices provide women with options that allow them to make responsible choices that relate to their needs, past experiences, culture, values, spirituality, abilities, and skills. Unfortunately, a history of dependence (e.g., alcohol or drugs, men, financial assistance) has denied many women this opportunity. It is further argued that it is only through the provision of meaningful and responsible choices that women will take control of their lives and

Continued >

Box 11.5   Continued

thus increase self-esteem and become empowered.

Respect and dignity refer to the reciprocal respect that is needed between offenders, between staff, and between staff and offenders. Moreover, the principle acknowledges that respectful treatment naturally addresses unique cultural, religious, or spiritual needs of minority groups in a holistic manner.

Supportive environment reflects the need to provide services within a positive milieu. Environmental aspects include both physical elements (e.g., clean air, access to fresh air, light, adequate nutrition) and broader interpersonal and spiritual aspects (e.g., positive

social interactions characterized by mutual respect, opportunities to engage in spiritual and culturally relevant practices). Otherwise, the goals of empowerment, self-esteem enhancement, spiritual and personal development, and physical and psychological well-being will not be realized.

Shared responsibility refers to the suggestion that all levels of government, corrections, volunteer organizations, businesses, private sector services, and the community have a role to play in the development of support systems and continuity of service for federally sentenced women.

Source: Blanchette and Brown (2006)

Canadian provincial governments have begun to recognize that correctional service delivery must be responsive to girls. As such, several informal working groups and girl-focused conferences have emerged across the country. Similarly, various non-governmental agencies are developing formal gender-informed policies (e.g., Elizabeth

Box 11.6

Federally Sentenced Women in Canada: Past, Present, and Future Approaches

The first Canadian federal prison for adult females—the Prison for Women (P4W)—opened in Kingston, Ontario, in 1934. From the beginning, numerous investigations, commissions, and advocacy groups called for its closure. It was argued that P4W was problematic because it was a maximum security environment that housed all women regardless of their security level, it forced women to be geographically separated from their families

and support systems, the architecture of the building was inadequate, gender-informed programs were not provided, and culturally responsive programs for francophone or Aboriginal women were not available (CSC 2006).

In 1989, CSC established a Task Force on Federally Sentenced Women mandated to develop a comprehensive strategy for the treatment and management of federally

Box 11.6 Continued

Prison for Women, Kingston, Ontario. 1934-2000.

sentenced women. Importantly, this Task Force was co-chaired by CSC and the Canadian Association of Elizabeth Fry Societies and included representation from diverse stakeholders including the government, correctional practitioners, Aboriginal organizations, and women offenders. The Task Force produced a report entitled, "Creating Choices" published in 1990. This lengthy report provided several recommendations aimed at improving the manner in which CSC manages women under its care. One of these recommendations included the closure of P4W and the creation and subsequent opening of smaller, regional facilities and an Aboriginal healing lodge that could address the problems associated with P4W.

Between 1995 and 2004 five new regional institutions and a healing lodge for women were opened across Canada. Unlike P4W these facilities embrace a community-living environment as recommended in Creating Choices. Each facility is comprised of several stand-alone houses (up to 10 women live in each house) where the women are responsible for daily living needs such as cooking, cleaning, and laundry. Each house has a communal living area as well as a kitchen, dining area, bathroom, and laundry room. There is also a main building with offices for staff, program rooms, a health care unit, and a visit unit. Maximum security women are housed in secure units commensurate with traditional cells. These facilities can accommodate anywhere between 150 (Edmonton Institution for Women) and 44 women (Okimaw Ohci Healing Lodge). The Okimaw Ohci Healing Lodge is located in Saskatchewan. Structurally and operationally, it is based on Aboriginal spirituality and traditions. It can accommodate both minimum and medium security women.

The Arbour report "Commission of Inquiry into Certain Events at the Prison for Women" was released in April 1996. The Honourable Louise Arbour, who at the time was a judge in the Ontario Court of Appeal and now sits on the United Nations Human Rights Violation Tribunal, was tasked with investigating incidents that involved a violent confrontation between six women offenders and various correctional staff at the Prison for Women. The report also addressed the offenders' subsequent lengthy segregation, CSC's deployment of a male emergency response team, their role in strip-searching the women offenders,

Continued >

Box 11.6 Continued

and CSC's response (CSC 2006). Arbour ruled that many of the women's concerns were valid.

The CSC has advanced considerably since 1990, though critics argue that there is still room for improvement (Expert Committee Review of the CSC's Ten-Year Status Report on Women's Corrections 2006). The "Creating Choices Report" identified five guiding principles to serve as the foundation for a correctional strategy for women offenders: empowerment, meaningful and responsible choices, respect and dignity, supportive environ-

ment, and shared responsibility (see Box 11.5). CSC is considered a world leader in the provision and development of gender-informed programs for women. Not only does it offer programs that target risk factors directly related to criminal behaviour (e.g., the Women Offender Substance Abuse Program (WOSAP) and the Women's Violence Prevention Program (WVPP)), it also offers a number of programs that may be considered central to the criminal conduct of women (e.g., trauma programs and mother–child programs).

Fry Society of Peel-Halton Structured Decision Making Model for Girls in the Youth Justice System 2005). We are making progress, though our expertise in the area of female offender treatment pales in comparison that that of males. Let's review what we know, what we don't know, and where lead researchers in the field are headed.

Targets

Research has identified various correctional treatment targets for girls and women. Some are also considered risk factors and were described in the previous section "Factors Related to Female Offending." However, there are a number of additional treatment targets that are not traditionally considered risk factors but could be conceptualized as non-criminogenic responsivity factors—factors that may not be directly related to criminal recidivism but if left unaddressed may impede correctional treatment outcomes and therefore fail to enhance community reintegration.

Applied correctional feminists have emphasized the following areas as especially salient to girls and/or women: childcare and prenatal services, parenting programs, female-only group programs, trauma programming, substance abuse treatment, education and employment training, gender-responsive medical (e.g., gynaecological) and mental health care services (e.g., programming for borderline personality and depression), and service delivery that permits meaningful communication with staff characterized by empowerment and empathy (Ashley, Marsden, and Brady 2003; Bloom et al. 2003; Kennedy 2004; Koons et al.

1997; Morash, Bynam, and Koons 1998; Owen 1998; Richie 2001; Wellisch, Anglin and Prendergast 1993). Additional proposed targets are more relevant during incarceration, such as protection against sexual harassment and abuse from staff, while others are more relevant in the community, such as protection from abusive partners, provision of safe and affordable housing, access to reliable transportation, and access to staff after hours (Ashley et al. 2003; Bloom et al. 2003).

Researchers also advocate that successful programming for girls and women must become more holistic in at least two important ways. First, it must target multiple needs simultaneously (e.g., substance abuse and mental health). Second, treatment must occur in an environment that is empowering and as such affords girls and women a voice in a safe setting characterized by mutual respect and understanding. This translates into gender-responsive training for staff that targets stereotypical beliefs about girls and women—that they are whiny, emotionally draining to work with, manipulative, needy— and provides knowledge and skills for dealing with a traumatized population (Bloom et al. 2003; Gaarder, Rodriguez, and Zatz 2004).

To date, researchers have not had ample opportunity to thoroughly investigate the extent to which targeting these factors can reduce recidivism in girls or women. The evidence we do have is encouraging, however. Ashley et al. (2003) narratively reviewed 38 substance abuse treatment studies that examined one or more of the above-noted factors. The authors concluded that substance abuse programming for women is most effective when it concurrently provides prenatal care, mental health care, women-specific comprehensive programming (e.g., children are integrated into the treatment effort and live with their mothers in the therapeutic community), and women-specific supplemental services (e.g., targeting breast health, breast self-examination, sexual and reproductive anatomy, sexually transmitted diseases (STDs), HIV and AIDS prevention, assertiveness, and communication skills).

Although the development of programs built specifically for girls and women are in their infancy, there are a number of notable examples developed by Canadian researchers for both girls—Earlscourt Girls Connection program (EGC; Pepler, Walsh, and Levene 2004), Girls Moving On (Orbis Partners Inc 2007c)—and women— Women Offender Substance Abuse Program(WOSAP; Correctional Service of Canada 2007a) and Women's Violence Prevention Program (WVPP; Blanchette, personal communication, 2009). These programs adopt an integrated approach, blending elements from gender-neutral correctional treatment literature (e.g., grounded in social learning theory and cognitive behaviourism (see Chapter 3) and gender-responsive literature (e.g., afford voice and enhance empowerment)). Noteworthy, one of these programs has been evaluated and has shown some promising results (Pepler, Walsh, and Levene 2004).

Although rigorous evaluations are lacking for programs designed specifically for girls or women, Dowden and Andrews (1999) conducted a meta-analytic review of gender-neutral correctional treatment programs that have targeted female offenders. Specifically, they explored whether treatment programs targeting female offenders (adhering to the

Table 11.3 Mean Effect Size Corresponding to Each Correctional Treatment Principle

Treatment Principle	Principle Adhered To	
	Yes (k)[a]	No (k)
Risk		
Predominantly female	.19 (36)	−.04 (9)
Solely female	.24 (18)	−.04 (6)
Need		
Predominantly female	.26 (21)	.04 (24)
Solely female	.23 (13)	.09 (11)
Responsivity		
Predominantly female	.27 (15)	.08 (30)
Solely female	.25 (8)	.12 (16)

Note: [a]k refers to the number of studies that contributed to the mean effect size.

Source: Dowden and Andrews (1999)

principles of risk, need, and responsivity) yield greater reductions in criminal recidivism than those that do not. The authors identified 26 unique treatment outcome studies comprised entirely (16 studies) or predominantly (10 studies) of female offenders. The main results of the meta-analysis are presented in Table 11.3.

The study demonstrated that programs adhering to the general responsivity principle generated a 25 percent (solely female) to 27 percent (predominantly female) reduction in criminal recidivism. Similarly, programs adhering to risk and/or need principles reduced recidivism by 19 to 26 percent. Studies with male offenders revealed comparable data (Andrews et al. 1990). Dowden and Andrew's (1999) results are encouraging, but should be interpreted judiciously for a number of reasons. First, as the authors note, the meta-analysis was based on a considerably small number of studies relative to comparable research with male offenders (i.e., 500+). Second, most of the studies were comprised of youthful female offenders. The extent to which the results generalize to adult female offender samples is largely unknown. As well, the majority of studies were published prior to 1990, so the meta-analysis did not permit a "fair test" of contemporary approaches.

Criticisms of the Gender-Neutral Correctional Treatment Model

A number of feminist scholars have been highly critical of the responsivity model in its application to females. The first criticism asserts that it is problematic because it targets individual change while simultaneously ignoring an individual's ecology, both immediate (e.g. partner, family, friends) and distal (e.g., society, cultural, political, economic) (Covington and Bloom 2003; Hannah-Moffat 2004; Kendall 2004; Pollack 2005; Shaw and Hannah-Moffat 2004). The second criticism argues that the RNR model was empirically informed by quantitative meta-analytic results. Kendall (2002; 2004) contends that using meta-analytic results to inform women-specific treatment strategies is unreliable because qualitative and small-scale studies are excluded. A third criticism against cognitive behaviourism stems largely from Kendall's (2002; 2004) distrust of science, particularly psychology. Kendall argues that science and empiricism reflect the values of the dominant class in society; namely, white middle-class men from the Western world. It would appear that there is much to be done in the field of female treatment and that perhaps the best path is an integrated one (Blanchette and Brown 2006).

Below is a list of the top 10 issues and people to consider when thinking about female offending in Canada.

Top 10 List

Advances to Come, Debates, Ethical Conundrums, and People to Watch

1 Should youthful females who commit violent crimes be sentenced as adults?

2 Is female violent crime on the rise in Canada? What do the official versus the unofficial crime statistics tell us?

3 If mental health and trauma experiences are key risk factors for girls and women, is it ethical to incorporate them into risk-assessment tools if it means higher security placements and/or lengthier stays in prison?

4 How do we deal with over-classification without further marginalizing already marginalized groups such as Aboriginal girls and women?

5 More research is needed that integrates multidisciplinary theories (e.g., social learning theory and feminist pathways) and methods (quantitative and qualitative approaches).

6 How should society address feminist advocacy positions that argue women should rarely be imprisoned because they are first and foremost victims?

7 More research is needed to examine the after effects of prison-based mother/child programs.

8 Risk-assessment tools that have been built from the ground up for women (e.g., the SPIN) require further validation.

9 Rigorous evaluations of women-specific programs are required.

10 People to Watch: Marlene Moretti, Debra Pepler, Nadine Lanctôt, Candice Odgers, and Craig Schwalbe.

SUMMARY

1. Girls and women commit substantially less crime and particularly less violent and less serious crime compared to boys and men. This fact holds true regardless of who conducted the research, how it was conducted, or where it was conducted. When girls and women commit crime, their motivations and situational contexts are sometimes different from that of their male counterparts (e.g., more relational in nature, directed against intimate partners), but sometimes similar (e.g., driven by a need to "save face" or restore personal reputation/integrity).

2. Gender-neutral and female-centred theories have been proposed to explain female criminal behaviour. Both perspectives have merit.

3. Girls and women share a number of risk factors with their male counterparts, such as substance abuse and employment and education needs. However, there are a number of factors that appear to be more salient for females (e.g., drug abuse) and some that are less salient (e.g., traditional criminal attitudes). However, this research is tentative and requires further investigation.

4. Gender-neutral risk tools appear to predict criminal recidivism equally well for male and female offenders. The extent to which gender-responsive tools will rival or potentially surpass gender-neutral tools requires further investigation.

5. Girls and women have a number of programming needs that don't typically arise in the context of treating male offenders, such as protection from abusive partners or parenting needs. Although the number of gender-responsive programs is growing, they remain in their infancy. They have not been fully evaluated, so the extent to which they can reduce recidivism has not been fully investigated.

6. Although girls and women share a number of similarities, there are some important developmental differences that have yet to be fully explored.

Discussion Questions

1. Do we need female-specific theories of crime or are traditional theories enough?

2. What are the advantages and disadvantages associated with using gender-neutral risk-assessment tools such as the LS/CMI versus gender-responsive risk-assessment tools such as the SPIN?

3. Throughout the chapter, we explored what the research has to say about whether girls and women have unique risk factors and unique treatment needs. Much of the discussion suggests that girls and women have many of same risk and need factors as their male counterparts. In contrast, modern correctional agencies such as the CSC begin with the assumption that women have unique needs, as exemplified by statements such as, "While CSC has come far in addressing the unique needs of women offenders" (CSC 2006: 3). So if the real world has already decided that women have unique needs, should we continue our research?

4. Should women offenders be considered offenders or victims?

5. Should mother/child programs be allowed in prisons?

Additional Reading

Blanchette, K. and Brown, S.L. 2006. *The assessment and treatment of women offenders: An integrative perspective.* Chichester: John Wiley and Sons.

Correctional Service of Canada. 2006. *Ten-year status report on women's corrections (1996–2006).* Correctional Service of Canada: Author. Retrieved March 21, 2009 (www.csc-scc.gc.ca/text/prgrm/fsw/wos24/tenyearstatusreport_e.pdf).

Moffitt, T.E., Caspi, A., Rutter, M., and Silva, P.A. 2001. *Sex differences in antisocial behaviour: Conduct disorder, delinquency, and violence in the Dunedin longitudinal study.* Cambridge: Cambridge University Press.

Relevant Websites

Correctional Service of Canada
www.csc-scc.gc.ca/text/pblcsbjct-eng.shtml#women

Canadian Association of Elizabeth Fry Societies
www.elizabethfry.ca/

Chapter 12

Aboriginal Offenders

At the age of two, Victor Dellaire was removed from his parents' home by Child Welfare Services and spent the next 12 years in and out of foster homes, where he experienced serious physical abuse. At 14, Victor ran away from his foster home and lived on the city streets for two years. While he attended school regularly as a child, he rarely showed up for classes once he was older and was frequently suspended for truancy and fighting. School took a back seat in Victor's life and he eventually dropped out. Victor's life gradually became centred on crime and alcohol abuse. He was often involved in the criminal justice system as a result of committing a wide range of crimes and ultimately found himself in an Aboriginal healing lodge. While in the lodge, Victor took part in a number of treatment programs, some to tackle his substance abuse issues and others to help him control his anger. He also took part in a variety of programs that taught him about his Native culture, which he had little knowledge of. An Elder at the lodge befriended Victor and introduced him to drumming. They would speak about his upbringing, his experiences in foster care, and his ultimate path into crime. They would spend time in sweat lodges, smoke tobacco together, and talk about what Victor needed to do to return to the right path. Over time, Victor learned to embrace his culture and devoted himself to giving back to his people. Today, Victor works at the lodge where he spent several years. He not only constructs the drums that are used during drumming classes, he teaches classes and talks to the inmates about his life and how he turned it around.

Learning Objectives

1   Describe why Aboriginal people might be overrepresented in the criminal justice system.

2   Describe the various attempts that have been made to reduce Aboriginal overrepresentation.

3   Discuss the similarities and differences between Aboriginal and non-Aboriginal offenders with respect to their risk and need factors.

4   Discuss the applicability of traditional risk assessment instruments to Aboriginal offenders.

5   Explain the legal requirements to provide Aboriginal-specific correctional programs.

6   Describe what an Aboriginal healing lodge is and explain why such lodges are used.

INTRODUCTION

As you will see throughout this chapter, Victor is one of many Aboriginal offenders in Canada who has come into contact with the law. In fact, for a variety of reasons we will explore, Aboriginals are much more likely than non-Aboriginals to serve time in a Canadian correctional facility. And when Aboriginal offenders do serve time, many are exposed to the types of Aboriginal treatment programs described in the opening vignette. Like traditional correctional programs, the goal with Aboriginal treatment programs is to reform offenders so that they do not commit further crimes, but this is done (at least in part) by attempting to reconnect the offender with their Aboriginal culture. Not only is the provision of such programs to (appropriate) Aboriginal offenders a legal requirement in Canada, it reflects the generally held belief that loss of culture is at the heart of the Aboriginal offending problem.

In this chapter, we will examine Aboriginal offenders and offending. We will begin by exploring the issue of Aboriginal overrepresentation in the Canadian criminal justice system, specifically discussing why Aboriginal people may be more likely than non-Aboriginals to come into contact with the law, and we will examine various attempts that have been made (and are still being made) to reduce overrepresentation. We will then discuss the similarities and differences between Aboriginal and non-Aboriginal offenders with respect to childhood and adult risk factors and examine the applicability of traditional risk assessment instruments to Aboriginal offenders. Lastly, we will look at correctional treatment for Aboriginal offenders, including the need for Aboriginal-specific treatment programs, what some of these programs look like, and whether these programs are having their intended effects.

THE PROBLEM OF ABORIGINAL OVERREPRESENTATION

You may be wondering why we include a chapter dedicated solely to Aboriginal offenders. There are many potential answers to this question. However, perhaps the most obvious has already been alluded to: within Canada, Aboriginal offending represents a particularly serious problem and Aboriginal offenders are by far the most overrepresented group in our criminal justice system. This has been true for a long time, as it has been in other countries with indigenous populations, such as Australia and New Zealand (e.g., Broadhurst 1997; Doone 2002). Unfortunately, despite attempts to reduce overrepresentation in Canada, the matter does not appear to be drastically improving (Roberts and Melchers 2003). In fact, many people believe that **Aboriginal overrepresentation** is one of the most important problems facing our criminal justice system (LaPrairie 1996). Even the Supreme Court of Canada believes it represents a "crisis in the criminal justice system" (*R v. Gladue* 1999: paragraph 64).

One just has to look at the numbers to appreciate the magnitude of the problem. For example, according to recent statistics, Aboriginal people make up only about 3 percent of the general population in Canada. However, Aboriginal offenders make up approximately 16 percent of the federal inmate population and 20 percent of the provincial/territorial inmate population (Rugge 2006). In addition, Aboriginals represent approximately 12 percent of offenders who are serving sentences in the community (Trevethan, Moore, and Rastin, 2002). While the problem of Aboriginal overrepresentation in the criminal justice system is evident across the country, it is much more pronounced in certain regions. As can be seen in Figure 12.1, the problem is much more obvious in the western half of Canada, particularly in the Prairie region (Boe 2000; Johnson 2005; Trevethan et al. 2002).

Explaining Aboriginal Overrepresentation

Given the data in Figure 12.1, the obvious question is *why* Aboriginal people are overrepresented in the Canadian criminal justice system. Unfortunately, there is no easy answer. Historically, four potential explanations have been proposed:

1. A higher Aboriginal crime rate.
2. The commission by Aboriginal people of offences that are more likely to result in criminal justice processing.
3. Differential criminal justice processing as a result of racial discrimination.
4. Criminal justice policies and practices that have a differential impact on Aboriginal offenders due to their socio-economic conditions.

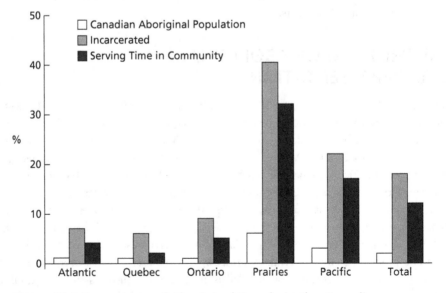

Figure 12.1 Percentage of Aboriginal People in the Canadian Population Serving Time in Prison and in the Community

Source: Trevethan, Moore, and Rastin (2002)

Higher Aboriginal Offending Rates There appears to be general agreement that the Aboriginal crime rate in Canada is significantly higher than the non-Aboriginal crime rate, especially when focusing on Aboriginal people living on reserves (Brzozowski, Taylor-Butts, and Johnson 2006). One previous estimate in Manitoba, for instance, put the 1989–1990 provincial crime rate (excluding reserves) at 1003 offences per 10 000 people, whereas the estimated crime rate on reserves was 1505 offences per 10 000 people (Aboriginal Justice Inquiry 1999). Another more recent estimate put the 1996–1997 crime rates in Saskatchewan at 1408 and 1407 offences per 10 000 people in urban and rural areas respectively (Quann and Trevethan 2000). The corresponding crime rate on reserves was 3054 offences per 10 000 people. If these numbers are accurate, it appears that one of the reasons for Aboriginal overrepresentation is that Aboriginal people simply commit more crime.

A Tendency to Commit More Violent Crime There also seems to be agreement among researchers that the types of crime committed by Aboriginal and non-Aboriginal offenders differ and that the types of crime committed by Aboriginal offenders are more likely to result in arrests and incarceration (Brzozowski et al. 2006; LaPrairie 1996; Moyer 1992). For example, compared to non-Aboriginal crime, significantly more Aboriginal crime is recorded as violent in nature. In Quann and Trevethan's (2000) study of recorded crime in Saskatchewan, for instance, on-reserve violent crime was five times higher than that in urban and rural areas. Most recently, a survey conducted by Statistics Canada indicated that rates of violent crime committed on reserves were eight times higher for assaults, seven times higher for sexual assaults, and six times higher for homicides than rates in the rest of Canada (Statistics Canada 2006). Given these findings, it is perhaps unsurprising that Aboriginal overrepresentation exists.

Discrimination in the Criminal Justice System Disagreement starts to emerge when attempts are made to understand the higher rate of recorded crime (particularly violent crime) for Aboriginal people. Does the data presented in the previous two paragraphs indicate that Aboriginal people actually commit more crime? Or does it just appear as if they do because of criminal justice practices, some of which might discriminate against Aboriginals? While there is insufficient space in this chapter to do justice to this topic, disagreement is apparent over the extent to which discrimination plays a role in Aboriginal overrepresentation.

There are clearly people who believe discrimination plays only a minor role in the overrepresentation problem. For example, according to Tonry (1994), the primary cause of overrepresentation is differences in offending patterns between Aboriginal and non-Aboriginal people, not racial discrimination. There is some empirical evidence to support this view. For instance, in contrast to what would be expected if discrimination was at play in the criminal justice system, a number of studies have found that, on average, Aboriginal offenders receive significantly shorter custodial sentences than non-Aboriginal offenders (LaPrairie 1990; 1996; Stenning and Roberts 2001; York 1995), although this may not be true at the provincial/territorial level (Trevethan, Tremblay, and Carter 2000).

This seems to be the minority view, however. Provincial and federal government inquiries (and numerous court rulings) have consistently concluded that the overrepresentation of Aboriginal Canadians in the criminal justice system is a result, to a significant degree, of discrimination (although not always overt discrimination) in the criminal justice system (e.g., Aboriginal Justice Inquiry 1991; Cawsey 1991; Indian and Northern Affairs Canada 1996; Rudin 2006). Aboriginal overrepresentation itself is typically used as evidence of this discrimination, but other potential sources have also been highlighted.

It has been argued, for example, that Aboriginal communities are subject to **overpolicing**, and that police officers use discretion differently depending on whether they are dealing with Aboriginal or non-Aboriginal people (Rudin 2006). Quigley's (1994) thoughts reflect a general concern voiced by many:

> Consider, for instance, the provincial offence of being intoxicated in a public place. The police rarely arrest whites for being intoxicated in public. No wonder there is resentment on the part of Aboriginal people arrested simply for being intoxicated. This situation very often results in an Aboriginal person being charged with obstruction, resisting arrest or assaulting a police officer. An almost inevitable consequence is incarceration ... Yet the whole sequence of events is, at least to some extent, a product of policing criteria that include race as a factor and selective enforcement of the law. (pp. 273–274; cited in Rudin 2007)

Many other signs of discrimination against Aboriginal offenders have also been recognized in other phases of the criminal justice system (e.g., in court, while incarcerated, after release). One inquiry found that, compared to non-Aboriginal inmates, Aboriginal inmates reported spending significantly less time with lawyers preparing their case and were more likely to appear in court without a lawyer (Aboriginal Justice Inquiry 1991). The same inquiry found that Aboriginal offenders are often detained for longer periods of time before their trial begins. In fact, provincial court data from Winnipeg reveals that Aboriginals spend more than twice as long in pre-trial detention as non-Aboriginals.

Other potential signs of discrimination toward Aboriginal offenders will be discussed throughout the chapter (e.g., the over-classification of female Aboriginal offenders with respect to security level placements) (Webster and Doob 2004).

The Socio-Economic Disadvantage of Aboriginal People

There seems to be little doubt that as a group, Aboriginal Canadians are more disadvantaged socio-economically than non-Aboriginal Canadians (Weinrath 2007). In contrast to other Canadians, data clearly indicate that the unemployment rate is significantly higher for Aboriginal people and that Aboriginal people earn significantly smaller incomes on average (Mendelson 2006; Perusse 2008). Aboriginal people are also less educated than non-Aboriginal people, with a much smaller number of Aboriginals finishing high school and very few completing a post-secondary degree (Hull 2005; Mendelson 2006).

There also seems to be agreement that these socio-economic disadvantages make Aboriginal people more vulnerable to certain criminal justice practices. Consider the issue of fine defaults as an example. Monetary fines are the most common legal sanction used in Canada (John Howard Society 1999). If offenders are unable to pay their fine, refuse to work it off in a fine option program, and other more serious sanctions are not appropriate for the offender, they can be sent to prison. Empirical data supports the view that compared to non-Aboriginal offenders, more Aboriginal offenders serve time for fine default, thus explaining to some extent their overrepresentation in the prison system (Aboriginal Justice Inquiry 1991; Haslip 2001; LaPrairie 1996).

Root Causes of Aboriginal Overrepresentation

While these issues may help explain Aboriginal overrepresentation, it is important to understand that they are simply symptoms of much larger, more serious social problems. In other words, while it is useful to know that Aboriginal people may commit more crime than non-Aboriginal people, or that Aboriginal people may be more socio-economically disadvantaged, it is more important to understand how this state of affairs came to be in the first place. If Aboriginal overrepresentation is to be adequately dealt with, we must understand the root causes of these problems. There is reason to believe that by dealing with these root causes, we will have the largest impact on Aboriginal overrepresentation (LaPrairie 1996).

Unfortunately, we still don't fully understand why these problems exist, although we have some good ideas (Rudin 2006). Culture clash seems to play an important role, for as Rudin argues, there is no question " . . . that Aboriginal concepts of justice and Western concepts of justice are very different" (p. 22). These differences may in part lead to Aboriginal overrepresentation in the criminal justice system. Consider Table 12.1, which lists some of the major conflicts between Aboriginal and non-Aboriginal values in a court setting. It is not difficult to imagine scenarios whereby Aboriginal offenders would be at a distinct disadvantage compared to non-Aboriginal offenders (see Ross 1992). For instance, the Aboriginal view that maintaining eye contact with a person of authority can be a sign of disrespect could make Aboriginals seem more guilty (or at least more deceptive) in the eyes of Western jurors and judges.

However, while there is no doubt some merit to this line of thinking, the concept of culture clash fails to explain certain realities of the criminal justice situation in Canada. For example, as Rudin (2006) points out, in contrast to what would be expected by a culture clash explanation, many Aboriginals incarcerated in Canadian prisons hold a distinctly Western view of justice. Surveys of these individuals have found that they often possess little knowledge of Aboriginal traditions and have little contact with Aboriginal communities, likely because many were uprooted as children (e.g., placed in foster care; Rudin 2006).

The impact of colonialism has also been proposed as a root cause of overrepresentation. As Rudin (2006) explains,

> . . . colonial governments prior to 1867 and Canadian governments since that time pursued a generally single-minded policy aimed at ensuring the disappearance of Aboriginal people in Canada . . . Included in the process was the relocation of Aboriginal people to

Table 12.1 Conflicts between Aboriginal and Non-Aboriginal Concepts of Justice

	Western Justice	Aboriginal Justice
Justice system	Adversarial	Non-confrontational
Guilt	European concept of guilty/not guilty	No concept of guilty/not guilty
Pleading guilty	The accused has the right against self-incrimination (it is not seen as dishonest to plead not guilty when one has actually committed the offence).	It is dishonest to plead not guilty if one has committed the crime.
Testifying	As part of the process, witnesses testify in front of the accused.	Reluctance to testify (it is confrontational to testify against the accused while in his/her presence)
Truth	Expectation to tell the "whole truth"	It is impossible to know the "whole truth" in any situation.
Witnesses	Only certain people are called to testify in relation to specific subjects.	Everyone is free to give their say. Witnesses do not want to appear adversarial and often make every attempt to give answers that please counsel, thus changing their testimony.
Eye contact	Maintaining eye contact conveys that one is being truthful.	Maintaining eye contact with a person of authority can be a sign of disrespect.
Verdict	Accused is expected to show, upon a verdict of guilty, remorse and a desire for rehabilitation.	Accused must accept what comes to him/her without a show of emotion.
Incarceration/probation	Means of punishing/rehabilitating offender	Completely absolves Aboriginal offender of responsibility of restitution to victim
Function of justice	To ensure conformity, punish deviant behaviour, and protect society	To heal the offender and restore peace and harmony to the community

Source: Mount Pleasant-Jette (1993)

often marginal land bases, criminalization of spiritual practices, severe restrictions on fundamental rights and liberties of Aboriginal people with respect to freedom of speech and assembly, mobility, and voting. *Indian Act* provisions regarding enfranchisement forced Aboriginal people who had ambitions to move outside of the reserve community and to give up their status, and discriminated against Aboriginal women and their children on the basis of the status of the man the woman married. (pp. 25–26)

The favoured explanation for how colonialism has led to Aboriginal overrepresentation in the criminal justice system relates directly to the disadvantages experienced by Aboriginal people that resulted from these efforts to eradicate them (Royal Commission on Aboriginal People 1996). For example, consider the impact of residential schooling. As part of colonial efforts, countless Aboriginal children went through the residential school system, where an attempt was made to remove their Aboriginal self-identity and assimilate them into the non-Aboriginal culture. While there, many children suffered serious mistreatment, including physical and sexual abuse, and these experiences have had a long-lasting, negative impact on the lives of many Aboriginal people. While it is difficult to quantify the impact of colonialism on Aboriginal people today, it is also difficult to imagine that their long-term mistreatment does not play some role in explaining

As part of colonial efforts to assimilate Aboriginal people into the non-Aboriginal culture, many Aboriginal children were sent away to residential schools.

why Aboriginals currently face so many problems, including their disproportionate involvement in the criminal justice system.

Attempts to Reduce Aboriginal Overrepresentation

Gradually, researchers, practitioners, and policymakers have begun to recognize and understand the unique circumstances surrounding Aboriginal people, resulting in numerous initiatives to reduce the number of Aboriginals who come into contact with the law. Many changes to policing have been introduced (Clairmont 2006). The introduction of self-administered First Nations police services is one example, as is the creation in 2006 of senior posts in the Royal Canadian Mounted Police and the Ontario Provincial Police to oversee Aboriginal policing. As you will see in a later section of this chapter, policies have also been introduced to ensure that Aboriginal offenders are able to receive treatment that is culturally appropriate (Corrections and Conditional Release Act (CCRA) 1992: s. 80), and that Aboriginal offenders can be transferred to the Aboriginal community, where they can have access to services and programs that reflect their culture (CCRA 1992: s. 81). There is still insufficient research to determine if these changes have had their desired effect, but many people believe that things are moving in the right direction.

Changes have also been made to sentencing practices in Canada. For example, in 1996, Parliament introduced Bill C-41, which discusses the principles and purposes of sentencing and introduced new sentencing options, such as the conditional (community) sentence. In section 718.2(*e*) of Bill C-41, which deals with the use of incarceration, the

government included the qualification that "all available sanctions other than imprisonment that are reasonable in the circumstances should be considered for all offenders, *with particular attention to the circumstances of aboriginal offenders.*" As indicated in Box 12.1, the Supreme Court of Canada interpreted this section in *R v. Gladue* (1999) as an attempt to "ameliorate the serious problem of overrepresentation of aboriginal people in prison" (paragraph 93). One significant result has been the development of courts in Canada that focus on processing Aboriginal offenders. Some of these courts are known as **Gladue Courts.**

First Nations police services are now common in Canada.

RISK FACTORS ASSOCIATED WITH ABORIGINAL OFFENDERS

ONE OF THE GOALS OF FORENSIC PSYCHOLOGISTS WHO STUDY ABORIGINAL ISSUES IS TO understand "why Aboriginal offenders are so disproportionately involved in and vulnerable to the policies and practices of the criminal justice system" (LaPrairie 1996: 64). A significant part of this endeavour requires that we develop an understanding of the

---

Box 12.1

R v. Gladue (1999): A Turning Point in Aboriginal Corrections?

The trial of *R. v. Gladue* is often heralded as a turning point in Aboriginal justice. Jamie Tanis Gladue pleaded guilty to the manslaughter of her common-law husband, who she suspected was cheating on her. Gladue was under the influence of alcohol when she stabbed her husband, but it was clear she intended to harm him. Gladue was Cree, but at sentencing the trial judge held that she had been "living in an urban area and not 'within the aboriginal community as such'" (*R v. Gladue* 1999: paragraph 18). The judge also stated that " . . . there were not any special circumstances arising from their [the victim and the accused] aboriginal status that he should take into consideration" (paragraph 18) in deciding the appropriate sentence. For her crime, Gladue was sentenced to three years in prison. The case proceeded through the British Columbia Court of Appeal to Canada's highest court, the Supreme Court of Canada. As a result of the Supreme Court's ruling in this case, Aboriginal courts were created to focus on the processing of Aboriginal offenders. One such court was the Gladue Court in Toronto.

In an Aboriginal court, special cultural considerations and adverse background conditions are taken into account when assessing the case of an accused, which may work to mitigate or reduce the culpability of the offender. Examples of Gladue factors include, but are not limited to: substance abuse; poverty; racism; family breakdown; exposure to abuse; lack of employment; loss of identity, culture, and ancestral knowledge; family involvement in crime; and attendance at a residential school (Law Courts Education Society of B.C. 2009).

Consideration of these factors will sometimes result in the application of a restorative justice approach in order to heal those affected by the criminal act instead of using prison time as a deterrent (Law Courts Education Society of B.C. 2009; see Chapter 4 for a more thorough discussion of restorative justice principles). Restorative justice is more in line with traditional Aboriginal justice than conventional sentencing. However, a consideration of Gladue factors does not necessarily mean that Aboriginal offenders will always get off more lightly than non-Aboriginal offenders. For example, because the *Criminal Code* calls for more serious sanctions when serious crimes have been committed, restorative justice options may not be appropriate in these cases. Nevertheless, because Gladue factors will be considered in the majority of cases involving Aboriginal

Continued >

Box 12.1 Continued

offenders, Aboriginal courts are expected to help reduce the overrepresentation of Aboriginals in Canadian prisons.

Unfortunately, there are reasons to be pessimistic about the impact of the Gladue decision. While 1996 reforms introduced by Parliament led to a reduction in the use of prison sentences in general, Aboriginal overrepresentation in Canada's prison system continues to persist (Roberts and Melchers 2003). As Rudin (2006) points out, " . . . as the rate of incarceration drops, it is dropping faster for non-Aboriginal people than for Aboriginal people" (p. 47). Why the lack of a significant impact? One problem is that while Gladue emphasized the need for judges to pay attention to the life circumstances of Aboriginal offenders, the decision "did not . . . provide any sense of how this information was to come to the court" (Rudin 2006: 48). For example, it wasn't (and perhaps still isn't) clear "what process would be used to gather this information, synthesize it, and provide it to the sentencing judge" (p. 48).

In addition to this issue, factors working against all attempts to ameliorate Aboriginal overrepresentation are probably also having a detrimental impact on the effectiveness of Aboriginal courts. These include a disproportionate increase in the Aboriginal youth population in Canada compared to the non-Aboriginal youth population, a demographic group that is particularly likely to come into contact with the law, and a continual influx of Aboriginal people to urban areas from reserves, which is expected to increase the chances of Aboriginals entering the criminal justice system given that they may not have the necessary skills to succeed in the city (Boe 2000; LaPrairie 1992; 1996; 2002).

various risk factors possessed by Aboriginal offenders and determine how these risk factors influence their offending behaviour. Based on existing research, it is clear that Aboriginal offenders generally represent a high-risk group with respect to both their childhood and adult backgrounds, which leads to relatively high rates of offending and reoffending compared to their non-Aboriginal counterparts.

Childhood Risk Factors

When surveyed, a large proportion of Aboriginal offenders report serious childhood trauma that could potentially contribute to their later law-breaking behaviour. Disturbingly high levels of poverty are reported by Aboriginal offenders when recounting their childhood, for instance, as are high levels of parental absence, behavioural and learning problems, and abuse of all kinds (e.g., physical, sexual, and substance) (Johnston 1997; 2000).

While similar traumas are also experienced by non-Aboriginal offenders, they appear to be experienced to a lesser degree. For example, in a comparative study of 175 Aboriginal and 148 non-Aboriginal offenders serving time in federal institutions, Trevethan et al. (2002) found that a significantly higher number of Aboriginal offenders had been adopted or placed in foster or group homes at some point in their childhood

(63 versus 36 percent) and reported serious instability in their adolescent years (50 versus 32 percent). Reflecting this instability, a larger proportion of Aboriginal offenders reported that they had experienced a range of negative events while growing up, such as exposure to drugs, alcohol, and crime in the home environment (see Figure 12.2).

A much larger proportion of Aboriginal offenders are also known to suffer from disorders such as fetal alcohol syndrome (FAS), which is associated with a range of problems, including juvenile delinquency and adult criminal behaviour (Boland, Duwyn, and Serin 2002). This issue has recently been the focus of much attention and is discussed further in Box 12.2.

Adult Risk Factors

In adulthood, Aboriginal offenders also appear to exhibit a range of risk factors. However, many of these risk factors appear to be the same as those exhibited by non-Aboriginal offenders (Rugge 2006). Bonta, LaPrairie, and Wallace-Capretta (1997) set out to determine whether a risk-assessment tool developed on non-Aboriginal offenders—the Manitoba Risk-Needs Scale—could be used successfully with Aboriginal offender populations. They collected data from 390 Aboriginal and 513 non-Aboriginal offenders and

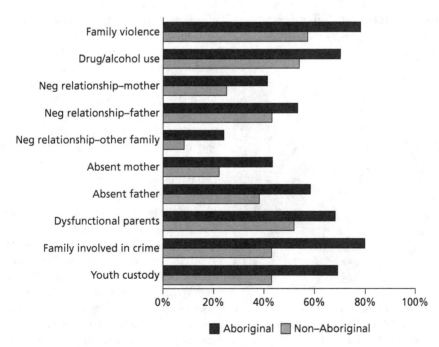

Figure 12.2 Percentage of Aboriginal and Non-Aboriginal Inmates Experiencing Serious Instability Factors in their Childhood

Source: Trevethan et al. (2001)

Box 12.2

The Role of Fetal Alcohol Syndrome in Aboriginal Offending

The consumption of alcohol by a woman when she is pregnant can cause serious problems for the unborn child, leading to long-lasting consequences after birth. One such problem that has implications for the criminal justice system is **fetal alcohol syndrome** (FAS) (Streissguth 1997). Fetal alcohol syndrome is diagnosed when the there is a history of maternal alcohol consumption during pregnancy in addition to three criteria: prenatal and/or postnatal growth delay, characteristic cranio-facial anomalies, and central nervous system impairments (Boland et al. 2002). A milder form of FAS known as **fetal alcohol effects** (FAE) only requires the presence of two of these three criteria.

Serena Nicotine was diagnosed with FAS at the age of 14 during her trial for the drowning death of a child.

The relevance of FAS to the criminal justice system becomes clear when one considers that individuals suffering from it are more likely to come into contact with the law and suffer a range of other serious problems. In a study by Streissguth, Barr, Kogan, and Bookstein (1997), data was collected from 251 adolescents and adults aged 12 to 51 who were suffering from FAS or FAE. According to the results, 95 percent of the sample had mental health problems (primarily depression), 60 percent had a disrupted school experience (e.g., suspensions), 35 percent had alcohol and other drug problems, and 49 percent had displayed inappropriate sexual behaviour (e.g., sexual touching). A full 60 percent had come into contact with the law, and 50 percent had been incarcerated.

The incidence rate of FAS in the Aboriginal population is much higher than it is in the non-Aboriginal population. Sandor et al.'s (1981) study in the Yukon and B.C. indicated a 10.9 to 1 ratio of Aboriginals with FAS to non-Aboriginals. A slightly more recent study in the same region (Asante and Nelms-Matzke 1985; cited by Bray and Anderson 1989) found that the prevalence rate of FAS and FAE in Aboriginal communities was 46 cases per 1000 people in the Yukon and 25 cases per 1000 in B.C. The prevalence rate for non-Aboriginals in these areas was .40 cases per 1000 people. An analysis of one Aboriginal reserve in B.C. found a prevalence rate of 190 cases per 1000 (Robinson, Conry, and

Conry 1987)! Given the link between FAS and crime, these figures represent a very serious problem for the Canadian criminal justice system and for the Aboriginal people of Canada.

Source: Brunet, n.d.

found that scores were significantly related to recidivism for both samples. In addition, they found that almost all of the scale items that predicted risk in the non-Aboriginal sample also predicted risk in the Aboriginal sample. Included among these factors were a history of substance abuse, prior criminal convictions, antisocial attitudes, and antisocial peers.

These findings suggest that predictors of recidivism may, at least to some extent, be independent of culture, as some researchers have argued (e.g., Andrews and Bonta 2006). This is not to say that Aboriginal-specific factors are totally unimportant, however. Recent research suggests there are a number of factors specific to Aboriginal offenders that may assist in predicting the likelihood of reoffending. For example, in a study by Sioui and Thibault (2002), participation in cultural and spiritual activities while incarcerated and involvement in Aboriginal-specific education and employment programs were related to decreases in recidivism for Aboriginal offenders.

RISK ASSESSMENT WITH ABORIGINAL OFFENDERS

AS INDICATED IN OTHER CHAPTERS, THERE ARE A NUMBER OF RISK-ASSESSMENT INSTRUMENTS currently in use. Here we will focus on ones that are regularly used to assess Canadian offenders, including Aboriginal offenders on occasion: the Level of Service Inventory–Revised (LSI-R), the Statistical Information on Recidivism Scale (SIR), and the Custody Rating Scale (CRS). Note that unlike the LSI–R and the SIR, the CRS is used for a very specific purpose (determining security classification), which is reflected in the type of risk it predicts (e.g., escape risk).

Level of Service Inventory–Revised (LSI–R)

The LSI–R is a 54-item risk-need assessment instrument designed for use with adult offenders (Andrews and Bonta 1995). The instrument taps into 10 dimensions related to risk and need factors (including the "Central Eight" items discussed in Chapter 1) and allows an offender's risk level to be categorized into five degrees, ranging from low to high. The LSI–R provides for professional discretion override, which allows administrators to consider special circumstances that may influence level of service decisions (Rugge 2006). Research has provided reasonably strong empirical support for the use of the LSI–R with non-Aboriginal offenders (e.g., Andrews 1982; Andrews and Robinson 1984; Bonta and Andrews 1993; Bonta and Motiuk 1985; Gendreau, Goggin, and Smith 2002). Although more limited, some research has examined the applicability of the LSI–R to the Aboriginal offender population.

Bonta (1989) studied 52 male Aboriginal offenders and 74 male non-Aboriginal offenders. His research indicated that the LSI–R was correlated with recidivism (i.e., re-incarceration) for both Aboriginals ($r = .35, p < .01$) and non-Aboriginals ($r = .50, p < .001$). Five of the 10 LSI–R sub-components predicted re-incarceration for both groups of offenders, while differences between the groups were found for four of the subcomponents (with each being predictive for the non-Aboriginal offenders only). The remaining subcomponent did not predict recidivism for either group.

More recently, Holsinger, Lowenkamp, and Latessa (2006) examined the predictive validity of the LSI–R for a number of different offender samples, including 264 white offenders and 140 American Aboriginal offenders (100 males and 40 females). While the total LSI–R score was found to correlate positively with reoffending for whites ($r = .23$), the results for the Aboriginal male subgroup indicated a weaker, non-significant relationship ($r = .19$). Even more discouraging was the non-significant, negative correlation found for the female Aboriginal subgroup ($r = -.13$). These results raise questions about the use of the LSI–R with American Aboriginal offenders, especially females. However, as the authors of this study point out, the findings may also reflect the fact that there are important differences between American and Canadian Aboriginal offenders that have yet to be fully understood.

Statistical Information on Recidivism (SIR) Scale

The SIR scale (Nuffield 1982) was developed to assist in parole decision making for federally sentenced offenders (Rugge 2006). The scale consists of 15 items, the majority of which are static (i.e., unchanging). Research has shown that the SIR scale demonstrates good psychometric properties with non-Aboriginal offenders, including reasonably high levels of predictive validity for general and violent recidivism (Bonta, Harman, Hann, and Cormier 1996; Hann and Harman 1989; Nafekh and Motiuk 2002; Nuffield 1982). In 1988, all non-Aboriginal offenders began being assessed using the SIR scale at intake (Rugge 2006). However, the SIR scale is typically not applied to Aboriginal offenders entering Correctional Service of Canada (CSC) institutions (Rugge 1996) due to a belief that it is not a valid risk-assessment instrument for this population (Nuffield, 1989).

Although the SIR scale is not used with Aboriginal offenders, some research has reported reasonable evidence that it can be usefully applied to this population. Hann and Harman (1989; cited in Rugge 1996) tested the scale's applicability to female and Aboriginal offenders and found that there was a general correspondence between risk category and recidivism, although the relationship was not as strong as that found for non-Aboriginal offenders. As a follow-up, Hann and Harman (1993; cited in Rugge 1996) conducted another study examining the applicability of the SIR scale to male Aboriginal offenders. According to Rugge (2006), the "results indicated that the SIR scale had predictive value for the general release risk of Aboriginal offenders, and that the predictive accuracy was comparable to the predictive accuracy of the scale for non-Aboriginal offenders" (pp. 17–18). Despite these results, the studies were not without limitation (e.g., small sample sizes) (Rugge 2006). As a result, the authors were cautious to recommend the widespread application of the scale to the Aboriginal offender population.

In 2002, Nafekh and Motiuk tested several versions of the SIR scale on male Aboriginal offenders. Specifically, because the scale is not regularly administered to Aboriginals, a SIR–Proxy scale was developed and used, whereby scoring was done using information from intake assessments of Aboriginal offenders that approximated items on the SIR scale (using a non-Aboriginal sample, the SIR scale and the SIR–Proxy were found to produce similar results). A version of the SIR–Proxy that was calibrated on the offenders examined in the study was also used (referred to as the Recalibrated SIR). Using receiver operating characteristic (ROC) analysis, tests of the SIR–Proxy on 6881 male non-Aboriginal offenders resulted in an area under the curve (AUC) of .75 for general recidivism and .73 for violent recidivism (no AUC could be calculated for sexual recidivism). The corresponding values on the SIR–Proxy for 1211 male Aboriginal offenders were .68 for general recidivism, .65 for violent recidivism, and .60 for sexual recidivism. With respect to the Recalibrated SIR, an AUC of .75 was found for non-Aboriginal offenders when predicting general recidivism. The corresponding accuracy value for the Aboriginal offenders was .72.

Most recently, Bonta and Rugge (2004; cited in Rugge 2006) examined the predictive accuracy of the SIR scale using data from 940 male Aboriginal offenders (despite CSC policy, the SIR scale is sometimes administered to Aboriginal offenders during the intake process, although it is not used in CSC decision making; Rugge 2006). Bonta and Rugge's results "indicated that the SIR scale scores predicted 'any reconvictions' and 'violent reconvictions' equally well for both Aboriginal and non-Aboriginal male offenders" (Rugge 2006: 18). However, "while the SIR scale predicted 'non-violent reconvictions' for both Aboriginal and non-Aboriginal males, results indicated that the prediction was better for non-Aboriginal males" (Rugge 2006: 18). See Table 12.2 for a summary of these results.

Custody Rating Scale (CRS)

The CRS was adopted by CSC in the early 1990s for the purpose of making institutional security classification decisions (i.e., minimum, medium, or maximum) (Blanchette, Verbrugge, and Wichmann 2002). The 12-item CRS consists of two subscales: the Institutional Adjustment (IA) subscale (including items such as history of institutional incidents and escape history) and the Security Risk (SR) subscale (including items such as number of prior convictions and severity of current offence) (Rugge 1996). The subscales consist of five items and seven items, respectively, with higher scores resulting in higher levels of classification. Since its implementation, there has been much debate as to whether the CRS is applicable for Aboriginal offenders (Rugge 2006), particularly females (Blanchette et al. 2002; Blanchette and Motiuk 2004; Canadian Human Rights Commission 2003; Webster and Doob 2004a; 2004b).

Table 12.2 Predictive Validity of the SIR Scale for Aboriginal and Non-Aboriginal Offenders

Criterion	Aboriginal	Non-Aboriginal
Any reconviction		
Correlation	−.42	−.46
AUC	.74	.77
Non-violent reconviction		
Correlation	−.27	−.38
AUC	.66	.73
Violent reconviction		
Correlation	−.21	−.19
AUC	.65	.65

Source: Rugge (2006)

In an early examination of male offenders, including 470 Aboriginals and 6679 non-Aboriginals, Luciani, Motiuk, and Nafekh (1996) studied a range of factors related to the CRS. Compared to non-Aboriginal offenders (IA = 36.9, SR = 74.7, overall = 111.6), Aboriginal offenders scored higher on the CRS (IA = 41.6, SR = 80.8, overall = 122.4). In addition, to examine the convergent validity of the CRS and its subscales, correlations between these scales, the SIR scale, and a risk/needs assessment completed at intake were calculated. All of the correlations were significant and in the expected direction for non-Aboriginal offenders. For Aboriginal offenders, all correlations were in the expected direction, but a significant number did not reach significance.

In a more recent study, Blanchette et al. (2002) examined the validity of using the CRS with female Aboriginal and non-Aboriginal offenders. Based on a sample of 68 Aboriginals and 266 non-Aboriginals, they found that the CRS designation distribution differed across Aboriginal and non-Aboriginal offenders, with Aboriginals being underrepresented in minimum security designations and overrepresented in both medium and maximum security designations. In addition, when the 12-item scores making up the two scales were examined, Aboriginals scored significantly higher on six of them (non-significant differences were found for the other six, although Aboriginal offenders scored higher on five of these items as well).

To examine the predictive accuracy of the CRS, Blanchette et al. calculated correlations between the scale scores and various outcome measures for 61 of the Aboriginal offenders and 230 of the non-Aboriginal offenders. The IA subscale was moderately correlated with violent and non-violent incidents for both Aboriginal (.39 and .47, respectively) and non-Aboriginal offenders (.19 and .21, respectively). On the other hand, the SR subscale was correlated with violent and non-violent incidents for non-Aboriginal offenders (.18 and .19, respectively), but not for Aboriginal offenders (.01 and .05, respectively).

As an additional sign of predictive accuracy, the percentage of women offenders who were involved in institutional incidents generally increased in the expected order for both Aboriginal and non-Aboriginal offenders at each CRS designation, although there were more reported incidents for Aboriginal offenders classified as a minimum security risk (28.6 percent) than a medium security risk (26.8 percent). While this general trend is encouraging, it seems that the CRS over-classifies Aboriginal offenders (i.e., a substantial portion of Aboriginal offenders are designated to higher security levels than they need to be based on their rates of institutional misconduct). For example, an examination of the data in Table 12.3 indicates that Aboriginal offenders are more likely to be assigned (and placed) in medium security even though they are less likely to be involved in institutional incidents at this security level (Blanchette, Verbrugge, and Wichmann 2002).

Fortunately, the situation for female Aboriginal offenders appears to be improving. Blanchette and Taylor (2007) evaluated a new instrument for reclassifying female offenders' security levels after their initial security classification. Known as the Security Reclassification Scale for Women (SRSW), the instrument includes nine items (i.e., serious disciplinary convictions, segregation during the review period, regular prosocial family contact, etc.). Based on data from 103 non-Aboriginal offenders and 45 Aboriginal offenders, Blanchette and Taylor examined the predictive validity of the SRSW by studying various institutional outcome measures (e.g., any misconduct within a three-month follow-up period). Based on the entire group, AUCs for the new scale were fairly impressive: .74 for major institutional misconduct, .75 for minor institutional misconduct, and .75 for any institutional misconduct. When the offenders were separated into Aboriginal and

Table 12.3 Percentage of Aboriginal and Non-Aboriginal Offenders Designated and Placed in Minimum, Medium, and Maximum Security

	Sub-group	Security Level			Total
		Minimum (%)	Medium (%)	Maximum (%)	
CRS designation	Aboriginal	20.6 [28.6]	70.6 [26.8]	8.8 [100]	100 (n = 68) [n = 61]
	Non-Aboriginal	55.3 [40]	42.8 [52.4]	1.9 [80]	100 (n = 266) [n = 230]
Actual placement	Aboriginal	29.4 [16.7]	60.3 [30.6]	10.3 [100]	100 (n = 68) [n = 61]
	Non-Aboriginal	55.3 [38.5]	42.1 [53.5]	2.6 [85.7]	100 (n = 266) [n = 230]

Note: Percentage of institutional incidents within each security level is provided in square brackets.

Source: Blanchette, Verbrugge, and Wichmann (2002)

non-Aboriginal samples the instrument was actually more accurate for Aboriginal offenders. The AUCs for minor misconducts were .72 and .75 for non-Aboriginal and Aboriginal offenders, respectively. For major misconducts, the difference was even more marked, with AUCs of .68 and .74 for non-Aboriginal and Aboriginal offenders, respectively.

Aboriginal-Specific Risk-Assessment Instruments

In light of the research described above, there is obviously some support for the use of traditional risk-assessment instruments with Aboriginal offenders (Rugge 2006). It appears that the LSI–R can potentially be used to predict recidivism for male Aboriginal offenders in Canada at moderate levels of accuracy, although this doesn't seem to be the case when the LSI–R is applied to indigenous populations in the U.S. (especially female samples). In addition, some studies have found that the SIR scale (or variations of this scale) has similar levels of predictive validity for Aboriginal and non-Aboriginal offenders, at least for predicting certain outcomes. While the CRS has been found to be problematic, especially when applied to female Aboriginal offenders, new risk-assessment tools for reclassifying female Aboriginal offenders appear to be more promising.

Thus, one potential path for individuals who are interested in assessing the risk of Aboriginal offenders is to continue with the type of research described above. In this way, additional support for the use of traditional risk-assessment tools with Aboriginal offenders may gradually accumulate. Another possible path also exists, however: to develop Aboriginal-specific risk assessment tools. Currently, very few Aboriginal-specific risk assessment instruments actually exist. Although there are some, they are somewhat different from the instruments we have discussed in the sense that they are not formal scientific instruments for predicting risk and do not necessarily treat recidivism as the primary outcome of interest (Boer, Couture, Geddes, and Ritchie 2003).

One such instrument, the Yókw'tól, is a risk-management guide for incarcerated male and female violent Aboriginal offenders (Boer et al. 2003). Yókw'tól is a native word meaning "the understanding of one is complete." Unlike the majority of traditional risk-assessment instruments, where item selection is based on rigorous statistical testing, the content of the Yókw'tól is based primarily on input from Aboriginal Elders, Aboriginal staff, and Aboriginal offenders (this is not to say that there isn't empirical evidence to support many of the items included in the guide). It was designed to "provide guidance for the effective management of the offender both in the institution and the community" (Boer et al. 2003: 7). The Yókw'tól consists of 20 items that summarize the issues that must be addressed by Aboriginal offenders in order to return home in a safe manner. As can be seen in Table 12.4, both static and dynamic items are included, some of which are unique to Aboriginal offenders.

Like other risk-assessment instruments, these factors can be coded for on a periodic basis. With this tool, this is done by conducting an interview with the offender and an Elder and by consulting the offender's institutional file (Boer et al. 2003). The resulting scores can be used to guide treatment and supervision strategies that are jointly agreed to by the offender, the assessor, and the Elder to ensure that the offender will realize their full potential. While the Yókw'tól could theoretically be validated in the same manner as the other instruments we discussed, such scientific validation efforts have not taken place yet, nor has there been a rush to conduct them by the authors of the guide. The authors of the Yókw'tól do not see it as a scientific "instrument" but as a guideline to help Aboriginal offenders take responsibility for what they have done and make positive changes in their lives (Boer et al. 2003). Neither do the authors necessarily see the prediction of recidivism as the only outcome of interest when working with Aboriginal offenders. For example, they suggest a range of other variables that may be important to consider, including " . . . the willingness of Aboriginal people to be assessed; the willingness of such offenders to be honest with the interviewer; and the opinion of the individual offender that he has been interviewed with questions that seem relevant to him" (Boer et al. 2003: 5).

Risk of Reoffending Among Aboriginal and Non-Aboriginal Offenders

The general finding of studies examining recidivism is that Aboriginal offenders tend to have higher recidivism rates than non-Aboriginal offenders (Bonta, LaPrairie, and Wallace-Capretta 1997; Bonta, Lipinski, and Martin 1992; Hann and Harman 1989; Rastin and Johnson 2002; Sioui and Thibault 2001). Sioui and Thibault (2002) examined the recidivism rates (i.e., technical violations and new offences) of 30 041 male offenders who were released on day parole, full parole, or statutory release from federal penitentiaries in Canada. Eighty-four percent were non-Aboriginal and the remaining

Table 12.4 Static and Dynamic Items Included in the Yókw'tól

1. Traditional teachings, ceremonies, and customs	11. Self-harm risk
2. Relationship of offender to heritage	12. Gains, insights, and behavioural changes
3. Child abuse history	13. Support for the victim(s)
4. Historical/generational issues	14. Support for the offender
5. Foster care history	15. Relevance of Sections 81/84 to offender
6. Family and marital relationships	16. Lifestyle stability
7. Alcohol and drug use	17. Self-support skills
8. Impulsive behaviour and violence	18. Supervision attitudes and compliance
9. Attitudes regarding offending	19. Risk-management plan
10. Psychological or psychiatric issues	20. Unique resiliency factors

Source: Adapted from Boer et al. (2003)

Box 12.3

Canadian Researcher Profile: Dr. Joseph Couture

In the area of Aboriginal mental health and corrections, Dr. Joseph Couture, a Cree Métis, is somewhat of a legend. Born in Edmonton and raised in Fort McMurray, Dr. Joe, as he was affectionately known, was the first Aboriginal person in Canada to receive a Ph.D. in psychology (University of Alberta, 1972). In the 1960s, Dr. Couture was a professor at Trent University, where he built (and chaired for several years) the first Native Studies program in Canada. This program is now emulated at universities across North America. During the 1970s and early 1980s, Dr. Couture "led the cultural, academic, and administrative development of the Nechi Institute, which has become a world-renowned indigenous-based training program

for addictions and recovery" (Retson 2007). More recently, Dr. Couture was an Elder and psychologist at the Pê Sâkâstêw Healing Centre in Hobbema, Alberta.

In his work with corrections, Dr. Couture brought together his skills as a Western-trained psychologist with Aboriginal understandings of holistic healing and wellness. His research was said to have broken " . . . new ground in the Native and non-Native mental health system by challenging long held views on healing and by combining traditional values with contemporary methods" (National Aboriginal Achievement Awards 2007). He helped transform Canadian prisons into places for healing and was involved in developing culturally sensitive assessment and treatment approaches for Aboriginal offenders. One of his last contributions to the field was the co-development of a risk management guide for Aboriginal Offenders, the Yókw'tól (described above). Many of his influential ideas can be found in his writings on Aboriginal corrections, healing, and spirituality.

For his significant accomplishments, Dr. Couture was awarded a 2007 National Aboriginal Achievement Award. At the ceremony, he was recognized for building bridges of understanding between two cultures and affecting "generations of educators and students with his straightforward and profound traditional healing methods" (National Aboriginal Achievement Awards 2007). Known as a respected Elder, cultural adviser, educator, academic, and psychologist, Dr. Couture died on June 15, 2008, at the age of 76 (Retson 2007).

Sources: National Aboriginal Achievement Foundation (2007); Retson (2007)

16 percent were Aboriginal. The researchers found that a larger proportion of Aboriginal offenders were re-admitted to a federal institution within six months (18 versus 11 percent for Aboriginal and non-Aboriginal offenders, respectively). This was true regardless of whether day parole (14 versus 7 percent), full parole (21 versus 9 percent), or statutory release (25 versus 21 percent) was examined.

These results are consistent with another large-scale recidivism study conducted by Bonta, Rugge, and Dauvergne (2003). Three cohorts of male offenders released from Canadian federal penitentiaries were examined, with recidivism defined as any new conviction for an offence committed within two years of release from prison. As is evidenced in Table 12.5, compared to non-Aboriginal offenders, a larger proportion of Aboriginal offenders in each cohort were re-convicted within two years post-release for both violent and non-violent crimes.

What is not yet clear is whether these findings for federal (i.e., more serious) offenders generalize to offenders serving time in provincial prisons. Bonta (1989) found only non-significant differences in re-incarceration rates for Aboriginal and non-Aboriginal offenders when he examined offenders released from provincial institutions (incarceration rates of 43.8 percent and 42.3 percent, respectively, one year after release). The reasons for the differences between federal and provincial offenders are not well understood.

Table 12.5 Percentage of Aboriginal and Non-Aboriginal Offenders Reconvicted (for Non-Violent and Violent Offences) within Two Years of Release

Type of Reconviction	Aboriginal	Non-Aboriginal
Any reconviction		
1994–95 cohort	58.3%	42.2%
1995–96 cohort	56.8%	41.2%
1996–97 cohort	52.7%	39.1%
Non-violent		
1994–95 cohort	36.9%	29.3%
1995–96 cohort	36.1%	29.1%
1996–97 cohort	33.1%	27.1%
Any violent		
1994–95 cohort	21.4%	12.9%
1995–96 cohort	20.7%	12.1%
1996–97 cohort	19.6%	12.0%

Note: Sample size for the 1994–95 cohort: Aboriginal = 961, non-Aboriginal = 6,018; for the 1995–96 cohort: Aboriginal = 919, non-Aboriginal = 2,362; for the 1996–97 cohort: Aboriginal = 1,046, non-Aboriginal = 2,334.

Source: Bonta, Rugge, and Dauvergne (2003)

TREATMENT OF ABORIGINAL OFFENDERS

Given that Aboriginal offenders are more likely to reoffend than non-Aboriginal offenders, there is great value in examining ways to reduce their likelihood of recidivism. For the most part, research examining this issue has focused on the treatment of Aboriginal offenders; specifically, whether culturally appropriate treatment programs (versus traditional correctional interventions) will help deal with the problem. As early as 1985, CSC began to introduce policies stressing the importance of Aboriginal culture, commenced an examination of the process Aboriginal offenders go through once they enter the criminal justice system, and started to work toward developing correctional programs that would meet the needs of these offenders. As discussed earlier, since 1992, the provision of Aboriginal-specific programs has been a requirement under the *Corrections and Conditional Release Act*. CSC's own policy also recognizes the need for Aboriginal programs, stating that " . . . differences in cultural approaches to learning require different techniques and stipulates the requirement for regions to provide Aboriginal offenders with culturally-specific programs, activities, and Elder services" (Trevethan, Moore, and Allegri 2005: 3).

The Treatment Needs of Aboriginal Offenders

A focus on Aboriginal treatment makes sense considering the treatment needs of this population. Although Aboriginal and non-Aboriginal offenders often exhibit similar types of treatment needs while incarcerated, the level of need does not appear to be the same (LaPrairie 1996). Studies have consistently shown that larger proportions of Aboriginal offenders are rated as being higher need than non-Aboriginal offenders. Trevethan, Moore, and Rastin (2002) examined the treatment needs of Aboriginal and non-Aboriginal offenders (primarily male) serving time in federal custody. As illustrated in Figure 12.3, Aboriginal offenders were rated as higher need across a range of domains, with the exception of antisocial attitudes.

Very similar differences in need ratings between Aboriginal and non-Aboriginal offenders emerge for both female offenders (Dell and Boe 2000) and young offenders (Corrado and Cohen 2002).

Aboriginal and Non-Aboriginal Treatment Programs

Given their serious treatment needs, CSC has dedicated a tremendous amount of energy into programming for Aboriginal offenders. As mentioned earlier, there is a belief in Canada that part of the cause of Aboriginal offending is loss of culture. Thus, re-establishing a connection with Aboriginal culture is viewed as part of the solution to the Aboriginal offending problem. A range of Aboriginal-specific treatment programs tailored to Aboriginal offenders in provincial and federal custody, as well as in the community, has been developed. For example, in addition to traditional correctional interventions such as anger management and substance abuse programs, Aboriginal offenders now have access to traditional

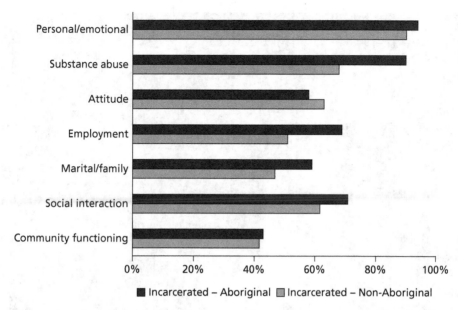

Figure 12.3 Need Ratings for Aboriginal and Non-Aboriginal Offenders in Federal Custody

Source: Trevethan, Moore, and Rastin (2002)

spiritual practices, Aboriginal literacy classes, sweat lodge ceremonies, drumming classes, etc. (LaPrairie 1996). In fact, in a relatively recent survey of Aboriginal-specific programs in Canada, 23 healing programs were identified (13 federal and 10 provincial) (Epprecht 2000). For a sense of what an Aboriginal treatment program looks like, the *In Search of Your Warrior* program is described in Box 12.4.

Aboriginal Healing Lodges

Section 81 of the *Corrections and Conditional Release Act* allows the Aboriginal community to take responsibility for overseeing Aboriginal offenders under certain conditions. This enables the provision of correctional services to Aboriginal offenders in a manner that respects their culture. These services are often provided in **Aboriginal healing lodges**. According to CSC (2009), healing lodges

> . . . offer services and programs that reflect Aboriginal culture in a space that incorporates Aboriginal peoples' tradition and beliefs. In the healing lodge, the needs of Aboriginal offenders serving federal sentences are addressed through Aboriginal teachings and ceremonies, contact with Elders and children, and interaction with nature. A holistic philosophy governs the approach, whereby individualized programming is delivered within a context of community interaction, with a focus on preparing for release. In the healing lodges, an emphasis is placed on spiritual leadership and on the value of the life experience of staff members, who act as role models. (p. 1)

Some Aboriginal-specific treatment programs include teaching offenders about drumming and encouraging them to learn traditional songs.

In Search of Your Warrior: A Violence Prevention Program for Aboriginal Offenders

The *In Search of Your Warrior* (ISOYW) program is a group-based, high-intensity violence prevention program designed by the Native Counselling Services of Alberta. It is intended to meet the needs of male Aboriginal offenders who have a history of violent behaviour (Laboucane-Benson 2002). The ISOYW program is based on the following guiding assumptions:

■ Human beings are part of a number of systems such as the family, community, and society at large. We affect these systems and, in turn, they affect us.

■ No matter how tortured an individual's history of violence may be, he is respected as a human being—one who has made "mistakes" from which he can and must learn.

■ Traditional Aboriginal teachings and culture will guide individuals back to a nonviolent way of life.

■ All human beings are inherently good, and their behaviour is shaped by their life experiences.

■ Personal change takes time and requires readiness, commitment, desire, and patience.

Box 12.4 Continued

- In order for healing to occur, the spiritual, emotional, physical, and psychological parts of the self must be engaged in the healing process (Laboucane-Benson 2002: 1).

Reflecting these assumptions, the program blends aspects of traditional Aboriginal spirituality with Western approaches to treatment.

The foundation for the program is clearly based in the culture, teachings, and ceremonies of Aboriginal people. For example, the program immerses participants in a holistic healing approach that encompasses all aspects of the Medicine Wheel (i.e., physical, emotional, spiritual, and mental well-being) with an emphasis on controlling violent and aggressive behaviour (Trevethan et al. 2005). With the assistance of an Aboriginal Elder, appropriate Aboriginal ceremonies and teachings are incorporated into the program and used to engage the offender in the healing process. While it is often delivered in a typical classroom setting, the program is occasionally delivered in the wilderness, reflecting the strong connection with nature that is part of Aboriginal culture.

The structure of the program is similar to traditional correctional programs that target violent offenders, as are many of its treatment targets. Indeed, the program relies heavily on the theories, principles, and processes of traditional violence prevention programs (Trevethan et al. 2005). Over the course of many weeks (up to 75 sessions), participants engage in group therapy targeting eight components: 1) anger awareness; 2) violence awareness; 3) family of origin awareness; 4) self awareness; 5) skill development; 6) group skill development; 7) cultural awareness; and 8) cognitive learning. The ultimate goal is to provide offenders with insight into their own behaviour and strategies for self-management so that violence can be reduced in their homes and communities upon release (Trevethan et al. 2005).

Source: Laboucane-Benson (2002); Trevethan, Moore, and Allegri (2005)

There are a number of healing lodges across Canada. Some are managed directly by CSC, and others are managed by Aboriginal agencies or communities. While each is unique, they all focus on providing correctional services that are respectful of Aboriginal culture (Crutcher and Trevethan 2002). One of these healing lodges, the Pê Sâkâstêw Healing Centre, is described in more detail in Box 12.5.

Does Paying Attention to Culture Matter?

While it is intuitively appealing to think that paying attention to culture matters in corrections, it is important that this issue be examined empirically. Do Aboriginal-specific treatment programs work? Do they work better than non-Aboriginal programs? What do we mean by "work"? It is possible for a program to "work" in the sense that it increases the connection that an Aboriginal offender feels to himself, his community, and/or his spirituality, but it may not actually lead to reductions in crime (i.e., the typical meaning of "work" in the Western correctional research tradition).

The Pê Sâkâstêw Healing Centre: Canada's First Healing Lodge for Aboriginal Men

The name of the Pê Sâkâstêw Centre (pronounced bay-saw-ga-stay-o) is derived from a term that means "new beginnings" in Cree. It was the first healing lodge in Canada built for Aboriginal men and was completed in August 1997. Located in Hobbema, Alberta, the centre is a federally owned, minimum-security facility consisting of 60 beds (CSC 2009). As evidenced in the picture, "the design of the facility reflects the Aboriginal world view—symbols that are significant to the Samson Cree First Nation, such as the medicine wheel, were integrated into the Centre's design" (CSC 2009). The services offered at Pê Sâkâstêw are based on the Aboriginal view that spirituality is central to the healing process of Aboriginal offenders. While traditional correctional programs are offered to inmates, a largely Aboriginal staff, including Elders, are heavily involved in delivering programs that instruct inmates in traditional values and spiritual practices (Trevethan, Crutcher, and Rastin, 2002). One such program is the popular ISOYW program

discussed in Box 12.4. It is believed that " . . . by integrating the concepts of self-motivated healing, cultural identity, spirituality, and community re-connection, the Centre helps rebuild connections between troubled individuals and the communities they have become alienated from" (Rashid 2004). Ultimately, it is hoped that this will reduce the likelihood of Aboriginal reoffending.

Sources: CSC (2009); Rashid (2004); Trevethan et al. (2002)

On the positive side, there are a range of studies that report encouraging results. When Aboriginal offenders are asked their views on the issue of culturally-based programming, it is clear that they appreciate their value (e.g., Trevethan et al. 2005). They report feeling more comfortable dealing with Aboriginal staff, for instance, and view them as more trustworthy than non-Aboriginal staff (Johnston 1997). Aboriginal offenders also feel as though they get a lot out of Aboriginal treatment programs. For example, one study found that Aboriginal offenders felt that culturally-based programs enable them to trust people more, stay out of trouble better, and deal more positively with their problems (Pfeifer and Hart-Mitchell 2001). Offenders in another study felt that Aboriginal programs helped them understand themselves better and were useful in alleviating anger and gaining control of their behaviour (Crutcher and Trevethan

2002). These findings are obviously important, but they are subjective in nature and should therefore be treated with some caution.

Studies have been conducted that have used more objective measures to demonstrate the benefits associated with Aboriginal treatment programs. These studies also reveal encouraging results. Aboriginal offenders appear more likely to complete treatment when they are participating in culturally-based programs (e.g., Ellerby and MacPherson 2002), which will potentially impact their likelihood of reoffending (Nunes and Cortoni 2006). Aboriginal offenders attending these programs also show improvement on treatment targets. In their study of a Native substance abuse pre-treatment program, for example, Weekes and Millson (1994) observed significant improvements on measures of knowledge and attitudes toward substance abuse, general problem-solving ability, and recognition of Native cultural factors. Likewise, in their evaluation of the ISOYW program, Trevethan et al. (2005) reported positive changes for offenders who had completed the program— these offenders demonstrated lower need ratings for personal distress, family issues, substance abuse, community functioning, employment, social interactions, and pro-criminal attitudes (see Bell and Flight 2006 for a similar study on female Aboriginal offenders).

These results all reflect positively on Aboriginal-specific programs. However, it is unclear whether they translate into lower levels of recidivism and, more specifically, whether they result in less recidivism than non-Aboriginal programs. This issue has not been extensively explored, but there are a few studies that have addressed these questions and the results are not always positive.

In an examination of the effectiveness of Aboriginal healing lodges to reduce reoffending, Trevethan et al. (2002) found a higher rate of recidivism (19 percent) among healing-lodge residents compared to a sample of Aboriginal offenders serving time in minimum security facilities (13 percent). Significant differences remained even when matching for risk to reoffend at intake. In addition, post-release, healing lodge residents were found to recidivate more quickly than Aboriginal offenders released from minimum security (275 days versus 338 days). While these results are not promising, it should be noted that recidivism rates differed significantly across healing lodges in the study, ranging from 12 percent (Okimaw Ohci) to 30 percent (Wahpeton). In another study, Trevethan, Moore, and Allegri (2005) examined the recidivism rate of offenders taking part in the ISOYW program (along with a matched comparison group that did not take part). No significant differences emerged between the two groups on re-admissions to federal custody at the end of a one-year follow-up, although a significantly smaller portion of ISOYW completers were re-admitted for new violent offences (see Table 12.6).

In contrast, however, other studies provide a more positive picture when it comes to reoffending rates following participation in Aboriginal-specific treatment programs (e.g., Ellerby and MacPherson 2001; Sioui and Thibault 2001). Ellerby and MacPherson (2001) found that traditional Aboriginal healing methods were more effective at reducing recidivism among Aboriginal sex offenders (8.1 percent) than non-Aboriginal approaches (25.5 percent). Sioui and Thibault (2001) found that Aboriginal offenders who participated in programs with cultural activities demonstrated significantly lower

Table 12.6 Recidivism Rates for Offenders Who Participated in the ISOYW Program and a Matched Comparison Group

Criteria	Participants	Comparison
Re-admitted to federal facility		
No	67%	78%
Yes—Technical violation	20%	11%
Yes—New offence	13%	11%
Yes—Other reason	1%	0%
Re-admitted for new violence offence		
No	93%	43%
Yes	7%	57%
Length of time (in months) to re-admission	5.9	5.8

Source: Trevethan, Moore, and Allegri (2005)

levels of recidivism (3.6 percent) compared to those who did not participate (32.5 percent). Furthermore, Aboriginal offenders who participated in programs that included Elder involvement reoffended significantly less (12.9 percent) than offenders who did not (26.8 percent). It is not yet clear why these programs were so effective compared to the programs discussed earlier. In the future, an increased understanding of this issue may lead to the creation of more effective programs for Aboriginal offenders, which may ultimately allow us control over the problem of Aboriginal overrepresentation.

Below is a list of the top 10 issues and people to consider when thinking about Aboriginal offending in Canada.

Top 10 List

Advances to Come, Debates, Ethical Conundrums, People to Watch

1. What role does colonialism play in the current Aboriginal overrepresentation problem?

2. How do we reduce Aboriginal overrepresentation given the variety of factors working against such efforts (e.g., increases in the at-risk Aboriginal youth population)?

3. What role do police practices play in the Aboriginal overrepresentation problem?

4. Should Aboriginal and non-Aboriginal offenders have access to the same sentencing and treatment options?

5. How do we decrease the prevalence of FAS/FAE in the Aboriginal population?

SUMMARY

1. There are four common explanations for Aboriginal overrepresentation. These include: 1) a higher Aboriginal offending rate; 2) the commission by Aboriginal offenders of crimes that are more likely to result in prison sentences; 3) criminal justice policies and practices that have a differential impact on Aboriginal offenders due to their socioeconomic conditions; and 4) differential processing through the criminal justice system as a result of discrimination.

2. A variety of attempts have been made to reduce Aboriginal overrepresentation in the criminal justice system, including various police reforms such as the introduction of First Nations police services, the creation of Aboriginal courts, and legislation that requires that Aboriginal offenders have access to culturally appropriate treatment programs.

3. The risk and need factors exhibited by Aboriginal and non-Aboriginal offenders appear to be similar, but Aboriginal offenders often exhibit more serious problems in these areas. For example, childhood trauma and instability is experienced by both groups, but to a greater extent and in more serious forms for Aboriginal offenders.

4. There is very limited research that has examined whether traditional risk-assessment instruments are applicable to Aboriginal offenders and there is much debate around this topic. The research that does exist produced mixed results—there is some evidence that traditional (i.e., non-Aboriginal) risk-assessment instruments can be used to predict risk among Aboriginal offenders, but other research does not support these findings. Most researchers recommend further study to clarify this issue and some efforts are being made to develop Aboriginal-specific risk-assessment tools. The predictive accuracy of these tools is not yet known.

5. In an attempt to deal with the problem of Aboriginal overrepresentation in the criminal justice system, a number of Canadian initiatives have been put into place

(e.g., Aboriginal courts such as the Gladue Court). In the mid 1980s, the CSC began to seriously examine the problem of Aboriginal overrepresentation and introduced programs that would better meet the needs of these individuals. By 1992, the *Corrections and Conditional Release Act* stated explicitly that CSC must provide a range of Aboriginal specific treatment programs. Currently, a range of such programs are available alongside more traditional correctional programs.

6. According to CSC, Aboriginal healing lodges offer services and programs to offenders that reflect Aboriginal culture in a space that incorporates Aboriginal traditions and beliefs. The delivery of such services is based on the belief that loss of culture is at the heart of Aboriginal offending and Aboriginal overrepresentation in the criminal justice system.

Discussion Questions

1. It is generally accepted that Aboriginal offenders exhibit a higher crime rate than non-Aboriginal offenders. Other than the obvious possibility that the higher crime rate actually represents a higher rate of crime commission, what other factors might explain the difference?

2. You are a judge in an Ontario court and the Supreme Court of Canada has just handed down their ruling in the case of *R v. Gladue* (1999), which indicates that you must consider alternatives other than incarceration when sentencing offenders and must pay particular attention to the circumstances of Aboriginal offenders. What challenges might you face when trying to implement this ruling? Are there things that could be done in Canada to overcome these challenges?

3. Should cultural, religious, and/or political orientations play a role in the treatment process for offenders? Why or why not?

4. Imagine you are a non-Aboriginal offender facing sentencing. Do you think you should be given the same sentencing options as an Aboriginal offender (e.g., the opportunity to serve your sentence in an Aboriginal healing lodge)? Why or why not?

5. CSC has just proposed a new treatment program for Aboriginal offenders serving time for violent offences. As a forensic psychology student doing a summer practicum with CSC, develop a study that would allow you to determine whether the new program is successful at reducing recidivism. What would this study look like?

Additional Reading

Dickson-Gilmore, J. and LaPrairie, C. 2005. *Will the circle be unbroken? Aboriginal communities, restorative justice, and the challenges of conflict and change.* Toronto: University of Toronto Press.

LaPraire, C. 1996. *Examining aboriginal corrections.* Ottawa: Solicitor General of Canada, Corrections Branch. (Available at www.eric.ed.gov/ERICDocs/data/ericdocs2sql/content_storage_01/0000019b/80/14/ba/6e.pdf)

Rugge, T. 2006. *Risk assessment of male aboriginal offenders: A 2006 perspective.* Ottawa: Public Safety and Emergency Preparedness Canada. (Available at http://dsp-psd.pwgsc.gc.ca/Collection/PS3-1-2006-1E.pdf)

Relevant Websites

Aboriginal Initiatives at the Correctional Service of Canada
www.csc-scc.gc.ca/text/prgrm/abinit/who-eng.shtml

Aboriginal Corrections at Public Safety Canada
www.publicsafety.gc.ca/prg/cor/ac/index-eng.aspx.

APPENDIX Thinking About a Career in Corrections?

The following hypothetical profiles are intended to provide the reader with a synopsis of different career options for students who continue in the field of criminal justice, either as a researcher, practitioner, or clinician. It is important to note that many staff conduct counselling with offenders, not just psychologists. For instance, all parole officers in Correctional Service of Canada (CSC) provide forms of counselling to offenders. CSC has nearly 1500 parole officers but only about 250 psychologists (full-time staff and contract), so with almost 20 000 offenders in prisons and the community, there is a clear need for many different staff to provide counselling services. As well, social workers and chaplains provide counselling services to offenders in both federal and provincial corrections. Observations and testimonials from "real" staff can be viewed at www.csc-scc.gc.ca/text/carinf/diversity-eng.shtml. It should be noted that there has been a significant influx of new staff in the past several years. The face of corrections staff is changing: it is younger, more diverse, and more gender equal. The profiles listed below attempt to reflect these changes.

CAREER PROFILES

Correctional Officer (Blended to Reflect Duties in Provincial and Federal Corrections)

Mary is a 29-year-old correctional officer working in a male offender medium security prison. She has an undergraduate degree in criminology and began in corrections three years ago, after volunteer work with the **John Howard Society** counselling ex-offenders. She enjoys her job and interacting with her fellow officers and believes she can make a difference because she interacts with offenders on a daily basis. Eventually, Mary hopes to become a parole officer. She realizes that security is a major part of her job, but she also likes the opportunity to talk to offenders. She sees herself as someone who does more than open locked doors and frisk inmates.

It took her a while to get used to working shifts, but now she finds real advantages in having time when others are working to get things done. One of the things Mary likes best about her job is the variety of the work. By being assigned different posts, she interacts with different people and gets a full appreciation for the workings of the prison. She might work at a control post one day, ensuring offenders have passes authorizing movement and keeping an area secure, while another day she might work in a unit, observing and interacting with offenders one on one. She always knew corrections was about people, necessitating good communication skills, but sometimes she has to make reports on offenders and now also realizes the importance of good writing skills.

Parole Officer (Federal, Institutional)

Fred is a 48-year-old parole officer who has seen many changes in his 20 years on the job. When he began his career, computers were just being introduced, and now everything regarding his interaction with an offender is entered into a computer. It is more efficient and permits tracking to ensure he meets his deadlines, but there are times when he wonders if computerization hasn't reduced the actual counselling contact he has with offenders. Fortunately, there are now correctional programs for offenders that are delivered by other staff. Fred is expected to meet regularly with all staff who interact with offenders on his caseload so that he is current regarding their adjustment in prison. The procedures he is required to follow are very detailed because of the need to meet legal requirements and the increased complexity of using different risk-assessment instruments. He has also noticed a change in the offender population: they have more serious criminal histories, are older on average, and have more serious mental health concerns. These issues make it more challenging for Fred to prepare offenders for release and to determine their suitability for transfer to reduced security.

Still, he loves his work. He has had the opportunity to work on some special assignments and he feels he makes a difference for those offenders who want to change. Yes, sometimes he might be yelled or sworn at, but in addition to the challenges, it is an interesting and rewarding career.

Probation Officer (Similar to a Federal Parole Officer in the Community)

Susan is a 32-year-old probation officer who worked as a substitute teacher for five years. She previously volunteered through her church to visit offenders at a minimum security prison. After years of trying to land a full-time teaching job, the chance came up to apply for the position of probation officer and she jumped at it. She loves it, but the shift in careers took some adjustment. She has always been a positive and people-oriented person. She now realizes that rehabilitation must be balanced with supervision. Not only is this required in terms of how her duties are defined, it also works best for offenders. Offenders need support and structure, and this is how Susan approaches her supervision of offenders in the community. Her days are varied. Some days she is in the office meeting clients; some days she sees various clients at different Tim Horton's, drinking way too much coffee; on other occasions she interviews employers and family members of an accused in order to complete presentence reports for the courts; and other days she goes to court to provide comments regarding the suitability for a sentenced offender to be placed on probation. It is the variety and connection to the community that she loves about her work.

There are disappointments, such as when she works very hard to assist an offender to make better decisions and the person still ends up returning to crime. She also finds it difficult to be in court, seeing the family wanting the offender home but recognizing that without significant changes, the offender is still a risk to the community and must be recommended to a term of imprisonment. Susan sees her job as helping offenders see that they have choices and are accountable for their actions.

Psychologist

Jane is a 35-year-old correctional psychologist who works at a medium security prison for male offenders. She completed her clinical psychology degree at the University of Saskatchewan, which included several placements at the Regional Psychiatric Centre in Saskatoon. While there, she gained invaluable experience completing risk assessments, conducting group treatment with offenders, and conducting research.

Since her early years as an undergraduate, Jane knew she wanted to work in corrections. She participated in a tour of a prison in Kingston that led her to volunteer with the Elizabeth Fry Society. She found this highly rewarding, and it solidified her interest in helping others, especially those who have been in conflict with the courts. Jane realizes that most offenders return to the community and that community support is vital to their success. While some see the role of psychology as simply conducting risk assessments, she sees risk assessment as the start of a process of change for the offender. She has a positive attitude, believing people can and do want to change, but knows change is difficult. Risk assessment helps the offender better understand the areas of their lives that must be addressed if they are to remain crime-free.

Jane realizes that further research is required to better understand offender change and crime desistance. She sees her role as a correctional psychologist as ideally situated to pursue such research.

Professor

At age 37, William has just been hired as an assistant professor in the Department of Psychology at a Canadian university. His area of expertise is sex offenders, and he has joined a small department that is interested in increasing the forensic psychology program, given its popularity with students. William's work has been mainly in the area of theory; that is, understanding models relating to why certain individuals (usually males) commit sexual crimes. Through his research, he has become expert in various assessments (static and dynamic risk, phallometrics) and has conducted research in both prisons and forensic hospitals, although he is not a clinical psychologist.

For the past several years, William has taught courses in forensic psychology and realizes it is a major reason he was hired. Through his teaching evaluations, he has learned of the need to make course material engaging (like showing movies) and to help students understand contemporary issues and current research topics. He realizes that not all undergraduates will wish to continue on to graduate school, but recognizes that it is important that he share his passion for the area, especially for those who may eventually choose a career in the field.

The past year has been hectic for William, to say the least. He has worked hard to prepare for his new courses, has been working on manuscripts from his recent doctoral thesis, and has been preparing grant applications. Without funding, it will be nearly impossible to continue his research on sex offenders because of the cost of the equipment and travel to prisons. William cannot remember when he last worked this hard! Nonetheless, he is excited about his new position and career.

A CAREER IN CORRECTIONS

FOR THOSE WHO FIND CORRECTIONS AND CRIMINAL JUSTICE TOPICS INTERESTING AND EXCITING, there are numerous career pathways to consider. Some require a degree in one of the social sciences and knowledge of the criminal justice system (i.e., relevant laws, **mission statements**, policy initiatives). Staff must be able to interact effectively with others, so good verbal and written communication skills are critical. In addition, recruitment notices for employment in corrections typically include such skills as the ability to motivate offenders to change antisocial behaviour, an interest in helping others, good analytic and problem-solving abilities, and knowledge of evidence-based practice (e.g., the information covered in this course!).

Table A.1 provides a summary that may be helpful in appreciating career paths in correctional psychology. These include academic professor and researcher, clinical forensic psychologist (private practice or within a corrections agency), government researcher, counsellor with a non-government organization such as the John Howard Society, correctional officer, probation or parole officer, and **project officer** in government. The minimum degree requirement for each career is provided, as is an estimate of salary level (note: some salaries are one or two years out of date due to contract negotiations with employers).

Context

In recent years, correctional agencies have significantly increased their recruitment efforts to attract university graduates. In addition to correctional officers, probation and parole officers are likely the most common entry-level clinical positions for graduates interested in working in the field of corrections. These positions require an undergraduate degree in any of the social sciences. There are more correctional officer positions (40 percent of all jobs in CSC are correctional officer positions; Public Safety 2008) than counsellor-type (e.g., parole officer, psychologist) jobs. Many individuals begin their careers as correctional officers and move into other positions over time. One of the unique advantages to a career in corrections is the opportunity to work in many different capacities. The current commissioner of CSC, Mr. Don Head, began his career as a correctional officer, and several of the assistant commissioners began as either correctional officers or parole officers. These backgrounds give senior staff a unique understanding of the challenges facing corrections, as well as its history and evolution.

There are other career paths available for graduates with a social science degree interested in criminal behaviour (see Table A.1). It is important to note that the competition for admission to graduate school in forensic psychology is very high for both clinical and experimental programs because the number of forensic graduate programs in Canada is very small. Competition for

Table A.1 Career Paths in Correctional Psychology

Type of Job	Degree Requirement and Number of Years to Obtain	Other Issues	Starting Salary
Professor	Ph.D.; typically completed in seven to eight years post-B.A.	Average age of new hires is 37, meaning several years seeking employment	Assistant professor in psychology ($60 000–70 000)
Clinical psychologist	Preferably Ph.D.; typically eight years post-B.A. Eligible for registration in province of practice (so could be an M.A. in some provinces)	In order to be licenced, one year of supervised practice is required	Salaries vary slightly between provincial and federal systems PS03 ($64 000–76,000, plus $12 000 terminable allowance and up to $2000 penological allowance)
Associate psychologist	M.A.; must be eligible to be registered in province of practice within two years	Two-year appointment	PS02 ($54 000, plus $12 000 terminable allowance and up to $2000 penological allowance)
Government researcher	M.A.; typically two years post-B.A.	Entry level	ES04 ($66 000)
	Ph.D.; typically completed in seven to eight years post-B.A	Senior researcher	ES05 ($75 000)

(continued)

Table A.1 (continued)

Counsellor in not-for-profit	B.A.; typically right out of school	Entry level (volunteer experience an asset)	Varies ($35 000–46,000) (some have benefits, shift work, etc.)
Correctional officer	High school	Entry level, differs by security level	CX1 ($52 300) CX2 ($55 500)
Parole or probation officer	B.A.; typically right out of school	Criminal justice experience an asset	WP04 ($57 600)
Administration officer	Secondary school degree	Entry level, bilingualism an asset.	AS02 ($51 000)
Project officer at NHQ	B.A.; typically right out of school	Entry level, bilingualism an asset.	AS03 ($54 500) AS04 ($59 500)

correctional positions (e.g., correctional officer, parole officer, probation officer) is also high. However, workforce demographics show high rates of retirement and many agencies are actively trying to fill vacancies. Unlike other employment sectors, downturns in the economy have less influence on hiring in corrections. Later we will discuss strategies for preparing for employment in corrections.

Descriptions of Different Jobs in Corrections

Correctional Officer—Group & Level CX-01 (Note: This material has been developed by CSC and as such reads much like a recruitment poster. Similar detailed descriptions for other positions are under development and will be available at www.csc-scc.gc.ca/text/emplo-eng.shtml.) Much of the material is appropriate for provincial correctional officer positions.)

What They Do

The Correctional Officer is vital to fulfilling the Correctional Service of Canada's (CSC) mission of enhancing public safety. As the primary contact for offenders, you will work with offenders on a continual basis developing in-depth knowledge of an offender's personality and behaviour. This work is vital to maintaining the safety and security of CSC's correctional institutions. By developing this knowledge, you will also support and assist in managing an offender's rehabilitation and eventual safe reintegration into the community. The work requires that you interact with offenders of various backgrounds, often within a confined and controlled setting for long periods of time.

Effective Correctional Officers exercise control while encouraging offenders to participate in their reintegration programs. As a Correctional Officer, you will be required to conduct rounds and counts of inmates, supervise inmate movement, escort inmates both inside and outside the institution, search cells, offenders, visitors, vehicles, living units and surrounding areas, extract inmates from cells and conduct security checks.

Correctional Officers also assess inmate activities, behaviours and attitudes for risk and take appropriate security measures when necessary to protect the safety of the institution and public. As a Correctional Officer your duties will include verifying your safety equipment on a daily basis, drafting daily logs, submitting reports and briefing visitors, volunteers and other criminal justice professionals entering the institution. You will work closely with colleagues, inmates, volunteers and visitors while conducting your day-to-day duties.

Diversity

The Correctional Service of Canada is committed to building a skilled, diverse workforce that is reflective of Canadian society. To fulfill this goal, we strongly encourage women and men representing all ethnicities and cultures, particularly Aboriginals and members of visible minorities, to seek employment as Correctional Officers. Preference will be given to Canadian citizens.

Training

Initial Correctional Officer training is intense. Training takes place in a variety of settings including classrooms, gymnasiums and exercise fields. As a Correctional Officer, you will be trained to handle a variety of weapons. You must be in good physical condition to participate in self defence and other physical aspects of Correctional Officer training. CSC conducts training at each of its five Regional Correctional Staff Colleges located at Memramcook, New Brunswick; Laval, Quebec; Kingston, Ontario; Saskatoon, Saskatchewan and Abbotsford, British Columbia.

There is no tuition fee or student allowance. Accommodation and meals are provided based on your residence location. The Correctional Training Program (CTP) includes four phases:

■ Phase 1: On-line training requiring four to eight weeks to complete.

■ Phase 2: Workbook assignments requiring approximately two to four weeks to complete.

■ Phase 3: Staff college training that includes training in security policies and practices, use of firearms, chemical agents, fire safety, self-defence and arrest and control techniques. Conflict management and defusing crisis situations are also addressed. This phase of training lasts eight weeks.

■ Phase 4: On the job training at a CSC institution will assess various skills. This phase lasts two weeks.

If you are successful in every aspect of the CTP, you will be offered a position at CSC. You will receive a letter of offer and will start your probationary period of employment in an institution.

Professional Development

CSC is a large government agency that hires a wide variety of occupations. Depending on your interest, you may go on to perform a variety of roles within the organization including Correctional Manager, Parole Officer, Warden, Project Officer, Staff College Instructor and Trainer. Career opportunities exist both within an institutional setting and at parole offices, Regional Headquarters or National Headquarters.

Work Environment

CSC has a presence from coast to coast to coast—from large urban centres with their diverse populations, to remote Inuit communities across the North. We operate under three levels of management: National, Regional, and Institutional/District Parole Offices. The National Headquarters in Ottawa performs overall planning and policy development for the Service, while each of the five regional offices implements CSC activities within the Pacific, Prairie,

Ontario, Quebec and Atlantic regions. CSC institutions operate 24 hours a day, seven days a week. As a result, Correctional Officers work shifts on weekends and statutory holidays. You may be required to work overtime.

Essential Qualifications

Education

To work as a Correctional Officer, you must possess one of the following educational qualifications:

- A secondary school diploma from a recognized educational institution, or;
- A satisfactory score on the Public Service Commission test, approved as an alternative to a secondary school diploma, or;
- Successful completion of a provincially or territorially approved secondary school equivalency test.

A secondary school education is considered graduation from an accredited Canadian institution or the alternatives, or proof of Canadian institution or the alternatives, or proof of Canadian accreditation of foreign credentials from a recognized Credential Assessment Service in Canada.

Visit the Public Service Commission website for information concerning the rest approved as an alternative to a secondary school diploma (General Intelligence Test 320). Visit the Canadian Information Centre for International Credentials website for additional information about accreditation.

Graduation from a recognized college or university in a field of study related to the position's duties is an asset. For example, graduation from a program related to the study of adult human behaviour would be considered an asset.

Please provide documentation verifying your education level when you apply.

Experience

Experience working with people in an educational, work or volunteer setting.

Please ensure you describe where you obtained your experience and how it relates to the position.

Abilities & Skills

Ability to identify and assess problems and conflict situations, determine viable solutions and recommend or take appropriate action

Ability to communicate effectively in writing

Ability to communicate effectively orally

Ability to summarize information accurately

Ability to motivate, positively influence and assist people

Personal Suitability

Respect

Initiative

Integrity

Results oriented

Ability to work as part of a team

Sensitivity to diversity

CSC respects and promotes positive values as per the Canadian Charter of Rights and Freedoms.

Other Essential Requirements

A valid Standard First Aid and Cardiopulmonary Resuscitation (CPR) "Level C" with Automated External Defibrilator (AED) Certificate from a qualified provider as approved by

Human Resources and Skills Development Canada, and in accordance with Part XVI of the Canada Occupational Health and Safety Regulations.

Possession of a valid unrestricted provincial or territorial driver's licence.

You must meet the medical requirements of Health Canada in accordance with Treasury Board Guidelines.

Security clearance: Reliability status

CSC offers positions representing a variety of official language profiles depending upon the position and location. Official language requirements are specific to individual job opportunities.

Compensation & Benefits

Correctional Officers are members of a labour union and enjoy compensation and benefits connected to union representation, including a collective agreement negotiated with the employer. Working as a Correctional Officer (CX-01) for CSC offers the following compensation package:

A competitive salary that includes an additional allowance for those working in a penitentiary setting.

Competitive vacation and family leave provisions

Medical, dental and other wellness provisions

Sick leave provisions that accumulate

Special provisions that allow for early retirement for long-term CSC employees who work in a penitentiary or parole office

Excellent learning opportunities

About the competitive job selection process

Job opportunities are posted on www.jobs.gc.ca. Applications are screened according to essential education, experience and asset criteria. Applicants must provide pertinent documentation including driver's licence, citizenship, CPR and First Aid certification. Applicants' abilities, skills and personal suitability are assessed during an interview. Those qualifying will be invited to attend CSC's Correctional Training Program (CTP). (MacDonald 2009)

Parole Officer/Probation Officer (CSC 2009)

Typically, probation officers are provincial employees and parole officers are federal employees. Probation occurs when an individual convicted of a summary offence is released into the community (either before or after serving time in custody). A probation officer will be assigned to the offender to ensure they follow conditions of the probation order. The length of the probation order is decided by the judge. Within provincial jails, classification officers function much like institutional parole officers in federal prisons.

The parole/probation officer is correctional agencies' key link with supervised offenders in the community and crucial to managing offender risk. The job is part police officer, part social worker. It demands diverse professional skills, sound professional judgment and strong personal commitment. Parole officers must be flexible, enforcing strict controls in some cases, acting as counsellors in others, depending on each offender's needs. They must be aware of threats to their own safety and take proper precautions, but not be immobilized by these concerns.

Parole work is based on a professional relationship with each offender and on a study of the risk factors that contribute to the individual's criminal behaviour. The parole officer ensures the offender follows his/her Correctional Plan by:

■ regular visits with the offender, with or without warning;

■ contacts with family, police and employers; and

■ checking with persons who may be assisting the offender in a program.

If the offender breaches parole conditions or seems likely to do so, the parole officer can take disciplinary measures, which include sending that person back to jail. Parole officers are guided in their work by rules and standards. As part of the routine, parole officers write reports on the progress of each offender and discuss cases which require additional attention with their supervisors. Officers work together with many community agencies to help secure stable housing, employment, income and positive personal contacts. Some officers also deliver group programs aimed at helping offenders cope with daily life, substance abuse or a tendency to commit sexual offenses.

Each parole officer is responsible for, on average, a caseload of 25 to 30 offenders. The caseload may be considerably lower, if the offenders require intensive supervision. It may be much higher if some of the day-to-day supervision is by a contracted agency such as the John Howard Society or the Salvation Army or by community volunteers. Contracted supervision is used most often in isolated locations. Some 20% of the 10,000 offenders under CSC jurisdiction are supervised through such contracts.

New parole officers usually must have a university degree, most commonly in criminology or social work. Many enter the parole field after extensive experience in related occupations. Once hired, initial and ongoing training is provided to keep staff current with new information and techniques.

Various provincial correctional agencies have formal job descriptions for parole and probation staff. An example of each is provided below. (CSC 2009)

Parole Officer Job Description (Alberta, 2009) Duties vary from one position to another but, in general, parole officers:

■ make recommendations regarding the initial placement of an offender in an appropriate federal penitentiary (for any offender who receives a sentence of two years or more, or a suspension of an original federal sentence)

■ investigate offenders' past and present behaviours by interviewing other inmates, institutional authorities, police, family and friends of the offender

■ plan programs for offenders during their imprisonment

■ assess the suitability of penitentiary inmates for release under parole and statutory release, and submit recommendations to the National Parole Board

■ develop liaisons and networks with other parole officers, social welfare and community agencies, staff in correctional institutions, psychiatric facilities and after care agencies

■ supervise those who have been released on parole, day parole or statutory release

■ offer guidance and direction to parolees in dealing with job related and personal problems.

Probation Officer Job Description (Alberta, 2009)

■ prepare presentence reports as requested by the court which describe the convicted offender's personal and social life, and make recommendations for sentence including conditions which may be imposed by a court order

■ gather information through interviews with offenders, police, family, friends, employers, school authorities and others as a basis for the court to determine appropriate sentences and to assist in casework and the supervision of offenders

■ supervise individuals who have been released on a pretrial release; sentenced by the court to probation, community service work or conditional sentences or supervision; or released by a correctional or young offender centre on a temporary pass

■ administer and supervise individuals accepted to the alternative measures, extra judicial sanctions and fine option programs.

Parole and probation officers must be aware of available community resources such as psychiatric services and addiction treatment centres in addition to having a working knowledge of client behaviour and motivation.

Working Conditions Parole and probation officers work in offices and courthouses and visit offenders' homes and workplaces. Parole officers also work in penitentiaries. Parole and probation officers sometimes work long hours, including evenings and weekends, to interview offenders and their associates.

Personal Characteristics Parole and probation officers need the following characteristics:

- maturity and good judgment
- strong interpersonal skills
- strong oral and written communication skills for writing and presenting reports.

They should enjoy dealing with and helping people, having clear rules and organized methods, and supervising others.

Educational Requirements Parole officers employed by the federal government must have at least a Bachelor of Arts (B.A.) degree with a specialization in sociology, psychology or criminology, or a Bachelor of Social Work (B.S.W.) degree. Some parole officers have a master's degree or equivalent.

Correctional Program Officer This is a somewhat unique position in CSC. Essentially, a **correctional program officer** is the individual who delivers correctional programs to offenders. In the past much of this work has been completed by psychologists, or in conjunction with psychologists. Increasingly, correctional programs are provided by specially trained para-professionals. Key is that the program is developed by experts and that detailed assessment and program manuals are provided. Moreover, there is a rigorous selection, training and certification process for CPOs, who are trained to complete specialized assessments for the specific program domain (i.e., substance abuse) as well as techniques to engage and motivate offenders to complete treatment. Programs with 10 or fewer offenders are typically delivered by a single CPO. Recently, CSC developed the **Generic Program Performance Measure** (Stewart and Price 2005) in order to better determine success in programming. The certification process for correctional program officers utilizes a review of videotaped program sessions and includes:

- successful completion of training on the theory and effective delivery of the program
- successful delivery of a minimum of one program to offenders
- successful completion all the requirements of the quality review process

For a certified correctional program officer, quality reviews are conducted at three and six years following certification, with additional reviews performed if needed. The quality review will end after the sixth year following certification, unless the need for improvement is identified. The review process evaluates a correctional program officer in the following areas:

- administration of the overall program
- program delivery
- assessment of offenders
- report writing

After the delivery of a correctional program, correctional program officers must produce a post-program report and input information into the offender management system, a centralized automated offender database (hence the need for staff to have good computer skills). The report, which is due immediately following the completion of the program, is limited to the following components:

■ attendance and participation

■ analysis of progress against program targets, taking into consideration the information generated by CX-02 level correction officers on the offender's progress in monthly structured casework records

■ psychological risk assessment, if required

■ recommendations regarding risk management strategies

Correctional Psychologist

The following description of psychological services is adapted from CSC policy directives (www.csc-scc.gc.ca/text/plcy/cdshtm/840-cde-eng.shtml). This description is similar to those in the United Kingdom and New Zealand. In the United States, greater emphasis is placed on prison-based crisis intervention and addressing the mental health needs of offenders and less emphasis is placed on risk assessments. The relative time allocated to these psychological services varies across settings and most recently, more emphasis has also been placed on addressing the mental health needs of offenders. Also, correctional agencies have both institutional and community-based psychologists.

The overarching theme to such policies is to ensure that psychological services, whether by full-time staff or contract, are provided to offenders in a manner consistent with professional standards in the community. Assessments and interventions shall be both culturally and gender sensitive. A major focus is to assist offenders in becoming law abiding citizens.

Types of psychological services

Primary psychological services for offenders include:

■ assessment;

■ therapeutic intervention;

■ crisis intervention;

■ program development, delivery and evaluation.

Psychological services focus on the needs of the offender, specifically the behaviour that contributed to criminal activity, on the assessment risk posed by the offender, and on strategies to reduce and/or manage risk.

The psychologist is one member of a multidisciplinary team responsible for the management of the offender's case.

Assessment

Assessments focus on offender risk, need, and responsivity and on the management of risk, utilizing a variety of scientifically validated assessment methodologies in an integrated process. These assessments occur at intake and throughout an offender's sentence, in prison, and during his or her community supervision.

Risk assessment reports typically provides an evaluation of the level of risk posed by the offender, options for the management of risk and the identification of problems that might be encountered, which would increase the risk. If the offender is being considered for release, the report includes specific recommendations concerning the continuing need for intervention in the community, including, but not limited to, psychological services.

Therapeutic intervention

Intervention is provided in priority to those offenders who require it most, with higher risk/higher need offenders receiving more intensive treatment. Problem behaviour directly related to criminality and essential mental health needs are the primary treatment targets.

Psychologists are expected to remain current in the research literature and deliver treatment matched to methods proven to be effective with offenders, subject to ongoing program development and innovation. Regarding counselling and treatment, psychologists provide treatment progress reports and/or treatment summaries as appropriate, in consultation with case management staff.

Other duties

Routinely, psychologists are also engaged in the following:

- conducting research
- providing consultation to senior management
- providing crisis debriefing to staff
- assisting in selection of new staff
- hostage negotiation
- providing staff training on a variety of topics
- testifying in court

Government Researcher The entry level for this position is typically ES03 or ES04, meaning preferably the candidate has an M.A. in a social science field (e.g., psychology, criminology, law, sociology, social work). Those with statistical skills (i.e., knowledge of **Statistical Program for the Social Sciences, meta-analysis**) will have a noticeable advantage with such employers as Justice Canada, Public Safety, and the CSC. Demonstration of writing skills and ability to conduct literature searches are also important.

An entry-level research position essentially involves conducting assigned research under the supervision of an experienced researcher. There is little independence, as the work is directly related to the annual workplan. Nonetheless, initiative and good time-management skills are essential (and appreciated).

Box A.1

A Day in the Life

A typical workday for a correctional psychologist begins at 8:00 or 8:30 a.m. If they work in a prison, they enter through various security checkpoints and screening machines en route to their office. Invariably, they meet staff members who may inquire about a particular offender and attempt to determine if the offender is making gains as a result of contact with the psychologist. Careful not to disclose confidential information, the psychologist will communicate relevant information and eventually proceed to his or her office.

It is not uncommon for the psychologist to be greeted by a crisis referral from the previous day. An offender (in the **general population** or in **segregation**) might have responded poorly to a specific situation and a staff member (i.e., health care worker, security guard, parole officer) has made a referral for the psychologist. This referral has multiple goals: 1) to assess the offender's current mental status; 2) to determine a need for more secure placement or a health care referral (perhaps relating to medication, since psychologists do not prescribe); 3) to assist

Continued >

the offender through crisis counselling to manage the situation, help reduce anxiety or depressive symptoms, and help implement short-term problem-solving steps; and 4) to communicate aspects of this information to the appropriate staff, including completing a **casework record** for placement on the offender's psychology file. (Most psychologists will also make working **clinical notes** for future reference.)

Next, the psychologist may have an offender scheduled to be seen (although this likely will have been delayed by the earlier crisis referral). If it is an assessment interview, the psychologist will review relevant documentation (e.g., psychological test results, file information) and follow a structured and fairly standardized process in terms of content (after making an initial effort to develop rapport through pursuing some less threatening topics). For a counselling session, the psychologist will review earlier clinical notes and determine a potential strategy before having the offender describe what has transpired since their last session. If homework was assigned, this would also be reviewed.

Somewhere during the process, the prison will close over the lunch hour. Offender movement is restricted, although it varies by security level, and a count will be taken to ensure there are no offenders unaccounted for. The afternoon will be a repeat of the morning, except the activities could include a meeting with a parole officer for a case management meeting to review an offender's progress; discussing a case with health care staff; or, if lucky, having the opportunity to review a report or read a technical research article.

It should be recognized that each day likely begins and ends with reviewing and responding to e-mails. By 4:00 or 4:30 p.m., the psychologist's workday comes to an end.

CHALLENGES FOR CORRECTIONAL AGENCIES

As noted in Chapter 1, public perception is a significant challenge for correctional agencies. At each level (institutional/community, regional, national), the day begins with a review of the previous day's headlines and issues. In some more serious cases, this involves staff compiling information and speaking notes for the commissioner and minister. Budget issues remain a constant concern (recently CSC has been criticized for cost overruns due to correctional officer use of overtime and failure to develop more cost-effective purchasing practices). Staff recruitment, selection, training, and retention are an ongoing challenge for correctional agencies. As well, correctional agencies continue to try and recruit staff to better reflect the gender and ethnic composition of the offender population (i.e., hiring more women and people of diversity). Recently, candidates for correctional officer positions must complete online surveys and tests in order to qualify to participate in the initial training, which they complete without remuneration in the hopes of gaining employment. The issue of staff training is critical given the influence it can have on correctional outcomes (see Chapter 4).

All correctional agencies strive to have better outcomes. This means they are constantly reviewing, evaluating, and refining policies and practices. For instance, the assessment measures and programming approaches utilized in 1995 are no longer used today. It has been said that every five years, assessment and programming must change to reflect changes in the offender population and evaluation data. Certainly this is the case in provincial and federal corrections in Canada, but it is only possible with strong evaluation and research capacity. The changing offender population is also a challenge for correctional agencies. Reports indicate increased rates of mental disorders, increased diversity, continued overrepresentation of Aboriginals, and a bimodal age distribution (larger numbers of younger and older offenders, with a mean age of approximately 35). Such population changes must be addressed in terms of both assessment (i.e., mental health screening) and intervention (i.e., specialized Aboriginal programs).

CONTEMPORARY ISSUES

Case Management

One key aspect of correctional practice is the parole/probation officer's role as a case manager. Initial assessments of criminogenic need and risk provide a backdrop against which the officer develops a case or correctional plan for each offender. This plan outlines the *who*, *what*, and *how* regarding the management of an individual offender. The *who* refers to which members of a **case management** team will be responsible for the different activities throughout the offender's sentence. The *what* refers to the type of programming required to reduce and manage risk. The *how* refers to responsivity: how to intervene to best engage the offender and yield change. It should be clear that case management is a team approach. The parole officer is the key person who manages the case, with consultation from other staff (e.g., psychologists, correctional officers, shop instructors, social workers, chaplaincy). Obviously, such a model requires excellent communication to ensure continuity of care and offender accountability.

In this manner, the psychologist is seen more as a specialist. Referrals to psychology for assessment are dictated by such things as evidence of mental health symptoms, violent and sexual offences, or challenges in terms of treatment engagement. Psychologists routinely meet with parole officers to discuss cases (this will be discussed later in terms of ethical considerations). The parole officer, however, is skilled and trained to manage an offender's risk and to influence change.

Another consideration of case management is the increasing emphasis on case formulation to complement more structured (i.e., actuarial) risk assessments (Boer, Thakker, and Ward 2009; Hart 2008). In general, case formulation or conceptualization involves two stages:

1. Part A:
   (a) Completing a file review and interviewing the offender to establish rapport
   (b) Developing a problem list (criminogenic needs)
   (c) Identifying core beliefs (antisociality, violence, sexual exploitation, etc.)
   (d) Identifying distal risk factors
   (e) Identifying precipitating and activating situations (dynamic risk factors)
   (f) Developing a working hypothesis

2. Part B:
   (a) Developing a treatment plan
   (b) Identifying obstacles to treatment and supervision (motivation, attitudes, peers)
   (c) Identifying potential protective factors (changed beliefs, prosocial peers, job, sobriety)
   (d) Overall analysis of the case
   (e) Written case formulation that captures key information
   (f) Monitoring and re-analyzing the case over time

Communication

Central to effective case management is effective communication. Some correctional agencies have automated databases where staff enter information (i.e., reports) regarding an offender. While there is often oversight and quality assurance regarding this information, it should not be a substitute for communication; not everyone will have access to or be able to review the material in a timely manner. For this reason, most corrections staff begin their shifts with a **briefing** of the key events that occurred in the preceding shift. In this manner, staff are alerted to important changes (i.e., the fact that a certain offender has recently received a distressing phone call) and can proceed accordingly. Some refer to this as **dynamic security**. Similarly, as noted in Chapter 4, the notion of dynamic risk assessment is gaining popularity in that it provides a more timely approach to risk management. Strategies to share relevant information (e.g., police to courts, courts to prisons, prisons to community) are in place to ensure that public safety is always paramount in decisions.

Offender Re-Entry and Community Aftercare

The transition from prison to the community is critical to an offender's successful **re-entry**. Recent surveys have identified challenges faced by offenders in their efforts to succeed (e.g., photo identification, transportation, gate money, public assistance access, prescription drug needs, health referrals, housing arrangements, and substance abuse treatment) (LaVigne, Davies, Palmer, and Halberstadt 2008). Brown (2002) notes that offenders who fail generally do so within the first three months of release, suggesting that initial release is a time of most acute risk. She also notes that the predictors of failure change over time, such that events and circumstances at one point are different than the next (i.e., dynamic risks change). Tamatea and Wilson (2009) contend that **protective factors** contribute to understanding offenders' successful desistance, even when static risk is controlled. In combination, these studies highlight the important of enlisting community support to assist offenders in their successful **desistance** from crime. The preoccupation with risk assessment that permeated the 1980s and 1990s has slowly given way to a more holistic view regarding offender re-entry—one where static risk informs the level of service delivery but where dynamic needs and aftercare are also important.

FOLLOWING GRADUATION

Entering the Job Market

Hettich (2008) describes how college or university and work are fundamentally different. He asserts that the knowledge a student acquires in university will be critical to their success, but the process of succeeding in the workplace is very different from that of university. Students often leave university with significant debt, so success in the workplace is paramount. Competition is high for jobs in the criminal justice field and preparation is essential. Table A.2 provides a summary of the differences between attending university and working in a career to help students prepare accordingly for job interviews.

For students planning to apply for corrections jobs with the government, it is critical to read the relevant documents (e.g., planning and priorities reports, mission statements, existing reviews of corrections, and perhaps auditor general and correctional investigator reports) to understand the key issues and legislative backdrop. Volunteer work can also greatly enrich a student's understanding and provide a context for the class materials.

According to Job Outlook (2008), organizations are looking for a different skill set for employees (e.g., communication and interpersonal skills, strong work ethic, teamwork, initiative) than might be seen in students (e.g., creative, sense of humour, outgoing, self-confident) (Michigan State University 2007). A successful transition from the university environment to the work environment requires preparation and an appreciation of the different goals of the two settings. One way to gain a fuller appreciation is to discuss the experiences of fellow graduates regarding their first full-time job interview. Good luck!

Table A.2 Graduates' Perceived Differences between University and the Workplace

University	Workplace
1. Frequent and concrete feedback	Feedback infrequent and not specific
2. Highly structured curriculum	Highly unstructured; fewer directions
3. Personally supportive environment	Less personal support
4. Few significant changes	Frequent and unexpected changes
5. Flexible schedule	Structured schedule
6. Frequent breaks and time off	Limited time off
7. Personal control over time	Responding to others' directions and interests
8. Intellectual challenge	Organizational and people challenges
9. Choose your performance level	A-level work required at all times
10. Focus on development/growth	Focus on getting results for organization
11. Create and explore knowledge	Get results with your knowledge
12. Individual effort	Team effort
13. "Right" answers	Few "right" answers
14. Independence of thinking	Do it the organization's way
15. Professors	Bosses
16. Less initiative required	Lots of initiative required

Source: Michigan State University (2007)

What about Graduate School? (aka Finding the Right Supervisor)

For students who aspire to go to graduate school in order to pursue careers as researchers or psychologists, the task can be daunting. First, there are few graduate programs in correctional/forensic psychology, so availability is limited. Second, this underscores the need for good grades; typically an A average is needed to get into a forensic psychology graduate program (some faculty may only look at psychology courses). Third, few undergraduate students fully know what they want to do in terms of research or careers, so some flexibility is required. These obstacles can be made easier by choosing the right supervisor. Helmus (2008) surveyed seven forensic psychology faculty to get the inside scoop on providing advice to students interested in graduate programs in psychology.

While hers is not an overly rigorous study from a large sample, it provides insights and helpful hints. For instance, while grades were obviously very important, other issues such as collegiality or "fitting in" were often considered a priority in determining whether to accept a potential student into a laboratory. As well, it is clear that preparation was important. Sending out a "Dear Professor X" form letter will yield few positive results, but a review of faculty research interests and recent publications can be very helpful to the prospective student. It demonstrates effort and interest. If you are going to commit to working with someone for up to seven or eight years (assuming you want to get your Ph.D.), you want to get it right! Table A.3 lists the most commonly cited factors relating to successful and unsuccessful applicants.

Table A.3 Reasons for Deciding on Graduate School Admissions

Major positive factors	Interest in conducting research within their area
	Passionate about (their) area
	Good fit
	Stellar GPA
Major negative factors	Applying to wrong program (clinical versus applied)
	Weak grades
	No forensic background
	Lack of preparation in application
Advice	Research the faculty
	Write a specific e-mail to each faculty, not a generic search and replace
	Check out their websites
	Read a few recent papers by preferred faculty
	Contact faculty—by e-mail, phone, in person (preferably)
	Get a good reference from your honours thesis supervisor
	Apply for a grant such as SSHRC/OGS

Source: Helmus (2008)

Box A.2

Ethics in Correctional Practice and Research

Case Study: Correctional Officer

Mary is a 29-year-old correctional officer working in a male offender medium security prison. She has become somewhat familiar with one particular offender, who has been having marital problems. The offender asks her to send a letter to his wife. He claims he doesn't want it vetted by other staff. What should she do?

- Read the letter, and if it is harmless, agree to send it?

- Report the offender to her supervisor?

- Charge the offender for contravening a rule?

Case Study: Psychologist

John is a correctional psychologist who has been seeing an offender for treatment for about 12 months. During their sessions, the offender completed various questionnaires and disclosed some fairly intimate aspects of his life, although none that are of significant concern in terms of his risk to harm himself or others. The offender has applied for parole and is requesting that John *not* complete a report for the National Parole Board because he is concerned that some of the intimate details will be revealed to staff. John doesn't believe his judgment is impaired due to his previous contact with the offender and in fact feels he can write a much more complete assessment because of their relationship. The psychology department is short-staffed, so having someone else complete the assessment would be a burden. Institutional policy is to have the offender sign a release form, but a consent form was completed at the initiation of treatment. What should John do?

- Complete the assessment but ensure the offender reads it prior to submitting to the National Parole Board?

- Conclude that treatment and risk assessment are uniquely different and refuse?

- Check with his chief or the regional psychologist?

ETHICS IN CORRECTIONS

WHEN HE WAS WARDEN AT KINGSTON PENITENTIARY, MONTY BOURKE WOULD TELL new staff, "Don't check your values at the front gate. Bring them with you. We need them in here."

The issue of ethics and ethical practice is of such importance to CSC that an entire edition of its popular *Let's Talk* magazine is devoted to this topic (www.csc-scc.gc.ca/text/pblct/lt-en/2008/32-2/index-eng.shtml). The focus is on real-life experiences and how to resolve ethical dilemmas, rather thanexamining a simple review of ethical principles.

Like any other federal department, CSC has masses of guidelines, directives, and standard operating procedures covering all kinds of conceivable situations; however, sometimes employees can still find themselves in an ethical grey area, where "going by the book" doesn't provide answers. For instance, a survey of corrections staff yielded more than 4500 comments and suggestions with six prominent themes: work environment, organizational culture, communications, leadership, consistency/fairness, and recognition.

Examples of ethical dilemmas in corrections include:

- loyalty to your team or to a colleague versus loyalty to the organization

- being torn between upholding the ethics of your own professional group and carrying out procedures required by the organization

- trying to balance the desire for open communication with privacy requirements

"We expect people to adhere to the rules," says Stephen Wilson, Director General of Values and Ethics, "but rules alone may not address all situations nor will they always provide answers when competing values are in play" (CSC 2008a). Following a national pilot study, CSC developed an ethics course to offer to staff at all levels. The general principle is that people have a moral compass and that, with training and awareness, adherence to ethics becomes empowering.

Ethics Means Doing the Right Thing

Wilson adds that ethics means much more than following laws and policies. "To me, it means doing the right thing. For example, if you obey the law, are you an ethical person? Many people would say 'I'm an ethical person because I don't break the law and I don't harm anyone.' But the truth is if you obey the law, it means you're not a criminal, but it doesn't mean you're an ethical person" (CSC 2008a).

Some Definitions

Values: Enduring beliefs that influence our opinions, actions, and choices.

Ethics: The dimension of human thought and behaviour guided by the standards and principles of "doing the right thing," independent of laws and regulations.

What is an ethical dilemma? It is a situation in which:

- You are unsure of the right thing to do.
- Two or more of your values may be in conflict.
- Some harm may be caused no matter what you do.

General Guidelines for Working Through Ethical Dilemmas (CSC, 2008b)

A ACT

- A decision-making grid—Alternative, Consequence, Tell your story

B Bell, Book and Candle

The bell

- Do any alarm bells go off in my head as I consider my choice of action?

The book

- Does my choice violate any laws, written policies, codes, etc.?

The candle

- Will my decision stand up in the light of day or media spotlight?

C Ethical Checklist

Is it legal?

- Does my decision violate any laws (e.g., *Criminal Code of Canada*, civil law, *Corrections and Conditional Release Act*), directives or policies? Just because it is legal doesn't mean it is ethical.

Is it fair?

- Is my decision fair to all?
- Does it promote "win-win" outcomes with all stakeholders?
- Do I have special information, because of my job, which gives me an unfair advantage over others?
- Is there a conflict between serving *my* interests and those of my organization or the community?

How will I feel afterwards?

- Will I be able to explain my actions so that my family, agency and others would be able to understand and support my decision?
- Would the greater community understand and agree with my choice?

D Ethical Deliberation–Decision-Making Model

1. **Establish the facts.**
   - What are the facts of the case? What values are involved?

2. **Identify values in conflict. Determine which one has the greatest authority and significance.**
   - What are the values which individuals involved in the case live by?
   - Which ones make conflicting demands?
   - Which have the greatest authority/significance in this case?

3. **Identify options and consequences of each option.**
   - Analyze and measure the impact of each option and consider the one that is the least damaging to the organization and the individuals involved, based on the conflicting values.

4. **Make a decision and take action.**
   - After ascertaining the facts, sorting and weighing the conflicting values and applying them to the case, make a decision based on what is right.
   - Be able to explain and justify the decision. (CSC 2008b)

Ethics is not a principle only for psychologists (although psychologists follow the Canadian Psychological Association Code of Ethics). Ultimately, individuals must make decisions to do the right thing. CSC's training and decision grid should assist staff in more smoothly navigating the complex challenges they face on a daily basis.

Below is a list of the top 10 issues to consider when thinking about careers in Canadian corrections.

Top 10 List

Advances to Come, Debates, and Ethical Conundrums

1 What are the elements that make up good case management?

2 Should clinicians conduct parole assessments (i.e., risk assessments) on offenders they are treating?

3 What do population demographics tell us about employment opportunities in corrections?

4 Which is the more important part of the job for a parole officer: public safety or rehabilitation?

5 Which is the more important part of the job for a correctional officer: public safety or rehabilitation?

6 Should a university degree be required for a correctional officer position? Explain.

7 For correctional staff, which is more important: personal suitability factors, knowledge, or abilities? Explain.

8 Why do correctional psychologists "treat" psychological symptoms such as anxiety or depression when they are not important criminogenic needs?

9 Based on the descriptions of different jobs, explain why staff are viewed as fundamental to effective corrections.

10 If you were to apply for a job in corrections, how would you proceed?

SUMMARY

The goal of this final chapter was to give students a flavour of the kinds of jobs available in corrections to better prepare them for career decisions. In addition to providing descriptive information, other useful details such as salaries and educational requirements were provided. It should be apparent that some jobs are specific to provincial (i.e., probation officer) and federal corrections (i.e., correctional program officer) and that preparation is key to obtaining employment. Some insight into the transition from university to the working world was reviewed to provide students with realistic expectations. The "day in the life" profile was intended to realistically depict the role of the correctional psychologist. Unlike on television, they are not all famous profilers who spend their time interviewing serial killers. They are, however, individuals committed to helping offenders progress toward a safe and productive return to the community. In terms of a career, it was noted that corrections provides considerable opportunity for working at different jobs. It can be challenging, rewarding, and interesting.

Another goal of this chapter was to illustrate the complementary roles played by different staff members with the overall objective of case management. The parole officer is the primary person responsible, but program staff and psychology contribute through meetings and reports. Effective communication, good case analysis (through case formulation), and a seamless transition from prison to the community contribute to improved outcomes for offenders (and the public!).

We also highlighted the importance of ethics in corrections. As noted earlier in the text, corrections is about people (not risk instruments, questionnaires, treatment manuals, and the like), so it is fitting that the book concludes with the observation that ethics is not just for psychologists; rather, it is about doing the right thing. It involves treating others (both offenders and colleagues) with dignity and respect.

Additional Reading

Helmus, L. 2008. "Advice for finding a thesis supervisor: What professors have to say." *Crime Scene*. 15, 38–41.

Relevant Websites

Public Service Commission of Canada—Careers in the Federal Public Service
http://jobs-emplois.gc.ca

Correctional Service of Canada—Careers
www.csc-scc.gc.ca/text/emplo-eng.shtml

Glossary

<div class="two-column">

[A]boriginal healing lodge A facility in which offenders can be exposed to correctional services in an environment that incorporates Aboriginal traditions and beliefs.

[A]boriginal overrepresentation Aboriginal people are incarcerated at levels higher than their proportion in the general population would predict.

[ac]ute dynamic risk factors Quickly changing risk factors (e.g., negative mood).

[A]cute–2007 Empirical actuarial scale designed to assess acute dynamic predictors of sexual recidivism.

[ad]aptation Evolutionary concept that refers to traits or characteristics that eventually become commonplace in a given species because they somehow enhanced reproductive success in an ancestral environment.

[ad]olescent-onset juvenile offenders Juvenile offenders who begin to show behavioural problems in their teen years.

[ag]gression (specifically human aggression) Refers to the intent and action of inflicting harm on others either through physical means (e.g., punching, gun, knife, slap) or indirect means (e.g., damaging someone's reputation with disparaging gossip).

[am]ino acids The basic proteins of life that are essentially the precursors to neurotransmitters. Amino acids are converted into neurotransmitters via enzymes.

[an]cestral environment An evolutionary term that refers to the hunter-and-gatherer era, from which most of our current-day adaptations are hypothesized to have evolved.

[an]drogens Steroidal hormones that play an important role in the development and growth of masculine characteristics (e.g., male sex organs, deepening voice, facial hair, muscle strength). They are also found females. The most well-known androgen is testosterone.

[an]tisocial behaviour Generic term that encompasses a wide range of behaviours (e.g., hitting, slapping, punching, lying, cheating, stealing, running away, breaking and entering, homicide, and so forth).

[an]tisocial orientation General term referring to a variety of antisocial characteristics and behaviours, such as antisocial personality disorder and psychopathy, self-regulation problems, impulsivity, hostility, employment instability, childhood behaviour problems, and violation of conditional release.

[an]tisocial path One of the main pathways influencing sexual aggression in Malamuth's Hierarchical-Mediational Confluence Model. Abusive home environments lead to early delinquent behaviour, which leads to impersonal sexuality, which in turn leads to sexual aggression.

[an]tisocial personality disorder (APD) Official diagnosis defined in the Diagnostic and Statistical Manual of Mental Disorders (DSM-IV), referring to a constellation of antisocial behaviours occurring during adulthood that have persisted for at least six months. Sometimes APD is used interchangeably with psychopathy, albeit incorrectly.

[att]achment Social bond proposed by Travis Hirschi in his social control theory, which refers to one's attachment to others (e.g., parents, friends, teachers).

[att]ention-deficit hyperactivity disorder (ADHD) Inattention and restlessness that is not developmentally appropriate.

[av]ersive conditioning Procedure whereby an unpleasant stimulus (e.g., an electric shock) is presented while an individual is engaged in problematic behaviour (e.g., experiencing sexual arousal while observing child pornography) with the goal of creating an aversion to the activity.

[be]havioural genetics A sub-discipline of biology that studies how genes in humans and animals influence behaviour.

[be]havioural treatments For sex offenders, treatments that use conditioning to reduce deviant sexual interests or increase appropriate sexual interests.

behaviourism A school of thought in psychology that emphasizes the view that all behaviour can be described and studied scientifically without reference to internal psychological constructs such as the mind.

belief Social bond proposed by Travis Hirschi in his social control theory, which refers to one's conviction to the view that people should obey common rules (e.g., the law).

Big Four The four most strongly correlated risk factors, as identified through meta-analysis.

biosocial theory of crime Theory of crime proposed by Hans Eysenck that suggests that people commit crime as a result of the interaction between biologically determined characteristics (e.g., nervous system processing) and environmental stimuli (e.g., parental discipline).

blockage Some people may be blocked from meeting their sexual and emotional needs in prosocial ways (e.g., consenting sexual contact with adults).

briefing In a prison, the sharing of key information with staff regarding events that have recently occurred in order to enhance dynamic security.

case management Coordination of offender services in prison and the community in order to manage risk and enhance rehabilitation.

casework record Document that reflects ongoing contact between an offender and correctional staff. Where there is an automated offender management system, the casework record is completed electronically.

causal mechanisms Processes that directly cause a behaviour (i.e., factor X causes factor Y). In order to confirm the existence of a causal mechanism, a research design is needed that allows for the independent variable to be manipulated by the experimenter. Ethically, however, we are unable to do this most of the time. For example, if we wanted to know beyond a doubt whether child abuse causes crime, we would have to randomly assign children to one of two conditions—an abuse and a non-abuse situation, and clearly this is not an option. There are reasonable proxy designs that get us closer to causality, such as treatment studies that use random assignment or comparison groups as well as longitudinal designs that examine whether naturally occurring changes in variable X are related to changes in variable Y.

Central Eight The eight most strongly identified risk factors, as identified through meta-analysis.

child abuse Any act or omission that results in harm or threatened harm to the health or welfare of a child.

child-onset juvenile offenders Juvenile offenders who have behavioural problems starting very early in childhood.

classical conditioning A form of learning that takes place when an unconditioned stimulus (e.g., food) that produces an unconditioned response (e.g., salivation) is paired with a conditioned stimulus (e.g., a tone) such that, over time, a conditioned response (e.g., salivation) is reproduced using only the conditioned stimulus.

clinical notes The working notes typically maintained by a clinical psychologist in a separate file to ensure confidentiality.

cognitive-behavioural therapy (CBT) Combines elements of cognitive and behavioural treatments to address psychological problems and abnormal behaviour.

cognitive distortions Beliefs that justify, excuse, or otherwise support sex offending.

cognitive social learning theory of crime A learning theory of crime that attends to both social and cognitive factors as well as behaviour.

commitment Social bond proposed by Travis Hirschi in his social control theory that refers to the time, energy, and effort one places in conventional behaviour (e.g., getting an education).

community notification Informing the public that a sex offender is being released to a particular city or neighbourhood.

</div>

community service Requirement by the courts to provide a form of service to the community (i.e., speaking to youth groups, cleaning up public sites, etc.) in lieu of incarceration. Could be performed in conjunction with a probation or community supervision order.

compensation Reimbursement for loss and/or harm experienced by being a victim of crime. Can be more inclusive than simple financial reimbursement for cost of loss.

conditioned response In classical conditioning, a response to a previously neutral stimulus turned conditioned stimulus (e.g., salivation is a conditioned response when it occurs after the presentation of a tone, which has become a conditioned stimulus by repeatedly pairing it with food, an unconditioned stimulus).

conditioned stimulus In classical conditioning, a previously neutral stimulus that comes to evoke a conditioned response after it is paired with an unconditioned stimulus (e.g., a tone becomes a conditioned stimulus that elicits a salivation response when repeatedly paired with food, an unconditioned stimulus).

Conduct Disorder (CD) Official diagnosis defined in the Diagnostic and Statistical Manual of Mental Disorders (DSM-IV). It refers to a constellation of antisocial behaviours (e.g., stealing, getting into fights, using a weapon during a fight) occurring during childhood that have persisted for at least six months.

Conflict Tactics Scale Scale designed to assess how a person and his or her partner resolve conflict; measures constructive problem solving, verbal aggression, and physical aggression.

conscience One component of the Freudian superego, which allows an individual to distinguish between right and wrong and inhibit id pursuits that are out of line with one's morals.

corporal punishment The deliberate infliction of pain intended to discipline or change a person's behaviour.

corporate crime Offences committed by organizations to advance their own interests.

correctional officer Person charged with the responsibility of the supervision, safety, and security of prisoners in a secure custody facility (i.e., jail, prison).

correctional program Structured set of methods and activities delivered by skilled staff to provide opportunities for offenders to gain new attitudes and skills in order to reduce the likelihood of reoffending. Also referred to as appropriate service delivery or treatment program.

correctional program officer Highly trained para-professional who delivers correctional programs to groups of offenders.

correctional psychology Application of psychology to the understanding of the assessment and management of individuals who engage in criminal behaviour.

Correctional Service of Canada Integrated prison and community correctional system responsible for supervising offenders who receive sentences of two years or greater.

correctional treatment plan Written plan that identifies an offender's criminogenic needs and treatment requirements. Typically includes the ranking of needs from most to least serious and an indication of the intensity of programming required based on risk assessment.

Corrections and Conditional Release Act Act brought into force on November 1, 1992, that governs corrections and the conditional release and detention of offenders. Its purpose is to contribute to the maintenance of a just, peaceful, and safe society by: (a) carrying out sentences imposed by courts through the safe and humane custody and supervision of offenders; and (b) assisting the rehabilitation of offenders and their reintegration into the community as law-abiding citizens through the provision of programs in penitentiaries and in the community.

crime desistance The cessation of criminal behaviour, most often described as a process of change rather than an instantaneous event.

criminal behaviour Intentional behaviour that, when detected, is sanctioned by the courts as a breach of society's established rules.

criminogenic needs/factors Changeable risk factors that, when reduced, result in reduced criminal behaviour. Sometimes referred to as dynamic risk factors.

cross-sectional research Type of research design whereby different groups people who differ on a variable of interest (e.g., involvement in del quent activity) are observed at a particular point in time to determi how they differ on some other variable (e.g., parental supervision) or of variables.

custody classification Method of initially assessing inmate risks that balanc security requirements with program needs. Placement considers both c tody level and area within a prison.

Custody Rating Scale Statistical scale used by CSC to determine secur placement.

delayed disclosure Victims of childhood sexual abuse often do not imme ately tell someone they have been abused.

delusion Erroneous beliefs that usually involve a misinterpretation of perce tions or experiences.

desistance The process by which an offender ceases their engagement in cri inal behaviour, usually as a function of internal and external changes.

deterrence Expectation that increased costs (i.e., longer sentences) by t courts will suppress the frequency and/or severity of crime. The impact these costs on the particular individual involved with the courts referred to as specific deterrence. The impact on the population as whole is referred to as general deterrence.

deviant identification The process of identifying with a deviant role mo (e.g., a criminal father).

Diagnostic and Statistical Manual of Mental Disorders Manual published the American Psychiatric Association that lists mental and personal disorders.

differential association theory Theory of crime proposed by Edwin Sutherla that suggests that people commit crime when they are exposed (e.g., in in mate group settings) to an excess of definitions (i.e., attitudes) that favourable to law-breaking versus definitions that are unfavourable law-breaking.

differential association-reinforcement theory Theory of crime proposed Robert Burgess and Ron Akers that combines operant conditioning pri ciples with differential association principles and suggests that peo commit crime when criminal behaviour is more reinforced (e.g., in in mate group settings) than non-criminal behaviour.

disinhibition In Finkelhor's model, he noted that inhibitions against ch sexual abuse are either circumvented or absent to allow an offender to on his or her sexual interest in children.

diversion A decision not to prosecute the young offender but rather ha him or her undergo an educational or community service program.

Domestic Violence Risk Appraisal Guide (DVRAG) Empirical actua risk-assessment instrument designed to estimate risk of spousal assa recidivism in adult male batterers.

Duluth Model Treatment program for male batterers that believes abusers overwhelmingly men who use violence to exercise control over women.

dynamic risk factors Risk factors that can change, unlike static factors, w such change related to reduced criminal behaviour.

dynamic security Maintaining the security of a prison through the use dynamic information such as offender–offender interactions rather th relying on static measures such as perimeter fences.

dysphoric/borderline batterer Male batterer who is depressed and has b derline personality traits, primarily exhibits violence toward his intim partner, and has problems with jealously and abandonment.

ecological model Model of family violence that examines the relationsh between multiple levels of influence, including individual, relationsh community, and societal levels, in understanding family violence.

economic crime Criminal offences where the primary motivation is e nomic gain.

effect size Outcome measure indicating the degree of the relationsh between two variables or the impact of an intervention.

ego The conscious part of the Freudian personality, which acts as the med tor between the instinctual demands of the id and the social restricti of the superego.

ego-ideal Component of the Freudian superego that represents the socia accepted standards that we all aspire to.

er maltreatment (or elder abuse) Any act or omission that results in harm or threatened harm to the health or welfare of an elderly person.

ectra complex A conflict, experienced in the phallic stage of development, whereby young females develop an unconscious desire for their father and hostility toward their mother.

otional congruence Perceived fit between an adult's emotional needs and a child's characteristics. Also referred to as emotional identification with children.

pirical actuarial approach Follows explicit rules about what factors to consider and how to combine those factors to arrive at a final estimate of risk. More specifically, a selection and combination of items are derived from their observed statistical relationship with recidivism. Provides tables linking scores to expected recidivism rates.

idemiological Refers to research designs that utilize large representative samples of the general population (or, in some cases, the entire population) in order to study the incidence, prevalence, and/or nature of a disease or a particular behaviour (e.g., crime).

ics That dimension of human thought and behaviour that is guided by standards and principles of "what is the right thing to do," independent of laws and regulations.

genics The belief that the evolution of the human species can be artificially improved by preventing individuals considered genetically "defective" from reproducing by methods such as forced sterilization.

idence-based practice Body of research and replicable clinical knowledge that describes contemporary correctional assessment, programming, and supervision strategies that lead to improved correctional outcomes such as the rehabilitation of offenders and increased public safety.

ibitionism An interest in exposing one's genitals to an unsuspecting stranger.

offender assistance Providing assistance in terms of accommodation, employment, and addictions counselling. Often provided by non-governmental agencies such as the Elizabeth Fry Society, the John Howard Society, and the St. Leonard's Society.

osure to parental violence Witnessing or knowledge of violence between parents as a child.

ernalizing problems Behavioural difficulties such as delinquency, fighting, bullying, lying, and destructive behaviour.

inction In classical conditioning, when the conditioned response no longer gets elicited by the conditioned stimulus as a result of the conditioned stimulus not being paired with an unconditioned stimulus (e.g., salivation—a conditioned response—no longer gets elicited by the presentation of a tone—a conditioned stimulus—because the tone has been repeatedly presented in the absence of the unconditioned stimulus, such as food).

rajudicial measures Community options and less serious alternatives than youth court.

se negative Occurs when it is predicted that an offender will not violently recidivate and actually does.

se positive Occurs when it is predicted that an offender will violently recidivate but actually does not.

iily-only batterer A male batterer who is typically not violent outside the home, has few psychopathological symptoms, and does not possess negative attitudes supportive of violence.

iily-supportive interventions Interventions that connect at-risk families to various support services (e.g., child care, counselling, medical assistance) that may be available in their community.

iily violence Any violence occurring between family members. Typically occurs in private settings

eral corrections The term used to describe correctional agencies for offenders serving two or more years. Includes prisons and parole offices in every region of the country.

erally sentenced women In Canada, offenders sentenced to periods of imprisonment of two years or more fall under federal jurisdiction. Those sentenced to less than two years are the responsibility of the provinces. Women sentenced to two years or more are collectively known as federally sentenced women.

ale salient predictor Risk factor that predicts recidivism in females and males but the strength of the association is significantly stronger for females.

feminism "A set of theories about women's oppression and a set of strategies for change" (Daly and Chesney-Lind: 502). The common theme that binds feminist theories of female crime is the assumption that the oppression of women plays a central role in the explanation and prediction of female criminal conduct.

fetal alcohol syndrome Disorder caused when a woman drinks alcohol during pregnancy. Diagnosed when the alcohol consumption results in prenatal and/or postnatal growth delay, characteristic cranio-facial anomalies, and central nervous system impairments. Prevalence rates of this disorder are known to be significantly higher in Aboriginal populations.

fetal alcohol effects Milder, more subtle form of fetal alcohol syndrome. Diagnosed when there is evidence of alcohol consumption by a woman when she is pregnant and any two of the following three criteria are present: prenatal and/or postnatal growth delay, characteristic cranio-facial anomalies, or central nervous system impairments. Prevalence rates of this disorder are known to be significantly higher in Aboriginal populations.

fetal alcohol spectrum disorder Umbrella term used to describe a range of disabilities that may affect people whose mothers drank alcohol during pregnancy.

financial abuse (material abuse) The illegal or improper exploitation and/or use of funds or resources.

first-degree murder Murder is first-degree when it is planned and deliberate or under any of the following conditions: (a) the victim is a peace officer (e.g., police officer) or prison employee (e.g., correctional officer, institutional parole officer); or (b) the victim's death is caused while committing or attempting to commit the hijacking of an aircraft, sexual assault, kidnapping, hostage taking, criminal harassment, terrorist activity, use of explosives in association with a criminal organization, or intimidation.

first-order correlate of crime Alternative term for major risk factors—the most important correlates of crime—based on empirical evidence.

forensic psychology Application of psychology to the legal system, intended to guide legal decision making.

frotteurism An interest in touching and rubbing against a non-consenting person.

gender informed Refers to research, risk tools, or treatment methods that were originally developed based on female-centred principles. The end result may or may not include hypothesized gender-specific factors (e.g., poverty) as well as gender neutral factors (e.g., criminal attitudes). Researchers and program developers initiated the process using contemporary female-focused theory and research. It doesn't matter if the final risk instrument, program, or policy resembles gender-neutral methods.

gender neutral Refers to research, risk tools, or treatment methods originally grounded in theories or research that either implicitly or explicitly excluded the female perspective. The assumption of gender-neutral approaches is that there are no differences between males and females.

gender responsive Describes correctional assessment and programming strategies that have been designed to address hypothesized female-specific risk factors, treatment targets, or responsivity factors.

gender specificity Term used to describe a situation in which a risk factor or treatment approach is unique to one gender but not the other. For example, a risk factor that predicts crime only for females but not at all for males would be taken as evidence of gender specificity, in this case in favour of females. Risk factors may also possess gender specificity for males as well.

general responsivity Refers to the principle of delivering treatment programs in a manner that is consistent with offenders' learning styles (i.e., skills-based, cognitive-behavioural).

General Social Survey (GSS) on Victimization A representative sample (territories excluded) of people over the age of 14 in 24 000 Canadian households is telephoned (via random-digit dialing) and surveyed about their criminal victimization experiences in the past 12 months.

general theory of crime Theory of crime proposed by Michael Gottfredson and Travis Hirschi that suggests that people do not commit crime because they possess high levels of self-control.

generally violent/antisocial A male batterer who is violent inside and outside the home; engages in other criminal acts; has drug, alcohol, and impulsive problems; and possesses violence-supportive attitudes.

general population The regular area of a prison, which can include dormitories (i.e., remand centres and provincial jails) or ranges with cells housing one or two offenders each (i.e., provincial jails and federal prisons).

Generic Program Performance Measure An interview-based rating scale completed by a correctional program officer before and after a program as a measure of program performance; taps into the construct of offender change.

genotype An individual's complete genetic makeup regardless of whether a particular gene has a visible influence on an individual's functioning or behaviour; what's on the "inside" versus the "outside."

Gladue Court An Aboriginal persons court, which performs the same duties as a regular court but in a way that is in line with Aboriginal beliefs and traditions.

Gladue decision The Gladue Court derives its name from the 1999 Supreme Court of Canada decision of *R v. Gladue*, which set out the parameters of section 718.2(e) of the *Criminal Code* regarding the sentencing of offenders and, in particular, Aboriginal offenders. All available sanctions other than imprisonment that are reasonable in the circumstances should be considered.

Good Lives Model–Comprehensive In addition to focusing on the usual risk management issues, this model emphasizes helping offenders identify and achieve healthy goals that promote psychological well-being. This is expected to increase the motivation of offenders to participate and engage in treatment, as well as reduce their likelihood of reoffending because they learn how to achieve fundamental human needs through prosocial means rather than through offending.

HCR-20 A structured professional judgement instrument designed to assess risk for violence.

hedonistic serial murderer In Holmes and DeBurger's (1988) typology, this type of serial murderer kills for sexual gratification or materialistic gains.

heterosocial competence The ability to competently interact with members of the opposite sex.

hostile aggression Impulsive reaction to some real or perceived provocation or threat that is ultimately aimed at harming the victim.

hostile masculinity path One of the main pathways influencing sexual aggression in Malamuth's Hierarchical-Mediational Confluence Model. Attitudes accepting violence toward women lead to narcissism, hostility toward women, and sexual dominance, which in turn lead to sexual aggression.

human trafficking The recruitment, transport, or harbouring of persons by means of threat, use of force, or other forms of coercion, abduction, fraud, or deception for the purpose of exploitation.

id The unconscious, instinctual part of the Freudian personality that seeks the immediate gratification of basic drives (e.g., aggression).

identity fraud The use of personal information without the person's knowledge or consent to commit various crimes under their name, such as fraud, theft, or forgery.

identity theft The collection, possession, and trafficking of personal information, which typically takes place independent of or in preparation for the commission of identity fraud.

incapacitation The incarceration of criminals to reduce the risk to the community.

idiographic An examination of individual cases in order to understand something.

incidence The number of *new* cases identified or reported at a given point in time, usually one year.

intimate partner violence Violence occurring between intimate partners who are living together or separated.

instigator In social learning theory, events in the environment or within the individual that act trigger violence.

instrumental aggression Premeditated aggression ultimately aimed at achieving some secondary goal beyond harming the victim (e.g., money).

interactive Effects that are known to be multiplicative, exponential, or synergistic rather than merely additive. Thus while psychopathy and sexual deviance

may elevate the risk of sexual recidivism by two points, in combination, t risk of sexual recidivism may increase by six points. Or, alternately, the no level generated by two young toddlers is interactive in that "one boy" pl "one boy" doesn't equal two boys playing but seems more like six toddlers

inter-individual differences Differences in criminal behaviour betwee individuals.

internalizing problems Emotional difficulties such as anxiety, depressic and obsessions.

intra-individual differences Differences in criminal behaviour over time a across situations for the same individual.

involvement Social bond proposed by Travis Hirschi in his social cont theory that refers to the time and energy one spends taking part activities that are in line with the conventional interests of socie (e.g., school).

longitudinal research Type of research design whereby a particular group individuals are observed repeatedly over time.

John Howard Society A non-governmental organization committed to t support and rehabilitation of individuals involved with the criminal ju tice system.

mandatory reporting Laws that require the reporting of suspected cases (child) abuse or neglect.

Massachusetts Treatment Centre: Child Molester Typology, Version (MTC:CM3) A typology developed to reflect the heterogeneity of ch molesters.

Massachusetts Treatment Centre: Rapist Typology A typology develop to reflect the heterogeneity of rapists.

mass murder Killing three or more victims in a single location with "cooling-off period" between murders.

mechanical approach Following explicit rules about what factors to consi and how to combine those factors to arrive at a final estimate of risk; t selection and combination of items are derived from theory or reviews the empirical literature and no tables are provided.

mediators Variables that explain the relationship between variable X and It might be concluded that variable X exerts its influence on variable through a third intervening variable—the mediator.

meta-analysis Quantitative method of combining the results of independe studies (usually drawn from published literature) and synthesizing su maries and conclusions that may be used to detect and evaluate trends

minor risk factors Risk factors with very weak association with crimir behaviour.

mission-oriented serial murderer In Holmes and DeBurger's (198 typology, this type of serial murderer is not psychotic and takes it up him- or herself to rid the world of a particular group of people he or s views as undesirable.

mission statement A statement of the guiding principles, values, and goals a correctional agency.

moderate risk factors Risk factors with moderate association with crimir behaviour; less strong than the Big Four.

moderators Variables that cause the relationship between variable A an to vary as a function of a third variable—the moderator.

money laundering The process whereby money received through ille activity is disguised to mask where it came from.

motivational interviewing Technique that focuses on the provision of nc judgmental feedback regarding an offender's risks and experience of pr lems. Avoids labels and confrontation and assists the offender to gener goals for behaviour change.

natural selection Primary mechanism through which evolution created species. Natural selection works by allowing the "trait" that bestowe reproductive fitness advantage to be "selected" for in the sense that th with the trait lived long enough to procreate and pass it on to the ne generation.

need Risk factor that is a treatment target. When the need relates to increa likelihood of criminal behaviour, it is referred to as criminogenic.

negative punishment In operant conditioning, a decrease in the likeliho of a behaviour being exhibited in the future due to the removal of a ple ant stimulus following the behaviour.

gative reinforcement In operant conditioning, an increase in the likelihood of a behaviour being exhibited in the future due to the removal of an aversive stimulus following the behaviour.

glect Intentional or unintentional refusal or failure of caregiver to provide proper shelter, safety, supervision, or nutritional needs.

urodevelopmental perturbation Early problems in brain functioning that may play a causal role in pedophilia.

urotic criminal An individual who commits crime as a result of a harsh superego, which is assumed to lead to pathological levels of unconscious guilt that can be resolved by receiving punishment (e.g., a legal sanction for a crime).

urotransmitters The chemical messengers of the brain.

mothetic An examination of group data regarding patterns and general trends in order to understand something.

t criminally responsible on account of a mental disorder Person who, due to a mental disorder at the time of an offence, is incapable of appreciating the nature and quality of the act or knowing that it was wrong.

servational learning Learning that occurs as a function of observing and often imitating behaviour exhibited by other people.

cupational crime Offences committed against businesses and government by those with a "higher" social status.

edipus complex A conflict experienced in the phallic stage of development whereby young males develop an unconscious desire for their mother and fear of retribution from their father.

fender classification Sometimes referred to as custody classification, this process involves the assessment of offender risk and need levels in order to determine the appropriate security placement of incarcerated prisoners.

fender rehabilitation The delivery of correctional programming that targets criminogenic needs for the purpose of reducing rates of reoffending by program completers.

erant conditioning A form of learning that takes place by experiencing environmental consequences caused by behaviour, especially reinforcement and punishment.

positional defiant disorder Pattern of negativistic, hostile, and defiant behaviour.

er-policing The practice of police targeting people of particular ethnic or racial backgrounds or who live in particular neighbourhoods.

raphilias Sexual disorders characterized by recurrent, intense, sexually arousing fantasies, sexual urges, or behaviours generally involving 1) non-human objects, 2) the suffering or humiliation of oneself or one's partner, or 3) children or other non-consenting persons that occur over a period of at least six months.

rent-focused interventions Interventions directed at assisting parents to recognize warning signs for later juvenile violence and/or training parents to effectively manage any behavioural problems that arise.

role officer With a background in social sciences, officers who supervise offenders, either in the community or federal prison, providing counselling and writing reports for various decision-makers (i.e., wardens, National Parole Board) regarding release suitability.

triarchal theory Theory that suggests violence of men against their female partners is rooted in a broad set of cultural beliefs and values that support the male dominance of women.

dophilia Sexual preference for children who have not yet begun puberty.

nile plethysmography (PPG) Measurement of penile tumescence (erection) during the presentation of various stimuli, such as descriptions of sexual activity. Deviant sexual interest is usually inferred from the amount of arousal in response to deviant stimuli relative to non-deviant stimuli.

rsonality disorders Maladaptive patterns of relating, perceiving, and thinking that are relatively inflexible and serious enough to cause distress or impaired functioning.

armacological treatments In the case of sex offenders, treatment with drugs, usually with the goal of reducing sex drive (e.g., desire, arousal).

enotypic An individual's observed properties or how one's genotype is actually expressed. For example, a genotype may have a recessive gene for blue eyes but a phenotype may be for brown eyes.

phi coefficient Measure of the degree of association between two binary variables. This measure is similar to the correlation coefficient in its interpretation.

physical abuse The infliction of physical pain or injury.

PIC–R An integrative and situational model of criminal behaviour that recognizes the influence of both historical and immediate factors in an individual arriving at the decision to engage in a criminal act and to view such behaviour as appropriate.

pleasure principle The driving force of the id, which leads people to seek immediate pleasure while trying to avoid pain.

polymorphism Biological term that refers to a situation where alternative versions of a discrete trait exist naturally in a given species. For example, a polymorphism exists for eye colour (e.g., blue eyes, brown eyes, green eyes) and blood type—A, B, AB, O). The contrasting forms are called morphs.

Ponzi scheme Pyramid investment scheme where no legitimate investment occurs and the money from later investors is used to pay earlier investors.

positive punishment In operant conditioning, a decrease in the likelihood of a behaviour being exhibited in the future due to the addition of an aversive stimulus following the behaviour.

positive reinforcement In operant conditioning, an increase in the likelihood of a behaviour being exhibited in the future due to the addition of a pleasant stimulus following the behaviour.

power/control serial murderer In Holmes and DeBurger's (1988) typology, this type of serial murderer desires the total capture of the victim and wants to hold the fate of the victim in his or her hands.

prevalence The *total* number of people who have experienced abuse or neglect in a specified time period.

price fixing Occurs when companies group together to sell the same product for the same price; there is no price variability for the consumer.

primary intervention strategies Strategies implemented prior to any violence occurring with the goal of decreasing its likelihood later.

proactive aggression Aggression directed at achieving a goal or receiving positive reinforcers.

probation officer Same as a parole officer, but probation officers supervise provincial offenders on a probation order prior to or after a period of incarceration.

professional override Provision within a decision-making process to permit trained staff, with well articulated reasons, to arrive at a decision different than that recommended by the results of a standardized risk measure.

program accreditation The process whereby correctional programs are reviewed by external experts in terms of theory, assessment, and outcome to determine if they meet contemporary standards of excellence.

project officer An entry position in government, usually involving the monitoring of progress on a specific project. This can involve gathering and collating information to communicate to supervisors and other employees.

prostitution The provision of sexual services in exchange for money.

protective factor Variable or factor that, if present, decreases the likelihood of a negative outcome such as antisocial behaviour and juvenile offending or increases the likelihood of a positive outcome.

provincial corrections Jail and probation services for youth and adults, the latter who receive sentences of less than two years.

psychodynamic A school of thought in psychology developed by Sigmund Freud that emphasizes the role of conscious and unconscious psychological forces (forming a dynamic personality system) in understanding human behaviour.

psychological abuse (emotional abuse) The infliction of mental distress.

psychopath A personality disorder defined by a cluster of interpersonal, affective, behavioural, and antisocial traits.

psychopathy Typified by a constellation of affective, interpersonal, and behavioural characteristics such as superficial charm, grandiosity, manipulation and lying, absence of remorse, inability to feel empathy, impulsivity, risk-taking, irresponsibility, and living a parasitic lifestyle.

psychosexual stages Distinct developmental stages proposed by Sigmund Freud that are characterized by conflicts that people must resolve in order to develop healthy personalities.

rape myths Beliefs that justify, excuse, or otherwise support rape.

reactive aggression An emotionally aggressive response to a perceived threat or frustration.

reality principle The driving force of the ego, which leads people to defer gratification until it is physically and socially safe to pursue it.

re-entry Involves the use of programs and community aftercare targeted at promoting the effective reintegration of offenders into communities upon release from prison.

regulator In social learning theory, the consequences of violence that result in an increase or decrease in the probability of future violence.

rehabilitative program See correctional program.

relapse prevention (RP) For sex offenders, RP focuses on addressing putative dynamic risk factors, identifying situational risk factors (e.g., high-risk situation), and developing ways to avoid or otherwise cope with these situational risk factors with the ultimate goal of avoiding recidivism.

reproductive fitness variance The range of possible offspring an organism can produce.

resilience The capacity for children to experience adverse events and yet not experience negative outcomes.

resilient A child who has multiple risk factors but can overcome them and prevail.

restitution Financial reimbursement for property damaged or lost by being a victim of crime.

restorative justice Emphasizes repairing the harm caused by crime. When victims, offenders, and community members meet voluntarily to decide how to achieve this, transformation can result.

restricted range Statistical situation whereby the lack of observed variance in a given variable is so small that it invalidates the statistical technique in question. Thus if we wanted to examine the correlation between grades in this course with your incoming GPA, but everyone received an A+ in this course, we would have a restricted range problem.

retribution Considered a morally acceptable response to crime intended to satisfy an aggrieved party, including society, through the application of punishment or other sanctions, if proportionate.

risk assessment The determination of risk or probability of reoffending through the systematic review of static and dynamic factors.

risk factors Measurable constructs (e.g., criminal history, employment stability) that predict future criminal reoffending. In order to be deemed a risk factor, the construct must be measured before criminal reoffending is assessed. Thus evidence for risk factors comes from predictive or longitudinal studies.

risk management The application of risk-assessment information to differentially allocate resources such as programming and supervision in order to manage changes in risk over time.

sanctions Terms used to describe punishment imposed by the courts.

secondary intervention strategies Strategies that attempt to reduce the frequency of violence.

segregation An area of a prison where there is greater security and in which prisoners are placed if there are concerns regarding safety. This can occur in instances where there are concerns for a prisoner's protection from others or because he or she is dangerous and poses a threat to others, including staff.

selection pressures Recurring conditions in the ancestral environment that favoured certain traits (in a reproductive fitness sense) and thus promoted their eventual conversion into adaptations.

Self-Appraisal Questionnaire (SAQ) A self-report empirical actuarial risk-assessment instrument developed to estimate risk of violent and non-violent recidivism.

serial murder Killing three or more people, usually in different locations, with a cooling-off period between murders.

sex offender registries In many jurisdictions, sex offenders are required to register with the police upon release and to maintain current information about their address.

Sex Offender Risk Appraisal Guide (SORAG) An empirical actuarial risk-assessment instrument designed to estimate risk of violent recidivism among adult sex offenders.

sexual abuse Any kind of sexual behaviour directed toward a child or unwant(ed) sexual behaviour directed toward an adult.

sexual deviancy A general term referring to a variety of deviant sexual inter(ests) and behaviours, such as sexual interest in children, sexual preoccupa(tion), and sex as coping.

sexual sadism Being sexually aroused and interested in inflicting humiliati(on) or pain on others.

sex tourism Going to other countries to seek (often child) prostitution.

Sexual Violence Risk–20 (SVR–20) A structured professional judgme(nt) instrument consisting of both static and putatively dynamic facto(rs) designed to estimate risk for sexual offending.

social control theory Theory of crime proposed by Travis Hirschi that su(g)gests that people don't commit crimes because of social controls or t(he) bonds people have to society.

social learning theory Theory of crime proposed by Ron Akers that sugge(sts) that people commit crime not only as a result of direct reinforcement (of) criminal behaviour through a process of operant conditioning but al(so) through vicarious reinforcement by observing others being rewarded (for) their criminal behaviour.

sociopathy A dated term previously used to describe psychopathy. Often us(ed) interchangeably though incorrectly with psychopathy and antisocial pe(r)sonality disorder.

sociopath Label used to describe individuals who commit antisocial ac(ts) because of family or environmental factors.

specific responsivity Principle of delivering treatment programs in a mann(er) that considers the unique aspects of the offenders, including gender, mo(ti)vation, and strengths.

Spousal Assault Risk Assessment Guide (SARA) A structured profession(al) judgment instrument consisting of both historical and dynamic risk facto(rs) designed to estimate risk for spousal assault recidivism.

spree murder Killing three or more victims at two or more locations with (a) cooling-off period between murders.

stable dynamic risk factors Slowly changing risk factors (e.g., sexu(al) preoccupation).

Stable-2007 An empirical actuarial scale designed to assess stable dynam(ic) predictors of sexual recidivism.

Static-99 An empirical actuarial risk-assessment instrument designed to es(ti)mate risk of sexual recidivism among adult sex offenders.

static risk factors Risk factors with a demonstrated correlation with crim(i)nal behaviour, but which cannot change over time or with interventio(n).

Statistical Package for the Social Sciences A computer program for statistic(al) analysis.

stigma Combination of stereotypes (i.e., cognitive labels used to describe (a) person), prejudices (i.e., negative emotions toward individuals), and d(is)crimination (i.e., curtailing the rights and opportunities of individua(ls) toward a specific group.

stimulus generalization In classical conditioning, the tendency for stimu(li) which are similar to a conditioned stimulus, to evoke similar respons(es) (e.g., fear occurring in response to the presentation of white furry anim(als) when the conditioned stimulus is a white rat).

structured professional judgment Incorporates features of both unstructur(ed) clinical judgment and the actuarial approach; there are explicit guidelin(es) for which factors to consider (although additional factors may also (be) considered) but their combination is left up to the discretion of the assess(or).

superego The part of the Freudian personality that acts as the moral reg(u)lator, making sure that we act in accordance with internalized gro(up) standards.

tertiary intervention strategies Strategies that attempt to prevent violen(ce) from reoccurring.

theory of maternal deprivation A theory of crime proposed by Jo(hn) Bowlby that suggests that if children are not exposed to consistent a(nd) constant maternal care in their early years they will experience diffic(ul)ties in developing the ability to establish meaningful prosocial relatio(n)ships and, as a result, will be more likely to exhibit antisocial patter(ns) of behaviour.

reat/control-override symptoms Psychotic symptoms in which an individual feels that their self-control is overridden by outside forces or feels they will be harmed by others.

eatment readiness Multidimensional construct that considers the contribution of individual (internal) and setting (external) factors in terms of an offender's potential for engagement in treatment.

ue negative Occurs when it is predicted that an offender will not violently recidivate and he or she in fact does not recidivate.

ue positive Occurs when it is predicted that an offender will violently recidivate and he or she in fact does so.

conditioned response In classical conditioning, an unlearned response that occurs automatically following the presentation of an unconditioned stimulus (e.g., salivation is an unconditioned response to the presentation of food).

conditioned stimulus In classical conditioning, a stimulus that unconditionally (i.e., automatically) triggers a response (e.g., food is an unconditioned stimulus that triggers salivation).

fit to stand trial Person who, due to a mental disorder, is unable to understand trial proceedings, interpret the consequences of a crime, or communicate with their counsel.

niform Crime Reporting (UCR) Survey Measures the incidence of crimes reported to police in a given year and some of the characteristics of those crimes. Includes offences against victims of all ages and incorporates the territories and the provinces.

structured clinical judgment Assessors arrive at an estimate of risk based on their own idiosyncratic decisions about what factors to consider and how to combine those factors.

values Enduring beliefs that influence our opinions, actions, and the choices we make.

vicarious conditioning A form of learning that takes place by observing the environmental consequences of other people's behaviour, especially reinforcement and punishment.

victim assistance Provision of information and support regarding the criminal justice process, which can occur from the time of an incident to the perpetrator's release into the community.

victim offender mediation Face-to-face meeting in the presence of a trained mediator between the victim of a crime and the person who committed it. The offender and victim talk to each other about what happened, the effects of the crime on their lives, and their feelings about it. They may choose to create a mutually agreeable plan to repair any damages that occurred as a result of the incident.

Violence Risk Appraisal Guide (VRAG) Empirical actuarial risk-assessment instrument designed to estimate risk for violent recidivism.

Violence Risk Scale–Sexual Offender version (VRS-SO) Actuarial instrument consisting of both static and putatively dynamic factors designed to estimate risk of sexual recidivism.

visionary serial murderer In Holmes and DeBurger's (1988) typology, this type of serial murderer is psychotic and is commanded to kill by an inner voice or apparition.

voyeurism An interest in observing unsuspecting people naked or engaging in sexual activity.

warden Person in charge of a federal prison; same as a superintendent in provincial corrections.

References

Aboriginal Justice Inquiry of Manitoba. 2009. *Report of the Aboriginal Justice Inquiry of Manitoba*. Retrieved January 12, 2009 (**www.ajic.mb.ca/volume.html**).

Abrahamsen, D. 1973. *The murdering mind*.New York, NY: Harper and Row, Publishers.

Abrahamsen, D. 1985. *Confessions of Son of Sam*. New York, NY: Columbia University Press.

Adler, F. 1975. *Sisters in crime*. New York, NY: McGraw-Hill.

Agnew, R. 1991. "A longitudinal test of social control theory and delinquency." *Journal of Research in Crime and Delinquency*. 28:126–156.

Agrell, S. 2003. "Liberals may shut youth boot camp." *National Post*. Retrieved June 1, 2004 (**www.nationalpost.com/components/printstory/printstory.asp?id=2520BBE9-64CE**).

Akers, C. and Kaukinen, C. 2009. "The police reporting behavior of intimate partner violence victims." *Journal of Family Violence*. 24:159–171.

Akers, R.L. 1973. *Deviant behavior: A social learning approach*. Belmont, CA: Wadsworth.

Akers, R.L. 1991. "Self-control as a general theory of crime." *Journal of Quantitative Criminology*. 7:201–211.

Akers, R.L. 1999. *Criminological theories: Introduction and evaluation*. 2nd ed. Los Angeles, CA: Roxbury.

Akers, R.L. 2009. *Social learning and social structure: A general theory of crime and deviance*. New Brunswick, NJ: Transaction Publishers.

Akers, R.L. and Jensen, G.F. 2006. "The empirical status of social learning theory: The past, present, and future." In F.T. Cullen, J.P. Wright, and K.R. Blevins, eds. *Taking stock: The status of criminological theory*. pp. 37–76. New Brunswick., NJ: Transaction Publishers.

Akers, R.L., Krohn, M.D., Lanza-Kaduce, L., and Radosevich, M. 1979. "Social learning and deviant behavior: A specific test of a general theory." *American Sociological Review*. 44:636–655.

Akers, R.L. and Sellers, C.S. 2004. *Criminological theories: Introduction, evaluation, and application*. 4th ed. Los Angeles, CA: Roxbury Publishing Company.

Alberta. 2009. "Probation parole officer occupational profile." Retrieved September 4, 2009 (**http://alis.alberta.ca/occinfo/Content/RequestAction.asp?aspAction=GetHTMLProfile&format=html&OCCPRO_ID=71001858**).

Alberta Adult Centres. Retrieved April 2, 2009 (**https://www.solgps.alberta.ca/programs_and_services/correctional_services/adult_centre_operations/Publications/Alberta%20Adult%20Centres.pdf**).

Alexander, F. 1935. *Roots of crime*. New York, NY: Knopf.

Amato, P.R. and Keith, B. 1991. "Parental divorce and the well being of children: A meta-analysis." *Psychological Bulletin*. 110:26–46.

American Psychiatric Association. 1994. *Diagnostic and Statistical Manual of Mental Disorders*. 4th ed. Washington, DC: Author.

American Psychiatric Association. 2000. *Diagnostic and Statistical Manual of Mental Disorders*. 4th ed., text revision. Washington, DC: Author.

Amstutz, L.S. and Zehr, H. 1998. *Victim offender conferencing in Pennsylvania's juvenile justice system*. Harrisonburg, PA: Eastern Mennonite University, Conflict Transformation Program (**www.emu.edu/cjp/pub/rjmanual.pdf**).

Andershed, H., Kerr, M., Stattin, H., and Levander, S. 2002. "Psychopath traits in non-referred youths: A new assessment tool." In E. Blaauw and Sheridan, eds. *Psychopaths—Current international perspectives*. pp. 131–15 Elsevier, The Hague.

Andersen, K., Wurmstedt, R.C., and Woodbury, R.C. 1981. "A drifter wh stalked success." Retrieved May 10, 2009 (**www.time.com/tim magazine/article/0,9171,954700-3,00.html**).

Anderson, G.S. 2007. *Biological influences on criminal behavior*. Boca Raton, F Simon Fraser University Publications, CRC Press, Taylor and Francis Grou

Anderson, C.A., Berkowitz, L., Donnerstein, E., Huesmann, L.R., Johnso J.D., Linz, D., Malamuth, N., and Wartella, E. 2003. "The impact of med violence on youth." *Psychological Science in the Public Interest*. 4:81–110.

Anderson, C.A. and Bushman, B.J. 2002. "Human aggression." *Annu Review of Psychology*. 53:27–51.

Anderson, C.A. and Dill, F.E. 2000. "Video games and aggressi thoughts, feelings, and behaviour in the laboratory and in life *Journal of Personality and Social Psychology*. 78:772–290.

Andrews, D.A. 1980. "Some experimental investigations of the principles differential association through deliberate manipulations of the stru ture of service systems." *American Sociological Review*. 45:448–462.

Andrews, D.A. 1982. *The Level of Supervision Inventory LSI: The first follow-* Toronto, ON: Ontario Ministry of Correctional Services.

Andrews, D.A. 1994. *An Overview of Treatment Effectiveness: Research a Clinical Principles*, Department of Psychology, Carleton University.

Andrews, D.A. 2001. "Principles of effective correctional programs." In L. Motiuk and R.C. Serin, eds. *Compendium 2000 on effective correction programming*. pp. 9–17. Ottawa, ON: Correctional Service of Canada

Andrews, D.A. and Bonta, J. 1995. *The Level of Service Inventory-Revise* Toronto, ON: Multi-Health Systems.

Andrews, D.A. and Bonta, J. 2006. *The psychology of criminal conduct*. 4th e Cincinnati, Ohio: Anderson Publishing.

Andrews, D.A., Bonta, J., and Wormith, S.J. 2004. *Level of Service/Co Management Inventory: An offender assessment system*. Toronto, O Multi-Health Systems.

Andrews, D.A., Bonta, J., Wormith, S.J., Guzzo, L., and Brews, A. 2008. T *relative and incremental predictive validity of gender-neutral and gend informed risk/need*. Unpublished Manuscript. Carleton University.

Andrews, D.A., Bonta, J., and Hoge, R.D. 1990. "Classification for effecti rehabilitation: Rediscovering psychology." *Criminal Justice and Behavi* 17:19–52.

Andrews, D.A. and Robinson, D. 1984. *The Level of Supervision Invento Second report*. Toronto, ON: Ontario Ministry of Correctional Servic

Andrews, D.A., Zinger, I., Hoge, R.D., Bonta, J., Gendreau, P., and Culle F.T. 1990. "Does correctional treatment work? A clinically relevant a psychologically informed meta-analysis." *Criminology*. 28:369–404.

Antiss, B. and Polaschek, D. in press. *Psychology, Crime and Law*.

Aos, S., Miller, M., and Drake, E. 2006. *Evidence-based public policy optic to reduce future prison construction, criminal justice costs and crime rat* Olympia: Washington State Institute for Public Policy.

Appel, A.E. and Holden, G.W. 1998. "The co-occurrence of spouse a physical child abuse: A review and appraisal." *Journal of Fam Psychology*. 12:578–599.

ppelbaum, P., Robbins, P., and Monahan, J. 2000. "Violence and delusions: Data from the MacArthur violence risk assessment study." *American Journal of Psychiatry*. 157:566–572.

rbour, L. 1996. "Commission of Inquiry into certain events at the Prison for Women in Kingston." Retrieved March 1, 2009 (**www.justicebehindthe walls.net/resources/arbour_report/arbour_rpt.htm**).

rcher, J. 1991. "The influence of testosterone on human aggression." *British Journal of Psychology*. 82:1–28.

rcher, J. 1999. "Assessment of the reliability of the conflict tactics scales: A meta-analytic review." *Journal of Interpersonal Violence*. 14:1263–1289.

rcher, J. 2002. "Sex differences in physically aggressive acts between heterosexual partners: A meta-analytic review." *Aggression and Violence Behavior*. 7:313–351.

rcher, J., Graham-Kevan, N., and Davise, M. 2005. "Testosterone and aggression: A reanalysis of Book, Starzyk, and Quinsey's 2001 study." *Aggression and Violent Behavior*. 10:241–261.

rnold, R. 1990. "Processes of victimization and criminalization of black women." *Social Justice*. 17:153–166.

sante, K. and Nelms-Matzke, J. 1985. *Report on the survey of children with chronic handicaps and fetal alcohol syndrome in the Yukon and Northwest British Columbia*. Whitehorse, YK: Council for Yukon Indians.

shford, J.B. and LeCroy, C.W. 1988. "Predicting recidivism. An evaluation of the Wisconsin juvenile probation and aftercare risk instrument." *Criminal Justice and Behaviour*. 15:141–151

hley, O.S., Marsden, M.E., and Brady, T.M. 2003. "Effectiveness of substance abuse treatment programming for women: A review." *American Journal of Drug and Alcohol Abuse*. 29:19–53.

e Associated Press. 2005. "Canadian gets 10 years for sex crimes." *The Seattle Times*. Retrieved December 21, 2009 (**www.thefreelibrary.com/Canadian +gets+10+years+for+sex+crimes.(Local+News)-a0132980734)**.

twood Strategy Corporation. 2002. *Canadian Police Survey on Youth Gangs*. Ottawa, ON: Public Safety Canada.

gimeri, L., Farrington, D., Koegl, C., and Day, D. 2007. "The SNAP under 12 outreach project: Effects of a community based program for children with conduct problems." *Journal of Child and Family Studies*. 16:799–807.

stin, J. 1983. "Assessing the new generation of prison classification models." *Crime and Delinquency*. 29:561–576.

stin, J. and McGinnis, K. 2004. *Classification of high-risk and special management prisoners: A National assessment of current practices*. Washington, DC: National Institute of Corrections.

ochishin, K. and Hanson, R.K. 2009. "Improving our talk: Moving beyond the 'Low,' 'Moderate,' and 'High,' typology of risk communication." *Crime Scene*. 161:11–14.

bcock, J.C., Green, C.E., and Robie, C. 2004. "Does batterers' treatment work? A meta-analytic review of domestic violence treatment." *Clinical Psychology Review*. 23:1023–1053.

ca-Garcia, E., Perez-Rodriguez, M.M., Basurte-Villamor, I., Fernandez del Moral, A,L., Gmenez-Arriero, M.A., Gonzalez de Rivera, J.L., Saiz-Ruiz, J., and Oquendo, M.A. 2007. "Diagnostic stability of psychiatric disorders in clinical practice." *British Journal of Psychiatry*. 190:210–216.

gley, C. and Young, L. 1987. "Juvenile prostitution and child sexual abuse. A controlled study." *Journal of Community Mental Health*. 6:5–26.

llargeon, J., Binswanger, I.A., Penn, J.V., Williams, B.A., and Murray, O.J. 2009. "Psychiatric disorders and repeat incarcerations: The revolving prison door." *American Journal of Psychiatry*. 166:103–109.

rd, C. 1981. "Probation and parole classification: The Wisconsin model." *Corrections Today*. 43:36–41.

Baker, M.W. 2007. "Elder mistreatment: Risk, vulnerability, and early mortality." *Journal of the American Psychiatric Nurses Association*. 12:13–321.

Bandura, A. 1965. "Influence of models' reinforcement contingencies on the acquisition of imitative responses." *Journal of Personality and Social Psychology*. 2:589–595.

Bandura, A. 1973. *Aggression: A social learning analysis*. Englewood Cliffs, NJ: Prentice Hall.

Bandura, A. 1977. *Social learning theory*. Orrville, OH: Prentice Hall.

Bandura, A. and Walters, R.H. 1963. *Social learning and personality development*. New York, NY: Holt, Rinehart and Winston.

Barbaree, H.E. and Marshall, W.L. 1991. "The role of male sexual arousal in rape: Six models." *Journal of Consulting and Clinical Psychology*. 59:621–630.

Barbaree, H.E. 2005. "Psychopathy, treatment behavior, and recidivism: An extended follow-up to Seto and Barbaree." *Journal of Interpersonal Violence*. 20:1115–1131.

Barkley, R.A. 1997. "Attention-deficit/hyperactivity disorder." In E.J. Mash, and L.G. Terdal, eds. *Assessment of childhood disorders*. pp. 71–129. New York: Guilford Press.

Baron, S. and Welty. A. 1996. "Elder abuse." *Journal of Gerontological Social Work*. 25:33–57.

Barnett, A., Blumstein, A., and Farrington, D.P. 1987. "Probabilistic models of youthful criminal careers." *Criminology*. 25:83–107.

Barrera, J. 2009. "Ont. wants federal clarity on medical pot." Canwest News Service. Available at **www.ottawacitizen.com/news/wants+ federal+clarity+medical/1381709/story.html**.

Barron, C. and Lacombe, D. 2005. "Moral panic and the nasty girl." *The Canadian Review of Sociology and Anthropology*. 42:51–69.

Barrowcliff, A.L. and Haddock, G. 2006. "The relationship between command hallucinations and factors of compliance: A critical review of the literature." *Journal of Forensic Psychiatry and Psychology*. 17:266–298.

Bartholow, B.D., Bushman, B.J., and Sestir, M.A. 2006. "Chronic violent video game exposure and desensitization to violence: Behavioral and event-related brain potential data." *Journal of Experimental Social Psychology*. 42:532–539.

Bartol, C.R. and Bartol, A.M. 2008. *Criminal behaviour: A psychosocial approach*. 8th ed. Pacific Grove, CA: Brooks/Cole.

Battin, S.R., Hawkins, J.D., Thornberry, T.P., and Krohn, M.D. 1998. *The Contribution of Gang Membership to Delinquency Beyond the Influence of Delinquent Peers*. Bulletin. Washington, DC: U.S. Department of Justice, Office of Justice Programs, Office of Juvenile Justice and Delinquency Prevention.

Beitchman, J.H., Zucker, K.J., Hood, J.E., DaCosta, G.A., Akman, D., and Cassavia, E. 1992. "A review of the long-term effects of child sexual abuse." *Child Abuse and Neglect*. 16:101–118.

Belknap, J. 2007. *The invisible woman: Gender, crime and justice*. 3rd ed. Belmont, CA: Thomson Wadsworth.

Belknap, J. 2001. *The invisible woman: Gender, crime, and justice*. 2nd ed. California: Wadsworth Publishing Company.

Bell, A. and Flight, J. 2008. *An evaluation of the Spirit of a Warrior program for women offenders*. Research Report No. R-180. Ottawa, ON: Correctional Service of Canada.

Benda, B.B. 2005. "Gender differences in life course theory of recidivism: A survival analysis." *International Journal of Offender Therapy and Comparative Criminology*. 493:325–342.

Benson, M.L. and Moore, E. 1992. "Are white-collar and common offenders the same? An empirical and theoretical critique of a recently proposed general theory of crime." *Journal of Research in Crime and Delinquency*. 29:251–272.

Berkowitz, L. 1994. "On the escalation of aggression." In M. Potegal and J. Knutson, eds. *The dynamics of aggression: Biological and social processes in dyads and groups.* pp. 33–41. Hillsdale, NJ: Erlbaum.

Bernstein, M.B. 2006. "The decision of the Supreme Court of Canada upholding the constitutionality of section 43 of the Criminal Code of Canada: What this decision means to the child welfare sector." *Family Court Review.* 44:104–118.

Birbaumer, N., Veit, R., Lotze, M., Herrmann, C., Erb, M., Grodd, W., and Flor, H. 2005. "Deficient fear conditioning in psychopathy: A functional magnetic resonance imaging study." *Archives of General Psychiatry.* 62:799–805.

Bjork, J.M., Dougherty, D.M., Moeller, F.G., and Swann, A.C. 2000. "Differential behavioural effects of plasma tryptophan depletion and loading in aggressive and nonaggressive men." *Neuropsychopharmacology.* 22:375–369.

Blackburn, R. 1995. *The psychology of criminal conduct: Theory, research and practice.* Chichester, UK: Wiley.

Blair, R.J.R. 2006. "Subcortical brain systems in psychopathy: The amygdala and associated structures." In C.J. Patrick, ed. *Handbook of the psychopathy.* pp. 296–312. New York, NY: Guilford Press.

Blair, R.J.R. 2007. "The amygdala and ventromedial prefrontal cortex in morality and psychopathy." *Trends in Cognitive Sciences.* 11:387–392

Blair, R.J.R., Colledge, E., Murray, L., and Mitchell, D.G.V. 2001. "A selective impairment in the processing of sad and fearful expressions in children with psychopathic tendencies." *Journal of Abnormal Child Psychology.* 294:491–498.

Blair, R.J.R., Jones, L., Clark, F., and Smith, M. 1997. "The psychopathic individual: A lack of responsiveness to distress cues." *Psychophysiology.* 34:192–198.

Blanchard, R., Christensen, B.K., Strong, S.M., Cantor, J.M., Kuban, M.E., Klassen, P., Dickey, R., and Blak, T. 2002. "Retrospective self-reports of childhood accidents causing unconsciousness in phallometrically diagnosed pedophiles." *Archives of Sexual Behavior.* 31:511–526.

Blanchette, K.D. and Brown, S.L. 2006. *The assessment and treatment of women offenders: An integrative perspective.* Wiley Series in Forensic Clinical Psychology. Chichester: John Wiley and Sons.

Blanchette, K. and Motiuk, L.L. 2004. "Taking down the straw man: A reply to Webster and Doob." *Canadian Journal of Criminology and Criminal Justice.* 46:621–630.

Blanchette, K.D. and Taylor, K.N. 2007. "Development and field test of a gender-informed security reclassification scale for female offenders." *Criminal Justice and Behaviour.* 34:362–379.

Blanchette, K. Verbrugge. P., and Wichmann, C. 2002. *The Custody Rating Scale, initial security placement, and women offenders.* Research Report No. R-127. Ottawa, ON: Correctional Service of Canada.

Blickle, G., Schlegel, A., Fassbender, P., and Klein, U. 2006. "Some personality correlates of business white-collar crime." *Applied Psychology.* 55:220–233.

Blitz, C.L., Wolff, N., and Shi, J. 2008. "Physical victimization in prison: The role of mental illness." *International Journal of Law and Psychiatry.* 31:385–393.

Bloom, B., Owen, B., and Covington, S.S. 2003. *Gender-responsive strategies for women offenders: Research, practice, and guiding principles for women offenders.* NIC Accession Number 018017. Retrieved August 15, 2005 (www.nicic.org).

Bloom, B., Owen, B., Rosenbaum, J., and Deschenes, E.P. 2003. "Focusing on girls and young women: A gendered perspective on female delinquency." *Women and Criminal Justice.* 14:117–136.

Bloom, B., Owen, B., and Covington, S.S. 2003. *Gender-responsive strategies for women offenders: Research, practice, and guiding principles for women offenders.* NIC Accession Number 018017. Retrieved August 15, 2005 (www.nicic.org).

Bonigen, D.M., Hicks, B.M., Krueger, R.F., Patrick, C.J., and Iacono, W.G. 2005. "Psychopathic personality traits: Heritability and genetic overlap with internalizing and externalizing psychopathology." *Psychological Medicine.* 35:637–648.

Bonigen, D.M., Hicks, B.M., Krueger, R.F., Patrick, C.J., and Iacono, W.G. 2006. "Continuity and change in psychopathic traits as measured via

normal-range personality: A longitudinal-biometric study." *Journal Abnormal Psychology.* 1:85–95.

Blum, J., Ireland, M., and Blum, R. 2003. "Gender differences in juven violence: A report from Add Health." *Journal of Adolescent Heal* 32:234–240.

Blumstein, A. and Cohen, J. 1987. "Characterizing criminal careers." *Scien* 237:985–991.

Boccaccini, M.T., Murrie, D.C., Clark, J.W., and Cornell, D.G. 2008. "Describi diagnosing, and naming psychopathy: How do youth psychopathy lab influence jurors?" *Behavioral Sciences and the Law.* 26:487–510

Boe, R. 2000. "Aboriginal inmates: Demographic trends and projection *Forum on Corrections Research.* 12:7–9.

Boe, R. 2002. "Future demographic trends may help Canada's Aborigi youth." *Forum on Corrections.* 14:13–16.

Boe, R. 2004. "Comparing Crime and Imprisonment Trends in the Unit States, England, and Canada from 1981 to 2001." Research Bri Correctional Service of Canada.

Boe, R., Motiuk, L.L., and Muirhead, M. 1998. "Recent Trends and Patter Shaping the Corrections Population in Canada: 1983/84 to 1996/9 Research Brief B-20. Correctional Service of Canada.

Boe, R. Motiuk, L.L., and Nafekh, M. 2004. "An examination of the avera length of prison sentence for adult men in Canada: 1994–200 Research Report R-136. Correctional Service of Canada.

Boe, R., Nafekh, M., Vuong, B., Sinclair, R., and Cousineau, C. 2003. "T Changing Profile of the Federal Inmate Population: 1997 and 200 Research Report R-132. Ottawa, ON: Correctional Service of Canad

Boer, D., Couture, J., Geddes, C., and Ritchie, A. 2003. *Yókw'tól: Risk ma agement guide for Aboriginal offenders.* Ottawa, ON: Correctional Serv of Canada.

Boer, D.P., Hart, S.D., Kropp, P.R., and Webster, C.D. 1997. *Manual for Sexual Violence Risk—20: Professional guidelines for assessing risk of sex violence.* Burnaby, BC: Mental Health, Law, and Policy Institute, Sim Fraser University.

Boer, D., Thakker, J., and Ward, T. 2009. "Sex offender Risk-Based Ca Formulation." In A. Beech, L. Craig, and K. Browne, eds. *Assessm and treatment of sex offenders: A handbook.* pp. 77–88. London: Jo Wiley and Sons, Ltd.

Boland, F.J., Burrill, R., Duwyn, M., and Karp, J. 1998. *Fetal Alco Syndrome: Implications for correctional service.* Research Report No. R- Ottawa, ON: Correctional Service of Canada.

Boland, F.J., Duwyn, M., and Serin, R. 2002. "Fetal alcohol syndron Understanding its impact." *Forum on Corrections.* 12:16–18.

Bonta, J. 2007. Unpublished training presentation, National Parole Board Canada.

Bonta, J., Bogue, B., Crowley, M., and Motiuk, L.L. 2001. "Implement offender classification systems: Lessons learned." In G.A. Bernfeld, D Farrington, and A.W. Leischied, eds. *Offender rehabilitation in practi Implementing and evaluating effective programs.* pp. 227–246. Chichest John Wiley and Sons.

Bonta, J., Harman, W.G., Hann, R.G., and Cormier, R.B. 1996. "The pred tion of recidivism among federally sentenced offenders: A re-validati of the SIR scale." *Canadian Journal of Criminology.* 38:61–79.

Bonta, J., LaPrairie, C., and Wallace-Capretta, S. 1997. "Risk prediction a re-offending: Aboriginal and non-aboriginal offenders." *Canad Journal of Criminology.* 39:127–144.

Bonta, J., Law, M., and Hanson, R.K. 1998. "The prediction of criminal a violent recidivism among mentally disordered offenders: A meta-analys *Psychological Bulletin.* 123:123–142.

Bonta, J., Lipinski, S., and Martin, M. 1992. "The characteristics Aboriginal recidivists." *Canadian Journal of Criminology.* 34:517–521 nta, J. and Motiuk, L.L. 1985. "Utilization of an interview-based classification instrument: A study of correctional halfway houses." *Criminal Justice and Behavior*. 12:333–352.

nta, J. and Rugge, T. 2004. *The prediction of recidivism with Aboriginal offenders*. Unpublished manuscript.

nta, J., Rugge, T., and Dauvergne, M. 2003. "The reconviction rate of federal offenders." User Report No. 2003-02. Ottawa, ON: Solicitor General Canada.

nta, J., Wallace-Capretta, S., and Rooney, J. 1998. *Restorative justice: An evaluation of the Restorative Resolutions Project*. Ottawa, ON: Solicitor General Canada.

nta, J., Wallace-Capretta, S., and Rooney, J. 2000. "A quasi-experimental evaluation of an intensive rehabilitation supervision program." *Criminal Justice and Behavior*. 27:312–329.

ok, A.S., Starzyk, K.B., and Quinsey, V.L. 2001. "The relationship between testosterone and aggression: A meta-analysis." *Aggression and Violent Behavior*. 6:579–599.

ok, A.S. and Quinsey, V.L. 2005. "Re-examining the issues: A response to Archer et al." *Aggression and Violent Behavior*. 10:637–646.

rduin, C.M., Henggeler, S.W., Blaske, D.M., and Stein, R. 1990. "Multisystemic treatment of adolescent sexual offenders." *International Journal of Offender Therapy and Comparative Criminology*. 34:105–113.

urgon, G. and Armstrong, B. 2005. "Transferring the principles of effective treatment into a 'real world' prison setting." *Criminal Justice and Behavior*. 32:3–25.

wlby, J. 1944. "Forty-four juvenile thieves: Their characteristics and home life." *International Journal of Psychoanalysis*. 25:19–53.

wlby, J. 1989. *The making and breaking of affectional bonds*. London, UK: Routledge.

wlby, J., Ainsworth, M., Boston, M., and Rosenbluth, D. 1956. "The effects of mother-child separation: A follow-up study." *British Journal of Medical Psychology*. 292:11–247.

yd, N. 2000. "The testosterone connection." In *The beast within: Why men are violent*. pp. 115–138. Vancouver, BC. New York: Greystone Books.

acey, D. 1979. *Baby pros: Preliminary profiles of juvenile prostitutes*. New York, NY: John Jay Press.

aithwaite, J. 1999. "Restorative justice: Assessing optimistic and pessimistic accounts." In M. Tonry, ed. *Crime and Justice: A Review of Research*. 25:1–127.

ame, B., Nagin, D.S., and Tremblay, R.E. 2001. "Developmental trajectories of physical aggression from school entry to late adolescence." *Journal of Child Psychology and Psychiatry*. 42:503–512.

ay, D.L. and Anderson, P.D. 1989. "Appraisal of the epidemiology of Fetal Alcohol Syndrome among Canadian Native peoples." *Canadian Journal of Public Health*. 80:42-45.

ennan, S. and Taylor-Butts, A. 2008. "Sexual assault in Canada: 2004 and 2007." Statistics Canada: Canadian Centre for Justice Statistics, Catalogue no. 85F0033M, no. 19.

ennan, T. 1998. "Institutional classification of females: Problems and some proposals for reform." In R.T. Zaplin, ed. *Female offenders: Critical perspectives and effective interventions*. pp. 179–204. Gaithersburg, MD: Aspen Publishers.

ennan, T. 2004. "The roles of objective classification in jail programming and internal management." *The Journal of Community Corrections*. 13:7–10.

ewer, D.D., Hawkins, J.D., Catalano, R.F., and Neckerman, H.J. 1995. "Preventing serious, violent, and chronic juvenile: A review of evaluations of selected strategies in childhood, adolescence, and, the community." In J.C. Howell, B. Krisberg, J.D. Hawkins, and J.J. Wilson, eds. *A Source Book: Serious, Violent, and Chronic Juvenile Offenders*. pp. 61–141. Thousand Oaks, CA: Sage.

Britten, R.J. 1986. "Rates of DNA sequences evolution differ between taxonomic groups." *Science*. 231:1393–1398.

Broadhurst, R. 1997. "Aborigines and Crime in Australia." *Crime and Justice: An Annual Review of Research*. 21:407–468.

Brochu, S., Cousineau, M.M., Gillet, M., Cournoyer, L.G., Pernanen, K., and Motiuk, L.L. 2001. "Drugs, alcohol, and criminal behaviour: A profile of inmates in Canadian federal institutions." *Forum on Corrections Research*. 133:20–24.

Brook, A.S., Starzyk, K.B., and Quinsey, V.L. 2001. "The relationship between testosterone and aggression: A meta-analysis." *Aggression and Violent Behaviour*. 6:579–599.

Broome, K.M., Simpson, D.D., and Joe, G.W. 2002. "The role of social support following short-term inpatient treatment." *The American Journal on Addictions*. 11:57–65.

Brown, G. R. 2004. "Gender as a factor in the response of the law-enforcement systems to violence against partners." *Sexuality and Culture*. 9:3–138.

Brown, S.L. 2002. "The dynamic prediction of criminal recidivism: A three-wave prospective study." *Forum on Corrections Research*. 141:24–27.

Brown, S.L. and Forth, A.E. 1997. "Psychopathy and sexual assault: Static risk factors, emotional precursors, and rapist subtypes." *Journal of Consulting and Clinical Psychology*. 65:848–857.

Brown, S.L., and Motiuk, L.L. 2005. "The Dynamic Factor Identification and Analysis DFIA component of the Offender Intake Assessment OIA process: A meta-analytic, psychometric and consultative review." Research Report R-164. Ottawa, ON: Research Branch, Correctional Service of Canada.

Brown, S.L. and Motiuk, L.L. 2008. "Using dynamic risk factors to predict criminal recidivism in a sample of male and female offenders." In K.D. Blanchette, chair. *Classification for the prediction of recidivism in girls and women*. Symposium conducted at the 2008 69th Annual Conference of the Canadian Psychological Association (CPA), Halifax, NS.

Browne, A. and Finkelhor, D. 1986. "Impact of child sexual abuse: A review of the research." *Psychological Bulletin*. 99:66–77.

Brunet, S. nd. *Fighting the 'hangover that lasts a lifetime'*. Retrieved January 14, 2009 (www.carleton.ca/jmc/cnews/18022000/n2.htm).

Brzozowski, J., Taylor-Butts, A., and Johnson, S. 2006. "Victimization and offending among the Aboriginal population in Canada." *Juristat*. 26.

Bumby, K.M. 1996. "Assessing the cognitive distortions of child molesters and rapists: Developments and validation of the MOLEST and RAPE scales." *Sexual Abuse: A Journal of Research and Treatment*. 8:37–54.

Bureind, J.W. and Bartusch, D.J. 2005. *Juvenile delinquency: An integrated approach*. Thousand Oaks, CA: Jones and Bartlett Publishers.

Burgess, R. and Akers, R.L. 1966. "A differential association-reinforcement theory of criminal behavior." *Social Problems*. 14:128–147.

Burnett, R. and McNeill, F. 2005. "The place of the officer-offender relationship in assisting offenders to desist from crime." *Probation Journal*. 52:221–242.

Bushman, B.J. and Anderson, C.A. 2001. "Media violence and the American public: Scientific facts versus media misinformation." *American Psychologist*. 56:477–489.

Bushman, B.J., and Anderson, C.A. 2001. "Is it time to pull the plug on the hostile versus instrumental aggression dichotomy?" *Psychological Review*. 108:273–279.

Buss, D.M. 2005. "Foundations of evolutionary psychology." In D.M. Buss, ed. *The handbook of evolutionary psychology*. pp. 5–145. Hoboken, New Jersey: John Wiley and Sons, Inc.

Butler, T., Andrews, G., Allnutt, S., Sakashita, C., Smith, N. E. and Basson, J. 2006. "Mental disorders in Australian prisoners: A comparison with a community sample." *Australian and New Zealand Journal of Psychiatry*. 40:272–276.

Byrne, M.K., and Howells, K. 2002. "The psychological needs of women prisoners: Implications for rehabilitation and management." *Psychiatry, Psychology, and Law.* 9:34–43.

Cacioppo, J.T., and Bernston, G.C., eds. 2005. *Social neuroscience: Key readings.* New York, NY: Psychology Press.

Cadoret, R.J., and Cain, C. 1980. "Sex differences in predictors of antisocial behavior in adoptees." *Archives of General Psychiatry.* 37:1171–1175.

Caldwell, M., Skeem, J., Salekin, R., VanRybroek, G. 2006. "Treatment response of adolescent offenders with psychopathy features: A 2-year follow-up." *Criminal Justice and Behavior.* 33:571–596.

Callahan, E.J. and Leitenberg, H. 1973. "Aversion therapy for sexual deviation: Contingent shock and covert sensitization." *Journal of Abnormal Psychology.* 81:60–73.

Campbell, A. 1984. *The girls in the gang: A report from New York City.* Oxford, UK: Blackwell.

Campbell, A. 1995. "A few good men: Evolutionary psychology and female adolescent aggression." *Ethnology and Sociobiology.* 16:99–123.

Campbell, A. 1999. "Staying alive: Evolution, culture, and women's intrasexual aggression." *Behavioural and Brain Sciences.* 22:203–252.

Campbell, A. 2002. *A mind of her own: The evolutionary psychology of women.* Oxford: Oxford University Press.

Campbell, A., Muncer, S., and Bibel, D. 2001. "Women and crime: An evolutionary approach." *Aggression and Violent Behavior.* 6:481–497.

Campbell, M. A., French, S., and Gendreau, P. 2009. "The prediction of violence in adult offenders: A meta-analytic comparison of instruments and methods of assessment." *Criminal Justice and Behavior.* 36:567–590.

Campbell, N.A., Reece, J.B., and Mitchell, L.G. 1999. *Biology.* 5th ed. Menlo Park, CA: Addison Wesley Longman.

Canadian Centre for Justice Statistics. 2004. *Canadian crime statistics.* Catalogue No. 85-205-XIE. Ottawa, ON: Statistics Canada.

Canadian Criminal Justice Association. 2000. *Aboriginal peoples and the criminal justice system.* Retrieved January 14, 2009 (**www.ccja-acjp.ca/en/aborit.html**).

Canadian Foundation for Children, Youth and the Law v. Canada. Attorney General [2004] 1 S.C.R. 76, 2004 SCC 4.

Canadian Human Rights Commission. 2003. "Protecting their rights: A systemic review of human rights in correctional services for federally sentenced women." Retrieved January 14, 2009 (**www.chrc-ccdp.ca/legislation_policies/consultation_report-en.asp**).

Canadian Institute for Health Information. 2006. "Health Care Spending to Reach $130 Billion This Year." Retrieved 21 March 2009 (**http://secure.cihi.ca/cihiweb/dispPage.jsp?cw_page=media_08dec2004_e**).

Canadian Institute for Health Information. 2007. "Health Care in Canada." Retrieved March 21, 2009 (**http://secure.cihi.ca/cihiweb/products/hcic2007_e.pdf**).

Canadian Paediatric Society. 2004. "Effective discipline for children." *Paediatrics and Child Health.* 9:37–41.

Canadian Press. 2006. "Peter Whitmore: Timeline of events." Retrieved August 13, 2009 (**www.ctv.ca/servlet/ArticleNews/story/CTVNews/20060803/whitmore_chronology_060803/20060804**).

Canadian Press. 2007. "Some key dates in the Pickton case." December 9, 2007. Retrieved August 13, 2009 (**www.ctv.ca/servlet/ArticleNews/story/CTVNews/20071209/pickton_keydates_071209/20071209**).

Canadian Psychological Association. 2009. "Canadian code of ethics for psychologists." 3rd ed. Electronic version available at **www.cpa.ca/cpasite/userfiles/Documents/Canadian%20Code%20of%20Ethics%20for%20Psycho.pdf.**

Canter, R. 1982. "Sex differences in self-report delinquency." *Criminology.* 20:373–393.

Cantor, J.M., Blanchard, R., Christensen, B.K., Dickey, R., Klassen, P.E. Beckstead, A.L., et al. 2006. "Intelligence, memory, and handedness pedophilia." *Neuropsychology.* 18:3–14.

Cantor, J.M., Blanchard, R., Robichaud, L.K., and Christensen, B.K. 200 "Qualitative reanalysis of aggregate data on IQ in sexual offender *Psychological Bulletin.* 131:555–568.

Cantor, J.M., Kabani, N., Christensen, B.K., Zipursky, R.B., Barbaree, H. Dickey, R., et al. 2008. "Cerebral white matter deficiencies pedophilic men." *Journal of Psychiatric Research.* 42:167–183.

Canwest News Service. 2008. "Police investigating brother in death seven-year-old Edmonton boy." *National Post.* Retrieved January 1, 20 (**www.nationalpost.com/scripts/story.html?id=1103251**).

Carlen, P. 1988. *Women, crime and poverty.* Milton Keynes: Open Universi Press.

Carlson, M., Mattos, J., and McDowell, J. 1995. "The real money trair Retrieved May 9, 2009 (**www.time.com/time/magazine/artic 0,9171,983811,00.html**).

Carney, M., Buttell, F., and Dutton, D. 2007." Women who perpetrate in mate partner violence: A review of the literature with recommendatio for treatment." *Aggression and Violent Behavior.* 12:108–115.

Carson, R.C. and Butcher, J.N. 1992. *Abnormal psychology and modern li* 9th ed. New York, NY: HarperCollins.

Caspi, A., McClay, J., Moffitt, T.E., Mill, J., Martin, J., Craig, I.W., Tayl A., and Poulton, R. 2002. "Role of genotype in the cycle of violence maltreated children." *Science.* 297:851–854.

Cassel, E. and Bernstein, D.A. 2001. *Criminal behavior.* Boston, MA: All and Bacon.

Cattaneo, L.B., Stuewig, J., Goodman, L. A., Kaltman, S., and Dutton, M. 2007. "Longitudinal helpseeking patterns among victims of intima partner violence: The relationship between legal and extraleg services." *American Journal of Orthopsychiatry.* 77:467–477.

Cawsey, Robert. 1991. *Justice on trial: Report of the task force on the crimi justice system and its impact on the Indian and Métis people of Alber* Edmonton, AB: Attorney General and Solicitor General of Alberta.

CBC News. 2008. "Man convicted of slaying girlfriend's family in Medici Hat." Retrieved August 4, 2009 (**www.cbc.ca/canada/calgary/sto 2008/12/04/steinke-murdertrial-verdict.html**).

CBC News. 2009. "Teen guilty of 1st-degree murder in death of Stefan Rengel, 14." Retrieved August 31, 2009 (**www.cbc.ca/canada/toron story/2009/03/20/murder-rengel-trial.html**).

CBC News. 2008. "Medicine Hat man plotted with girlfriend to kill fam Crown." Retrieved August 31, 2009 (**www.cbc.ca/canada/edmonte story/2008/11/17/steinke-medhat.html**).

Cernkovich, S.A. and Giordano, P.C. 1979. "A comparative analysis of m and female delinquency." *Sociological Quarterly.* 20:131–145.

Cernkovich, S.A., Lanctôt, N., and Giordano, P.C. 2008. "Predicting a lescent and adult antisocial behaviour among adjudicated delinque females." *Crime and Delinquency.* 54:3–33.

Chan, K.L., Straus, M.A., Brownridge, D.A., Tiwari, A., and Leung, W. 2008. "Prevalence of dating partner violence and suicidal ideati among male and female university students worldwide." *Journal Midwifery and Women's Health.* 53:529–537.

Chesney-Lind, M. 1986. "Women and crime: The female offender. Sign *Journal of Women in Culture and Society.* 121:78–96.

Chesney-Lind, M. and Irwin, K. 2008. *Beyond bad girls: Gender, violence a hype.* New York, NY: Taylor and Francis Group.

Chesney-Lind, M. and Paramore, V.V. 2001. "Are girls getting more violen *Journal of Contemporary Criminal Justice.* 17:142–166.

Chesney-Lind, M. and Rodriguez, N. 1983. "Women under lock and ke *Prison Journal.* 63:47–65.

hiffriller, S.H., and Hennessy, J.J. 2007. "Male batterer profiles: Support for an empirically generated typology." *Journal of Offender Rehabilitation*. 44:117–131.

hiffriller, S.H., Hennessy, J.J., and Zappone, M. 2006. "Understanding a new typology of batterers: Implications for treatment." *Victims and Offenders*. 1:79–97.

hoe, J.Y., Teplin, T.A., and Abram, K.M. 2008. "Perpetration of violence, violent victimization, and severe mental illness: Balancing public health concerns." *Psychiatric Services*. 59:153–164.

cchetti, D. and Rogosch, F.A. 1997. "The role of self-organization in the promotion of resilience in maltreated children." *Developmental Psychopathology*. 9:799–817.

airmont, D. 2006. "Aboriginal policing in Canada: An overview of developments in First Nations." Retrieved January 12, 2009 (**www.attorneygeneral.jus.gov.on.ca/inquiries/ipperwash/policy_part/research/pdf)./Clairmont_Aboriginal_Policing.pdf**).

eckley, H. 1941. *The mask of sanity: An attempt to clarify some issues about the so called psychopathic personality*. St. Louis: Mosby.

inard, M.B. and Quinney, R. 1967. *Criminal behavior systems: A typology*. New York, NY: Holt, Rinehart, and Winston.

hen, A.J., Adler, N., Kaplan, S.J., Pelcovitz, D., and Mandel, F.G. 2002. "Interactional effects of marital status and physical abuse on adolescent psychopathology." *Child Abuse and Neglect*. 26:277–288.

hen, J. 1988. *Statistical power analysis for the behavioural sciences*. Hillsdale, NJ: Lawrence Erlbaum Associates.

id, J., Yang, M., Ullrich, S., Zhang, T., Sizmur, S., Roberts, C., and Rogers, R.D. 2009. "Gender differences in structured risk assessment: Comparing the accuracy of five instruments." *Journal of Consulting and Clinical Psychology*. 77:237–348.

id, J., Yang, M., Ullrich, S., Roberts, A., and Hare, R.D. 2009. "Prevalence and correlates of psychopathic traits in the household population of Great Britain." *International Journal of Law and Psychiatry*. 32:65–73.

ker, A.L., Smith, P.H., Thompson, M.P., McKeown, R.E., Bethea, L., and Davis, K.E. 2002. "Social support protects against the negative effects of partner violence on mental health." *Journal of Women's Health and Gender-based Medicine*. 11:465–476.

ie, J.D., Belding, M., and Underwood, M. 1988. "Aggression and peer rejection in childhood." In B.B. Lahey and A.E. Kazdin, eds. *Advances in clinical child psychology*. Vol. II. pp. 125–158. New York, NY: Plenum.

leman, C. and Norris, C. 2000. *Introducing criminology*. Devon, UK: Willan Publishing.

llins, J.M. and Schmidt, F.L. 1993. "Personality, integrity, and white-colllar crime. A construct validity study." *Personnel Psychology*. 46:295–311.

llege of Nurses of Ontario. 1993. "Abuse of clients by RNs and RNAs." Report to Council on Result of Canada Health Monitor Survey of Registrants. Toronto, ON: Author.

nroy, M.A. and Murrie, D.C. 2007. *Forensic assessment of violence risk*. Hoboken, NJ: Wiley.

rnell, D., Warren, J., Hawk, G., Stafford, E., Oram, G., and Pine, D. 1996. "Psychopathy in instrumental and reactive violent offenders." *Journal of Consulting and Clinical Psychology*. 64:783–790.

rrado, R.R. and Cohen, I.M. 2002. "Needs profile of serious and/or violent Aboriginal youth in prison." *Forum on Corrections Research*. 14:20–24.

rrectional Service of Canada. 1992. "Corrections and Conditional Release Act 1992." Electronic version available at **www.canadianprisonlaw.com/ccra/frontpage.htm**.

rrectional Service of Canada. 1994. "Psychological Services." Commissioner's Directive #840. Retrieved January 7, 2010 (**www.csc-scc.gc.ca/text/plcy/cdshtm/840-cde-eng.shtml**).

Correctional Service of Canada. 1999. *An outcome evaluation of CSC substance abuse programs: ASAP, ALTO, and Choices*. Ottawa, ON: Correctional Service of Canada.

Correctional Service of Canada. 2006. "Ten-year status report on women's corrections 1996–2006." Correctional Service of Canada: Author. Retrieved March 21, 2009 (**www.csc scc.gc.ca/text/prgrm/fsw/wos24/tenyearstatusreport_e.pdf**).

Correctional Service of Canada. 2007. "Women Offender Substance Abuse Program (WOSAP)." Retrieved July 6, 2009 (**www.csc-scc.gc.ca/text/prgrm/fsw/fsw-eng.shtml**).

Correctional Service of Canada. 2007. "Careers: Diversity @ Work." Retrieved August 31, 2009 (**www.csc-scc.gc.ca/text/carinf/diversity-eng.shtml**).

Correctional Service of Canada. 2008. "Corrections and Conditional Release Statistical Overview, Annual Report: Public Safety Canada." Retrieved March 21, 2009 (**www.publicsafety.gc.ca/res/cor/rep/2008-04-ccrso-eng.aspx**).

Correctional Service of Canada. 2008a. "Let's Talk: When Rules Are Not Enough." Retrieved August 31, 2009 (**www.csc-scc.gc.ca/text/pblct/lt-en/2008/32-2/2-eng.shtml**).

Correctional Service of Canada. 2008b. "Let's Talk: Tools for Working Through Ethical Dilemmas." Retrieved August 24, 2009 (**www.csc-scc.gc.ca/text/pblct/lt-en/2008/32-2/8-eng.shtml**).

Correctional Service of Canada. 2009. "Protecting society through community corrections." Retrieved July 16, 2009 (**www.csc-scc.gc.ca/text/pblct/protect/broch-eng.shtml**).

Correctional Service of Canada. 2009. "Correctional Programs: Sexual Offender Programs." Retrieved August 14, 2009 (**www.csc-scc.gc.ca/text/prgrm/sexoff-eng.shtml**).

Correctional Service Canada. 2009. *Healing lodges for Aboriginal federal offenders*. Ottawa, ON: Correctional Service Canada.

Correctional Service of Canada. 2009. "Correctional Programs: Violence Prevention Programs." Retrieved August 13, 2009 (**www.csc-scc.gc.ca/text/prgrm/vp-eng.shtml**).

Correctional Service of Canada. 2009. "Report on Planning and Priorities: 2008–09." Retrieved March 21, 2009 (**www.tbs-sct.gc.ca/rpp/2008-2009/inst/pen/pen-eng.pdf**).

Correctional Service of Canada. 2009. "Correctional Programs: Substance Abuse Program." Retrieved August 6, 2009 (**www.csc-scc.gc.ca/text/prgrm/sub-eng.shtml**).

Correctional Service of Canada. 2009. "Careers." Retrieved January 5, 2010 (**www.csc-scc.gc.ca/text/emplo-eng.shtml**).

Correctional Service of Canada. 2009a. "Restorative Justice." Retrieved August 1, 2009 (**www.csc-scc.gc.ca/text/rj/bckgrndr-eng.shtml**).

Correctional Service of Canada. 2009b. "Correctional Programs." Retrieved August 1, 2009 (**www.csc-scc.gc.ca/text/prgrm/st-eng.shtml#2**).

Correctional Service of Canada. 2009c. "Correctional Programs: Program Evaluation and Accreditation." Retrieved August 1, 2009 (**www.csc-scc.gc.ca/text/prgrm/eval-eng.shtml**).

Correctional Service of Canada. 2009d. "Commissioner's Directive: Review of Offender Security Classification." Retrieved August 1, 2009 (**www.csc-scc.gc.ca/text/plcy/cdshtm/710-6-cd-eng.shtml**).

Correctional Service of Canada. 2009e. "Commissioner's Directive: Security Classification and Penitentiary Placement." Retrieved December 11, 2009 (**www.csc-scc.gc.ca/text/plcy/cdshtm/705-7-cd-eng.shtml**).

Cortoni, F., Nunes, K., and Latendresse, M. 2006. *An examination of the effectiveness of the Violence Prevention Program*. Research Report No. R-178. Ottawa, ON: Correctional Service of Canada.

Cotton, D. 2004. "The attitudes of Canadian police officers towards the mentally ill." *International Journal of Law and Psychiatry*. 27:135–146.

Costa, D.M., and Babcock, J.C. 2008. "Articulated thoughts of intimate partner abusive men during anger arousal: Correlates with personality disorder features." *Journal of Family Violence*. 23:395–402.

Covington, S.S. 2003. "A woman's journey home: Challenges for female offenders." In J. Travis and M. Waul, eds. *Prisoners once removed: The impact of incarceration and reentry on children, families, and communities*. pp. 67–103. Washington, DC: The Urban Institute.

Covington, S.S. and Bloom, B.E. 2003. "Gendered justice: Women in the criminal justice system." In B.E. Bloom, ed. *Gendered justice: Addressing female offenders*. pp. 3–23. Durham, NC: Carolina Academic Press.

Coy, E., Speltz, M.L., DeKlyen, M., and Jones, K. 2001. "Social-cognitive processes in preschool boys with and without oppositional defiant disorder." *Journal of Abnormal Child Psychology*. 29:107–119.

Crick, N.R. and Dodge, K.A. 1994. "A review and reformulation of social information-processing mechanisms in children's social adjustment." *Psychological Bulletin*. 115:74–101.

Criminal Intelligence Service Canada. 2008. Report on organized crime.

Crutcher, N. and Trevethan, S. 2002. "An examination of healing lodges for federal offenders in Canada." *Forum on Corrections Research*. 14:52–54.

Cullen, D. 1999. "Columbine killers thank gun providers on video." Retrieved May 10, 2009 (**www.salon.com/news/feature/1999/11/12/videos/**).

Cullen, F.T., Link, B.G., and Polanzi, C.W. 1982. "The seriousness of crime revisited: Have attitudes toward white-collar crime changed?" *Criminology*. 20:83–102.

Cullen, F.T., Wright, J.P., and Blevins, K.R. 2006. *Taking stock: The status of criminological theory*. New Brunswick, NJ: Transaction Publishers.

Cullen, F.T., Wright, J.P., Gendreau, P., and Andrews, D.A. 2003. "What correctional treatment can tell us about criminological theory: Implications for social learning theory." In R.L. Akers and G.F. Jensen, eds. *Social learning theory and the explanation of crime: A guide for the new century*. pp. 339–362. New Brunswick, NJ: Transaction Publishers.

Cumming, E., Cumming, I., and Edell, I. 1965. "Police as philosopher, guide and friend." *Social Problems*. 12:276–286.

Cummings, E.M., Davies, P.T., and Campbell, S.B. 2000. *Developmental psychopathology and family process: Theory, research, and clinical implications*. New York, NY: Guilford Press.

Cunningham, S.M. 2003. "The joint contribution of experiencing and witnessing violence during childhood on child abuse in the parent role." *Violence and Victims*. 186:619–639.

Dahlberg, L.L., and Krug, E.G. 2002. "Violence—A global health problem." In E. Krug et al., eds. *World report on violence and health*. pp. 1–56. Geneva, Switzerland: World Health Organization.

Daigle, L.E., Cullen, F.T., and Wright, J.P. 2007. "Gender differences in the predictors of juvenile delinquency: Assessing the generality-specificity debate." *Youth Violence and Juvenile Justice*. 5:254–286.

Daly, K. 1992. "Women's pathways to Felony court: Feminist theories of lawbreaking and problems of representation." *Review of Law and Women's Studies*. 2:11–52.

Daly, K. 1994. *Gender, crime and punishment*. New Haven, CT: Yale University Press.

Daly, M. and Wilson, M. 1988. *Homicide*. New York, NY: Aldine De Gruyter.

Darwin, C.R. 1859. *The origin of species*. London: John Murray.

Dauvergne, M. 2008. "Crime statistics in Canada, 2007." *Juristat*. 287:1–17. Catalogue no. 85-002-X. Ottawa, ON: Statistics Canada.

Davidson, W.S. and Redner, R. 1988. "The prevention of juvenile delinquency: Diversion from the juvenile justice system." In R.H. Price, E.L. Cowen, R.P. Lorion, and J. Ramos-McKay, eds. *Fourteen ounces of prevention: A casebook for practitioners*. pp. 123–137. Washington, DC: American Psychological Association.

Davis, S.M. and Pollock, J.M. 2005. "The continuing myth of the viole female offender." *Criminal Justice Review*. 30:5–29.

Dawkins, R. 1989. *The selfish gene*. 2nd ed. Oxford: Oxford University Pre

Dawson, D. and Reiter, J. 1998. "Juvenile violence overview: An introd tion to the available literature." *American Academy of Psychiatry a Law Newsletter*. 23:10–11.

Dean, K, and Malamuth, N.M. 1997. "Characteristics of men who aggr sexually and of men who imagine aggressing: Risk and moderati variables." *Journal of Personality and Social Psychology*. 72:449–455.

DeFries, J.D. and Fulker, D.W. 1985. "Multiple regression analysis of tw data." *Behaviour Genetics*. 15:467–473.

Dell, C.A., and Boe, R. 2000. An examination of Aboriginal and Caucas women offender risk and needs factors. Research Report No. R-9 Ottawa, ON: Correctional Service of Canada.

Department of Justice Canada. 2009. "Youth Risk/Need Assessment: A Overview of Issues and Practices." Retrieved March 21, 2009 (**www justice.gc.ca/eng/pi/rs/rep-rap/2003/rr03_yj4-rr03_jj4/a3.html**).

Diefenbach, D.L. 1997. "The portrayal of mental illness on prime time te vision." *Journal of Community Psychology*. 25:289–302.

DeKeseredy, W.S., Schwartz, M. D., and Alvi, S. 2008. "Which women a more likely to be abused? Public housing, cohabitation, and separate divorced women." *Criminal Justice Studies*. 21:283–293.

Dekovic, M. 1999. "Risk and protective factors in the development of probl behavior during adolescence." *Journal of Youth and Adolescen* 28:667–685.

DeMatteo, D. and Marczyk, G. 2005. "Risk factors, protective factors, and prevention of antisocial behavior among juveniles." In K. Heilbr N. Goldstein, and R. Redding, eds. *Juvenile Delinquency: Prevention, ass ment, and intervention*. pp.19–44. New York, NY: Oxford University Pre

Denham, S. and Almeida, M. 1987. "Children's social problem solving sk behavioral adjustment, and interventions: A meta-analysis evaluat theory and practice." *Journal of Applied Developmental Psycholo* 8:391–409.

Department of Health and Human Services. 2001. *Youth violence: A repor the surgeon general*. Rockville, MD: Author.

Devlin, M., et al. 2006. *Drug Treatment Court of Vancouver Progr Evaluation Final Evaluation Report*. National Crime Prevention Cent

Dixon, L. and Browne, K. 2003. "The heterogeneity of spouse abuse: review." *Aggression and Violent Behavior*. 8:107–130.

Dobash, R. and Dobash, R.E. 1979. *Violence against wives: The case against patriarchy*. New York, NY: Free Press.

Dobash, R.P., Dobash, R.E., Wilson, M., and Daly, M. 1992. "The myth sexual symmetry in marital violence." *Social Problems*. 39:71–91.

Dodge, K.A. 1991. "The structure and function of reactive and proac aggression." In D. Pepler and K. Rubin, eds. *The development and treatm of childhood aggression*. pp. 201–218. Hillsdale, NJ: Earlbaum.

Dodge, K.A. 2000. "Conduct disorder." In A.J. Sameroff, M. Lewis, and S Miller, eds. *Handbook of developmental psychopathology*. 2nd ed. pp. 447–463. New York, NY: Kluwer Academic/Plenum Publishers.

Dodge, K.A., Lochman, J.E., Harnish, J.D., Bates, J.E., and Pettit, G.S. 19 "Reactive and proactive aggression in school children and psychia cally impaired chronically assaultive youth." *Journal of Abnor Psychology*. 106:37–51.

Doob, A. and Sprott, J.B. 1998. "Is the quality of youth violence becom more serious?" *Canadian Journal of Criminology and Criminal Just* 40:185–194.

Doone, P. 2002. "Report on combating and preventing Maori crime: F WHAKARURUTANGA MO TE AO." Retrieved January 14, 2 (**www.justice.govt.nz/pubs/reports/2000/doone_rpt/index.html**).

ren, D. 2002. *Evaluating sex offenders: A manual for civil commitments and beyond.* Thousand Oaks, CA: Sage.

uglas, K.D. 2009. *What Should the Next Generation of Violence Risk Assessment and Management Look Like? Building on Current Knowledge to Advance the Field.* Keynote presentation at the International Association of Forensic Mental Health Services, Edinburgh, June.

uglas, K.S., Cox, D.N., and Webster, C.D. 1999. "Violence risk assessment." *Legal and Criminological Psychology.* 4:149–184.

uglas, K.S., and Skeem, J.L. 2005. "Violence risk assessment: Getting specific about being dynamic." *Psychology, Public Policy, and Law.* 11:347–383.

uglas, K.S., Yeomans, M., and Boer, D.P. 2005. "Comparative validity analysis of multiple measures of violence risk in a sample of criminal offenders." *Criminal Justice and Behavior.* 32:479–510.

wden, C. and Andrews, D.A. 1999. "What works for female offenders: A meta-analytic review." *Crime and Delinquency.* 45:438–452.

wden, C. and Andrews, D.A. 2000. "Effective correctional treatment and violent reoffending." *Canadian Journal of Criminology.* 42:449–467.

wden, C. and Andrews, D.A. 2004. "The Importance of staff practice in delivering effective correctional treatment: A meta-analytic review of core correctional practice." *International Journal of Offender Therapy and Comparative Criminology.* 482:203–214.

wden, C. and Brown, S.L. 2002. "The role of substance abuse factors in predicting recidivism: A meta-analysis." *International Journal of Crime, Psychology, and Law.* 8:243–264.

eznick, M.T. 2003. "Heterosocial competence of rapists and child molesters: A meta-analysis." *The Journal of Sex Research.* 40:170–178.

chesne, D. 1997. "Street Prostitution in Canada." *Juristat.* Catalogue no. 85-002-XPE. Ottawa, ON: Statistics Canada.

ncan, E.A.S., Nicol, M.M., Ager, A., and Dalgleish, L. 2006. "A systematic review of structured group interventions with mentally disordered offenders." *Criminal Behaviour and Mental Health.* 16:271–241.

nford, F.W. 2000. "The San Diego Navy Experiment: An assessment of interventions for men who assault their wives." *Journal of Consulting and Clinical Psychology.* 68:468–476.

ntley, J.D. and Buss, D.M. 2008. "The origins of homicide." In J.D. Duntley and T.K. Shackelford, eds. *Evolutionary forensic psychology: Darwinian foundations of crime and law.* pp. 41–64. Oxford, NY: Oxford University Press.

tton, D.G. 1995. *The domestic assault of women: Psychological and criminal justice perspectives.* Vancouver, BC: UBC Press.

tton, D.G. and Browning, J.J. 1988. "Concern for power, fear of intimacy, and aversive stimuli for wife assault." In G.J. Hotaling, D. Finkelhor, J.T. Kirkpatrick, and M.A. Strausm, eds. *Family abuse and its consequences: New directions in research.* pp. 163–175. Newbury Park, CA: Sage.

tton, D.G. and Corvo, K. 2006. "Transforming a flawed policy: A call to revive psychology and science in domestic violence research and practice." *Aggression and Violent Behavior.* 11:457–483.

tton, D.G. and Corvo, K. 2007. "The Duluth Model: A data-impervious paradigm and a failed strategy." *Aggression and Violent Behavior.* 16:658–667.

er, C.B., Pavlik, V.N., Murphy, K.P., and Hyman, D. J. 2000. "The high prevalence of depression and dementia in elder abuse or neglect." *Journal of the American Geriatrics Society.* 48:205–208.

lscourt Child and Family Centre. 2001a. *SNAP children's group manual.* Toronto, ON: Earlscourt Child and Family Centre.

lscourt Child and Family Centre. 2001b. *SNAP parent group manual.* Toronto, ON: Earlscourt Child and Family Centre.

teal, P. 1991. "Premenstrual syndrome (PMS) in the courtroom." *Women and the Law.* 165–172.

Ebata, A.T., Peterson, A.C., and Conger, J.J. 1990. "The development of psychopathology in adolescence." In J. Rolf, A.S. Masten, D. Cicchetti, K. Nuechterlein, and S. Weintraub, eds. *Risk and protective factors in the development of psychopathology.* pp.308–333. Cambridge, MA: Cambridge University Press.

Edens, J.F., Campbell, J.S., and Weir, J.M. 2007. "Youth psychopathy and criminal recidivism: A meta-analysis of the Psychopathy Checklist measures." *Law and Human Behavior.* 31:53–75.

Edens, J.F., Guy, L.S. and Fernandez, K. 2003. "Psychopathic traits predict attitudes toward a juvenile capital murderer." *Behavioral Sciences and the Law.* 21:807–828.

Edens, J.F., Skeem, J.L., Cruise, K.R., and Cauffman, E. 2001. "Assessment of 'juvenile psychopathy' and its association with violence: A critical review." *Behavioral Sciences and the Law: Special Issue: Youth Violence.* 19:53–80.

Elbogen, E.B. and Johnson, S.C. 2009. "The intricate link between violence and mental disorder." *Archives of General Psychiatry.* 66:152–161.

Elizabeth Fry Society of Peel-Halton. *Structured Decision Making Model for Girls in the Youth Justice System.* 2005

Ellerby, L.A. and MacPherson, M. 2001. *Exploring the profile of Aboriginal sex offenders: Contrasting Aboriginal and non-Aboriginal sexual offenders to determine unique client characteristics and potential implications for sex offender assessment and treatment strategies.* Research Report No. R-122. Ottawa, ON: Correctional Service Canada.

Elliott, D.S., Huizinga, D., and Ageton, S.S. 1985. *Explaining delinquency and drug use.* Thousand Oaks, CA: Sage.

Ellis, D. 1989. "Male abuse of a married of a married or cohabiting female partner: The application of sociological theory to research findings." *Violence and Victims.* 4:235–255.

Ellis, L. and Walsh, A. 1997. "Gene-based evolutionary theories in criminology." *Criminology.* 35:229–276.

Ellis, L. and Walsh, A. 2000. *Criminology: A global perspective.* Boston: Allyn and Bacon.

Epprecht, N. 2000. "Programs for Aboriginal offenders: A national survey." *Forum on Corrections Research.* 12:45-47.

Erickson, P.G. and Butters, J.E. 2006. "Youth, weapons, and violence in Toronto and Montreal." Report prepared for Public Safety Canada, Ottawa.

Esposito, R., Harper, E., and Sauer, M. 2009. "Bernie Madoff pleads guilty to ponzi scheme, goes straight to jail, says he's deeply sorry." ABC World News. Retrieved March 12, 2009 (http://abcnews.go.com/blotter/wallstreet.story?id=7066715andpage=1).

Ewen, R.B. 2003. *An introduction to theories of personality.* 6th ed. Mahwah, NJ: Lawrence Erlbaum Associates.

Expert Committee Review of the Correctional Service of Canada's Ten-Year Status Report on Women's Corrections. 2006. *Moving Forward with Women's Corrections.* Retrieved March 20, 2008 (www.csc-scc.gc.ca/text/prgrm/fsw/wos29/wos29_e.pdf).

Eysenck, H.J. 1964. *Crime and personality.* 1st ed. Boston, MA: Houghton Miffin.

Eysenck, H.J. 1977. *Crime and personality.* 2nd ed. London, UK: Routledge.

Eysenck, H.J. and Gudjonsson, G.H. 1989. *The causes and cures of criminality.* New York, NY: Plenum.

Fagan, A.A., Lee Van Horn, M., Hawkins, J.D., and Arthur, M.W. 2007. "Gender similarities and differences in the association between risk and protective factors and self-reported serious delinquency." *Prevention Science.* 8:115–124.

Fagot, B.I. and Kavanagh, K. 1990. "The prediction of antisocial behaviour from avoidant attachment classifications." *Child Development.* 61:864–873.

Falconer, D.S. 1965. "The inheritance of liability to certain diseases, estimated from the incidence among relatives." *Annuals of Human Genetics.* 29:51–76.

Fals-Stewart, W., Birchler, G.R., and Kelley, M.L. 2003. "The timeline follow back spousal violence interview to assess physical aggression between intimate partners: Reliability and validity." *Journal of Family Violence*. 18:131–142.

Farr, K.A. 2000. "Classification of female inmates: moving forward." *Crime and Delinquency*. 461:3–17.

Farrell, A. and Bruce, S. 1997. "Impact of exposure to community violence on violent behavior and emotional distress among urban adolescents." *Journal of Clinical Child Psychology*. 26:2–14.

Farrington, D.P. 1989. "Early predictors of adolescent aggression and adult violence." *Violence and Victims*. 4:79–100.

Farrington, D.P. 1995. "The development of offending and antisocial behavior from childhood: Key findings from the Cambridge Study in Delinquent Development." *Journal of Child Psychology and Psychiatry*. 36:929–964.

Farrington, D.P. 2003. "Key results for the first forty years of the Cambridge Study in Delinquent Development." In T.P. Thornberry and M.D. Krohn, eds. *Taking stock of delinquency: An overview of findings from contemporary longitudinal studies*. New York, NY: Kluwer Academic/Plenum Publishers.

Farrington, D.P. and Hawkins, D. 1991. "Predicting participation, early onset and later persistence in officially recorded offending." *Criminal Behavior and Mental Health*. 1:1–33.

Farrington, D.P. and Painter, K.A. 2004. "Gender differences in offending: Implications for risk-focused prevention." Retrieved August 22, 2005 (www.homeoffice.gov.uk/rds/pdfs2/rdsolr0904.pdf).

Farrington, D.P. and West, D.J. 1993. "Criminal, penal and life histories of chronic offenders: Risk and protective factors and early identification." *Criminal Behaviour and Mental Health*. 3:492–523.

Fazel, S. and Danesh, J. 2002. "Serious mental disorder in 23,000 prisoners: A systematic review of 62 surveys." *Lancet*. 359:545–550.

Fazel, S. and Grann, M. 2004. "Psychiatric morbidity among homicide offenders: A Swedish population study." *American Journal of Psychiatry*. 161:2129–2131.

Federal Bureau of Investigation. 2002. "Crime in the United States 2002." Uniform Crime Reporting Program. Retrieved September 15, 2005 (www.fbi.gov/ucr/cius_02/html/web/arrested/04-NC.html).

Feinman, C. 1986. *Women in the criminal justice system*. 2nd ed. New York, NY: Praeger Publishers.

Feldman, M.P. 1977. *Criminal behavior: A psychological analysis*. Hoboken, NJ: John Wiley and Sons, Inc.

Felitti, V.J., Anda, R.F., Nordenberg, D., Williamson, D.F., Spitz, A. M. and Edwards, V. 1998. "Relationship of childhood abuse and household dysfunction to many of the leading causes of death in adults: The Adverse Childhood Experiences ACE Study." *American Journal of Preventive Medicine*. 144:245–258.

Felson, R.B. and Cares, A.C. 2005. "Gender and the seriousness of assaults on intimate partners and other victims." *Journal of Marriage and Family*. 675:182–195.

Fergusson D.M., and Horwood, L.J. 1998. "Early conduct problems and later life opportunities." *Journal of Child Psychology and Psychiatry*. 39:1097–1108.

Fergusson, D.M., Horwood, L.J. and Lynskey, M.T. 1996. "Childhood sexual abuse and psychiatric disorder in young adulthood: II. Psychiatric outcomes of childhood sexual abuse." *Journal of the American Academy of Child and Adolescent Psychiatry*. 3510:1365–1374.

Fergusson, D.M, and Lynskey, M.T. 1997. "Early reading difficulties and later conduct problems." *Journal of Child Psychology and Psychiatry*. 38:899–907.

Fergusson, D.M. and Woodward, L.J. 2000. "Educational, psychological, and sexual outcomes of girls with conduct problems in early adolescence." *Journal of Child Psychology and Psychiatry*. 41:779–792.

Feshbach, S. 1964. "The function of aggression and the regulation of aggressive drive." *Psychological Review*. 71:257–272.

Finckenauer, J. 1982. *Scared Straight and the Panacea Phenomenon*. Englewood Cliffs, NJ: Prentice Hall.

Finkelhor, D. 1984. *Child sexual abuse: New theory and research*. New York, NY: Free Press.

Fiske, S. and Taylor, S. 2007. *Social cognition: From brains to culture*. New York, NY: McGraw-Hill.

Flannery, D.J. and Williams, L. 1999. "Effective youth violence prevention." In T. Gullotta and S.J. McElhaney, eds. *Violence in homes and communities: Prevention, intervention, and treatment*. Thousand Oaks, CA: Sage.

Flight, J.I. and Forth, A.E. 2007. "Instrumentally violent youths: The roles psychopathic traits, empathy, and attachment." *Criminal Justice and Behavior*. 34:739–751.

Foglia, W.D. 1997. "Perceptual difference and the mediating effect of internalized norms among inner-city teenagers." *Journal of Research in Crime and Delinquency*. 34: 414–42.

Foley, D.L., Eaves, L.J., Wormley, B., Silberg, J.L., Maes, H.H., Kuhn, J., and Riley, B. 2004. "Childhood adversity, monoamine oxidase A genotype, and risk for conduct disorder." *Archives of General Psychiatry*. 61:738–744.

Follingstad, D.R., Helff, C.M., Binford, R.V., Runge, M.M., and White, J. 2004. "Lay persons' versus psychologists' judgments of psychological aggressive actions by a husband and wife." *Journal of Interpersonal Violence*. 19:916–942.

Fontaine, R.G., Burks, V.S., and Dodge, K.A. 2002. "Response decision processes and externalizing behavior problems in adolescents." *Development and Psychopathology*. 14:107–122.

Food and Drugs Act, R.S., 1985, c. F-27. Retrieved August 31, 2005 (www.wipo.int/clea/en/details.jsp?id=605).

Forsman, M., Lichtenstein, P., Andershed, H., and Larsson, H. 2008. "Genetic effects explain the stability of psychopathic personality from mid- to late adolescence." *Journal of Abnormal Psychology*. 117:606–617.

Forth, A.E., Kosson, D.S., and Hare, R.D. 2003. The Psychopathy Checklist Youth Version. Toronto, ON: Multi-Health Systems.

Fowles, D.C. 1980. "The three arousal model: Implications of Gray's two-factor learning theory for heart rate, electrodermal activity, and psychopathy." *Psychophysiology*. 17:87–104.

Fowles, D.C. 1988. "Psychophysiology and psychopathology: A motivational approach." *Psychophysiology*. 25:373–391.

Fox, L. and Sugar, F. 1990. *Survey of Federally Sentenced Aboriginal Women in the Community*. Ottawa, ON: Correctional Service of Canada.

Frazzetto, G., Lorenzo, G.D., Carola, V., Proietti, L., Sokolwska, E., Siracusano, A., Gross, C., and Troisi, A. 2007. "Early trauma and increased risk for physical aggression during adulthood: The moderating role of MAOA genotype." *PLoS ONE*, 5, e486. Available at www.pubmedcentral.nih.gov/picrender.fcgi?artid=1872046andblobtype=pdf.

Freeman, R.B. 1996. "Why do so many young American men commit crimes and what might we do about it?" *Journal of Economic Perspectives*. 10:25–42.

Gricar, B. 1983. "A preliminary theory of compliance with OSHA regulation." *Research in Corporate Social Performance and Policy*. 5:121–141.

French, S. and Garneau, P. 2003. "Safe and Humane Corrections Through Effective Treatment, Correctional Service of Canada." Research Report R-139.

Freud, S. 1953. *A general introduction to psychoanalysis*. New York, NY: Permabooks.

Freud, S. 1901. *The psychopathology of everyday life*. New York, NY: Macmillan.

Freud, S. 1916. "Some character types met with in psychoanalytic work." *Standard Edition*. 14:309–336.

eud, S. 1923. *The ego and the id.* London, UK: Hogarth Press.

eud, S. 1938. *The basic writings of Sigmund Freud.* New York, NY: Modern Library.

ick, P.J. 1994. "Family dysfunction and the disruptive disorders: A review of recent empirical findings." In T.H. Ollendick and R.J. Prinz, eds. *Advances in clinical child psychology.* Vol. 16. New York, NY: Plenum.

ick, P.J., and Hare, R.D. 2001. *The Antisocial Process Screening Device.* Toronto, ON: Mental Health Systems.

ick, P.J., Kimonis, E.R., Dandreaux, D.M. and Farrell, J.M. 2003. "The 4 year stability of psychopathic traits in non-referred youth." *Behavioral Sciences and the Law.* 21:1–24.

ick, P.J., Lahey, B.B., Loeber, R., Stouthamer, M., Christ, M.A.G., and Hanson, K. 1992. "Familial risk factors to oppositional defiant disorder and conduct disorder: Parental psychopathology and maternal parenting." *Journal of Consulting and Clinical Psychology.* 60:49–55.

ick, P.J., and Marsee, M.A. 2006. "Psychopathic traits and developmental pathways to antisocial behavior in youth." In C. J. Patrick, ed. *Handbook of psychopathy.* pp. 355–374. New York, NY: Guilford Press.

lero, S. 1995. "Review of the Hare Psychopathy Checklist-Revised." In J.C. Conoley, and J.C. Impara, eds. *Twelfth Mental Measurements Yearbook.* pp. 453–454. Lincoln, NE: Buros Institute Mental Measures.

lmer, T. 2000. "Elder neglect assessment in the emergency department." *Journal of Emergency Nursing.* 26:436–443.

arder, E. and Belknap, J. 2004. "Little women: Girls in adult prison." *Women and Criminal Justice.* 152:5–80.

arder, E., Rodriguez, N., and Zatz, M. 2004. "Criers, liars, and manipulators: Probation officers' views of girls." *Justice Quarterly.* 21:547–578.

bora, N., Stewart, L., Lilley, K., and Allegri, N. 2007. *A profile of female perpetrators of intimate partner violence: Implications for treatment.* R-175. Ottawa, ON: Correctional Services of Canada.

nnon, M. and Mihorean, K. 2005. "Criminal victimization in Canada, 2004." *Juristat.* 257:1–27. Catalogue no. 85-002-XPE. Ottawa, ON: Statistics Canada.

nnon, T.A. 2009. "Social cognition in violent and sexual offending: An overview." *Psychology, Crime, and Law.* 15:97–118.

rbarino, J. 2006. *See Jane Hit: Why girls are growing more violent and what we can do about it.* New York, NY: Penguin Books.

rmezy, N. 1985. "Stress-resistant children: The search for protective factors." In J.E. Stevenson, ed. *Recent research in developmental psychopathology.* pp. 213–233. New York, NY: Pergamon.

rmezy, N. 1991. "Resilience in children's adaptation to negative life events and stressed environments." *Pediatric Annuals.* 20:460–466.

rtner, R., Hussemann, J., and Kruttschnitt, C. 2008. "Female violent offenders: Moral panics or more serious offenders?" *Australian and New Zealand Journal of Criminology.* 41:9–35.

riépy, J.-L., Lewis, M.H., and Cairns, R.B. 1996. "Genes, neurobiology, and aggression: Timeframes and functions of social behaviors in adaptation." In D.M. Stoff, and R.B. Cairns, eds. *Aggression and Violence.* pp. 41–48. Mahawah, NJ: Lawrence Erlbaum.

uce, A.M., Cormer, J.P., and Schwartz, D. 1987. "Long term effects of a systems oriented school prevention program." *American Journal of Orthopsychiatry.* 57:125–131.

ylord, M.S., and Galliher, J.F. 1988. *The criminology of Edward Sutherland.* New Brunswick, NJ: Transaction Publishers.

ndreau, P., French, S., and Gionet, A. 2004. "What works (What doesn't work): The principles of effective correctional treatment." *Journal of Community Corrections,* XIII (Spring Edition). pp. 4–30.

ndreau, P. French, S., Taylor, A. 2002. *What Works What Doesn't Work.* Invited Submission to the International Community Corrections Association Monograph Series Project.

Gendreau, P., Andrews, D.A., Goggin, C., and Chanteloupe, F. 1992. *The development of clinical and policy guidelines for the prediction of criminal behaviour in criminal justice settings.* Unpublished manuscript, University of New Brunswick, St. John, NB.

Gendreau, P., Goggin, C., and Cullen, F. 1999. "The effects of prison sentences on recidivism." Ottawa, ON: Solicitor General Canada.

Gendreau, P., Goggin, C., Cullen, F.T., and Paparozzi, M. 2001. "The effects of community sanctions and incarceration on recidivism." In L.L. Motiuk and R.C. Serin, eds. *Compendium 2000 on effective correctional programming.* Ottawa, ON: Correctional Service of Canada.

Gendreau, P., Goggin, C., and Smith, P. 2002. "Is the PCL-R really the 'unparalleled' measure of offender risk?" *Criminal Justice and Behaviour.* 29:397–426.

Gendreau, P., Little, T., and Goggin, C. 1996. "A meta-analysis of predictors of adult offender recidivism: What works!" *Criminology.* 34:575–607.

Gendreau, P. and Ross, R.R. 1979. "Effective correctional treatment: Bibliotherapy for cynics." *Crime and Delinquency.* 25:463–489.

Gershoff, E.T. 2002. "Corporal punishment by parents and associated child behaviors and experiences: A meta-analytic and theoretical review." *Psychological Bulletin.* 128:539–579.

Gewirtz, A.H., and Edleson, J.L. 2007. "Young children's exposure to intimate partner violence: Towards a developmental risk and resilience framework for research and intervention." *Journal of Family Violence.* 22:151–163.

Gilfus, M. 1992. "From victims to survivors to offenders: Women's routes of entry into street crime." *Women and Criminal Justice.* 4:63–89.

Glaser, D. 1956. "Criminality theories and behavioral images." *American Journal of Sociology.* 61:441.

Gleuck, S. and Glueck, E. 1950. *Unravelling juvenile delinquency.* Cambridge, MA: Harvard University Press.

Glueck, S. and Glueck, E. 1968. *Delinquents and non-delinquents in perspective.* Cambridge, MA: Harvard University Press.

Goffman, E. 1963. *Stigma: Notes on the management of spoiled identity.* Englewood Cliffs, JH: Prentice Hall.

Gobéil, R. and Blanchette, K. 2007. "Re-validation of a gender-informed security classification scale for women inmates." *Journal of Contemporary Criminal Justice.* 23:296–309.

Golding, S.L., Eaves, D., and Kowaz, A.M. 1989. "The assessment, treatment, and outcome of insanity acquittees: Forensic history and response to treatment." *International Journal of Law and Psychiatry.* 12:149–179.

Gondolf, E.F. 1985. *Men who batter: An integrated approach for stopping wife abuse.* Holmes Beach, CA: Learning Publications.

Gondolf, E.F. 1988. "Who are those guys? Toward a behavioral typology of batterers." *Violence and Victims.* 3:187–203.

Goode, E., ed. 2008. *Out of control: Assessing the general theory of crime.* Palo Alto, CA: Stanford University Press.

Gottfredson, M.R., and Hirschi, T. 1990. *A general theory of crime.* Stanford, CA: Stanford University Press.

Gottman, J.M., Jacobson, N.S., Rushe, R.H., Shortt, J., Babcock, J., La Tailade, J.J,. et al. 1995. "The relationship between heart rate reactivity, emotionally aggressive behavior, and general violence in batterers." *Journal of Family Psychology.* 9:227–248.

Government of British Columbia. 2006. "Corrections." Retrieved April 2, 2009 (**www. pssg.gov.bc.ca/corrections/site-map/index.htm**).

Government of Canada. 2009. "National Victims of Crime Awareness Week." Retrieved January 25, 2009 (**www.victimsweek.gc.ca/archives_2006/fact-sheets/p2.html**).

Government of Newfoundland and Labrador. n.d. "Adult Custody." Retrieved April 2, 2009 (**www.justice.gov.nl.ca/just/Strategic%20Planning/PUBLICPR/INSTSRV.htm**).

Government of Nova Scotia. 2007. "Correctional Services Division." Retrieved April 2, 2009 (http://gov.ns.ca/just/Corrections/_docs/OrgChart.pdf).

Government of Prince Edward Island. 2009. "Attorney General: Community and Correctional Services." Retrieved April 2, 2009 (www.gov.pe.ca/oag/cacs-info/index.php3).

Government of Saskatchewan. n.d. "Adult Correctional Facilities." Retrieved April 2, 2009 (www.cpsp.gov.sk.ca/Adult-Correctional-Facilities).

Governor General of Canada. 2007. "Governor General to invest 41 recipients into the Order of Canada." Retrieved July 17, 2009 (www.gg.ca/media/doc.asp?DocID =5048andlang=e).

Grant, B.A., Kunic, D., MacPherson, P., McKeown, C., and Hansen, E. 2003. "The High Intensity Substance Abuse Program HISAP: Results from the Pilot Programs." Research Report R-140: Correctional Service of Canada.

Grasmick, H.G., Tittle, C.R., Bursik, R.J., and Arneklev, B.J. 1993. "Testing the core empirical implications of Gotteredson and Hirschi's general theory of crime." Journal of Research in Crime and Delinquency. 30:5–29.

Gray, J.A. 1987. "Perspectives on anxiety and impulsivity: A commentary." Journal of Research in Personality. 21:493–509.

Gray, J.A., and McNaughton, N. 2000. The neuropsychology of anxiety: An enquiry into the functions of the septohippocampal system. 2nd ed. Oxford: Oxford University Press.

Green, L. and Campbell, M.A. 2006. "Gender influences and methodological considerations in adolescent risk-need assessment: A meta-analysis." Paper presented at the 67th annual meeting of the Canadian Psychological Association, Calgary, Alberta.

Greenfeld, L.A., and Snell, T.L. 1999. Women offenders. Special Report NCJ 175688. Bureau of Justice Statistics, U.S. Department of Justice. Retrieved Sept. 15, 2005 (www.ojp.usdoj.gov/bjs/abstract/wo.htm).

Greiner, L., Brown, S.L. and Jones, N. 2009. Do criminal attitudes predict re-offending for youthful female delinquents? Manuscript submitted for publication.

Griffiths, A.J.F., Wessler, S.R., Lewontin, R.C., Gelbart, W.M., Suzuki, D.T., and Miller, J.H. 2005. Introduction to Genetic Analysis. 8th ed. New York, NY: W.H. Freeman and Company.

Grimes D.A., and Schultz K.F. 2002. "Uses and abuses of screening tests." Lancet. 359:881–884.

Grossman, R. 2008. "Psychiatric manual's update opens openness, critics say." Chicago Tribune. December 27.

Grove, W.M., Eckert, E.D., Heston, L., Bouchard, T.L., Segal, N., and Lykken, D.T. 1990. "Heritability of substance abuse and antisocial behavior: A study of monozygotic twins reared apart." Biological Psychiatry. 27:1293–1304.

Grove, W.M., Zald, D.H., Lebow, B.S., Snitz, B.E., and Nelson, C. 2000. "Clinical versus mechanical prediction: A meta-analysis." Psychological Assessment. 121:19–30.

Guy, L.S., Edens, J.F., Anthony, C., and Douglas, K.S. 2005. "Does psychopathy predict institutional misconduct among adults? A meta-analytic investigation." Journal of Consulting and Clinical Psychology. 73:1056–1064.

Hall, G.C.N. and Hirschman, R. 1991. "Towards a theory of sexual aggression: A quadripartite model." Journal of Consulting and Clinical Psychology. 59:662–669.

Hall, G.C.N. and Hirschman, R. 1992. "Sexual aggression against children: A conceptual perspective of etiology." Criminal Justice and Behavior. 19:8–23.

Hamberger, J.E. and Hastings, L.K. 1994. "Psychosocial modifiers of psychopathology for domestically violent and nonviolent men." Psychological Reports. 74:112–114.

Hamberger, L.K., Lohr, J.M., Bonge, D., and Tonlin, D.F. 1996. "A large empirical typology of male spouse abusers and its relationship to dimensions of abuse." Violence and Victims. 11: 277–292.

Hann, R.G. and Harman, W.G. 1989. Release risk prediction: Testing the Nuffi scoring system for Native and female inmates. User Report No. 1989 Ottawa, ON: Solicitor General Canada.

Hann, R.G. and Harman, W.G. 1993. Predicting release risk for Aboriginal pe itentiary inmates. User Report No. 1993-12. Ottawa, ON: Solicit General Canada.

Hannah-Moffat, K. 2004. "Gendering risk at what cost: Negotiations of ge der and risk in Canadian women's prisons." Feminism and Psycholo, 142:243–249.

Hannah-Moffat, K. and Maurutto, P. 2003. "Youth Risk/Need Assessme. An overview of issues and practices." Department of Justice Cana Youth Justice Research. RR03YJ-4e.

Hansberry, M.R., Chen, E. and Gorbien, M.J. 2005. "Dementia and el abuse." Clinics in Geriatric Medicine. 21:315–332.

Hanson, R.K. 1997. The development of a brief actuarial risk scale for sex offense recidivism. Ottawa, ON: Ministry of Public Safety.

Hanson, R.K. 2008. "What statistics should we use to report predictive acc racy." Crime Scene. 151:15–17.

Hanson, R.K., Bourgon, G., Helmus, L., and Hodgson, S. 2009. The princip of effective correctional treatment also apply to sexual offenders: A me analysis. Manuscript submitted for publication.

Hanson, R.K., Bourgon, G., Helmus, L., and Hodgson, S. 2009. A me analysis of the effectiveness of treatment for sexual offenders: Risk, need, c responsivity. Corrections Research User Report No. 2009-01. Ottaw ON: Public Safety Canada.

Hanson, R.K., Broom, I., and Stephenson, M. 2004. "Evaluating commun sex offender treatment programs: A 12-year follow-up of 724 offender Canadian Journal of Behavioural Science. 36:87–96.

Hanson, R.K., and Bussière, M.T. 1998. "Predicting relapse: A meta-analy of sexual offender recidivism studies." Journal of Consulting and Clin Psychology. 66:348–362.

Hanson, R.K., Gizzarelli, R., and Scott, H. 1994. "The attitudes of inc offenders: Sexual entitlement and acceptance of sex with childre Criminal Justice and Behavior. 21:187–202.

Hanson, R.K., Gordon, A., Harris, A.J.R., Marques, J.K., Murphy, ` Quinsey, V.L., and Seto, M.C. 2002. "First report of the collaborat outcome data project on the effectiveness of treatment for s offenders." Sexual Abuse: A Journal of Research and Treatme 14:169–194.

Hanson, R.K., Harris, A.J.R., Scott, T.-L., and Helmus, L. 2007. Assessing risk of sexual offenders on community supervision: The Dynamic Supervis Project. Ottawa, ON: Public Safety Canada.

Hanson, R.K., Helmus, L., and Bourgon, G. 2007. The validity of risk asse ments for intimate partner violence: A meta-analysis. Public Safety Can 2007-07.

Hanson, R.K., and Morton-Bourgon, K.E. 2004. Predictors of sexual recidivi An updated meta-analysis. Ottawa, ON: Public Safety Canada.

Hanson, R.K. and Morton-Bourgon, K.E. 2009. "The accuracy of recidiv risk assessments for sexual offenders: A meta-analysis of 118 predict studies." Psychological Assessment. 21:1–21.

Hanson, R.K., and Thorton, D. 2000. "Improving risk assessments for offenders: A comparison of three actuarial scales." Law and Hur Behavior. 24:119–136.

Hardyman, P.L. 2001. Validation and refinement of objective prison classifica systems for women: The experience of four states and common the Washington, DC: The Institute on Crime, Justice and Correctic National Institute of Corrections.

Hardyman, P. and Van Voorhis, P. 2004. Developing gender specific classifica systems for women offenders. Washington, DC: National Institute Corrections.

are, R.D. 1978. "Electrodermal and cardiovascular correlates of psychopathy." In R.D. Hare and D. Schalling, eds. *Psychopathic behavior: Approaches to research.* pp. 107–144. New York, NY: Wiley.

are, R.D., Clark, D., Grann, M., and Thornton, D. 2000. "Psychopathy and the predictive validity of the PCL-R: An international perspective." *Behavioral Sciences & the Law.* 18:623–645.

arlow, C.W. 1999. *Prior abuse reported by inmates and probationers. Bureau of Justice Statistics: Selected Findings.* Report No. NCJ 172879. U.S. Department of Justice: Office of Justice Programs.

are, R.D. 2003. *Hare Psychopathy Checklist-Revised (PCL-R).* 2nd ed. Toronto, ON: Multi-Health Systems.

arper, R, and Murphy, R. 2000. "An analysis of drug trafficking." *British Journal of Criminology.* 40:746–749.

arris, B. 1979. "Whatever happened to Little Albert?" *American Psychologist.* 34:151–160.

arris, G.T., Rice, M.E. and Cormier, C.A. 1991. "Length of detention in matched groups of insanity acquittees and convicted offenders." *International Journal of Law and Psychiatry.* 14:223–236.

arris, G.T., Rice, M.E., and Lalumière, M. 2001. "Criminal violence: The roles of psychopathy, neurodevelopmental insults, and antisocial parenting." *Criminal Justice and Behavior.* 28:402–426.

arris, G.T., Rice, M.E., and Quinsey, V.L. 2001. "Criminal violence: The roles of neurodevelopmental inslues, psychopathy, and antisocial parenting." *Criminal Justice and Behavior.* 28:377–394.

arris, G.T., Rice, M.E., and Quinsey, V.L. 1993. "Violent recidivism of mentally disordered offenders: The development of a statistical prediction instrument." *Criminal Justice and Behavior.* 20:315–335.

arris, G.T., Rice, M.E., Quinsey, V.L., and Chaplin, T.C. 1996. "Viewing time as a measure of sexual interest among child molesters and normal heterosexual men." *Behavior Research and Therapy.* 34:389–394.

arris, G.T., Rice, M.E., Quinsey, V.L., Lalumière, M.L., Boer, D., and Lang, C. 2003. "A multi-site comparison of actuarial risk instruments for sex offenders." *Psychological Assessment.* 15:413–425.

arris, S.B. 1996. "For better or worse: Spousal abuse grown old." *Journal of Elder Abuse and Neglect.* 8:1–33.

rt, S., Cox, D., and Hare, R.D. 1995. *Manual for the Psychopathy Checklist: Screening Version PCL: SV.* Toronto, ON: Multi-Health Systems.

rt, S.D. 2008. *The Future of Violence Risk Assessment and Management: From Prediction to Prevention, from Formula to Formulation.* Keynote presentation at the International Association of Forensic Mental Health Services, Vienna, June.

rt, S.D., Watt, K.A. and Vincent, G.M. 2002. "Commentary on Seagrave and Grisso: Impressions of the state of the art." *Law and Human Behavior.* 26:241–245.

slip, S. 2001. "Conditional sentencing and the overrepresentation of Aboriginal offenders in penal institutions." *Gonzaga Journal of International Law.* 5:1–40.

rtley, C.C. 2002. "The co-occurrence of child maltreatment and domestic violence: Examining both neglect and child physical abuse." *Child Maltreatment.* 7:349–358.

wkins, J.D., Herrenkohl, T.I., Farrington, D.P., Brewer, D., Catalano, R.F., Harachi, T.W., et al. 2000. *Predictors of youth violence.* Juvenile Justice Bulletin. Washington, DC: U.S. Department of Justice, Office of Justice Programs, Office of Juvenile Justice and Delinquency Prevention.

zardous Products Act, R.S., 1985, c. H-3. Retrieved from (http://laws.justice.gc.ca/en/H-3/index.html).

alth Canada. 2003. *The consequences of child maltreatment: A reference guide for health practitioners.* Report prepared by Jeff Latimer. Ottawa, ON: Health Canada.

Helmus, L. 2008. "Advice for finding a thesis supervisor: What professors have to say." *Crime Scene.* 15:38–41.

Helzer, J.E., Kraemer, H.C., and Kruger, R.F. 2007. "The feasibility and need for dimensional psychiatric diagnoses." *Psychological Medicine.* 36:1671–1680.

Hendley, N. 2000. "The shine is off boot camps." *Eye Weekly.* January 20. Retrieved June 1, 2004 (www.eye.net/eye/issue/issue_01.20.00/news/bootcamp.html).

Henggeler, S.W. 1991. "Multidimensional causal models of delinquent behaviour and their implications of treatment." In R. Cohen and A.W. Siegel, eds. *Context and development.* pp. 211–231.

Henggeler, S.W. and Borduin, C.M. 1990. *Family therapy and beyond: A multisystemic approach to treating the behavior problems of children and adolescents.* Pacific Grove, CA: Brooks/Cole.

Henggeler, S.W., Melton, G.B., and Smith, L.A. 1992. "Family preservation using multisystemic therapy: An effective alternative to incarcerating serious juvenile offenders." *Journal of Consulting and Clinical Psychology.* 60:953–961.

Henggeler, S.W., Schoenwald, S.K., Borduin, C.M., Rowland, M.D., and Cunningham, P.B. 1998. *Multisystemic treatment of antisocial behavior in children and adolescents.* New York, NY: Guilford Press.

Henggeler, S.W., Schoenwald, S.K., and Pickrel, S.A.G. 1995. "Multisystemic therapy: Bridging the gap between university and community bad treatment." *Journal of Consulting and Clinical Psychology.* 63:709–717.

Henry, B., Avshalom, C., Moffitt, T.E., and Silva, P.A. 1996. "Temperamental and familial predictors of violent and non-violent criminal convictions." *Developmental Psychology.* 32:614–623.

Henry, B. and Moffitt, T.E. 1997. "Neuropsychological and neuroimaging studies of juvenile delinquency and adult criminal behaviour." In D.M. Stoff, J. Breiling, and J.D. Maser, eds. *Handbook of Antisocial Behavior.* pp. 280–287. New York, NY: Wiley.

Herrenkohl, E.C., Herrenkohl, R.C. and Egolf, B.P. 1994. "Resilient early school-age children from maltreating homes: Outcomes in late adolescence." *American Journal of Orthopsychiatry.* 642:301–309.

Herrenkohl, E.C., Herrenkohl, R.C., Egolf, B.P., and Russo, M.J. 1998. "The relationship between early maltreatment and teenage parenthood." *Journal of Adolescence.* 21:291–303.

Herrenkohl, T., Maguin, E., Hill, K., Hawkins, J., Abbott, R., and Catalano, R. 2000. "Developmental risk factors for youth violence." *Journal of Adolescent Health.* 26:176–186.

Herrenkohl, T.I., Sousa, C., Tajima, E.A., Herrenkohl, R.C., and Moylan, C.A. 2008. "Intersection of child abuse and children's exposure to domestic violence." *Trauma, Violence, and Abuse.* 9:84–99.

Herrenkohl, T.I., Tajima, E.A., Whitney, S.D. and Huang, B. 2005. "Protection against antisocial behavior in children exposed to physically abusive discipline." *Journal of Adolescent Health.* 36:457–465.

Hersh, K. and Borum, R. 1998. "Command hallucinations, compliance, and risk assessment." *Journal of the American Academy of Law.* 26:353–359.

Hessing, D., Junger, M., Pickering, L., and Vazsonyi, A. 2001. "An empirical test of a general theory of crime: A four-nation comparative study of self-control and the prediction of deviance." *Journal of Research in Crime and Delinquency.* 38:91–131.

Hickey, E.W. 2006. *Serial murderers and their victims.* Belmont, CA: Wadsworth.

Hill, C., Kelley, P., Agle, B., Hitt, M., and Hoskisson, R. 1992. "An empirical examination of the causes of corporate wrongdoing in the United States." *Human Relations.* 45:1055–1076.

Hill, K.G., Howell, J., Hawkins, J., and Battin-Pearson, S. 1999. "Childhood risk factors for adolescent gang membership: Results from the Seattle Social Development Project." *Journal of Research in Crime and Delinquency.* 36:300–322.

Hilton, N.Z. 1993. "Childhood sexual victimization and lack of empathy in child molesters: Explanation or excuse?" *International Journal of Offender Therapy and Comparative Criminology*. 37:287–296.

Hilton, N.Z., Harris, G.T. and Rice, M.E. 2001. "Predicting violence by serious wife assaulters." *Journal of Interpersonal Violence*. 16:408–423.

Hilton, N.Z., Harris, G.T., Rice, M.E., Houghton, R.E. and Eke, A.W. 2008. "An in-depth risk assessment for wife assault recidivism: The Domestic Violence Risk Appraisal Guide." *Law and Human Behavior*. 32:150–163.

Hilton, N.Z., Harris, G.T., Rice, M.E., Lang, C., Cormier, C.A., and Lines, K.J. 2004. "A brief actuarial assessment for the prediction of wife assault recidivism: The Ontario Domestic Assault Risk Assessment." *Psychological Assessment*. 16:267–275.

Hindelang, M.J. 1973. "Causes of delinquency: A partial replication and extension." *Social Problems*. 20:471–487.

Hinshaw, S.P. 1992. "Externalizing behavior problems and academic underachievement in childhood and adolescence. Causal relationships and underlying mechanisms." *Psychological Bulletin*. 111:127–155.

Hinshaw, S.P. and Stier, A. 2008. "Stigma as related to mental disorder." *Annual Review of Psychology*. 4:367–393.

Hinshaw, S.P., Lahey, B.B., and Hart, E.K. 1993. "Issues of taxonomy and comorbidity in the development of conduct disorder." *Development and Psychopathology*. 5:31–49.

Hipwell, A.E. and Loeber, R. 2006. "Do we know which interventions are effective for disruptive and delinquent girls?" *Clinical Child and Family Psychology Review*. 9:221–255.

Hirschi, T. 1969. *Causes of delinquency*. New Brunswick, NJ: Transaction Publishers.

Hirschi, T. 2002. *Causes of delinquency*. New Brunswick, NJ: Transaction Publishers.

Hirschi, T. and Selvin, H.C. 1967. *Delinquency research: An appraisal of analytic methods*. New York, NY: The Free Press.

Hobson, J., Shine, J. and Roberts, R. 2000. "How do psychopaths behave in a prison therapeutic community." *Psychology, Crime, and Law*. 6:139–154.

Hodgins, S. 1992. "Mental disorder, intellectual deficiency, and crime: Evidence from a birth cohort." *Archives of General Psychiatry*. 49:476–483.

Hodgins, S. 1987. "Men found unfit to stand trial and/or guilty by reason of insanity. Recidivism." *Canadian Journal of Criminology*. 29:451–70.

Hodgins, S., Hiscoke, U., and Freese, R. 2003. "The antecedents of aggressive behavior among men with schizophrenia: A prospective investigation of patients in community treatment." *Behavioral Sciences and the Law*. 21:523–546.

Hodgins, S., Mednick, S.A., Brennan, P., Schulsinger, F. and Engberg, M. 1996. "Mental disorder and crime: Evidence from a Danish birth cohort." *Archives of General Psychiatry*. 53:489–96.

Hodgins, S., Tengström, A., Eriksson, A., Österman, R., Kronstrand, R., Eaves, D., et al. 2007. "A multisite study of community treatment programs for mentally ill offenders with major mental disorders: Design, measures, and forensic sample." *Criminal Justice and Behavior*. 34:211–228,

Hoffman, P.B. and Beck, J.L. 1984. "Burnout: Age at release from prison and recidivism." *Journal of Criminal Justice*. 12:617–623.

Hoge, R.D. and Andrews, D.A. 1996. *Assessing the youthful offender: Issues and techniques*. New York, NY: Plenum.

Hoge, R.D., and Andrews, D.A. 2002. *The Youth Level of Service/Case Management Inventory*. Toronto, ON: Multi-Health Systems.

Hoge, R.D., Andrews, D.A., and Leschied, A.W. 1996. "An investigation of risk and protective factors in a sample of youthful offenders." *Journal of Child Psychology and Psychiatry*. 37:419–424.

Hollin, C.R. 1989. *Psychology and crime: An introduction to criminological psychology*. London, UK: Routledge.

Hollin, C.R. and Palmer, E.J. 2006. "Criminogenic need and women offenders: A critique of the literature." *Legal and Criminological Psychology*. 11:179–195.

Holmes, R.M. and DeBurger, J. 1988. *Serial murder*. Newbury Park, CA: Sage.

Holmes, R.M. and Holmes, S.T. 1998. *Serial murder*. 2nd ed. Thousand Oaks, CA: Sage.

Holsinger, A.M., Lowenkamp, C.T., and Latessa, E.J. 2006. "Exploring the validity of the Level of Service Inventory–Revised with Native American offenders." *Journal of Criminal Justice*. 34:331–337.

Holsinger, K., Belknap, J., and Sutherland, J. 1999. *Assessing the gender specific program and service needs for adolescent females in the juvenile justice system*. Columbus, OH: Office of Criminal Justice Services.

Holtfreter, K. 2005. "Is occupational fraud 'typical' white-collar crime? A comparison of individuals and organizational characteristics." *Journal of Criminal Justice*. 33:353–365.

Holtfreter, K. and Cupp, R. 2007. "Gender and risk assessment." *Journal of Contemporary Criminal Justice*. 23:363–382.

Holtfreter, K. and Morash, M. 2003. "The needs of women offenders: Implications for correctional programming." *Women and Criminal Justice*. 14:137–160.

Holtfreter, K., Reisig, M.D., and Morash, M. 2004. "Poverty, state capital, and recidivism among women offenders." *Criminology and Public Policy*. 32:185–208.

Holtfreter, K., Van Slyke, S., Bratton, J., and Gertz, M. 2008. "Public perceptions of white-collar crime and punishment." *Journal of Criminal Justice*. 36:50–60.

Holtzworth-Munroe, A. and Meehan, J.C. 2004. "Typologies of men who are martially violent: Scientific and clinical implications." *Journal of Interpersonal Violence*. 19:1369–1389.

Holtzworth-Munroe, A., Meehan, J.C., Herron, K., Rehman, U. and Stuart, G.L. 2003. "Do subtypes of martially violent men continue to differ over time." *Journal of Consulting and Clinical Psychology*. 714:728–740.

Holtzworth-Munroe, A. and Stuart, G.L. 1994. "Typologies of male batterers: Three subtypes and the differences among them." *Psychological Bulletin*. 116:476–497.

Hood, R. 2002. *The Death Penalty: A Worldwide Perspective*. 3rd ed. Oxford: Oxford University Press.

Hubbard, D. and Matthews, B. 2008. "Reconciling the differences between the 'gender responsive' and the 'What Works' literature to improve services for girls." *Crime and Delinquency*. 54:225–258.

Hubbard, D.J. and Pratt, T.C. 2002. "A meta-analysis of the predictors of delinquency among girls." *Journal of Offender Rehabilitation*. 34:1–13.

Huesmann, L.R., Eron, L.D., Lefkowitz, M.M., and Walder, L.O. 1984. "Stability of aggression over time and generations." *Developmental Psychology*. 20:1120–1134.

Hughes, P. and Mossman, M.J. 2001. "Re-thinking Access to Criminal Justice in Canada: A Critical Review of Needs and Responses." Unpublished paper for the Department of Justice Canada.

Hughes, H.M., Parkinson, D., and Vargo, M. 1989. "Witnessing spouse abuse and experiencing physical abuse: A "double whammy"?" *Journal of Family Violence*. 4:197–209.

Hull, J. 2005. *Post-secondary education and labour market outcomes Canada, 2001*. Ottawa, ON: Minister of Indian Affairs and Northern Development.

Hunnicutt, G. and Broidy, L.M. 2004. "Liberation and economic marginalization: A reformulation and test of formerly? competing models." *Journal of Research in Crime and Delinquency*. 412:130–155.

Huss, M.T. 2009. *Forensic psychology: Research, clinical practice and applications*. Chichester: Wiley-Blackwell.

ussong, A.M., Curran, P.J., Moffitt, T.E., Caspi, A., and Carrig, M.M. 2004. "Substance abuse hinders desistance in young adults' antisocial behavior." *Development and Psychopathology*. 16:1029–1046.

uizinga, D., Esbensen, F., and Weiher, A.W. 1991. "Are there multiple paths to delinquency?" *Journal of Criminal Law and Criminology*. 82:83–118.

amarigeon, R., ed. 2006. *Women and girls in the criminal justice system*. Kingston, NJ: Civic Research Institute.

mmigration and Refugee Protection Act, S.C., 2001, c. 27. Retrieved from **http://laws-lois.justice.gc.ca/PDF/Statute/I/I-2.5.pdf**.

ciardi, J., Lockwood, D., and Pottieger, A.E. 1993. *Women and crack-cocaine*. New York, NY: Macmillan.

come Tax Act. 1985, c. 1, 5th Supp. Retrieved from **http://laws-lois.justice. gc.ca/PDF/Statute/I/I-3.3.pdf**.

dian and Northern Affairs Canada. 1996. *Report of the Royal Commission on Aboriginal Peoples*. Ottawa, ON: Canada Communication Group.

ternational Network for the Prevention of Elder Abuse. 2009. Retrieved August 31, 2009 (**www.inpea.net/weaad/weaad2009paris.html**).

ffee, S.R., Caspi, A., Moffitt, T.E., Dodge, K.A., Rutter, M., Taylor, A., et al. 2005. "Nature X Nurture: Genetic vulnerabilities interact with physical maltreatment to promote conduct problems." *Development and Psychopathology*. 17:67–84.

mes, D.V., Mullen, P.E., Pathé, M.T., Meloy, J.R., Farnham, F.R., Preston, L., and Darnley, B. 2008. "Attacks on British Royal Family: The role of psychotic illness." *Journal of American Academy of Psychiatry and Law*. 36:59–67.

mes, D.V., Mullen, P.E., Meloy, J.R. Pathé, M.T., Farnham, F.R., and Damley, B. 2007. "The role of mental disorder in attacks on European politicians 1994–2004." *Acta Psychiatrica Scandinavica*. 116:334–344.

mes, J. and Meyerding, J. 1977. "Early sexual experiences and prostitution." *American Journal of Psychiatry*. 134:1381–1385.

assen, Marthan. 1983. "Crazy." In *Silent Scream*. Minneapolis, MN: Augsburg.

ey, M.L. and Stewart, M.A. 1985. "Psychiatric disorder in the parents of adopted children with aggressive conduct disorder." *Neuropsychobiology*. 13:7–11.

fery, C.R. 1965. "Criminal behavior and learning theory." *Journal of Criminal Law, Criminology, and Police Science*. 56:294–300.

spersen, A.F., Lalumière, M.L., and Seto, M.C. 2009. "Sexual abuse history among adult sex offenders and non-sex offenders: A meta-analysis." *Child Abuse and Neglect*. 33:179–192.

ssor, R., Van Den Bos, J., Vanderryn, J., Costa, F.M., and Turbin, M.A. 1995. "Protective factors in adolescent problem behavior: Moderator effects and developmental change." *Developmental Psychology*. 31:923–933.

hn Howard Society. 1999. *Sentencing in Canada*. Toronto, ON: John Howard Society.

b Outlook. 2008. "Class of 2008 Steps Into Good Job Market." Retrieved August 31, 2009 (**www.jobweb.com/studentarticles.aspx?id=1219**).

hnson, H. 1996. *Dangerous domains: Violence against women in Canada*. Scarborough, ON: Nelson.

hnson, H. 2006. "Concurrent drug and alcohol dependency and mental health among incarcerated women." *Australian and New Zealand Journal of Criminology*. 1–22. Retrieved April 11, 2009 (**http://findarticles.com/p/ articles/mi_hb3370/is_2_39/ai_n29294216/pg_2/?tag=content;col1**).

hnson, R.E. 1979. *Juvenile delinquency and its origins*. Cambridge, UK: Cambridge University Press.

hnson, S. 2005. "Returning to correctional services after release: A profile of Aboriginal and non-Aboriginal adults involved in Saskatchewan corrections from 1999/00 to 2003/04." *Juristat*. 25.

hnston, J.C. 1997. *Aboriginal offender survey: Case files and interview sample*. Research Report No. R-61. Ottawa, ON: Correctional Service of Canada.

Johnston, J.C. 2000. "Aboriginal federal offender surveys: A synopsis." *Forum on Corrections Research*. 12:25–27.

Jolliffe, D. and Farrington, D.P. 2007. *A systematic review of the national and international evidence on the effectiveness of interventions with violent offenders*. Ministry of Justice Research Series 16/07.

Jones, E. 1953. *Sigmund Freud: Life and work Volume 1: The young Freud 1856–1900*. London, UK: Hogarth Press.

Jones, E. 1955. *Sigmund Freud: Life and work Volume 2: The years of maturity 1901–1919*. London, UK: Hogarth Press.

Jones, E. 1957. *Sigmund Freud: Life and work Volume 3: The last phase 1919–1939*. London, UK: Hogarth Press.

Jones, S. and Cauffman, E. 2008. "Juvenile psychopathy and judicial decision making: An empirical analysis of an ethical dilemma." *Behavioral Science and the Law*. 26:151–165.

Junginger, J. 1995. "Command hallucinations and the prediction of dangerousness." *Psychiatric Services*. 46:911–914.

Junginger, J., Claypoole, K., Laygo, R., Crisanti, A. 2006. "Effects of serious mental illness and substance abuse on criminal offences." *Psychiatric Services*. 57:879–882.

Kalmus, E. and Beech, A.R. 2005. "Forensic assessment of sexual interest: A review." *Aggression and Violent Behavior*. 10:193–396.

Kalmuss, D.S. 1984. "The intergenerational transmission of marital aggression." *Journal of Marriage and the Family*. 46:11–19.

Kandel, D.B. and Adler, I. 1982. "Socialization into marijuana use among French adolescents: A cross-cultural comparison with the United States." *Journal of Health and Social Behavior*. 23:295–309.

Kandel, E. and Freed, D. 1982. "Frontal-lobe dysfunction and antisocial behavior." *Journal of Clinical Psychology*. 45:404–413.

Kandel, E., Mednick, S.A., Kikegaard-Sorensen, L., Hutchings, B., Knop, J., Rosenberg, R., et al. 1988. "IQ as a protective factor for subjects at high risk for antisocial behavior." *Journal of Consulting and Clinical Psychology*. 56:224–226.

Kantor, G.K. Jasinski, J.L., and Aldaraondo, E. 1994. "Sociocultural status and incidence of marital violence in Hispanic families." *Violence and Victims*. 9:207–222.

Kaplan, H.S. and Gangestad, S.W. 2005. "Life history theory and evolutionary psychology." In D.M. Buss, ed. *The handbook of evolutionary psychology*. pp. 68–118. Hoboken, NJ: John Wiley and Sons, Inc.

Kazdin, A.E. 1996. *Conduct disorders in childhood and adolescence*. 2nd ed. Thousand Oaks, CA: Sage.

Kazdin, A.E., Kraemer, H.C., Kessler, R.C., Kupfer, D.J., and Offord, D.R. 1997. "Contributions of risk factor research to developmental psychopathology." *Clinical Psychology Review*. 17:375–406.

Kendall, K. 2004. "Dangerous thinking: A critical history of correctional cognitive behaviouralism." In G. Mair, ed. *What matters in probation*. pp. 53–89. Cullompton, Devon, UK: Willan Publishing.

Kendall, K. 2002. "Time to think again about cognitive behavioural programmes." In P. Carlen, ed. *Women and punishment: The struggle for justice*. pp.182–198. Cullompton, Devon, UK: Willan Publishing.

Kendell, R. and Jablensky, A. 2003. "Distinguishing between the validity and utility of psychiatric diagnoses." *American Journal of Psychiatry*. 160:2–12.

Kennedy, S.M. 2004. "A practitioner's guide to responsivity: Maximizing treatment effectiveness." *Journal of Community Corrections, XIII*. 7–9:22–30.

Kerbaj, R. March 16, 2009. "Thousands of girls mutilated in Britain." *The Times*.

Kershaw, C. 1999. *Reconviction of offenders sentenced or released from prison in 1994*. Research Findings 90. London: Home Office Research, Development and Statistics Directorate.

Kessler, R.C., McGonagle, K.A., and Zhao, S. 1994. "Lifetime and 12-month prevalence of DSM-III-R psychiatric disorders in the United States: results from the National Comorbidity Survey." *Archives of General Psychiatry*. 51:8–19.

Kiehl, K.A. 2006. "A cognitive neuroscience perspective on psychopathy: Evidence for paralimbic system dysfunction." *Psychiatry Research*. 142:107–128.

Kiehl, K.A., Smith, A.M., Hare, R.D., Forster, B.B., Brink, J. and Liddle, P.F. 2001. "Limbic abnormalities in affective processing by criminal psychopaths as revealed by functional magnetic resonance imaging." *Biological Psychiatry*. 50:677–684.

Kim, T.E., and Goto, S.G. 2000. "Peer delinquency and parental social support as predictors of Asian American adolescent delinquency." *Deviant Behavior*. 21:331–348.

Kimonis, E.R., Frick, P.J., Fazekas, H. and Loney, B.R. 2006. "Psychopathic traits, aggression, and the processing of emotional stimuli in non-referred children." *Behavioral Sciences and the Law*. 24:21–37.

Klemke, L.W. 1982. "Reassessment of Cameron's apprehension-termination of shoplifting finding." *California Sociologist*. 5.88–95.

Kong, R. and AuCoin, K. 2008. "Female offenders in Canada." *Juristat*. Catalogue no. 85-002-XIE. Ottawa, ON: Statistics Canada.

Koons, B.A., Burrow, J.D., Morash, M., and Bynum, T. 1997. "Expert and offender perceptions of program elements linked to successful outcomes for incarcerated women." *Crime and Delinquency*. 434:515–532.

Knight, R.A. 2010. "Typologies for rapists: The generation of a new structural model." In A. Schlank, ed., *The sexual predator* (vol. IV). Kingston, NJ: Civic Research Institute.

Knight, R.A., Carter, D.L., and Prentky, R.A. 1989. "A system for the classification of child molesters: Reliability and application." *Journal of Interpersonal Violence*. 4:3–23.

Knight, R.A., and Prentky, R.A. 1990. "Classifying sexual offenders: The development and corroboration of taxonomic models." In W.L. Marshall, D.R. Laws, and H.E. Barbaree, eds. *The handbook of sexual assault: Issues, theories, and treatment of the offender*. pp. 23–52. New York, NY: Plenum Press.

Kochanska, G. 1993. "Toward a synthesis of parental socialization and child temperament in early development of conscience." *Child Development*. 64:325–347.

Kochanska, G. 1994. "Beyond cognition: Expanding the search for the early roots of internalization and conscience." *Developmental Psychology*. 30:20–22.

Kochanska, G., Murray, K.T. and Coy, K.C. 1997. "Inhibitory control as a contributor to conscience in childhood: From toddler to early school age." *Child Development*. 68:263–277.

Kockler, T. and Meloy, J.R. 2007. "The application of affective and predatory aggression to psycholegal opinions." In R. C. Browne, ed. *Forensic psychiatry research trends*. pp. 63–83. New York, NY: Nova.

Kropp, P.R., Hart, S.D., Webster, C.D., and Eaves, D. 1999. *Manual for the Spousal Assault Risk Assessment Guide*. 3rd ed. Toronto, ON: Multi-Health Systems.

Kruttschnitt, C. 2001. "Gender and violence." In C.M. Renzetti and L. Goodstein, eds. *Women, crime, and criminal justice: Original Feminist Readings*. pp. 77–92. Los Angeles: Roxbury Publishing Company.

Kumpfer, K.L. and Alvarado, R. 2003. "Family- strengthening approaches for the prevention of youth problem behaviors." *American Psychologist*. 58:457-465.

Kunic, D. and Grant, B.A. 2006. "The computerized assessment of substance abuse CASA: Results from the demonstration project." Addictions Research Centre, Research Branch, Correctional Service of Canada. Available at **www.csc-scc.gc.ca/text/rsrch/reports/r173/r173-eng-shtml**.

LaBoucane-Benson, P. 2002. "In Search of Your Warrior program." *Forum on Corrections Research*. 14:40–41.

Lachs, M.S. and Pillemer, K. 2004. "Elder abuse." *Lancet*. 364994 1263–1272.

Lachs, M.S., Williams, C., O'Brien, S., Hurst, L. and Horwitz, R. 1997. "R factors for reported elder abuse and neglect: A nine-year observation cohort study." *Gerontologist*. 374:469–474.

Lader, D., Singleton, N., and Meltzer, H. 2003. "Psychiatric morbidity amo young offenders in England and Wales." *International Review Psychiatry*. 15:144–147.

LaGrange, R.L. and White, H.R. 1985. "Age differences in delinquency: test of theory." *Criminology*. 23:19–45.

Lahey, B.B., Waldman, I.D., and McBurnett, K. 1989. "The development antisocial behaviour: An integrative causal model." *Journal of Cl Psychology and Psychiatry*. 40:669–682.

Laird, R.D., Jordan, K.Y., Dodge, K.A., Petit, G.S., and Bates, J.E. 200 "Peer rejection in childhood, involvement with antisocial peers in ea adolescence and the development of externalizing behavior problem *Development and Psychopathology*. 13:337–354.

Lalumière, M.L., Harris, G.T., Quinsey, V.L., and Rice, M.E. 2005. *The cau of rape: Understanding individual differences in male propensity for sex aggression*. Washington, DC: American Psychological Association.

Lalumière, M.L., Harris, G.T., and Rice, M.E. 2001. "Psychopathy and dev opmental instability." *Evolution and Human Behaviour*. 22:75–92.

Lalumière, M.L., Mishra, S., and Harris, G.T. 2008. "In cold blood: The ev lution of psychopathy." In J.D. Duntley and T.K. Shackelford, e *Evolutionary forensic psychology: Darwinian foundations of crime and la* pp. 176–197. Oxford, NY: Oxford University Press.

Lalumière, M.L., and Quinsey, V.L. 1994. "The discriminability of rapists fr non-sex offenders using phallometric measures: A meta-analys *Criminal Justice and Behavior*. 21:150–175.

Lalumière, M.L., Quinsey, V.L., Harris, G.T., Rice, M.E., and Trautrimas, 2003. "Are rapists differentially aroused by coercive sex in phallomet assessments?" In R. Prentky, E. Janus, and M.C. Seto, eds. *Sexually cc cive behavior: Understanding and management*. pp. 211–224. New Yc NY: Annals of the New York Academy of Sciences.

Lambert, M.J. 1992. "Psychotherapy outcome research: Implications for integ tive and eclectical therapists." In J.C. Norcross and M.R. Goldfried, e *Handbook of psychotherapy integration*. pp. 94–129. New York, NY: Ba Books, Inc.

Lange, P.J. 1994. "The varieties of emotional experiences: A mediation James-Lange theory." *Psychological Review*. 101:211–221.

Langton, C.M., Barbaree, H.E., Harkins, L. and Peacock, E.J. 2006. "S offenders response to treatment and its association with recidivism a function of psychopathy." *Sexual Abuse: A Journal of Research Treatment*.181:99–120.

Lanier, M.M. and Henry, S. 2004. *Essential criminology*. 2nd ed. Boulder, C Westview Press.

LaPrairie, C. 1989. *The role of sentencing in the over-representation of aboriginal ple in correctional institutions*. Ottawa, ON: Department of Justice Cana

LaPrairie, C. 1990. "The role of sentencing in the over-representatior Aboriginal people in correctional institutions." *Canadian Journal Criminology*. 32:429–440.

LaPrairie, C. 1992. "Aboriginal crime and justice: Explaining the prese exploring the future." *Canadian Journal of Criminology*. 34:281–298.

LaPrairie, C. 1996. *Examining Aboriginal corrections*. Ottawa, ON: Solic General Canada.

LaPrairie, C. 2002. "Aboriginal over- representation in the criminal justice tem: A tale of nine cities." *Canadian Journal of Criminology*. 44:181–2C

Larsson, H., Andershed, H. and Lichtenstein, P. 2006. "A genetic fac explains most of the variation in the psychopathic personality." *Jour of Abnormal Psychology*. 115:221–230.

timer, J., and Desjardins, N. 2007. "The 2007 National Justice Survey: Tackling crime and public confidence." Research Report 07-4e. Ottawa, ON: Department of Justice.

timer, J., Dowden, C., and Muise, D. 2005. "The effectiveness of restorative justice practices: A meta-analysis." *The Prison Journal.* 85:127–44.

timer, J. and Kleinknecht, S. 2000. *The effects of restorative justice programming: A review of the empirical research literature.* Ottawa, ON: Research and Statistics Division, Department of Justice Canada.

timer, J., Kleinknecht, S., Hung, K., and Gabor, T. 2003. *Self-reported delinquency in Canada: An analysis of the National Longitudinal Survey of Children and Youth.* Ottawa, ON: Department of Justice.

timer, J. and Lawrence, A. 2006. *The Review Board Systems in Canada: An overview of results form the mentally disordered accused data collection study.* RR06-1E. Research and Statistics Division: Department of Justice Canada.

ub, J.H. and Sampson, R.J. 1988. "Unraveling families and delinquency: A reanalysis of the Gluecks' data." *Criminology.* 26:355–380.

ub, J.H., and Sampson, R.J. 1991. "The Sutherland-Glueck debate: On the sociology of criminological knowledge." *American Journal of Sociology.* 96:1402–1440.

idet, A.B., Savage, R., and Mahmood, D.J. 2002. "Pathways to Long-term Recovery: A Preliminary Investigation." *Journal of Psychoactive Drugs.* 343:305–311.

Vigne, N.G., Davies, E., Palmer, T., and Halberstadt, R. 2008. "Release planning for successful re-entry: A guide for corrections, service providers and community groups." Urban Institute. Retrieved July 20, 2009 (www.urban.org/publications/411767.html).

w Courts Education Society of B.C. 2009. *Gladue and Aboriginal sentencing.* Retrieved January 14, 2009 (http://216.197.122.213/gladue_sentencing).

ws, D.R., Hanson, R.K., Osborn, C.A., and Greenbaum, P.E. 2000. "Assessment of sexual arousal and a self-report measure of sexual preference." *Journal of Interpersonal Violence.* 15:1297–1312.

ws, D.R. and Marshall, W.L. 1990. "A conditioning theory of the etiology and maintenance of deviant sexual preference and behaviour." In H.E. Barbaree, W.L. Marshall, and D.R. Laws, eds. *Handbook of sexual assault: Theories and treatment of the offender.* pp. 209–229. New York, NY: Plenum.

ws, D.R., Meyer, J., and Holmen, M.L. 1978. "Reduction of sadistic arousal by olfactory aversion: A case study." *Behaviour Research and Therapy.* 16:281–285.

adbeater, B.J., Kuperminc, G.P., Blatt, S.J., and Hertzog, C. 1999. "A multivariate model of gender differences in adolescents' internalizing and externalizing problems." *Developmental Psychology.* 35:1268–1282.

e, L.C., Kotch, J.B. and Cox, C.E. 2004. "Child maltreatment in families experiencing domestic violence." *Violence and Victims.* 19:573–591.

e, R. and Coccaro, E.R. 2007. "Neurobiology of impulsive aggression: Focus on serotonin and the orbitofrontal cortex." In D.J. Flannery, A.T. Vazsonyi, and I.D. Waldman, eds. *The Cambridge handbook of violent behavior and aggression.* pp. 170–186. New York, NY: Cambridge University Press.

e, T., Chong, S.A., Chan, Y.H., and Sathyadevan, G. 2004. "Command hallucinations among Asian patients with schizophrenia." *Canadian Journal of Psychiatry.* 49:838–842.

eder, E., ed. 2004. *Inside and out: Women, prison, and therapy.* Binghamton, NY: Haworth Press, Inc.

stico, A.R., Salekin, R.T., DeCoster, J., and Rogers, R. 2008. "A large-scale meta-analysis relating the Hare measures of psychopathy to antisocial conduct." *Law and Human Behavior.* 32:28–45.

mgruber, J. 2001. "Women in the criminal justice system." In N. Ollus and S. Nevala, eds. *Proceedings of the workshop held at the Tenth United Nations Congress on the preventions of crime and the treatment of offenders:* Volume 36. *Women in the criminal justice system: International examples and national responses.* pp. 59–67. Helsinki, Finland: European Institute for Crime Prevention and Control.

Lenzner, R. 2008. "Bernie Madoff's $50 billion Ponzi Scheme." December 12, 2008. *Forbes Magazine.* Retrieved August 31, 2009 (www.forbes.com/2008/12/12/madoff-ponzi-hedge-pf-ii-in_rl_1212croesus.inl.html).

Leonard, E. 1982. *Women, crime and society.* New York, NY: Longman.

Leschied, A.W. and Cunningham, A. 2002. *Seeking effective interventions for serious young offenders: Interim results of a four-year randomized study of multisystemic therapy in Ontario, Canada.* London, ON: Centre for Children and Families in the Justice System.

Levenson, J.S., D'Amora, D.A., Hern, A.L. 2007. "Megan's Law and its impact on community re-entry for sex offenders." *Behavioral Sciences and the Law.* 25:587–602.

Levenson, J.S., Brannon, Y.N., Fortney, T., and Baker, J. 2007. "Public perceptions about sex offenders and community protection policies." *Analyses of Social Issues and Public Policy.* 7:137–161.

Leventhal, J.M. 1996. "Twenty years later: We do know how to prevent child abuse and neglect." *Child Abuse & Neglect.* 20:647–653.

Li, G. 2008. "Homicide in Canada, 2007." *Juristat.* 289:1–26. Ottawa, ON: Statistics Canada Catologue no. 85-002-X.

Liebling, A. 2006. "Why fairness matters in criminal justice." In N. Padfield, ed. *Who to Release? Parole, fairness and criminal justice.* pp. 63–71. Portland, Oregon: Willan Publishing.

Lilienfeld, S.O. and Andrews, B.P. 1996. "Development and preliminary validation of a self-report measure of psychopathic personality traits in noncriminal populations." *Journal of Personality Assessment.* 66:488–524.

Lilienfeld, S.O., and Fowler, K.A. 2006. "The self-report assessment of psychopathy: Problems, pitfalls, and promises." In C.J. Patrick, ed. *Handbook of the psychopathy.* pp. 107–132. New York, NY: Guilford Press.

Lilienfeld, S.O. 1992. "The association between antisocial personality and somatization disorders: A review and integration of theoretical models." *Clinical Psychology Review.* 12:641–662.

Lilly, J.R., Cullen, F.T., and Ball, R.A. 2006. *Criminological theory: Context and consequences.* 4th ed. Thousand Oaks, CA: Sage.

Link, B., Andrews, A., and Cullen, F. 1992. "The violent and illegal behavior of mental patients reconsidered." *American Sociological Review.* 57:275–292.

Link, B. and Stueve, A. 1994. "Psychotic symptoms and the violent/illegal behavior of mental patients compared to community controls." In J. Monahan and H. Steadman, eds. *Violence and mental disorder: Developments in risk assessment.* pp. 137–159. Chicago, IL: University of Chicago Press.

Link, B., Monahan, J., Stueve, A., and Cullen, F. 1999. "Real in their consequences: A sociological approach to understanding the association between psychotic symptoms and violence." *American Sociological Review.* 64:316–332.

Link, B. and Stueve, A. 1994. "Psychotic symptoms and the violent/illegal behavior of mental patients compared to community controls." In J. Monahan and H. Steadman, eds. *Violence and mental disorder.* Chicago, IL: University of Chicago Press.

Link, B., Stueve, A., and Phelan, J. 1998. "Psychotic symptoms and violent behaviors: Probing the components of 'threat/control-override' symptoms." *Social Psychiatry and Psychiatric Epidemiology.* 33:S55–S60.

Linnoila, M., Virkkunen, M., Scheinin, M., Nuutila, A., Rimon, R., and Goodwin, F.K. 1983. "Low cerebrospinal fluid 5-hydroxyindolacetic acid concentration differentiates impulsive from non-impulsive violent behavior." *Life sciences.* 33:2609–2614.

Lipsey, M.W. and Derzon, J.H. 1998. "Predictors of violent or serious delinquency in adolescence and early adulthood: A synthesis of longitudinal research." In R. Loeber and D.P. Farrington, eds. *Serious and Violent*

Juvenile Offenders: Risk Factors and Successful Interventions. pp. 86–105. Thousand Oaks, CA: Sage.

Lipsey, M.W. and Wilson, D.B. 1993. "The efficacy of psychological, educational, and behavioral treatment: Confirmation from meta-analysis." *American Psychologist*. 48:1181–1209.

Lipsey, M.W. and Williams, D.B. 1998. "Effective intervention for serious juvenile offenders: A synthesis of research." In R. Loeber and D.P. Farrington, eds. *Serious and violent juvenile offenders: Risk factors and successful interventions*. pp. 313–345. Thousand Oaks, CA: Sage.

Lipton, D.S., Pearson, F.S., Cleland, C.M., and Yee, D. 2002. "The effects of therapeutic communities and milieu therapy on recidivism." In J. McGuire, ed. *Offender rehabilitation and treatment: Effective programmes and policies to reduce re-offending*. Chichester: Wiley.

Liska, A.E. and Reed, M.D. 1985. "Ties to conventional institutions and delinquency: Estimating reciprocal effects." *American Sociological Review*. 50:547–560.

Lloyd, C. 1995. "To scare straight or educate? The British experience of day visits to prison for young people." Home Office Research Study no. 149. London: Home Office.

Lloyd, C.D. 2009. *Age–Crime Curve and Effect of Substance Abuse*. Unpublished class notes.

Lloyd, C., Mair, G., and Hough, M. 1994. *Explaining reconviction rates: A critical analysis*. Home Office Research Study 136. London: HMSO.

Lochman, J.E., Whidby, J.M., and Fitzgerald, D.P. 2000. "Cognitive-behavioural assessment and treatment with aggressive children." In P. Kendall, ed. *Child and Adolescent Therapy: Cognitive Behavioural Procedures*. 2nd ed. pp. 31–87. New York, NY: Guilford Press.

Loeber, R. and Farrington, D.P. 1998a. "Never too early, never too late: Risk factors and successful interventions for serious and violent juvenile offenders." *Studies on Crime and Crime Prevention*. 7:7–30.

Loeber, R. and Farrington, D.P. 1998b. *Serious and violent juvenile offenders: Risk factors and successful interventions*. Thousand Oaks, CA: Sage.

Loeber, R. and Farrington, D.P. 2000. "Young children who commit crime: Epidemiology, developmental origins, risk factors, early interventions, and policy implications." *Development and Psychopathology*. 12:737–762.

Loeber, R., and Farrington, D.P., eds. 2001. *Child delinquents: Development, intervention, and service needs*. Thousand Oaks, CA: Sage.

Loeber, R., Pardini, D.A., Stouthamer-Loeber, M., and Raine, A. 2007. "Do cognitive, physiological, and psychological risk and promotive factors predict desistance from delinquency in males?" *Development and Psychopathology*. 19:867–887.

Loeber, R. and Stouthamer-Loeber, M. 1986. "Family factors as correlates and predictors of juvenile conduct problems and delinquency." In M. Tonry and N. Morris, eds. *Crime and justice: An annual review of research*. Volume 7. pp. 29–159. Chicago, IL: Chicago University Press.

Lombroso, C. and Ferrero, G. 2004. *Criminal Woman, the Prostitute, and the Normal Woman*. N.H. Rafter and M. Gibson, Trans. Durham and London: Duke University Press. Original work published 1893.

Lombroso, C. and Ferrero, W. 1895. *The female offender*. London: T. Fisher Unwin.

Loney, B.R., Frick, P.J., Clements, C.B., Ellis, M.L. and Kerlin, K. 2003. "Callous/unemotional traits, impulsivity, and emotional processing in antisocial adolescents." *Journal of Clinical Child and Adolescent Psychology*. 32:66–80.

Loos, M.E. and Alexander, P.C. 1997. "Differential effects associated with self-reported histories of abuse and neglect in a college sample." *Journal of Interpersonal Violence*. 12:340–360.

Lopez, J.M.O., Redondo, L.M., and Martin, A.L. 1989. "Influence of family and peer group on the use of drugs by adolescents." *The International Journal of the Addictions*. 24:1065–1082.

Lorber, M.F. 2004. "Psychophysiology of aggression, psychopathy, an conduct problems: A meta-analysis." *Psychological Bulleti* 130:531–552.

Lösel, F. 1995. "The efficacy of correctional treatment: A review and synth sis of meta-evaluations." In J. McGuire, ed. *What Works: Reduci Re-offending. Guidelines from research and practice*. Chichester: Wiley.

Lösel, F. and Schmucker, M. 2005. "The effectiveness of treatment for sex al offenders: A comprehensive meta-analysis." *Journal of Experimen Criminology*. 1:117–146.

Low, B.S. 2000. *Why sex matters*. Princeton, NJ: Princeton University Pre

Lowenkamp, C.T., Holsinger, A.M., and Latessa, E.J. 2001. "Risk/ne assessment, offender classification, and the role of childhood abuse *Criminal Justice and Behavior*. 285:543–563.

Lowenkamp, C.T., Latessa, E.J., and Smith, P. 2006. "Does correctional pr gram quality really matter? The importance of adhering to the princip of effective intervention." *Criminology and Public Policy*. 5:201–220.

Lowenkamp, C.T., Smith, P., Latessa, E.J., and Cullen, F.T. 2009. *Can 14,7 women be wrong? A meta-analysis of the LSI-R and recidivism for fem offenders*. Manuscript submitted for publication.

Loza, W. 2005. *The Self-Appraisal Questionnare SAQ: A tool for assessing vi lent and non-violent recidivism*. Toronto, ON: Multi-Health Systems.

Loza, W., Dhaliwal, G., Kroner, D. G., and Loza-Fanous, A. 200 "Reliability, construct, and concurrent validities of the Self-Apprais Questionnaire: A tool for assessing violent and nonviolent recidivism *Criminal Justice and Behavior*. 27:356–374.

Luciani, F. 2001. "Initiating safe reintegration: A decade of Custodial Rati Scale results." *Forum on Corrections Research*. 13:8–10.

Luciani, F.P., Motiuk, L.L., and Nafekh, M. 1996. *An operational review of t custody rating scale: Reliability, validity and practical utility*. Researc Report No. R-47. Ottawa, ON: Correctional Service Canada.

Luke, K.P. 2008. "Are girls really becoming more violent?" *Journal of Wom and Social Work*. 23:38–50.

Lykken, D.T. 1995. *The antisocial personalities*. Mahwah, NJ: Erlbaum.

Lynam, D.R. 1997. "Pursuing the psychopath: Capturing the fledgli psychopath in a nomological net." *Journal of Abnormal Psycholog* 106:425–438.

Lynam, D.R., Loeber, R., and Stouthamer-Loeber, M. 2008. "The stability psychopathy from adolescence into adulthood: The search for moder tors." *Criminal Justice and Behavior*. 35:228–243

Lyons, M.J. 1996. "A twin study of self-reported criminal behavior." *Ci Foundation Symposium*. 194:61–70.

MacDonald, L. 2009. Personal correspondence June 30, 2009

MacKenzie, D.L., Wilson, D.B., and Kider, S.B. 2001. "Effects of correctio al boot camps on offending." *Annals of the American Academy of Politi and Social Science*. 578:126–43.

Magaletta, P. and Boothby, J. 2002. In T.J. Fagan and R.K. Ax, e *Correctional Mental health handbook*. Sage.

Magdol, L., Moffitt, T.E., Caspi, A. and Silva, P.A. 1998. "Developmen antecedents of partner abuse: A prospective -longitudinal study." *Jour of Abnormal Psychology*. 1073:375–389.

Maidment, M.R. 2006. "'We're not all that criminal': Getting beyond t pathologizing and individualizing of women's crime." In E. Leeder, e *Inside and out: Women, prison, and therapy*. pp. 35–56. Binghamton, N York, NY: Haworth Press, Inc.

Malamuth, N.M. 1986. "Predictors of naturalistic aggression." *Journal Personality and Social Psychology*. 50:26–49.

Malamuth, N.M. 2003. "Criminal and noncriminal sexual aggressors: Integrati psychopathy in a hierarchical-mediational confluence model." In R. Prentky, E.S. Janus, and M.C. Seto, eds. *Annals of the New York Academy*

Sciences. Vol. 989. "Sexually coercive behavior: Understanding and management." pp. 35–58. New York, NY: New York Academy of Sciences.

alamuth, N.M., Sockloskie, R.J., Koss, M.P., and Tanaka, J.S. 1991. "Characteristics of aggressors against women: Testing a model using a national sample of college students." *Journal of Consulting and Clinical Psychology*. 59:670–681.

aletzky, B. 1991. *Treating the sexual offender*. Newbury Park, CA: Sage Publications.

anitoba Justice. "Criminal Legal Process: Corrections." Retrieved April 2, 2009 (**www.manitoba.ca/justice/corrections/index.html**).

ann, R., Webster, S., Wakeling, H., and Marshall, W. 2007. "The measurement and influence of child sexual abuse supportive beliefs." *Psychology, Crime and Law*. 13:443–458.

arriage, K., Fine, S., Moretti, M.M, and Haley, G. 1986. "Relationship between depression and conduct disorder in children and adolescents." *Journal of the American Academy of Child Psychiatry*. 25:687–691.

arshall, T.F. 1996. "The evolution of restorative justice in Britain." *European Journal of Criminal Policy and Research*. 4:21–42.

arshall, W.L. 1971. "A combined treatment method for certain sexual deviations." *Behaviour Research and Therapy*. 9:292–294.

arshall, W.L. 1973. "The modification of sexual fantasies: A combined treatment approach to the reduction of deviant sexual behavior." *Behaviour Research and Therapy*. 11:557–564.

arshall, W.L. and Barbaree, H.E. 1990. "An integrated theory of the etiology of sexual offending." In W.L. Marshall, D.R. Laws, and H.E. Barbaree, eds. *Handbook of sexual assault: Issues, theories, and treatment of the offender*. pp. 257–275. New York, NY: Plenum.

arshall, W.L. and Fernandez, Y.M. 2000. "Phallometric testing with sexual offenders: Limits to its value." *Clinical Psychology Review*. 20:807–822.

arshall, W.L. and Lippens, K. 1977. "The clinical value of boredom: A procedure for reducing inappropriate sexual interests." *Journal of Nervous and Mental Diseases*. 165:283–287.

arshall, W.L., and Marshall, L.E. 2007. "The utility of the random controlled trial for evaluating sexual offender treatment: The gold standard of an inappropriate strategy?" *Sexual Abuse: A Journal of Research and Treatment*. 19:175–191.

arshall, W.L. and Marshall, L.E. 2008. "Good clinical practice and the evaluation of treatment: A response to Seto et al." *Sexual Abuse: A Journal of Research and Treatment*. 20:256–260.

arshall, W.L., Serran, G., Moulden, H., Mulloy, R., Fernandez, Y.M., Mann, R.E., and Thornton, D. 2002. "Therapist features in sexual offender treatment: Their reliable identification and influence on behaviour change." *Clinical Psychology and Psychotherapy*. 9:395–405.

arshall, W.L., Serran, G.A., Fernandez, Y.M., Mulloy, R., Mann, R.E., and Thornton, D. 2003. "Therapist characteristics in the treatment of sexual offenders: Tentative data on their relationship with indices of behaviour change." *Journal of Sexual Aggression*. 9:25–30.

arshall, W.L. and Serran, G.A. 2004. "The role of the therapist in offender treatment." *Psychology, Crime and Law*. 10:309–320.

arshall, W.L., Ward, T., Mann, R.E., Moulden, H., Fernandez, Y.M., Serran, G., and Marshall, L.E. 2005. "Working positively with sexual offenders: Maximizing the effectiveness of treatment." *Journal of Interpersonal Violence*. 20:1096–1114.

artin, S.E., Annan, S., and Forst, B. 1993. "The special deterrent effects of a jail sanction on first-time drunk drivers: A quasi experimental study." *Accident Analysis and Prevention*. 25:561–8.

rtinson, R. 1974. "What works? Questions and answers about prison reform." *The Public Interest*. 10:22–54.

runa, S. 2001. *Making good: How ex-convicts reform and rebuild their lives*. Washington, DC: American Psychological Association.

Masten, A. and Coatsworth, J. 1998. "The development of competence in favourable and unfavourable environments: Lessons from research on successful children." *American Psychologist*. 53:205–220.

Mathews, R. 1987. *Familiar strangers: A study of adolescent prostitution*. Toronto, ON: Central Toronto Youth Services.

McDermott, R., Tingley, D., Cowden, J., Frazzetto, G., and Johnson, D.D.P. 2009. "Monoamine oxidase A gene MAOA predicts behavioural aggression following provocation." *Proceeds of the National Academy of Sciences of the United States of America*. 106:2118–2123.

Matsueda, R.L. 1988. "The current state of differential association theory." *Crime and Delinquency*. 34:277–306.

Matsueda, R.L. 1989. "The dynamics of moral beliefs and minor delinquency." *Social Forces*. 68:428–457.

Matthiessen, P. 1962. *Under the mountain wall: A chronicle of two seasons in the stone age*. New York, NY: Viking.

McCabe, K.M., Lucchini, S.E., Hough, R.L., Yeh, M. and Hazen, A. 2005. "The relation between violence exposure and conduct problems among adolescents: A prospective study." *American Journal of Orthopsychiatry*. 754:575–584.

McCloskey, L.A. and Lichter, E.L. 2003. "The contribution of marital violence to adolescent aggression across different relationships." *Journal of Interpersonal Violence*. 1840:390–412.

McCord, J. 1999. "Interventions: Punishment, diversion, and alternative routes to crime prevention." In A.K. Hess and I.B. Weiner, eds. *The handbook of forensic psychology*. 2nd ed. pp. 559–579. New York, NY: Wiley.

McCord, W. and McCord, J. 1959. *Origins of crime*. New York, NY: Columbia University Press.

McGuire, J. 2001. "Defining correctional programs." In L.L. Motiuk and R.C. Serin, eds. *Compendium 2000 on effective correctional programming*. Ottawa, ON: Correctional Service of Canada.

McGuire, J. 2002. "Criminal sanctions versus psychologically-based interventions with offenders: A comparative empirical analysis." *Psychology, Crime, and Law*. 8:183–208.

McGuire, J. 2004. *Understanding psychology and crime: Perspectives on theory and action*. New York, NY: McGraw Hill.

McGuire, R.J., Carlisle, J.M. and Young, B.G. 1965. "Sexual deviation as conditioned behaviour: A hypothesis." *Behaviour Research and Therapy*. 2:185–190.

McLeer, S.V., Dixon, J.F., Henry, D., Ruggiero, K., Escovitz, K. and Niedda, T. 1998. "Psychopathology in non-clinically referred sexually abused children." *Journal of the American Academy of Child and Adolescent Psychiatry*. 3712:1326–1333.

McMahon, R.J. 1994. "Diagnosis, assessment, and treatment of externalizing problems in children: The role of longitudinal data." *Journal of Consulting and Clinical Psychology*. 62:901–917.

McMurran, M. 2003. "Alcohol and crime." *Criminal Behaviour and Mental Health*. 13:1–4.

McMurran, M. and Gilchrist, E. 2008. "Anger control and alcohol use: Appropriate interventions for perpetrators of domestic violence." *Psychology, Crime and Law*. 142:107–116.

McMurran, M. and Priestley, P. 2001. *Addressing substance-related offending ASRO*. London: Home Officer Probation Directorate.

McNeil, D.E. and Binder, R.L. 2007. "Effectiveness of a mental health court in reducing criminal recidivism and violence." *American Journal of Psychiatry*. 164:1395–1403.

McNeill, F. 2004. "Desistance, rehabilitation and correctionalism: Developments and prospects in Scotland." *Howard Journal of Criminal Justice*. 43:420–436.

Mears, D.P., Ploeger, M., and Warr, M. 1998. "Explaining the gender gap in delinquency: Peer influence and moral evaluations of behaviour." *Journal of Research in Crime and Delinquency*. 35:251–266.

Mednick, S.A., Gabrielli, W.F.J., and Hutchings, B. 1984. "Genetic influences in criminal convictions: Evidence from an adoption cohort." *Science*. 224:891–894.

Mednick, S. and Kandel, E. 1988. "Congenital determinants of violence." *Bulletin of the American Academy of Psychiatry and the Law*. 16:101–109.

Medical Marijuana Information Resource Centre. 2009. "Medical Marijuana in Canada." Retrieved August 31, 2009 (**www.medical-marijuanainformation.com/incanada**).

Meloy, J.R., and Gacono, C.B. 1997. "A neurotic criminal: 'I've learned my lesson . . .' ". In J.R. Meloy, M.W. Acklin, C.B. Gacono, J.F. Murray, and C.A. Peterson, eds. *Contemporary Rorschach interpretation*. pp. 289–300. Mahwah, NJ: Lawrence Erlbaum Associates.

Melton, G.B., Petrila, J., Poythress, N.G., and Slobogin, C. 1997. *Psychological evaluations for the courts: A handbook for mental health professionals and lawyers*. 2nd ed. New York, NY: Guilford Press.

Mendelson, M. 2006. *Aboriginal peoples and postsecondary education in Canada*. Ottawa, ON: The Caledon Institute of Social Policy.

Merton, R. 1938. "Social structure and anomie." *American Sociological Review*. 3:672–682.

Merton, R.K. 1957. *Social Theory and Social Structure*. New York, NY: Free Press.

Meyer, W.J.J.I. and Cole, C.M. 1997. "Physical and chemical castration of sex offenders: A review." *Journal of Offender Rehabilitation*. 25:1–18.

Michigan State University. 2007. "From moving up or moving out of the company? Factors that influence the promoting or firing of new college hires." Research Brief 1-2007. Michigan State University Collegiate Employment Research Institute.

Miller, E. 1986. *Street woman*. Philadelphia: Temple University Press.

Miller, M. and Neaigus, A. 2002. "An economy of risk: Resource acquisition strategies of inner city women who use drugs." *International Journal of Drug Policy*. 13:409–418.

Millon, T., Simonsen, E., Birket-Smith, M., and Davis, R.D. 1998. *Psychopathy: Antisocial, criminal, and violent behaviour*. New York, NY: Guilford Press.

Miller, S.L. and Burack, C. 1993. "A critique of Gottfredson and Hirschi's general theory of crime: Selective inattention to gender and power positions." *Women and Criminal Justice*. 4:115–134.

Millon, T., Simonsen, E., and Birket-Smith, M. 2002. "Historical conceptions of psychopathy in the United States and Europe." In T. Millon, E. Simonsen, M. Birket-Smith, and R.D. Davis, eds. *Psychopathy: Antisocial, criminal, and violent behaviour*. pp. 3–31. New York, NY: Guilford Press.

Mishra, S. and Lalumière, M.L. 2008. "Risk-taking, antisocial behavior, and life histories." In J.D. Duntley and T.K. Shackelford, eds. *Evolutionary forensic psychology: Darwinian foundations of crime and law*. pp. 139–159. Oxford, NY: Oxford University Press.

Mitchell, K.J. and Finkelhor, D. 2001. "Risk of crime victimization among youth exposed to domestic violence." *Journal of Interpersonal Violence*. 16:944–964.

Mitchell, S. and Rosa, P. 1979. "Boyhood behavior problems as precursors of criminality: A fifteen-year follow-up study." *Journal of Child Psychology and Psychiatry*. 22:19–33.

Moffitt, T.E. 1983. "The learning theory model of punishment: Implications for delinquency deterrence." *Criminal Justice and Behavior*. 10:131–158.

Moffitt, T.E. 1993. "Adolescence-limited and life-course-persistent antisocial behavior: A developmental taxonomy." *Psychological Bulletin*. 100:674–701.

Moffitt, T.E. 2005. "The new look of behavioural genetics in development psychopathology: Gene-environment interplay in antisocial behaviour." *Psychological Bulletin*. 131:533–554.

Moffitt, T.E., Brammer, G.L., Caspi, A., Fawcett, P., Raleigh, M., Yuwiler, a Silva, P. 1998. "Whole blood serotonin relates to violence in an epiderm ological study." *Biological Psychiatry*. 43:446–457.

Moffitt, T.E. and Caspi, A. 2001. "Childhood predictors differentia life-course persistent and adolescence-limited antisocial pathwa among males and females." *Development and Psychopatholog* 13:355–375.

Moffitt, T.E., Caspi, A., Harrington, H., and Milne, B.J. 2002. "Males the life-course-persistent and adolescence limited antisocial pathwa Follow-up age 26 years." *Development and Psychopatholog* 14:179–207.

Moffitt, T.E., Caspi, A., Rutter, M., and Silva, P.A. 2001. *Sex difference antisocial behaviour: Conduct disorder, delinquency, and violence in Dunedin Longitudinal Study*. Cambridge: Cambridge University Press.

Moffitt, T.E. and Henry, B. 1989. "Neurological assessment of executive fur tions in self-reported delinquents." *Developmental and Psychopatholog* 1:105–118.

Molnar, B.E., Buka, S.L., Brennan, R.T., Holton, J.K., and Earls, F. 2003. multilevel study of neighborhoods and parent-to-child physical aggre sion: Results from the Project on Human Development in Chica neighborhoods." *Child Maltreatment*. 8:84–97.

Monahan, J. Steadman, H.J., Silver, E., Appelbaum, P.S., Robbins, P.C Mulvey, E.P., et al. 2001. *Rethinking risk assessment: The MacArthur stu of mental disorder and violence*. New York, NY: Oxford University Pres

Moore, T.M., Scarpa, A., and Raine, A. 2002. "A meta-analysis of serotor metabolite 5-H1AA and antisocial behavior." *Aggressive Behavio* 28:299–316.

Monahan, E.J. 1995. "The Fabrikant case at Concordia University: Some le sons for the better management of universities and improved academ ethics." *Minerva*. 33:129–148.

Monahan, J. 1997. "Major mental disorders and violence to others." In D. Stoff, J. Breiling, and J.D. Maser, eds. *Handbook of antisocial behavio* pp. 92–100. New York, NY: John Wiley.

Morash, M., Bynam, T.S., and Koons, B.A. 1998. *Women Offende Programming Needs and Promising Approaches*. Research in Bri Washington, DC: National Institute of Justice.

Moretti, M.M., Catchpole, R.E.H., and Odgers, C. 2005. "The dark side girlhood: Recent trends, risk factors, and trajectories to aggression a violence." *Canadian Child and Adolescent Psychiatry Review*. 14:21–25

Moretti, M.M., Obsuth, I., Odgers, C.L., and Reebye, P. 2006. "Exposure maternal vs. paternal partner violence, PTSD, and aggression in adol cent girls and boys." *Aggressive Behavior*. 32:385–395.

Moretti, M.M., Odgers, C.L., and Jackson, M.A. 2004. "Girls and aggression point of departure." In M.M. Moretti, C.L. Odgers and M.A. Jackson, e *Girls and aggression: Contributing factors and intervention principles*. pp. 1– New York, NY: Kluwer Academic/Plenum Publishers.

Morgan, A.B., and Lilienfeld, S.O. 2000. "A meta-analytic review of relation between antisocial behavior and neuropsychological measu of executive function." *Clinical Psychology Review*. 20:113–136.

Morgan, P. 1975. *Child care: Sense and fable*. London, UK: Temple Smith.

Morris, R.R. 1987. *Women, crime and criminal justice*. Oxford: Basil Blackwe

Morse, S.J. 2008. "Psychopathy and criminal responsibility." *Neuroeth* 1:205–212.

Mossman, D. 1994. "Assessing predictions of violence: Being accurate abo accuracy." *Journal of Consulting and Clinical Psychology*. 62:783–792.

Motiuk, L.L. 1997. "Classification for correctional programming: The Offen Intake Assessment OIA process." *Forum on Corrections Research*. 9:18–

otiuk, L.L., Cousineau, C. and Gileno, J. 2005. *The Safe Return of Offenders to the Community Statistical Overview*. Correctional Service of Canada.

otiuk, L.L., Luciani, F., Serin, R.C., and Vuong, B. 2001. "Federal Offender Population Movement: A Study of Minimum-security Placements." Research Report R-107. Correctional Service of Canada.

otiuk, L.L. and Porporino, F.J. 1991. *The prevalence, nature and severity of mental health problems among federal male inmates in Canadian penitentiaries*. R-24. Ottawa, ON: Correctional Service of Canada.

otiuk, L. and Nafekh, M. 2000. "Aboriginal offenders in federal corrections: A profile." *Forum on Corrections Research*. 12:10–15.

oyer, S. 1992. "Race, gender, and homicide: Comparisons between Aboriginals and other Canadians." *Canadian Journal of Criminology*. 34:387–402.

uncie, J. 2001. "The construction and deconstruction of crime." In J. Muncie and E. McLaughline, eds. *The problem of crime*. 2nd ed. London, Sage Publications in association with the Open University.

uller, J.L., Sommer, M., Wagner, V., Lange, K., Taschler, H. and Roder, C.H. 2003. "Abnormalities in emotion processing within cortical and subcortical regions in criminal psychopaths: Evidence from a functional magnetic resonance imaging study using pictures with emotional content." *Biological Psychiatry*. 54(2):152–162.

ulti-Health Systems. 2005. *Controlling Anger and Learning to Manage It CALM Program: Corrections Version*. Winogron, Van Dieten, Gauzas, and Grisim.

ulvey, E. 2005. "Risk assessment in juvenile justice policy and practice." In K. Heilbrun, N. Goldstein, and R. Redding. eds. *Juvenile Delinquency: Prevention, Assessment, and Intervention*. pp. 209–231. New York, NY: Oxford University Press.

ulvey, E.P., Arthur, M.W., and Reppucci, N.D. 1993. "The prevention and treatment of juvenile delinquency: A review of the research." *Clinical Psychology Review*. 13:133–167.

uñoz, L.C., and Frick, P.J. 2007. "The reliability, stability, and predictive utility of the self-report version of the Antisocial Process Screening Device." *Scandinavian Journal of Psychology*. 48:299–312.

unroe, A. 1994. "Affect, verbal content, and psychophysiology in the arguments of couples with a violent husband." *Journal of Consulting and Clinical Psychology*. 625:982–988.

urnen, S.K., Wright, C., and Kaluzny, G. 2002. "If 'boys will be boys,' then girls will be victims? A meta-analytic review of the research that relates masculine ideology to sexual aggression." *Sex Roles*. 46:359–375.

urray, L., and Fiti, R. 2004. *Arrests for notifiable offences and the operation of certain police powers under PACE: England and Wales, 2003/2004*. London: Home Office. Retrieved Sept. 15, 2005 (www.homeoffice.gov.uk/rds/arrests1.html).

urrie, D.C., Boccaccini, M.T., McCoy, W. and Cornell, D. 2007. "Diagnostic labeling in juvenile court: How do psychopathy and conduct disorder findings influence judges." *Journal of Clinical Child and Adolescent Psychology*. 36:228–241

urrie, D.C., Cornell, D.G. and McCoy, W. 2005. "Psychopathy, conduct disorder, and stigma: Does diagnostic labeling influence juvenile probation officer recommendations." *Law and Human Behavior*. 29:323–342.

don, S.M., Koverola, C., and Schludermann, E.H. 1998. "Antecedents to Prostitution: Childhood victimization." *Journal of Interpersonal Violence*. 13:206–221.

ffine, N. 1987. *Female crime: The construction of women in criminology*. Sydney: Allen and Unwin.

afekh, M. and Motiuk, L. 2002. *The Statistical Information on Recidivism–Revised 1 SIR-R1 Scale: A psychometric examination* Research Report No. R-126. Ottawa, ON: Correctional Service of Canada.

Nathanson, C., Paulhus, D.L. and Williams, K.M. 2006. "Predictors of a behavioral measure of scholastic cheating: Personality and competence but not demographics." *Contemporary Educational Psychology*. 31:97–122.

National Aboriginal Achievement Foundation. 2007, "National Aboriginal achievement awards." Retrieved January 14, 2009 (www.naaf.ca/html/dr_j_couture_e.html).

National Center on Elder Abuse. 1998. *National Elder Abuse Incidence Study*. Washington, DC: U.S. Department of Health and Aging.

National Crime Prevention Council. 1995. *Risk or threat to children*. Ottawa, ON: National Crime Prevention Council.

National Crime Prevention Council 1997. *Preventing crime by investing in families and communities: Promoting positive outcomes in youth twelve- to eighteen-years-old*. Ottawa, ON: National Crime Prevention Council.

National Victims of Crime, 2007. Retrieved August 24, 2007. (www.victimsweek.gc.ca/archives_2006/fact-sheets/p2.html).

Needlemann, H., Riess, J., Tobin, M., Biesecker, G., and Greenhouse, J. 1996. "Bone lead levels and delinquent behavior." *Journal of the American Medical Association*. 275(5):363–369.

Newburn, T. 2007. *Criminology*. Cullompton, UK: Willan Publishing.

Newman, J.P., Brinkley, C.A., Lorenz, A.R., Hiatt, K.D., and MacCoon, D.G. 2007. "Psychopathy as psychopathology: Beyond the clinical utility of the *Psychopathy* Checklist-Revised." In H. Hervé and J.C. Yuillle, eds. *The psychopath: Theory, research, and practice*. pp. 173–206. Mahwah, NJ: Lawrence Erlbaum.

Newman, J.P. and Wallace, J.F. 1993. "Psychopathy and cognition." In P.C. Kendall and K.S. Dobson, eds. *Psychopathology and cognition*. pp. 293–349. New York, NY: Academic Press.

Newell, P. 1989. *Children are people too: The case against physical punishment*. London: Bedford Square Press.

Newman, G. 1976. *Comparative deviance: Perception and law in six cultures*. New York, NY: Elsevier.

Newman, G. 1977. "Social institutions and the control of deviance: A cross-national opinion survey." *European Journal of Social Psychology*. 7:39–59.

Niehoff, D. 1999. "Seeds of controversy." In *The biology of violence: How understanding the brain, behaviour and environment can break the vicious circle of aggression*. pp. 1–30. New York, NY: Free Press.

Northwest Territories Department of Justice. 2009. "Corrections: Custody/Institutional Services." Retrieved April 2, 2009 (www.justice.gov.nt.ca/facilities/Corrections_Institutions.shtml).

Nuffield, J. 1982. *Parole decision-making in Canada: Research towards decision guidelines*. Ottawa, ON: Supply and Services Canada.

Nuffield, J. 1982. *Parole decision-making in Canada*. Ottawa, ON: Solicitor General Canada.

Nuffield, J. 1989. "The SIR scale: Some reflections on it applications." *Forum on Corrections Research*. 1.

Nunavut Department of Justice. 2008. "Corrections." Retrieved April 2, 2009 (www. justice.gov.nu.ca/i18n/english/corrections.shtm).

Nunes, K.L. and Cortoni, F.A. 2006. *The heterogeneity of treatment non-completers*.Research Report No. R-176. Ottawa, ON: Correctional Service of Canada.

Nunes, K.L., Cortoni, F, and Serin, R.C. 2009. "Screening offenders for risk of dropout and expulsion from correctional programs." *Journal of Legal and Criminological Psychology*.

Nunes, K.L. and Cortoni, F. 2008. "Dropout from sex offender treatment and dimensions of risk of sexual recidivism." *Criminal Justice and Behavior*. 35:24–33.

Nunes, K.L. Firestone, P., Wexler, A.F., Jensen, T.L., and Bradford, J.M. 2007. "Incarceration and recidivism among sexual offenders." *Law and Human Behavior*. 31:305–318.

Nunes, K.L., Hanson, R.K., Firestone, P., Moulden, H.M., Greenberg, D.M., and Bradford, J.M. 2007. "Denial predicts recidivism for some sexual offenders." *Sexual Abuse: A Journal of Research and Treatment.* 19:91–105.

Nye, F.I. 1982. *Family relationships: Rewards and costs.* Beverly Hills, CA: Sage Publications.

Ogborne, A., Smart, R., and Adlaf, E. 2000. "Self reported medical use of marijuana: a survey of the general population." Retrieved August 31, 2009 (www.cmaj.ca/cgi/content/full/162/12/1685).

Odgers, C.L., Moretti, M.M., Burnette, M.L., Chauhan, P., Waite, D., and Reppucci, N.D. 2007. "A latent variable modeling approach to identifying subtypes of serious and violent female juvenile offenders." *Aggressive Behaviour.* 33:1–14.

Odgers, C.L., Moretti, M.M., and Reppucci, N.D. 2005. "Examining the science and practice of violence risk assessment with female adolescents." *Law and Human Behaviour.* 29:7–27.

Offord, D.R., Boyle, M.H., Szatmari, P., Rae, Grant, J.L., Links, P.S., Cadman, D.T., Byles, J.A., Crawford, J.W., Blum, H.M. Byrne, C., Thomas, H., and Woodward, C.A. 1987. "Ontario Child Health Study: II Six month prevalence of disorder and rates of service utilization." *Archives of General Psychiatry.* 44:832–836.

Offord, D.R., Lipman, E.L., and Duku, E.K. 2001. "Epidemiology of problem behaviour up to age 12 years." In R. Loeber and D.P. Farrington, eds. *Child Delinquents.* pp. 95–234. Thousand Oaks, CA: Sage.

Ogborne, A.C., Smart, R.G., and Adlaf, E.M. 2000. "Self-reported medical use of marijuana: a survey of the general population." *Canadian Medical Association Journal.* 16212. Available at www.cmaj.ca/cgi/content/full/162/12/1685.

Olver, M.E. and Wong, S.C.P. 2009. "Therapeutic responses of psychopathic sexual offenders: Treatment attrition, therapeutic change, and long-term recidivism." *Journal of Consulting and Clinical Psychology.* 77:328–336.

Olver, M.E., and Wong, S.C.P. 2006. "Psychopathy, sexual deviance, and recidivism among sex offenders." *Sexual Abuse: A Journal of Research and Treatment.* 18:65–82.

Olver, M.E., Wong, S.C.P., Nicholaichuk, T., and Gordon, A. 2007. "The validity and reliability of the Violence Risk Scale–Sexual Offender Version: Assessing sex offender risk and evaluating therapeutic change." *Psychological Assessment.* 19:318–329.

O'Malley, P., Coventry, G., and Walters, R. 1993. "Victoria's Day in Prison Program: An evaluation and critique." *Australian and New Zealand Journal of Criminology.* 26:171–83.

Ontario Ministry of Community Safety and Correctional Services. 2009. "Correctional Services." Retrieved April 2, 2009 (www. mcscs.jus.gov. on.ca/english/corr_serv/adult_off/facilities/corr_centres/corr_centres .html).

Ontario Network for the Prevention of Elder Abuse. 2009. "About Elder Abuse." Retrieved August 28, 2009 (www.onpea.org/english/elderabuse/faq.html).

Orbis Partners. 2007a. *Girl's Youth Assessment Screening Inventory G-YASI.* Ottawa, ON: Author.

Orbis Partners. 2007b. *Service Planning Inventory for Women SPIN-W.* Ottawa, ON: Author.

Orbis Partners. 2007c. *Girls Moving On.* Ottawa, ON: Author.

Ogrodnik, L. 2008 *Family violence in Canada: A statistical profile 2008.* Statistics Canada: Ministry of Industry.

Ortiz, J. and Raine, A. 2004. "Heart rate level and antisocial behavior in children and adolescents: A meta-analysis." *Journal of the American Academy of Child and Adolescent Psychiatry.* 43:154–162.

Owen, B. 2001. "Perspectives on women in prison." In C.M. Renzetti and L. Goodstein, eds. *Women, crime, and criminal justice: Original feminist readings.* pp. 243–254. Los Angeles: Roxbury.

Owen, B. 1998. *In the mix: Struggle and survival in a women's prison.* Albany State University of New York Press.

Oxford, M.C., Cavell, T.A., and Hughes, J.N. 2003. "Callous/unemotional traits moderate the relation between ineffective parenting and child externalizing problems: A partial replication and extension." *Journal Clinical Child and Adolescent Psychology.* 32:577–585.

Palmer, T. 1975. "Martinson re-visited." *Journal of Research in Crime and Delinquency.* 12:133–52.

Palumbi, S.R. 2002. *The evolution explosion: How humans cause rapid evolutionary change.* New York: Norton, W.W. and Company Inc.

Paolucci, E.O., Genuis, M.L., and Violato, C. 2001. "A meta-analysis of the published research on the effects of child sexual abuse." *The Journal Psychology.* 135:17–36.

Pardini, D.A., Lochman, J.E. and Frick, P.J. 2003. "Callous/unemotional traits and social cognitive processes in adjudicated youth." *Journal of the American Academic of Child and Adolescent Psychiatry.* 42:364–371.

Parker, J.G. and Asher, S.R. 1987. "Peer relations and later personal adjustment: Are low accepted children at risk?" *Psychological Bulletin.* 102:357–389.

Passingham, R.A. 1972. "Crime and personality: A review of Eysenck's theory." In V.D. Nebylitsyn and J.A. Gray, eds. *Biological basis of individual behavior.* New York, NY: Academic Press.

Patterson, G.R. 1982. *Coercive family process.* Eugene, OR: Castalia.

Patterson, G.R., Reid, J.B., and Dishion, T.J. 1998. *Antisocial boys.* Eugene OR: Castalia.

Paulhus, D.L., Hemphill, J.F, and Hare, R.D. (in press). *Manual for the Self Report Psychopathy Scale.* Toronto, ON: Multi-Health Systems.

Paulhus, D.L. and Williams, K.M. 2002. "The dark triad of personality: Narcissism, Machiavellianism, and psychopathy." *Journal of Research Personality.* 36:556–563.

Pearson, F.S., Lipton, D.S., Cleland, C.M., and Yee, D.S. 2002. "The effects behavioral-cognitive-behavioral programs on recidivism." *Crime and Delinquency.* 48:476–496.

Pepler, D.J., Walsh, M.M., and Levene, K.S. 2004. "Intervention for aggressive girls: Tailoring and measuring the fit." In M.M. Moretti, C.L. Odgers, and M.A. Jackson, eds., *Girls and Aggression: Contributing factors and intervention principles.* pp. 131–145. New York, NY: Kluwer.

Perel-Levin, S. 2008. *Discussing screening for elder abuse at primary health care level.* World Health Organization, Geneva.

Pernanen, K., Cousineau, M.M., Brochu, S., Sun, F. 2002. *Proportions crimes associated with alcohol and drugs in Canada.* Ottawa, ON: Canadian Centre on Substance Abuse.

Perrone, D., Sullivan, C.J., Pratt, T.C., and Margaryan, S. 2004. "Parental efficacy, self-control, and delinquency: A test of general theory of crime on a nationally representative sample of youth." *International Journal of Offender Therapy and Comparative Criminology.* 48:298–312.

Perusse, D. 2008. *Aboriginal people living off-reserve and the labour market: Estimates from the Labour Force Survey, 2007.* Ottawa, ON: Statistics Canada.

Petersilia, J. and Turner, S. 1993. "Intensive probation and parole." *Crime and Justice: A Review of Research.* 17:281–335.

Petrosino, A., Turpin-Petrosino, C., and Buehler, J. 2003. "Scared straight and other juvenile awareness programs for preventing juvenile delinquency: A systematic review of the randomized experimental evidence." *Annals of the American Academy of Political and Social Science* 589:41–62.

Petrosino, A. 2000. "Answering the why question in evaluation: The causal model approach." *Canadian Journal of Program Evaluation.* 15:1–24.

Pfeifer, J. and Hart-Mitchell, R. 2001. *Evaluating the effect of healing lodge residency on adult offenders.* Regina, SK: Canadian Institute for Peace, Justice and Security, University of Regina.

helan, J.C., Link, B.G., Stueve, A., and Pescosolido, B.A. 2000. "Public conceptions of mental illness in 1950 and 1996: What is mental illness and is it to be feared?" *Journal of Health and Social Behavior.* 41:188–207.

illips, L.R., de Ardon, E.T., and Briones, G.S. 2000. "Abuse of female caregivers by care recipients: Another form of elder abuse." *Journal of Elder Abuse and Neglect.* 12:123–143.

lemer, K. and Moore, D.W. 1989. "Abuse of patients in nursing homes: Findings from a survey of staff." *Gerontologist.* 29(3):314–320.

hers, W.D. 1990. "Relapse prevention with sexual aggressors: A method for maintaining therapeutic gain and enhancing external supervision." In W.L. Marshall, D.R. Laws, and H.E. Barbaree, eds. *Handbook of sexual assault: Issues, theories and treatment of the offender.* pp. 343–361. New York, NY: Plenum.

hers, W.D., Marques, J.K., Gibat, C.C., and Marlatt, G.A. 1983. "Relapse prevention: A self-control model of treatment and maintenance of change for sexual aggressives." In J. Greer, and I.R. Stuart, eds. *The sexual aggressor: Current perspectives on treatment.* pp. 292–310. New York, NY: Van Nostrand Reinhold.

quero, A.R. 2008. "Taking stock of developmental trajectories of criminal activity over the life course." In A.M. Liberman, ed. *The long view of crime: A synthesis of longitudinal research.* New York, NY: Springer.

quero, A.R., Blumstein, A., Brame, R., Haapanen, R., Mulvey, E.P., and Nagin, D.S. 2001. "Assessing the impact of exposure time and incapacitation on longitudinal trajectories of criminal offending." *Journal of Adolescent Research.* 16:54–74.

omin, R., DeFries, J.C., McClearn, G.E., and McGuffin, P. 2001. *Behavioral Genetics.* 4th ed. New York, NY: Worth.

dnieks, E., Pillemer, K., Nicholson, J., Shillington, T. and Frizzel, A. 1990. *National survey on abuse of the elderly in Canada: Final report.* Toronto, ON: Ryerson Polytechnical Institute.

laschek, D.L.L., and Collie, R.M. 2004. "Rehabilitating serious violent adult offenders: An empirical and theoretical stocktake." *Psychology, Crime and Law.* 10:321–334.

ldrack, R.A. 2009. "Neuroimaging: Separating the Promise from the Pipe Dreams, Dana Foundation." Retrieved July 8, 2009 (**www.dana.org/ news/cerebrum/detail.aspx?id =22220**).

llack, O. 1950. *The criminality of women.* Philadelphia: University of Philadelphia Press.

llock, S. 2005. "Taming the shrew: Regulating prisoners through women-centered mental health programming." *Critical Criminology.* 13:71–87.

rter, S., Birt, A.R. and Boer, D.P. 2001. "Investigation of the criminal and conditional release histories of Canadian federal offenders as a function of psychopathy and age." *Law and Human Behavior.* 25:647–661.

stmus, J.L., Severson, M., Berry, M., and Yoo, J.A. 2009. "Women's experiences of violence and seeking help." *Violence Against Women.* 15:852–868.

zulo, J., Bennell, C., and Forth, A.E. 2008. *Forensic psychology.* Toronto, ON: Pearson.

tt, T.C. and Cullen, F.T. 2000. "The empirical status of Gottfredson and Hirschi's general theory of crime: A meta-analysis." *Criminology.* 38:931–964.

tt, T.C., Sellers, C.S., Cullen, F.T., Winfree, L.T., and Madensen, T.D. 2005. *The empirical status of social learning theory: A meta-analysis.* Unpublished manuscript. Washington State University, Pullman, Washington.

ntky, R.A. and Knight, R.A. 1991. "Identifying critical dimensions for discriminating among rapists." *Journal of Consulting and Clinical Psychology.* 59:643–661.

cewaterhouseCoopers 2007. "Economic crime: People, culture, and controls. Ottawa, Canada." Retrieved August 31, 2009 (**www.pwc.com/en_CA/ca/ risk/forensic-services/publications/economic-crime-2007-en.pdf**).

Prochaska, J.O., DiClemente, C.C., and Norcross, J.C. 1992. "In search of how people change: Applications to addictive behaviors." *American Psychologist.* 47:1102–14.

Proudfoot, S. 2009. "Girl violence increasing in 'lethality', experts say." *Ottawa Citizen.* March 21.

Public Safety Canada. 2006. *Corrections and Conditional Release Statistical Overview.* Government Services of Canada.

Public Safety Canada. 2007. *Corrections and conditional release statistical overview.* Retrieved March 20, 2009 (**www.publicsafety.gc.ca/res/cor/ rep/ccrso2007-eng.aspx**).

Quann, N. and Trevethan, S. 2000. *Police-reported Aboriginal crime in Saskatchewan.* Ottawa, ON: Statistics Canada.

Queen's University. 2006. "Canadian Public Opinion Trends." Retrieved March 21, 2009 (**www.queensu.ca/cora/_trends/mip_2006.htm**).

Queen's University. 2006. "Canadian Public Opinion Trends: Federal Government Spending—The Justice System." Retrieved March 21, 2009 (**www.queensu.ca/cora/_trends/Spend_Justice.htm**).

Quigley, T. 1994. Some issues in sentencing Aboriginal offenders. In R. Gosse, J. Henderson, and R. Carter, eds., *Continuing poundmaker and Riel's quest.* pp. 273–274. Saskatoon, SK: Purich Publications.

Quinsey, V.L. 2002. "Evolutionary theory and criminal behaviour." *Legal and Criminological Psychology.* 7:1–13.

Quinsey, V.L., and Ambtman, R. 1979. "Variables affecting psychiatrists' and teachers' assessments of the dangerousness of mentally ill offenders." *Journal of Consulting and Clinical Psychology.* 47:353–362.

Quinsey, V.L., Bergersen, S.G., and Steinman, C.M. 1976. "Changes in physiological and verbal responses of child molesters during aversion therapy." *Canadian Journal of Behavioral Science.* 8:202–212.

Quinsey, V.L. and Chaplin, T.C. 1982. "Penile responses to nonsexual violence among rapists." *Criminal Justice and Behavior.* 9:312–324.

Quinsey, V.L., Chaplin, T.C., and Varney, G. 1981. "A comparison of rapists' and non-sex offenders' sexual preferences for mutually consenting sex, rape, and physical abuse of women." *Behavioral Assessment.* 3:12.

Quinsey, V.L., Coleman, G., Jones, B., and Altrows, I.F. 1997. "Proximal antecedents of eloping and reoffending among supervised mentally disordered offenders." *Journal of Interpersonal Violence.* 12:794–813.

Quinsey, V.L., Harris, G.T., Rice, M.E., and Cormier, C.A. 2006. *Violent offenders: Appraising and managing risk.* 2nd ed. Washington, DC: American Psychological Association.

Quinsey, V.L., Jones, G.B., Book, A.S., and Barr, K.N. 2006. "The dynamic prediction of antisocial behaviour among forensic psychiatric patients: A prospective field study." *Journal of Interpersonal Violence.* 21:1539–1565.

Quinsey, V.L., Skilling, T.A., Lalumière, M.L., and Craig, W. 2004. *Juvenile delinquency: Understanding individual differences.* Washington, DC: American Psychological Association.

Rabinovitch, J. and Strega, S. 2004. "The PEERS story: Effective services sidestep the controversies." *Violence against women.* 10:140–159.

R. v. Demers. 2004. 2 S.C.R. 489, 2004 SCC 46.

R. v. Gladue. 1999. 1 S.C.R. 688.

R. v. M'Naughton. 1843. 8 Eng. Rep. 718.

R. v. Swain. 1991. 63 C.C.C. 3d 481 SCC 13

Raine, A. 1993. "Genetics and Crime." In *The psychopathology of crime: Criminal behaviour as a clinical disorder.* pp. 47–78. San Diego, CA: Academic Press.

Raine, A. 1997. "Crime, conditioning, and arousal." In H. Nyborg, ed. *The scientific study of human nature: Tribute to Hans J. Eysenck.* pp. 122–141. Oxford, UK: Elsevier.

Raine, A. 2008. "From genes to brain to antisocial behaviour." *Current Directions in Psychological Science.* 17:323–328.

Raine, A. and Venables, P.H. 1981. "Classical conditioning and socialization—A biosocial interaction." *Personality and Individual Differences*. 2:273–283.

Raine, A. and Yang, Y. 2006. "Neural foundations to moral reasoning and antisocial behaviour." *Social Cognitive and Affective Neuroscience*. 1:203–213.

Ramsland, K. 2009. *School killers*. Retrieved May 9, 2009 (**www.trutv.com/library/crime/serial_killers/weird/kids1/index_1.html**).

Rappaport, J. 1987. "Terms of empowerment/exemplars of prevention: Toward a theory for community psychology." *American Journal of Community Psychology*. 15(2)1:21–148.

Rashid, A. 2004. *A visit to the Pê Sâkâstêw healing centre: Not your ordinary prison*. Retrieved January 14, 2009 (**http://maritimes.indymedia.org/news/2004/01/7234.php**).

Rastin, C. and Johnson, S. 2002. "Inuit sexual offenders: Victim, offence, and recidivism characteristics." *Forum on Corrections Research*. 14.

Reiss, A.J. 1951. "Unraveling juvenile delinquency. II. An appraisal of the research methods." *American Journal of Sociology*. 57:115–120.

Reis, M. and Nahmiash, D. 1995. "Validation of the Caregiver Abuse Screen CASE." *Canadian Journal on Aging*. 14:45–60.

Reis, M. and Nahmiash, D. 1998. "Validation of the Indicators of Abuse IOA screen." *Gerontologist*. 38:471–480.

Reisig, M.D., Holtfreter, K., and Morash, M. 2006. "Assessing recidivism risk across female pathways to crime." *Justice Quarterly*. 23:384–405.

Renner, L.M., and Slack, K.S. 2006. "Intimate partner violence and child maltreatment: Understanding intra- and intergenerational connections." *Child Abuse and Neglect*. 30:599–617.

Resick, P.A. 1993. "The psychological impact of rape." *Journal of Interpersonal Violence*. 8:223–255.

Retson, D. 2007. "Dedicated Dr. Joe 'followed the courage of his convictions.'" July 11. Retrieved January 14, 2009 (**www.canada.com/edmontonjournal/news/cityplus/story.html?id=5d3ddcff-42d0-4ae7-983e-62140d7e9069**).

Rex v. Hadfield.1800. 27 St. tr. 1281.

Rhee, S.H. and Waldman, I.D. 2002. "Genetic and environmental influences on antisocial behavior: A meta-analysis of twin and adoption studies." *Psychological Bulletin*. 128:490–529.

Rice, M.E., Chaplin, T.C., Harris, G.T., and Coutts, J. 1994. "Empathy for the victim and sexual arousal among rapists and nonrapists." *Journal of Interpersonal Violence*. 9:435–449.

Rice, M.E. and Harris, G.T. 1997. "Cross-validation and extension of the Violence Risk Appraisal Guide or child molesters and rapists." *Law and Human Behavior*. 21:231–241.

Rice, M.E. and Harris, G.T. 1997. "The size and sign of treatment effects in therapy for sex offenders." In R. Prentky, E. Janus, and M.C. Seto, eds. *Sexually coercive behavior: Understanding and management*. pp. 428–440. New York, NY: Annals of the New York Academy of Sciences.

Rice, M.E., and Harris, G.T. 2005. "Comparing effect sizes in follow-up studies: ROC area, Cohen's *d*, and *r*." *Law and Human Behavior*. 295:615–620.

Rice, M.E., Harris, G.T. and Cormier, C.A. 1992. "An evaluation of a maximum security therapeutic community for psychopaths and other mentally disordered offenders." *Law and Human Behavior*. 16:399–412.

Rice, M.E., Harris, G.T., Lang, C., Cormier, C. 2006. "Violent sex offenses: How are they best measured from official records?" *Law and Human Behavior*. 30:525–541.

Richie, B. 2001. "Challenges incarcerated women face as they return to their communities: Findings from life history interviews." *Crime and Delinquency*. 47:368–389.

Richie, B.E. 1996. *Compelled to crime: The gender entrapment of black battered women*. New York, NY: Routledge.

Roberts, A.R. 2007. "Domestic violence continuum, forensic assessment, a crises intervention." *Families in Society: The Journal of Contemporary Soc Services*. 88:30–43.

Roberts, A.R. and Roberts, B. 2005. *Ending intimate abuse: Practical guidar and survival strategies*. New York, NY: Oxford University Press.

Roberts, J.V. and Melcher, R. 2003. "The incarceration of Aboriginal offen ers: An analysis of trends, 1978–2001." *Canadian Journal of Criminolc and Criminal Justice*. 45:211–242.

Roberts, J.V., Crutcher, N. and Verbrugge, P. 2007. "Public attitudes to se tencing in Canada: Exploring recent findings." *Canadian Journal Criminology and Criminal Justice*. 491:75–107.

Roberts, A., Yang, M., Zhang, T., and Coid, J. 2008. "Personality disord temperament and childhood adversity: Findings from a cohort prisoners in England and Wales." *Journal of Forensic Psychiatry a Psychology*. 19:460–483.

Robins, L.N. 1986. "The consequences of conduct disorder in girls." In Olweus, J. Block, and M. Radke-Yarrow, eds. *Development of antisoc and prosocial behaviour*. pp. 385–408. New York, NY: Academic Press.

Robins, L.N., and Hill, S.Y. 1966. "Assessing the contribution of fam structure, class and peer groups to juvenile delinquency." *Journal Criminal Law, Criminology, and Police Science*. 57:325–334.

Robinson, G.G., Conry, J.L., and Conry, R.F. 1987. "Clinical profile a prevalence of fetal alcohol syndrome in an isolated community British Columbia." *Canadian Medical Association Journal*. 137:203–2C

Robinson, D. and Porporino, F.J. 2001. "Programming in cognitive skills: T reasoning and rehabilitation program." In C.R. Hollin, ed. *Handbook offender assessment an treatment*. London: Wiley.

Robinson, D. and Taylor, J. 1995. *Incidence of family violence perpetrated by f eral offenders: A file review study*. FV-03. Correctional Services of Cana

Rockett, J., Murrie, D.C. and Boccaccini, M.T. 2007. "Diagnostic labeling juvenile justice settings: Do psychopathy and conduct disorder findi influence clinicians." *Psychological Services*. 4:107–122.

Rodriguez, M.A., Wallace, S.P., Woolf, N.H. and Mangione, C.M. 20 "Mandatory reporting of elder abuse: Between a rock and a hard plac *Annals of Family Medicine*. 4:403–409.

Roesler, T.A. and Weissman-Wind, T.W. 1994. "Telling the secret: Ad women describe their disclosures of incest." *Journal of Interperso Violence*. 9:327–338.

Rogers, R., Gillis, R., Turner, R., and Frise-Smith, T. 1990. "The clini presentation of command hallucinations in a forensic populatio *American Journal of Psychiatry*. 147:1304–1307.

Rosenbaum, J.L., and Lasley, J.R. 1990. "School, community context, and del quency: Rethinking the gender gap." *Justice Quarterly*. 7:493–513.

Rosoff, S.M., Pontell, H.N., and Tillman, R.H. 2002. *Profit without hon White-collar crime and the looting of America*. Upper Saddle River, I Prentice-Hall.

Ross, R. 1992. *Dancing with a ghost: Exploring Indian reality*. Markham, C Reed Books Canada.

Rotter, M., Way, B., Steinbacher, M., Sawyer, D., and Smith, H. 20 "Personality disorders in prison: Aren't they all antisocial?" *Psychia Quarterly*. 73:337–349.

Royal Canadian Mounted Police. 2006. "Drug situation in Canada – 20C Retrieved December 21, 2009 (**www.rcmp-grc.gc.ca/drugs-drogu drg-2006-eng.htm**).

Royal Commission on Aboriginal Peoples. 1996. *Bridging the cultural div A report on Aboriginal people and the criminal justice system in Cana* Ottawa, ON: Ministry of Supply and Services.

Rudin, J. 2006. *Aboriginal peoples and the criminal justice system*. Retrieved Janu 12, 2009 (**http://74.125.113.132/search?q=cache: Jwb3MjRPcTC www.attorneygeneral.jus.gov.on.ca/inquiries/ipperwash/policy_pa**

research/pdf/Rudin.pdf+Aboriginal+peoples+and+ the+criminal+justice+system+attorney+general&cd=2&hl=en&ct=clnk&gl=ca&client=firefox-a).

...dolph, K.D. and Asher, S.R. 2000. "Adaptation and maladaptation in the peer system: Developmental processes and outcomes." In A.J. Sameroff, M. Lewis, and S.M. Miller, eds. *Handbook of developmental psychopathology*. 2nd ed., pp. 157-175. New York, NY: Kluwer Academic/Plenum Publishers.

...gge, T. 2006. "Risk assessment of male Aboriginal offenders: A 2006 perspective." User Report No. 2006-01. Ottawa, ON: Public Safety Canada.

...msey, J.M. and Rapoport, J.L., eds. 1983. *Nutrition and the Brain*. New York, NY: Raven Press.

...tter, M. 1981. *Maternal deprivation reassessed*. 2nd ed. Harmondsworth, UK: Penguin.

...tter, M. 1990. "Psychosocial resilience and protective mechanisms." In J. Rolf, A.S. Masten, D. Cicchetti, K. Nuechterlein, and S. Weintraub, eds., *Risk and protective factors in the development of psychopathology*. pp. 181–214. Cambridge, MA: Cambridge University Press.

...tter, M., ed. 1995. *Psychosocial disturbances in young people: Challenges for prevention*. Cambridge, MA: Press Syndicate of the University of Cambridge.

...mpson, R.J. and Laub, J.H. 1995. *Crime in the making: Pathways and turning points through life*. Cambridge, MA: Harvard University Press.

...mpson, R.J. and Laub, J.H. 2005. "A life-course view of the development of crime." *Annals of the American Academy of Political and Social Science*. 602:12–45.

...mpson, R.J., Raudenbush, S.W., and Earls, F. 1997. "Neighbourhoods and violent crime: A multilevel study of collective efficacy." *Science*. 277:918–924.

...ndler, J.C., Freeman, N.J., Socia, K.M. 2008. "Does a watched pot boil? A time-series analysis of New York State's sex offender registration and notification law." *Psychology, Public Policy, and Law*. 14:284–302.

...ndor, S., Smith, D., MacLeod, P. Tredwell, S., Wood, B., and Newman, D. 1981. "Intrinsic defects in the Fetal Alcohol Syndrome: Studies of 76 cases from B.C. and the Yukon." *Neurobehavioral Toxicology and Teratology*. 3:145–152.

...nders, B.E. 2003. "Understanding children exposed to violence: Toward an integration of overlapping fields." *Journal of Interpersonal Violence*. 18:356–376.

...voie, J. 2007. "Youth self-reported delinquency, Toronto, 2006." *Juristat*. 27:6. Canadian Centre for Justice Statistics. Catalogue no. 85-002-XPE. Ottawa, ON: Ministry of Industry.

...hmitt, D.P. 2005. "Sociosexuality from Argentina to Zimbabwe: A 48-nation study of sex, culture, and strategies of human mating." *Behavioural Brain Sciences*. 28:247–311.

...hoenthaler, S.J. 1983. "Diet and crime, an empirical examination of the value of nutrition in the control and treatment of incarcerated juvenile offenders." *International Journal of Biosocial Research*. 4:25–39.

...hoepfer, A., Carmichael, S. and Piquero, N.L. 2007. "Do perceptions of punishment vary between white-collar and street crimes?" *Journal of Criminal Justice*. 35:151–163.

...hulz, S. 2006. *Beyond self-control: Analysis and critique of Gottfredson and Hirschi's general theory of crime*. Berlin, Germany: Duncker and Homblot.

...hwalbe, C.S. 2008. "A meta-analysis of juvenile justice risk assessment instruments." *Criminal Justice and Behaviour*. 35:1367–1381.

...hwartz, D., Dodge, K.A., Coie, J.D., Hubbard, J.A., Cillessen, A.H.N., Lemerise, E.A., and Bateman, H. 1998. "Social-cognitive and behavioral correlates of aggression and victimization in boys' play groups." *Journal of Abnormal Child Psychology*. 26:431–440.

Seagrave, D. and Grisso, T. 2002. "Adolescent development and the measurement of juvenile psychopathy." *Law and Human Behavior*. 26:219–239.

Seguin, J., Pihl, R., Harden, P., Tremblay, R., and Boulerice, B. 1995. "Cognitive and neuropsychological characteristics of physically aggressive boys." *Journal of Abnormal Psychology*. 104:614–624.

Sellers, C.S. and Akers, R.L. 2005. "Social learning theory: Correcting misconceptions." In S. Henry, and M. Lanier, eds. *The essential criminology reader*. pp. 89–99. Boulder, CO: Westview Press.

Serial Killers. 2008. "Serial Killers Paul Kenneth Bernardo and Karla Homolka." Retrieved January 25, 2009 (www.serialkillers.ca/bernardo-homolka.htm).

Serin, R.C., Mailloux, D. L., Kennedy, S. M. 2007. "Development of a clinical rating scale for offender readiness: Implications for assessment and offender change." *Issues in Forensic Psychology*. 7:70–80.

Serin, R.C. and Lloyd, C.D. 2009 "Examining Models of Offender Change: Bridging the Process from Antisocial to Prosocial." *Psychology, Crime and Law*. 15:347–364.

Serin, R.C. and Shturman, M. 2007. "Correctional Staff's Important Contribution to Effective Corrections." *Corrections Today*. 5.

Seto, M.C. 2008. *Pedophilia and sexual offending against children: Theory, assessment, and intervention*. Washington, DC: American Psychological Association.

Seto, M.C. and Lalumière, M.L. 2009. *What is so special about male adolescent sexual offending? A review and test of explanations using meta-analysis*. Manuscript submitted for publication.

Seto, M.C., Marques, J. K., Harris, G.T., Chaffin, M., Lalumière, M.L., Miner, M.H. et al. 2008. "Good science and progress in sex offender treatment are intertwined: A response to Marshall and Marshall 2007." *Sexual Abuse: A Journal of Research and Treatment*. 20:247–255.

Shapiro, C.M., Federoff, J.P., and Trajanovic, N.N. 1996. "Sexual behavior in sleep: A newly described parasomnia." *Sleep Research*. 25:367.

Shapiro, C.M., Trajanovic, N.N., and Federoff, J.P. 2003. "Sexomnia—a new parasomina?" *Canadian Journal of Psychiatry*. 48:311–317.

Shapland, J., Atkinson, A., Atkinson, H., Dignan, J., Edwards, L., Hibbert, J., Howes, M., Johnstone, J., Robinson, G., and Sorsby, A. 2008. "Does restorative justice affect reconviction? The fourth report from the evaluation of three schemes." Ministry of Justice Research Series 10/08: National Offender Management Service (www.justice.gov.uk/publications/docs/restorative-justice-report_06-08.pdf).

Shaw, M. 1991. *Survey of Federally Sentenced Women: Reports to the Task Force on Federally Sentenced Women on the Prison Survey*. User Report 1991–4. Ottawa, ON: Ministry of the Solicitor General.

Shaw, M. and Hannah-Moffat, K. 2004. "How cognitive skills forgot about gender and diversity." In G. Mair, ed. *What matters in probation*. pp. 90–121. Cullompton, Devon: Willan Publishing.

Short, J.F. 1957. "Differential association and delinquency." *Social Problems*. 4:233–239.

Shurman, L.A. and Rodriguez, C.M. 2006. "Cogntive-affective predictors of women's readiness to end domestic violence relationships." *Journal of Interpersonal Violence*. 21:1417–1439.

Siegal, H.A., Li, L., and Rapp, R.C. 2002. "Case Management as a Therapeutic Enhancement: Impact on Post-treatment Criminality." *Journal of Addictive Disorders*. 214:37–46.

Signorelli, N. 1989. "The stigma of mental illness on television." *Journal of Broadcasting and Electronic Media*. 33:325–331.

Silbert, M.H. 1982. "Prostitution and sexual assault: Summary of results." *International Journal for Biosocial Research*. 3:69–71.

Silbert, M.H. and Pines, A.M. 1981. "Sexual abuse as an antecedent to prostitution." *Child abuse and Neglect*. 5:407–411.

Simkins, S. and Katz, S. 2002. "Criminalizing abused girls." *Violence Against Women*. 8:1474–1499.

Simon, R.J. 1975. *Women and crime.* Lexington, MA: Lexington Books.

Simon, T.R., Anderson, M., Thompson, M.P., Crosby, A.E., Shelley, G., and Sacks, J.J. 2001. "Attitudinal acceptance of intimate partner violence among US adults." *Violence and Victims.* 16:115–126.

Silver, E., Cirincione, C., and Steadman, J.J. 1994. "Demythologizing inaccurate perceptions of the insanity defence." *Law and Human Behavior.* 18:63–70.

Simourd, L. and Andrews, D.A. 1994. "Correlates of delinquency: A look at gender differences." *Forum on Corrections Research.* 61:26–31.

Simourd, L. and Andrews, D.A. 1994. "Correlates of delinquency: A look at gender differences." *Forum on Corrections Research.* 6:26–31.

Simpson, D. W. and Christensen, A. 2005. "Spousal agreement regarding relationship aggression on the Conflict Tactics Scale-2." *Psychological Assessment.* 17:423–432.

Sinclair, R.L. and Boe, R. 2002. *Canadian federal women offender profiles: Trends from 1981 to 2002 Revised.* Research Report R-131. Ottawa, ON: Research Branch, Correctional Service of Canada.

Singular, S. 2008. *When men become Gods: Mormon polygamist Warren Jeffs, his cult of fear, and the women who fought back.* New York, NY: Macmillan

Sioui, R. and Thibault, J. 2001. *Pertinence of cultural adaptation of Reintegration Potential Reassessment RPR scale to Aboriginal context.* Research Report No. R-109. Ottawa, ON: Correctional Service Canada.

Sioui, R. and Thibault, J. 2002. "Examining reintegration potential for Aboriginal offenders." *Forum on Corrections Research.* 14:49–51.

Sirdifield, C., Gojkovic, D., Brooker, C., and Ferriter, M. 2009. "A systematic review of research on the epidemiology of mental health disorders in prison populations: A summary of findings." *Journal of Forensic Psychiatry and Psychology.* 20:S78–S101.

Skeem, J., Eno Louden, J., Polasheck, and Cap, J. 2007. "Relationship quality in mandated treatment: Blending care with control." *Psychological Assessment.* 19:397–410.

Skeem, J., and Manchak, S. 2008. "Back to the future: From Klockars' model of effective supervision to evidence-based practice in probation." *International Journal of Offender Rehabilitation.* 47:220–247.

Skeem, J., Schugert, C., Odgers, C., Mulvey, E., Garnder, W., and Lidz, C. 2006. "Psychiatric symptoms and community violence among high-risk patients: A test of the relationship at the weekly level." *Journal of Consulting and Clinical Psychology.* 74:967–979.

Skinner, B.F. 1953. *Science and human behavior.* New York, NY: Macmillan.

Smart, C. 1976. *Women, crime and criminology: A feminist critique.* London: Routledge and Kegan Paul.

Smart, C. 1982. "The new female offender: Reality or myth?" In B.R. Price and N. Sokoloff, eds. *The criminal justice system and women.* pp. 105–116. New York, NY: Clark Boardman.

Smigel, E.O. 1956. "Public attitudes toward stealing as related to the size of the victim organization." *American Sociological Review.* 21:3–20.

Smigel, E.O., and Ross, H.L. 1970. *Crimes against bureaucracy.* New York, NY: Van Nostraand Reinhold.

Smith, C. and Thornberry, T.P. 1995. "The relationship between childhood maltreatment and adolescent involvement in delinquency." *Criminology.* 33:451–481.

Smith, D.W., Letourneau, E.J., Saunders, B.E., Kilpatrick, D.G., Resnick, H.S., and Best, C.L. 2000. "Delay in disclosure of childhood rape: Results from a national survey." *Child Abuse and Neglect.* 24:273–287.

Smith, P., Cullen, F.T., and Latessa, E.J. 2009. "Can 14,737 women be wrong? A meta-analysis of the LSI-R and recidivism for female offenders." *Criminology and Public Policy.* 8:183–208.

Smith, P., Gendreau, P., and Swartz, K. 2009. "Validating the principles of effective intervention: A systematic review of the contributions of meta-analysis in the field of corrections." *Victims and Offenders.* 4:148–169.

Smith, P., Goggin, C., and Gendreau, P. 2002. *The effects of prison sentenc and intermediate sanctions on recidivism: General effects and individu differences.* Ottawa, ON: Public Safety Canada.

Snodgrass, J. 1972. *The American criminological tradition: Portraits of men a ideology in a discipline.* Unpublished Ph.D. Dissertation, University Pennsylvania.

Snyder, H.N., and Sickmund, M. 2006. *Juvenile Offenders and Victims: 200 National Report.* Washington, DC: U.S. Department of Justice, Office Juvenile Justice and Delinquency Prevention.

Sorbello, L., Eccleston, L., Ward, T., and Jones, R. 2002. "Treatment nee of female offenders: A review." *Australian Psychologist.* 37:196–205.

Statistics Canada 1999. *General Social Survey*

Statistics Canada 2004. *General Social Survey.*

Statistics Canada. 2005. "International Criminal Victimization Survey ar European Survey on Crime and Safety." Retrieved March 21, 200 (www.statcan.gc.ca/pub/85-002-x/2008010/article/10745-eng.htm#a1

Statistics Canada. 2005. "Adult Correctional Services in Canad 2003–2004." Retrieved April 2, 2009 (www.statcan.gc.ca/pub/85-21 x/85-211-x2004000-eng.pdf).

Statistics Canada. 2006. "Youth Crime in Canada, 2006." *Juristat.* Catalog no. 85-002-XIE, Vol. 28, no. 3.

Statistics Canada. 2006. Aboriginal people as victims and offenders. T *Daily.* Retrieved January 14, 2009 (www.statcan.gc.ca/daily-quotidie 060606/dq060606b-eng.htm).

Statistics Canada. 2007. "CANSIM Summary Tables." Retrieved February 1 2009 (www40.statcan.gc.ca/z01/cs0002-eng.htm).

Statistics Canada. 2008. *The Daily.* May 16. Retrieved December 8, 200 (www.statcan.gc.ca/daily-quotidien/080516/dq080516a-eng.htm).

Statistics Canada. 2008. "Youth Court Statistics, 2006/2007." *Jurista* Canadian Centre for Justice Statistics. Catalogue no. 85-002-XIE, no.

Statistics Canada. 2009. *Measuring Crime in Canada: Introducing the Crin Severity Index and Improvements to the Uniform Crime Reporting Surve* Retrieved June 10, 2009 (www.statcan.gc.ca/pub/85-004-x/85-00 x2009001-eng.pdf).

Steffensmeier, D. and Allan, E. 1996. "Gender and crime: Toward a ge dered theory of female offending." *Annual Sociological Revie* 22:459–487.

Steffensmeier, D., Schwartz, J., Zhong, H., and Ackerman, J. 2005. "A assessment of recent trends in girls' violence using diverse longitudir sources: Is the gender gap closing?" *Criminology.* 43:355–406.

Steinberg, L. 2002. "The juvenile psychopath: Fads, fictions, and fact *National Institute of Justice Perspectives on Crime and Justice: 2001 Lectu Series.* Vol. V.:35–64.

Stenning, P. and Roberts, J.V. 2001. "Empty promises: Parliament, t Supreme Court, and the sentencing of Aboriginal offender *Saskatchewan Law Review.* 64:137–168.

Stevenson, D.B. 2001. *Freud's psychosexual stages of development.* Retriev December 17, 2009 (www.victorianweb.org/science/freud/develop.htm

Stevenson, J. 2007. "Alberta girl found guilty in bloody murders of parer and younger brother." Retrieved August 4, 2009 (www.redorbit.co news/health/994904/alberta_girl_found_guilty_ir bloody_murders_of_parents_and/index.html).

Stewart, L. and Price, L. 2005. *Generic Program Performance Measu* Unpublished document. Ottawa, ON: Correctional Service of Canad

Stewart, L., Gabora, N., Kropp, R., and Lee, Z. 2008. *Family violence progra ming: Treatment outcome for Canadian federally sentenced offende* Correctional Service of Canada R-174.

Stompe, T., Ortwein-Swoboda, G., and Schanda, H. 2004. "Schizophren delusional symptoms, and violence: The threat/control-override conce reexamined." *Schizophrenia Bulletin.* 30:31–44.

orms, M.D. 1981. "A theory of erotic orientation development." *Psychological Review*. 88:340–353.

raus, M.A. 1977. "A sociological perspective on the prevention and treatment of wife beating." In M. Roy, ed. *Battered women*. pp. 194–239. New York, NY: Van Nostrand Reinhold.

raus, M.A. 1979. "Measuring intrafamily conflict and violence: The conflict tactics CT scales." *Journal of Marriage and the Family*. 41:75–88.

raus, M. 2007. *Prevalence and effects of mutuality in physical and psychological aggression against dating partners by university students in 32 nations*. International Family Aggression Society conference, Lancashire, England.

raus, M.A. 2008. "Dominance and symmetry in partner violence by male and female university students in 32 nations." *Children and Youth Services Review*. 30:252–275.

raus, M.A., Gelles, R.J., and Steinmetz, S. 1980. *Behind closed doors: Violence in the American family*. Garden City, NY: Anchor/Doubleday.

raus, M.A., Hamby, S.L., Boney-McCoy, S., and Sugerman, D.B. 1996. "The revised conflict tactics scale CTS2: Development and preliminary psychometric data." *Journal of Family Issues*. 17:283–316.

raus, M.A. and Stewart, J.H. 1999. "Corporal punishment by American parents: National data on prevalence, chronicity, severity, and duration, in relation to child and family characteristics." *Clinical Child and Family Psychology Review*. 2:55–70.

preme Court of Texas. 2008. Texas Department Family and Protective Services. No. 08-0391.

reissguth, A.P. 1997. *Fetal Alcohol Syndrome: A guide for families and communities*. Baltimore, MD: Pearl H. Brooks Publishing Company.

reissguth, A.P., Barr, H.M., Kogan, J., and Bookstein, F.L. 1996. *Understanding the occurrence of secondary disabilities in clients with FAS and FAE*. Seattle, WA: University of Washington Publication Services.

rve, G.J., MacKenzie, D.L., Gover, A.R., and Mitchell, O. 2000. "Perceived conditions of confinement: A national evaluation of juvenile boot camps and traditional facilities." *Law and Human Behavior*. 24:297–308.

therland, E.H. 1939. *Principles of criminology*. 3rd ed. Philadelphia, PA: J.B. Lippincott Company.

therland, E.H. 1947. *Principles of criminology*. 4th ed. Philadelphia, PA: J.B. Lippincott Company.

therland, E.H. 1949. *White-collar crime*. New York, NY: Dryden Press.

therland, E.H. and Cressey, D.R. 1970. *Principles of criminology*. 6th ed. New York, NY: Lippincott.

anson, J., Borum, R., Swartz, M., and Monahan, J. 1996. "Psychotic symptoms and disorders and the risk of violent behavior in the community." *Criminal Behaviour and Mental Health*. 6:309–329.

anson, J., Estroff, S., Swartz, M., Borum, R., Lachicotte, W., Zimmer, C., and Wagner, R. 1997. "Violence and severe mental disorder in clinical and community populations: The effects of psychotic symptoms, comorbidity, and lack of treatment." *Psychiatry*. 60:1–22.

anson, J.W., Van Dorn, R.A., Swartz, M.S., Smith, A., Elbogen, E.R., and Monahan, J. 2008. "Alternative pathways to violence in persons with schizophrenia: The role of childhood antisocial behavior problems." *Law and Human Behavior*. 32:228–240.

anson, J.W., Swartz, M.S., Van Dorn, R.A., Elbogen, E.B., Wagner, H.R., Rosenheck, R., Stroup, S., and Liberman, J. 2006. "A national study of violent behavior in persons with schizophrenia." *Archives of General Psychiatry*. 63:490–499.

anson, J., Holzer, C., Ganju, V., and Jono, R. 1990. "Violence and psychiatric disorder in the community: Evidence from the Epidemiological Catchment Area Surveys." *Hospital and Community Psychiatry*. 41:761–770.

ima, E.A. 2004. "Correlates of the co-occurrence of wife abuse and child abuse among a representative sample." *Journal of Family Violence*. 19:399–410.

Tamatea, A. and Wilson, N. 2009. *Dynamic Risk Assessment for Offender Re-entry DRAOR: A Pilot Study*. New Zealand Department of Corrections. Unpublished paper.

Tarling, R. 1993. *Analysing crime: Data, models and interpretations*. London: Home Office.

Task Force on Federally Sentenced Women. 1990. "Creating choices: Report of the Task Force on Federally Sentenced Women." Retrieved March 20, 2009 (**www.csc-scc.gc.ca/text/prgrm/fsw/choices/toce-eng.shtml**).

Taxman, F.S., Shepardson, E.S., Delano, J., Mitchell, S., Byrne, J.M., Gelb, A., and Gornik, M. 2004. *Tools of the trade*. Washington, DC: National Institute of Corrections.

Taylor, I., Walton, P., and Young, J. 1973. *The new criminology*. London, UK: Routledge and Kegan Paul.

Taylor, J., Iacono, W.G., and McGue, M. 2000. "Evidence for a genetic etiology of early-onset delinquency." *Journal of Abnormal Psychology*. 1094:634–643.

Taylor, J., Loney, B.R., Bobadilla, L., Iacono, W.G., and McGue, M. 2003. "Genetic and environmental influences on psychopathy trait dimensions in a community sample of male twins." *Journal of Abnormal Child Psychology*. 31:633–645.

Taylor, N. and Bareja, M. 2002. *2002 National Police Custody Survey*. Canberra: Australian Institute of Criminology. Retrieved September 15, 2005 (**www.aic.gov.au/publi cations/tbp/tbp013/**).

Taylor, S.M. and Dear, M.J. 1981. "Scaling community attitudes towards the mentally ill." *Schizophrenia Bulletin*. 7:226–240.

Teasdale, D., Silver, E., and Monahan, J. 2006. "Gender, threat/control-override delusions and violence." *Law and Human Behavior*. 30:649–658.

Teplin, L.A. 1984. "Managing disorder: Police handling of the persons with mental illness." In L. Teplin, ed. *Mental health and criminal justice*. pp. 157–175. Beverly Hills, CA: Sage.

Thomas, W.I. 1923. *The unadjusted girl*. Boston, MA: Little, Brown and Company.

Thornberry, T.P. 1996. "Toward an interactional theory of delinquency." In P. Cordella and L. Siegel, eds. *Readings in contemporary criminological theory*. pp. 223–239. Boston, MA: Northeastern University Press.

Thornberry, T.P., Huizinga, D., and Loeber, R. 1995. "The prevention of serious delinquency and violence: Implications from the program of research on the causes and correlates of delinquency." In J.C. Howell, B. Krisberg, J.D. Hawkins, and J.J. Wilson, eds. *A Sourcebook: Serious, Violent, and Chronic Juvenile Offenders*. pp. 213–237. Thousand Oaks, CA: Sage.

Thornberry, T.P. and Krohn, M.D., eds. 2003. *Taking stock of delinquency: An overview of findings from contemporary longitudinal studies*. New York, NY: Kluwer Academic.

Thorndike, E.L. 1898. "Animal intelligence: An experimental study of the associative processes in animals." *Psychological Review Monograph Supplement*. 2:1–109.

Thornton, D., Beech, A., and Marshall, W.L. 2004. "Pretreatment self-esteem and posttreatment sexual recidivism." *International Journal of Offender Therapy and Comparative Criminology*. 48:587–599.

Thornton, D. and Laws, D.R. 2009. *Cognitive approaches to the assessment of sexual interest in sexual offenders*. Chichester, UK: Wiley.

Thornton, D., Mann, R., Webster, S., Blud, L., Travers, R., Friendship, C., and Erikson, M. 2003. "Distinguishing and combining risks for sexual and violent recidivism." In R.A. Prentky, E.S. Janus and M.C. Seto, eds. *Sexually coercive behavior: Understanding and management*. pp. 225–235. Annals of the New York Academy of Sciences, Volume 989. New York, NY: New York Academy of Sciences.

Tierney, J.P., Grossman, J.B., and Resch, N.L. 1995. *Making a difference: An impact study of Big Brothers Big Sisters*. Philadelphia, PA: Public/Private Ventures.

Tittle, C.R., Villimez, W.J., and Smith, D.A. 1978. "The myth of social class and criminality: An empirical assessment of the empirical evidence." *American Sociological Review*. 43:643–656.

Toch, H.H. 1988, *Violent Men: An inquiry into the psychology of violence*. Chicago: Aldine Publishing Co.

Tong, L.S.J. and Farrington, D.P. 2006. "How effective is the "Reasoning and Rehabilitation" programme in reducing reoffending? A meta-analysis of evaluations in four countries." *Psychology, Crime and Law*. 12:3–24.

Tonry, M. 1994. "Editorial: Racial disparities in courts and prisons." *Criminal Behaviour and Mental Health*. 4:158–162.

Tooby, J. and Cosmides, L. 2005. "Conceptual foundations of evolutionary psychology." In D.M. Buss, ed. *The handbook of evolutionary psychology*. pp. 5–67. Hoboken, NJ: John Wiley and Sons, Inc.

Torre, P. 2009. *Beavis and Butthead*. Retrieved May 9, 2009 (www.museum.tv/ archives/etv/B/htmlB/beavisandbu/beavisandbu.htm).

Toth, S.L., Cicchetti, D. and Kim, J. 2002. "Relations among children's perceptions of maternal behavior, attributional styles, and behavioral symptomatology in maltreated children." *Journal of Abnormal Psychology*. 30:487–501.

Tran, T.T., Chowanadisai, W., Lonnendal, B., Le., L., Parker, M., Chicz-Demet, A., and Crinella, F.M. 2002. "Effects of neonatal dietary manganese exposure on brain dopamine levels and neurocognitive functions." *Neurotoxicology*. 145:1–7.

Trasler, G. 1987. "Some cautions for the biological approach to crime causation." In Mednick, S.A., Moffitt, T.E., and Stach, S.A., eds. *The causes of crime: New biological approaches*. pp. 7–24. Cambridge: Cambridge University Press. Proceedings NATO Conference, Skiathos Greece, Sept. 20–24, 1982.

Travis, J., Solomon, A.L., and Wahl, M. 2001. *From Prison to Home: The Dimensions and Consequences of Prisoner Reentry*. The Urban Institute (www.urban.org/url.cfm?ID=410098.html).

Trevethan, S., Crutcher, N., and Rastin, C.J. 2002. *An examination of healing lodges for federal offenders in Canada*. Research Report No. R-130. Ottawa, ON: Correctional Service of Canada.

Trevethan, S., Moore, J., and Allegri, N. 2005. *The "In Search of Your Warrior" program for Aboriginal offenders: A preliminary evaluation*. Research Report No. R-172. Ottawa, ON: Correctional Service of Canada.

Trevethan, S., Auger, S., Moore, J.P., MacDonald, M., and Sinclair, J. 2001. "The Effect of Family Disruption on Aboriginal and Non-Aboriginal Inmates." Research Report No. R-113. Ottawa, ON: Correctional Service of Canada.

Trevethan, S., Moore, J., Auger, S., MacDonald, M., and Sinclair, J. 2002. "Childhood experiences affect Aboriginal offenders." *Forum on Corrections Research*. 14:7–9.

Trevethan, S., Moore, J., and Rastin, C.J. 2002. "A profile of Aboriginal offenders in federal facilities and serving time in the community." *Forum on Corrections Research*. 14:17–19.

Trevethan, S., Tremblay, S., and Carter, J. 2000. *The over-representation of Aboriginal people in the justice system*. Ottawa, ON: Statistics Canada.

Trevino, L.K. and Victor, B. 1992. "Peer reporting of unethical behavior: A social context perspective." *Academy of Management Journal*. 35:38–64.

Trivers, R.L. 1972. "Parental investment and sexual selection." In B. Campbell, ed. *Sexual selection and the descent of man*. pp.1871–1971. Chicago, IL: Aldine.

Trocmé, B.N., Fallon, B., MacLaurin, B., Daciuk, J., Felstiner, C., Black, T., Tonmyr, L., Blackstock, C., Barter, K., Turcotte, D., and Cloutier, R. 2005. *Canadian Incidence Study of Reported Child Abuse and Neglect–2003: Major Findings*. Minister of Public Works and Government Services Canada.

Turnbull, S.R., 2004. *Genghis Khan and the Mongol conquests, 1190–140* New York, NY: Routledge.

United Nations. 2005. *World population prospects: the 2004 revision highligh* New York, United Nations.

United States Department of Justice. 2005. "Fiscal year 2005 budget and pe formance summary." Retrieved August 31, 2009 (www.usdoj.gov/jm 2005summary).

Vale, E.L.E. and Kennedy, P.J. 2004. "Adolescent drug trafficking trends the United Kingdom—a 10-year retrospective analysis." *Journal Adolescence*. 27:749–754.

Vance, J.P. 2001. "Neurobiological mechanisms of psychosocial resilienc In J.M. Richman and M.W. Fraser, eds. *The context of youth violen Resilience, risk, and protection*. pp. 43–81. Westport, CN: Praeger.

Van Ness, D. and Strong, K.H. 1997. *Restoring justice*. Cincinnati, O Anderson.

Van Voorhis, P., Salisbury, E., Wright, E., and Bauman, A. 2008. "Achievi accurate pictures of risk and identifying gender responsive needs: T new assessments for women offenders. National Institute Corrections." Retrieved September 02, 2008 (http://community.nic org/files/folders/tools_for_evidence_based_decisio making_in_local_justice_systems/entry7534.aspx).

Wadsworth, M.E.J. 1976. "Delinquency, pulse rates, and early emotional de rivation." *British Journal of Criminology*. 16:245–256.

Wellisch, J., Anglin, M.D., and Prendergast, M.L. 1993. "Treatment stra gies for drug-abusing women offenders." In J.A. Inciardi, ed. *Drug tre ment and criminal justice*. pp. 5–25. Newbury Park, CA: Sa Publications.

Vidal, S. and Skeem, J.L. 2007. "Effect of psychopathy, abuse, and ethnicity juvenile probation officers decision-making and supervision strategie *Law and Human Behavior*. 31:479–498.

Viding, E., Blair, R.J.R., Moffitt, T.E., and Plomin, R. 2005. "Evidence substantial genetic risk for psychopathy in 7-year-olds." *Journal of Ch Psychology and Psychiatry*. 46:592–597.

Vitacco, M.J., Neumann, C.S., Caldwell, M.F., Leistico, A.M., and V Rybroek, G.J. 2006. "Testing factor models of the Psychopat Checklist: Youth Version and their association with instrumen aggression." *Journal of Personality Assessment*. 87:74–83.

Vitacco, M.J., Van Rybroek, G.J., Rogstad, J.E., Erickson, S.K., Tripp, Harris, L., and Miller, R. 2008. "Developing services for insanity acqu tees conditionally released into the community: Maximizing success a minimizing recidivism." *Psychological Services*. 5:118–125.

Wahl, O.F. 1995. *Media madness: Public images of mental illness*. N Brunswick, NJ: Rutgers University Press.

Wakefield, J.C. 2006. "High mental disorder rates are based on invalid mea ures: Questions about claimed ubiquity of mutation-induced dysfur tion." *Behavioral and Brain Sciences*. 298:424–426.

Wallace, J. 2006. "Even inmates eat better than seniors in nursing home *Kingston Whig Standard*. Thursday, August 10, 2006, p. 4.

Wallace, J.F., and Newman, J.P. 2004. "A theory-based treatment mo for psychopathy." *Cognitive and Behavioral Practice*. 11:178–189.

Walsh, A. and Beaver, K.M., 2008. "The promise of evolutionary psycholc for criminology: the examples of gender and age." In J.D. Duntley T.K. Shackelford, eds. *Evolutionary forensic psychology: Darwinian foun tions of crime and law*. pp. 20–40. Oxford, NY: Oxford University Pres

Walters, G.D. 2003a. "Predicting criminal justice outcomes with t Psychopathy Checklist and Lifestyle Criminality Screening form: meta-analytic comparison." *Behavioral Sciences and the Law*. 21:89–1

Walters, G.D. 2003b. "Predicting institutional adjustment and recidivism w the Psychopathy Checklist factor scores: A meta-analysis." *Law a Human Behavior*. 27:541–558.

ard, T., Day, A, Howell, K., and Birgden, A. 2004. "The multifactor offender readiness model." *Aggression and Violent Behavior*. 9:645–673.

ard, T. and Gannon, T.A. 2006. "Rehabilitation, etiology, and self-regulation: The comprehensive good lives model of treatment for sexual offenders." *Aggression and Violent Behavior*. 11:77–94.

ard, T. and Hudson, S.M. 1998. "A model of the relapse process in sexual offenders." *Journal of Interpersonal Violence*. 13:700–725.

ard, T. and Marshall, W.L. 2007. "Narrative Identity and Offender Rehabilitation." *International Journal of Offender Therapy and Comparative Criminology*. 51:279–297.

ard, T., Melser, J., and Yates, P.M. 2007. "Reconstructing the risk-need-responsivity model: A theoretical elaboration and evaluation." *Aggression and Violent Behavior*. 12:208–228.

arren, J.I., Burnette, M., South, S.C., Chauhan, P., Bale, R., and Friend, R. 2002. "Personality disorders and violence among female prison inmates." *Journal of the American Academy of Psychiatry and Law*. 30:502–509.

aschbusch, D.A. 2002. "A meta-analytic examination of comorbid hyperactive-impulsive-attention problems and conduct problems." *Psychological Bulletin*. 128:118–150.

ashington Post. September 5, 2006, NIMH Administrator, Wayne S. Fenton, 53.

atkins, R.E. 1992. "An historical review of the role and practice of psychology in the field of corrections." Research Report No. R-28. Ottawa, ON: Correctional Service of Canada.

atson, J.B., and Rayner, R. 1920. "Conditioned emotional reactions." *Journal of Experimental Psychology*. 3:1–14.

ebb, R.C. 1999. *Psychology of the consumer and its development: An introduction*. New York, NY: Kluwer Academic.

eber, S., Habel, U., Amunts, K., and Schneider, F. 2008. "Structural brain abnormalities in psychopaths—A review." *Behavioral Sciences and the Law*. 26:7–28.

ebster, C.M. and Doob, A.N. 2004. "Classification without validity or equity: An empirical examination of the Custody Rating Scale for federally sentenced women offenders in Canada." *Canadian Journal of Criminology and Criminal Justice*. 46:395–421.

ebster, C.M. and Doob, A.N. 2004. "Taking down the straw man or building a house of straw? Validity, equity and the Custody Rating Scale." *Canadian Journal of Criminology and Criminal Justice*. 46:631–638.

ebster, C.D., Douglas, K.S., Eaves, D., and Hart, S.D. 1997. *HCR-20: Assessing risk for violence*. Version 2. Burnaby, BC: Mental Health, Law, and Policy Institute, Simon Fraser University.

ebster-Stratton, C. 1992. *The incredible years: A trouble shooting guide for parents of children ages 3-8 years*. Toronto, ON: Umbrella Press.

ebster-Stratton, C. and Hammond, M. 1997. "Treating children with early-onset conduct problems: A comparison of child and parenting training interventions." *Journal of Consulting and Clinical Psychology*. 65:93–109.

eekes, J. and Millson, W. 1994. *The Native offender substance abuse pre-treatment program: Intermediate measures of program effectiveness*. Research Report No. R-35. Ottawa, ON: Correctional Service of Canada.

einrath, M. 2007. "Sentencing disparity: Aboriginal Canadians, drunk driving, and age." *Western Criminology Review*. 8:16–28.

eisburd, D. and Chayet, E. 1995. "Specific deterrence in a sample of offenders convicted of white-collar crimes." *Criminology*. 33:587–607.

eisburd, D., Wheeler, S., Waring, E., and Bode, N. 1991. *Crimes of the middle-classes: White-collar offenders in the federal courts*. New Haven, CT: Yale University Press.

ells, E. and Rankin, J. 1991. "Families and delinquency: A meta-analysis of the impact of broken homes." *Social Problems*. 38:71–90.

Werner, E. 2000. "Protective factors and individual resilience." In J. Shonkoff and S. Meisels, eds. *Handbook of Early Childhood Intervention*. 2nd ed. Cambridge: Cambridge University Press.

Westhead, R. 2007. "Court report could mean 7-year terms for Black." *Toronto Star*. Retrieved August 31, 2009 (www.thestar.com/news/world/article/280603).

Westhead, R. 2007. "Black sentenced to 6.5 years." *Toronto Star*. Retrieved August 31, 2009 (www.thestar.com/news/world/article/284155).

Wheeler, S., Weisburd, D., Waring, E., and Bode, N. 1988. "White-collar crimes and criminals." *American Criminal Law Review*. 25:331–357.

Whitaker, D.J., Le, B., Hanson, R.K., Baker, C.K., McMahon, P.M., Ryan, G., et al. 2008. "Risk factors for the perpetration of child sexual abuse: A review and meta-analysis." *Child Abuse and Neglect*. 32:529–548.

White, R.J., and Gondolf, E.W. 2000. "Implications of personality profiles for batterer treatment." *Journal of Interpersonal Violence*. 15:467–486.

Wichmann, C., Serin, R.C., Motiuk, L.L. 2000. "Predicting Suicide Attempts Among Male Offenders in Federal Penitentiaries." Research Report No. R-91. Ottawa, ON: Correctional Service of Canada.

Widom, C.S. 1989. "The cycle of violence." *Science*. 244:160–166.

Widom, C.S. 1997. "Child abuse, neglect and witnessing violence." In D.M. Stoff, J. Breiling, and J.D. Maser, eds. *Handbook of Antisocial Behavior*. pp. 159–170. New York, NY: Wiley.

Widom, C.S. 2000. "Understanding the consequences of childhood victimization." In R.M. Reece, ed. *Treatment of child abuse: Common ground for mental health, medical, and legal practitioners*. pp. 339–361. Baltimore, MD: Johns Hopkins University Press.

Wille, R. and Beier, K.M. 1989. "Castration in Germany." *Annals of Sex Research*. 2:103–134.

Williams, S.L. and Frieze, I.H. 2005. "Patterns of violent relationship, psychological distress, and marital satisfaction in national sample of men and women." *Sex Roles*. 52:771–785.

Wilson, J.Q. and Herrnstein, R.J. 1985. *Crime and human nature*. New York, NY: Simon and Schuster.

Winfield, L. 1994. *NCREL Monograh: Developing resilience in urban youth*. NCREL: Urban Education Monograph Series.

Winko v. British Columbia. 1999. 2 S.C.R. 625.

Wolfgang, M.E. 1958. *Patterns in criminal homicide*. Philadelphia, PA: University of Pennsylvania Press.

Wong, S. and Hare, R.D. 2005. *Guidelines for a psychopathy treatment program*. Toronto, ON: Multi-Health Systems.

Wong, S., Olver, M.E., Nicholaichuk, T.P., and Gordon, A. 2003. *The Violence Risk Scale – Sexual Offender version VRS–SO*. Saskatoon, SK: Regional Psychiatric Centre and University of Saskatchewan.

Wooldredge, J.D. 1988. "Differentiating the effects of juvenile court sentences on eliminating recidivism." *Journal of Research in Crime and Delinquency*. 25:264–300.

Wootton, J.M., Frick, P.J., Shelton, K.K. and Silverthorn, P. 1997. "Ineffective parenting and childhood conduct problems: The moderating role of callous-unemotional traits." *Journal of Consulting and Clinical Psychology*. 65:301–308.

Wootton, B. 1962. "A social scientist's approach to maternal deprivation." In *Deprivation of maternal care: A reassessment of its effects*. pp. 255–266. Geneva: World Health Organization, Public Health Papers, No. 14.

World Health Organization. 2005. *WHO multi-site study on women's health and domestic violence against women*. Geneva: World Health Organization

Wright, R.A. and Miller, J.M. 1998. "Taboo until today? The coverage of biological arguments in criminology textbooks, 1961–1970 and 1987–1996." *Journal of Criminal Justice*. 26:1–19.

Yukon Department of Justice. 2008. "Community and Correctional Services." Retrieved April 2, 2009 (www.justice.gov.yk.ca/prog/cor/index.html).

Xantidis, L. and McCabe, M.P. 2000. "Personality characteristics of male clients of female commercial sex workers in Australia." *Archives of Sexual Behavior.* 29:165–176.

Yaffe, M. 2004. *Development and validation of a suspicion index for elder abuse for physicians' use: Results and implications.* Invited presentation to the Ageing and Life Course unit of World Health Organization, Montreal, Quebec.

Yessine, A. and Kroner, D.G. 2004. "Altering Antisocial Attitudes among Federal Male Offenders on Release: A Preliminary Analysis of the Counter-Point Community Program." Research Report No. R-152. Ottawa, ON: Correctional Service of Canada (www.csc-scc.gc.ca/text/rsrch/reports/r152/r152_e.pdf).

Yllo, K. and Straus, M.A. 1990. "Patriarchy and violence against wives: The impact of structural and normative factors." In M. Straus and R. Gelles, eds. *Physical violence in American families.* pp. 383–399. New Brunswick, JH: Transaction.

York, P. 1995. *The Aboriginal offender: A comparison between Aboriginals and non-Aboriginal offenders.* Ottawa, ON: Solicitor General of Canada.

Young, N.K., Boles, S.M., and Otero, C. 2007. "Parental substance use disorders and child maltreatment: Overlap, gaps, and opportunities." *Child Maltreatment.* 12:137–149.

Zehr, H. 1999. "Restoring Justice." In Lisa Barnes Lampman, ed. *God and the victim: Theological reflections on evil, victimization, justice and forgiveness.* p. 131–159. B. Eerdmans Publishing. The poem by Martha Janssen is on p. 137–38 of this chapter.

Zerjal, T. et al. 2003. "The genetic legacy of the Mongols." *American Journal of Genetics.* 72:717–721.

Zevitz, R.G. 2006. "Sex offender community notification: Its role in recidivism and offender reintegration." *Criminal Justice Studies.* 19:193–208.

Zickefoose, S. 2008. "Boyfriend guilty of killing girlfriend's family." *Calgary Herald,* Canwest News Service. December 5, 2008. Retrieved August 2009 (www.calgaryherald.com/news/alberta/Boyfriend+guilty+killing+girlfriend+family/1037369/story.html).

Zillmann, D. 1994. "Cognition-excitation interdependencies in the escalation of anger and angry aggression." In M. Potegal and J. Knutson, eds. *The dynamics of aggression: Biological and social processes in dyads and groups.* p. 33–41. Hillsdale, NJ: Erlbaum.

Zimmerman, C., Hossain, M., Un, K., Gajdadziev, V., Guzun, M., Tchomarova, M., Ciarrocchi, R.A., Johansson, A., Kefurtova, A., Scodanibbio, S., Motus, M., Roche, B., Morison, L., and Watts, C. 2008. "The health of trafficked women: A survey of women entering posttrafficking services in Europe." *American Journal of Public Health.* 98:55–59.

Zinger, I. and Forth, A.E. 1998. "Psychopathy and Canadian criminal proceedings: The potential for human rights abuses." *Canadian Journal Criminology.* 40:237–276.

CREDITS

Text, Tables, and Figures

Chapter 1 *Page 4*: Figure 1.1, Department of Justice Canada, *The National Justice Survey: Tackling Crime and Public Confidence*. Department of Justice Canada, 2007, Figure 4, p. 14. http://justice.gc.ca/eng/pi/rs/rep-rap/2007/rr07_4/rr07_4. f. Reproduced with the permission of the Minister of Public Works and Government Services Canada, 2009; *p. 8*: Rice, M.E. & Harris, G.T. (1995). olent recidivism: Assessing predictive validity. *Journal of Consulting and inical Psychology*, 63(5): 737-748. © 1995 American Psychological ssociation. Reprinted with permission; *p. 11*: Table 1.1, Bonta, James (2007). npublished training presentation, National Parole Board of Canada. Used th permission of James Bonta; *p. 12*: Table 1.2, Andrews, D. A., & Bonta, J. 006). *The psychology of criminal conduct* (4th ed.), Cincinnati, OH: Anderson, 64. Reprinted from *The Psychology of Criminal Conduct*, Fourth Edition, with rmission. Copyright 2006 Matthew Bender & Company, Inc., a member of e LexisNexis Group. All rights reserved; *p. 13*: Table 1.3, Adapted from ndrews, D.A., & Bonta, J. (2006). *The psychology of criminal conduct* (4th ed.), ncinnati, OH: Anderson (Table 2.5, p. 66). Reprinted from *The Psychology of riminal Conduct*, Fourth Edition, with permission. Copyright 2006 Matthew nder & Company, Inc., a member of the LexisNexis Group. All rights served; *p. 17*: Table 1.6, Corrections and Conditional Release Statistical verview, Annual Report, 2008. www.publicsafety.gc.ca/res/cor/rep/_fl/2008- -ccrso-eng.pdf; Report on Planning and Priorities, Correctional Service of anada, 2008-09; *p. 18*: Figure 1.3, Data is based on Statistics Canada, Uniform ime Reporting Survey, Canadian Centre for Justice Statistics, Statistics anada. Retrieved on Infrastructure Canada, Public Safety Canada Portfolio orrections Statistics, *Corrections and Conditional Release Statistical Overview*, 08. Cat. No. PS1-3/2008E, Fig. A1, www.publicsafety.gc.ca/res/ r/rep/_fl/2008-04-ccrso-eng.pdf. Reproduced with the permission of the inister of Public Works and Government Services Canada, 2009; *p. 19*: ble 1.7, Data is based on Statistics Canada, Uniform Crime Reporting Survey, nadian Centre for Justice Statistics, Statistics Canada. Retrieved on frastructure Canada, Public Safety Canada Portfolio Corrections Statistics, rrections and Conditional Release Statistical Overview, 2008. Cat. No. PS1- 008E, Fig. A5 and A11, www.publicsafety.gc.ca/res/cor/rep/_fl/2008-04- rso-eng.pdf. Reproduced with the permission of the Minister of Public Works d Government Services Canada, 2009; *p. 20*: Figure 1.4, Statistics Canada, verall Crime Severity Index and traditional crime rate, Canada, 1998 to 07," in Statistics Canada publication, *Measuring Crime in Canada: Introducing Crime Severity Index and Improvements to the Uniform Crime Reporting Survey*, 09, Cat. No. 85-004-X, Chart 1.1, p. 14. http://statcan.gc.ca/pub/85-004-x/ 004-x2009001-eng.pdf; *p. 21*: Table 1.8, Department of Justice Canada, *The tional Justice Survey: Tackling Crime and Public Confidence*. Department of stice Canada, 2007, Table 3, p. 13. http://canada.justice.gc.ca/eng/pi/rs/rep- /2007/rr07_4/rr07_4.pdf. Reproduced with the permission of the Minister of blic Works and Government Services Canada, 2009; *p. 22*: Figure 1.5, partment of Justice Canada, *The National Justice Survey: Tackling Crime and blic Confidence*. Department of Justice Canada, 2007, Figure 2, p. 11. http:// nada.justice.gc.ca/eng/pi/rs/rep-rap/2007/rr07_4/rr07_4.pdf. Reproduced with e permission of the Minister of Public Works and Government Services nada, 2009; *p. 24*: Figure 1.6, Data is based on Statistics Canada, Uniform ime Reporting Survey, Canadian Centre for Justice Statistics, Statistics nada. Retrieved on Infrastructure Canada, Public Safety Canada Portfolio rrections Statistics, *Corrections and Conditional Release Statistical Overview*, 08. Cat. No. PS1-3/2008E, Fig. A9, www.publicsafety.gc.ca/res/cor/rep/_fl/ 08-04-ccrso-eng.pdf. Reproduced with the permission of the Minister of blic Works and Government Services Canada, 2009; *p. 25*: Figure 1.7, Data based on Statistics Canada, Uniform Crime Reporting Survey, Canadian ntre for Justice Statistics, Statistics Canada. Retrieved on Infrastructure

Canada, Public Safety Canada Portfolio Corrections Statistics, *Corrections and Conditional Release Statistical Overview*, 2008. Cat. No. PS1-3/2008E, Fig. A2, www.publicsafety.gc.ca/res/cor/rep/_fl/2008-04-ccrso-eng.pdf. Reproduced with the permission of the Minister of Public Works and Government Services Canada, 2009; *p. 26*: Figure 1.8, *World Prison Population List*, 8th edition. International Centre for Prison Studies, 2008, www.prisonstudies.org.

Chapter 2 *Page 38*: Figure 2.1, Adapted from Caspi, A., et al. (2002). Role of genotype in the cycle of violence in maltreated children. Science, 297(2): 851-854, Figure 2, p. 852. Reprinted with permission from AAAS; *p. 45*: Table 2.1, Adapted from Lorber, M.F. (2004). "Psychophysiology of aggression, psychopathy, and conduct problems: A meta-analysis." *Psychological Bulletin*, 130: 531-552.

Chapter 3 *Page 70–71*: Excerpt from pp. 9-10 from *The Murdering Mind* by David Abrahamsen, M.D. Copyright © 1973 by David Abrahamsen, M.D. Reprinted by permission of HarperCollins Publishers; *p. 86–87*: Excerpt from Raine, A. (1997). Crime, conditioning, and arousal. In Nyborg, H. (Ed), *The Scientific Study of Human Nature: Tribute to Hans J. Eysenck*, Oxford, UK: Elsevier, pp. 123-124. Copyright 1997 by Emerald Group Publishing Limited. Reproduced with permission of Emerald Group Publishing Limited via Copyright Clearance Center; *p. 88*: Figure 3.1, Raine, A., & Venables, P.H. (1981). Classical conditioning and socialization - A biosocial interaction? *Personality and Individual Differences*, 2: 273-283, Figure 1, p. 280, with permission from Elsevier. Copyright © 1981 Published by Elsevier Science Ltd. All rights reserved; *p. 97*: Excerpt from Akers, R. L., Krohn, M. D., Lanza-Kaduce, L., & Radosevich, M. (1979). Social learning and deviant behavior: A specific test of a general theory. *American Sociological Review*, 44(4) (August 1979): 636-655, p. 638. Used with permission of the American Sociological Association.

Chapter 4 *Page 108*: Table 4.1, Andrews, D. A., & Bonta, J. (2006). *The psychology of criminal conduct* (4th ed.), Cincinnati, OH: Anderson, p. 373. Reprinted from *The Psychology of Criminal Conduct*, Fourth Edition, with permission. Copyright 2006 Matthew Bender & Company, Inc., a member of the LexisNexis Group. All rights reserved; *p. 111*: Table 4.2, Gendreau, P., Goggin, C., & Cullen, F. (1999). "The Effects of Prison Sentences on Recidivism." User Report: 1999-3, p. 40. Ottawa, ON: Solicitor General Canada; *p. 112*: Table 4.3, Gendreau, P., Goggin, C., Cullen, F., Andrews, D., *Compendium 2000 on Effective Correctional Programming*, Correctional Service of Canada, 2001, Table 31. Reproduced with the permission of the Minister of Public Works and Government Services Canada, 2009; *p. 114*: Table 4.4, © Boe, R., "Research Brief: Comparing Crime and Imprisonment Trends in the United States, England, and Canada from 1981-2001," Correctional Service of Canada, 2004, Table 2. www.csc-scc.gc.ca/text/rsrch/ briefs/b29/b29_e.pdf. Reproduced with the permission of the Minister of Public Works and Government Services Canada, 2009; *p. 114*: Figure 4.1, © Boe, R., "Research Brief: Comparing Crime and Imprisonment Trends in the United States, England, and Canada from 1981-2001," Correctional Service of Canada, 2004, Figure 1. www.csc-scc.gc.ca/text/rsrch/briefs/b29/b29_e.pdf. Reproduced with the permission of the Minister of Public Works and Government Services Canada, 2009; *p. 115*: *Silent Scream* by Martha Janssen copyright © 1983 Fortress Press. Reproduced by special permission of Augsburg Fortress Publishers; *p. 119*: Table 4.5, Latimer, J., Dowden, C., & Muise, D. (2005). The effectiveness of restorative justice practices: A meta analysis. *The Prison Journal*, 85: 127-144. Copyright © 2005 Sage Publications. Reprinted by permission of Sage Publications; *p. 122*: Figure 4.2, Adapted from Bonta, J., Wallace-Capretta, S., & Rooney, J. (2000).

A quasi-experimental evaluation of an intensive rehabilitation supervision program. *Criminal Justice and Behavior*, 27: 312-329, Table 2, p. 324. Copyright © 2000, International Association for Correctional and Forensic Psychology. Reprinted by permission of Sage Publications; *p. 123*: Table 4.6, Adapted from Andrews, D. A., & Bonta, J. (2006). *The psychology of criminal conduct* (4th ed.), Cincinnati, OH: Anderson, Table 13.2, p. 451. Reprinted from *The Psychology of Criminal Conduct*, Fourth Edition, with permission. Copyright 2006 Matthew Bender & Company, Inc., a member of the LexisNexis Group. All rights reserved; *p. 123*: Figure 4.3, Gendreau, French, and Taylor (2002). *What Works (What Doesn't Work)* Revised 2002. Invited Submission to the International Community Corrections Association Monograph Series Project. Used with permission of Dr. Paul Gendreau; *p. 124*: Figure 4.4, Andrews, D.A. 1994. *An Overview of Treatment Effectiveness. Research and Clinical Principles*, Department of Psychology, Carleton University. Used with permission of Dr. Paul Gendreau; *p. 124*: Figure 4.5, Andrews, D. A., & Bonta, J. (2006). *The psychology of criminal conduct* (4th ed.), Cincinnati, OH: Anderson, Figure 2.2 p. 73. Reprinted from *The Psychology of Criminal Conduct*, Fourth Edition, with permission. Copyright 2006 Matthew Bender & Company, Inc., a member of the LexisNexis Group. All rights reserved; *p. 132*: Table 4.7, © *Commissioner's Directive 705-7: Security Classification and Penitentiary Placement*, Correctional Service of Canada website, 2009. www.csc-scc.gc.ca/text/plcy/cdshtm/705-7-cd-eng.shtml. Reproduced with the permission of the Minister of Public Works and Government Services Canada, 2009; *p. 133*: Table 4.8, © Luciani, F., *Initiating Safe Reintegration: A Decade of Custodial Rating Scale Results*, Correctional Service of Canada, 2001, Table 2. www.csc-scc.gc.ca/text/pblct/forum/e131/131c_e.pdf. Reproduced with the permission of the Minister of Public Works and Government Services Canada, 2009; *p. 136*: Figure 4.6, Unpublished figure from teaching notes, Carleton University, 2009. Used with permission of Caleb Lloyd.

Chapter 5 *Page 146*: Table 5.2, Adapted from Statistics Canada, Canadian Centre for Justice Statistics, "Youth Court Statistics, 2006/2007," *Juristat*, Cat. No. 85-002-XIE, no. 4, Table 1, p. 11. Source: Youth Court Survey, 2008. www.statcan.ca/pub/85-002-x/85-002-x2008004-eng.pdf; *p. 146*: Figure 5.1, Statistics Canada, *The Daily*, May 16, 2008. Retrieved Dec. 8, 2008 from www.statcan.gc.ca/daily-quotidien/080516/dq080516a-eng.htm; *p. 154*: Table 5.3, Estimated Number of Youth Gangs and Youth Gang Members, Nationally and by Province, 2002, in "Youth Gangs in Canada: What Do We Know" (2007), Table 2, p. 4, found at www.publicsafety.gc.ca/prg/cp/bldngevd/_fl/2007-YG-1_e.pdf. Reproduced with the permission of the Minister of Public Works and Government Services, 2009; *p. 159*: Table 5.4, Adapted with kind permission from Springer Science+Business Media from Fagan, A.A., Lee Van Horn, M., Hawkins, J.D., & Arthur, M.W. (2007). Gender similarities and differences in the association between risk and protective factors and self-reported serious delinquency. *Prevention Science*, 8: 115-124, Table 3, p. 120. Copyright © 2007, Springer Netherlands.

Chapter 6 *Page 187*: Table 6.2, "Potential Drug Proceeds Net at Street Level for 2006," from RCMP Criminal Intelligence, *Drug Situation Report 2006*, Table 1, p. 27. © (2006) Her Majesty the Queen in right of Canada as represented by the Royal Canadian Mounted Police (RCMP). Reprinted with permission of the RCMP; *p. 192*: Table 6.3, Criminal Intelligence Service Canada, *Organized Crime and Domestic Trafficking in Persons in Canada*, 2008, Appendix 1.1 "Profit Table." www.cisc.gc.ca/products/services/domestic_trafficking_persons/persons_e.html. Reproduced with the permission of the Minister of Public Works and Government Services Canada, 2009; *p. 196*: Figure 6.1, © Substance Abuse Program: Treatment Model Diagram, Correctional Service of Canada website, 2009. www.csc-scc.gc.ca/text/prgrm/sub-eng.shtml. Reproduced with the permission of the Minister of Public Works and Government Services Canada, 2009.

Chapter 7 *Page 204*: Figure 7.1, Statistics Canada, Canadian Centre for Justice Statistics (2008), "Crime Statistics in Canada, 2007," *Juristat*, Cat. no. 85-002-X, vol. 28, no. 7, Chart 1 (right), p. 3. Source: Uniform Crime Reporting Survey. www.statcan.gc.ca/pub/85-002-x/85-002-x2008007-eng.pdf; *p. 205*: Figure 7.2, Statistics Canada, Canadian Centre for Justice

Statistics (2008), "Crime Statistics in Canada, 2007," *Juristat*, Cat. no. 85-002-X, vol. 28, no. 7, Chart 5, p. 5. Source: Uniform Crime Reporting Survey. www.statcan.gc.ca/pub/85-002-x/85-002-x2008007-eng.pdf; *p. 205*: Figure 7.3, Statistics Canada, Canadian Centre for Justice Statistics (2008), "Crime Statistics in Canada, 2007," *Juristat*, Cat. no. 85-002-X, vol. 28, no. 7, Chart 11 (right), p. 8. Source: Uniform Crime Reporting Survey. www.statcan.ca/pub/85-002-x/85-002-x2008007-eng.pdf; *p. 206*: Figure 7.4, Statistics Canada, Canadian Centre for Justice Statistics (2005), "Criminal Victimization in Canada, 2004," *Juristat*, Cat. no. 85-002-XPE, vol. 25, no. 7, Figure 1, p. 4. Source: General Social Survey, 1993, 1999 and 2004. www.statcan.gc.ca/pub/85-002-x/85-002-x2005007-eng.pdf; *p. 208*: Figure 7.5, Statistics Canada, Canadian Centre for Justice Statistics (2005), "Criminal Victimization in Canada, 2004," *Juristat*, Cat. no. 85-002-XPE, vol. 25, no. 7, Figure 8, p. 12. Source: General Social Survey, 1993, 1999 and 2004. www.statcan.gc.ca/pub/85-002-x/85-002-x2005007-eng.pdf; *p. 211*: Figure 7.6, Anderson, C.A., & Bushman, B.J., Human aggression. *Annual Review Psychology*, 53 (February): 27-51, Figure 2, p. 34. Copyright 2002 by Annual Reviews Inc. Reproduced with permission of Annual Reviews Inc. via Copyright Clearance Center; *p. 216*: Table 7.1, Adapted from Quinsey, V. L., Harris, G.T., Rice, M.E., & Cormier, C.A. (2006), Exhibit 8.1, p. 161. *Violent offenders: Appraising and managing risk.* © 2006 American Psychological Association. Adapted with permission; *p. 216*: Figure 7.7, Adapted from Harris, G.T., Rice, M.E., & Quinsey, V.L. (1993). "Violent recidivism of mentally disordered offenders: The development of a statistical prediction instrument." *Criminal Justice and Behavior*, 20: 315-335, Figure 1, p. 327. Copyright © 1993, International Association for Correctional and Forensic Psychology. Reprinted by permission of Sage Publications; *p. 221*: Table 7.2, Adapted from Loza, W., Dhaliwal, G., Kroner, D.G., & Loza-Fanous, A. (2000). "Reliability, construct, and concurrent validities of the Self-Appraisal Questionnaire: A tool for assessing violent and nonviolent recidivism." *Criminal Justice and Behavior*, 27: 356-374, Table 2, p. 366. Copyright © 2000, International Association for Correctional and Forensic Psychology. Reprinted by permission of Sage Publications; *p. 221*: Table 7.3, Adapted from Campbell, M.A., French, S., & Gendreau, P. (2009). "The prediction of violence in adult offenders: A meta-analytic comparison of instruments and methods of assessment." *Criminal Justice and Behavior*, 567-590, p. 575. Copyright © 2009, International Association for Correctional and Forensic Psychology. Reprinted by permission of Sage Publications; *p. 226*: Figure 7.8, Jolliffe, D., & Farrington, D.P. (2007). *A systematic review of the national and international evidence on the effectiveness of interventions with* violent offenders. Ministry of Justice Research Series 16/07, Figure 2, p. 14. www.justice.gov.uk/publications/docs/review-evidence-violent.pdf. Reproduced under the terms of the Click-Use Licence; *p. 226*: Table 7.5, Adapted from Jolliffe, D., & Farrington, D.P. (2007). *A systematic review of the national and international evidence on the effectiveness of interventions with violent offenders.* Ministry of Justice Research Series 16/07, Tables 2 and 3, pp. 20-21. www.justice.gov.uk/publications/docs/review-evidence-violent.pdf. Reproduced under the terms of the Click-Use Licence; *p. 228*: Figure 7.9, Statistics Canada, Canadian Centre for Justice Statistics (2008), "Homicide in Canada, 2007," *Juristat*, Cat. no. 85-002-X, vol. 28, no. 8, Chart 1, p. 6, www.statcan.gc.ca/pub/85-002-x/2008009/article/10671-eng.pdf, Interpol Ottawa, and national statistical office websites; *p. 229*: Figure 7.10, Statistics Canada, Canadian Centre for Justice Statistics (2008), "Homicide in Canada, 2007," *Juristat*, Cat. no. 85-002-X, vol. 28, no. 8, Chart 2, p. 7. Source: Homicide Survey. www.statcan.gc.ca/pub/85-002-x/2008009/article/10671-eng.pdf; *p. 231*: Figure 7.11, Statistics Canada, Canadian Centre for Justice Statistics (2008), "Homicide in Canada, 2007," *Juristat*, Cat. no. 85-002-X, vol. 28, no. 8, Chart 6, p. 11. Source: Homicide Survey. www.statcan.gc.ca/pub/85-002-x/2008009/article/10671-eng.pdf; *235*: Excerpt from *Serial Murder*, 2nd edition (paper) by Holmes, R.M., Holmes, S.T., pp. 43-44. Copyright 1998 by Sage Publications Inc. Books. Reproduced with permission of Sage Publications Inc. Books via Copyright Clearance Center.

Chapter 8 *Page 241*: Figure 8.1, Dahlberg, L.L., and Krug, E.G. (2002). Violence—A global public health problem. In E. Krug et al. (Eds.), *World report on violence and health*. Geneva, Switzerland: World Health ganization, p. 12. http://who.int/violence_injury_prevention/violence/ rld_report/en/full_en.pdf, Accessed October 15, 2009. Used with permis- n; *p. 244*: Table 8.2, Adapted from Chan, K.L., Straus, M.A., Brownridge, A., Tiwari, A., & Leung, W.C. (2008). "Prevalence of dating partner vio- ce and suicidal ideation among male and female university students rldwide." *Journal of Midwifery & Women's Health*, 53: 529-537, Tables 2 and pp. 532-533. Copyright © 2008 American College of Nurse-Midwives blished by Elsevier Inc., with permission from Elsevier; *p. 258*: Table 8.4, lapted from "The average weighted accuracy (d) of individual risk meas- es for the prediction of spousal assault recidivism," in Hanson, K.R., elmus, L., & Bourgon, G. (2007). *The validity of risk assessments for intimate rtner violence: A meta-analysis*. Public Safety Canada (2007-07), Table 2, . 20-21, found at: www.publicsafety.gc.ca/res/cor/rep/_fl/vra_ipv_200707_ df. Reproduced with the permission of the Minister of Public Works and vernment Services, 2009; *p. 261*: Table 8.5, Adapted from Trocmé, N. al. (2005). *Canadian Incidence Study of Reported Child Abuse and Neglect— 03: Major Findings*, Table 9-3, p. 96. www.phac-aspc.gc.ca/cm-vee/ a-ecve/pdf/childabuse_final_e.pdf. © Public Health Agency of Canada 09. Adapted and reproduced with the permission of the Minister of Public orks and Government Services Canada, 2009; *p. 263*: Table 8.6, Adapted m Trocmé, N. et al. (2005). *Canadian Incidence Study of Reported Child use and Neglect—2003: Major Findings*, Table 4-4(a), p. 52. www.phac- c.gc.ca/cm-vee/csca-ecve/pdf/childabuse_final_e.pdf. © Public Health ency of Canada 2009. Adapted and reproduced with the permission of the nister of Public Works and Government Services Canada, 2009; *p. 274*: le 8.8, Adapted from Perel-Levin, S. (2008). *Discussing screening for elder use at primary health care level*. World Health Organization, Geneva, p. 16. w.who.int/ageing/publications/Discussing_Elder_Abuseweb.pdf, cessed October 15, 2009. Used with permission.

apter 9 *Page 284*: Figure 9.1, Statistics Canada, Canadian Centre for tice Statistics Profile Series (2008), "Sexual Assault in Canada, 2004 and 07" Cat. no. 85F0033M, no. 19, Chart 1, p. 9. Source: Uniform Crime porting Survey. www.statcan.gc.ca/pub/85f0033m/85f0033m2008019-eng. ; *p. 288*: Figure 9.2, Malamuth, N.M. (2003). "Criminal and noncriminal ual aggressors: Integrating psychopathy in a hierarchical-mediational con- ence model." In R.A. Prentky, E.S. Janus, & M.C. Seto (Eds.), *Annals of New York Academy of Sciences*, vol. 989 (June). "Sexually coercive behav- Understanding and management," pp. 33-58, Figure 1, p. 40. Used with mission of Wiley-Blackwell Publishers; *p. 291*: Figure 9.3, Seto, M.C. 08). *Pedophilia and sexual offending against children: Theory, assessment, and rvention*, p. 95. © 2008 American Psychological Association. Reprinted h permission; *p. 293*: Figure 9.4, Knight, R.A., Carter, D.L., & Prentky, A. (1989). "A system for the classification of child molesters: Reliability application." *Journal of Interpersonal Violence*, 4: 3-23, p. 8. Copyright © 39, Sage Publications. Reprinted by permission of Sage Publications; 294: Figure 9.5, © 2010 Civic Research Institute. Adapted with permis- n from Figure 17.1 in Knight, R. (2010) "Typologies for rapists: The eration of a new structural model." In A. Schlank (Ed.), *The sexual pred- r* (vol. IV). Kingston, NJ: Civic Research Institute; *p. 295*: Figure 9.6, 010 Civic Research Institute. Adapted with permission from Figure 17.6 Knight, R. (2010) "Typologies for rapists: The generation of a new struc- al model." In A. Schlank (Ed.), *The sexual predator* (vol. IV). Kingston, Civic Research Institute; *p. 300*: Figure 9.7, Lalumière, M.L., Quinsey, ., Harris, G.T., Rice, M.E., & Tautrimas, C. (2003). "Are rapists differen- ly aroused by coercive sex in phallometric assessments?" *Annals of the New k Academy of Sciences*, Volume 989, Issue June 2003: 211-224, Figure 2, 218. Used with permission of Wiley-Blackwell Publishers; *p. 305*: le 9.1, "The predictive accuracy of the main categories of risk factors." In nson, R.K., & Morton-Bourgon, K.E. (2004). *Predictors of sexual recidi- m: An updated meta-analysis*, Table 1, p. 9, www.publicsafety.gc.ca/res/cor/ _fl/2004-02-pred-se-eng.pdf. Reproduced with the permission of the nister of Public Works and Government Services Canada, 2009.

apter 10 *Page 329*: Table 10.1, Adapted from Butler, T.G., Andrews, G., nut, S., Sakashita, C., Smith, N., and Basson, J. (2006). "Mental disorders Australian prisoners: A comparison with a community sample." *Australian*

and New Zealand Journal of Psychiatry, 40: 272-276, Table 2, p. 275. Used with permission of Wiley-Blackwell Publishers; *p. 338*: Table 10.4, Department of Justice Canada, "Report: The Review Board Systems in Canada: An Overview of Results from the Mentally Disordered Accused Data Collection Study." Department of Justice Canada, 2006, (Table 4, p. 14, Table 6, p. 16, Table 8, p. 17, and Table 10, p. 20). http://canada.justice.gc.ca/eng/pi/rs/rep- rap/2006/rr06_1/rr06_1.pdf. Reproduced with the permission of the Minister of Public Works and Government Services Canada, 2009; *p. 341*: Table 10.5, Hodgins, S., Mednick, S. A., Brennan, P., Schulsinger, F. & Engberg, M. (1996). "Mental disorder and crime: Evidence from a Danish birth cohort." *Archives of General Psychiatry*, 53: 489-96, Table 1, p. 491, and Table 4, p. 494. Used with permission of the American Medical Association; *p. 356*: Table 10.6, Adapted from Guy, L. S., Edens, J. F., Anthony, C., & Douglas, K. S. (2005). "Does psychopathy predict institutional misconduct among adults? A meta-analytic investigation." *Journal of Consulting and Clinical Psychology*, 73: 1056-1064, pp. 20, 22, and Edens, J.F., & Campbell, J.S. (2007). Identifying youths at risk for institutional misconduct: A meta- analytic investigation of the psychopathy checklist measures. *Psychological Services*, 4: 13-27, p. 1060. Both © American Psychological Association. Adapted with permission; *p. 358*: Table 10.8, Adapted from Boccaccini, M.T., Murrie, D.C., Clark, J.W., & Cornell, D.G. (2008). "Describing, diag- nosing, and naming psychopathy: How do youth psychopathy labels influ- ence jurors?" *Behavioral Sciences & the Law*, 26 (4):487-510, p. 489. Used with permission of Wiley-Blackwell Publishers; *p. 360*: Figure 10.2, Adapted from Kochanska, G. (1993). "Toward a synthesis of prenatal socialization of child temperament in early development of conscience." *Child Development*, 64, 325-347, pp. 328-329. © 1993 American Psychological Association. Adapted with permission; *p. 363*: Table 10.10, Adapted from Raine, A. (2008). "From genes to brain to antisocial behaviour." *Current Directions in Psychological Science*, 17(5), 323-328, p. 326, and Weber, S., Habel, U., Amunts, K., & Schneider, F. (2008). "Structural brain abnormalities in psychopaths—A review." *Behavioral Sciences & the Law*, 26, 7-28, p. 24. Used with permission of Wiley-Blackwell Publishers.

Chapter 11 *Page 376*: Figure 11.1, Adapted from Statistics Canada, Canadian Centre for Justice Statistics (2008), "Female Offenders in Canada," *Juristat*, Cat. No. 85-002-XIE, vol. 28, no. 1, Chart 5 (left), p. 7, www.statcan.gc.ca/pub/ 85-002-x/85-002-x2008001-eng.pdf; *p. 377*: Figure 11.2, Adapted from Statistics Canada, Canadian Centre for Justice Statistics (2008), "Female Offenders in Canada," *Juristat*, Cat. No. 85-002-XIE, vol. 28, no. 1, Chart 5 (right), p. 7, www.statcan.gc.ca/pub/85-002-x/85-002-x2008001-eng.pdf; *p. 391*: Table 11.2, Adapted from Blanchette, D.K., & Taylor, K.N. (2007). "Development and field test of a gender-informed security reclassification scale for female offenders." *Criminal Justice and Behaviour*, 34, 362-379, p. 366. Copyright © 2007, International Association for Correctional and Forensic Psychology. Reprinted by permission of Sage Publications; *pp. 393–394*: Box 11.5, Blanchette, K.D., & Brown, S.L. (2006). *The assessment and treatment of women offenders: An integrative perspective*. Wiley Series in Forensic Clinical Psychology. Chichester: John Wiley and Sons. Used with permission of Wiley- Blackwell Publishers; *p. 398*: Table 11.3, Dowden, C., & Andrews, D.A. (1999). "What works for female offenders: A meta-analytic review." *Crime and Delinquency*, 45, 438-452, p. 455. Copyright © 1999, Sage Publications. Reprinted by permission of Sage Publications.

Chapter 12 *Page 404*: Figure 12.1, © Trevethan, S., Moore, J.P., & Rastin, C., "FORUM—A Profile of Aboriginal Offenders in Federal Facilities and Serving Time in the Community," Correctional Service of Canada, 2002, (Figure 1). www.csc-scc.gc.ca/text/pblct/forum/e143/e143f-eng.shtml. Reproduced with the permission of the Minister of Public Works and Government Services Canada, 2009; *p. 408*: Table 12.1, Corinne Mount Pleasant-Jette, "Creating a Climate of Confidence: Providing Services Within Aboriginal Communities," in *National Round Table on Economic Issues and Resources* (Royal Commission on Aboriginal Issues: Ottawa, April 27–29, 1993) at 11. www.ccja-acjp.ca/ en/abori4.html. Reproduced with the permission of the Minister of Public Works and Government Services Canada, 2009; *p. 413*: Figure 12.2, © Trevethan, S., Auger, S., Moore, J.P., MacDonald, M., Sinclair, J., *The Effect of Family Disruption on Aboriginal and Non-Aboriginal* Inmates, Correctional

Service of Canada, 2001, Figure 3, p. 25. http://198.103.98.138/text/rsrch/reports/r113/r113_e.pdf. Reproduced with the permission of the Minister of Public Works and Government Services Canada, 2009; *p. 418*: Table 12.2, Rugge, T. (2006). "Risk assessment of male Aboriginal offenders: A 2006 perspective" (User Report No. 2006-01), Table 3, p. 19, found at: http://dsp-psd.pwgsc.gc.ca/Collection/PS3-1-2006-1E.pdf. Reproduced with the permission of the Minister of Public Works and Government Services, 2009; *p. 419*: Table 12.3, © Blanchette, K., Verbrugge, P., & Wichmann, C.,*The Custody Rating Scale, Initial Security Placement, and Women Offenders*, Correctional Service of Canada, 2002, Tables 1, 2, 9. www.csc-scc.gc.ca/text/rsrch/reports/r127/r127_e. pdf, Reproduced with the permission of the Minister of Public Works and Government Services Canada, 2009; *p. 423*: Table 12.5, Bonta, J., Rugge, T., & Dauvergne, M. (2003). "The reconviction rate of federal offenders" (User Report No. 2003-02), Table 6. p. 13, found at www.publicsafety.gc.ca/res/cor/rep/_fl/2003-02-rec-rte-eng.pdf. Reproduced with the permission of the Minister of Public Works and Government Services, 2009; *p. 425*: Figure 12.3, © Trevethan, S., Moore, J.P., Rastin, C., "FORUM—A Profile of Aboriginal Offenders in Federal Facilities and Serving Time in the Community," Correctional Service of Canada, 2002, Figure 2. www.csc-scc.gc.ca/text/pblct/forum/e143/e143f-eng.shtml. Reproduced with the permission of the Minister of Public Works and Government Services Canada, 2009; *p. 430*: Table 12.6, © Trevethan, S., Moore, J.P., & Allegri, N., "The 'In Search of Your Warrior' Program for Aboriginal Offenders: A Preliminary Evaluation," Correctional Service of Canada, 2005, Table 9. www.csc-scc.gc.ca/text/rsrch/reports/r172/r172-eng.shtml. Reproduced with the permission of the Minister of Public Works and Government Services Canada, 2009.

Appendix *Page 444*: Correctional Service of Canada, 1994. "Psychological Services." Commissioner's Directive #840. www.csc-scc.gc.ca/text/plcy/cdshtm/840-cde-eng.shtml. Reproduced with the permission of the Minister of Public Works and Government Services Canada, 2010; *p. 449*: Table A.2, Adapted from Gardner, Phil (2007). "Moving up or moving out of the company? Factors that influence the promoting or firing of new college hires." *Research Brief* 1-2007, p. 6. www.ceri.msu.edu/publications/pdf/brief1-07 pdf. Adapted with permission of Michigan State University Collegiate Employment Research Institute; *p. 450*, Table A.3, Helmus, L. (2008). "Advice for finding a thesis supervisor: What professors have to say." *Crime Scene*, 15(1), pp. 38-40. http://cpa.ca/cpasite/userfiles/Documents/Criminal%20Justice/Crime%20Scene%202008-04.pdf. Adapted with permission of Leslie Helmus, Carleton University; *p. 452*: © Oliver, C.R., *Tools for Working Through Ethical Dilemmas*, Correctional Service of Canada, 2008, www.csc-scc.gc.ca/te? pblct/lt-en/2008/32-2/8-eng.shtml. Reproduced with the permission of t? Minister of Public Works and Government Services Canada, 2010.

Photographs and Cartoons

Chapter 2 *Page 32* © Mary Evans Picture Library/Alamy; *p. 41* © Dorli? Kindersley; *p. 47* © Dorling Kindersley; *p. 50* The Canadian Press (Je? Tavin/Everett Collection); *p. 55* Courtesy of Dr. Martin Lalumière; *p. 61* Jim Sizemore, www.Cartoonstock.com; *p. 62* Pearson Learning Photo Stud? **Chapter 3** *Page 78* Steve Agan Photography; *p. 80* Dennis the Menace? North America Syndicate; *p. 84* © Hagen, www.Cartoonstock.com; *p. ?* Courtesy of Ron Akers; *p. 95* © Creatas Images/Jupiter Images; *p. ?* Courtesy of Dr. Don Andrews.**Chapter 4** *Page 113* © 2005 Bob Englehar? The Hartford Courant/Cagle.com; *p. 128* Courtesy of Dr. Paul Gendrea? **Chapter 5** *Page 150* Courtesy of Dr. Marlene Moretti; *p. 157* © Pixlar? Jupiter Images; *p. 161* Steve Skjold/Getstock.com. **Chapter 6** *Page 1?* Angela Hampton/Alamy/Getstock.com; *p. 187* © iStockphoto; *p. ?* Courtesy of John Weekes. **Chapter 7** *Page 213* Courtesy of Dr. Vern? Quinsey; *p. 232* The Canadian Press (La Voix de l'Est - Alain Dion); *p. 2?* Andy Clark/Reuters/Landov. **Chapter 8** *Page 249* Courtesy of Dr. Don? Dutton; *p. 262* Department of Justice Canada Publication: "Abuse is wro? www.phac-aspc.gc.ca/ncfv-cnivf/pdfs/fem-abus-wrg-eng.pdf. Department? Justice Canada, 2009. Reproduced with the permission of the Minister? Public Works and Government Services Canada, 2009; *p. 271* BananaStock/Thinkstock **Chapter 9** *Page 304* The Canadian Press (Toror? Star/John Mahler); *p. 309* Courtesy of R. Karl Hanson, Ph.D.; *p. 3?* Courtesy of the Rockwood Psychological Services. **Chapter 10** *Page 3?* Courtesy of Dr. Sheilagh Hodgins; *p. 345* The Canadian Press/Richard Lan? **Chapter 11** *Page 373* The Canadian Press (Adrian Wyld); *p. 379* Ceza? Gesikowski/Correctional Services Canada; *p. 395* The Canadian Pr? (Kingston Whig-Standard/Ian MacAlpine. **Chapter 12** *Page 409* Library a? Archives Canada/PA-042133; *p. 410* The Canadian Press (Troy Fleec? *p. 414* Richard Marjan/The StarPhoenix; *p. 422* Courtesy of the Natio? Aboriginal Achievement Foundation, www.naaf.ca; *p. 426* Gunter Ma? Alamy/Getstock.com; *p. 428* © Correctional Service Canada. Reproduc? with permission of the Minister of Public Works and Government Servi? Canada, 2009.

Name Index

Brewer, D.D., 153
Brews, A., 385
Brinkley, C.A., 361
Briones, G.S., 274
Broadhurst, R., 403
Brochu, S., 13–14
Broidy, L.M., 378, 380, 387
Brooker, C., 330
Broom, I., 321
Brown, G.R., 251
Brown, S.L., 13, 31, 39, 63, 129, 355, 371, 380, 383, 384, 386, 387, 390, 394n, 399
Browne, A., 284
Browne, K., 252
Browning, J.J., 247
Bruce, S., 153
Brunet, S., 414n
Bryne, M.K., 387
Brzozowski, J., 405
Buehler, J., 166
Buka, S.L., 265
Bumby, K.M., 302
Burack, C., 383
Bureind, J.W., 79
Burgess, R., 93–94
Burks, V.S., 149
Burrow, J.D., 383
Bursik, R.J., 82
Bushman, B.J., 151, 204, 208, 210
Buss, D.M., 50, 51, 62
Bussière, M.T., 305, 307, 308, 309, 314
Butcher, J.N., 152, 156, 157
Butler, T., 328
Buttell, F., 250, 251
Butters, J.E., 155
Bynam, T.S., 397
Bynum, T., 383

C

Cacioppo, J.T., 91
Cadoret, R.J., 149
Cain, C., 149
Caldwell, M., 364
Caldwell, M.F., 209, 355
Callahan, E.J., 317
Campbell, A., 63, 373
Campbell, J.S., 355
Campbell, M.A., 138, 214, 221, 221n, 383, 384–385, 387, 390
Campbell, N.A., 37, 39, 41, 43, 50, 51, 59, 63
Campbell, S.B., 152
Canter, R., 372
Cantor, J.M., 303
Cap, J., 135
Cares, A.C., 251
Carlen, P., 380
Carlisle, J.M., 85
Carlson, M., 95
Carmichael, S., 179
Carney, M., 250–251
Carrig, M.M., 5
Carson, R.C., 152, 156, 157
Carter, D.L., 292, 293n

Carter, J., 405
Caspi, A., 5, 37, 38n, 56, 148, 250, 269, 372
Cassel, E., 83, 95
Cattaneo, L.B., 253
Cauffman, E., 357
Cavell, T.A., 361
Cawsey, R., 406
Cernkovich, S.A., 372, 385
Chan, K.L., 243–244
Chan, Y.H., 349
Chanteloupe, F., 93
Chaplin, T.C., 299, 300
Chayet, E., 111
Chen, E., 274
Chesney-Lind, M., 377, 378, 380
Chiffriller, S.H., 253
Choe, J.Y., 340, 341, 346
Chong, S.A., 349
Christensen, A., 243
Cicchetti, D., 269
Clairmont, D., 410
Clark, F., 360
Claypoole, K., 341
Cleckley, H., 360, 364
Cleland, C.M., 13, 98, 351
Clements, C.B., 361
Clinard, M.B., 176
Coatsworth, J., 162
Coccaro, E.R., 43
Cohen, I.M., 424
Cohen, A.J., 152
Cohen, J., 5, 42, 224, 225
Coid, J., 330, 352, 383
Coie, J.D., 153
Coker, A.L., 254
Cole, C.M., 39
Coleman, C., 91
Coleman, G., 222
Colledge, E., 361
Collie, R.M., 224
Collins, J.M., 178
Conger, J.J., 160
Conry, J.L., 415
Conry, R.F., 415
Cormer, J.P., 167, 364
Cormier, R.B., 416
Cormier, C.A., 138, 307, 337
Corrado, R.R., 424
Cortoni, F., 228, 321
Cortoni, F.A., 429
Corvo, K., 248, 259
Cosmides, L., 51
Costa, D.M., 247
Costa, F.M., 157
Cotton, D., 344
Cournoyer, L.G., 13
Cousineau, C., 5, 383
Cousineau, M.M., 13–14
Coutts, J., 300
Couture, J., 420
Coventry, G., 166
Covington, S.S., 378, 383, 389, 393, 399
Cowden, J., 37

Cox, C.E., 264
Cox, D., 354
Cox, D.N., 139
Coy, K.C., 361
Craig, W., 50, 212, 290
Cressey, D.R., 5
Crick, N.R., 149
Crisanti, A., 341
Crowley, M., 133
Cruise, K.R., 357
Crutcher, N., 23, 428
Cullen, F, 96, 101, 222, 314, 349
Cullen, F.T., 81, 82, 98, 178, 383, 385, 387, 3?
Cumming, E., 344
Cumming, I., 344
Cummings, E.M., 152
Cunningham, A., 168
Cunningham, S.M., 268
Cupp, R., 389
Curran, P.J., 5

D

D'Amora, D.A., 314
Dahlberg, L.L., 241, 241n
Daigle, L.E., 385
Dalgleish, L., 351
Daly, K., 380
Daly, M., 51, 61, 63, 242, 373
Dandreaux, D.M., 359
Danesh, J., 328
Darwin, C.R., 50
Dauvergne, M., 204, 204n, 423
Davidson, W.S., 168
Davies, P.T., 152
Davis, R.D., 352
Dawkins, R., 53
Day, A., 134
Day, D., 167
Dean, K., 288
Dear, M.J., 344
de Ardon, E.T., 273–274
DeBurger, J., 235
DeCoster, J., 357
DeFries, J.C., 34
DeFries, J.D., 34
DeKeseredy, W.S., 243
Dekovic, M., 152
Dell, C.A., 424
DeMatteo, D., 156, 164
Denham, S., 167
Derzon, J.H., 153
Deschenes, E.P., 380
Desjardins, N., 3, 21, 22, 22n, 23, 25–26, 11?
Devlin, M., 197
Dhaliwal, G., 217
DiClemente, C.C., 134
Diefenbach, D.L., 346
Dill, F.E., 151
Dishion, T.J., 55, 152
Dixon, L., 252
Dobash, R.E., 242, 247
Dobash, R.P., 242, 247
Dodge, K.A., 149
Doob, A., 377

Hanson, R.K., 9, 137, 138, 214, 221, 258, 299,
    302, 303, 305–307, 308, 309, 310, 311,
    312–314, 321–322
Harden, P., 152
Hafdyman, P., 389, 392
Hare, R.D., 87, 257, 352, 353, 354, 355, 360,
    364, 383
Harkins, L., 364
Harlow, C.W., 385
Harman, W.G., 416, 421
Harper, E., 176n
Harper, R., 186
Harrington, H., 148
Harris, A.J.R., 306
Harris, B., 84
Harris, G.T., 9, 54, 56, 57, 59, 138, 212,
    215, 216n, 290, 299, 300, 307,
    321–337, 364
Harris, S.B., 271
Hart, E.K., 148, 311
Hart, S., 354
Hart, S.D., 216, 257, 307, 357
Hart-Mitchell, R., 428
Hartley, C.C., 264
Haslip, S., 407
Hastings, L.K., 252
Hawkins, J.D., 151, 152, 153, 157, 158
Hazen, A., 268
Helff, C.M., 251
Helmus, L., 9, 258, 306, 322
Helzer, J.E., 328
Hemphill, J.F., 353
Hendley, N., 170, 170n
Henggeler, S.W., 168, 169
Hennessy, J.J., 253
Henry, B., 46, 47, 149, 153
Hern, A.L., 314
Herrenkohl, E.C., 268
Herrenkohl, R.C., 264
Herrenkohl, T.I., 151, 264, 269
Herrnstein, R.J., 91
Hersh, K., 349
Hessing, D., 81
Hiatt, K.D., 361
Hickey, E.W., 233
Hicks, B.M., 361–362
Hill, C., 177
Hill, K.G., 153
Hill, S.Y., 77
Hilton, N.Z., 256–257, 297
Hindelang, M.J., 79
Hinshaw, S.P., 148, 153, 346
Hipwell, A.E., 385, 390
Hirschi, T., 75, 77, 78, 79, 80, 81, 82, 98, 101,
    371, 383
Hirschman, R., 287
Hiscoke, U., 349
Hitt, M., 177
Hobson, J., 364
Hodgins, S., 222, 337, 340, 349, 351
Hodgson, S., 9, 322
Hoffman, P.B., 136
Hoge, R.D., 101, 152, 156, 157, 225, 322, 388

Holden, G.W., 263
Hollin, C.R., 87, 387
Holmen, M.L., 317
Holmes, R.M., 235
Holmes, S.T., 235
Holsinger, A.M., 385, 416
Holsinger, K., 377
Holtfreter, K., 175, 177, 178, 387, 389
Holton, J.K., 265
Holtzworth-Munroe, A., 251, 252
Holzer, C., 222
Hood, R., 112–113
Horwitz, R., 274
Horwood, L.J., 153, 158, 268
Hoskisson, R., 177
Hough, R.L., 268
Howell, J., 153
Howell, K., 134
Howells, K., 387
Huang, B., 269
Hubbard, D.J., 383, 385, 387, 390
Hudson, S.M., 318
Huesmann, L.R., 150
Hughes, P., 114, 263, 361
Huizinga, D., 112, 150, 152
Hull, J., 406
Hung, K., 155
Hunnicutt, G., 378, 380, 387
Hurst, L., 274
Huss, M.T., 5
Hussong, A.M., 5
Hutchings, B., 35
Hymann, D.J., 274

I

Iacono, W.G., 36, 361–362
Immarigeon, R., 387
Inciardi, J., 384
Ireland, M., 153
Irwin, K., 377

J

Jablensky, A., 327
Jackson, M.A., 380
Jaffee, S.R., 36
James, D.V., 350
James, J., 380
Janssen, M., 115
Jarey, M.L., 149
Jasinski, J.L., 256
Jeffery, C.R., 90, 91
Jensen, G.F., 93
Jensen, T.L., 314
Jespersen, A.F., 297, 298
Jessor, R., 157–158
Johnson, D.D.P., 37
Johnson, H., 242, 384, 385
Johnson, R.E., 93
Johnson, S., 404, 405, 421
Johnson, S.C., 340, 346–347, 347n, 348
Johnston, J.C., 412, 428
Jolliffe, D., 224, 225, 226, 226n,
    227, 228, 229

Jones, B., 222
Jones, E., 70
Jones, G.B., 138
Jones, L., 360
Jones, N., 383–384
Jones, R., 387
Jono, R., 222
Junginger, J., 341, 349

K

Kalmus, E., 299
Kalmuss, D.S., 248
Kaltman, S., 253
Kaluzny, G., 302
Kandel, D.B., 98
Kandel, E., 48, 49, 152, 156, 157
Kantor, G.K., 256
Kaplan, H.S., 54
Katz, S., 380
Kaukinen, C., 245
Kavanagh, K., 152
Kazdin, A.E., 151, 168
Keith, B., 152
Kelley, M.L., 243
Kelley, P., 177
Kendall, K., 389, 399
Kendell, R., 327
Kennedy, P.J., 186
Kennedy, S.M., 134, 396
Kerlin, K., 361
Kerr, M., 354
Kershaw, C., 111
Kessler, R.C., 151
Kider, S.B., 112
Kiehl, K.A., 362–363
Kim, J., 269
Kim, T.E., 98
Kimonis, E.R., 359, 361
Klein, U., 178
Kleinlnecht, S., 117, 155
Klemke, 112
Knight, R.A., 292, 293n, 294, 295, 295n
Kochanska, G., 360, 361
Kockler, T., 208
Koegl, C., 167
Kogan, J., 414
Kong, R., 371, 372, 375, 376n, 377n,
    383, 392
Koons, B.A., 383, 396
Koss, M.P., 287
Kosson, D.S., 355
Kotch, J.B., 264
Koverola, C., 184
Kowaz, A.M., 337
Kraemer, H.C., 151, 328
Krohn, M.D., 97, 385
Kroner, D.G., 125, 217
Kropp, P.R., 257, 307, 311
Kropp, R., 260
Krueger, R.F., 361–362
Krug, E.G., 241, 241n
Kruger, R.F., 328
Kruttschnitt, C., 373, 380

Subject Index

discrimination in criminal justice system, 405–406
disinhibition, 286
diversion, 143
diversion programs, 168
dizygotic (DZ) twins, 34
domestic violence. *See* family violence; intimate partner violence
Domestic Violence Risk Appraisal Guide (DVRAG), 256–257
Doob, Anthony, 27
dopamine, 42–43
Douglas, Kevin, 236
Drug Abuse Screening Test (DAST), 194
drug trade, 186–188, 192–193
drug trafficking, 374
drug treatment courts, 197–198
Duluth Domestic Abuse Intervention Project (DAIP), 259
Duluth model, 259
Dutton, Donald, 249–250, 277
dynamic risk, 137–313
dysfunctional family history, 385
dysphoric-borderline batterer, 252

E

Earlscourt Girls Connection Program, 397
early sexual intercourse, 57
ecological niche, 54
economic crime
    corporate crimes, 175
    defined, 175
    drug trade, 186–188
    fraud, 180–182
    introduction, 174–175
    occupational crimes, 175
    organized crime, 188–193
    prostitution, 182–186
    punishment of white-collar criminals, 178–179
    theft, 179–180
    top ten list, 198–199
    types of, 175–182
    typical white-collar offenders, 176–178
    white-collar crime, 175–179
economic marginalization, 380, 386–387
Ecstasy, 193
education, and white-collar offenders, 177
effect sizes, 8–9, 225–226, 226f
ego-ideal, 71
elder abuse. *See* elder maltreatment
elder maltreatment
    adult guardianship laws, 276
    adult protection laws, 276
    consequences, 275
    defined, 271
    described, 271
    examples of, 272
    financial abuse, 240–241
    institutional caregiver abuse, 273
    laws that protect, 276
    neglect, 240
    perpetrators, 272
    prevalence, 272

risk factors, 275
    screening for elder abuse, 273–275
electronic surveillance, 112
Elizabeth Fry Society, 117, 396
Ellard, Kelly, 372
emotion, 360, 360f
emotional abuse, 298
emotional congruence, 285
emotional funnel system, 248
empirical actuarial instruments, 215, 307
employment difficulties, 386
empowerment, 393
encounter, 116
endocrine system, 38
epidemiological, 37
eugenics, 32
evaluation of correctional programs, 127
evidence-based practice, 139
    see also correctional practice
evolutionary theories of crime, 50–64
    criticisms, 52–53
    determinism, 52
    evolution, and crime, 53
    female-perpetrated crime, 63–64
    homicide, 60–63
    life history theory, 54–58
    natural selection, 52–53
    naturalistic fallacy, 52
    psychopathy, 58–59
    rape, 288–290
    researching, 53–64
    risk-taking, 54–58
    violent crime, 211–212
ex-offender assistance, 117
exhibitionism, 285
external punishment, 248
externalizing problems, 160
extrajudicial measures, 144
Eysenck, Hans, 86

F

F test (ANOVA), 9
Fabrikant, Valery, 232, 233
familial protective factors, 157
familial risk factors, 152
family functioning, and sexual offenders, 298
family-only batterer, 251–252
family-oriented strategies, 165
family-supportive interventions, 165
family violence
    background issues, 239–241
    child abuse, 260–270
    defined, 239–240
    ecological model, 241, 241f
    elder maltreatment, 271–276
    intimate partner violence, 241–256
    introduction, 239
    neglect, 240
    psychological abuse, 240–241
    risk assessment, 256–260
    top ten list, 276–277
    types of, 240
Family Violence Prevention Program, 259
"father of criminology," 32

federal corrections, 15–16
federally sentenced women, 391
female genital mutilation (FGM), 267–268
female infidelity, 246
The Female Offender (Lombroso and Ferrero), 37
female offenders
    Aboriginal offenders, 419–420
    antisocial personality, 383
    applied correctional feminists, 396
    background, 370–378
    classification, 387–392
    community functioning, 386
    community-wide factors, 386–387
    criminal attitudes, 383
    criminal history, 382
    criticisms of gender-neutral instruments, 389–390
    dis-empowerment, 383–384
    domestic homicide, 374
    drug trafficking, 374
    dysfunctional family history, 385
    economic marginalization, 386–387
    employment difficulties, 386
    empowerment, 393
    familial assault, 374
    federally sentenced women, 391, 394–395
    female-centred theories, 378–382
    female-perpetrated crime, 63–64
    female-salient predictor, 385
    feminist pathways research, 380
    fraud, 374
    gender-informed risk-assessment instruments, 390–391
    gender-neutral risk-assessment instrume 388–390
    gender-responsive services, 393
    general responsivity principle, 398
    girls, and violent crime, 375–377, 376f, 377f
    high risk female offender, 382–383
    historical context, 370–371, 394–395
    holistic programming, 397
    impulsivity, 383
    infanticide, 375
    integrated liberation and economic marginalization theory, 380–381
    interpersonal factors, 385–386
    intrapersonal factors, 382–385
    introduction, 370
    length of sentences, 23
    Level of Supervision/Case Management Inventory (LS/CMI), 388–389
    meaningful and responsible choices, 393
    mental health issues, 384
    nature of female-perpetrated crime, 371–373
    negative relationships, 385–386
    over-classification hypothesis, 392
    patriarchy, 386–387
    personal, interpersonal, and community-reinforcement theory (PIC-R), 381–3
    prevalence of female-perpetrated crime, 371–373
    principles of programming for women, 393–396